THE INSTITUTE FOR POLISH–JEWISH STUDIES

The Institute for Polish–Jewish Studies in Oxford and its sister organization, the American Association for Polish–Jewish Studies, which publish *Polin*, are learned societies that were established in 1984, following the International Conference on Polish–Jewish Studies, held in Oxford. The Institute is an associate institute of the Oxford Centre for Hebrew and Jewish Studies, and the American Association is linked with the Department of Near Eastern and Judaic Studies at Brandeis University.

Both the Institute and the American Association aim to promote understanding of the Polish Jewish past. They have no building or library of their own and no paid staff; they achieve their aims by encouraging scholarly research and facilitating its publication, and by creating forums for people with a scholarly interest in Polish Jewish topics, both past and present.

To this end the Institute and the American Association help organize lectures and international conferences. Venues for these activities have included Brandeis University in Waltham, Massachusetts, the Hebrew University in Jerusalem, the Institute for the Study of Human Sciences in Vienna, King's College in London, the Jagiellonian University in Kraków, the Oxford Centre for Hebrew and Jewish Studies, the University of Łódź, University College London, and the Polish Cultural Institute and the Polish embassy in London. They have encouraged academic exchanges between Israel, Poland, the United States, and western Europe. In particular they seek to help train a new generation of scholars, in Poland and elsewhere, to study the culture and history of the Jews in Poland.

Each year since 1986 the Institute has published a volume of scholarly papers in the series *Polin: Studies in Polish Jewry* under the general editorship of Professor Antony Polonsky of Brandeis University. Since 1994 the series has been published on its behalf by the Littman Library of Jewish Civilization, and since 1998 the publication has been linked with the American Association as well. In March 2000 the entire series was honoured with a National Jewish Book Award from the Jewish Book Council in the United States. More than twenty other works on Polish Jewish topics have also been published with the Institute's assistance.

Further information on the Institute for Polish–Jewish Studies can be found on its website, <www.polishjewishstudies.co.uk>. For the website of the American Association for Polish–Jewish Studies, see <www.aapjstudies.org>.

THE LITTMAN LIBRARY OF
JEWISH CIVILIZATION

Dedicated to the memory of
LOUIS THOMAS SIDNEY LITTMAN
*who founded the Littman Library for the love of God
and as an act of charity in memory of his father*
JOSEPH AARON LITTMAN
and to the memory of
ROBERT JOSEPH LITTMAN
who continued what his father Louis had begun
יהא זכרם ברוך

'Get wisdom, get understanding:
Forsake her not and she shall preserve thee'

PROV. 4: 5

*The Littman Library of Jewish Civilization is a registered UK charity
Registered charity no. 1000784*

POLIN
STUDIES IN POLISH JEWRY

VOLUME FOUR
Poles and Jews
Perceptions and Misperceptions

Edited by
WŁADYSŁAW T. BARTOSZEWSKI

Published for
The Institute for Polish–Jewish Studies

The Littman Library of Jewish Civilization
in association with Liverpool University Press

*The Littman Library of Jewish Civilization
in association with Liverpool University Press
4 Cambridge Street, Liverpool* L69 7ZU, UK
www.liverpooluniversitypress.co.uk/littman

Managing Editor: Connie Webber

*Distributed in North America by
Oxford University Press Inc., 198 Madison Avenue,
New York,* NY 10016, USA

*First published in hardback 1989 by Basil Blackwell Ltd
First published in paperback 2004*

© *Institute for Polish–Jewish Studies 1989*

*All rights reserved.
No part of this publication may be reproduced,
stored in a retrieval system, or transmitted, in any form or by
any means, without the prior permission in writing of
The Littman Library of Jewish Civilization*

*The paperback edition of this book is sold subject to the condition
that it shall not, by way of trade or otherwise, be lent, re-sold,
hired out or otherwise circulated without the publisher's prior consent
in any form of binding or cover other than that in which it is published
and without a similar condition including this condition
being imposed on the subsequent purchaser*

*Catalogue records for this book are available from the
British Library and the Library of Congress*

*ISSN 0268 1056
ISBN 978-1-904113-19-5*

*Publishing coordinator: Janet Moth
Cover design: Pete Russell, Faringdon, Oxon.*

In memory of
MARCELL AND MARIA ROTH
Polish Jews dedicated to the preservation of their heritage

The Institute for Polish–Jewish Studies, which sponsors *Polin*, has also benefited from the support of the following:

Mrs Irene Pipes; the Jewish Presence Foundation;
the M. B. Grabowski Fund; the American Jewish Committee;
the Polish American Congress; the Anti-Defamation League of B'nai B'rith;
Commentary magazine; *Present Time* magazine;
Gadsby & Hannah; Paisner & Co.; Edmund Gibbs & Co.; and
the American Foundation for Polish–Jewish Studies.

Editors and Advisers

EDITORS

Monika Adamczyk-Garbowska, *Lublin*
Israel Bartal, *Jerusalem*
Antony Polonsky (Chair), *Waltham, Mass.*
Michael Steinlauf, *Philadelphia*
Jerzy Tomaszewski, *Warsaw*

REVIEW EDITORS

Władysław T. Bartoszewski, *Warsaw*
ChaeRan Freeze, *Waltham, Mass.*
Joshua Zimmerman, *New York*

EDITORIAL BOARD

Chimen Abramski, *London*
David Assaf, *Tel Aviv*
Władysław T. Bartoszewski, *Warsaw*
David Engel, *New York*
David Fishman, *New York*
Józef Gierowski, *Kraków*
Jacob Goldberg, *Jerusalem*
Yisrael Gutman, *Jerusalem*
Jerzy Kłoczowski, *Lublin*
Ezra Mendelsohn, *Jerusalem*

Elchanan Reiner, *Tel Aviv*
Jehuda Reinharz, *Waltham, Mass.*
Moshe Rosman, *Tel Aviv*
Henryk Samsonowicz, *Warsaw*
Robert Shapiro, *New York*
Adam Teller, *Haifa*
Daniel Tollet, *Paris*
Piotr S. Wandycz, *New Haven, Conn*
Jonathan Webber, *Birmingham, UK*
Steven Zipperstein, *Stanford, Calif.*

ADVISORY BOARD

Władysław Bartoszewski, *Warsaw*
Jan Błoński, *Kraków*
Abraham Brumberg, *Washington*
Andrzej Chojnowski, *Warsaw*
Tadeusz Chrzanowski, *Kraków*
Andrzej Ciechanowiecki, *London*
Norman Davies, *London*
Victor Erlich, *New Haven, Conn.*
Frank Golczewski, *Hamburg*
Olga Goldberg, *Jerusalem*
Feliks Gross, *New York*
Czesław Hernas, *Wrocław*
Maurycy Horn, *Warsaw*
Jerzy Jedlicki, *Warsaw*
Andrzej Kamiński, *London*
Hillel Levine, *Boston*

Lucjan Lewitter, *Cambridge, Mass.*
Stanisław Litak, *Lublin*
Heinz-Dietrich Löwe, *Heidelberg*
Emanuel Meltzer, *Tel Aviv*
Czesław Miłosz (Hon. Chair), *Berkeley*
Shlomo Netzer, *Tel Aviv*
David Patterson, *Oxford*
Zbigniew Pełczyński, *Oxford*
Szymon Rudnicki, *Warsaw*
Alexander Schenker, *New Haven, Conn*
David Sorkin, *Madison, Wisc.*
Edward Stankiewicz, *New Haven, Conn*
Norman Stone, *Ankara*
Shmuel Werses, *Jerusalem*
Jacek Woźniakowski, *Lublin*
Piotr Wróbel, *Toronto*

CONTENTS

STATEMENT FROM THE EDITORS ... 1

Leszek Kołakowski National Stereotypes ... 3
Władysław T. Bartoszewski Poles and Jews as the 'Other' ... 6

ARTICLES
Janusz Tazbir Images of the Jew in the Polish Commonwealth ... 18
Murray J. Rosman A Minority Views the Majority: Jewish Attitudes towards the Polish Lithuanian Commonwealth and Interaction with Poles ... 31
Chava Turniansky Yiddish 'Historical' Songs as Sources for the History of the Jews in Pre-Partition Poland ... 42
Israel Bartal Non-Jews and Gentile Society in East European Hebrew and Yiddish Literature 1856–1914 ... 53
Magdalena Opalski Trends in the Literary Perception of Jews in Modern Polish Fiction ... 70
Frank Golczewski Anti-Semitic Literature in Poland before the First World War ... 87
Michael C. Steinlauf Mr Geldhab and Sambo in *Peyes*. Images of the Jew on the Polish Stage, 1863–1905 ... 98
Eugenia Prokopówna The Image of the *Shtetl* in Polish Literature ... 129
Norman Davies Ethnic Diversity in Twentieth Century Poland ... 143
Andrzej Chojnowski The Jewish Question in the Work of the *Instytut Badań Spraw Narodowościowych* ... 159
Anna Landau-Czajka The Ubiquitous Enemy. The Jew in the Political Thought of Radical Right-Wing Nationalists in Poland, 1926–1939 ... 169
Pawel Korzec and Jean-Charles Szurek Jews and Poles under Soviet Occupation (1939–1941): Conflicting Interests ... 204

Antony Polonsky Polish-Jewish Relations and the Holocaust	226
Władysław Bartoszewski The Founding of the All-Polish Anti-Racist League in 1946	243
Krystyna Kersten and Jerzy Szapiro The contexts of the so-called Jewish Question in Poland after World War II	255
Julian Ilicki Changing Identity among Younger Polish Jews in Sweden after 1968	269

NOTES

Iwona Irwin-Zarecka Problematizing the 'Jewish Problem'	281
Nechama Tec Of Help, Understanding and Hope: Righteous Rescuers and Polish Jews	296
Stefan Kieniewicz Jews in Jarmolińce	311

PERSONAL VIEW

Roman Zimand Wormwood and Ashes (Do Poles and Jews Hate Each Other?)	313

EXCHANGE

Stanislaus A. Blejwas Polemic as History: Shmuel Krakowski, *The War of the Doomed. Jewish Armed Resistance in Poland, 1942–1944*	354
Shmuel Krakowski Response to Blejwas	363
Stanislaus A. Blejwas Reply to Krakowski	368

REVIEW ARTICLES

Andrzej Bryk The Struggles for Poland	370
Gershon C. Bacon Unchanging View: Polish Jewry as Seen in Recent One-Volume Histories of the Jews	390
Anna Radziwiłł The Teaching of the History of the Jews in Secondary Schools in the Polish People's Republic, 1949–88	402
David Engel Works in Hebrew on the History of the Jews in Inter-War Poland	425
Peter Pulzer *Ostjuden*	434
Sergiusz Michalski On Zweig	438
Tomasz Gąsowski Reading Ringelblum	442
Adam A. Hetnal Recent Publications on the Plight of the Jews in Occupied Poland	449
M. R. D. Foot Resistance to Tyranny	457
Michael Burleigh Nazi Social Policies	462
Alexandra Reiche History, Holocaust and German National Identity	467
Jack Kugelmass A Look at the Last Jews of Poland	474

REPORT
Anna Izydorczyk, Ewa Pankiewicz Scholarly Conference—500
  Years of Jewish Settlement in Podlasie   482

CONTRIBUTORS   488
OBITUARY   495
Shmuel Ettinger

POLIN

'... The place is specially intended for Jews. When the Gentiles had greatly oppressed the exiled Jews, and the Divine Presence saw that there was no limit and no end to the oppression and that the handful of Jews might, God forbid, go under, the Presence came before the Lord of the Universe to lay the grievance before Him, and said to Him as follows: "How long is this going to last? When You sent the dove out of the ark at the time of the flood, You gave it an olive branch so that it might have a support for its feet on the water, and yet it was unable to bear the water of the flood and returned to the ark; whereas my children You have sent out of the ark into a flood, and have provided nothing for a support where they may rest their feet in their exile." Thereupon God took a piece of Eretz Yisroel, which he had hidden away in the heavens at the time when the Temple was destroyed, and sent it down upon the earth and said: "Be My resting place for My children in their exile." That is why it is called Poland (Polin), from the Hebrew *poh lin*, which means: "Here shalt thou lodge" in the exile. That is why Satan has no power over us here, and the Torah is spread broadcast over the whole country. There are synagogues and schools and Yeshivahs, God be thanked.

'And what will happen in the great future when the Messiah will come? What are we going to do with the synagogues and the settlements which we shall have built up in Poland?' asked Mendel ...

'How can you ask? In the great future, when the Messiah will come, God will certainly transport Poland with all its settlements, synagogues and Yeshivahs to Eretz Yisroel. How else could it be?'

Sholem Asch *Kiddush ha-Shem*

STATEMENT FROM THE EDITORS

> O wad some Pow'r the giftie gie us
> *To see oursels as others see us!*
> It wad frae monie a blunder free us
>   An' foolish notion.
>   Robert Burns

This special issue of *POLIN*, edited by Władysław T. Bartoszewski, is devoted to stereotypes: how they arise, how they develop and how they are perpetuated. Its theme is how Poles came to see Jews and Jews Poles and it describes the evolution of attitudes as Poland developed from a pre-modern to a modern society. In the pre-modern period, the basic division was between Jews and Christians and both groups were determined to maintain their separateness and to uphold their basically incompatible views of the world. As the pre-modern, agrarian and static society was transformed under the impact of western political ideas and economic forces, religion lost some of its hold and modern concepts of national identity became established. Anti-judaism was transformed, first in Germany and then over the whole of Europe, into anti-semitism. On the lands of the Polish-Lithuanian Commonwealth, new nationalisms – Byelorussian, Ukrainian, Lithuanian – developed leaving the Jews in an awkward position between the Poles and these groups. New social forces, first marxism and then communism further complicated inter-ethnic relations. With the apparent failure of assimilation by the end of the nineteenth century, the Jews were transformed from a religious community into a proto-nation with many of the characteristics of the other nations of eastern Europe. A new division, no longer between Christians and Jews but between Poles and Jews became established. The relations between these groups were drastically transformed by the traumatic impact of the Nazi holocaust and the imposition of communist rule in Poland. As a result, organized Jewish life has virtually ceased on Polish soil and the issues discussed in this volume are almost entirely historical in character. Nevertheless, we believe that they have a relevance which extends considerably beyond the actual bounds of the subject investigated, revealing much about the character of modern nationalism and the emergence of anti-semitism as a European phenomenon. It should be stressed that many of the topics discussed are controversial and disputed and that the contributors speak only for themselves. The articles by Murray Rosman, Frank Golizewski, Norman Davies, Władysław Bartoszewski and Krystyna Kersten and Jerzy Szapiro were all first presented at the International Conference on the History and Culture of Polish Jews held in Jerusalem in February 1988. The article by Anna Landau-Czajka is a revised version of one which appeared in *Przegląd Historyczny* in 1988.

This issue is special in another sense, in that although it contains review essays, it includes no book reviews. These will again be a feature of volume V. Since a number of questions have been asked about our book reviewing policy, we feel it is desirable to explain the principles on which it is based. We include only articles which are directly relevant to the history of Jews on the lands of the Polish-Lithuanian Commonwealth. In the case of books, however, we regard as legitimate subjects for review any volumes which help us directly or indirectly to understand that history. In particular, we are interested in highlighting developments elsewhere which illuminate those in Poland and believe strongly in the value of a comparative approach to our subject.

Our editorial board was sadly impoverished by the death last year of one of the most distinguished modern Jewish historians, Professor Shmuel Ettinger of the Hebrew University, whose obituary appears in this issue. His always sagacious counsel will be sorely missed. Professor Chimen Abramsky and Dr Łukasz Hirszowicz of London have joined our editorial board. We hope to make full use of their expertise, as well as that of the other members of the editorial board and all our well-wishers and subscribers.

The editor of this volume would like to thank Steven Zipperstein, the co-author of the idea behind this volume, Magdalena Opalski, who contributed many suggestions, and Antony Polonsky without whose generous help this project could not have been realized.

NATIONAL STEREOTYPES
Leszek Kołakowski

Only infrequently do we notice that a great deal of our mental universe, our images and our reactions to the world and to other people is made of, or caused by, stereotypes, that is to say spontaneously shaped, quasi-empirical generalizations which, once established, are hardly corrigible by subsequent experience. This is a natural and perhaps, as a whole, beneficial arrangement of mind; the stereotypes – of things, people, nations, places – may be plausible, half-true or simply false, but because they are indispensable for our mental security, they usually survive the counter-experience unless they bring obviously harmful effects. If they are wrong but practically innocuous, they persist because it is mentally safer for us to stick to stereotypes even if false than to be incessantly watchful, to correct them and thus to keep our mind in a state of never-ending uncertainty and disarray.

National stereotypes do not differ from others in this respect. Any example will do. England, for instance, has the reputation of a rainy country. This reputation is not based on our study of meteorological statistics, but on a spontaneous quasi-generalization. Once the reputation has been established, a peculiar logic – or illogical mechanism – is at work. When it rains in France, it just rains. But each rainy day in England provides us with a confirmation of the stereotype: this is a rainy country. But not conversely: a sunny day in England is then logically irrelevant, it does not disturb the reputation. Our normal, incurable daily-life thinking does not and probably never will abide by the sensible Popperian rules: we need stereotypes because on balance we are mentally better off if we keep them intact.

This applies to national stereotypes. Each tribe or nation invariably produces stereotypes – often half-respectful and half-scornful – of its neighbours and of more or less acquainted tribes. And so we 'know', for instance, that Germans are disciplined and humourless, English people are reliable and narrow-minded, Poles are courageous and disorganized,

Jews clever and tactless, Americans friendly and naive, Czechs hard-working and mean, and so on. There is never a shortage of examples, and the counter-examples never count; the stereotypes are always safe and, if we are challenged, we have always an infallible safety-net: 'oh, yes, I know that there are exceptions', 'some of my best friends . . .', etc.

The study of stereotypes is very important not because it may destroy them: most likely it cannot help in shattering deeply ingrained images. Those images do change not as a result of rational arguments and statistics, but because social conditions require another image. It is not plausible that the massacre of Jews by the Nazis can be accounted for by the negative stereotypes of the Jews that had been in existence previously. To be sure, the Nazis skilfully and efficiently exploited and reinforced those stereotypes when, as it turned out, the Germans needed a scapegoat which they could blame for their misery; but it was this misery and despair which made the Nazi genocidal programme acceptable.

National stereotypes do not necessarily carry the seeds of hatred; some do, some do not. They are converted into a deadly weapon when other factors – in particular a war or a war-threat – require it. Countries which have never been at war, or not for a very long time, tend to form more benign, though rarely quite innocent or entirely positive stereotyped images of each other.

The Jews, in so far as they lived in almost all European countries, were, so to say, in a 'privileged' position: they were stereotyped everywhere. How those images differed from each other depending on local and historical circumstances is a matter for a separate study. One should admit, however, that those stereotypes often, albeit not always, included, next to unflattering descriptions which are more or less normal in tribal animosities, some horrifying and potentially deadly accusations, especially that of ritual murder. And, in particular among peasants, one could occasionally find truly impressive and astonishing stories: as a 10-year-old boy I was told by another boy that the Jews do not see the sun; when I asked why they wear sun-glasses, he replied: they pretend (incredible but true, I swear).

If, however, we leave aside the blood libel and similar horror stories or just absurd superstitions, the stereotyped pictures of foreign nations usually include a grain of truth. More often than not they are not whimsical products of sheer fantasy, concocted *ex nihilo*, but rather simplified, petrified and inflated records of experience. There is, after all, such an entity as the historically shaped 'national character' which is never made of unadulterated virtues. Even though it obviously cannot be imputed to individuals ('every Pole is courageous and disorganized', 'every Jew is clever and tactless'), it can reasonably be studied by analysis of typical patterns of behaviour. And many nations have mirrored their own, unedifying qualities in literature, art and jokes (Jewish humour and modern Yiddish literature are an inexhaustible treasury of knowledge about the Jews' none too flattering self-perception; and Polish 'national vices' have for centuries been one of the favourite targets of Polish writers and publicists).

The investigation of national stereotypes, a particular branch of social anthropology, may greatly contribute to our insight into what the 'national character' is: not because our stereotypes deliver an undistorted image of other peoples, which they certainly do not, but because by judging the others we involuntarily disclose our own patterns of perception and thus our own vices and virtues. In other words: those stereotypes perhaps say no less about their holders than about their targets. Even though it is not likely that the examination of stereotypes will make them disappear, it may have a practical significance: by knowing how the others see us, we certainly get a better insight into ourselves, even if we think (as we usually do) that this counter-image is unjust. It is not only the case that one can recognize oneself in a distorted looking-glass (a caricature is good if it really resembles the original) but the distortion itself, by exaggerating some features of the object, can be useful and can contribute to our self-understanding.

POLES AND JEWS AS THE 'OTHER'
Władysław T. Bartoszewski

When describing mutual perceptions of Poles and Jews over the centuries one enters the realm of prejudices, stereotypes, and convictions. Almost all the articles in the present volume of *POLIN* deal with perceptions which the Jews had of the Poles, and which the Poles had of the Jews. In order to understand this relationship it is useful to start by examining such theoretical concepts as 'stereotypes', the 'other' or the 'stranger', as well as traditional belief systems.

In pre-modern times, the dominant attitude of the Jews and the Poles towards one another was similar to that which characterises the relationship of ideas in a system of religious belief. Both communities held convictions about the world, and beliefs about 'strangers' – whether Jewish, Polish, or others – which formed part of their respective cosmologies. These were organised according to the ethnocentric principle of relations between ethnic groups, first established by the American anthropologist McGee in 1900.[1] As Sumner, the creator of the first theory of ethnocentrism, stated: 'Ethnocentrism is the technical name for this view of things in which one's own group is the center of everything, and all others are scaled and rated with reference to it ... Each group nourishes its own pride and vanity, boasts itself superior, exalts its own divinities, and looks with contempt on outsiders'.[2] The application of this principle can be seen clearly in this volume in the articles of Janusz Tazbir and Murray Rosman. As they show, the Poles looked at the Jews as servants of the Devil as they had 'lost contact with God', who at any rate was probably Polish. The Jews, on the other hand, considered all other nations to have been created for their benefit – 'were it not that there is some good [that comes from them] they would not have been created at all' – preached Rabbi Levi Yitshak of Berdichev to his followers at the end of the eighteenth century. Polish peasants in the nineteenth and early twentieth century mocked the gods of others which they compared unflatteringly with the Polish god:

> 'At Kraków's castle, gods fought there,
> Our Jesus Lord broke the legs of the German god!'³

and,

> 'On a bridge of Kraków two gods got together,
> Our Jesus Lord wanted to break the legs of the Jewish god'.⁴

These stereotypes did not apply simply to Poles or Jews; indeed one of the characteristic features of traditional beliefs about the 'other' is that all the strangers are put in the same category. Convictions held by the Poles about the Jews did not substantially differ from those they held about the Turks, Gypsies, Tartars, and so on, or even of Poles in other regions. Such was the case with the belief that Jewish children were born blind like some animals; a belief which was extended to include the Polish inhabitants of the Mazowsze region. Similar views were held by the Jews, who regarded all Gentiles as dangerous, demonic and devilish, and were accordingly convinced of Jewish superiority, even if for pragmatic reasons they chose to keep this to themselves.

Attitudes toward the 'stranger' were not, however, simply negative. Another typical feature of ethnocentric beliefs is their ambiguity, which makes them akin to the 'numinotic' experience of the sacred, a concept developed by Rudolf Otto.⁵ There is in the stranger a fascinating element which makes him, at the same time, evil and attractive, strange and admirable. This element is particularly noticeable in some popular convictions which have persisted among Polish peasants from at least the nineteenth century to the present. One could argue that peasants experienced strangers in a way comparable to the way numinous feeling is experienced. Zbigniew Benedyktowicz, a Polish anthropologist and phenomenologist, has proposed a division into two stages of the morphology of the attitude towards strangers. In the first, he claimed, strangers appear simultaneously as sacred (divine) and devilish. In the second stage, a rationalisation takes place, and the strangers lose their divine characteristics and their contact with God. This phenomenon is alluded to by Janusz Tazbir in his article. (pp. 18–30)

The first stage is characterised by respect for the unknown. The second stage involves ridicule and caricature of the strangers, which deprives them of their fearful power. Numerous megalomaniac stories produced by various groups about others, and beliefs in the monstrosity of strangers are part of this second stage.⁶ One could easily document the second stage by invoking numerous caricatures, jokes and proverbs related to the Jews throughout Europe.

The first stage, in which the stranger is in some way seen connected with divinity, has often been overlooked by those who study ethnic groups. However, as Gerardus van der Leeuw remarked in his classic study on religion: 'For, taking everything into consideration, no essential difference can be admitted between demon and god; the idea of god certainly has many other roots besides belief in demons, but one of these may become a god – if he does not become a devil'.[7] There is indeed a *coincidentia oppositorum* between the divine and the demonic, which is clearly to be seen in Slavonic mythology. This mythology borrowed some elements from Iranian in a way which has been described by Roman Jakobson as constituting a kind of religious revolution. Both Iranians and proto-Slavs removed from their religious vocabulary the proto-Indo-European *dieus* meaning 'heaven' and 'god of clear heaven'. They substituted for *dieus* a word previously meaning 'cloud' – Iranian *nebah*, Slavonic *nebo*, Polish *niebo*. The adjective *deiwos*, retained in other Indo-European languages to denote everything heavenly and divine, Iranians and Slavs use in relation to demonic creatures, or peculiar and stupendous beings. (Iranian *daeva*, Slavonic *divъ*, appearing in Slavonic mythology also as *divožena*, Polish *dziwożona*).[8]

Julian Pitt-Rivers has also commented on the ambiguity of strangers: 'The stranger belongs to the "extra-ordinary" world, and the mystery surrounding him allies him to the sacred and makes him a suitable vehicle for the apparition of God, the revelation of a mystery'. He discusses situations in which God takes the form of the stranger:

> Therefore, to put it in the phrasing of the popular epigram, it was not in the least odd of God to choose the Jews, but on the contrary exactly what the anthropologist should expect of him. The ambiguity of their status, as at the same time belonging and not belonging, within the gates yet beyond the pale, and their reputation as the possessors of cryptic knowledge, the initiates of the mysteries of finance and of precious metals, made them strangers par excellence, perfectly endowed to be chosen to remain thereafter as his renegade kin. For this reason they were the 'sacred of the left hand' and the natural associates of the fallen angel. That these 'internalised strangers' should have served for centuries as the focus of the ambivalences of their Christian neighbours is in no way surprising; what is surprising is that psychological studies of anti-semitism should not all start with a profile of the mythological character of Jewry.[9]

The stranger can be both a stranger-enemy (Latin *hostis*) and a stranger-guest, a friend (*hospes*). Both imply inequality of status. Georg Simmel, in his famous essay published in 1908, noticed an element of strangeness which is very applicable to the Jews in Poland: 'The stranger is by nature no "owner of soil" – soil not only in the physical, but also in the figurative sense of a life-substance which is fixed, if not in a point in space, at least in an ideal point of the social environment.'[10]

Both for the *szlachta*, who, as Tazbir quotes, considered that 'it is a sin and shame to trade', and for the peasants, who looked at farming as the only proper occupation ('the Jews did not work – they only traded'), the Jews constituted a group of 'internal strangers'. Moreover, the non-agricultural professions were ascribed to them permanently: 'Not now, not ever, there will be farmer from a Jew' was the prevailing peasant view. As Ludwik Stomma has concluded: 'The stranger was always to remain one. Such was simply the order of the peasants' world'.[11]

The general attitude of Poles and Jews in pre-modern times, and much later in the case of the peasants, as well as Hassidic and other traditional Jews, was that each group occupied a particular place in what they perceived to be the universal order of things and that each group should stay there. For traditional societies, as for Bruno Schulz, 'the essence of reality is Meaning or Sense. What lacks Sense is, for us not reality. Every fragment of reality lives by virtue of partaking in a universal Sense'.[12] Thus the efforts to 'emancipate' or to modernise the population were resisted by many members of both communities. One of the reasons for this resistance was the perception that the world, in this case Poland, was created together with all groups and nations included in it as part of an unchangeable landscape. As Jerzy Wasilewski pointed out: 'The holistic vision of the world in traditional cultures assumes that human actions should follow the pattern designated by the universe, otherwise the disturbance of the cosmic order will take place, and man will bear the consequences. This *Elementargedanken* is realised in varying degrees by different cultures'.[13]

Indeed as late as the 1970s, as Alina Cała has established, the extermination of the Jews in Poland was explained by the peasants in terms of God's interference in His own order which without Him could not have been changed.[14]

Some elements of this traditional *Weltanschauung* have been carried into late 19th century and early 20th century attitudes as well. For example, the non-agricultural occupations of the Jews in Poland were criticised both in 19th-century Polish fiction, described in this volume by Magdalena Opalski, and in the publicistic works analysed by Frank Golczewski. These authors show that in the 1870s and 1880s, an in some cases even later, the Jews were urged to undertake ' "real", or productive work' (although there were simultaneous voices advocating involvement in commercial activities for the Poles). There were both Jews and Poles who fought against what they considered to be a backward traditional society. The Jewish *haskala*, whose intellectual pre-occupations are described by Yisrael Bartal, and Polish Positivism, which is discussed by Opalski, Golczewski and Steinlauf, shared this negative perception of traditional life, especially in the economic sphere. Paradoxically the economy became, however, an area of intensified competition, to which many images of the 'other' were closely related. These images could be called, after Walter Lippmann, 'images in our heads', or ethnic stereotypes.[15]

Virtually all articles included in this volume of *POLIN* describe the various forms such stereotypes have taken throughout the history of Polish-Jewish contacts. As in Plato's *Republic*, the reality of these contacts has been apprehended through images. Like the shadows for the people in the cave, they were the images of objects (and subjects) which were accepted as reality and not the reality itself. People were more inclined to believe in the strongly established images than in reality if they were in the end confronted with it.[16]

Benedyktowicz has shown that a stereotype is a mixture of both critical and emotional thinking in which the subject attempts to arrange expressions of experience and sensation in concept-like terms. 'There is a tendency amongst people to treat the symbol in a way which confuses and identifies the image with that which the image represents. Stereotype, like symbol, possesses the dual character of reality and unreality'.[17] There is no agreement as to what the stereotype really is and how to define it. There are, however, certain traits common to all stereotypes.[18]

Stereotypes have a social character and origin. Their objects are entire groups of people. For example *all* the Jews, or *all* the Poles share the same features according to national stereotypes. Stereotypes are expressions of public opinion transmitted through upbringing and education in which personal experiences have marginal significance. Therefore, we may come across statements such as 'some of my best friends are Jewish' which usually suggests that the speaker has just expressed or is about to express some anti-semitic views, or 'there are some Poles who do not hate the Jews', which implies that most Poles do. Both statements imply that there are exceptions to an otherwise general and universally applicable rule. Personal encounters with people who do not confirm the stereotypical view of the 'other' are dismissed as irrelevant or unrepresentative.

Stereotypes are simplified generalisations and are often misrepresentations of reality. Proponents of the 'kernel of truth' theory are not necessarily correct, so that in some cases it is futile to search for the 'rational' or 'logical' roots of the image. Stereotypes often develop from minor features of the 'stranger' which, through a little understood process, take on a significance which is in no way proportional to their real importance, but which nevertheless come to define the group as a whole.

Stereotypes undergo no mutation or re-evaluation for long periods of time, as those who use them tend to reject empirical evidence. This is partially due to the emotional nature of these images, which are usually framed in an unequivocal 'positive' or 'negative' way. They are always bound with a name or an expression which immediately conveys its meaning and is understood by the group which uses it. These may be 'everyday' words which carry no particular significance outside the group.

Some negative examples of this include those conveyed by the use of words such as: *Żydziak, gudłaj, shiksa* or *kapornik*. The same applies to expressions like *cyganić* (to cheat – etymologically related to *Cygan* – Gypsy) or '*iść na Żyda*' – to lie and cheat shamelessly like a Jew. In this volume, linguistic aspects of stereotypical perceptions of the Poles by the Jews are discussed by Bartal.

One could say that stereotypes are an attempt to rationalize the beliefs about other ethnic groups or nations. Stereotypes help to link the mythical reality (which was *the* reality for groups such as peasants and probably some traditional Jews as well), with social reality. Their main function seems to be a defense of a group's values and judgments, and the group's position in society. Stereotypes simplify the world and save the group from the effects of having to see the world in its complexity.

In the modern period Polish stereotypes of the Jews have oscillated between those which regarded them as romantic, noble, spiritually rich, patriotic heroes, and those which portrayed them as demonic, evil and depraved exploiters of the Polish masses. During the interesting interlude of the Positivist period (which lasted approximately from 1863 to 1885), the ideals of capitalism started to become accepted and were positively contrasted with the traditional, rural *ethos* of both the nobility and the peasants. This meant that the enterprising Jewish representatives of a newly emerging middle-class became glorified as harbingers of economic progress. Such a perception of capitalism and of the Jews did not last long, since, as Opalski correctly points out, it went against the traditional value system of the Poles and did not take into account the important issue of lost independence. The January uprising of 1863-64, in which some Jews participated, resulted in the emergence of very positive stereotypes of Jews-Polish patriots. Opalski has pointed out in vol. I of *POLIN* that these perceptions did not last long.[19] Here it may be noted that despite the Polish-Jewish *rapprochement*, during the 1860s and 1870s, in these years Jewish descriptions of Russian officials became eulogistic, and although this changed somewhat later, that change, according to Bartal, was ambiguous. He regards this attitude towards the Russians as a continuation of the past alliance between the Jewish *maskilim* and the upper-class Gentiles against the traditional Jewish society. In the eyes of many Poles, this kind of attitude was perfectly acceptable as long as the upper-class was Polish. Once the support for authority was transferred onto the Russians – a change which had to be followed by the abandonment of support for Polish independence – the Jews risked being branded as unpatriotic. This accusation has been a constant one throughout the twentieth century and was to intensify with the emergence of a concept of communist-Jewish alliance, commonly refered to as *Żydokomuna* (Judeo-Communism).

The Jewish perceptions of the Poles in the modern period were, as

Bartal shows, equally schematic, and consisted of a mixture of the traditional Jewish view of the Gentile world with some new elements. According to the latter, all non-Jewish figures should be divided into revolutionary philo-semites and reactionary anti-semites.

The articles by Opalski, Bartal and Steinlauf demonstrate the co-existence of the traditional mythical image of the 'other' with these modern stereotypes. They also show the change of Polish and Jewish societies during the transformation from the feudal system of complementary estates to our modern world characterized by the growth of nationalism, industrial development and economic competition. This process ended with the emergence of the multi-ethnic Second Polish Republic after 1918, described by Norman Davies. The difficult adaptation to the new socio-economic structure raised a variety of problems including the acculturation, assimilation and secularization of the Jews, which raised fundamental questions about national identity: who is a Jew?, and who is a Pole? The newly emerging national identities caused problems which are discussed by both Golczewski and Davies. They also strengthened a negative emotional response which is discussed by Anna Landau-Czajka in her article on the Polish radical Right, and which one may, after Max Scheler, call *ressentiment*.[20] The extreme nationalists held an image of the Jews which concentrated almost exclusively on their alleged negative qualities. They minimised any positive traits, and embodied a hatred which was directed not against some transitory attributes, but against the Jewish very essence and being.[21]

This volume does not contain any material dealing with Jewish ultra-nationalists. However, as Ezra Mendelsohn has pointed out in *POLIN*[22] the relations between majority and minority groups are not necessarily based on a symmetry of feelings and actions. At the same time there is no reason to assume that such attitudes were restricted to the Poles only. Indeed some problems analysed by Paweł Korzec and Jean-Charles Szurek, Krystyna Kersten and Jerzy Szapiro, and Roman Zimand suggest that there were also among the Jews, those whose attitudes towards the Poles were prejudiced and characterised by *ressentiment*.

Nothing influenced the mutual perceptions of Jews and Poles more than the mass-murder of the Jews which took place on Polish soil during the Second World War. As Antony Polonsky points out, the fact that an almost equal number of Polish Jews and Polish Gentiles died during the war did not avert the intensification of fear, hatred, suspicion, and general divisions between the two communities. There are numerous reasons for this, many of which have been discussed in earlier volumes of *POLIN*.

It should be stressed that the memory of the Holocaust and the Second World War in general is very different for Jews and for Poles. The Jews tend to look at the war (and indeed even at pre-1939 history) through the prism of the *Shoah*, and to stress that their fate was not comparable to that of other groups. In consequence, they resent any attempts to 'relativise' their suffering. The non-Jewish Poles who were decimated during the war, who witnessed the large-scale destruction of their country, particularly the almost total destruction of Warsaw, often do not regard the Jews as a special case. For a variety of reasons, Polish historiography after the war 'polonised' the Holocaust. The Jews were usually described as Poles, which enabled the official historians and propagandists to talk about the six million Poles killed during the war. Technically speaking, this is correct, since the almost three million Polish Jews killed were legally Polish citizens. It was, however, an unreasonable and insensitive claim considering the very different fate which befell the Jews and the Poles. These two nations did not have an equal status during the Nazi occupation of Poland, their destiny – as planned and implemented by the Germans – was different, and in reality they suffered not together, but separately. An overwhelming majority of the Polish Jews had a feeling of being isolated from the rest of society, of being marginalised and degraded. They went to their deaths alone. The reasons for this are complex. As Ewa Berberyusz suggested, some Poles regarded the Job-like state of the Jews as placing them 'beyond the pale of human solidarity'.[23]

A clear example of differing perceptions of Jews and Poles is the case of Auschwitz. This camp, which has become the symbol of the destruction of European Jewry, is not regarded as a particularly 'Jewish' camp by the Poles. They remember that about 340,000 prisoners died in the *KL* Auschwitz, most of whom were Polish. Moreover, when the camp was opened in June 1940 it was intended primarily for the members of the Polish intelligentsia, and was later used also for Soviet POWs. The first Jewish transport arrived in the camp on 26 March 1942, after it had been open for over 18 months. Auschwitz had already come to be known as a place of death for thousands of Poles. This perception does not take into account that, despite the fact that the Jews were sent to the camp much later, they were sent to Auschwitz-Birkenau, a sub-camp which was an *extermination*, and not a concentration camp. Auschwitz-Birkenau was to claim three million Jewish victims. Nevertheless many Poles object to those Jews who perceive Auschwitz as a purely Jewish camp. This incompatibility of views has resulted in a well-known controversy concerning the fate of the Carmelite convent situated in the camp area.[24]

Further examples of different perceptions of events, and also of the attitudes, especially of the Home Army towards the Jews, are discussed in the volume. One such case is illustrated in the exchange between Stanislaus Blejwas and Shmuel Krakowski. In her essay about a meeting between Jewish survivors and their rescuers, Nechama Tec shows how such incompatible views can be held even by the people who were ready to risk their lives to help and those who were helped.

The state of Polish-Jewish debate about the Holocaust, including interesting exchanges following an essay of Jan Błoński, 'The Poor Poles look at the Ghetto' (printed in *POLIN* vol. 2), is comprehensively presented by Antony Polonsky. One can only speculate as to the extent to which Poles felt that the Jews as a nation did not fully belong to Polish society. This notion was encouraged, however, by both Polish and Jewish traditional views of the world, in which Poles and Jews lived side by side but not together, and the subsequent stereotypical views, which in some ways reinforced (even if at the same time distorted) the mythical image, diminishing the sensitivity towards Jewish losses and suffering. It is, however, clear that the 'Jewish problem' did not disappear despite the extermination of almost the entire Jewish population of Poland.

As Landau-Czajka demonstrates, using pre-war material, there were many small radical rightist parties which contained in their xenophobic ideologies a stereotyped view of the Jew-communist (*Żydokomuna*). This view, which was to some extent accepted by the less marginal political parties and by a considerable proportion of the Polish population, seemed to gain some credibility after the Soviet invasion of Poland and the ensuing communist occupation of the eastern borderlands. As Korzec and Szurek admit, the Jewish youth and proletariat played an important ('although not exclusive') rôle in the apparatus of oppression, and implemented the 'class struggle' directed primarily against the Poles with 'revolutionary intransigence'. At the same time, the Jewish community structure was destroyed, and eventually the non-communist political leaders and various socially active Jews were arrested and sent into the Soviet Union by the predominantly Jewish local militia. The Jewish response was not uniformly pro-communist and as a result many Jews were also deported. Korzec and Szurek try to explain why so many Jews were sympathetic to the Soviet Union and why some actively participated in its most objectionable policies. Despite the lack of specific studies of this problem, various sources suggest that, for the majority of Poles, such behaviour was tantamount to treason. The Jews were Polish citizens (even if sometimes treated as second class citizens) and the cooperation of some of them in introducing Stalinist terror in eastern Poland was seen by others as acting against the vital interests of the state and its citizens. As Aleksander Smolar observed:

> In no other European country during the war was there such a dramatic collision of interests and attitudes between the Jews and the nation among which they lived, as during the Soviet occupation 1939–41. Elsewhere Jews had discordant interests with a part of the society around them (for example with collaborators), but in solidarity, in a relationship with the rest of society. In eastern Poland, however, it was the Jews who were perceived as collaborators.[25]

A number of issues emerge from this. First is the problem of how to judge the extensive (although not precisely established) Jewish cooperation with the Soviet officials and the NKVD in 1939–1941. Here Korzec and Szurek object to the use of terms like 'betrayal' and 'collaboration', which many Poles would consider appropriate. Secondly, is the problem of stereotypical generalisation which would blame *all* the Jews for those acts committed by some of them. Thirdly, there is a distinction which should be made between those who supported and joined the communist party and even became its propagandists and activists, and those who were directly involved in the security apparatus. The latter meant participation in arrests and interrogations, and thus torture, deportations, and, in some instances, killing of the civilian population.

Similar situations arose after the war, at a time when one could have expected the emergence of a more positive perception of the Jews by the Poles. As Władysław Bartoszewski comments, the stereotype of the Jew-communist:

> was unexpectedly and spectacularly replenished by the public activity of those Jewish communists who played an important rôle in the so-called security and propaganda apparatus, at the time when the majority of Polish society was inclined to see this activity as action taken in the direct interests of the USSR. A dangerous, and morally absolutely unacceptable tendency was born to indiscriminately burden the Jews in Poland *en masse* with the responsibility for the mass repression of human rights by the apparatus of the new so-called 'people's' authorities and for the misfortune of the nation which felt robbed of its independent status, despite nominally winning the war, as one of the Allies, against Germany. It should be added that we do not see a tendency of principled generalisation regarding members of the security apparatus who were *not* Jewish.

Again, a general, stereotypical view of the 'other', which was supposed to protect Polish values and national cohesion dictated that the brutal torturers of the *UB* and *MBP*[26] could *only* be Jewish, since no Pole could conceivably have done such things to his (and often her) compatriots. This view is challenged in Bartoszewski's article which shows that there was a liberal reaction against the anti-semitic stereotypes. A similar rejection of the stereotypes which foster a sense of collective responsibility can be found in an interview given by Simon Wiesenthal on his eightieth birthday:

> Then the war came. It is at times like these that the lower elements in society surface – the *szmalcownicy* (blackmailers) who would betray Jews for a bottle of vodka or a pair of shoes. That was one aspect. On

the other hand the thirty or forty thousand Jews who survived, survived thanks to help from Poles. This I know. But on the other hand whenever I am talking on this subject I always say that I know what kind of rôle Jewish communists played in Poland after the war. And just as I, as a Jew, do not want to shoulder responsibility for the Jewish communists, I cannot blame 36 million Poles for those thousands of *szmalcownicy*.[27]

The purpose of this volume is to emphasise the importance of studying stereotypes and mutual perceptions. In order fully to understand the complex relationship between Poles and Jews, one must look not only at traditional sources of historical research, but must also take into account the pervasive nature of traditional beliefs and stereotypes of the 'other' which have characterised Polish-Jewish relations for centuries. It is only then that the complex and many-sided nature of this relationship will become clear.

NOTES

1 W. J. McGee, 'Primitive Numbers', *Nineteenth Annual Report of the Bureau of American Ethnology to the Secretary of the Smithsonian Institution*, 1897–98, pp. 825–851.
2 W. G. Sumner, *Folkways and Mores*, 2nd edition, (New York, 1907), p. 13.
3 J. Świętek, 'Zwyczaje i pojęcia prawne ludu nadrabskiego', *Materyjały antropologiczno-archeologiczne i etnograficzne*, 1897, vol. 2, p. 269.
4 W. T. Kosiński, 'Parodye i żarty w rzeczach religijnych', *Materyjały antropologiczo-archeologiczne i etnograficzne*, 1910, vol. 11, p. 119.
5 Rudolf Otto, *The Idea of the Holy*, (London, 1923).
6 Zbigniew Benedyktowicz, 'O niektórych zastosowaniach metody fenomenologicznej w studiach nad religią, symbolem i kulturą', Part I, *Etnografia Polska*, 1980, 24, 2, pp. 9–46, and private communication with the author.
7 G. van der Leeuw, *Religion in essence and manifestation*, vol. 1, (Gloucester, Mass., 1967), p. 139.
8 A. Gieysztor, *Mitologia Słowian* (Warsaw, 1982), pp. 34–35.
9 J. Pitt-Rivers, 'The Stranger, the Guest and the Hostile Host', in J.-G. Peristiany (ed), *Contributions to Mediterranean Sociology*, (Paris, 1968), p. 20.
10 Georg Simmel, 'The Stranger', in K. H. Wolf (ed), *The Sociology of Georg Simmel* (Glencoe, Illinois, 1950), p. 403.
11 L. Stomma, *Campagnes insolites. Paysannerie polonaise et mythes européens* (Paris, 1986), p. 35.
12 B. Schulz, 'The Mythologizing of Reality', in J. Ficowski (ed) *Letters and Drawings of Bruno Schulz with selected prose* (New York, 1988), p. 115.
13 J. S. Wasilewski, 'Symboliczne uniwersum jurty mongolskiej', *Etnografia Polska*, 1977, 21, 1, p. 112.
14 Alina Cała, 'Stosunek swój-obcy w kulturze ludowej', *Etnografia Polska*, 1983, 26, 2, pp. 204–214; see also her article 'The Question of the Assimilation of Jews in the Polish Kingdom (1864–1897)', *POLIN*, vol. 1, (1986), pp. 148–150.
15 W. Lippmann, *Public Opinion* (New York, 1961).
16 Plato, *Rzeczypospolita* (Kraków, 1928), pp. 100–102.

17 Z. Benedyktowicz, 'Kategoria "swój-obcy" w kulturze ludowej, a niektóre problemy identyfikacji etnicznej i kulturowej', paper delivered at a conference on the ethnogenesis of Slavs, Warsaw, October 1978, p. 10.
18 The summary of the characteristic features of stereotypes is a modified version of that included in A. Schaff, 'Stereotyp: Definicja i teoria', *Kultura i społeczeństwo*, 1978, 22, 3, p. 77.
19 M. Opalski, 'Polish-Jewish relations and the January uprising: the Polish perspective', *POLIN*, vol. 1 (1986), pp. 68–80.
20 M. Scheler, *The Ressentiment* (New York, 1961).
21 Ibid., p. 75.
22 E. Mendelsohn, 'Response to Majchrowski', *POLIN*, vol. 3 (1988), pp. 309–313.
23 E. Berberyusz, 'Wina przez zaniechanie', *Tygodnik Powszechny*, 22 February 1987.
24 This particular issue was resolved after lengthy negotiations between representatives of European Jewish organizations and the Catholic Church. The Geneva Declaration of February 1987 containing the compromise reached between the parties was printed in full in *Christian Jewish Relations* (London), vol. 20, no.2 (1987), pp. 56–59.
25 A. Smolar, 'Tabu i niewinność', *ANEKS*, 41/42 (London, 1986), p. 98.
26 *UB – Urząd Bezpieczeństwa* was a political security police; *MBP – Ministerstwo Bezpieczeństwa Publicznego*, (the Ministry of Public Security). After 1956 both were renamed.
27 Interview with Simon Wiesenthal, RFE, 7 January 1989.

IMAGES OF THE JEW IN THE POLISH COMMONWEALTH
Janusz Tazbir

The sources and literature for the theme of this study[1] present particular difficulties. The former consist largely of pamphlets, texts which have to be approached with great care. The same can be said of the literature on the subject, which is often far from objective. With a few commendable exceptions,[2] there is a dearth of studies on attitudes to Jews in the context of attitudes to outsiders in general, although it is clear from many pre-partition Polish sources that the commercial activities of Armenians, Scots, Italians and Germans were often criticized in much the same way. Accusations were not only levelled against Judaism, but also against Islam (practised by Tatars settled in the noble Republic) or supporters of the Reformation who, it was claimed, secretly wanted to destroy both human souls and the Republic itself. The writers who made these accusations were often the same people who were offended by every 'outsider', that is by anyone different from them in language, traditions or religion. The Jews, although settled in Poland since the Middle Ages, represented a classical and principal example of such an outsider.

It was claimed that Jews, by not eating pork and practising circumsion, 'in many of their rites resemble the Turks'. They were also said to follow the wishes of the Turks by abducting Christian children and then taking them to the sultan after circumcising them. Although in the first half of the 18th century fear of Turkish invasion had subsided, the accusation that 'they pass all state secrets to other countries and make pacts with enemies of the Republic . . .'[3] continued to be levelled at Jewish society.

The heretic, the Jew, the witch, all of them, since they had lost contact with God, were considered to be servants of the devil. It is not surprising that there was a proverb that a Jew feared holy water as much as Satan did. It was claimed that all of them used charms, in case of need, to cause personal misfortunes, natural disasters (particularly epidemics), cattle plagues and even Tatar invasions. Gypsies and Tatars who had settled in the Grand Duchy of Lithuania were also accused of practising witchcraft.

It was widely believed, although the clergy denied it, that Jewish practices included drawing blood from the host and from Christian children, because Jews were born blind and could only see after rubbing their eyes with this blood. (In many regions of the noble Republic it was claimed that the inhabitants of Mazowsze were also born blind and could only see nine days later.) Jews were also accused of having an unpleasant smell. This was caused by Jewish people eating large amounts of onions or garlic ('the smell of garlic spreads over a quarter of a mile'). Italian culinary tastes were also criticized, but with the crucial difference that the Italians failed to convert the Poles to their salads, whereas certain elements of Jewish cooking acquired citizen's rights within Polish national cuisine. Despite this, the general image of the Jew was of someone who loved garlic, in much the same way as the present-day image of the Frenchman is someone who eats snails or of the Italian as someone who eats pasta.

The Jews stood out from the rest of the population above all by their dress. The difference in their clothes and features could prompt certain associations, since many paintings showed the devil with a hooked nose and curly hair. Furthermore, Jewish dress was mainly black and this colour also evoked comparison with the forces of hell. In the popular imagination, a heretic was a strange foreigner in German dress. The impression of strangeness was accentuated by the Jews' distinctive hairstyle and particularly their side-locks. These were the principal distinguishing features, as beards were also worn by the Christian population. The Jews also stood out by their specific mannerisms: their nervous gestures, continually emphasizing the spoken word, and their characteristic feverish haste, an inevitable product of the way they lived. The excitable temperament of these voluble southerners always contrasted with the more languid disposition of the Christian population, as did their exaggerated oriental way of speaking.

Their incomprehensible language was dismissed as gibberish, which was found as irritating as the German from which Yiddish had, after all, largely developed. This was linked with a phenomenon which can be described as 'linguistic xenophobia', since almost all languages apart from one's own would be considered inferior, peculiar, ugly to hear or even odious. Latin, of course, was an exception, as this was the language used to communicate with God, as were written Greek and Hebrew, which were known from the Scriptures. However, the spoken Hebrew used during Jewish services was found irritating.

The Jew as a blasphemer, who denied the divinity of Christ, an economic rival, an onerous creditor, accused of arrogance and impudence, also appeared as a buffoon character, clumsy, mangling the Polish language, and willing to suffer any humiliation for even a small gain. He provided the comic element in many plays: in nativity plays 'a Jew and Jewess, and a Jewish dance, were always a source of general and perpetual amusement'.[4] This picture of the Jew was used to show the difference between the value-system recognised (though not always realised in practice) by aristocratic society, and those features considered dominant in the Jewish racial character. High in the scale of values, not only among the *szlachta*, were chivalrous ones: skill in battle, courage, physical strength, and not showing fear even in moments of mortal danger. On the other hand every Jew was generally held to be a weak and cowardly person who fled not only from an armed enemy but even from a dog. A Jew setting off for war was also the subject of jokes, situation comedies and proverbs, just as a servant of the church was.

Even if the *szlachta* sometimes engaged in trade, they never considered this their main activity; in *szlachta* circles it was often repeated emphatically that 'It is a sin and shame to trade'.[5] In the opinion of this estate, every merchant whether Italian, German or Jewish, whether dealing on a large scale or merely from house to house (the latter were mainly Scots) was by nature a swindler, deceiver and criminal. Although it had long been held that religious minorities provided necessary service industries, which the native population either could not or did not wish to undertake, –nevertheless, these alien religious (or racial) groups did not enjoy social approval.

The Jews were widely considered harmful or parasitic, partly because of the belief that their occupations did not deserve to be called 'work'. Only agriculture was worthy of this description, unlike trade, credit deals or 'rocking' over the Talmud. Talmudic studies were doubly discredited: on the one hand Jews were thought to blaspheme against the true God in pursuing these studies, and on the other hand there could be no respect for occupations which involved working with books (the analysis and commentary of texts). The fame which the noble Republic's rabbinical schools enjoyed all over Europe until the mid-17th century was of little interest to anyone. One exception was Szymon Starowolski, who reported in 1632 that the Jews in Brześć, Lithuania, ran 'their own school. It was famous throughout Europe and people come from Italy, Germany, Moravia, and Silesia to study and to advance themselves by becoming rabbis and on returning to their own lands being able to direct synagogues'.[6]

Hostile views of Jews appeared as soon as printing began to develop. But they were found even earlier, as in the 15th century, in Jan Długosz who wrote with approval of bloody pogroms in Prague (1389) and Kraków (1407). The forge where these anti-Jewish pamphlets were fashioned was the 16th-century Polish capital of Kraków. These works not only repeated individual opinions about the Jews, but also created a kind of picture of them as a group, a register of accusations. This served at the same time as a tool for the further development of opinions decidedly hostile towards followers of Judaism. These pamphlets came mainly from burgher circles but were also written by minor clergy or poor *szlachta*. The authors did not include members of the wealthier landowning class, nor better-known writers: Jews do not seem to have interested Jan Kochanowski at all; Mikołaj Rej criticized them, but only in passing. Scholars point out that at a time when there was an incredibly large and varied anti-Jewish literature in Western Europe (particularly Germany), there were strikingly few Polish works containing occasional attacks on Jews or dedicated specifically to them, while the content of those that do exist is also comparatively restrained. Hardly thirty appeared in the years 1588-1668, 90 per cent of which were produced during the reigns of the first two Vasa monarchs (1587-1648). Their contents were unspeakably monotonous, repeating the same arguments.[7]

The principal image was that of the Jew as a dangerous economic rival, increasing his wealth quickly, *per fas et nefas*, at the expense of the Christian. It was no accident that the wave of pamphlets which reached its apogee at the close of the 16th century and in the first half of the 17th century, coincided with the beginning of the decline of Polish towns. In a situation where market outlets for goods were contracting and the chances for trade decreasing, and with restrictions on credit, burgher writers became very sensitive to every sign of competition.

There was general anxiety at the rapid growth of the Jewish population, caused in part by the influx of immigrants from Germany, Italy and even Spain. 'All these exiles have one goal before them, and that is Poland', wrote Majer Bałaban, adding that 'the destruction of any larger commune in the West' meant a growth of the Jewish population in Poznań, Kraków, Lublin, Lwów, or 'even distant Wilno'.[8] Another reason was the way Jews reproduced. As Sebastian Miczyński wrote: none of them dies in war or of the plague; furthermore they marry when they are twelve and so ... multiply rampantly'.[9] At the close of the Middle Ages the Jews made up 0.6 per cent of the population of Poland and Lithuania; in the mid-17th century there were half a million of them and therefore 5 per cent of all inhabitants of the Republic. This figure amounted to 30 per cent of the whole Jewish diaspora. Their economic activity also developed rapidly and was all the more noticeable compared with the general decline in prosperity.

Both in the works dedicated specifically to Jews and in tracts concerning the principal grievances of the noble Republic, we find, almost without exception and repeated with a certain monotony, a list of profitable leases and positions which ought to be removed from Jewish hands. Some of these even included inns and mills. Appropriate proposals were made at the *szlachta sejm* and the regional diets by representatives of the middling, and particularly the poorer *szlachta*, who felt threatened by Jewish financial competition and by the leasing of toll-posts and custom-houses as well as land and salt-mines. Jews were also accused of counterfeiting and exporting money, of practising usury at the expense of the Christian population, of systematically evading civic taxes and military service.

It should be mentioned that while the regional diets often simply reported the complaints of the towns about economic competition from the Jewish tradesmen and craftsmen, they also protected Jews, condemning the sporadic pogroms, and granted Jews privileges such as trade with the East.

The *szlachta* moreover cannot have been very concerned about the Jews taking over commerce and crafts or their activities in the area of free trade of which the burgher writers complained so often and with such passion. The latter described the particular ways in which Jews brought about the ruin of Christian master-craftsmen and so on. However, the Hungarian Martin Csombor, who travelled round Poland at the beginning of the 17th century, wrote: 'The Jews are very active in trade which, though sometimes causing losses for the burghers, is also convenient for the latter, as one can buy any commodity from a Jew, so that it has become common to say: "If you can not find something at a Jew's, you will search for it in vain elsewhere".'[10] Christian competitors obviously had a different opinion of this 'convenience'.

The *szlachta* viewed foreigners in a similar way to that in which Polish burghers regarded the Jews. Foreigners, thanks to the protection of the king, seemed to wrest profitable leases and well-paid posts from deserving citizens and, furthermore, ruined them by dishonestly trading in luxury goods (at which the Italians supposedly excelled). The only difference was that the king supported foreigners to the detriment of the *szlachta* whereas the noble gentlemen – it was claimed – protected Jews at the expense of the lower sections of society, the poor and oppressed Christians. The latter 'must revere them (the Jews), respect and even bow down to the ground before them when requesting something from them', claimed the Jesuit Mateusz Bembus.[11]

Just as the *szlachta* showed their xenophobia in criticizing the foreigners coming to court, and thus indirectly the monarch who protected them, anti-magnate or even anti-*szlachta* feelings were also expressed by writing about Jewish competitors 'lording it' on magnates' estates. The basic contradiction within these various positions came from the fact that for the burgher estate (the Germans, Ruthenians and Armenians as well as Poles) the Jews were a harmful element in economic life, while the magnates or wealthy *szlachta* saw Jewish activities fitting into the model of the state envisaged by its noble owners. For in their eyes they alone made up the nation: the role of the other sections of society was purely one of service. The *szlachta* was, on the whole, indifferent to the descent, language or faith of the people who sold them goods or worked the land, especially since neither the peasants nor the burghers were entirely of Polish descent. The magnates willingly employed those who were dependent only on them.

And the Catholic clergy could rage in vain that Jews 'are a nation dear to many lords'. 'Who has easiest access to the lord? The Jew. Who is most trusted at the manor house? The Jew', wrote Szymon Starowolski.[12]

The Jews were necessary to the magnates and to the *szlachta* as tenants, innkeepers, moneylenders and merchants. The Jew represented an indispensable intermediary in the economic system of the time: he provided large and small amounts of credit and he helped the landowner in many trading activities. He also frequently kept him informed of what was happening in the wider world, shaved and nursed him, and played at his receptions and weddings (Jewish barbers, surgeons and musicians appear in many memoirs, and have also been immortalised in paintings and engravings). In a variety of ways the Jew helped overcome the isolation of thousands of *szlachta* farms, scattered throughout the huge noble Republic. In the eyes of the magnate or wealthy member of the *szlachta*, the Jew was sometimes an irritating creature – more often simply funny –, but indispensable none the less. The Jews acted as intermediaries in the feudal exploitation of the peasant. Above all they could be blamed for the various levies imposed by the magnates and *szlachta* on their subjects.

It is not strange, then, that Jews were found intolerable by the Orthodox and Ruthenian peasantry in the Ukrainian lands belonging to the Republic. Conditions prevailing there 'allowed Jews to conduct forms of exploitation impossible elsewhere'.[13] In some areas they apparently even leased sources of church income, namely payments for christenings, weddings and funerals. Economic conflicts overlapped with racial and religious differences; thus the image of the Jew in Ukrainian popular writing of the 17th to 18th centuries is a far more hostile one than in Polish literature of the same period. Equally the great Cossack Uprising under Bohdan Chmielnicki (1648) and the rebellions of the so-called *hajdamaki* (Kolivshczyzna) in the following century, were conducted under the slogans of slaughtering the *Lachy* (masters), Jews, and Catholic priests, that is those groups held responsible for political, economic and religious oppression. The Jewish settlements in the east of the noble Republic paid for their close economic cooperation with the *szlachta* and magnates with thousands of victims (in the mid-17th century 100,000 Jews were to die, victims of the Cossack knife and lance). Mass pogroms erupted in those lands vacated by the Polish armies and authorities.

The image of the Jew held by the magnates and *szlachta* was opposed by the most radical writers, who had a vision of the Republic without Jews whose activities harmed the whole state materially (for example by counterfeiting and ruining money and taking it out of the country). In the credit sphere – they wrote – Christians could easily take the place of the Jews or special institutions could be established to do so (*montes pietatis*). The most radical views came primarily from burgher circles; very few members of the *szlachta* demanded the expulsion of the Jews from Poland.

Some writers, however, demanded that they should be made to work on the land. Clerical writers hoped that in this way the Jewish population could be gradually persuaded to be christened. These arguments were welcomed in burgher circles, where Jews were called 'cruel beasts', 'locusts', 'venomous reptiles and foul vermin'.

Both Polish publicists and foreigners travelling in the noble Republic believed the Jews made up a kind of separate estate because of the privileges they enjoyed. The Jewish settlements did indeed enjoy considerable legal autonomy, guaranteed and observed by the state authorities and local feudal lords.

Most accusations levelled against Jewish merchants, artisans or moneylenders, tended to owe more to class criticism than to anti-semitism. This trend emerged constantly in feudal society, and a much larger volume could be compiled from the criticisms of peasants, burghers and *szlachta* than that produced seventy years ago by Kazimierz Bartoszewicz on anti-semitism in pre-partition Polish literature.[14]

From the 16th century the image of the Jew in Polish literature was linked with a particular social issue, although it was not possible at the time to identify it. Although it was known that the population was steadily increasing (which caused some anxiety), this did not seem then to be the most important issue in the multi-racial Republic. The most crucial cause for concern was the obvious decline in the overall economic situation. The signs could be read by everyone and easily enumerated, but the causes were far less clear. Burgher writers in particular explained the decline partly by the growing role of Jews in the economy. The more this economic decline increased, the more it was written about and explained by the activities of a specific group rather than through particular economic mechanisms. The Jew became a 'scapegoat', a guilty party (if not the principal culprit), for the economic decline of the noble Republic. With every subsequent financial crisis the ones chiefly to blame were identified as foreigners, more frequently Jews than, for example, Italians, who also managed the mint.

Public opinion did not consider Jewish innkeepers, tenants, moneylenders or merchants the descendants of David, Solomon, Jeremiah, let alone of the apostles, the Holy Family and Christ. They had crucified him and were still blind to the light of true faith. They were ungrateful sinners, and, for this, God, 'in whose eyes nothing is more ugly than ingratitude', had turned away from them.[15] What is worse, the Jews continued to repeat the deicide they had committed centuries ago. They profaned the host of the living God and murdered innocent children who were the image of the Saviour (hence the frequent motif of crucifixion of the victim in trials over alleged ritual murders).

The memory of their role as murderers of Christ was revived in presentations of the Passion during Holy Week, or in works on the

Suffering of Christ. In the second half of the 17th century there was an increase in the number of paintings representing the judgement of Christ and his suffering. The members of the Sanhedrin and those responsible were usually portrayed dressed as wealthy Jewish merchants. In one of these paintings (in the cloisters of the Dominican Fathers at Janów Podlaski) the Jewish wise men are shown plotting against the Christian faith. Anti-Jewish features were also present in paintings depicting Christ's casting out of the merchants from the temple. The message was clearly aimed 'first at merchants, but also at Jews engaged in trade and usury'.[16]

The regional diet in Łęczyca in 1669 even demanded that the Jews should be held collectively responsible for desecrating the host and for ritual murders: all Jews from one province should be punished by expulsion and the confiscation of their property. Severe punishments were also demanded by other regional diets. Belief in these accusations led to trials described in many publications. They served to develop an image of the Jew as a dangerous enemy of all Christians, whose blood was supposedly used for the practice of his religion. These beliefs encouraged hanging paintings in churches and monasteries (e.g. in Sandomierz cathedral, the Bernardine Fathers in Kalwaria Zebrzydowska), showing scenes of ritual murder, woodcuts of similar design and coffins depicting the remains of murdered children. There were, however, no written works on this theme.

Similar propaganda was received best in the towns; there above all (and not on the estates of the *szlachta* or on royal property) anti-Jewish trials took place. The crucial role played by economic antagonism is shown, because in some instances these cases preceded the expulsion of the Jewish population from a town. The *Sejm* and other authoritative bodies tried to prevent these accusations: only royal and *sejm* courts, not municipal courts, could examine them. However, this was not adhered to in practice. Sigismund III in 1618 banned the publication and distribution of Sebastian Miczyński's pamphlet *Zwierciadło Korony Polskiej* (Mirror of the Polish Crown), as a work which could, by discussing ritual murder, provoke religious outrage and anti-Jewish rioting.

For three hundred years (from the 16th to 18th century) very few authors attempted to present the image of the Jews in a better light, or even to show any understanding for their situation. However, in 1517 Maciej Miechowita had written that in Lithuania or Russia one meets many Jews, 'not the exploitative types found in Christian countries, however, but working farmers and great merchants, often running customs and tax offices'. He had also praised them for taking up 'the humanistic sciences, astronomy and medicine'.[17] At the beginning of the following century Jan of Kijan (in the poem *Lichwa polska* [Polish usury]) had argued that Jews practising usury were less insensitive than their Christian colleagues. Similarly,

Daniel Bratkowski (1697) had written that in collecting their percentage the Christian pupils outdid their Jewish teachers.

In popular literature one can also find some traces of compassion towards Jews persecuted by students. These may be rare but they do appear in dramas such as P. Baryka's *Z chłopa król* (From Peasant to King) (1637) or Fr D. Neserowicz's *Świat na opak wywrócony* (The World Turned Upside Down) (1663), where Jews demand compensation from the students, while berating them for stealing and participating in pogroms. Similarly, Pęski, a Jesuit and member of the *szlachta*, in his quarrel with those who called the Republic a paradise for Jews, wrote that he himself would flee such a paradise if he had to go about in tattered clothes, to buy protection from persecution or to be victimized by schoolboys.

These voices begin to increase under the gradual influence of the Enlightenment. Bishop Józef Andrzej Załuski, for example, appealed for a whole nation not to be blamed for a crime (the crucifixion of Christ) committed by individuals centuries ago. Józef Pawlikowski, one of the most vociferous and influential polemicists of the time, warned against imitating the treatment meted out to Jews earlier by the fanatical Spaniards. The Jews were also defended by such journals appearing in the second half of the 18th century as *Monitor* or P. Świtkowski's *Pamiętnik Polityczny i Historyczny*.

In the noble Republic Jews had become, as it were, a part of the human landscape, one of the most permanent colours in the palate of a multiracial community. In the second half of the 18th century the painter's brush incorporated them into the portrayal of the general ruin of Polish towns (B. Vogel did this with great panache, cf. the view of the market square in Olkusz and other works by this artist), who depicted these wretched abodes, worthy of 'the peasant and the Jew', to quote the words of the poet, Ignacy Krasicki. Immortalised in paintings and engravings also were the Jewish inn and its owners, the synagogue with the faithful returning home, Jewesses dressed for holy days and Jewish children outside the *heder* and, finally, Kazimierz near Kraków, which was inhabited mainly by Jews. We owe most of these works to the talent of Piotr Norblin who frequently, with obvious pleasure and the eye of a true reporter, portrayed Jews trading, haggling fiercely with noble or peasant.

Foreigners visiting Poland were surprised at the size of the Jewish population (some even wrote exaggeratedly that it reached 2 million), their privileges, which gave them greater freedom than 'anywhere else in the world except Holland and England', and their dress and traditions which differed completely from those in Western Europe. Some above all noted the wealth of Jewish merchants or the flourishing state of their affairs, while others only saw poor Jews, dressed in black tattered robes. Some recognised their indispensability in the economic system of the noble Republic, while others blamed them for the economic ruin of the state, the decline of the towns and the universal drunkenness (particularly among the peasants), and accused them of benefiting from commercial fraud, usury and swindling. In sum, their opinions largely matched the image of the Jew in Polish sources. It should be remembered, however, that foreign travellers used the works of Polish writers (the marginalia of foreign accounts refer to them), and they must also surely have discussed the theme with native Poles. Paradoxically, the travellers in Poland stressed that on Saturday evenings only Jews remained sober (indeed Jews were the only group in the Polish Commonwealth whom nobody accused of drunkenness).

Jewish omnipresence, their monopoly of most areas of economic life (crafts as well as trade) and their close links with the *szlachta* were noted by almost all foreigners. This, in their view, reflected badly on the Jews as well as on the Poles themselves, or rather on the 'fecklessness and apathy of the *szlachta*', 'the oppressed peasant', and the inertia of the native burgher class. All these indulged in drink and allowed themselves to be exploited, but could not conduct trade themselves, run inns or engage in credit activities, areas where English, French and German merchants had not allowed themselves to be ousted by foreign immigrants.[18]

Returning to the image of the Jew held by the Poles themselves, it should be mentioned that it was formed through economic contacts and religious conflicts, those areas where they appeared rivals. The stereotype was developed therefore in very unfavourable circumstances, in the area of contact between a merchant (or moneylender) and his client (or debtor). Jews were not encountered, however, in political life, in their traditional or family life, as might be the case, for example, with the *szlachta*, who belonged to various Christian denominations. Furthermore, only a tiny percentage of Jews was Polonized and assimilated into the nationalities then living in the noble Republic. Whereas in the 16th and 17th centuries Germans, Ruthenians, Armenians and Lithuanians, and even the Tatar *szlachta* living in the Grand Duchy began to be assimilated, the Jews – apart from a few individuals – remained completely resistant to this process. It was not until the second half of the 18th century that the so-called Frankists began the assimilation of Polish Jewry; their descendants played a significant role in the cultural history of the 19th century. The promoters of the Polish Enlightenment were also moving in the same direction. On the one hand they demanded the Polonization of the Jewish population by gradually limiting publications in Hebrew, abandoning distinctions in dress, and introducing compulsory education and even military service. On the other, they demanded that Jews should be productive (which involved removing them from usury and trade and directing them towards work in agriculture and manufacturing). This was to be accompanied by lifting all legal barriers dividing the Jews from the rest of society. No follower of the Enlightenment favoured expelling the Jews from Poland. There was also anger at their persecution at the hands of town mobs. 'How can we suffer this barbaric vestige of older practices and allow this banditry which brings shame on a great nation and age', wrote Piotr Świtkowski in *Monitor* (1783).[19] Accusations of ritual murder or desecration of the host also became less and less frequent at this time.

In conclusion, let us try to discover the image of the Poles and the noble Republic which appeared in the consciousness and literature of its Jewish inhabitants. It is difficult to give a complete answer without studying Hebrew writings. We know, from much later translations, that Polish tolerance was praised, a tolerance which allowed Jews expelled from beyond the Warta, Vistula and Dniepr to find food and freedom of worship. It was for this reason that David Gans, a Jewish chronicler from Prague, mourned the 'righteous' King Sigismund Augustus. The Hebrew poets often took up the same theme, and the famous religious polemicist, Izaak ben Abraham of Troki, contrasted the religious tolerance at the end of the 16th century in the 'state without stakes' with the religious persecution in Western Europe. He wrote that in England the 'papists' were treated with such cruelty that it 'made one's hair stand on end', and that in France and Spain Protestants were dealt with in the same way. This was God's punishment, for all three states had once persecuted Jews, and then expelled them completely. In Poland, however, the followers of Judaism were protected. 'And that is why God has granted this land great power and such peace that those of different faiths are not enemies and do not fight each other'.[20] In the mid-16th century Moses Isserles, an outstanding Jewish scholar who found refuge in Kraków, wrote to one of his pupils that it was better to be satisfied with a piece of dry bread and live peacefully in Poland than to live in Germany where Jews were surrounded by universal hatred.

A hostile image of the Jew is also found in French, German and English writing of the 16th to 18th centuries; Polish literature was not therefore an exception. Furthermore, as far as the *szlachta* was concerned, and they were the ones with whom Jews had most contact, it was more a question of anti-Judaism than anti-semitism, if the question arose. As soon as the disciples of Moses were christened they were regarded as citizens with full rights; for as soon as they did so they ceased to be Jews. Converts were not reminded of their non-Christian descent, as was the case in Spain, for example. Moreover, in the Grand Duchy of Lithuania between 1588–1764, Jewish converts were made members of the *szlachta*, although no statute provided for this for burghers or peasants. Polish members of the *szlachta* knew that there were many assimilated newcomers in their midst, ranging from Christians whose mother tongue was German, Lithuanian or Ruthenian, to former adherents of Islam (the Tatars) or Judaism (the Jews). The *szlachta* was unconcerned about this; at the most it was occasionally mentioned in anecdotes about new Christians. The burghers looked on these matters rather differently, writing with hostility about the Frankists.

To conclude, the image of the Jew throughout the three centuries covered in this study is a very stable one, a feature of all stereotypes. This was because of the influence of the Church, which did not revise its approach to the Jewish question until the 20th century, and because of the inertia and size of Jewish centres. In the 16th and 17th centuries the noble Republic held the largest concentration of Jews outside the Ottoman Empire, and on a scale unprecedented in Western Europe: 44 per cent of the Jewish diaspora lived in the lands of the former Polish state in 1800. This must have had definite repercussions on attitudes to Jews; the popular view was that of someone who was an outsider, and such a person is never represented very positively in any country. Neither the Reformation nor the Enlightenment brought about any radical changes: the only difference lay in the fact that the future of the Jews was perceived in a different way from the traditional view. In the 16th and 17th centuries Catholics and Protestants hoped that at least some Jews would be gradually absorbed into society through conversion, whereas in the following century it was not hoped there would be racial assimilation. However, no one approached the problem from a wider social perspective: arguments for granting the Jewish population equal rights were not broached until the 19th century.

NOTES

1 This article is a shortened version of a longer study in German ('Das Judenbild der Polen im 16-18 Jahrhundert', *Acta Poloniae Historica*, vol. 50 (1984), pp. 29-56) and French ('Les Juifs vus par l'opinion polonais des XVIe, XVIIe et XVIIIe siècle', *Literary Etudes in Poland*, vol. 19 (1988), pp. 41-77).
2 These include the excellent collection of studies by A. Hertz, *Żydzi w kulturze polskiej* (Paris, 1961) (particularly pp. 224 ff.: 'Obraz Żyda'). Cf. also J. Goldberg, 'Poles and Jews in the 17th and 18th Centuries. Rejection or Acceptance', *Jahrbücher für Geschichte Osteuropas*, vol. 22 (1974), no.2, and M. Fuks, Z. Hoffman and J. Tomaszewski, *Die Juden in Polen. Geschichte und Kultur* (Warsaw, 1982).
3 W. Konopczyński, *Polscy pisarze polityczni XVIII w.* (Warsaw, 1966), p. 30.
4 J. St. Bystroń, *Dzieje obyczajów w dawnej Polsce, wiek XVI- XVIII*, vol. 1 (Kraków, 1932), pp. 65-5.
5 J. Tazbir, *Świat panów Pasków. Eseje i studia* (Łódź, 1986), p. 217. Ibid. 'Żydzi w opinii staropolskiej', pp. 213 ff.
6 Sz. Starowolski, *Polska albo opisanie położenia Królestwa Polskiego* (Warsaw, 1976), p. 88.
7 Cf. D. Tollet, 'La litérature antisémite polonaise de 1588 à 1668', *Revue française d'histoire du livre*, no. 14 (1977) and in a separate edition (Bordeaux, 1977).
8 M. Bałaban, 'Umysłowość i moralność żydowstwa polskiego XVI w.', *Kultura staropolska* (Kraków, 1932), p. 607.
9 S. Miczyński, *Zwierciadło Korony Polskiej*... (Kraków, 1618), p. 3.

10 M. Csombor, *Podróż po Polsce* (Warsaw, 1961), p. 101.
11 M. Bembus, *Kometa, to jest pogrożka z nieba* (Kraków, 1619), p. 36.
12 Sz. Starowolski, *Wady staropolskie*. A shortened version of the work: *Robak sumienia złego* . . . (Kraków, 1853), pp. 86-7.
13 J. St. Bystroń, op. cit., vol. 1, p. 68.
14 K. Bartoszewicz, *Antysemityzm w literaturze polskiej XV-XVII w.* (Warsaw, 1914).
15 J. Tazbir, op. cit., p. 229.
16 M. Gutowski, *Komizm w polskiej sztuce gotyckiej* (Warsaw, 1973), pp. 169 and 203.
17 M. Miechowita, *Opis Sarmacji azjatyckiej i europejskiej*, (Wrocław, 1972), pp. 62-3 and 71.
18 Cf. J. Tazbir, op. cit., pp. 235-7.
19 W. Smoleński, *Przewrót umysłowy w Polsce wieku XVIII* (Warsaw, 1979), p. 386.
20 M. Bersohn, *Tobiasz Kohn, lekarz polski w XVII wieku* (Kraków, 1872), pp. 32-33.

A MINORITY VIEWS THE MAJORITY: JEWISH ATTITUDES TOWARDS THE POLISH LITHUANIAN COMMONWEALTH AND INTERACTION WITH POLES*

M. J. Rosman

The behaviour of the various subordinate minorities of the Polish Lithuanian Commonwealth towards Polish hegemony covers the entire theoretical spectrum: from rebellious through resigned, to accepting, to assimilationist.[1] At one extreme are the Germans, Scots, and others who reached an accommodation with Polish domination that resulted in their eventual assimilation and integration. At the other extreme are the Arians, whose failure to submit to the demands of subordinate status led in 1667 to their expulsion. Somewhat different was the response of the Cossacks and, at times, the Ruthenian peasants. The posture they maintained was frequently one of antagonism and conflict, and even led to militant secessionist tendencies as expressed in various uprisings.

The Jews' position was between the extremes. Polish society supported the Jews' communal institutions, tolerated their cultural differences, and offered opportunities for successful articulation with the general economic order. In exchange, the Jews resigned themselves to domination and, by and large, remained within the bounds of the economic, social, and political roles that the majority defined for them. Significantly, the first act of the umbrella institution of Jewish autonomy, the Council of Four Lands, was intended to guarantee that Jewish economic activity would not infringe on the prerogatives of Poles. This decree, issued in 1580, forbade Jews to lease royal concessions in the western parts of Poland. The probable reason for the Council taking such action was the fear that competition with Polish noblemen for these leases might elicit a reaction that would endanger all Jews.[2]

* This article, based on a lecture I delivered at the Conference on Polish-Jewish History held in Jerusalem in February 1988, was completed during my tenure as a visitor in the Department of History at the University of Michigan. I would like to express my gratitude to the Department and the University for their hospitality.

The Jews were generally supporters of the political *status quo*. As I have pointed out elsewhere, Jewish leaders were convinced that the graciousness of kings and nobility was what guaranteed their security and prosperity.[3] They regarded the Polish kings as the guarantors of the Jews' safety and freedom and generally perceived their interests as being linked with those of the king or local magnate.[4] The clearest expressions of Jewish support for the Polish political order come from the period of the Chmielnicki uprising (1648–57). The Jews were not passive observers waiting for the accursed houses of the protagonists to be put in order so that Jewish suffering would cease; rather, they were active allies of the Commonwealth. In Tulczyń, for example, according to the Jewish chronicler, Meir of Szczebrzeszyn,[5] writing no later than 1650:

> About 600 courageous men, the nobles, barricaded themselves in the fortress. Approximately 2,000 of the scattered sheep [the Jews], accurate marksmen, joined them. The noblemen received them and they joined together, making an honest covenant between them; each would help the other. The noblemen were deployed inside the fortress; the Jews stood around on the battlements, on guard with bow and arrow. When the smouldering butts [Cossacks and Tartars] attacked, they shot at them with arrows and flames. The Greeks recoiled in fear and trembling and the noblemen and Jews chased them, smiting a mighty blow against the rebels.

The Polish anti-rebel forces, according to Frank Sysyn, 'depicted the revolt as a bloody *jacquerie* against society and civilization. They condemned the Cossacks as the driving force of the revolt and portrayed the uprising as a rebellion of subjects against their lawful masters.'[6] The Jews certainly shared this view. Obviously, it was in the interests of the Jews to support the *Rzeczpospolita* against those who had targeted them, along with the Polish side, as objects of their resentment. What is interesting, however, is how the Jews explained their own support of the Poles to themselves. For the most part, they did not see the alliance in pragmatic terms, but supported the Poles because right was on the Polish side. While some of them expressed awareness of the heavy price the feudal yoke exacted from the Ruthenian peasantry,[7] they still regarded the existing structure of the Commonwealth as right and proper. In the Jews' opinion, the rebels who intended to create a new order were clearly in the wrong. As the chronicler Shabbetai HaKohen asserted, the Ruthenian villains (whom he also styles 'Greeks' and 'Cossacks'), were 'a contemptible nation ... vile, base, unreliable and vacuous ... Peasants and farmers gathered from near and far and raised their hand against the king, his noblemen and retainers, a great and powerful nation, like the giants'.[8] R. Meir of Szczebrzeszyn was no less hostile in his assessment. 'Cruel men, the sons of cruel men, as they have been for generations ... their words appear sincere, but their intentions (are) to spill blood in stealth and to destroy cities ... They all revolted; betraying their Catholic masters ... Slaves ruled over masters'.[9] Gabriel Shusberg's reaction to Jan Kazimierz's predicament at Zbaraż and subsequent compromise settlement with the Cossacks at Zborów would have been appropriate from an anti-rebel nobleman:

> But the King, the royal officials and the noblemen were forced to fulfil all of [the rebels'] desires, handing over a large ransom. Then, after an agreement was reached, the Greek [i.e. Cossack] hetman and Tartar king returned in great honour to their land; they had almost attained sovereignty. What humiliation and disgrace.[10]

Jews not only supported the Polish political constellation. Some also displayed an interest in Polish history. David Ganz, a German Jew who had studied in Poland as a young man, wrote a chronicle of world and Jewish history that was published in Prague in 1592, which treats Poland as a major power and its political history as an important part of world history.[11] Nathan Hannover, a Jewish chronicler writing in the early 1650s about the roots of Cossack Polish antagonism, displayed a fairly sophisticated understanding of the far-reaching changes in Polish society wrought by Zygmunt III, champion of the Counter-Reformation. Hannover related how Zygmunt III abandoned the tradition of treating noblemen equally, regardless of their religious faith, and favoured the Catholics; he also attempted to induce the Ruthenian nobility to abandon their faith and embrace Catholicism. Subsequently, the Ruthenians were impoverished and relegated to a wretched and lowly status. The exceptions to this were the registered Cossacks charged with protecting the south-eastern border against the Tatars, in return for which they were granted special privileges.[12]

The Jewish chronicler most familiar with Polish history, government, and society at this time was the eighteenth-century wine merchant, Dov Ber of Bolechów. Despite certain *lacunae*, he was acquainted with such events as the post-Altranstadt machinations involving the supporters of King Augustus II and their rivals supporting Leszczyński; Count Poniatowski's rise to power; Moscow's intervention in favour of the election of Augustus II; Frederick William of Prussia's role in aggravating Polish inflation; and the Confederation of Bar. In the light of such knowledge, it is hardly surprising that he also understood the workings of such Polish institutions as the *Sejm* and High Tribunal at Lublin.[13] He held the High Tribunal in great esteem:

> This Tribunal was the supreme court over all the courts which existed in each *starostwo*. Each province and district used to elect a

number of wealthy noblemen, learned in the law, who assembled at Warsaw, the capital of Poland, and there the Diet chose from among them men known for their high character, fear of God, love of truth and incorruptibility.[14]

While the Jews may have generally supported the Polish political configuration, and individuals among them may have taken an interest in Polish history and institutions, for the most part Jewish political involvement was marginal. There were, it is true, some instances of successful Jewish lobbying at the *Sejm* and regional *Sejmiki* (dietines), but this was in an attempt to defeat specifically anti-Jewish legislation or to prevent an increase in the taxes on Jews.[15] The Jews may have shown political astuteness in securing their own interests,[16] but they held no formal political positions and played no defined role.[17]

The Jews were resigned to their relative exclusion from the formal political process before partition and never attempted to do more than lobby behind the scenes. By the eighteenth century, however, in the classic fashion of subordinate minority groups, discontent began to be apparent in their literature and folklore. The Jews, like most minority groups, tended to interpret the political history of their country ethnocentrically.[18] Thus, typically, the Jews who called the Polish kings 'hasid' were motivated to do so by their favourable assessment of the royal policy on Jews. Shabbetai Hakohen, for example, said that Władysław IV was worthy of being numbered among the righteous because of his graciousness and fidelity to the Jews.[19] But not all Jews held favourable views of the Commonwealth. Dov Ber of Bolechów, for example, claimed that the partitions of Poland came as a punishment for the dissolution of the Council of Four Lands:

> Then the Polish people and their kingdom were deprived of all honour, and the verse was fulfilled: 'And I will lay vengeance upon Edom . . . by the hand of my people Israel'; that is to say that as they had dealt with Israel so were they dealt with. All the honour of their country was taken away from them, and they were enslaved forever. And so perish our foes who denounce us![20]

Jewish fantasies also embroidered their own role in the political process: the Polish government held the power – legitimately, one might add – and Jews wanted to share in it. The most famous example of this type of thinking is the legend of a Jew called Saul Wahl, which was first written down in 1733 but is probably much older. According to the various versions of this legend, Wahl, who won the admiration of the *Sejm*, became Polish regent for a day; while ruling justly over the Poles, he instituted legislation favourable to the Jews, and finally crowned Zygmunt III king of Poland.[21] Similarly, later Hasidic legend asserted that the founder of

Hasidism, the Baal Shem Tov, had intervened to assure victory for a cossack ('Greek') ruler over a Tatar ('Ishmaelite') in order to prevent suffering for the Jews.[22] Another Hasidic legend reported that the election of Stanisław August Poniatowski was merely a confirmation of a choice made by the Maggid of Międzyrzecz in consultation with R. Pinhas of Korzec.[23]

Pinhas of Korzec (d. 1790) claimed that the Jews had a stake in preserving Poland because 'the exile (in Poland) is less bitter than anywhere else'. Thus, as long as R. Nahman Horodenker prayed to keep the Russians out of Poland, the power of his prayer was sufficient to assure it. But when in 1764 R. Nahman left for the Land of Israel, the Russians succeeded in crossing the Dniepr in order to act against the Confederation of Bar. After that, R. Pinhas himself worked to limit the effects of partition; only following his death was Poland completely dismembered.[24]

A clear instance of Polish Jews' insistence on their central importance in the country, despite the apparent reality, is to be found in a statement made by Rabbi Levi Yitshak of Berdichev to his followers in the late eighteenth century:

> Know that all of the nations that were created were created for the sake of Israel, for the good of Israel; for sometimes, for some reason, good comes to Israel from the nations. Thus their sustenance is from a holy source; were it not that there is some good [that comes from them] they would not have been created at all ... And know that each ruler of the nations must serve our God who is the God of gods and the Lord of lords ...[25]

The fact that Dov Ber of Bolechów and Pinhas of Korzec held different attitudes towards the partition of Poland raises another subject for examination: Jewish attitudes towards Poland and their opinions on how Jews should interact with Poles were not monolithic. It has long been accepted that Polish attitudes towards Jews in the pre-partition period varied with social groups. Thus, although certain religiously-based and other Jewish stereotypes were widespread, Jacob Goldberg, for one, has demonstrated that the stances of magnates, *szlachta*, townsmen, peasants, and high and low clergy each bore characteristically distinguishing features.[26] By contrast, Jewish historians portraying the Jewish attitude towards Poles under the Commonwealth have tended to postulate a general position. Bernard Weinryb, for example, although recognising negative reactions among Polish Jews holds that the prevailing attitude among at least the élite of the Jewish community, was one of sympathy with the Poles and trust, confidence, and even pride in Poland.[27] Jacob Katz subsumes Polish Jewry under the general rubric of Ashkenazic Jewry, thereby implying that there was no attitude towards the Gentiles around them particular to Polish Jews. He posits, rather, that the attitude of Ashkenazi Jewry towards all non-Jews was directly linked to the norms of Jewish religious law, and it was this that resulted in the Jewish stance of isolation and estrangement throughout Central and Eastern Europe.[28]

In my opinion, the distance between these apparently opposed viewpoints can be bridged if one concedes that in the Jewish community, there was not a single 'Jewish attitude' towards Poles, but rather a spectrum of attitudes, which depended on their holders' vantage points within society no less than they derived from traditional norms. While on the face of it this proposition seems logical, the scarcity of Jewish sources that document attitudes makes it difficult to substantiate. Only in the eighteenth century does one find sufficient sources to permit the identification of different approaches to Poles on the part of Jews from different sectors of the Jewish community.

The first is the best known and represents the view of what sociologists might term the 'accommodation-leadership', those charged with liaising with the majority.[29] In the case of the Polish-Jewish interaction, these were the *kahal* leaders. Their attitude towards the Polish environment can be seen in the legislation that they passed and which appears in the communal record books that have survived. One of the important features of their legislation was prohibitions on individuals from entering into politically or economically significant relationships with Poles.[30] These prohibitions demonstrate that their authors were convinced that powerful Poles and Polish institutions represented a potential threat to the stability of the Jewish community and the prerogatives of the autonomous Jewish institutions. They never challenged the legitimacy of Polish authority; their approach was to accept Polish authority as a given, to negotiate with it when possible, but to minimize its impact (and preserve their own status) by restricting contact between Jews and Poles or Polish institutions.[31] Loans, tax payments, business partnerships, adjudication before non-Jewish authorities, *arenda* leases and political lobbying efforts were all to be mediated, or at least approved by the *kahal*. By limiting contact to routine bureaucratic channels, Polish influence on the Jewish community could be anticipated, controlled, and reduced to the minimum extent possible.

A different approach was advocated, in the eighteenth century at least, by some who were not part of the *kahal* establishment and managed to establish close relationships with powerful Poles (and after partition with Germans, Austrians, and Russians). People like Dov Ber of Bolechów, or later Moshe Wasserzug, saw close relationships with powerful non-Jews as potentially advantageous, rather than potentially dangerous. All that was necessary, they said, was to keep one's wits about one and know how to deal properly with such people. Both men took obvious pride in their relationships with powerful Gentiles – relationships which, while based on utilitarian considerations, clearly acquired other significance. Dov Ber goes to great lengths to impress upon his readers – his family – how he had genuinely friendly relations with certain noblemen, while several Jews cheated him and caused him trouble. Far from avoiding relations with Poles, then, such men were eager to develop economic, social, and even cultural ties with them.[32]

More complex than either the attitudes of the official leadership or the individuals with special relations with Poles was the attitude expressed in early Hasidic sources. *Shivhei Ha-Besht* (first published in 1814) is the earliest collection of oral traditions concerning the activities of the founder of Hasidism, Israel ben Eliezer Baal Shem Tov (died 1760) and some of his disciples.[33] It is imbued with a sense of the demonic character of non-Jews and the dangers inherent in encounters with them. One of the most common motifs is how in situations where contacts between Jew and non-Jew – Cossack, robber, nobleman, peasant, priest, or sorcerer – could result in the victimization of the Jew, the Baal Shem Tov's intervention could assure a happy ending.[34]

Alongside the belief in the non-Jews' demonic nature and the fear and mistrust of Gentile society, some of these tales hint at a very different evaluation of the theological-moral standing of the non-Jew. According to Jacob Katz, given the religious rivalry between Judaism and Christianity, the members of each group adopted a double standard of morality towards each other. There was no religious rationale for treating outsiders according to ethical norms. Jews frowned on mistreating or cheating non-Jews not on moral grounds but from enlightened self-interest: such behaviour would bring Jews into disrepute and result in sanctions or even violence being brought to bear against them.[35]

In *Shivhei Ha-Besht* other considerations seem to come into play. In one story, the Baal Shem Tov's disciple Jacob Joseph of Polnoye has a dream in which he enters a palace in paradise. There Satan accused an *arendator* of defrauding the villagers in his area. This sin was deemed to outweigh the fact that the man 'studied constantly' and gave money to charity. A punishment was decreed, and on earth the lord of the estate confiscated the *arendator*'s possessions and put him and his family in jail. The moral of the story is actually spelled out: 'From this it can be seen that one should refrain from robbing the Gentiles, since, as it is written in the books, Satan deducts this sin from one's holy merits, God forbid'.[36] The point here, then, is not that one should deal honestly with Gentiles out of consideration of expediency in this world, but that cheating non-Jews is a sin that will be punished by the heavenly court. Thus, in another story, the Baal Shem Tov tells his disciples how 'he saw that in heaven Jews who live in the villages were accused of cheating the Gentiles in their accounts'.[37] The warning is clear.

When the question of interaction with Poles was considered at greater remove, as in the case of eighteenth-century Polish Jews who had emigrated and had been influenced by Western European culture, attitudes could be more extreme. Such men seem to have absorbed the deprecatory attitudes towards Poland common in the West and mince no words in their description of Poles (and Polish Jews as well). The physician Tobias Kohn, born in Poland, but educated in universities in Italy and Germany, wrote in 1707 concerning causes of *plica polonica* (trichosis or elflock), a disease of the hair and scalp for which there was no known cure in Poland.[38] He noted that, as a young man in Poland, he had seen at first hand:

> ... this country is more fertile than all the other lands of the nations,[39] but it is full of filth and offal ... people's homes stink and their clothes are dirty. They do not comb their hair or beards even once a year ... Their diet is bizarre, mainly beans, pickles and, on an empty stomach, radishes, onions and garlic. They drink liquor that burns the heart and the soul as well and mead and beer and other unhealthy drinks that unquestionably cause serious diseases ... so there is no wonder that they suffer such illnesses due to their bad habits ... [Furthermore] even if demons had never been created they would have had to have been created for the people of this country; for there is no land where they are more occupied with demons, talismans, oath formulas, mystical names and dreams ...

If Tobias criticized Polish hygiene and superstition, Solomon Maimon, who had attached himself to the intellectual circles of Berlin, recorded his negative opinion of Polish political, economic, and social organization. According to Maimon, Poland's political policies were informed by ignorance, and its non-Jewish and non-serf population were distinguished by laziness.[40] I have not found such negative statements as these made by Jews who were living in Poland, even in texts intended for a Jewish readership.

The Jews' accommodation to their political status in Poland combined moderation on the practical level with an imaginative interpretation of reality that gave expression to their desire for power and their belief in their ultimate superiority. By contrast, attitudes towards interaction with Poles and other non-Jews were rooted more in the actual experiences and position of the members of the various Jewish sub-groups within society. Thus, Jewish emigrés, who no longer had any ongoing relationship with Poles, criticized them. The representatives of the institutional establishment, who wanted to consolidate their power within the Jewish community, saw Poles as a threat to their position. This threat could best be managed by maintaining correct relations between Polish and Jewish institutions and maximum distance between Polish and Jewish societies. Jews who benefited from close relationships with non-Jews tended to admire their interlocutors and take pride in such relationships. One of the characteristics of early Hasidism may have been an attempt by a leadership sensitive to the unpredictability and possible violence of everyday encounters with Gentiles to explore new bases for the relationship between Jew and non-Jew. From this variety of attitudes, it is evident that, although Jews' reactions to minority status were typical and predictable, their stance towards interaction with the non-Jewish environment cannot be characterized by one paradigm only, and was connected closely enough to reality as to be susceptible of change.

NOTES

1 For a description of the typology of responses see Floyd James David, *Minority-Dominant Relations: A Sociological Analysis* (Arlington Heights, III: 1978); Minako Kurokawa, ed., *Minority Responses* (New York, 1970); cf. P.R. Brass, ed., *Ethnic Groups and the State* (Totowa, N.J., 1985), pp. 34–47, 171–173, 184–186; W.F. Mackey and W. Verdoodt, eds., *The Multinational Society* (Rowley, Mass., 1975), pp. 329–353.
2 Israel Halpern (ed.), *Pinkas Va'ad Arba Aratsot* (Jerusalem, 1945), p. 1. For an analysis of the background to this declaration see S.A. Cygielman, 'Leasing and contracting interests (public incomes) of Polish Jewry and the foundation of *Vaad Arba Aratsot*', *Tsion*, vol 47, (1982) pp. 112–144. For other examples of the Jews' conviction that they must keep a low profile and conform to the requirements of the majority, see M.J. Rosman, 'Jewish Perceptions of Insecurity and Powerlessness in 16th-18th century Poland', *Polin*, vol I, pp. 19–27.
3 Rosman, 'Perceptions', p. 23. For a discussion of how Jewish political consciousness in Poland developed in post-Partition times see: Jack Kugelmass, 'Native Aliens', unpublished Ph.D. dissertation (New School for Social Research, New York, 1980), esp. pp. 52–54, 253–54.
4 B.D. Weinryb, *The Jews of Poland* (Philadelphia, 1973), pp. 165–167; Rosman, 'Perceptions', pp. 20–22.
5 *Tsok Ha-Itim* (Kraków, 1650, new edition, Jerusalem, 1981), p. 6. Other Hebrew chronicles contain several mentions of Jews' fighting alongside Poles against the rebels; e.g. Shabbatai Ha-Kohen, *Megilat Eifa* (Amsterdam, 1651, reprinted in *Beit Yisrael Be-Polin*, I. Halpern, ed. vol. 2, Jerusalem, 1953), p. 253; Nathan Hannover, *Yeven Metsula* (Venice, 1953, translated *Abyss of Despair* by A.J. Mesch, New York, 1950, reprinted New Brunswick, N.J., 1983), pp. 54, 63, 80..
6 F.E. Sysyn, 'Seventeenth-Century Views on the Causes of Khmel'nysts'kyi Uprising: An Examination of the "Discourse on the Present Cossack or Peasant War"', *Harvard Ukrainian Studies* 5 (1981), p. 446.
7 See Hannover, pp. 27–28, 38.
8 Ha-Kohen, p. 252. See also Weinryb, *The Jews of Poland*, p. 200. The terms used by Shabbetai and other Jewish chroniclers to describe the Ukrainians are parallel to those used by Poles; compare the Hebrew *nivzim* (contemptible), *shefalim* (base), *pohazim* (fickle), *raikim* (vacuous) with the Polish *swawolny* (dissolute), *zdrajca* (traitor), *niecnota* (scoundrel), *hultaj* (good-for-nothing). See: A.Z. Baraboy, et al., eds., *Dokumenty osvoboditelnoi voine Ukrainskovo naroda* (Kiev, 1965), passim.
9 Meir ben Samuel, p. 3.
10 Gabriel ben Joshua Shusberg, *Petah Teshuvah* (Amsterdam, 1651), p. 12b.

11 David Ganz, *Zemah David*, M. Breuer, ed. (Jerusalem, 1983), pp. 314. See the index under Poland for other events of Polish history reported in the book.
12 N.N. Hannover, pp. 27-28.
13 Ber Birkenthal, *The Memoirs of Ber of Bolechow*, M. Vishnitzer, ed. (London, 1922, reprinted New York, 1973) pp. 52-53, 73-74, 125, 127, 131-2, 150, 172.
14 Ber Birkenthal, p. 124. Note that the Hebrew terms used here to characterise the members of the High Tribunal (see Hebrew edition of the memoirs, p. 75) are the same ones employed in the Bible to describe the type of people Jethro told Moses to pick to serve as judges in the courts of Biblical Israel (*Exodus* 18, 21).
15 Isaac Lewin, *The Jewish Community in Poland* (New York, 1985), pp. 67-96; Birkenthal, p. 143.
16 Rosman, 'Perceptions', pp. 19-20.
17 Dov Ber of Bolechów did several times house the officer who brought money from Paris for the support of the Confederation of Bar (Birkenthal, p. 92 [Hebrew Edition]; Vishnitzer's translation, p. 150, is not accurate on this point). Sometimes non-Polish Jews did play a role in high level Jewish politics; see Cecil Roth's articles: 'Dr. Solomon Ashkenazi and the Election to the Throne of Poland', *Oxford Slavonic Studies* 9 (1960), pp. 8-20; 'A Mantuan Jewish Consortium and the Election to the Throne of Poland in 1587' [Hebrew], *Yitzhak F. Baer Jubilee Volume*, S.W. Baron, et al., eds. (Jerusalem, 1960), pp. 291-296. On the role of the German Court Jew, Berend Lehmann, in the election of August II, see Selma Stern, *The Court Jew* (Philadelphia, 1950), pp. 80-82.
18 On covert aggression of minority groups against the dominant group see Davis, pp. 50, 131-132, 138, 145. Particularly relevant for our discussion is the notion of expressive hostility (p. 138).
19 *Ha-Kohen*, p. 252.
20 Birkenthal, p. 149-151.
21 P. Bloch, 'Die Sage von Saul Wahl, dem Eintags König von Polen', *Zeitschrift den Historischen Gessellschaft für die Provinz Posen* 4 (1889) p. 234ff; Majer Balaban, *Yidn in Poyln* (Wilno, 1930), pp. 17-38; there is also the legend of Prochownik which while it may date from an earlier period does not appear until the nineteenth century: see B. Weinryb, *The Beginnings of East European Jewry in Legend and Historiography* (Leiden, 1962), pp. 1-11.
22 Dov Ber ben Samuel, *Shivhei ha-Besht: In Praise of the Ba'al Shem Tov*, D. Amos and J. Mintz, trans. and eds., (Bloomington, Indiana, 1972) (henceforth SB) No.174; the Baal Shem Tov also supposedly brought about the wartime destruction of the town of Balta. (SB No.45).
23 A.J. Heschel, *The Circle of the Baal Shem Tov*, (Chicago, 1985), p.22.
24 Heschel, p. 40-43.
25 Levi Yitshak of Berdichev, *Kedushat Levi* (Slavita, 1798), p. 106. On Levi Yitshak's political activism under both Polish and Russian rule see I. Halpern, *Yehudim Ve-Jahadut be-Mizrah Europa*, (Jerusalem, 1968), p. 340-47.
26 J. Goldberg, 'Poles and Jews: in the 17th and 18th centuries. Rejection or Acceptance' in *Jahrbücher für Geschichte Osteuropas*, vol. 22 (1974) No.2, pp. 248-82. See also R. Mahler, *History of the Jews in Poland* (Hebrew), (Merhavia, 1946) pp. 164-188. For discussion of some of the stereotypical ideas about Jews, see A. Kamiński, 'Poland as a Host Country of the Jews' *Proceedings of the Conferences on Poles and Jews: Myth and Reality in Historical Context*, J. Micgiel et al, eds. (New York, 1986), p. 16-31 and M.J. Rosman, *The Lords' Jews* (Cambridge, Mass., 1989), Conclusion.
27 The Jews of Poland, pp. 165-176.
28 J. Katz, *Exclusiveness and Tolerance* (New York, 1952), pp. 56-7; idem., *Tradition and Crisis* (New York, 1971), pp. 18-42. Cf. Kugelmass, p. 254.

29 Davis, pp. 133-5.
30 For examples see: *The Lords' Jews*, Chapter 7, 'The Magnates and the Jewish Community', notes 1, 8, 9.
31 For modern examples of minority accommodation leadership acceding to the essential legitimacy of the majority-dominated political system see: *Brass*, pp. 34-35, 39; M.S. Dhami, *Minority Leaders' Image of the Indian Political System* (New Delhi, 1975), pp. 27-28, 35, 57. For a discussion of the threat that the power of the state represents to ethnic élites in modern developing countries, see: *Brass*, pp. 27-36.
32 Birkenthal, pp. 55-57, 65-67, 75, 89, 94, 102, 107, 120, 135, 148-149, 152, 156-158, 162, 167-168, 176-177 (Dov also has some uncomplimentary things to say about particular noblemen of his acquaintance, see pp. 74, 85, 106-107, 170); *Korot Moshe Wasserzug* (The Life of Moshe Wasserzug), H. Loewe, ed. (Berlin, 1911) pp. 6, 15-17, 19, 23-27.
33 Despite its relatively late date, there are good grounds for believing that many of the traditions recounted in Shivhei Ha-Besht are authentic; see M.J. Rosman, 'Międzybóż and Rabbi Israel Ba'al Shem Tov' (Hebrew), *Tsion* 52 (1987), pp. 177-189; idem, 'The Quest for the Historical Ba'al Shem Tov,' *Tradition and Crisis Revisited* (Harvard Center for Jewish Studies: in preparation).
34 SB Nos.4, 23, 30, 41, 69, 77, 82, 103, 123, 150, 167, 171, 180, 198, 218, 224, 229, 232, 235.
35 *Exclusiveness and Tolerance*, pp. 56-63; *Tradition and Crisis*, pp. 35-42.
36 SB, No.90.
37 SB, No.236.
38 *Ma'ase Tuviah* (The Exploits of Tobias), (Venice, 1707), p. 110d.
39 Earlier in the text Tobias had remarked that Poland had a large population and was richly endowed with water resources.
40 *The Autobiography of Solomon Maimon*, J. Clark Murray, trans. (London, 1888, reprinted 1954), pp. 11-13.

YIDDISH 'HISTORICAL' SONGS AS SOURCES FOR THE HISTORY OF THE JEWS IN PRE-PARTITION POLAND

Chava Turniansky

The 'historical' song (*'historish' lid*), a song which describes a recent event, is one of the outstanding genres of Yiddish literature of the pre-partition period. The authors of these songs did not intend to describe past events for posterity. They did not possess even the limited historical consciousness which motivated the average chronicler of the Middle Ages. Their purpose was an immediate, realistic portrayal of an event for a contemporary public. This purpose places the 'historical' song in a category similar to that of the newspaper of today which, while it can at some point be used as a historical source, cannot be classified as a historiographical work. For more than a decade, a research project, sponsored by the Israel Academy of Sciences and Humanities has sought, under the direction of Professor Chone Shmeruk and myself, within the framework of the Yiddish Department of the Hebrew University, to prepare and publish a complete critical edition of all such Yiddish *'historishe' lider* – 'historical' songs – from the 17th and 18th centuries.

Unlike *pieśni historyczne* in Poland, these Yiddish songs do not fall within the category of folklore. There is no evidence of their ever having been or become part of the oral tradition, or of having been converted into folksongs, or of undergoing popular abridgements or adaptations. They were meant to spread information regarding current events as did the Polish *pieśni nowiniarskie*, and the ways of their distribution seem to have been similar to those of the *pieśni jarmarczne* or the *pieśni kramarskie*. They were mainly lengthy songs, with tens of stanzas, at times over a hundred, which combined elements of the German parallel genre – the *neue Zeitungen* or *neue Lieder* – with elements of Hebrew elegies and prayers. The songs were mainly printed a short time after the event they described and, in most cases, quickly forgotten.

This literary genre is almost the only kind of Yiddish literary expression of the 17th and 18th centuries which deals directly and in its entirety with contemporary events. The aim of this article is, thus, twofold. Firstly, to draw the attention of scholars to the significance of these songs as a historical source, and, secondly, to seek for the help of Polish historians in the search for Polish documentary material related to the events dealt with in the songs, as well as in the proper interpretation of these documents.

'Historical' songs are known in European literature from the 16th century, after the spread of printing and the decrease in its costs. In Yiddish, however, this kind of song is known only from the beginning of the 17th century. The earliest three were printed in 1616 and 1617. From the following thirty years, a time of war, not one song of this kind has reached us, but from the period between 1648 and 1721 we know of thirty songs, and from then until the end of the 18th century, an additional thirteen songs have come down to us. The songs were mainly printed in small, cheap booklets of four, eight or twelve octavo-size pages. Almost all of them are preserved in one single copy, more than half of them in the Bodleian Library in Oxford as part of the collection of one man, Reb Dovid Oppenheimer of Prague, whose activity as a collector of Jewish books and manuscripts ceased around 1720.

The forty-six songs we have today are only a small part of a larger number of Yiddish ballads which appeared in the 17th and 18th centuries but did not reach us. The reasons for this are various: the size and quality of the editions of these songs; the short-lived interest they aroused owing to the fleeting nature of the events they dealt with; the insecurity of Jewish life and the need to preserve books of greater value, mainly in Hebrew. These and other factors seem to explain why the Oppenheimer collection lacks even songs printed during the collector's lifetime, and even in his own city. The fact that each discovery of a collection of Yiddish books of this period – such as the recent discoveries in the University libraries of Erlangen and Rostock and the latest findings in the genizah in Veitshochheim – reveals hitherto unknown songs or editions, strengthens our assumption that in Yiddish, as in other literatures, the number of 'historical' songs must have reached into hundreds.

The songs we have deal mainly with events occurring in one or more of the Jewish communities in Germany, Holland, Poland, Lithuania, Bohemia or Moravia, embracing, in fact, the entire Ashkenazi territory, that is, the whole Yiddish-speaking area, from Amsterdam and Metz in the West, to Wilno and Uman in the East. The events dealt with are mainly fires and plagues, sufferings in time of siege and war, persecutions and expulsions, trials and executions, natural disasters and other calamities, and even the deaths of famous rabbis or other important persons. The authors, mainly religious functionaries such as scribes, preachers, beadles, teachers or cantors, were quite often eye-witnesses to the events they described, for the most part writing only in Yiddish but sometimes in bilingual form with parallel Hebrew and Yiddish versions.

While only a few songs are written in rhymed prose, the great majority make use of various kinds of stanzaic structures. Some of the songs are accompanied by a refrain, and many of them are explicitly intended to be sung with a well-known tune, taken at times from the Jewish context (such as the tune of the *Akeyda*, a liturgical poem on the sacrifice of Isaac, or of the prayer *El mole rakhamim*) and, at times, from German popular songs (such as *Die Schlacht von Pavia*, or *Der Graf von Rom*).

In accordance with the journalistic purposes of the genre – and whether the authors were eye-witnesses of the events or not – the songs were mainly written immediately after the event occurred and printed very soon afterwards. This despite the fact that Prague and Amsterdam served as printing places for most of the songs, even those which described events which took place far away from these cities.

Although not one of the Yiddish ballads was printed in Poland, we know of a Polish Jew, one Haim ben Sholem of Poland, who was the author of a song of this kind which describes the trial and execution of two Jewish thieves in Prostits (Prostejow), Moravia, in 1684.[1] This song is quite remarkable in the context of the genre for his finely developed balladic elements.

On at least two other occasions Polish Jews are mentioned in songs dealing with events with took place outside Poland. A song from 1675 tells us about a Polish Jewish woman who was deserted by her husband.[2] She travels first to Amsterdam, where she finds out his whereabouts in Germany, and then to Hamburg, where she finds him and succeeds, after many trials and tribulations, in getting a divorce. In another song, which deals with the suffering of the Jewish community of Ungarish-Brod at the time of the Turkish invasion in 1683,[3] there is a brief description of the killing, during the raid, of Natan Hannover, the Wolhyn-born author of the famous Hebrew chronicle *Yeveyn Metsula* on Chmielnicki's massacres. The devastation caused by bubonic plague in Poland at the end of the first decade of the 18th century is mentioned in another song, which describes a fire in Altona in 1713.[4]

Of the forty-six Yiddish 'historical' songs of the 17th and 18th centuries that are in our possession, nine – that is, about one fifth-deal directly with events which took place within the borders of the Polish Commonwealth over a period of one hundred and twenty years – from 1648 to 1768.[5] Only two of these belong to the 18th century. The first, *Di bashraybung fun gzeyres kak Pozne* (Note 5H)[6] about the ordeal of the Jews in Poznan during the summer of 1716, is incomplete. Only a few pages have been preserved in the binding of a Hebrew book printed one year later in Berlin. The second one, a lamentation for the sufferings caused by deeds of the Cossack Ivan Gonta in Uman in 1768 (5I), is known only in a 19th-century reprint.[7] A unique copy of each of the remaining seven songs which deal with events in Poland, as well as a second edition of one of them,[8] is to be found in the

Oppenheimer collection in Oxford, including one that has reached us only in manuscript form (5C).

All of these songs were written and printed during a period of less than fifty years, from 1648 to 1696. The year of publication, lacking in all but two, can be determined by the dates referred to one way or another in the songs themselves, and by consideration of the basic principle, in this genre, of immediate printing. A reference made in one song to the events described in another, which lacks any specific detail of time, is helpful in fixing at least a *terminus ad quem*. Although the place of publication, Prague or Amsterdam, is given in only a few songs, there are very good reasons to believe that the others were also printed in one of these cities.

A fairly superficial comparison between songs on Polish events and those dealing with events in other places reveals, besides many similarities, some quite striking differences. For example, the term *lid* and its variations: *sheyn lid*, *nay lid*, *sheyn nay lid*, *nay kloglid*, *sreyfe lid*, and so on, which are so common in the titles of songs from Western and Central Europe, do not appear in the songs from Poland, except for *gzeyre lid* in the second edition of one of them.[8] Other terms appear instead, such as *kina* – elegy or lamentation – which is quite rare in the other songs, and the terms *bikhl* (= booklet) and *bashraybung* (= description), which are not used in them at all.

While most of the other songs are written in stanzaic strophes and only a few present defective structures or a leaning towards rhymed prose, for the songs concerning events in Poland the opposite is true. More than half are written in rhymed prose or display defective structures, so much so that it is difficult at times to tell which pattern the author meant to use. Only two songs indicate a tune (5A and 5F) and another two (5B and 5E) are accompanied by a refrain, both of them of Jewish origin. One of the songs is bilingual (5G) and four (5A, 5B, 5D and 5F) have an acrostic; both features are found here to a far higher degree than in the other Yiddish 'historical' songs.

These and other facts of the same kind indicate that certain characteristics of the genre's tradition, which crystallised in Western and Central Europe through close contact with the popular literature of the German environment, were changed, distorted or lapsed in the course of the absorption of the genre in Eastern Europe. It seems that the lack of direct contact with the German language and its popular literature led not only to a greater reliance on elements from within the Jewish context, but also to a weakening of earlier aesthetic criteria. Nevertheless, the basic twofold dependence of the songs upon the Hebrew elegy, the *kina*, on one hand, and upon the devices of the genre as known in German-speaking countries on the other, remained unchanged. No signs have been found of any link or contact between Yiddish songs on Polish events and the parallel genre known in Poland, the reason for this probably being the language barrier.

The main difference between Yiddish songs on Polish events and songs dealing with events that occurred in other places, lies in their themes, that is, in the kinds of events described. Not one of the nine songs deals with a fire, a plague, an expulsion, a natural disaster or the natural death of an important personage. All nine songs are concerned with persecutions and assaults, or with trials and executions of Jews. Although there is no doubt that it was only chance that determined which songs were to be preserved and which lost, it seems, nevertheless, that the thematic contrast between the two groups of songs reflects the outstanding events in the historical reality of each area.

Persecutions and assaults on Jewish communities in Poland in the course of invasion, war or rebellion, are the themes of four of our songs. The first (5A) describes episodes during the Chmelnicki uprising of 1648, while the last (5I) depicts the deeds of Gonta and the Haydamaks in Uman in 1768. The sufferings of the Jews in Lithuania and White Ruthenia, in Lublin and Lwów during the Muscovite invasion in 1655 are registered in one song (5B), and what befell the Jews of Poznań during the attack of the Tarnogród Confederation in 1716 is recorded in another (5H).

A song (5G) concerning events in Poznań in 1695 differs significantly from the other songs not only for its subject – the history of a blood-libel which threatened disaster for all the Jews of the city and its environs – but also for its bilingual nature and its unusually broad perspective, forty-four closely printed pages. The song describes in great detail the convoluted turn of events which led to an upsurge of passions that endangered the entire community, who were threatened by a blood-thirsty mob. Investigation and a vigorous search by Jews and non-Jews alike for the real murderer were successful. The threat was averted as a result of the arrest of the murderer and his confession. It is not surprising, therefore, that the author – who believed that a different turn of events would have endangered all Jews in Poland – entitled his work *Sefer ge'ules Yisroel* (The Book of the Redemption of Israel).

All four remaining songs (5C, 5D, 5E and 5F) deal with trials of Jews in Poland, leading to the death sentence and execution. Similar episodes outside Poland – in Hanau in 1617 and in Prostejov in 1684 – were also recorded in Yiddish 'historical' songs.[9] In both of these cases, the Jews were accused of theft and sentenced to death. They were tortured in order to force them to convert, an act that would save them from death. Having refused to convert in spite of torture, they died and earned the epithet of *kodesh* (martyr) in the songs telling their stories.

The earliest song we know about this sort of trial in Poland was written in 1682 (5C), and entitled *Dos bikhl fun dem kodesh Reb Shakhne* (The booklet of the martyr Reb Shakhne). This is the only one of the Yiddish songs preserved in manuscript and the only one published so far, in a detailed article by Professor Shmeruk, after a careful analysis and comparison with accounts of the event found in Hebrew sources.[10] It tells of a Jew of Kraków, who was arrested and sentenced to death for purchasing sacred objects stolen from a church by two non-Jewish youngsters, who confessed and were put to death. Reb Shakhne suffered various tortures designed to make him convert, but withstood them all and was executed. The song ends with a severe warning not only against the purchase of sacred objects, but of stolen goods in general, stating clearly that such acts are liable to endanger the whole community. The severity of the warning seems to attest to the frequency of transactions of this nature. A similar case, regarding the goldsmith Volf of Kraków, who was accused of buying objects stolen from a church in 1676, is registered in Majer Bałaban's history of the Jews in this city,[11] where the historian makes it clear that such accusations, made by non-Jewish goldsmiths *after* the thief was arrested, were quite common.

Bałaban does not mention our Reb Shakhne. Nor do we know from other sources about the similar case of one Avrom of Mościsk, whose trial and execution are described in an undated Yiddish song entitled *Kidush ha- shem ha-meyukhed shel Reb Mates ve-Reb Pinkhes ve-Reb Avrom* (5E) (The sanctification of the Only One by Reb Mates and Reb Pinkhes and Reb Avrom). Avrom of Mościsk was, according to the song, victim of an *aliles sheker lekhem hago'el* (A false libel of the Holy Host). We are told that a thief, captured for stealing church objects, was induced by the people of the town to lay blame on the Jews in return for false promises of reward and freedom.

It is not clear why the thief chose to accuse Reb Avrom of Mościsk – who is portrayed as an honourable and well-loved person for his good deeds towards Jews and non-Jews alike – as well as his employee, a respectable Jewish widow whose name does not appear in the text. The *porets* (nobleman), who was ordered to turn Reb Avrom over to the authorities, obstinately refused to do so; in the end, however, he was forced to agree. Both of the accused were brought for trial to Lublin, where the woman was tortured first in order to obtain her confession which would thereby prove Reb Avrom's guilt. Her resistance to torture and her pleas of innocence until the end did not save her from being burnt to ashes in the marketplace. Nor did it save Reb Avrom's life. After having refused to convert in order to be granted an easier death, he was also condemned to perish by fire.

The same song tells the case of Reb Pinkhes of Tomaszów, an ascetic dedicated entirely to the study of the Torah, who also fell victim to a false libel of the Holy Host and was burned at the stake. The narration of the trial indicates that at a certain stage the accused was transferred to the Tribunal in Lublin. A plot to prove his guilt with the help of false evidence from a servant girl, and torture to force a confession from him, failed. Reb

Pinkhes withstood the tortures and denied until the end all the accusations against him.

Somewhat different is the case of Reb Mates of Kraków. According to the song, the libel is born out of the anger of certain priests, who used to engage in discussions on matters of religion with Reb Mates, an extremely learned man. When the priests saw that he was unconvinced by their arguments and that he always won the debates, they decided to take revenge. They composed and signed in his name a forged document which insulted Christianity, and hung it in various churches. Reb Mates was arrested and, although he refused to confess under terrible torture, was condemned to death by fire.

While the anonymous author of this song about the three martyrs seems to have lived in Lublin during the events described, there is no doubt concerning Reb Shmuel Ben Dovid in the Auerbach family. Reb Shmuel 'called by all Reb Shmuel of Lublin', was the author of a song (5F) on the trial of one Reb Shloyme of Krzeszów. He was accused and condemned to death in 1692 for something which the song does not make clear. He withstood torture and the temptation to convert, and was executed by hanging. The author of the song, who also wrote a commentary in Hebrew on the Book of Genesis,[12] included at the end of his song a long sermon on martyrdom.[13] Linking it to the biblical verse 'For Thy sake we are slain all the day long, and accounted as sheep for the slaughter' (Psalms XLIV, 22), he describes the torture of a series of martyrs in which, in addition to Reb Avrom of Mościsk, Reb Pinkhes of Tomaszów and Reb Mates of Kraków, other *kdoyshim* are mentioned: Reb Avrom of Lublin, Reb Yehuda of Przemyśl, Reb Binyomen and Reb Pinkhes Zelig of Luków, Reb Nakhman of Maków and Reb Shmuel of Ir Khodosh (Nowe Miasto or Nowy Dwór). He does not mention – nor does any other source we know – the three Jews of Wilno who were accused of killing a Christian child in 1690. Their trial and execution are depicted in another Yiddish 'historical' song entitled *Dos bilbl is oyf di dray kdyoshim be-kak Vilne* (This blood libel is on the three martyrs in the Holy Community of Vilna).

All these Yiddish songs combine to form a sort of scroll of martyrology of the Jews of Poland in the late 17th century. They display, each in its own way, varied and different sides of the events dealt with. Besides the incident itself, its time, place and duration, as well as the names of the victims, we are informed in the course of the song, for instance, of the efforts made by the community to save the life of the accused or at least to grant him an easier or less shameful death, to alleviate his torture, to aid him to die in purity and to bury his body according to Jewish law. All this is done out of deep fear, not only for the fate of the accused – who is never abandoned – but also for the fate of the entire community. The songs also depict, in a non-stereotyped way, the behaviour of groups or individuals among the general population, such as priests and rulers, nobles and common folk, witnesses and hangmen.

Two matters occupy a central place in these songs. One: the comprehensive and extremely detailed account of the terrible tortures suffered by the accused, sometimes along with shorter descriptions of the tortures inflicted upon Jewish and non-Jewish witnesses – all of which make the reader shudder; and two: the depiction of the proud stance of all the accused Jews, without respect to sex, age, social standing or education, in the face of such terrible suffering, their staunch refusal to confess to deeds they did not commit and their uncompromising denial of all tempting offers to convert.

Their devotion to their religion, their readiness to die for *kiddush ha-shem* and their attempt stringently to adhere to all the commandments on the subject, are quite often expressed by way of direct speech by the accused, whether in the form of a monologue during or after torture, or when about to be executed, or in the form of a dialogue with the priests over their offers of conversion, or with the people of the community who come to hear the last requests of the condemned.

Although in most cases the authors of the songs were present at the time of the event they describe, it is doubtful whether one can attribute to these speeches a stenographic reliability, or regard the detailed description of the torture as an accurate picture of reality. However, there is no doubt that despite the fact that the songs respond to literary traditions and conventions or the tastes of the period, they *do* reflect the thoughts and feelings of the authors, who express the stance, feelings, fears and hopes of the community in general, including the further audience to whose taste and viewpoint the authors adapted. In addition, the language of the songs, spoken and understood by all, depicts events in a more concrete and detailed way than would a Hebrew elegy (*Kina*) or prayer on the same subject.

However, the value of these Yiddish songs as historical sources for the events described is not exhausted with the glimpse they provide of diverse aspects of the spiritual world of the time or the details of everyday life. In order properly to evaluate the significance of the songs as historical documents, each song must of course be considered separately. There is no doubt that from the viewpoint of the historian, the most important songs are those which describe an event hitherto unknown to historical research. The song concerning the blood libel in Wilno in 1690 belongs to this category. All attempts to trace the event in other contemporary sources have been in vain, apart from one obscure sentence in the *Pinkas* (Minute Book) of *Va'ad Medinat Lita* (The Lithuania Council) concerning a payment for 'a bad business' in Wilno, the meaning of which was discovered only thanks to the Yiddish song.[14] In the case of another unknown event, the trial and execution of Reb Shakhne of Kraków in 1682, the search for traces of the event led to the *Pinkas* of the burial society of this community, and it became clear that the Yiddish song mentioned significant essential details – such as the purchasing of stolen church objects – that were not mentioned at all, either in the *Pinkas* or in the special *El mole rakhamim* prayer which was composed in the memory of Reb Shakhne.

Even where the historical events are well known, like Chmielnicki's massacres, or the invasion of the Muscovites, or the blood libel in Poznań in 1696, or the persecutions of Gonta in the Ukraine, the songs serve to expand or enrich our knowledge, to a greater or lesser degree, in different ways. They may add hitherto unknown details, as well as clarify or explain the known ones. They may bring to light aspects that have not been displayed in other sources, or shed a new light, from a different perspective, on the others.

The Yiddish song about the Chmielnicki massacres serves as an instructive example. Its publication date, September 1648, just before the Jewish New Year and right in the middle of the massacres, makes it the earliest document we have on these events since the Hebrew *Kina* it mentions as sources has not reached us. The song preserves, naturally, not only fresh reactions and evaluations different from those preserved in the chronicles which were written and published later, but also details and descriptions which, while scant, differ from those that appear in the chronicles. On the other hand, a great deal of the later descriptions seem to have their roots in the Hebrew source of this Yiddish song, where they were first registered.

There is no doubt as to the importance for historical research of the Yiddish 'historical' songs in general, and among them, those which deal with events within the boundaries of Poland in the 17th and 18th centuries. Recourse to them for research purposes and preparing their critical edition, as a first step in this direction, cannot be done properly, however, without careful examination of all the existing documents relevant to the events discussed in the songs. This has proved to be a vital necessity in our work on the songs dealing with events in Western and Central Europe, where chronicles in various languages, archival documents, pamphlets, broadsheets and illustrations of the time, and even German songs about the same event have explained, confirmed, corrected or filled in the details preserved in the Yiddish song, and by their illumination of the event from other perspectives helped us to understand it properly and fully, both in itself and within the general historical context. This was pointed out, as early as 1927, by Max Weinreich who, in a survey of Yiddish 'historical' songs on events in Poland from the second half of the 17th century,[15] asserted that in order to advance research in this area, it is necessary to find and examine the relevant official documents in the state archives of Poland. He pointed specifically to the records of trials which took place in the Tribunal of Lublin.

Weinreich's view is just as valid today. The scope of the *desiderata* should however be expanded in terms of place, as well as in terms of the types of documents and testimonies sought. We need to investigate, in addition to Lublin, the relevant archives or libraries in Kraków and Wilno, as well as those in the smaller localities that are mentioned in the songs, and to look at, not only legal documents of various kinds, but also historiographical material, such as chronicles, diaries and memoirs, and even Polish *pieśni nowiniarskie* on the same or similar events. There is no way of knowing, of course, what this research will uncover, perhaps even hitherto unknown Yiddish 'historical' songs. There is no doubt that such investigations must be undertaken, in the hope that they will be fruitful and that their findings will shed light on the various unknown or little-known episodes of the history of Jews in Poland, which were registered in nine contemporary 'historical' songs in Yiddish.

NOTES

1 *Eyn sheyn lid oyf shney kdoyshim . . . be-kak Prostitz . . . be-nign Akeyde oder be-nign Broyneslid* [Prague 1684?]; see M. Steinschneider, *Catalogus Librorum Hebraeorum in Bibliotheca Bodleian*, Berolini 1852–1860 (= *Cat. Bodl.*), No.3692.

2 *Eyn sheyn lid vos tsu Hamburg iz geshen*, Amsterdam 1675, *Cat. Bodl.*, No.3636.

3 *Khurbn godl she-hoyo be-kak Ungarish-Brod* [Prague 1683?], *Cat. Bodl.*, no.3526.

4 See: Chava Turniansky, 'Yiddish Song as Historical Source Material: Plague in the Judenstadt of Prague in 1713', *Jewish History, Essays in Honour of Chimen Abramsky*, London 1988, p. 189, note 3.

5 The songs in chronological order of the events described in them, are: A) *Kine al gzeyres kak Ukraine* [Prague], 1648, *Cat. Bodl.* No.3693.

A A second edition appeared shortly afterwards, see note 7 below.

B [*Kine*], s.l.e.a. [1655], *Cat. Bodl.*, No.3651.

C *Das bikhl fun dem kodesh Reb Shakhne* (manuscript), 1682; see M. Steinschneider, 'Jüdish-Deutsche Literatur und Jüdish-Deutsch', *Serpaeum* XXV (1864), no.320.

D *Dos bilbl iz oyf di dray kdoyshim be-kak Vilne*, Amsterdam [1682?], *Cat. Bodl.*, No.4028.

E *Kidesh ha-shem ha-meyukhed shel Reb Mates ve-Reb Pinkhes ve-Reb Avrom . . . be-medines Poyln*, s.l.e.a. [166–1692?], *Cat. Bodl.*, No.4030.

F *Min ha-kodesh Reb Shloyme*, s.l.e.a. [Amsterdam? 1692–1699?], *Cat. Bodl.*, No.3691.

G *Seyfer ge'ules Yisroel*, Prague [1696?], *Cat. Bodl.*, No.5392. H) *Die bashraybung fun gzeyres kak Pozne*, see note 5 below.

I *Kine al gzeyres Ukraine* [1768?], see note 6 below.

6 See: 'Notizen aus Einbanden und gedrückten Büchern, mitgetheilt A. Neubauer', *Israelitische Letterbode* XI pp. 166–169; A.E. Cowley, *A Concise Catalogue of the Hebrew Printed Books in the Bodleian Library*, Oxford 1971, p. 531.

7 Menakhem Nokhem Litinsky, 'Tsu di geshikhte fun di yidn in Podolien – nokh eyn dokument tsu gzeyres Gonte in Ukraine', *Der hoyzfraynd* III (1894), pp. 188–191.

8 *Gzeyre lid*, Amsterdam s.e., a second edition of the song mentioned above, note 5A; see *Cat. Bodl.*, No.3694. This edition seems to have adapted the language for the

Western European Yiddish reader by changing the syntax and omitting or replacing Slavic elemnets for German ones.

9 One is entitled: *Des kodesh fun Hena zayn Lid* (see *Cat. Bodl.*, No.3689) and the other is mentioned above, see note 1.
10 See: Khone Shmeruk, 'Ha-kadosh Reb Shakhne, Krakow 1682 – rishum be-pinkas shel ha-khevre kadisha leumat "shir histori"', *Galed, on the History of the Jews in Poland*, VII-VIII, Tel Aviv 1985, pp. 57–69.
11 See: M. Bałaban, *Historia Żydow w Krakowie i na Kazimierzu, 1304– 1868*, vol. II, Kraków 1936, p. 94.
12 *Sefer khesed Shmuel . . . al sefer be-reyshit*, Amsterdam 1699, see A.E. Cowley (note 5 above), p. 607.
13 An abridged Hebrew version of this sermon was printed at the end of his commentary (note 12 above).
14 See S. Dubnow, *Pinkas ha-medina*, Berlin 1925, p. 217, No.1009, and I. Halperin, 'Tosafot "Lemiluim Pinkas Medinat Lita¿', in *Horev*, II, Jerusalem 1935, pp. 23–24.
15 Max Weinrich, *Shturemvint*, Vilna 1927, pp. 165–220, and his claim alluded to on p. 169.

NON-JEWS AND GENTILE SOCIETY IN EAST EUROPEAN HEBREW AND YIDDISH LITERATURE 1856–1914*

Israel Bartal

The evolution of Jewish literature in Eastern Europe was closely related to the social, economic and cultural changes which took place in the contacts between Jewish society and the non-Jewish population. These changes, which were part of the 'modernisation' process in Eastern Europe, influenced literary creation, whether in Galicia under Austrian rule or in the Congress Kingdom, Lithuania or Volhynia under Russian rule. This extra-literary reality not only found expression in the literary material, but also determined the manner of characterisation and form, for the world of the ideas of the writers and their emotional load mingled with the literary traditions and determined their use of conventions, literary patterns and modes of formation. An analysis of the changes which took place in the image of the non-Jews and their society in relation to the historical background has to be an inter-disciplinary study which touches the realms of sociology, linguistics and folklore.

The changes which took place in the way the non-Jewish environment and its socio-historical background was described in literature are a part of a cultural-linguistic polysystem which evolved over a specific period. In this sketch, I want to deal with the period which begins with the reign of Tsar Alexander II (1856) and which ends with the outbreak of the First World War. During this period there was an intensification of contact between the Jews of Eastern Europe and the non-Jewish population. Social and cultural processes which had already begun in the first half of the nineteenth century were accelerated, and literature evolved in Hebrew, Yiddish, Russian, German and Polish, in which expression was given to the image of the non-Jewish environment in relationship to these changes. This was a transitional period at the start of which a system of contacts and

---

* This article is a summary of the main themes set out in my forthcoming book on this subject, to be published shortly by Hebrew Union Col'ege.

relationships of a medieval character was dominant between Jews and Gentiles. By its end, a number of different views of the relations between Jews and Gentiles competed for dominance in the Jewish environment. These ranged from the acceptance of the conceptual and literary influences of the outside world while rejecting assimilation, to the negation of a specific Jewish identity.

The Jewish literature produced in this period is a prime historical source for the clarification of the sociological phenomenon involved in the changes in the relationship of the Jews to their environment in Eastern Europe. It is possible to learn from this literature how non-Jewish society came to be seen as a model for those absorbing its cultural and intellectual influences, to elicit from it the image of the various ethnic layers or social *strata* which made up the surrounding society, to examine the abstract conceptual view of the world which underlay trends toward integration or separation and to observe how a group of writers, all of whom were born within a traditional Jewish environment, underwent a similar process of estrangement from this environment, but failed to integrate into the non-Jewish environment, whether Russian or Polish. The acquaintance of these writers with non-Jewish society was, of course, mainly literary and abstract, and they treated only the social sectors familiar to them. Moreover, they relied upon literary models and conventions which, in themselves, and in the way they were used, were a product of their spiritual attitudes. These Jewish writers were 'transitional' writers, sociologically speaking: they observed the passage from Jewish traditional society, with its long-established relationship with the world of the 'goyim', to the 'maskilic' or 'national' society of the future. There is a strong continuity between the writers of the 1860s and those of the 1880s or of the early 1900s. Their reliance upon fixed literary models built on conceptual analyses or common traditional images, led to the preservation of such models for the figure of the Russian or Polish hero, even though the ideological and political background changed continually.

This literary phenomenon, which is of central sociological significance for the understanding of the spiritual world of the Jewish intelligentsia in Eastern Europe, is not peculiar to the society we are discussing or to any specific period. There is a typological similarity between the subject we are examining here and the form of the 'Jewish figure' in European literature during the seventeenth and eighteenth centuries. The transition from an essentially religious stereotype to new models, whether an essentially negative socio-economic stereotype, or the positive exemplary figure based on the principles of rationalism, was one of the reflections of the changing character of social contacts between Jews and their environment. In Eastern Europe, a similar phenomenon can be observed in Russian and Polish literature in the nineteenth century. Jewish society, too, when it found itself in a situation in which it was forced to make contact with the

Gentile environment at various levels of intensity, revealed its expectations, suspicions and familiarity through literary modes. In traditional Jewish society, there were defined patterns of thought and behaviour for explaining and dealing with phenomena and individual types in the non-Jewish environment. In Eastern Europe, these were preserved until the twentieth century and found expression in language, folklore, *halakhic* literature and other facets of human behaviour. Deviations from these patterns, one of the obvious signs of the disintegration of the traditional social systems, evolved mainly as a result of conscious conceptual justification. But alongside this consciously new pattern of thought, the older patterns in language and literature were preserved for a time, and sometimes came to the fore as authentic, complex manifestations of Jewish attitudes, as the Jew emerged from his traditional environment and encountered Gentile society. Thus, in Jewish literature, there existed, side by side, both a rational-universal trend and a deeply rooted heritage of traditional characterisation. The relative strengthening or weakening of these two components, the rational-universal trend and the traditional characterisation, can be compared to the historical model proposed by Shmuel Ettinger for explaining the extent of openness on the part of Russian society to the integration of the Jews. In his view, this was related to the strengthening or weakening of 'westernising' influences as against the Christian-Slavic components in the Russian tradition. The period between 1856 and 1914 extends between two high points of increased 'westernising' influence: the reforms of Alexander II in the first years of his reign and the political ferment of the beginning of the twentieth century.

The Jewish attitude toward the non-Jew in literature can be examined simultaneously on three planes, interrelated and of mutual influence:

(a) the non-Jewish figure as a *literary* problem;
(b) the non-Jewish figure and his society as an *anthropological-sociological* problem; and
(c) the form of the non-Jewish figure and his society as a *historical* problem.

The emergence from traditional society in modern Jewish history involved an actual relationship, or at least an abstract-ideal one, with a specific sector of the surrounding society. This relationship also found literary expression, whether directly or through the adoption of formal and linguistic features and their association with the integrated or assimilated Jewish character. Whereas in Central Europe, the bourgeoisie was the only social class which served as a model for integrated Jews in the eighteenth and nineteenth centuries, this class occupies only a marginal position in Eastern European literature. Of the sectors of the population living alongside the Jews, or coming into contact with them, in the Jewish literature of our period, a relationship exists only with three basic groups, whose literary form depicts the full range of attitudes toward the non-Jewish historical reality: the *authorities*, whose literary manifestation can be seen in the depiction of Russian or Austrian officialdom; the *Polish nobility*, whose principal literary manifestation is the image of the *porets*; and the *peasantry*, which is made up of various ethnic elements (Ukrainian, Polish, Byelorussian, Lithuanian). The changes in the depiction of these three groups should be discussed not on the one-dimensional, apologetic-national plane, which is still occasionally found in scholarship, but in a broader socio-historical context.

The Jewish literature of this period, whether in Yiddish or in Hebrew, contains partial manifestations of other trends of development and further possibilities, which were sometimes realised in the creation of literary works. It is particularly in literary creation that the complexity of spiritual attitudes toward figures and situations within Gentile society can be detected. The mode used by writers to deal with the raw material of reality is often more significant than their declared attitudes in digressions within a given work or in journalistic writing. The large gap between the *centrality* of the confrontation between Jews and surrounding world, and the *marginality* of the literary involvement which depicts that encounter, is obvious to the reader of the literature we are discussing. Calls for integration with the environment are rarely accompanied by the presentation of a literary picture of that society. Indeed, negation and contrast are usually perceptible not in a rich, detailed literary reality, but rather by symbolic form or by digression.

Despite the infrequent treatment in literary criticism of the question of the image of the non-Jews in Hebrew and Yiddish literature, it is possible to find a certain 'image' of the non-Jewish image in criticism: there is almost no treatment of its historical development, whereas the 'traditional' context of the relationship of Jewish society to the outside world or its neo-romantic and symbolistic metamorphosis is emphasised. The reason for this seems to be connected with an anachronistic attitude toward nineteenth century literature, influenced by the impact of the pogroms of the beginning of the century and the massacres in the Ukraine following the First World War. The beginning of the twentieth century provides a clear chronological limit for studying the literary depiction of non-Jews and their society; on the one hand, the relationship between Jews and their surroundings was intensifying, as was their familiarity with the surrounding cultures and even their identification with conceptual trends and political parties. Yet, on the other hand, pogroms were taking place, supported by broad segments of non-Jewish society. Familiarity was increasing, as were withdrawal and suspicion. This was the backdrop to the zenith and decline of the use of certain literary patterns and modes of characterisation which had already begun in the 1860s, alongside new modes and different thematics, the appearance of which also constitute a borderline.

The key Jewish writers of the years 1856 to 1914 link, both historically and literally, the period of the beginning of the changes in the contacts of the Jews with their environment and the high points of intensive contact on the eve of the First World War: Gottlober, Dik and Mapu represent, in their anachronistic mode of writing, the conceptual world of the *maskilim* of the first half of the nineteenth century, whereas Sholem-Aleichem and Peretz are confronted with the Revolution of 1905, the pogroms of the beginning of the century and the spiritual and political trends within Russian and Polish society on the eve of the First World War. The centrality of the three classic writers, Abramovitz (Mendele Mokher Seforim), Sholem-Aleichem and Peretz, who all wrote in both Yiddish and Hebrew and who all derived from the *haskala* traditions while also rejecting much of their central concerns, enable us to find, within their *oeuvre*, texts which represent either a pessimistic assessment of social development in relation to the external environment or modes of literary struggle with the non-Jewish world. Their literary creativity extends beyond the limits of the two chronological and literary 'generations' which began in the years when Mapu's *The Hypocrite* and Abramovitz's *Fathers and Sons* were written and ends with the literary works of the period prior to the First World War. As a result, their absorption of influences stemming from the central spiritual trends both within Jewish society and within the neighbouring cultural environment, enables us to see clearly the way the literary picture of the non-Jewish world developed in this period.

The literary works of the period of Alexander II are concerned principally with the image of the higher social *strata* of non-Jewish society and, only to a much lesser extent, that of the lower classes. The Ukrainian peasants, the Byelorussians or the Lithuanians came into close daily contact with broad strata of the Jewish population, but the literary and ideological interest of Jewish writers in these *strata* was rather limited. They were depicted as part of the existing Jewish social milieu, serving as a part of the landscape, as a backdrop for the plot. Only toward the 1870s is there an increasing interest in them, an ideological attitude in which the impact of the positive image of the Russian 'people', as it appears in Russian literature and journalism is evident. Most of the descriptions of the non-Jewish environment are built on two ethnic-social groups which, for the Eastern European Jew, were the politically, culturally and economically élite *strata*; the Polish nobility and the Russian cadre of officials. The depictions of these *strata* underwent changes and developments which were related to political and social processes within Polish society in the areas of Jewish settlement. But an examination of the formation of the images and situations clearly indicates that the ideological element – and, in its wake, the literary conventions of the *maskilic* tradition, whether in Hebrew or Yiddish – was decisive in the development of the image of the Russians and Poles. The various images which appear in these works, repeat almost constant character traits and are integrated within plots in similar modes. Despite the fact that these images are sometimes represented negatively and sometimes almost entirely positively – the logic of the ideological form can clearly be seen.

The depiction of the Russian official as a positive social exemplar, in Hebrew and Yiddish literature of the 1860s and early 1870s, is related to the continuation of the literary conventions within *haskala* literature from the days of Perl on; the alliance of Jewish *maskilim* with '*maskilim*' within the upper classes of the non-Jewish society, against the vices of the traditional society. This theme recurred in the works of Gordon, Gottlober and Linetzky. Thus Gordon's Hebrew short story 'Two days and one night in an inn', written in 1871, contains a highly stylised eulogistic description of a Russian government official:

> Out of the carriage stepped a man dressed in an official uniform, looking like an army officer. I heard him speaking the language of Russia and I felt secure enough to approach him. The Russians are a people of modest mien and genuine feeling and they adhere to the tradition of their Slavic ancestors of making foreigners welcome and receiving them hospitably ... The Russian responded to me with a smile and answered me politely. 'I am going to Warsaw, Sir ... Very good, Sir,' continued the good-hearted official. 'I will be happy to keep you company because I am travelling alone ... I know you are a Hebrew (Evrei).' He said to me, 'You cannot go on your way because it is still the Sabbath. I shall wait for you until nightfall.'

In the 1870s, one notices the disappearance of the image of the positive official, as is evident in the novels of Smolenskin and Braudes. But the change is ambiguous, except in *The Nag (Di Kliatshce)* by Abramovitz in which the abandonment of this literary convention is implicitly presented as a consequence of concrete historical reality. Similarly the literary characterisation of the Polish nobility, between the 1860s and the 1870s, ranged from the unreservedly positive to the complete negation of the ethics and morals of this social class. The absolutely positive manifests itself as an outcome of the *haskala* ideology of exemplary images, which are identified with historical examples of enlightened Polish nobles who were in accord with the trends of enlightened absolutism in Russia and Austria. Thus in his Hebrew novel, *The Hypocrite* (1854), Mapu depicts the salon of a Lithuanian magnate, in which enlightened Poles and Jews meet and discuss Voltaire, philosophy and the Jews. 'The Count's wife and her daughter are well-disposed: they do not distinguish between members of different nations but only between good and bad people.' The Countess introduces the Jewish hero and heroine, 'These are the young people of the new generation, filled with knowledge and reason.'

In sharp contrast to this idyllic picture is the negative characterisation of the aristocracy derived essentially from the traditional Jewish milieu and reflected in the folkloristic depiction of the *porets*. A good example is contained in Gordon's story 'Two days and one night in an inn' where the arrogance and condescension of a Polish nobleman contrasts strongly with the idealised picture of the Russian official we have already cited. In this incident, the aristocratic Pole is receiving a Jewish pedlar:

> The nobleman sat on his chair, like an officer in front of his regiment. He sipped from the full glass in front of him and shook his head at everything the pedlar took from his basket to show he did not want his wares ... The Jew showed the Pole all his treasures, exhausting his soul by his efforts and trying to induce him to buy with all the adjurations in the *Torah*. But the nobleman did not choose any of his wares. He criticised and cursed him and all the Jews, and when he was wearied with all the trinkets set before him, drove the pedlar away.

The last positive *maskilic* image appears in the works of Smolenskin, whereas the negative characterisation – the 'national' one – can be encountered in the literature of the 1880s and, albeit with modifications, becomes linked with social-radical influences in the depiction of Polish society and its attitude toward the Jews.

The literary formation of peasants in the 1860s and 1870s is strongly influenced by the literary criteria of Russian criticism in the 1860s, which made its impact on Jewish literature through the writings of Kovner, Abramovitz and Paperna. Beyond revealing understanding and sympathy for the reasons underlying the economic and social conditions of the peasants, their characterisation is linked to their image within traditional society and to a limited and fixed repertory of realia of contacts between Jews and peasants in the *shtetl* environment. Thus, for all the sympathy he would like to display towards the peasants, they remain for Abramovitz primitive and prone to violence. His novella *The Nag* is an allegory, in which the peasant's broken-down horse represents the suffering Jewish people, the peasant, the popular persecutor of the Jews, the narrator a typical Jewish radical of the '70s, and the Devil, who rides the nag, the Russian government. The encounter between the narrator, Yisrolik and a peasant is described as follows:

> A few minutes later, a peasant came out of the woods with a large cart, which was being pulled by a broken-down nag. He shouted and screamed, cursed and hit the horse, which could barely drag along

the heavy cart, as if he wanted to kill it. From time to time, unable to go on, the horse stopped . . .

I went to the peasant and said, 'Listen, why are you hitting the horse like that. Have pity. You shouldn't hit him like that.' 'Why do you say I can't,' the *goy* [*orel* – an even more derogatory term. The reply is also clearly shown to be in Ukrainian] responded, rather surprised, and again attacked the horse . . . A peasant always remains a peasant. He wanted to beat me.

Abramovitz's literary activity had begun early in the reign of Alexander II. In his novel *Fathers and Sons*, he continued the well-known *haskala* convention of the *maskil* struggling against traditional society and its institutions, assisted by a Russian official. This convention enjoyed a lifespan corresponding almost exactly to that of *haskala* literature itself in Eastern Europe, from Perl to Gordon, Gottlober and Smolenskin. The first version of this novel (1862) was, in general, steeped with a passionate love for Russia and for the Russians. In the late 1860s and early 1870s, the more Abramovitz abandoned his former optimism about government intentions, the greater was the change in his literary stance vis-à-vis this particular convention. In *The Nag*, as we have seen, the Russian government is depicted allegorically as the Devil who exploits the people of Israel. Cooperation between a Jewish *maskil* and the authorities is now presented as something indecent and quite unacceptable. Yisrolik, the narrator, strongly objects to serving as a *baal toyve* ('benefactor' or 'informer' for the authorities), a position which, in much *maskilic* literature, would have been looked on with understanding and even with favour. 'I will not do it,' he protests. 'I cannot cooperate with them.'

This change, which led Abramovitz to regard the officials as an element hostile to the Jews and to Russian society, finds its literary expression in the refusal of the *maskil* to serve the authorities. Similar examples could be adduced from other *haskala* writers of the late 1870s. As far as Abramovitz is concerned, he now develops a preoccupation to depict the typical non-Jewish character from a *shtetl*, who is to be seen as part of the literary picture of that environment. A single central non-Jewish type now becomes dominant in his works between the 1870s and the Hebrew reworkings of his material: the peasant 'goy' from *shtetl* or village. This characterisation is derived from two main sources: Abramovitz's social world-view, expressed in digressions in the style of Russian populism and in positive elements in the image of the peasant, and in contrast, the image of the peasant and the *shtetl* 'goy' in the traditional Jewish model – stereotypic, comic and typified by peasant traits (crudeness, drunkenness, violence, dullness and the like). The image of the peasant serves Abramovitz as an element in Jewish social criticism, and the point of contact with the 'goy' emphasises also the author's ambivalent attitude toward Jews.

His story *The Secret Place of Thunder*, (*Be-Seter Ra'am*, 1886), written in reaction to the pogroms of 1881–82, contains most of the components of his image of the peasant and his contact with Jews. The conceptualisation of the 'setting' with all its typical components does not, in the first instance, castigate the violence against the Jews, but rather the social and political conditions which Abramovitz continued to oppose, in his manner of the 1870s. It is clearly a characterisation much more favourable than that to the found in *The Nag*. Thus, in this story, the narrator asks a group of peasants, 'Why do you blame the Jews for what are in fact the consequences of the economic system?' One of them, Vlas, replies as if from a text book of Marxist political economy,

> There is no work and no demand for production and the wages in our town have fallen to miserable levels since men have begun to dominate men to do them wrong [i.e. since the introduction of capitalism]. Many of the merchants are impoverished and go hungry. When men are idle, what have they to do but drink?

Sholem-Aleichem considerably expanded the social backdrop and filled it with a broader range of the non-Jewish characters. At a certain stage in his work, he abandoned the ideological-*maskil* tradition in describing the social milieu and brought greater unity to the Jewish traditional and literary images of the *shtetl* and peasant 'goy'. The conflict between Jew and 'goy' in his writings is much sharper than in the works of Abramovitz and the stereotypic traits of the non-Jew within the milieu – the quantitative and qualitative richness of which is also greater – are more absolute and are not blurred by ideological digressions or by traits imposed upon the characters. But Sholem-Aleichem sought to come to terms with the changing reality, which Abramovitz consciously and openly ignored, and he abandoned the image of the 'goy' of the *shtetl* milieu. In his novelistic and dramatic *oeuvre*, he created several images of non-Jews from the 'young intelligentsia' of the early twentieth century. These characters, such as the Ukrainian lover of Chave, Tevye's daughter, or Romanienko, the revolutionary in the novel *In Shturm*, are constructed in a shallow manner around social, ideological models derived from Sholem-Aleichem's world-view and the literary-political images of reality as he saw them. The shallow, positive model of the non-Jewish revolutionary – set in antithesis to the shallow, negative model of the non-Jewish anti-semite – was a sort of return to the commonplace gentile '*maskil*' as depicted by Abramovitz in the 1860s. The only difference is that instead of the enlightened Russian official, we find the radical member of the intelligentsia.

Sholem-Aleichem's portrait of the radical Romanienko is hardly less idealised than Gordon's view of the enlightened Russian official, willing to wait until the end of the Sabbath to accompany a Jew to Warsaw. Romanienko is half-Polish and half Ukrainian. His mother is a well-meaning, distinguished and liberal Polish lady, his father a brutal Ukrainian anti-semite. Sholem-Aleichem describes him as follows:

> Anyone who knows the events of recent times will understand the meaning of the phrase 'eternal student'. He is, indeed, one of the best children of this land, he has in his heart a warm love, a pure conscience, lofty ideals and was full of goodwill to do everything possible for the hungry and unhappy people ... In short, not only does he hold revolutionary and socialist views, he is also an organiser and activist, the creator of a whole group.

Peretz, too, fluctuated early in his writings between the ideal image of the Pole of the 'intelligentsia' with a radical-social world-view (and the obverse of the negative, stereotypic anti-semite) and the image of the Polish peasant, whose formulation was also influenced by ideology. Most of the common ground with the peasants in his social stories in realistic style is economic, and the contrast between Jew and peasant is blurred and almost non-existent. The character of the provincial professional is tailored according to the cut of the positivist trend in Polish literature, and served Peretz as an antithetic figure to the provincial Jew, whose life and opinions are subjected to penetrating social scrutiny. Thus the story, *In the Post Carriage* (*In postvogn*, 1891), is a sympathetic portrait of Janek Polyniewski, a radical member of the intelligentsia who has abandoned the study of medicine to become a provincial pharmacist. The character owes much to Konopnicka, Prus and Żeromski and his largely positive depiction is used to set off the aesthetic and moral flaws in Jewish society. Peretz cannot, however, stop himself from recoiling instinctively when Polyniewski displays interest in a Jewish woman. He observes: 'A Jewish woman? Why not? Once it was a religious duty to baptize them, now they aim merely to make a Jewish woman rebel against her God, her parents, her husband and her whole life.'

In his later folk-like stories in neo-Romantic style, Peretz created a Jewish reality, supposedly historical, in which the antagonism between Israel and the Nations is absolute and unbridgeable. Much of these stories is built on the constellation of relationships between the Polish nobility and their Jewish lessees: the Polish nobleman represents the uncleanness, the lust and the violent nature of the gentile world. The Polish noblewoman is the epitome of sexual attractiveness and lasciviousness, and can be resisted by the Jew only with difficulty:

> On market days, especially on the days of their festivals, they drive about in their carriages, all decked out, splendid, and accompanied

by the cossacks of their courts, through the towns and villages. When they see a handsome and comely Jew, they call the cossacks... [And the Jew] is filled with fear and awe before the lady whom he had glimpsed and seen that she was very beautiful, splendidly dressed and ornamented.

In most of Peretz's stories, the Polish peasant appears in a more positive light, sharing the suffering of the Jews. In *The Fur Hat* (*Dos shtrayml*, 1893), a Jewish tailor feels sympathy for his peasant clients:

I used to enjoy making peasant coats.
First, why not?
Second, I thought to myself, 'The peasant gives us bread, he does hard and bitter work in the summer and he cannot protect himself against the sun, so he should at least be protected from the cold, during the winter, when he rests'.

Indeed, the non-Jewish characters in Peretz's stories are mostly stereotypic, whether they are constructed according to ideological conventions or based mainly in the social milieu or representative of the impure gentile world which is to be totally rejected. In their stereotyped essence, they stand in ironic contract to Peretz's literary criticism of the one-dimensional depiction – lacking in internal comprehension – of the Jewish character in Polish literature. Yet, as he shows in his writings, he was not over-keen to dispel this ignorance. In one of his reviews, he wrote:

From time to time, the Polish press complains 'We don't know the Jews at all. The Jews are familiar with us and with our life. Polish literature is known to every member of the Jewish intelligentsia, while we hear from the Jews only what they want to tell us. The Jew, who has lived with us, in our neighbourhood, for centuries is a closed book, an unsolved riddle'. When this gap is mentioned, there rush in writers who have been sitting on the fence, Poles who (with the help of a little Jew) know some Yiddish, like Klemens Junosza. The Jews also write in Polish, but not all of them. Those who have any talent or gift do not want to sell their Jewishness. On the contrary, they try to purify it with holy water, or at least to throw away the Jewishness, lest it be used against them.

Several central trends are common to the position of the non-Jew and his society within Jewish literature throughout the period under discussion. The social *strata* which were best represented in literature are those which had traditional ties with the Jews and their environment: the

Polish nobility; the Slavic and other ethnic villagers; the Russian or Austrian authorities. Attempts to form other images from social realms outside the recognised system of contacts do not diverge in most cases from a simplistic ideological mode or from adherence to known material. Even though most of the writers were long resident in the larger cities (St. Petersburg, Odessa, Kiev, Warsaw, Wilno), they were close to the *shtetl* milieu and the associated surrounding society. The social class of which the Jews were a part-the various sub-groups of townfolk – occupied a marginal position, both as a group embodying a cultural mode and as an entity which was in daily contact with the Jews. Yet the description of this group is less stereotypic and its literary application is less loaded with symbolism and ideological meanings, apologetic or mythical. Adherence to a basic ethnic-class group was a result of the social-demographic structure of Eastern Europe and of the role of the Jews within it. Yet changes in this structure are largely interpreted and distorted through its own concepts and terms, as can be seen *inter alia* in the facility in which the writers depict the 'milieu', in contrast to the constant difficulties created when they attempt to go beyond the small town or *shtetl* environment.

Socio-cultural change is conceived in terms of the traditional environment or, conversely, through the application of ideologies which demand an approach to the environment. These find expression in fixed models whose relationship to historical reality is weak or even contradictory. Traditional situations involving the contact between Jews and their environment, which had been part of a fixed and defined system, also evolve toward attempts to define the changes, and are revealed in the continued application of earlier patterns and conventions. The literary encounter with the 'goy' in the city is often the continuation of the familiar encounter in the *shtetl* or in its environment. When a new social possibility emerges, such as the meeting of youth of various ethnic origins in the context of radical activity, national or social, similar patterns recur, from Smolenskin to Sholem-Aleichem. These have at their base the tension between the rationalistic-universal concept and the persistence of the traditional aversion to direct contact between Poles, Ukrainians, Russians and Jews.

These repeated literary patterns are typical of the range of contacts between Jewish society and the non-Jewish environment. They are closely tied to the geographical, historical, economic and linguistic reality. In this sense, there is no difference between the *haskala* literature of the 1860s and 1870s and the works of the 1880s and later. The meanings, the modes of characterisation, the style and language change – but the fixed models of the Jewish-Gentile encounter remain intact, from Mapu and Dik almost to the last works of Abramovitz, Peretz and Sholem-Aleichem.

The ideological changes modify meanings, but the possibilities of contact with the environment remain limited. The *haskala* conventions of the struggle of an enlightened government and its officials with a backward traditional society lose their force during the 1880s. An encounter of the police with the *Hasidim*, a frequent occurrence in *maskilic* literature, intended to display Hasidic backwardness, evolves into Peretz's story *Khsidish*, which depicts Hasidism in a much more favourable, neo-romantic manner. A Jewish youth in the 1870s turns to Polish liberal nationalism, which he associates with the idealised literary image of a Polish girl-friend. In the 1880s and 1890s, the Jews seek Liberty, Art or Self-Identity in the companionship of a nobleman or official. At the beginning of this century, they are carried away by revolutionary-radical fervour and join the Russian revolutionary movement. Yet, in all these instances, the meeting is formed on similar lines, partly derived from Jewish popular writing, the repetition of an almost fixed pattern. The Polish nobleman who tempts the Jewess, in a tavern in Smolenskin's novel *The Reward of the Righteous* (1876), behaves like the nobleman who wins the heart of the daughter of the Jewish landowner in Ben-Avigdor's *Eliakim the Madman* (1889) and like the customs official who courts the Jewess in Sholem-Aleichem's *Moshkale Ganev* (1903). The possibility of replacing each text with another (taking into account the differences in language), reveals just how strong is the one-dimensional adherence to an almost inflexible form.

The demographic situation of the Eastern European Jews – a large population centred in areas of settlement in which they often comprised a decided majority or at least, a large sector of the population-finds expression throughout the period under discussion. The sense of the Jews as a weighty demographic entity with an autonomous socio-cultural existence, almost entirely independent of its immediate surroundings, is typical both of the *haskala* attitude and of the changing characterisation of the 'milieu'. Even when the 'autonomous' Jewish milieu is rejected, the historical reality of a large social body is recognised, one in which the non-Jews are numerically insignificant, and culturally of no influence. Models for 'departure' from this traditional realm are also literary projects of a historical-biographical situation linked with a consciousness of the strength and the size of traditional Jewish society.

The non-Jewish socio-cultural model with which the Jewish writer in Eastern Europe was faced, constitutes a continuing problem. The gap between the abstract idealisation of social *strata* and direct familiarity with them within the reality of the Congress Kingdom, Lithuania or the Ukraine constitutes a literary *problem* and a *subject* for developing conflicts. The solutions, in most instances, involve reservations about the ideal model of depiction of non-Jewish figures or frustration of any approach to them by literary means within the plot. In any event, the ideal model of the images from the upper social classes (up to the 1880s) is related to Gentiles whose culture is dominant in the Jewish environment – Russian or Polish – and not to the peoples living in that geographical environment and maintaining daily economic contacts with Jews. Until the beginning of the twentieth century, at least, the positive ideological relationship was connected with 'the Russian people', as a general concept, with no other, specific national designation noted. It is only from the linguistic reality that the non-Russian identity of the non-Jew is revealed.

The linguistic differentiation between the various national groups – which is well developed in Yiddish prose but which penetrated Hebrew writing only belatedly – in *haskala* literature simultaneously serves a didactic purpose and is a literary means making possible the 'realistic' characterisation of the non-Jewish figures. The first trend is weakened, though it does not disappear, in the various language transitions, while the second trend is expanded (less so in the works of Peretz, more so in those of Sholem-Aleichem), and reveals the very wide possibilities existing in the multi-lingual system. The general model related to the socio-ethnic structure of Eastern Europe is preserved from the 1860s until the beginning of the twentieth century; the 'high' non-Jewish language, that of culture and the authorities (Russian, Polish); the 'low' non-Jewish language, that of the peasants and the *shtetl* 'goyim' (Ukrainian-Byelorussian); the Jewish diglossia in its relationship to the non-Jewish languages ('Holy language' i.e. Hebrew; Yiddish). Both because of the direct relationship with the 'milieu' and because of the literary addressee of the Jewish *oeuvre*, the 'low' non-Jewish language occupies the principal quantitative position in the texts examined. A large part of the use of Polish, Russian, Ukrainian or Byelorussian is limited to a vocabulary typifying the regular contacts between Jews and their environment and related to the fixed figures characterised in it.

In Sholem-Aleichem, there is a special language used by the *shabbes-goy*, by the non-Jewish maid who serves in a Jewish house, by the non-Jewish healer in the *shtetl*, by the village policeman, by the anti-semitic postman, by the Justice of the Peace and by the village priests whether Catholic or Orthodox. All of them use a fixed vocabulary with many Ukrainian or Russian words, when talking to Jews or about Jews. Thus, Sholem-Aleichem writes of Hapke, a Ukrainian maid in a Jewish household that, 'Hapke spoke Yiddish like a Jew and used in her speech a mass of phrases in *loshn-koydesh* [literally 'holy language' – Jewish religious terms, usually Hebrew or Aramaic derived]. When she spoke of Hveydor [another servant], she referred to him as a *kapoemik* [a derogatory term for non-Jew].

A decidedly negative stance toward Christianity, both Polish Catholicism and Greek Orthodoxy (Russian, Ukrainian or Byelorussian) is revealed in the characterisation of the clergy. Deviations from this attitude occur only when a priest (exclusively Catholic!) is characterised as enlightened, with a universal attitude differing from the medieval posture of the Church toward the Jews; or when 'realistic' figures are depicted derived from the realm of economic contacts between Jews and clergy.

Izaak Meir Dik's story *Zafrona* illustrates maskilic attitudes to enlightened churchmen. Writing of a senior figure in the Catholic hierarchy, he observes:

> He was one of the most distinguished of all the priests of the region, he knew oriental languages, Hebrew and Arabic, was a great engineer and scientist and knew history. His wealth corresponded to his wisdom, since, the descendant of great ancestors, he owned much property. Despite his wealth he was modest with all people of the town ... They [the bishop and the Jewish narrator] both had benevolent feelings for both Jews and Christians. At one table they, each for his part, spoke peace and truth [traditional *haskala* catchphrases]. The difference of religion did not separate their hearts.

Peretz distinguished between the pre-modern setting in which Catholic priests were a positive force and friendly towards the Jews, and the modern period, when the priest is frequently an anti-semite. Peretz depicts more than once the transition from a 'positive' to a 'negative' priest. Thus in *The Stake* (*Der drong*):

> Previously there had been a good priest, roly-poly, smiling, with red cheeks and laughing grey eyes ... He was friendly with the Jews ... He used to lend a ruble from time to time against some pawn and without high interest ... Before the Sabbath and holidays he was a redeemer and saviour ... 'Take pity on Moyshe Khaym, an abhorred Christ-hater, but who has a wife and children, and lend him a few coins ...'
> While the old priest had maintained good economic relations with the Jews, the new one was active in boycotting them. The new priest was infected with anti-semitism and preached against economic contacts with the Jews. He often referred to that story, the old tale of the hanged man [i.e. Jesus] ... 'Be careful,' he says, 'you should not deal with any Jew, neither buy nor sell.' If they don't listen, he refuses confession, won't grant absolution. 'Let their souls burn in hell for ever,' he says.

Jewish hostility is also evident in the anxiety provoked by Christian worship and its symbols, by churches, by monasteries and by the objects connected with them. The transfer of the Jewish-Christian encounter to the plane of an ideal confrontation or the symbolic link with materials derived from Jewish mysticism expresses this attitude. Christian themes, even at the beginning of the twentieth century, were regarded as taboo, beyond the realms already depicted in literature, and outside the frame of reference of *maskil*-radical attitudes, which linked the Church with reaction and modern anti-semitism.

The rise of this modern anti-semitism in Eastern Europe had a decisive influence on the literary depiction of non-Jewish society and on its image. The struggle with modern anti-semitism, in the works we have described, was also carried out with *haskala* conceptual tools, according to which this ideology was conceived as the reactionary antithesis of the progressive elements in Russian and Polish society. The apologetic element was still central in Jewish writing and, parallel to it, literary conventions were developed to describe the anti-semitic non-Jewish figure, which are the exact opposite of the traits and concepts which characterise the enlightened non-Jew, whether *maskil* or revolutionary. There seem to be only two ideological possibilities for characterising the modern non-Jewish figure: the revolutionary philo-semite or the reactionary anti-semite. These figures perpetuate ideological attitudes and literary analyses from the 1860s and 1870s. The difference between Abramovitz and Sholem-Aleichem, in their application of these patterns, is related *inter alia* to the extent of their attachment to particular *strata* within non-Jewish society. Abramowitz derived his universalism from the influence of Russian literature and criticism of the 1860s and 1870s, but his contacts with the radical Russian intelligentsia were quite limited. Sholem-Aleichem, on the other hand, came into contact at the beginning of the twentieth century with several radical Russian writers, and even absorbed something of the 'optimism' which typified the Russian intelligentsia of the period. Peretz, in contrast, was influenced by Polish positivism and absorbed something of the pessimistic spirit. Yet he also stood apart, early in the century, from the unambiguous assimilatory trend with which radical Polish philo-semitism was marked. Certainly, some of the most striking differences between the image of non-Jews in the works of Sholem-Aleichem and those of Peretz are related to their different relationships to the two sources of literary ideological influence – Russian and Polish. In spite of these differences, what is striking is the persistence of literary images derived either from the *haskala* or from the traditional Jewish view of the non-Jewish world, which retained their force on the eve of the First World War. Neither modern ideologies, nor modern literary trends could erase these deeply-rooted images. This was, of course, not only a literary but also a social and political phenomenon, the reflection of the ambiguous character of the Jewish encounter with the modernising societies of Eastern Europe.

The ambivalent feelings widely felt about this process in the Polish environment were well articulated by Peretz in his article 'I give up', written in 1911:

> It was not I who allowed Poland to be partitioned, because of family intrigue and hope of material gain. It was not I who put foreign rulers

on the Polish throne . . . It was not I who brought modern civil law from Paris. It was not I who brought religion and the Jesuits from Rome. It was not I who delayed the emancipation of the peasants, so that it had to come from Petersburg. Dear nobleman, this culture, with all its virtues and mistakes, is *yours* [. . .] my only sorrow is that in this Poland which is *yours*, besides me, who works and trades in the town, so, also, the peasant, who ploughs and sows had no share! There is also no place in *that* culture which you have created with foreign ideologies and laws for those who feel and act in a human (*menshlekh*) and not in an aristocratic (*pritsish*) way. I know, too, that in the Poland that is coming, there will be a place for the humanist, for the peasant and for me.

TRENDS IN THE LITERARY PERCEPTION OF JEWS IN MODERN POLISH FICTION
Magdalena Opalski

1. TOWARD LITERARY EMANCIPATION OF THE JEW. CLASSICIST AND ROMANTIC TRADITIONS

In the early 1840s Michał Grabowski, a conservative literary critic, deplored a Polish writer's 'serious' that is, non-comical that is, non-comical, treatment of his Jewish characters. Grabowski blamed the romantics, against whom he campaigned on a number of ideological fronts, for much of this new 'seriousness' in depicting the Jewish world. Specifically, he linked this new approach to the figure of Jankiel in Adam Mickiewicz's *Pan Tadeusz*. Although Grabowski devoted only limited space to comments on Polish literary perceptions of the Jews, he was in fact responding to a major socio-literary trend.[1]

In the mid-nineteenth century, the social horizons of Polish literature were rapidly widening. This process expressed itself in the massive introduction of lower-class themes which were until then regarded unfit for artistic treatment. The literary advancement of peasant, bourgeois, Jewish and other plebeian motifs was accompanied by the gradual abandonment of comicality as the standard approach to non-noble characters. The appearance of 'serious' Jewish characters in non-satirical contexts, an approach offensive to Grabowski's understanding of literature, echoed the emergence of new literary perceptions of non-noble groups in Polish society.[2]

In other words, the classicist convention in depicting social reality was crumbling. The Jew's place in this convention was determined by the role which classicist aesthetics assigned to literary characters in general. Treating them as mutations of a basically unchangeable 'human nature', classicist writers credited fictional figures with features which, while universal, were 'typical' of groups rather than individuals. As an element in the classicist panoply of plebeian types, the Jew was to remain on the periphery of high culture. The collective features which he personified such as greed, shrewdness and social exclusivism made him instrumental in the classicists' selective criticism of the basically immutable social order. Although this enlightened didacticism became less pronounced in the following period, the comical Jewish villain established himself as a stock figure in Polish literature and folklore.

Grabowski was correct in blaming the romantics for altering this classicist pattern. They did so by establishing a link between the degradation of the contemporary Jew and the glory of his biblical ancestors. The biblical connection increased the dramatic potential of Jewish characters and cleared the way for their selective literary 'rehabilitation'.[3] This growth in stature, occasionally reaching pathetic dimensions, and the more prominent roles assigned to Jewish characters, coincided with a gradual shift away from group stereotypes, and toward a more individualised approach. Indeed Jankiel in *Pan Tadeusz* (1834), Judyta in Słowacki's *Ksiądz Marek* (Father Marek) (1843), Rachel in Hołowiński's *Rachel* (1847) and Jews appearing in the works of Jan Czyński, Teodor Tomasz Jeż, Józef Ignacy Kraszewski – were full-fledged romantic heroes who drew much of their spiritual resources from the past greatness of the Jewish tradition. However, the new emphasis on Jewish spirituality, and the resulting marked psychological dualism of the Jew, were instrumental in both ennobling and demonising Jewish characters.

From the sociological point of view, early and mid-century Polish writers typically focused on the economic role of the Jew in the life of Poland's landed nobility. The relationship between the landlord and his Jewish tavern-keepers and creditors, loyal or disloyal to the noblemen in managing his finances or dealing with his peasants, remained the single most common 'Jewish' theme.[4] If this approach mirrored the prevailing feudal pattern of the Polish-Jewish encounter, the new stereotype emerging in mid-19th century emphasised the Jews' link to the expanding capitalist economy and the modernisation of their way of life. Mid-century writers focused on the upward mobility of the assimilating *stratum* of Jewish society and the increasingly visible process of osmosis between Polish and Jewish societies. While romantic literature dealt with the traditional Jews, its more realistic successor stressed the growing cultural and social differentiation of Jewish society. This diversification, complicated by the emergence of a sphere of mixed Polish-Jewish cultural influences, further undermined the classicist concept of the Jews as a social 'type'.

In the mid-nineteenth century, the proliferation of Jewish themes was not limited to literature. In many other spheres of cultural life, Jewish themes as well as Jewish contributors to Polish culture dramatically increased their visibility. Both these forms of Jewish cultural 'invasion', which intensified in the following decades, are crucial to our understanding of the subsequent transformations of the Polish image of the Jews.

Mid-century literature took note of the appearance of the Jew in many new social roles. For example, in *Sfinx* (Sphinx) (1846), Kraszewski introduced the first figure of a Jewish painter to appear in Polish fiction. The arrival in Wilno of this highly idealised character causes a sensation in the city's artistic community: 'A Jewish painter! – said Jan with amazement – something strange indeed! Indeed, an uncommon phenomenon!'[5] To understand the novelty of the phenomenon over which Kraszewski's interlocutors marvel, we should remember, that in the mid-nineteenth century not only Jewish painters but also non-biblical Jewish themes in the fine arts were an unheard of violation of the artistic conventions of the time. Nineteenth century Polish reviews of art exhibits illustrate the Polish audiences' ambivalent responses to the proliferation of Jewish themes, not to mention works by Jewish painters.[6] The resistance which this increased Jewish presence met, and the clash between the traditional and modern approaches, was echoed in Daniel Zgliński's play *U wspólnego stołu* (At the Common Table) (1833). In the play, a noble woman who watches her daughter draw a figure of a lamenting Jew, makes the following comment:

> I must admit, I am surprised by your choice of topic. In the final analysis, despite the great sorrow expressed in the features of your Israelite, your picture as a whole makes a comical impression. The looks of a Jew are always comical, even in tragedy. You would do better to leave drawing Jews and peasants to Kostrzewski. I am free of aristocratic prejudice and I share the democratic ideals of my husband, but this is not to say that I am delighted to see my daughter drawing lapserdak-wearing figures.[7]

The anachronism of the artistic conventions used to depict the Jewish world found its first critic in Józef Ignacy Kraszewski. Unusually sensitive to new cultural trends, Kraszewski contrasted the wooden vagueness of Jewish characters and the stereotypical situations in which they appeared with the picturesque richness of real Jewish life. In *Latarnia czarnoksięska* (The Magic Lantern) (published in 1843, simultaneously with Grabowski's essays), Kraszewski called for more realism in rendering contemporary social life, including Jewish society.

> Why, in depicting the Jew, do writers content themselves with hanging on beards and sidelocks and putting a *yarmulke* on the Jew's head ..., portraying always in the same way and with the same monotony our Jewry, so diverse and full of character? There are Jews and there are Jews, as different as earth and sky.[8]

Kraszewski's 'Historia Herszka' (The story of Hersz), included in *Latarnia*, a picturesque story of a Jewish smuggler whose wife runs away with a nobleman, translated into literary practice Kraszewski's desire to break with the dominant convention by providing the reader with a 'photograph' of Jewish life. Kraszewski's theoretical remarks seem to be rooted in the emerging realist rather than the romantic worldview. However, they passed over in silence the predominantly negative or comical features attributed to Jews in earlier Polish fiction, a fact acknowledged by some contemporary intellectuals. Newer historical research confirms that nineteenth century writers were aware of that negative image, but held divergent views on how to interpret it.[9] Waleria Marrené, the first Polish writer to deal systematically with the literary perceptions of the Jew, characterised his prevailing image in pre-positivist literature in the following manner:

> For many years a Jew appearing in a literary work represented, with very few exceptions, the negative or the comical element. (...) Our writers depicted Jewish society mainly in its relationship to the Christians. Not surprisingly, then, Jewish middlemen, cheats and moneylenders were introduced as being representative of the Jewish population. Portraying the Jews in the standard role which they played in relation to the non-Jewish world, literature presented this role as either base or comical, but invariably humiliating. (...) In that way fiction exacerbated mutual irritation instead of diffusing it. After the country's prosperity decreased and the discussion of financial matters gradually came to be accepted in *belles lettres*, Jewish characters appeared more frequently. The more realistically the novel mirrored real life, the greater the frequency of these appearances.[10]

In a series of essays published by *Tygodnik Ilustrowany* in 1879 Marrené not only noted the negative stereotype of the Jew rooted in the classicist and romantic traditions, but tried to explain it in terms of the prevailing pattern of Polish-Jewish encounters. This pattern, according to Marrené, exposed the Poles to the least attractive elements of Jewish society, the more positive features of which remained hidden from Polish eyes. Marrené did not question the legitimacy of this perception. At the same time, however, she correctly observed the increasing visibility of the Jews in contemporary Polish literature and linked this growing visibility to the expansion of the capitalist economy on the one hand, and to changing literary trends on the other.

2. THE RISE OF A MODERN JEWISH HERO

The impact of these combined factors expressed itself in the confusion surrounding the Jew's place in the social structure, a confusion that intensified as the Jewish quest for improved social status grew stronger. Signs of diversification in Jewish themes in literature appeared sporadically in the 1840s. For instance, a number of ideologically diverse authors[11] dealt with the question of intermarriage, a theme that became one of the most frequently treated 'Jewish' motifs in the post-1863 period.[12] All of these authors discussed possible matches between a Pole of noble ancestry and a totally assimilated, well-to-do and sympathetic convert to Christianity, or a Christian-born child of converted Jewish parents. Although – characteristically enough – none of these love stories ends happily, the large-scale introduction of the intermarriage theme reflected major changes in the Polish-Jewish encounter. These new patterns could hardly be served by literary techniques which, by promoting the idea of the immutability of the social order, petrified obsolete feudal structures.[13]

The number of Jewish characters deviating from the stereotypical figure with *yarmulke* and sidelocks continued to grow rapidly in the two decades preceding the January uprising. In addition to Kraszewski's previously mentioned Jewish painter, an important role in Józef Korzeniowski's *Kollokacja* (The Liquidation) (1847) is played by a gifted young Jew, Szloma, the Polish-educated son of a well-known Jewish physician. Several Jewish doctors appeared in mid-19th century Polish literature, ranging from unscrupulous and money-minded figures in Kraszewski's *Metamorfozy* (Metamorphoses) (1856) and Korzeniowski's *Nowe wędrowki oryginala* (New Journeyings of an Eccentric) (1858), to the ideal of selflessness in August Wilkonski's *Szlachetny nieznajomy* (The Noble Stranger) (1846). A Jewish actress of extraordinary beauty and great spiritual richness, played a leading role in Kraszewski's *Powieść bez tytułu* (A Story without a Title) (1853–4). Among this first generation of emancipated Jews to appear in Polish literature were also Jewish landowners with freshly acquired aristocratic titles and considerable fortunes, and Jewish bankers such as the pretentious Baron Geldson and the more amiable Olkuski (a former 'Żydek z Olkusza': a little Jew from Olkusz) in Korzeniowski's *Krewni* (Relatives) (1856).

Individual departures from the traditionally Jewish way of life continued to attract Polish attention in the years preceding the January uprising, giving birth to a gallery of increasingly acculturated Jewish characters. In Kraszewski's *Jermola* (1856), for instance, a rich Jewish tavern-keeper in Eastern Poland, 'having filled his purse and feeling the importance of his condition, slowly began to suffer from lordly pretensions.'[14] Among the characteristic symptoms of the Jew's 'sickness' is his large, recently built tavern, whose architectural features and interior decor are clearly reminiscent of a typical nobleman's manor. In Ludwik W. Anczyc's *Flisacy* (Raftsmen) (1855), both of the play's Galician-Jewish characters deviate from the traditional stereotype of a rural Jew. The acculturation of the more conservative of them, Chaim, is symbolised by a red umbrella that he carries with his traditional black dress. The pitilessly ridiculed cultural ambitions of the second Jew in the play, Edelstein, reach much farther. They include attending the theatre and opera, subscribing to Viennese newspapers and art periodicals, reading the Polish-language *Czas*, playing the violin, having affairs with women from various social strata and, generally speaking, pursuing the way of life characteristic of a well-to-do Polish nobleman. In the novel *Powieść bez tytułu* (A Novel without a title) (1853-4), Kraszewski presents a complex and unbiased portrayal of a well-to-do Wilno Jewish family, whose three generations represent three different cultural worlds.

The literature of the 1850s recorded, in addition to individual attempts by Jews to break away from the ghetto, another important development: the rise of a rich, secular and assimilated Jewish bourgeoisie. Literary portrayals of this new élite soon became a major 'Jewish' theme of Polish fiction. The first depictions of this milieu appeared in the 1850s with the publication of novels such as Kraszewski's *Dwa światy* (Two Worlds) (1851), *Choroby wieku* (Illnesses of our Age) (1856), *Metamorfozy* (Metamorphoses) (1958), Korzeniowski's *Nowe wędrówki oryginała* (New Journeyings of an Eccentric) (1851), *Krewni* (Relatives) (1856) and Niemcewicz's *Rok 3333 czyli sen niesłychany* (The Year 3333 or a Nightmare) (1858). These works introduced the Jewish bourgeoisie as a standard element of the social landscape portrayed in literature and consolidated the Jewish banker's status as a villain in Polish fiction.[15]

These novels articulated, on the one hand, the accumulating resentment which the accomplishments of this highly visible group generated in various *strata* of Polish society. On the other hand, they betrayed a preoccupation with the upward mobility of Jews in general. In fact, in that time of accelerated social change, the upward mobility of the Jews attracted more attention than that of any other group. The concern with their increased 'pushiness' found its characteristic reflection in scenes such as the dramatic description of Warsaw's Saxon Gardens being 'invaded' by the public from the nearby Jewish quarters in a 'takeover' compared to the biblical siege and fall of Jericho.[16] An even more dramatic takeover, presented as a nightmare (*sen niesłychany*) from which the narrator awakens in terror, was recounted in Niemcewicz's *Rok 3333*. In the story, whose distinctly 'classicist' comicality derives from the reversal of the established social hierarchies, a mafia of superficially modernised Jews takes over Warsaw, now renamed Moszkopolis after its Jewish ruler. The preoccupation with the advancement of the Jews was also mirrored in expressions such as *Żyd szejne morejne*, referring to a Jew whose modern urban 'elegance' distinguished him from his more traditional coreligionists, and *chorować na morejnë*, meaning 'suffering from exaggerated lordly ambitions'. Jermola's tavern-keeper is not alone among the previously discussed characters in being described in terms of one or both of these expressions.[17] Both these and many similar terms which entered the mid-century Polish vocabulary were applied exclusively to Jews.

Many nineteenth century writers, and particularly Kraszewski, associated the capitalist transformations in Polish society, including the growing power of money, with the irreversible destruction of the old world. In *Choroby wieku*, *Wieczory wołyńskie* (Volynian Evenings) (1959), *Metamorfozy* and other writings of that period, he obsessively depicts the disappearance of the old civilization in catastrophic terms.[18] Kraszewski was not alone in perceiving the Jews – and more precisely the most modernised strata of Jewish society – not only as a force rising on the ruins of the old social order (whose fall it previously accelerated) but also as one which successfully imposed its own values upon European culture. Such ideas were echoed even by writers who showed a considerable understanding of economic matters and were more differentiated in their responses to capitalist changes in Polish society. But even Józef Korzeniowski, a writer commonly considered a forerunner of Polish positivism, unequivocally associates the Jews with 'easy' money, the morally ambiguous wealth generated by unproductive financial operations. The opposition between money created by productive and by unproductive labour, and the author's contempt for the latter, provides the plot structure for several of Korzeniowski's literary works.[19]

3. JEWS IN POST-1863 POLISH LITERATURE

The immediate post-insurrectionary and the following Positivist periods brought about crucial changes in Polish literary perceptions of the Jewish world.[20] The basic impulse behind these changes came from a new ideological scheme which became influential in the late 1860s, and found its most mature literary expression in the following decade. The political depression which followed the defeat of the January uprising turned the attention of a new generation of liberally-minded writers to the question of Poland's economic and social well-being. Post-1863 literature, characterised by a more down-to-earth approach to social reality, called for a Western-style modernisation of Polish society as the only means of ensuring the nation's survival. It advocated a re-channelling of social energy away from the dream of Poland's independence, which was considered utopian, towards attainable goals: the satisfaction of basic needs and human welfare.

These writers evaluated individuals and groups according to their productivity, and in order to promote the latter, advocated individual liberty and equality of rights, opportunities and duties within society. Overcoming the traditional anti-urban and anti-capitalist bias, the positivists looked for a way of strengthening the entrepreneurial and middle-class element in Polish society and assigned an important role in this process to the Jews. However, they saw no possibility of using their potential without the immediate and complete Polonisation of the recently emancipated Jewish masses. Overestimating both the readiness of the Jews to surrender their cultural distinctiveness, and the willingness and ability of the Poles to integrate them, they advocated the dissolution of Jewish 'separatism' while appealing to the Poles for compassion and tolerance. Intended to be bias-free, many works which this assimilationist ideology inspired were, in fact, *romans à thèse* promoting various enlightened 'solutions' to the Jewish question in Poland.

On the other hand, the positivists' perceptions of Jewish society were shaped by the actual patterns of Polish-Jewish relations, which in many instances ran counter to their ideologically-motivated expectations. They took shape at a time when the acquisition of civil rights in the 1860s abolished most of the obsolete social barriers between Poles and Jews, while creating new areas of tension between them. It is true that instances of co-operation during the January uprising improved the climate of interethnic relations, generating hopes that the troublesome 'Jewish question' in Poland could be solved or at least substantially eased. This mood expressed itself, for example, in the popularity in the 1860s of the messianic motif of 'the two Israels' – a vision of the parallel destinies of Polish and Jewish nations, chosen by God for the accomplishment of crucial historical missions. In the long run, however, these gains were offset by the intensifying economic competition and Polish concerns about Jewish political loyalties at a time when Polish society faced strong denationalisation pressures. This climate was neither eased by the rise of militant nationalisms in the late 19th century, nor by multiplying indications that the dissolution of Jews in a sea of ethnic Poles was not likely to occur.

The positivists' massive literary 'discovery' of the Jewish world produced a body of writings dealing with various aspects of Jewish life which, marking the beginning of 'Jewish' topical specialisation in Polish fiction, further increased the overall visibility of the 'Jewish question' in Poland. Going far beyond occasional glimpses of Jewish life, the positivist interest in Jewish matters widened to include all of Poland's Jewish society, whose internal structure and grievances became the subject of literary investigation. The most ambitious of them placed the plots of their Jewish stories in a purely or predominantly Jewish environment, enriching Polish literature with a hitherto unheard of variety of human types. Many of these works focused, as did the most famous 'Jewish' novel of that period, Eliza Orzeszkowa's *Meir Ezofowicz* (1878), on the struggle between traditionalists and the pro-Polish forces of progress in Jewish society. Others, such as Przyborowski's *Hinda* (1869), Asnyk's *Żyd* (The Jew) (1874), Lubowski's *Żyd* (The Jew) (1868), Bałucki's *Żydówka* (The Jewess) (1869) i *Za winy nie popełnione* (For an uncommitted fault) (1871), Jeż's *Urocza* (The Charmer)

(1866), Orzeszkowa's *Eli Makower* (1874), set in a mixed or predominantly non-Jewish cultural environment, explored the conditions which encouraged or discouraged the integration of Jews into Polish society. It is noteworthy that this preoccupation with acculturation and assimilation of Jews retained its prominence long after the assimilationist ideology of Polish positivism was declared bankrupt. Free of the unrealistic optimism of the 1870s, works such as Prus's *Lalka* (The Doll) (1995), Maciejowski's *Zyzma* (1896), Konopnicka's *Mendel Gdański* (Mendel of Gdańsk) (1893), continued to focus on the pattern of Polish-Jewish interaction along the lines established by positivist writers.

Emphasising the need for greater Jewish participation in public life, 'classical' positivist fiction depicted mutually-enriching encounters between Poles and Jews. In *Ogniwa* (The Links), for instance, Orzeszkowa brings together an old Polish nobleman and a Jewish watchmaker and makes them discover the amazing similarity of their respective human experiences. In *Gedali*, the wonderful Talmudic parables told by a poor village pedlar meet with the love and gratitude of his gentile audiences. In Prus's *Anielka*, a village tavern-keeper is the only constructive force in the troubled life of a bankrupt nobleman and his children. No justice can be done to these works without mentioning the genuine human warmth permeating many of these images, and their well-documented ability to move both the Polish and Polish-Jewish readers for whom they were intended.

On the other hand, the early realists developed and broadened the scope of 'Jewish' themes introduced in the 1850s. Their discussion of the social progress of the Jew and its implications for the non-Jewish environment, acquired new political undertones. The post-1863 images of Jewish life were also characterised by a gradual shift from rural to urban surroundings. The heavy emphasis on the Jew's role in the capitalist economy overshadowed other 'Jewish' themes which, like inter-generational conflict in Jewish families, mixed marriages, scenes from the life of the Jewish bourgeoisie and other aspects of the osmosis occurring between the two societies, still inspired a substantial literary output.

In literary terms, these developments were made possible by the continuing advances of realism, which from timid non-romantic subcurrents evolved into the dominant literary trend in the late positivist period. In fact, the most widely-read 'Jewish' novels, Eliza Orzeszkowa's *Eli Makower* (1874) and *Meir Ezofowicz* (1878) and Aleksander Świętochowski's *Chawa Rubin* (1879) also helped shape the model of a realist novel. Reaching maturity in the late 1870s, realism remained a constant factor in Poland's literary life to the end of the period under study. Its internal evolution progressed from the tendentiousness characteristic of the positivist period, to an objective and mature form of realism, contributing to the continuous widening of the social horizons of Polish literature.

As the 'invasion' of creative arts by popular themes and characters continued, the literary and journalistic exploration of lower-status groups became the centrepiece of the positivist programme.

> From the moment when journalism poked its head out of the salons of its sponsors and looked at the world around, the time of Arcadian articles was over. It became clear that, in addition to people living off their capital, which, as is generally known, helps keep up spirits and preserve virtue, in addition to serious matrons, innocent virgins and vigorous young men 'gracefully mounting their steeds', there existed a different form of mankind: the world of parvenus and starvelings, of swindlers and murderers, of malicious old ladies and licentious young women. In this ocean of misery and bitter struggle for survival the world of good tone and good manners, with its livery and optimism, constituted only a tiny island. Moreover, this island was not beyond the reach of the poisonous breath of the crowds, and it occasionally happened that some of the island's inhabitants rolled down to the common den.[21]

In general, for the remaining part of the nineteenth century, the growing visibility of the Jew in Poland's social life led to an increased demand for fictional and non-fictional literature dealing with Jewish matters, and the number of such publications rose considerably. In *belles lettres*, there was a significant broadening of the reading public. As the popularity of Jewish themes increased in Polish literature as a whole, much of this growing demand was satisfied by 'professionals', writers like Klemens Junosza-Szaniawski, Artur Gruszecki and Tadeusz Jeske-Choiński, who partially built their careers on the basis of their literary depictions of Jewish society. Junosza-Szaniawski's reception by contemporary critics indicates that his colourful depictions of Jewish life account for most of his considerable popularity with Polish readers.[22]

A bibliographical survey I have undertaken can provide the basis for a rough estimate of the rising visibility of the Jew in Polish literature. The survey includes slightly less than 700 fictional works written between 1820 and 1905. Imperfect as it may be, this sample clearly shows the growing frequency with which Jewish themes are treated in Polish fiction of the late 19th century. While the period up to 1863 accounts for less than 10 percent of the works listed, those published during the positivist period (1863–1885) comprise close to 30 percent. For the following two decades (1885 to 1905), the figure is slightly more than 50 percent of the total. If we consider the quality of the works surveyed, and the prominence of Jewish motifs in their plots, this increase is even more significant. While few lengthy 'Jewish' novels were published in the years 1820–1863, the abundant production of poetry in the early 1860s represents an important part of the 10 percent recorded for the first period. The positivist discovery of the Jewish world as a subject of literary exploration alters these proportions. In general, Jewish motifs move to the foreground while works devoted primarily to the Jews grow both in volume and in literary importance. The output of such 'heavyweight' fiction becomes more significant in the mid-1870s and reaches its peak in the last decade of the 19th century.

4. THE TURN OF THE CENTURY

The great novelty of the positivist period was undoubtedly its idealisation of capitalism, an approach which paved the way for a more positive evaluation of the Jewish role in Polish society. This idealisation of capitalism, however, turned out to be short-lived and ran against values deeply rooted in the national tradition. The pragmatism of positivist writers failed to address the painful issue of Poland's lost political independence. Moreover, the Warsaw anti-Jewish riots of 1881 eroded what was still left of the assimilationist hopes for the massive, quick and painless Polonisation of the Jewish masses. In the course of the following decade, opposition to the 'shamefaced materialism' inherent in the positivist ideology continued to grow. Looking back at the failure of this positivist ideal, Ignacy Matuszewski, a well-known literary critic of the turn of the century, observed:

> Alas! The golden age remained a dream: the heroic engineers, praised by contemporary writers, were transformed into legal bandits. [Organic] work, which was to raise the spirits of the individual and of the collective, changed into a nightmare which preyed on the sweat of the poor and the brains, nerves and hearts of the rich and those determined to become rich.[23]

The reaction against the 'materialist' orientation of the positivists, marked by the transformation of 'heroic engineers' into 'legal bandits', was bound to affect literary perceptions of the Jew. In fact, in the last two decades of the 19th century, the image of capitalism, including its specifically Jewish face, becomes darker and more threatening. This trend continued to prevail in the early 20th century. Klemens Junosza-Szaniawski's *W pajęczej sieci* (In the Spider's Web) (1896), *Pod wodę* (Under Water) (1899), *Pająki* (Spiders) (1894), *Czarnobłoto. Pająki wiejskie* (Rural Spiders) (1895), Kazimierz Laskowski's *Zrośli z ziemią* (They have grown from this Land) (1913), *Pamiętnik eks-dziedzica z dopiskami eks-pachciarza* (The Memoirs of an ex-Landlord, taken from the Notes of a Jewish ex-tenant) (1904), Artur Gruszecki's *Szachraje* (Swindlers) (1899), *Dla miliona*

(For a Million) (1900), Władysław Reymont's *Ziemia obiecana* (The Promised Land) (1899), Teodor Jeske-Choiński's *Na straconym posterunku* (At a Lost Outpost) (1891), Michal Bałucki's *W żydowskich rękach* (In Jewish Hands) (1884), *Przeklęte pieniądze* (Cursed Money) (1899), Jozef Rogosz's *W piekle galicyjskim* (In the Galician Hell) (1896) – this is just a small sample of turn-of-the-century works which stress the dark side of capitalist society. Most of them are lengthy novels which focus on the unsuccessful efforts of Polish characters to free themselves from the capitalist cobwebs that entangle them. In all cases, the 'flies' are ultimately strangled and become the prey of a swarm of Jewish 'spiders'.

Maria Konopnicka's short story *Nasza szkapa* (Our Nag) (1893) offers an example of this approach. Described with exceptional detachment, its Jewish hero is typical of Jewish figures found in most works of this group in his lack – if not a total absence – of any non-pecuniary traits. This petty merchant, characteristically nicknamed Handel (trade), appears on the scene in order to deprive a debt-ridden worker's family of yet another of its few remaining necessities. His appearances divide the plot into segments and mark consecutive stages in the family's realistically depicted physical, economic and social decline. The child who narrates the story does not resent Handel as an individual. He sees the Jew as a tool in the hands of impersonal forces which, destructive as they may be, appear to him to be self-explanatory, necessary and constant elements of life. The naïveté and fatalism inherent in the narrator's perspective enable Konopnicka to pass over in silence the nature of the threat and to give it the appearance of invisibility. This literary trick, however, does not make the danger hanging over the boy's head less real. In the final analysis, the perspective of the narrator reinforces rather than tones down the naturalistic cruelty and sadness of *Nasza szkapa*.

It is noteworthy that in the post-positivist period interest in Jewish matters was particularly pronounced among writers with naturalist leanings. Although a distinctly naturalist school remained on the periphery of mainstream Polish realism, both currents absorbed-to varying extents and in various ways – the experiences of Zola and the French naturalists. In fact, all of the most prominent representatives of naturalism, such as Junosza-Szaniawski, Gruszecki, Gabriela Zapolska and Ignacy Maciejowski (Sewer), devoted substantial attention to the Jews. Jewish society appears to have provided them with a theme particularly fit to illustrate their pessimistic vision of social reality based on biological determinism.

As with the overall vision of capitalism, an optimistic interpretation of the bonds tying individuals and groups to their respective environments and backgrounds was gradually replaced by a more pessimistic view. The optimistic interpretation of determinism expressed itself in the form of a positivist faith in the magical power of education as a tool for the transformation of human societies. The positivist writers' emphasis on the harmonious and self-regulatory nature of social evolution accounts for their persistent reluctance to confront the issue of anti-semitism. A more pessimistic view of determinism is echoed in the previously quoted passage by Prus: a bitter struggle for survival governs the 'other mankind', the world of 'parvenus, starvelings, swindlers and murderers'. This vision of human relations as conflict-ridden is a typical feature of mature realism and naturalism. In general, the naturalists tended to view conflicts pitting various human groups against each other as an integral, 'natural' and necessary element of social life.

Analogies between the patterns of animal and human behaviour underlie many naturalist depictions of the tension between Poles and Jews. The following scene from Dygasiński's story of animal life, *Wilki, psy i ludzie* (Wolves, Dogs and Men) (1883), provides a particularly illuminating example of this way of thinking. It discusses the nature of the hostility between the narrator's dog and a young domesticated wolf. At first the narrator spontaneously intervenes in defence of the wolf, offering him protection against the dog's aggression. On second thought, however, deeper 'philosophical and historical' reflection makes the narrator refrain from interfering in the animals' affairs. Comparing the dogs' instinctive hostility towards wolves to the antagonism between Jews and non-Jews, he recognises the 'natural' character of human and animal aggression.

> Although anti-semitism did not yet exist at the time when I raised Buta (the wolf), even then the Christians held the Jews in contempt. Such and similar reflections cooled down my anger at the hound. How can you expect animals to achieve equality, I thought, if humans seem unable to achieve it? Let my wolf experience the bitterness of civilised life in his youth: let him have some tragic memories.[24]

From the 1890s onward the realist and naturalist depictions of Jewish society – now reaching their peak of popularity – were shaped by yet another literary factor. Individual psychology and the 'metaphysical essence' of the Jew became the focus of modernism, a current which placed the individual quest for the absolute, and devotion to pure art, at the heart of its artistic credo. The gloomy and decadent moods of the Polish modernists were fed by a strong perception of the decline of modern civilisation, a vision which was spreading throughout *fin-de-siècle* Europe.

The modernist taste for the esoteric and the irrational is exemplified by the psychological portrayals of Jewish women at the turn of the century. Thus Rachela, a thoroughly acculturated young Jewess with a deep interest in Polish literature, personifies the magic power of poetry in Stanisław Wyspiański's *Wesele* (The Wedding) (1901). At a wedding party which brings together all strata of Polish society, Rachela establishes contact with the world beyond. At her invitation the spirits of Polish history join the living, thereby initiating a confrontation between Poland's present and past which is at the very heart of Wyspiański's masterpiece.

But while Rachela's poetic visions play a constructive role in *Wesele*, dark and destructive sensuality is the dominant feature of Jewish heroines in Kazimierz Tetmajer's *Panna Mary* (Miss Mary) (1899), Zofia Nałkowska's *Węże i róże* (Serpents and Roses) (1913) and Jozef Weyssenhoff's *Hetmani* (The Hetmans) (1911). All these rich and spoiled young women emanate a striking lack of moral sensitivity. The two former characters' obsessive love of riches is equalled by the latter's hunger for political power. Although on the surface their alienation from the Jewish tradition is complete, the 'southern blood', the mysterious power of heredity, ties these three women to various aspects of Jewishness. In *Hetmani* this atavism expresses itself in the form of Hala's political support for the Jewish cause, which ranges from diplomatic intrigue to political terrorism. The Jewish roots of the two other heroines, who live in the twilight zone between the realities of contemporary Poland and biblical Palestine, are far more esoteric. The key to their psychology lies in the latter world, full of strange animals, of exotic plants and precious stones, and permeated by an intense eroticism.

On the whole, post-positivist Polish literature legitimised greater brutality in the depiction of conflicts between Jews and their gentile surroundings. This phenomenon can be explained in terms of the trends which marked the evolution from positivism to mature realism and naturalism. Among these features were the shift from a materialist to an idealist trend and the evolution from an optimistic to a pessimistic interpretation of determinism, a vision which reached fatalist dimensions in the literary output of the Polish naturalists. This evolution was also encouraged by a shift of emphasis from the harmony between the interests of an individual and his community to the vision of society as conflict-ridden and, finally, from the tendentiousness of positivist literature to an objective and more mature form of realist.[25]

At one pole, we have Orzeszkowa's *Eli Makower*, a novel depicting the conflict of economic interests with a realism and explicitness rarely found in the positivist *romans à thèse*. Ideological considerations, however, imposed an artificially happy ending on Orzeszkowa's realistically depicted conflict. By uniting Poles and Jews around common goals, the author restores the natural harmony of the social organism. At the other pole we have the basically conflict-ridden social reality of the 'cobweb' novels. All of them depict confrontations between two antagonistic human species, presented in their respective roles of 'flies' and 'spiders'. Together with the modernist exploration of Jewish spirituality, which removed much of the previous restraint on fantasising about Jews and their culture, these trends reinforced the perception of the Jews as an alien and threatening group.

5. CONCLUSIONS

The highly eclectic image of the Jew in modern Polish literature can only be studied as a complex interplay of social, literary and ideological factors. Its relatively short formative phase was marked by a rapid succession of diverse, sometimes conflicting, trends. The lives of writers who shaped Polish perceptions of the Jew stretched over several periods dominated by 'romantic', 'positivist', 'realist' and other literary conventions, techniques and topics. Formed under the combined impact of rapid social change and political instability, their views of Jewish society went through several equally distinct phases. While the erosion of liberal values and the failure of an integrationist ideology characterised the post-positivist period as a whole, the evolution of Świętochowski's or Bałucki's views illustrates what radical forms such a reorientation of Polish intellectuals could assume.

While the literary image of the Jew grew out of contributions made by various literary currents, periods marked by an unquestionable dominance of one of them were few and short. Rather, it reminds one of a *pot pourri* in which old and new elements, integrated around some obsessively recurring social themes, constantly change their place and functions within the broader framework of a literary tradition. For example, the appearance of 'serious' Jewish characters noted by Grabowski did not eliminate their classicist predecessor, the 'comical' Jew. Rather, it relegated it to the periphery of mainstream Polish literature, where it continued to thrive, indeed blossom, in second-rate fiction, mass-produced popular literature and folklore. Also, the longevity of some artistically and socially obsolete themes was due to the political connotations which they acquired. This politicisation of certain positivist and romantic themes is best exemplified by the figure of Jankiel in Mickiewicz's *Pan Tadeusz*. Countless imitations of Jankiel, a symbol of the retrospectively idealised golden times of Polish-Jewish relations, as well as his vicious caricaturing by writers supporting or opposing various 'solutions' to the Jewish question, Poles and Jews alike, indicate his continuing importance as a political symbol in the late 19th and early 20th century.

NOTES

1 Michal Grabowski, *Korespondencja literacka M..G..*, Wilno 1842, part I, pp. 75–78. Grabowski's views are discussed by Eugenia Prokopówna, in 'Śmiech szlachecki w

satyrycznych obrazach żydowskiego świata', in *Studenckie Zeszyty Polonistyczne*, no.4, *Ironia, Parodia, Satyra*, Krakow 1988, pp. 131-135.
2 See W. Wolk-Gumplowiczowa, 'Chłopi, mieszczaństwo i szlachta w powieści polskiej w pierwszej połowie 19-go wieku', *Przegląd Socjologiczny*, 7 (1938), p. 226; R. Czepulis, 'Uwarstwienie społeczne Królestwa Polskiego w świadomości współczesnych', in *Społeczeństwo Królestwa Polskiego*, Warsaw, vol. 1, pp. 356-376.
3 A characteristic example of such romantic ennoblement is the motif of the Sabbath and, in general, of the praying Jew. See Eugenia Prokopówna, 'The Sabbath Motif in Interwar Polish-Jewish Literature', in *The Jews of Poland Between Two World Wars*, University Press of New England, Hanover, 1989.
4 See Madgalena Opalski, *The Jewish Tavern-Keeper and His Tavern in Nineteenth-Century Polish Literature*, Center for Research on the Culture and History of Polish Jews at the Hebrew University of Jerusalem, Jerusalem 1986.
5 J.I. Kraszewski, *Sfinx* (1846), Poznań 1874, pp. 127-128.
6 An extensive discussion of the emergence of Jewish themes in Polish fine arts, and of Polish reception of the first Jewish contributors to Polish visual arts, can be found in an unpublished essay by Aleksander Żyga, 'Kraszewski and the Jewish Iconography'.
7 Daniel Zgliński, *U wspólnego stołu*, Warsaw 1883, pp. 7-8.
8 J.I. Kraszawski, *Latarnia czarnoksięska*, Kraków 1978, vol. 1, p.219.
9 Such opinions were expressed by Warsaw Jewish assimilationists centred around Daniel Neufeld's *Jutrzenka*. Aleksander Kraushar, 'Wspomnienia. Kartka z niedawnej przeszłości', in *Książka jubileuszowa dla uczczenia pięćdziesięcioletniej działalności J.K. Kraszewskiego*, Warsaw 1880, p. 508; W. Marrené, 'Kwestia żydowska w powieści współczesnej', *Tygodnik Ilustrowany* 199 (1879), p. 253; H. Galle, 'Żydzi w belletrystyce dzisiejszej', *Biblioteka Warszawska*, vol. 1 (1905), pp. 138-150: see also Czepulis, op.cit., pp. 275-380.
10 W. Marrané, op.cit., p. 253.
11 A. Wilkoński, *Szlachetny nieznajomy* (1846), J. Korzeniowski, *Żydzi* (1843); I. Hołowiński, *Rachel* (1847).
12 J. Szacki, 'Asnyk a Żydzi', *Nasz Kurier*, 22 August 1922.
13 On the socially conservative character of the classicist typology of literary figures in Polish literature, see S. Pietraszko, *Doktryna literacka polskiego klasycyzmu*, Wroclaw 1966, pp. 615-17.
14 J.I. Kraszewski, *Jermoła* (1856), Wrocław 1948, p. 49.
15 R. Czepulis, op.cit., p. 358.
16 *Szkice i obrazki. Fizjologia Saskiego Ogrodu*, Warsaw 1858, p. 77.
17 The importance of the socio-cultural information conveyed in these terms is best illustrated by Korzeniowski's introduction of Szloma in *Kollokacja*: 'Closer to the door stood Szloma Krzemieniecki. Szloma was an educated and *szejne morejne* (type of) Jew.'
18 A discussion of this vision in Kraszewski's *Wieczory wołyńskie* (1859) can be found in W. Danek, 'Kraszewskiego droga do pisania *Rachunków*', in *Pamiętnik Literacki*, vol. 1 (1956), pp. 27-30: for Kraszewski's view of the Jewish role in this process see also A. Eisenbach, *Kwestia równouprawnienia Żydów w Królestwie Polskim*, Warsaw 1971, pp. 263-265.
19 See J. Bachórz, *Realizm bez 'chmurnej' jazdy. Studia o powieściach Józefa Korzeniowskiego*, Warsaw 1979, pp. 75-76.
20 My discussion of the positivism is to a large extent based on my earlier essay, 'The Concept of Jewish Assimilation in Polish Literature of the Positivist Period', *The Polish Review*, vol. 32, no.4 (1987).
21 Bolesław Prus, *Kroniki*, vol. 7, p. 103; the column was originally published in *Kurier Warszawski*, no.123 (1894).

22 (A. Świętochowski), 'Klemens Junosza-Szaniawski. Wspomnienie pozgonne', in *Prawda* no.13 (1898); 'Liberum veto', *Prawda* no.39 (1893). See also A. Dąbrowski, 'Klemens Junosza-Szaniawski. Portret literacki', *Świat*, nos.3 and 5 (1899); M.b. (M. Blumberg), 'Klemens Junosza-Szaniawski jako żydoznawca', *Izraelita* nos.17–19 (1911) and T. Jeske-Choiński, 'Klemensa Junoszy nowele i opowieści żydowskie', in *Żyd w powieści polskiej*, Warsaw 1914, pp.61–68.
23 I. Matuszewski, 'Przemyśl w powieści', *Tygodnik Ilustrowany* no.48 (1899).
24 A. Dygasinski, *Wilki, psy i ludzie* (1883) in *Wybór nowel*, Warsaw 1973, p. 65. The wolf was found by the narrator in 1866.
25 H. Markiewicz, 'The Dialectic of Polish Posivitism', in *Literary Studies in Poland. Études littéraires en Pologne*, vol. 6, *The Positivism. Le positivisme*, Wrocław 1980, p. 27.

ANTI-SEMITIC LITERATURE IN POLAND BEFORE THE FIRST WORLD WAR
Frank Golczewski

In the not-so-distant past merely to mention Polish anti-semitism was considered a *faux pas*. The reason was that after the German atrocities in World War II the suggestion of any similarity by using a term like 'Polish anti-semitism' would reduce German responsibility for what culminated in the Holocaust. These views have changed somewhat: diagnosing the phenomenon of anti-semitism in another society has no direct connection with the guilt of German National Socialists for what happened during their short reign. Moreover anti-Jewish political statements certainly *have* played an important role in shaping Polish history.

Two prominent scholars from different parts of the world – Andrzej Chojnowski from Warsaw and Edward Wynot from Tallahassee, Florida[1] – have argued that the anti-Jewish aspect of inter-war Poland (as well as other nationality problems) was one of the main causes for the weakness of its policy and one of the main sources of internal conflict.

This does not eliminate another interpretation – that measures against non-Polish nationalities helped consolidate what would have been a greatly divided Polish society under the well-worn banner of attacking an internal enemy.[2]

Christian and Jewish Poles lived together in one country. Life and culture, political strife and alliances of both Orthodox and liberal Jews in Poland (both of those considered Jews by non-Jews) took place on a political, cultural and social stage shaped by developments not directly related to Jewish internal affairs.

To understand modern Polish politics it is important to consider the image that politically important Poles had of themselves. This was connected with their historical self-image, with the common aims of a society with a national identity, with the equation of 'Poland' with Catholicism, and resulting hostility towards various materialist doctrines, Soviet Bolshevism being only the most prominent of these. But all these points are not self-evident and are also specifically linked to the 'Jewish question'.

Poland was the most important home for Jews in the world: they were one of the more numerous 'nationalities' and they seemed to be everywhere. Unlike other 'alien' minorities, Jews were not restricted to specific border areas. They lived in towns and for historical reasons were in continuous contact with all other economically-active groups in Polish society. Consequently they had an important place in religious, political and economic thought. Thus any study of Polish politics has to take this into account, although this was usually not the case for much of the past.

Playing down the anti-Jewish theme in Polish political thinking limits our understanding of some crucial aspects of Polish history. Twentieth-century anti-semitic measures were explained merely as peculiar peripheral acts of unimportant personalities, although these phenomena were in fact a response to a quite important tradition in Polish political thought. At whatever point you look at modern Polish history, a specific 'Judeocentrism' (not always the same as anti-semitism) can be observed – most of all in the National Democrats, but in other political groups as well.

It is only now that an important book has been published in Poland that relates the question of late nineteenth-century Polish anti-semitism to the quarrels between Polish positivists and conservatives.[3] I do not intend to discuss Andrzej Jaszczuk's findings here, but the very fact that the problem of relations between Jews and non-Jews in Poland is discussed together with the struggle between two of the most important theoretical groupings in partitioned Poland hints at the relevance of the anti-semitic aspect of the moves for Polish independence before World War I.

We will try to look at some aspects of the Polish anti-Jewish arguments of an era when the issue of a national uprising was a dead one, but when, nevertheless, the desire for an independent state and the popularity of the 'Polish issue' corresponded with other aspirations in East-Central Europe, and when the resurrection of a Polish state was not considered totally impossible.

At that time – in a very modern way – the question of economic behaviour was linked with national aspirations. Not only the 'organic-work' representatives, but other thinkers and politicians as well, made much of the social question which had a totally different character in Poland than elsewhere in Europe. The question of economic activities was discussed in connection with achieving independence – and thus the Jews, to whom a specific kind of economic activity was ascribed were inevitably part of this discussion.

What I have in mind is not a specific '*Polish* anti-semitism' (which is a question of national categorization I do not accept) but the arguments of specific interest groups within Polish society who mixed foreign and domestic topics in order to support a particular political programme which appealed to them.

The increase in anti-Jewish writing and activities in Poland in the early

1880s is not an isolated phenomenon. In the West (including Germany) the economic crisis of these years, together with a growing conflict between liberals and conservatives, led to the formulation of racist theories, to the expansion of distinctly anti-Jewish parties and the invention of the term 'anti-semitism' to show that the current anti-Jewish feeling was different from *religious* prejudices. The new argument for hatred of Jews based on scholarly and scientific, rather than religious, grounds was most clearly visible in the dispute between the history professors Heinrich von Treitschke and Theodor Mommsen in Berlin.

In Russia after the success of increasing anti-Jewish legislation, anti-semitism was less based on 'scholarly' arguments than on political pragmatism. The pogroms of the 1880s and of the first years of the twentieth century, and the Beilis case later on, seemed to the enlightened intelligentsia, as to Western observers, indications of the backwardness and ruthlessness of the Russian Tsarist state.

Poland's particular role in European history is sometimes neglected. Pogroms in the Russian part are mostly seen as an outgrowth of Russian *ochrana* activities, and anti-Jewish populist activities in Galicia as a less important factor in the movement to politicise the Polish peasants. Anti-semitism in Poznania and western Prussia is 'explained away' by the fact that most Jews there felt more attracted to the German world, so that it was a sideshow in the German-Polish 'war' for domination there.[4]

But this is not sufficient. From the *żydocentryzm* of the National Democrats through Jabłonna, Przytyk, the ghetto benches, the activities of the *Narodowe Siły Zbrojne* (*NSZ*) to the absence of any serious reactions in 1968 and the Grunwald statements in more recent times, there are indications that the 'Jewish question' *cannot* be explained only in terms of 'foreign influence'. That is why it is important to look at the printed sources of anti-semitism of that period.

Akin to similar developments in the West, a little newspaper was published in Warsaw in 1883 which became a focal point for anti-semitic ideas. This was the *Rola* of Jan Jeleński (1845–1909), who had previously published a book called *The Jews, the Germans and Us*.[5]

Jeleński's approach differed from Western and Russian anti-Jewish forms: in his first statements he did not use openly racist or archaic religious arguments. In fact, in these first years he seemed only concerned with the 'completion' of Polish society. This was not very different from the political aims of the 'Positivists', and this is probably why Positivists – including Bolesław Prus – considered it worth arguing with Jeleński.

Jeleński at that time felt the 'intelligentsia in the middle' were a positive Jewish group, unlike the 'money aristocracy' and the 'superstitious lower strata'.[6] Following the Polish reformer Stanisław Staszic's demands for the improvement of the Jews he wanted to assimilate them with the Poles by mixing their economic activities; the Poles should become commercial middlemen like the Jews, and the Jews should undertake 'real', that is productive, work.[7] Before the 1880s Jeleński was definitely against any 'social barrier' between Poles and Jews: on the contrary, his was an ideology of assimilation, at least as far as certain kinds of Jews were concerned.

This changed somewhat, but not completely, with the foundation of *Rola*. In the first editorial Jeleński, as in his book, saw the Jews and the Germans as two 'tribes' (*plemiona*) that *dominated* the Poles. Describing the Jews he wrote:

> There is a tribe for whom disasters became harvests; a resourceless ness and a certain softness of character in [Polish] society, was the guarantee that the caste would fulfill its aspirations . . . The granting of equal rights [in Poland] gave this tribe dual rights: those of the caste, and those of the society.[8]

Reactions to this state of affairs were 'pessimistic'. The situation which he deplored was caused by the basic indifference of the non-Jewish Poles:

> And also mistaken would be he who, even for a moment, presumed that we want to put the entire blame for what has happened on the Jews and the Germans. No, we ourselves are guilty and our guilt is great.[9]

Thus anti-semitic arguments, which soon became a marked feature of *Rola*, were aimed at 'reconstructing' Polish society. They did not become a weapon for defending pogroms, but an argument for being aware of 'foreign' influence in Polish society. Without losing its anti-semitic character, Jeleński wanted to reach a state similar to that desired by the Positivists, but his arguments were different: besides being aware of an external enemy, Poles should watch out for an internal one as well.

Though this might seem less relevant, the result of such thinking is important. Where the 'Positivists' argued for moving forward into a void, into the unknown, a development which seemed to have risks, Jeleński's approval provided a feeling of 'security'. The enemy was visible and weak (though he was sometimes described as being strong), and – most important of all – he already established positions that waited only to be taken. The 'pioneering' factor lost its element of risk and encouraged the more timid Poles to set out in the required direction. This might be a reason why the Polish intelligentsia preferred 'Positivism' (its members had enough phantasy in their make-up), while the petty bourgeoisie found more avowedly anti-semitic arguments preferable.

We should remember that at that time (before the Dreyfus affair in France) there were voices in the Socialist movement, too, that were not against different approaches to creating a particular state of consciousness: the definition of anti-semitism as 'Sozialismus des dummen Kerls' carried no strange undertones then.[10]

By starting his *Rola* newspaper, Jan Jeleński filled a gap in the Warsaw newspaper world. Unlike the liberals, he did not criticize the landowners, professed an outspoken Catholic point of view and succeeded in rousing public interest.

Jeleński's political background comes as no surprise. He came from an impoverished landowner's family. He was mostly self-educated and he had to work hard in his early years. A short publication produced after his death mentions that he worked as a builder's labourer.[11] Though this is not mentioned explicitly, he may have worked on houses owned by Jews. This may have helped shape his later ideology into its paranoid belief that the Jews were in dominant positions in Poland, whereas non-Jewish Poles were only labourers and poor peasants. Later he managed to find jobs as a train-conductor and railway-telegraphist, which brought him into the world of the petty bourgeoisie – the breeding-ground for anti-semitism in all countries.

Though he did little writing in his *first* years of political activity, he argued fiercely with what he called the 'liberal-non-religious' press.[12]

He soon won the support of Jan Matejko, the painter, who was at loggerheads with Jewish financiers. Matejko, well-known in Poland even today, wrote to *Rola*'s editor:

> Our concessions at every step and in all areas; a great decline in our energy and spirit; sluggishness in social matters and a passive, and I would even say servile surrender to Hebrew influences; have caused the disciples of the Talmud to look at us as if we were walking corpses whom they may even torment – these are frightening developments.[13]

As mentioned above, Jeleński's first book in 1876 still favoured some aspects of assimilation. It was when he was strongly criticized from various sides that he started to abandon assimilation and to defend 'Polish' interests, moves which led to the founding of *Rola*. Once again I should like to stress that this development corresponded with that of other 'progressives'. Positivists also, later on – because of the refusal of Polish Jews to give up their own cultural identity, and the rise of Jewish nationalism (whether Zionist or Bundist) – gave up assimilationist ideas and developed an anti-Jewish stand not very different from Jeleński's. Aleksander Świętochowski is only the most well-known example of this.[14]

Thus Jeleński and his associates can be seen as forerunners of an ideological development that was not unusual in Polish society. This makes it interesting to consider their arguments in this context.

In 1887 Konstanty Wzdulski, a frequent contributor of articles to *Rola*, published a book called *The Polish Jews in a True Light*.[15] Wzdulski argued that only those having had commercial and financial dealings with Jews were entitled to write about them, rather than Jews themselves and their partisans, whose evidence could have no real meaning for an 'objective person'.[16] He therefore limited the perspective of a 'correct' observer to an economic one. As any economic perspective is inevitably primarily affected by competition, we might expect his statements to be hostile ones. However, here we can analyze priorities in this avowedly anti-semitic sphere. To the author economic behaviour is the most important one. Nonetheless Wzdulski was not overly concerned with economic factors. His starting point was the specific character traits which he ascribed to the Jews. The stereotypes used were very similar to those common throughout the ages.

The Jews' main trait was their astuteness — he declared that no other nation (yes, nation in 1887!) equalled the Jews in this 'and you can state openly that in this sense they really are a chosen people'.[17] The 'second important trait' — which he declared to be a 'terrible fault' (*straszliwa wada*) — was their 'avarice and boundless desire to get rich quickly'. And then like all non-Christian peoples (except for the Hindus) they were cunning, false, malicious, and vindictive. Unlike all other foreigners who settled in Poland, only they did not become acculturated. Wzdulski compared the Jews with the Armenians, whom he falsely claimed were also Semites, thus hinting that these statements, though using similar words to contemporary German or French writers, were not basically racist. Just the opposite: he regretted that the Polish 'power of assimilation which affects other nationalities, proved too weak in relation to the Jews'.[18]

He contrasted an image of the Poles with that of the Jews. According to him, the Slavic character expressed friendship towards everybody. That was why all kinds of persecuted people came to Poland from the Middle Ages to modern times, including the Jews who were '*cudzoziemcy duchem*' (strangers by spirit).[19] Wzdulski believed it was not the Jews' fault that they could not change their 'asiatic nature', but that of 'our forefathers', who allowed a 'foreign element' to rise that 'poisoned the moral health of society and destroyed its material welfare wherever this element settled in very great numbers'.[20]

Here we have a basic element of this kind of anti-semitism: the Jews are stronger than we are, and it is our group's fault that they were allowed to rise. The maxim derived from this statement is that in order to change the situation, i.e. to improve the position of the Poles, one has to consider that basic historical mistake and rectify it.

We can easily compare Wzdulski's position with that of Wilhelm Marr in Germany.[21] Like Wzdulski, Marr also warned that the Jewish race was going to triumph over the Teutonic one. This led directly to rationalizing the necessity for self-defence. But whereas Marr is considered to be one of the first German militant racists, Wzdulski did not advocate violence.

Self-defence in Poland should not be violent. Wzdulski declared his total opposition to the 'deplorable events of the Jewish pogrom in Warsaw in 1881'.[22] Not only did he use the word 'pogrom' which Poles later tried to avoid in relation to Polish events,[23] he also called it a 'shocking and inherently foolish act that was justly criticized and condemned in the press'.[24] He criticized, too, those Poles who tried to blame foreigners (i.e. the Russians) for the events.

The lesson Wzdulski learned from the pogroms of 1881 was that there *was* a Jewish problem. Bolesław Prus's analysis was not very different from that. The basic responsibility for the pogrom, according to Wzdulski, belonged to the Jews: 'Don't use the law to beat them, then they won't beat you illegally'.[25] And as the Jews (because of their 'character') would never stop their anti-Polish activities, he described the way the Poles would have to act to obtain the desired results: giving the Jews equal rights he believed to be the wrong way – the Wielopolski reforms were described as opening the floodgate for Jewish domination of the Polish economy.[26] Many years, even centuries, would be needed to 'repair what centuries have destroyed'.[27] As the main result of 'Jewish activity' was the destruction of the Polish aristocracy and it was now the peasants' turn to be destroyed,[28] Wzdulski's book was intended to persuade Polish society to analyze its position and to begin to cure it – if only the *Rola* circles would suggest some kind of practical solution not based on anti-Jewish or anti-German sentiment.

Here we have the principal difference with the Warsaw Positivist thinkers of the 19th century: they intended a total restructuring of the Polish economy and thought in terms of a modern 'national economy' that would include all inhabitants of Poland. Anti-Jewish tirades were not to come till later, when some Positivists seemed to have realized that many Jews rejected the riches of Polish culture, were opposed to national assimilation, and were starting to profess a separate national identity. The *Rola* anti-semites spoke earlier – though not from the beginning - of the basic impossibility of assimilation. To them – basing it on a cliché about the weakness of their own group – the main point was not to build their 'own' economic position but the easier way of taking over those existing already.

One should be very careful about condemning them on these grounds alone. A take-over (though not in nationality terms) is one of the basic modes of action in Marxist thought, and liberal capitalism is not a stranger to this procedure either.

What happened to the *Rola* anti-semites when the Positivists (or Progressivists) also incorporated anti-Jewish elements into their ideology? They rejoiced in finding their long-held theories had finally proved acceptable. We will take the example of a book by Teodor Jeske-Choiński, published in 1912 just after the Duma elections which sent a Socialist candidate from Warsaw to the assembly through Jewish votes. This led to the declaring of a wide-spread boycott of Jewish businesses in Poland.[29] Teodor Jeske-Choiński was a mediocre writer, but nevertheless he had a following in Poland's cultural world. He was one of the 'theoreticians' of Polish anti-semitism. Though Jaszczuk does not even mention him in his list of the *Rolarze* (*Rola* writers) he was one of their main representatives. The *Rola* jubilee book described him as somebody who 'from the beginning was a *Rola* associate, who sincerely professed the programme and the slogans of anti-semitism. At the same time he was a fighter against Warsaw Positivism, who enriched the volumes of *Rola* with many valuable studies . . .'[30]

His book *Poznaj Żyda!* is a kind of synthesis of this kind of anti-semitism from before World War I; that is, before it was augmented by the prospects of Polish national independence, the Bolsheviks' victory in Russia and direct accusations of collaboration with the Nation's enemies, the Germans. Even though the concepts mentioned there were not held by all and it is still difficult to count its adherents and adversaries, they were nevertheless held by enough people for them to be found among some individuals even today.

What was it? Like Wzdulski[31] Jeske-Choiński set out to prove the great 'unknown' – the role of Jews in history and more important, in the present.[32] This was not a unique approach. Most writers used and still use this stock theme to prove the importance of their own findings. But when combined with anti-semitism this approach has a different quality. It seems to emphasize that there is indeed an 'anonymous empire' whose proceedings are hidden from ordinary people and which only a perceptive few, including the author, can describe. From the start the author made a second point to stress his own importance. Though Jews were mostly the objects of ridicule and comedy,[33] they were in fact 'Jehovah's chosen people'. Their pride was only 'kept in check by their willpower'; they were full of 'unlimited hatred for the power of all foreigners' and this would have had serious consequences, 'if they ever ruled'.[34] Later on Jewish rule was identified with that of the Bolsheviks: the Tharauds called their book on Bela Kun and Hungary *Quand Israël est Roi*,[35] and my own copy of Jeske-Choiński's book has numerous hand-written comments by a Polish reader of the 1920s referring to *Trockij* at relevant points. But before World War I this was still an unknown perspective.

It must be emphasized that Jeske-Choiński was not a very original thinker. Most of his statements are clearly recognizable quotations from foreign sources, especially German and French ones. This is an important point. More often than not those who stress the harmlessness of Polish anti-semitism indicate its 'non-racist' quality. As the German and French 'thinkers' were racist from a very early stage this cannot always be true. Jeske-Choiński's book is full of racist undertones, whether he is describing the 'Semite', whose qualities are said to dominate the Jews,

> The Jew, from the Semite, Hittite and in part Amorite mould, a new racial creation preserves the stubbornness and the energy of his distant ancestors – the will of a Semite.[36]

or when he is distinguishing between the 'better' Israelites from Galilee ('where the primeval Semites were swamped completely by the Hittite elements'[37]) and the Jews from Judea who 'blackened the Israelites' later.[38] It does not seem necessary to stress that these arguments coincided with numerous Western ones – from revised Gobineauism to some 'defenders' of Christianity who tried to make Jesus an Aryan from Galilee and who came into their own in Germany after 1933.

In his criticism of the Talmud he relied on the Münster theologian Rohling, and his claim that the stock exchange was a sign of the 'judaisation' of commerce was also unoriginal. More important was his criticism (common in contemporary nationalist German circles) of the German Jewish poet Heinrich Heine, who was supposed to have 'introduced into German and world literature a special kind of humour, or rather joke, unknown in Aryan societies till then'. According to Jeske-Choiński it lacked 'both German *Gemütlichkeit*, French *esprit* and Polish joviality'. It was cynical, full of (negative) self-irony and lacked the most important aim of Aryan satire: *castigare mores*. It was nevertheless found in plenty in Warsaw.[39]

Unlike Wzdulski's limited approach, which seemed only concerned with Poland's economy, Jeske-Choiński tried an all-embracing one. After having stated that the Jews were taking over numerous aspects of Polish public and cultural life, he dwelt at length on how different peoples had reacted to similar moves. Remarking that anti-semitism was present in medieval and early-modern Poland (though more 'innocent' than the West and Central European kind)[40] and having 'exposed' assimilationism as merely tactical, he was not prepared even to accept the fledgling Zionist movement as a solution: for nine-tenths of the Jews their aim was not settlement in Palestine but the imposition of 'Jewish nationalism on foreign garbage'.[41]

Here was a call for action: Wielopolski's assimilationist drive had evidently blinded Polish society for decades,[42] while only a few declared anti-semites had remained true to the doctrines – Jan Jeleński, Teodor Jeske-Choiński and Roman Dmowski.[43]

This is not the place to describe the historical development of the Polish national democrats, but one should remember that anti-semitism did not become a part of the *Endeks*' official programme before 1906. Polish *Rola* anti-semitism was not primarily a conservative one before then: some of its efforts to stimulate economic modernisation were directed against 'old' Polish *szlachta* values. But a change in the argument developed: national thinking of the Dmowski kind joined forces with that of *Rola*. Eventually, the *Endeks* would take the lead in an anti-semitic role. Publication of *Poznaj Żyda* coincided with the start of the *Gazeta Poranna 2 Grosze* – the *Endek* instrument for organizing the biggest anti-Jewish boycott campaign to date. And, as the Positivists, who were not anti-Jewish, also revised their stand under the impact of Jewish anti-assimilationism and nationalism of various groups, an unholy alliance came into being, joined together chiefly by one thing – respectable anti-semitism.

From a supposed economic issue, anti-semitism had developed into a more comprehensive one: all modernisms had 'led to ruins, ruins, the same ruins...'.[44] The time had come to look back, to 'cleanse the Polish soul',[45] to use anti-semitism as a means of 'economic and spiritual self-defence'.[46]

Rola and those who wrote for it were certainly not the leading contemporary politicians or journalists. But they were successful in not having to wait too long (though Jeleński died before he was triumphant – Jeske-Choiński's own words)[47] to see their wishes come true. Politically-motivated anti-Jewish feeling – the kind they sponsored – became an accepted issue in parts of Polish 'good society'. Though the *Rolarze* were swamped in the *Endek* ocean, their demands were taken over – and passed on to Piłsudski's successors in the 1930s. Though sometimes said to be of minor importance, the *Rolarze* were a very significant aspect of Polish political thought.

NOTES

1 Andrzej Chojnowski, *Koncepcje polityki narodowościowej rządów polskich w latach 1921-1939* (Wrocław, 1979); Edward D. Wynot, *Polish Politics in Transition* (Athens, Georgia, 1974).
2 For the conservatives in most European countries this movement served to explain the social process that led to a new capitalist civilization – and thus destroyed the old order. This explanation by Franz Neumann, 'Angst und Politik' (1954) in his *Demokratischer und autoritärer Stat* (Frankfurt, 1st ed., 1967), p. 203, is not sufficient for the militant non-conservative anti-semites. Here it was not so much the fear of destruction of older social structures but an attempt at social reconstruction. It was only later that this kind of Polish anti-semitism came together with the broader clerical and nationalist *Endek* movement.
3 Andrzej Jaszczuk, *Spór pozytywistów z konserwatystami o przyszłość Polski 1870-1903* (Warsaw, 1986).
4 Cf. William W. Hagen, *Germans, Poles, and Jews. The Nationality Conflict in the Prussian East 1772-1914* (Chicago/London, 1980), pp. 288-319; Rudolf Jaworski, *Handel und Gewerbe im Nationalitätenkampf. Studien zur Wirtschaftsgesinnung der Polen in der Provinz Posen (1871-1914)* (Göttingen, 1986), pp. 132-6.
5 Jan Jeleński, *Żydzi, Niemcy i My* (Warsaw, 1876).

6 Ibid., pp. 12, 39.
7 Ibid., p. 19.
8 'Czego chcemy?', *Rola* 1/6.1.1883.
9 Ibid.
10 In Poland similar views were advanced by Wacław Nałkowski in his book *Jednostka i ogół* (Kraków, 1904).
11 Antoni Skrzynecki (Werytus), *Jan Jeleński i Jego hasła ku odrodzeniu narodu* (Warsaw, 1910), p. 7. Jaszczuk, *Spór*, pp. 211–2, also writes about his conservative tendencies which he could not live up to, because of his difficulties in being accepted by the upper class. To him this is the main reason for Jeleński's efforts to drive towards a specific kind of emancipation of the Polish bourgeoisie.
12 Jaszczuk's position is that Jeleński stressed a Catholic approach so as not to be confused with 'liberals and free- thinkers' (ibid., p. 213); the anti-semitic movement became clearly clerical after the merger with the *Endeks*.
13 Jan Matejko in *Rola* 6/1883.
14 Cf. Frank Golczewski, *Polnisch-jüdische Beziehungen 1881–1922* (Wiesbaden, 1981), pp. 92–6.
15 Konstanty Wzdulski, *Żydzi polscy w świetle prawdy* (Warsaw, 1887).
16 Ibid., p. 5.
17 Ibid., p. 11.
18 Ibid., p. 18.
19 Ibid., p. 15.
20 Ibid., pp. 10–11.
21 Wilhelm Marr, *Der Sieg des Judenthums über das Germanenthum. Vom nicht confessionellen Standpunkt aus betrachtet* (Bern, 1879).
22 Cf. Wzdulski, *Żydzi*, p. 19.
23 Cf. Golczewski, *Beziehungen*, p. 7.
24 Cf. Wzdulski, *Żydzi*, p. 119
25 Ibid.
26 Cf. ibid., p. 22.
27 Ibid., p. 41.
28 Cf. ibid., p. 28.
29 Cf. Golczewski, *Beziehungen*, pp. 101–20.
30 *Ćwierćwiecze walki. Księga pamiątkowa Roli* (Warsaw, 1910), p. 98.
31 Cf. Wzdulski, *Żydzi*, p. 17.
32 Cf. Teodor Jeske-Choiński, *Poznaj Żyda!* (Warsaw, 2nd ed., 1912), p. 5.
33 Cf. Magdalena Opalski, *The Jewish Tavern-Keeper and his Tavern in Nineteenth-Century Polish Literature* (Jerusalem, 1986), passim.
34 Cf. Jeske, p. 6.
35 Jérôme & Jean Tharaud, *Quand Israël est Roi* (Paris, 1921).
36 Jeske, p. 12.
37 Ibid., p. 16.
38 Ibid., p. 17.
39 Cf. ibid., pp. 130–1.
40 Cf. ibid., p. 191.
41 Ibid., p. 171.
42 Cf. ibid., p. 198.
43 Cf. ibid., p. 201.
44 Ibid., p. 221.
45 Ibid.
46 Ibid., p. 238.
47 Cf. ibid., p. 201.

MR. GELDHAB AND SAMBO IN *PEYES* IMAGES OF THE JEW ON THE POLISH STAGE, 1863-1905

Michael C. Steinlauf

Introducing his study of the Jewish character in Polish literature, Yekhezkl Viltshinski concludes: 'In researching the portrayal of Jews in world literature, we discover indeed that no literature has occupied itself so much with Jews as Polish literature.'[1] If this statement, a measure of the fascination with which generations of Polish writers meditated upon the peculiar nation which lived among them for nearly a millennium, is a fair assessment of the situation in Polish literature as a whole, one would expect it to be especially so in the realm of theatre. For the encounter between actors and audience particularly lends itself to the creations of the collective imagination, to the 'figure', the stereotype, and therefore, one would expect, to the Jew, for centuries perceived by Poles not as an individual, but as a 'type'. Moreover, the essence of theatre is to act, play, take on a role, in a word – to become other than one is. Should this not assume a special significance in relation to the Jew, that paradigmatic 'other' for Polish society? Furthermore, in a world in which, even in the nineteenth century, literacy was the property of a small élite, Polish theatre offered participation to a considerably wider audience, whose needs, in turn, shaped this theatre. It follows that the Jew on the Polish stage, reflecting the experiences and values of varying strata of Polish society, should reveal even more faces than the Jew in Polish literature.

As with so many other facets of Polish-Jewish relations, the question before us is fascinating, enormously complicated, and barely touched by scholarship. While the stage Jew in Western European theatre has received a respectable amount of attention, there has not been one comparable study of the rich sources relating to the image of the Jew in Polish theatre.[2] The present article, intended as a modest introduction to the subject, focuses on the stage Jew during one decisive period and primarily in one key city: Warsaw between the last Polish uprising against the Tsars and the first Russian Revolution.[3]

Following the failure of the 1863 Uprising and Russia's emancipation of the peasants, Polish society, particularly in Congress Poland, began to undergo rapid economic transformation. A centuries-old feudal order began to crumble, while Polish cities, with Warsaw in the lead, developed into modern urban centres. Change was accompanied on one hand by a crisis in the ruling values of society. Messianic insurrectionary politics and aristocratic values tied to land and lineage proved helpless in the face of aggressive capitalist expansion. On the other hand, within the crucible of the cities, a new urban society began to take shape. Polish cities now became a magnet for ruined gentry, freed peasants and Jews from throughout the Russian Empire, and the dynamics of urban life began to bring them into contact with each other in numerous ways. This was a period of social flux, of a naive curiosity about life-styles and cultures, and was accompanied by the emergence of ideologies suggesting the possibility of new alliances, new kinds of co-existence towards the building of a modern Polish society. Specifically, both Jews and peasants were understood to have a role to play in the development of a modern Poland. With respect to Jews, however, by the early twentieth century the situation had changed again: new Polish and Jewish national ideologies, and particularly the rise of political anti-semitism, began to harden attitudes on both sides. To focus therefore on the last decades of the nineteenth century is to examine Polish society at the moment of its greatest cultural fluidity and openness to both Jews themselves and their imaginative representation. During these decades, a dense panorama of 'Jews' crowded the Polish stage, and indeed, the stage Jew reached the climax of his development. Neither before nor after this period was the 'Jew' so everpresent, so diversely represented, and, as we shall see, so essentially linked to the fundamental functions of theatre.

A clear sign of the times is that, for the first time, it is necessary to speak not of one, but two sorts of theatre: the well-established Polish State Theatres (*Teatry Rządowy*),[4] and the newly developing popular establishments known as 'garden theatres' (*teatrzyki ogródkowe*). The State Theatres traced their lineage directly back to the National Theatre (*Teatr Narodowy*) which had been founded by King Stanisław August Poniatowski during the last years of Polish independence. In contrast to the situation in most of Western Europe, this was a theatre 'without a powerful popular-national base, without native theatrical traditions, without a native repertoire developed over preceding centuries.'[5] For decades, the State Theatres staged a repertoire of opera, ballet and drama which, strongly influenced by Western European, especially French, models, and strictly controlled by the Russian censor, catered primarily to Warsaw 'high society' – Polish aristocracy, wealthy merchants, Russian officers and officials. During the period we are examining, this theatre developed increasing cultural and national importance. First of all, in the aftermath of the failed insurrection, the Tsarist authorities powerfully repressed Polish cultural institutions. Theatre, in common only with the Church, remained an exception, and as a result, attained near-religious significance, sharing only with the Church the status of being 'the last bastion of the living mother tongue.'[6] In practice, veneration of the theatre most often vented itself in worship of its stars, who were typically showered with flowers, mobbed in the streets, the smallest details of their lives the subject of avid public attention. This fashionable 'theatre-mania' was linked to changes in both the State Theatres' repertoire and audiences. On one hand, a new generation of Polish playwrights, creators of the new genre of bourgeois drama, began to find their plays more welcome in the State Theatres than French comedies.[7] On the other hand, a new middle class which was particularly attracted by plays reflecting its own milieu, and for whom attendance at theatre, as in Western Europe, was an emblem of status, began to fill the State Theatres' expensive seats, while in the galleries, a less prosperous audience howled enthusiasm or derision at the stage. Increasingly in evidence among these new audiences, as, indeed, among the new Warsaw bourgeoisie as a whole, were Jews. In their vanguard was a new generation of Jewish financiers and industrialists who developed into a Jewish plutocracy of an unprecedented sort: seeking entrance into Polish aristocratic society through education, as well as, to an extent, intermarriage and conversion, they identified themselves with Polish cultural values, and became patrons of Polish literature, art, music, opera and theatre.

At the same time, in the years immediately following 1863, Warsaw garden theatres – popular open-air establishments linked to restaurants and cafés – began to provide a different sort of entertainment for a different audience: the new urban masses who, during their free hours in the summer, while the State Theatres were closed and their actors and upper class audiences abandoned Warsaw for fashionable spas, crowded the boulevards and squares of Warsaw looking for inexpensive diversion. These impulses among the mass of uprooted, restless, new urban dwellers were no different from those which led to the rise, during the same period, of comparable forms of popular entertainment elsewhere, vaudeville in the United States, for example.[8] The ubiquitous farces, melodramas and operettas, for the most part free of tendentious and didactic impulses, attracted a certain share of artisans and workers, but also the Warsaw *demi-monde*, and most of all, the clerks and shopkeepers of the lower middle class. This was a young, exuberant and extremely varied audience: 'a mixture of voices, languages, social class, manners, moods; a veritable Tower of Babel of people linked only by the hope of relaxation, freedom and entertainment.'[9] Prominent among these theatregoers were Yiddish-speaking, traditionally dressed Jews (whose considerable appetite for theatre beginning in the late 1870's also brought them to the new Yiddish theatre). Jews, in addition, were also in evidence in Polish theatre as performers and particularly as singers and musicians accompanying performances. Indeed, in no other realm of culture during this period was there greater contact between Poles and Jews than in Polish theatre, both 'high' and 'low'.[10]

What sort of 'Jew', then, did these new audiences see on the stage? As a first approximation, let us broadly differentiate between two kinds of representation: on one hand, the traditional comic personage of the *żydek* (little Jew, pl. *żydki*), a figure profoundly rooted in Polish folklore and feudal society, and on the other, images influenced by European cultural currents and reflecting contemporary Polish social reality. Certainly, both sorts of representation were to be found on the stages of all Warsaw theatres, and indeed there was even a degree of interchange between the repertoires of 'high' and 'low' theatres.[11] Nevertheless, in the last decades of the nineteenth century, the comical *żydek*'s characteristic abode was the garden theatre stage, while the 'new Jew' was most often, and certainly first seen, in the State Theatres. Let us begin with the latter.

In order to understand the changes that brought the Jew centre-stage in Polish dramatic theatre, it is useful to examine a work which prefigured these changes. This is Józef Korzeniowski's play, *Żydzi* (Jews), which premiered in 1843.[12] True to its title, *Żydzi* is filled with Jews: there are street peddlers hawking their wares; there is an itinerant bookseller; there is the convert Baron Izajewicz, a wealthy landowner and merchant; and there is, finally, the moneylender Aron Lewe and his assistants. Nevertheless, *Żydzi* is not really about Jews; set amidst the Polish landed aristocracy of the Russian-Polish borderlands, the play documents, in the figure of the unscrupulous Count Ponicki, the moral decay of a class which, faced by economic decline, resorts to brutal swindles in order to maintain its extravagant life-style. Alongside Ponicki, and equally detestable, is the parvenu Zadzirnowski, a local official who has exploited his position to become a ruthless moneylender. These villains' victims are the Staroświęcki [of Old Faith] family, small gentry who are the perpetuators of the authentic, old-fashioned aristocratic values of honour, loyalty and lineage.

Compared to Ponicki and Zadzirnowski, the Jews in Korzeniowski's play manifest dignity and a considerable sense of honour. This is particularly true of Aron Lewe who, frequently mentioned throughout the play, finally appears, white-bearded and patriarchal, in the final act to save the Staroświęckis from ruin by offering them a low-interest loan. Aron Lewe is a hard-headed businessman, yet he is nevertheless capable of returning a favour done him long ago by old Staroświęcki; Aron Lewe, therefore, like the Staroświęckis, is a man of honour. The title of Korzeniowski's play, therefore, is ironic, and underscores a world that has started to go awry: it is the landowners and the Polish parvenus who are now the 'real Jews'. Reproached by Zadzirnowski for being a Jew when he refuses to take him on as a partner, Aron makes Korzeniowski's moral explicit:

> I, a Jew? Well, what's wrong with that since I was born a Jew? ... A Jew likes money. Certainly he likes money because a Jew without money isn't a human being ... If a Jew doesn't have money, he stands on the other side of the door until he's pushed out ... But what do you call someone who has honours and offices and land, to whom no one would dare say a word, at whom no one would dare point a finger, and yet he loves money more than brother or sister?[13]

Żydzi was an important prefiguration of things to come. What is new in this play is the setting of Jews amidst a deteriorating feudal world in which money is becoming the measure of all things. The Jew, who in his middleman role within traditional society was intimately associated with money, still maintains his association to it, and, indeed, the Jew is used as a standard against which to measure Polish corruption. Nevertheless, the meaning of money has begun to transcend its association with the Jew. At the same time, the wealthy apostate Baron Izajewicz, to whom the Ponickis attempt to wed their niece, offers a foretaste of a whole genre. Yet Baron Izajewicz's role in *Żydzi* is limited; it is Aron Lewe, with his traditional ties to the aristocracy and the feudal order, a stable feature in a changing landscape, who is the dominating Jewish figure in this play. More generally, *Żydzi*, whose world is entirely rural, and whose heroes exemplify pure 'old Polish' values, is still a major step from the cynical urban environment of post-1863 bourgeois drama.

Despite (or perhaps because of) its old-fashioned values, and certainly because of its sympathetic portrayal of Jews, *Żydzi* attained great popularity and maintained it for several generations of audiences, among whom, understandably, Jews were particularly well represented.[14] The role of Aron Lewe attracted the greatest stars of Polish theatre, including the celebrated Alojzy Żółkowski Jr., who premiered in the role in Warsaw and developed it over the course of forty-five years.[15] Jewish critics often saw *Żydzi* as a model for 'Jewish plays'. Ignacy Suesser, for example, a nineteenth century critic uniquely sensitive to Jewish matters, wrote as follows: 'For the first time in our dramatic literature appeared a Jew, not in the figure of a buffoon, not to please the crowd, but in his everyday attire, in a true, unfalsified form neither disfigured nor embellished.'[16] As late as the turn of the century, a Jewish critic noted the 'unusual interest' in the play displayed by the 'younger generation'.[17] This interest, however, was doubtless primarily nostalgic, for already by the 1870s a stage figure such as Aron Lewe was decidedly anachronistic.

In the aftermath of the 1863 Uprising, the nationally-minded Polish intelligentsia began the work of learning hard political and economic lessons from the last and most catastrophic of the insurrectionary débacles. What was the point of the conspiratorial, messianic politics championed by the nobility, indeed, what was the point of Romanticism with its noble posturing? What good had it brought the Polish nation? The landowning class of Russian Poland was ruined, its political power broken by Russian reprisals, its economic base shattered by large-scale migrations to the cities. Furthermore, who *was* the Polish nation, anyway? Did it include the peasants, who had often denounced their insurrectionist landlords to the Russian authorities, did it include women, did it include Germans and Jews, engaged in factory and railroad construction throughout Poland? Answering such questions led in the 1860s and 70s to the creation of a new and highly influential school of thought: Polish Positivism. Drawing on the ideas of Auguste Comte and the English utilitarians, the Positivists adopted as their motto the term 'organic work'. The nation, for the Positivists, was an organism, whose growth could only proceed gradually, and through harmony among all its constituent parts. Not the noble gesture, but the patient, rational development of industry and culture was to be the measure of the nation's progress. Money, that assassin of traditional values, had its place in the new world – what mattered was how it was made and how it was used.

The period as a whole seemed to bode well for Polish-Jewish relations. Polish attitudes to Jews, first of all, were influenced by the widespread perception that many Jews, and not just those from assimilated families, had identified with the Polish cause and in various ways supported the uprising. The central symbol of this cooperation was Dov Ber Meisels, the Chief Rabbi of Warsaw at the time of the revolt, an orthodox Jew who aligned himself with the insurrectionary movement and preached Jewish support for Polish national demands.[18] Moreover, in the aftermath of the uprising, could not the Jews serve as a model for maintaining national integrity in the absence of political independence? Furthermore, and for the Positivists this was the key factor, were not Jews, after all, in the vanguard of precisely those economic transformations which the Positivists acclaimed? In an ironical reply to a chauvinistic pamphleteer, Aleksander Świętochowski, principal voice of the Warsaw Positivists, well defined the new attitude to Jews and also suggested its contradictions:

> Jew or German, tenant, huckster, pedlar, broker of any kind, loosely linked to the nation, this is our consolation or at least a petty nuisance, but Jew or German as manufacturer, merchant, who raises up the nation's industry, who puts a thousand hands to work, with good merchandise for the people, this is true defeat, this is a corrupter. If not for such defeats and such corrupters, there would reign among us, particularly for our lower classes, the most perfect paradise: we would lack cord, flannel, calico, linen, the poor and the modestly affluent would have every opportunity to walk about like our first parents, while fig leaves would be supplied them by some aristocrat who, emerging from a long line of generations engaged in

sport, ballet and cards or tiring of other sorts of diversion, would set up a factory on his property. Isn't it worthwhile longing for such a state?[19]

For Świętochowski, attempting to wrench the basis for an optimistic liberal orientation out of Polish conditions, it made sense to bracket together Jews and Germans; differences of religion and cultural tradition took second place to economic facts: both Jews and Germans were in the vanguard of capitalist development. Yet this very fact suggests the Polish complication. In the West, a gradually expanding native bourgeoisie, anchored in long-established urban centres, confronted and finally vanquished the landed aristocracy. But for Świętochowski at the end of the nineteenth century, the idea of a Polish factory owner is still a joke. In Poland, capitalist development, nowhere in nineteenth century Europe a very pretty thing, would be mirrored not just in class, but in national antagonisms. And, through the eyes of its proliferating Polish critics, whose gentry origins were never distant, capitalism would be seen as particularly ugly, particularly disorienting, and inevitably – un-Polish. These are some of the contradictions which lay at the basis of the new and highly popular genre of bourgeois drama, which one Polish critic outlined as follows:

> The most important questions for it: money, possessions, business (*geszeft*); then the moral side: making use of this money, exploitation; then the social: the relationship of the new class, the bourgeoisie, to the old landed aristocracy and the gentry, the struggle for social position; finally, the complication of these relationships as a result of the national and racial antagonisms which exist in our land ...[20]

As in other areas of nineteenth-century Polish culture, but particularly theatre, Polish bourgeois drama was strongly influenced by French models, especially the plays of Émile Augier, Alexandre Dumas *fils*, and Victorien Sardou. During the years of economic expansion of the Second Empire, these playwrights had established the middle class on the French stage, and while mocking its pretensions and excesses, and a world in which money was becoming the measure of all things (including love and matrimony), reserved their sharpest barbs for the old aristocracy. The 'well-made play', which offered its bourgeois audiences the pleasures of tight plot construction embellished with unexpected twists, discovered its master in Sardou. In Poland in the period after 1863, numerous playwrights turned to the genre; in Warsaw the most successful were: Zygmunt Sarnecki (1837–1922), Edward Lubowski (1837–1923) and Kazimierz Zalewski (1849–1919).

What these playwrights had in common was, first, an association with large cities, primarily Warsaw. Their plays, staged in the State Theatres but also in the 'better gardens', were usually set in cities, but even if not, urban rhythms predominate. All were also journalists in the Positivist press, published stories, theatre and literary criticism, and translated the works of their French counterparts into Polish. All reached the peak of their creativity early, and by the beginning of the twentieth century, when the radically new currents of Polish neo-Romanticism began to dominate theatre, their playwriting had come to an end.[21] Not just today, but already by the 1920s, these playwrights were quite forgotten in Polish letters, and indeed, the genre they represented, cosmopolitan, often flighty and cynical, stands outside the context of values which subsequent Polish writers have used to evaluate the past.[22] Yet in their time, Sarnecki, Lubowski and Zalewski were not only extremely popular, but highly regarded by critics. Moreover, their appearance in Warsaw represented a victory for Polish culture: the conquest of the Polish stage for works by Polish authors. As one critic, writing in 1882, noted: 'We remember ourselves that (c. 1865) a poster announcing an original play ... was an obstacle for the public, [a sign] that there was no reason to attend ... today ... a poster announcing an original play attracts masses, [who are] less eager when it comes to a foreign work'.[23]

At the centre of the world of bourgeois drama, underlying every dramatic intrigue, is money: *Febris aurea* (Gold Fever), the title of one of Sarnecki's plays, might well stand as the motto of all the characters in these plays. Gold fever crushes and transforms, sets all things in motion: money becomes the common denominator of all values. 'Money,' explains the Baroness in one of Lubowski's plays, 'baptizes anew, gives beauty to the ugly, gives sense, imagination and wit to the stupid, health to the sick, comfort to the wretched.'[24] In *Febris aurea*, everyone is constantly shaking hands, but, as one character remarks early in the play: 'It's not the person, but the business you're greeting amicably.'[25] As a result, the solidity of land and lineage is replaced by ambiguous mixtures, a half-world of dubious moral substance: 'We must accept whatever we can grasp: half-principled people, half-virtuous spouses, half-mixed salons. We are an agent of decomposition in the dregs of that world which is arising from the misalliance of the new principles with the old.'[26] This loss of boundaries, indeed, extended onto the stage itself: contemporary critics complained of a genre that, by banishing the comic from comedy, had eradicated traditional distinctions between 'comedy' and 'drama'.[27] An ideal context for mirroring such changes is the institution of marriage. In a world ruled by exchange value, the most apparently natural of liaisons becomes the ultimate exchange. The aristocrat seeks money without work, the parvenu Jewish or German millionaire seeks a noble title, that is, 'Polishness': a straightforward business transaction satisfies both sides. 'Mixed marriages' are as essential to the landscape of the bourgeois drama as the noble's manor house was in earlier genres. And in a good number of plays, they are at the centre of the action: for example, in Zalewski's extremely popular *Nasi zięciowie* (Our Sons-in-Law),[28] whose title refers to the young noblemen to whom Jews have married their richly dowered daughters, and in Sarnecki's *Zemsta pani hrabiny* (The Countess's Revenge), in which a young noblewoman is enjoined by her mother to 'Christian sacrifice', to 'turn your thought toward Him who suffered for the whole world', and marry the financier Goldberg.[29]

For all the Positivist stress on industry and productive capitalism, there is rarely a sense in these plays that money produces anything of social value. One never sees the inside of a factory, while enormous fortunes, the products of speculation, appear and disappear overnight. Certainly, attempts are made to distinguish 'good' money from 'bad', yet such distinctions are generally either lip-service or highly problematic. In *Febris aurea*, the hero Juljusz demands of the parvenu Gałdzyński: 'Yes, little ducat, what is your birth: work and virtue, or usury and crime?' A Positivist slogan, that is, is encased in an aristocratic metaphor: this 'Positivist' hero can only grasp good and bad in terms of lineage. Moreover, in the following scene, the phrase, 'What is your birth, little ducat' (*Kto cię rodzi, dukaciku?*) is appropriated and debased by Gałdzyński and his equally despicable rival, who employ it to escalate their exchange of insults.[30] The ability to conceive of capitalism on its own terms flounders in these plays because even its Polish defenders have only their own gentry background on which to draw. In contrast, it is the non-Polish characters, and above all, the Jews, who, cut off from their past, seem capable of representing the new world in all its ambiguity. Furthermore and more profoundly, the sense of Korzeniowski's *Żydzi* now suffuses an entire genre: this world is very 'Jewish'.

Throughout these plays, Jews are everpresent. First of all, they appear in traditional roles, as moneylenders, brokers, matchmakers, inevitably scheming to make money out of the financial woes of some aristocrat. Yet often, as in *Żydzi*, such Jews simply underline the even worse behaviour of Poles. Furthermore, even when Jews are not physically present on the stage, the Jewish presence is inescapable. Early in *Febris aurea*, for example, the stage is set for Gałdzyński's appearance through allusions to the source of his money: he is said to have been married to a Jewish woman, daughter of a liquor distiller (*dzierżawca propinacji*) whose fortune Gałdzyński wrested from her family after her father's death. And more generally, such words as *handel* (trade) and *Aby handel szedł* (Business as usual), mouthed by a vast succession of Jewish characters throughout Polish literature, pervade the dialogue of these plays.

Alongside the 'old' Jew, and in a number of cases, standing at the centre of the play, is the 'new' Jew: banker, speculator, factory-owner, usually a convert and generally married into the aristocracy. Such a figure was hardly unknown to Polish audiences. Aleksander Fredro's classic comedy *Pan Geldhab* (Mr. Havemoney), for example, first staged in 1821, created the Polish stereotype of the vulgar parvenu. *Pan Geldhab* remained extremely popular throughout the century, and although the character was originally played as a German, in our period Mr. Geldhab often became a Jew.[31] Furthermore, during the first half of the century, a number of Polish comedies and farces derided the invasion of Polish society by specifically Jewish parvenus. Among them was a one-act play entitled *Nasze przebiegi* (Our Intercourse) which, translated from the German by and starring Aloyzy Żółkowski Sr., was popular in Warsaw beginning in 1818. In the 1840s this play was revived as a satire on the powerful Epstein family.[32] It is in the period after 1863, nevertheless, that the 'new' stage Jew achieved his greatest prominence. Let us examine several plays in which such a Jew is a central figure.

Zygmunt Sarnecki's play *Słonecznik* (The Sunflower) contains a specific response to the Russian pogroms of 1881. One of the main characters in the play is the Jewish convert Merker, a financier who identifies himself as a cosmopolitan, with Kościuszko who, according to Merker, was 'a great man before he was a great Pole'. But when Merker learns that his father, whose house was destroyed by rioting mobs in Kiev, was saved from death by a Pole, his attitude changes profoundly. 'I have stopped being a cosmopolitan,' he declares, 'I am a Pole.' He will now rededicate himself to the common cause 'not in order to gain power, not to marry my daughter to a prince, but to be worthy of the sacrifice which saved my father and redeemed me.'[33] For Sarnecki, therefore, assimilation is the solution to the 'Jewish problem'. Moreover Merker, the capitalist whose morality is no worse than that of any Pole in this play, and considerably above that of its despicable protagonist, must nevertheless spend considerable energy apologizing for his wealth.

Edward Lubowski's interests were very different. In his plays he devoted particular attention to the way in which class and traditional divisions interfered with the development of the Polish 'organism'. In *Przesądy* (Prejudices), for example, an aristocrat and a Polish factory owner (one of the rare examples in our repertoire of a Pole as authentic bourgeois) learn to overcome their mutual antipathies and realize that 'these prejudices disappear when two honest men come together'.[34] But in Lubowski's melodrama, *Żyd* (The Jew), things turn out rather differently. When Goldstein, who has loyally managed the finances of the aristocratic family which his father served before him, learns that his only daughter Elka and young Count Adam have fallen in love, he resolves on revenge: the financial ruin of the young aristocrat. Even Adam's offer to convert to Judaism is of no use, and Goldstein too is destroyed when he learns that Elka has fled from it all and chosen to spend her life in a nunnery. Although Lubowski also demonstrates the prejudices of the other side –

Adam is thrown out of his house by the Countess when she learns of his love for a Jewess – it is Goldstein's transformation into a demonic avenger which is at the heart of the play. 'O, be cursed from my entire heart!' Goldstein shrieks at Adam in the last act.

> O, may that word die on your lips, may the arm which reaches for your lover's embrace wither, may your cheeks shrivel, and your eyes collapse deep into caverns, to appal God's creatures! May your heart break in grief and despair, you accursed enemy of our faith, degenerate seducer of the daughters of Israel.[35]

Lubowski's was hardly the only case of a play in which the Jew, however 'modern', under emotional pressure suddenly manifests a hatred of Christian society. In the poet Adam Asnyk's work, *Żyd*, a wealthy convert has done everything possible to be accepted in gentile society, but as a result has become filled with hatred. Spurned as a Jew by the woman he loves, he attempts to revenge himself on her lover, and ends by destroying himself.[36] Not far from the surface in many a 'modern' stage Jew, therefore, lurked the familiar presence of Shylock, who appeared as well in more traditional incarnations. Thus, in Wacław Szymanowski's *Salomon*, set in the sixteenth century, the eponymous usurer and kabbalist murders his daughter when he learns of her love both for a Pole and for the Gospel of Love.[37] The original Shylock was introduced to Warsaw audiences at this time, apparently first in an opera, and then played frequently thereafter.[38] One measure of how deeply rooted in Polish consciousness the notion of Jewish vengefulness continued to be, is an innocent remark of the actor Wincenty Rapacki. In his memoirs, Rapacki describes learning to play the role of Shylock after entering a synagogue, apparently on Yom Kippur, and witnessing 'these old men, so serious, so calm a moment ago, suddenly transformed into thundering titans awakening heaven in order to rouse it to vengeance with them.'[39] Given such astounding (and momentous) misconceptions among even the Polish intelligentsia, one can understand the basis for frequent Jewish complaints about the Polish stage; as a theatre critic in the Polish-language Jewish weekly *Izraelita* put it: 'eternally and to the point of boredom one and the same theme – Jewish fanaticism and vengefulness in the struggle with the spirit of love and forbearance.'[40]

Kazimierz Zalewski was the most staged playwright of the period, and also the one most thoroughly committed to a liberal version of Positivism. In *Górą nasi* (Up with Our Side) the central figure is Pomper, a powerful banker and director of a railroad, a converted Jew who has married into the aristocracy. Pomper's business methods are no better nor worse than those of this Polish counterparts, and he knows it. His associate Szwindelman, however, provides a shady contrast. The plot turns around Pomper's attempt to gain the presidency of the city council, in the course of which he demonstrates a modern talent for manipulating influence, including the press. Accused of belonging to a 'nation of financiers', Pomper too must offer an apologia, but one that must have greatly pleased the new Jewish plutocrats in the audience. Listing the many attempts which Jews had made to enter Polish society, including conversion, and the rejections these had provoked from Poles, he concludes: 'The only weapon we have against you is money; do not wonder that making it is our one goal in life, since within these bounds you've locked our entire life and all our activity.'[41] Predictably, Pomper loses the election to a champion of typical Positivist ideology: 'organic work of the whole nation straining in one direction, economic and spiritual rebirth, the fusion of all elements in united work under the common banner of love for everything that's ours.'[42] Yet Pomper loses by only a few votes, the struggle as a whole has been one between equals, and Pomper and his opponent shake hands at the end. Even the liberal Zalewski, however, could not resist giving the last word to Szwindelman, who exclaims: 'Up with our side!' and then explains that 'whoever wins, that's our side.'

In *Małżeństwo Apfel* (Mr. and Mrs. Apfel), Zalewski presented his audiences with an entirely sympathetic modern Jewish hero: Ernest Apfel. Ernest, too, has married into an aristocratic Polish family, but in distinct contrast to other such situations, including another one in this play, Ernest really loves his wife Zofia, and that is why old Apfel permitted the marriage. On the other hand, Zofia's family, who move in with the Apfels, look down on them, and Zofia herself, indifferent to Ernest, takes a lover. But old Apfel goes bankrupt, and Ernest turns his own fortune over to his father to cover his losses. This understandably provokes a storm from the in-laws. Zofia's mother insists that the marriage be annulled, that if her daughter married 'a newly baptized Apfel, it was not in order for her to eat poverty and drink misery and go with him into private service.' To which old Apfel, with considerable dignity, responds:

> If I understand you correctly, you are presenting the problem very straightforwardly. We had merchandise for sale and you purchased it. Today you don't have the money to pay for it, so begone. But it seems to me that that is precisely the way in which tradesmen and shopkeepers behave.[43]

As in Korzeniowski's *Żydzi*, but here amidst a cosmopolitan, money-hungry urban world, the question is clearly posed: what constitutes nobility, and who, after all, are the real 'Jews'? Having made his point, Zalewski extracts a happy ending. Zofia suddenly comes to Ernest's side, ready to love the poor husband whom she did not love when he was rich. Even in this play, however, the Jew must apologize: at the play's conclusion, old Apfel suddenly realizes how little love there has been in his capitalist's heart and, moved by the young couple's love, declares: 'For the first time I believe in people, but it's already too late for me.'[44]

In Western Europe, from the Renaissance on, the history of the theatre and the history of the market have been intimately intertwined. As the physical marketplace became increasingly abstract and 'placeless', as it invaded human relations to a greater and greater degree, as traditional social signs and symbols increasingly took on the quality of commodities, the resulting 'general crisis of representation' nowhere found a better reflection than on the stage. This is because 'the new drama showed, as no other genre could, how precarious social identity was, how vulnerable to unexpected disruptions and disclosure it was, and therefore how deeply theatrical it was.'[45] Such connections apply particularly well to newly urbanizing Poland, where the crisis of representation was not only best reflected on the stage, and in the cult of stars and the 'theatre-mania' associated with it, but precisely in the stage Jew. For in Poland, the development of the 'placeless' market to a great extent *was* the movement of the Jew from *shtetl* marketplace to urban finance. As nowhere else then, the 'new' stage Jew represents actual changes: the development of market forces and the bewildering transformations of consciousness which accompany them. The Jewish Mr. Geldhab on the Polish stage, uniting in his own person theatre and market in a particularly concrete way, uniquely fascinated an entire generation of Polish audiences. Whilst this 'Jew' strode dramatic stages, however, the antics of a very different personage dominated the 'gardens'.

In attempting to sketch the everpresent stage Jew of Polish popular theatre, we encounter a number of significant difficulties. There is, first, a problem of documentation. A large portion of the repertoire of the garden theatres was never published, while theatre reviews, planted in the world of high culture, typically dismiss such productions as unworthy of attention. Moreover, and here we confront a problem of interpretation as well, even when we possess the text of the play, how are we to 'read' it? How are we to imagine its actual production and its meaning for its audience? This is a problem in any historical study of theatre, but it becomes particularly acute in the case of popular theatre. For the popular stage is supremely a world of 'types' shaped by theatrical conventions which precede and may well confound the apparent meaning of any particular text. Texts, that is, become pretexts for 'simple entertainment,' an experience, of course, which we can scarcely take for granted, and which is hardly simple.

Approaching the image of the Jew in the Polish popular theatre of our period solely from the texts of plays can easily become an exercise in accumulating long lists of 'positive' and 'negative' characters. And indeed the latter, it is soon apparent, greatly outweigh the former. Can we then conclude that what we have here is a Polish variant of the Western

European stage Jew, a personage one theatre historian has aptly described as 'everybody's bogeyman'?[46] In Western Europe, this stage Jew, metaphysical miscreant or common knave, emerged at a time when the Jew's actual involvement in Western European economies was diminishing, in most cases, indeed, after the Jew's physical expulsion from these societies. Western theatre, therefore, was free to develop its Jews 'into forms and shapes limited only by the human imagination.'[47] But in Poland, the Jew's relationship to the larger society was entirely different, and here we must begin in order to approach the complexity of the Polish stage Jew.

In Poland, centuries of co-existence under feudal conditions had made the Jew a fixture of the Polish landscape, as familiar an element of the natural order as the peasant village or the landowner's manor, and linked to both through networks of mutual economic dependence. This was a world, nevertheless, so profoundly divided into its three constituent 'estates' that one popular conception identified them with the races descended from the sons of Noah: landowner as Japhet, peasant as Ham, Jew as Shem.[48] Three separate races, that is, yet bound together through a common father. How then did Ham and Japhet conceive of their brother Shem? Specifically, what form did his representation assume in the traditional theatre of peasant and gentry? Although this large question cannot as yet be definitely answered, recent scholarship offers some important clues.

In her studies of the figure of the Jew in Polish folk theatre, Olga Goldberg-Mulkiewicz notes, first, the extraordinary prevalence of the Jewish figure, and second, its widespread association with laughter and entertainment.[49] In the various genres of spectacle performed annually by players from local villages, the Jew appears in a variety of important roles: as a biblical figure (Herod or sage in the puppet show known as *jasełka*), as a masked figure leading a ceremonial animal into homes at New Year (a ritual known as *herody*), and as himself, that is, as a type recognised by the local community (in the interludes of the *jasełka*, for example). In the latter case, the Jew's function is invariably comic, and includes gesticulation, shouting and wailing, often over imaginary wrongs suffered at the hands of other characters in the play or those in the audience. Dressed in an outlandish version of his distinctive attire (long beard, *peyes* [earlocks], *kapote* [long black coat], furred hat), often with a hump, speaking a deformed Polish, the Jew also sings and dances, and indeed, his appearance often closes with a dance, frequently solo. Furthermore, even in those cases where the Jew's function is initially serious, as when he represents a biblical figure, in the course of the play his *persona* usually disintegrates and concludes by disrupting the seriousness of the proceedings, transforming it into laughter. The role of entertainer distinguishes the Jew, moreover, from other ethnic stereotypes in these performances: just as Tatar is equated with warrior, so Jew is equated with jester. Finally, this function of the Jewish figure, in at least one important case, expanded in response to social change: in the nineteenth century, when purchase of a bride by a groom's family had lost its legal meaning, that portion of the marriage ceremony was retained, but began to include the figure of a Jewish pedlar, who substituted jest for outmoded rituals. The figure of the Jewish entertainer, therefore, was not only deeply rooted in peasant performance rituals, but seems to have been highly adaptable as well.

Let us be careful, however, not to oversimplify. Within the complex structure of Polish peasant culture, the image of the Jew was laden with the contradictory meanings customarily associated with the role of the 'other' within a closed society.[50] Perceived as both holy and demonic, powerful and powerless, the Jew's 'otherness' was also shaped by specific sociocultural factors. For example, the Jew was uniquely linked to trade: as late as the 1930s, a Jew in traditional dress might be addressed by the formula, '*Czego kupiec tu szuka?*' (What does the tradesman want here?)[51] The Jew, accordingly, was associated with the character traits typical of the pre-capitalist conception of trade: craftiness, deceit and miserliness. The Jew was also connected with wisdom: frequently portrayed in folk sculpture carrying a book, he was assumed to be privy to various sort of 'knowledge'.[52] Furthermore, in contrast to the fighting, drinking and carousing in which peasants, and in their own manner the gentry as well, indulged, the Jew in peasant eyes was characteristically sober, chaste and non-violent, and therefore associated with the conventional traits of unmanliness. And, of course, in dress, speech, customs and religion, the Jew was supremely alien, and, moreover, specifically implicated, as Church doctrine never allowed the peasant to forget, in deicide. Future research will have to relate these and other elements to the Jew's role in performance rituals. For the time being, let us tentatively suggest a connection between the image of the Jew as entertainer and his 'otherness' in peasant society. Within the cyclical theatrical rituals, which reaffirm the abiding order of a closed peasant society, disorder, it seems, is first introduced and then defused in laughter by the gaily cavorting *żydek*. This bizarre yet completely commonplace figure – the perfect domestic 'other' – thereby functions to reassert the mythic order of the peasant universe.

By nearly any measure of customs, values, daily life, even language, the Polish manor was a universe far removed from the peasant villages which served it. Nevertheless, the Jew as reflected in the literature of the Polish gentry, particularly in works for the theatre, bears notable similarities to the Jew in Polish folk theatre. In a recent study, Eugenia Prokopówna has examined the conventional representation of the Jew in the literary tradition of the Polish manor.[53] Within this tradition the Jew emerges not just as invariably comical, but as necessarily, inherently so. On one hand, here parallel to the peasant's perception, the Jew is the ideal 'other';

indeed, the 'unmanly' Jew, associated with the 'dishonorable' activity of trade, specifically contradicted the gentry's ethos of honour, manliness and courage. The Jew, therefore, was supremely suited to the creation of a comic image characterized by 'imperfection, disharmony, incongruity'.[54] On the other hand, the vision of the Jew as inherently comical reflects the influence of classical literary conventions which required the comical representation of the lower classes. For the gentry, in this respect, both Jews and peasants ('our Jews' and 'our peasants') could be similarly represented. Peasants, however, could also be depicted according to pastoral conventions; in the case of the Jew the only alternative was the comic. And therefore the development in gentry writing, as early as the sixteenth century, and particularly in theatrical interludes, monologues, farces, sketches, of a convention which linked 'the representation of the alien and the plebeian'[55] in the figure of the comical *żydek*. In Polish interludes, Jews are 'figures of amusement, constantly enacting arguments and fights. They are a kind of comic accessory, the subject of entertainment, generally divested of didactic intentions'. The convention particularly emphasizes the figure's plebeian aspect: 'The Jewish heroes of the interludes are generally poor peddlers, with little in their purses, which are frequently the object of attacks by soldiers (*hajducy*) and students (*żaki*) . . . [they are] little people, comical in their exertions.'[56] This comic convention undercut the literary possibilities for demonizing the Jew, and even for literary satire, whose intentions are critical and didactic. Negative Jewish stereotypes were certainly perpetuated, but primarily in non-literary genres such as the pamphlet. In literary and theatrical works, however, where laughter and the Jew were inseparable, criticism was overshadowed by entertainment.

The convention of the comical Jew rooted in the Polish manor lived on well into the nineteenth century; its most secure home was doubtless the stage. The most celebrated Polish comic actors of the period were skilled purveyors of the *żydek*: in the case of the Żółkowskis, Aloyzy Sr. (1777–1822) and Aloyzy Jr. (1814–89), the tradition was passed down from father to son.[57] It also developed 'specialists', foremost among them, Aleksander Ładnowski (1815–91), who in the course of a long career of wandering provincial stages accompanied by his acting family, developed the stylized Jew into a distinct theatrical genre. This was a skit or monologue, of the form known as *farsa* or *krotochwila* (from '*krótka chwila*', meaning 'brief moment'), exclusively devoted to the antics of a Berek, Mosiek or Icek.[58] Ładnowski's chief creation was the impoverished pipe salesman Berek Kugelman (Yiddish for Noodle puddingman), 'a gullible, hen-pecked unfortunate, a bungler falling into the most varied predicaments, cheated, ridiculed, threatened, the personification of persecuted innocence'.[59] Ładnowski's acting, which in other roles was criticized for its exaggeration and buffoonery, was perfectly suited to his Jewish characters, which attained great popularity. In a typical contemporary account, Ładnowski's extemporaneous performance of his *Berek zapieczętowany* (Berek Sealed) is credited with relieving the 'great boredom' of the previous pieces; indeed, his works were often substituted at the last moment for failing productions.[60]

By the end of the nineteenth century, the *żydek* as a literary convention was an anachronism: from Adam Mickiewicz to Eliza Orzeszkowa, the portrayal of the Jew in Polish literature had assumed entirely new dimensions of depth and seriousness. In theatre, however, and especially on the popular stage, the *żydek* comes into his own. He appears, first of all, in his own skits, Ładnowski's perennial favourites and numerous others with titles such as *Wesele Ojzerka i Ryfki* (Little Oyzer and Ryfka's Wedding) and *Żydek wesoły* (The Merry Little Jew).[61] More importantly, the *żydek* pervades the popular stage because nearly all of the many Jewish characters, major and minor, 'positive' and 'negative', who appear on that stage, are to a greater or lesser extent 'done' as *żydki*. No better example can illustrate this than the fate of Shylock on the 'garden' stage: when excerpts from the *Merchant of Venice* were produced at the Tivoli garden theatre in 1871, Polish reviewers protested the 'painful parody', and declared that 'this was not Shylock, but simply Icek'.[62]

But who exactly *was* Icek? A Polish theatre historian's comment situates him as a response to the demands of the new audiences, genteel romantic conventions making way for something else: 'the "coarse comedian" became more useful than the "tragic lover", the ability to "do a Jew" was valued more highly than the melodramatic talent of "turning up the eyes." '[63] 'Doing the Jew', termed *żydłaczenie*,[64] involved costume, make-up, gestures, facial expressions, and all aspects of speech. Polish sources, however, are silent about what this was actually like: Icek is Icek – what need is there to describe a figure so commonplace? Only at the turn of the century, amidst an attempt to stage serious 'Jewish plays' in Polish popular theatre, do Jewish critics in *Izraelita* denounce the convention, and thereby identify it: 'the crooked nose, and impossibly long *peyes* ... grabbing at one's beard, ... drawling out vowels', 'holding one's belly, endlessly grimacing', and the interminable use of the interjection *'aj waj!'*[65] Another critic inveighs against characters with 'grotesque physiognomies' who speak 'a language which according to the author is supposed to be Jewish, or biblical, but is rather Chinese-barbarian-idiotic',[66] and was in fact, a mixture, sometimes barely comprehensible, of broken Polish and stylized 'Yiddish'. This stage speech was, indeed, part of a considerably wider phenomenon: an upsurge of popular literature (novels, stories, songs, sketches, jokes, poems) written partly or exclusively in Polish-Jewish dialect.[67] Summing up the stage situation, a critic protests: 'Every Jew ... on stage offends with his tasteless garish attire, clownishly deformed speech and prodigious hooked nose'. And, emphasizing Icek's presence in all the genres of popular theatre, the critic concludes: 'In farce, this "artistic" exaggeration may perhaps be allowed to pass, but in a work of literary character – never!'[68] Indeed, these conventions were so deeply associated with the stage representation of the Jew, that even in the absence of traditional Jewish dress, żydłaczenie of speech and gesture was commonly used to identify a character's Jewish origin. And as late as the interwar period, well-intentioned attempts to present serious Jewish characters on the Polish stage were marred by the actors' ingrained inclination to speak with 'typically Jewish' accents and intonations.[69]

Icek was not only funny, he was also merry, and performed as a singer and a dancer. Music, which played a major role in garden theatre productions, was of course also a fundamental feature of traditional Jewish culture. Cantorial singing, *klezmer* bands and especially hasidic dancing had long been remarked by Poles, and music, indeed, was one of the oldest channels of Polish-Jewish cultural contact. In the 'gardens', to the accompaniment of bands which included numerous Jewish musicians, and were sometimes all-Jewish, Icek performed a customary song-and-dance known as *majufes*.[70] The etymology of this word is revealing: it derives from the opening words of a popular Sabbath hymn, '*Ma-yafit*' ('How fair thou art'), or in Central Polish pronunciation, '*ma-yufes*', which Poles came to associate with Jewish liturgical music as a whole. Behind this was doubtless the landowner's custom, in feudal Poland, of having his Jewish lessee 'sing and dance *majufes*' for him, that is, having him perform on command. I have been unable to discover descriptions of what the *majufes* actually looked like on stage. There are, however, numerous complaints in the Polish-Jewish press attesting to its pervasiveness. Singing-and-dancing by Icek and company was greatly in demand, and was conventionally inserted into productions whether 'appropriate' or not. Thus one critic, reviewing a serious attempt at 'Jewish folk theatre', ruefully adds:

> The success of the play was undoubtedly due to the 'songs and dances', served up in substantial quantity, which are apparently supposed to add interest to the drama. The fans of this kind of display will find a profusion of tasteless couplets, Jewish can-cans and other ... *majufesy*. But this is already a necessary sacrifice brought to the altar of ... a rather suspect sort of muse who reigns in Warsaw's summer shrines.[71]

Earlier in this article, attempting to understand the ubiquity of the 'new' stage Jew, the figure I have called 'Mr. Geldhab', we examined certain changes which particularly affected the rising bourgeoisie. Mr. Geldhab, certainly, was no stranger to popular theatre, yet his characteristic home was the dramatic theatre of the upper middle class. Similarly, in attempting to account for Icek's remarkable prevalence on the Polish stage of this period, we must reflect on the audience that was most his own: the new mass urban audience. In one respect, this was a very 'un-Polish' audience: while for the new bourgeoisie, eagerly assimilating old gentry culture, and steered by Positivist ideologues, questions of 'Polishness' and 'national values' played a significant role, this was hardly the case for the rootless new urban dwellers, of various class and national backgrounds, who sought entertainment in the garden theatres. Indeed, this audience at this time – and I stress 'at this time' because its 'national attitudes' were soon to change – was the most cosmopolitan public in Poland, and most resembled its emerging counterparts in Western Europe and America. The analogy to America is particularly fruitful. In America, the 1860s witnessed the destruction of a long-established feudal order, one whose lifeways and myths had powerfully imprinted themselves in the national imagination. To be sure, the Old South was not all of America, yet the centuries-old stability of its social and cultural institutions had played a key role in shaping the image of American rural life. The destruction of the plantation system combined with waves of foreign immigration (partly from the same areas that swelled Warsaw's population) to fuel the rapid industrialization and urbanization of the northern cities. Within the cities, new forms of entertainment arose, and indeed an entire culture, to serve the needs of an extraordinarily diverse mass public. And, 'every nook and cranny' of this popular culture disclosed a unique figure, reigning supremely on the stage, but found as well in 'journals, weeklies, newspapers, magazines, travel reports, diaries, brochures . . . novels, short stories, children's tales, dime novels, essays, pamphlets, and leaflets . . . in posters, on sheet music covers, postcards, wooden pegboards, in illustrations, paintings, cartoons, comic strips, children's games, on postage stamps, in advertisements, on magazine covers, playing cards, stereoscopic slides . . . place mats, wooden coins, whisky pourers, kitchen reminders, trays, shoehorns, belt buckles, tea sets, goblets, pillows.'[72] This was Black Sambo, the quintessential American jester.

Sambo, first of all, was 'naturally', inherently comical, and this reflected a fundamental White perception: 'Have you ever seen a negro in the street and thought how funny he looked, with his thick lips, his sooty face, and his woolly black hair? I dare say you have – and, perhaps, laughed out loud, too – and wondered why some people are made of such very queer faces!'[73] Sambo's speech, a dialect which inspired a vast and diversified genre of popular literature, was as comical as his physical appearance. Sambo, moreover, was also a bit of a folk philosopher, as well as a natural coward, quaking, rolling his eyes and fleeing ('Feets don't fail me now!') at the slightest hint of trouble. And, of course, Sambo was pre-eminently associated with singing and dancing. If these traits suggest parallels with Icek, so do Sambo's origins: the Southern planation. From within the manor, be it in Virginia or Poland, both 'our darky' and 'our *żydek*' are at once supremely alien and completely familiar. The threat which each, in his own way, poses to the master's chivalric world is neutralized through the master's laughter and also through his voyeurism: the 'exotic' and 'soulful' singing and dancing of the oppressed unfailingly arouse the master. Born in the plantation, by the early nineteenth century Sambo had given birth to the first indigenous American theatre, the minstrel show, 'a white imitation of a black imitation of a contented slave'.[74] Minstrelsy was so quickly and intuitively accepted as *the* American entertainment, that in 1854, to celebrate the signing of the first trade treaty with Japan, while their hosts staged performances of sumo wrestling and ceremonial dance, American sailors put on a shipboard minstrel show.[75] Without drawing too strong a parallel, pointing out a certain correspondence is irresistible. Denouncing the supplanting of Polish by German theatre in Kraków in the very year 1854, the pioneering theatre historian, Karol Estreicher, intending no irony, hails Aleksander Ładnowski for being the single exception: reintroducing the sacred Polish language onto the stage with – his 'supremely entertaining monodrama *Berek zapieczętowany*'.[76]

Rooted in the most fundamental social division in America, that of race, Sambo proved far more durable than any other American comic figure (frontiersman, Yankee peddler, various 'ethnic' types).[77] In his *persona* of happy country bumpkin, Sambo incarnated for his urban audiences the comforting myth of a stable rural America, a refuge from the new turmoil of city streets. In this respect, Icek's relationship to the needs of his Polish audiences was, if anything, an even more perfect match. For to a new Italian or Polish immigrant in America, Sambo was a figure without immediate associations, whereas in contemporary Warsaw, no popular audience was quite so diverse that the sight of Icek did not inspire instant recognition. Whether of gentry or peasant background, Polish audiences saw in Icek a reassuring apparition out of the past, a guarantee that beneath all the pandemonium of daily life, some basic order yet prevailed. As long as Icek remained Icek, Poland could be Poland.

Once transported into the city, however, Sambo and Icek could not but take on new roles. Popular culture, like the unconscious, is at home to opposites: nudged by actual social changes – the increasing urbanization of both Blacks and Jews – the traditional figure generates a parallel *persona*, supremely cosmopolitan. Sambo and Icek doff country tatters and *kapote*, respectively, and become paradigmatic insiders: foppish urban dandies, privy to all the good-time secrets of the modern city. To appreciate the form this transformation took in Poland, we must turn to the forgotten work of Feliks Szober (1846–70), the single most popular playwright of the garden theatres, who created to order for one of its impresarios, 'like a suit ... from a tailor', a series of 'urban folk plays' in which the Warsaw audience 'beheld, for the first time, itself on the stage'.[78] The model for these plays, first staged before audiences of two thousand at the Tivoli in 1876, was *Podróż po Warszawie* (A Journey through Warsaw),[79] a sequence of sketches in which Barnaba Fafuła, a provincial lad from the town of Woli Ogon (Ox Tail),[80] is guided through the urban *demi-monde* by Józio Grojseszyk, a high-spirited hustler who knows all the ins and outs of Warsaw street life. Józio, whose last name means 'big chic' in 'Yiddish-Polish', and who poses in a contemporary photograph attired in a plaid suit, holding up a massive walking stick and enormous cigar,[81] is a master of yiddishized satirical couplets. While the press railed against Szober's 'messageless' entertainments as 'theatrical humbug', Warsaw coachmen would ask the actor who played Fafuła, 'Where to, Sir Fafuła?' (*'Gdzie mam jechać, jaśnie panie Fafuła?'*), and Jews would point out 'Józio' on the street and exclaim, *'Kikste, Józio!'* ('Look, Józio!' in Warsaw Yiddish).[82] Szober capitalized on his success with a sequel entitled *Fafuła i Grojseszyk na wystawie paryskiej* (Fafuła and Grojseszyk at the Paris Fair),[83] and after his untimely death, for decades his characters reappeared in revivals of his plays as well as in numerous sequels and adaptations.[84] In addition, Szober authored one popular play 'with a message'. Subtitled a 'comic-fantastic operetta', *Piekło* (Hell) specifically addresses the 'Jewish question': poor Chaim, father of a huge family, declares, for example, that 'not all Jews are bankers, and I out of poverty cry out: *aj, waj*'.[85]

Modern mass culture arises out of the fragmentation of traditional cultures and itself further stimulates this process. In return, however, it creates new genres, contexts and symbols that begin to bind together what one historian has termed a 'New Folk'.[86] Atomization provokes interest in the alien: in both turn-of-the-century America and Poland, for example, popular culture refracted the new science of ethnography into fascination with foreign, but also domestic 'others'. Yet, and here the analogy we have been pursuing breaks down: in America, racism locked the Black out of American society, even out of the otherwise hospitable New Folk. Sambo therefore, relatively undisturbed, could develop his career into radio, movies and even early television. In Poland things developed quite differently.

As we have seen, in Poland by the late nineteenth century Jews were both a major constituent of the new bourgeoisie and of the New Folk. They were major consumers of the new popular culture; indeed, by the turn of the century, the fortunes of many garden theatres were dependent on their Jewish audiences.[87] The result was a fluid and highly ambiguous situation, remarkably open and remarkably tense. Let us consider the complex matter of humour. In the words of the Polish sociologist Kazimierz Żygulski:

> The processes of emancipation and assimilation in the nineteenth century ... led to the creation in Poland of a large ... Polish-Jewish

cultural borderland; it was the producer and consumer of a specific type of humour... The humour of the borderland often entertained both communities, and at the same time integrated them, eased, rather than impeded, co-existence.[88]

True enough: such humour was not as a rule the work of Julius Streicher prototypes; the upsurge of Jewish jokes, cartoons and literary parodies doubtless helped discharge many psycho-social tensions, and in themselves reflected a degree of Polish-Jewish familiarity. Nevertheless, more remains to be said. Writing at the turn of the century, the Polish-Jewish critic Alfred Lor offers us rare and perceptive glimpses of the *Jewish* consumers of this culture. Describing a type of popular Polish calendar filled with jokes in which 'everything turns around a long nose and a Jewish accent or a more or less raised woman's skirt', and illustrated with caricatures of Jews, Lor concludes: 'And, what is strangest is that Jews undoubtedly purchase a major portion of these "little calendars", behind the window of every Jewish bookseller we see the numerous colourful pornographic covers of these publications.'[89] One year later, he returns to the calendars: 'I would not mention this fact if it were unique. But who goes to the theatre for anti-semitic plays?... Jews. Who scrambles in sweet-shops for *Rola* and *Niwa* (anti-semitic papers)?... Jews.'[90] The twofold function of a humour which both 'eases co-existence' with one's neighbours *and* reflects self-hatred should come as no surprise to viewers of Mel Brooks films. Musing on the Jewish audience at a performance of popular theatre, Lor declares: 'What quiet tragedy must quaver in the heart of the Jewish spectator, when his mouth despite itself is twisted by laughter, yet his consciousness ceaselessly repeats: who are you laughing at? At yourself, and falsely depicted and publicly abused to boot! Strangely painful then is the smile!'[91]

Sambo's centuries-long career was finally terminated in the 1960s through the initiative of Black people themselves. In Poland, where modern social divisions never approximated the rigidity of American racism, and where the stage Jew, after all, was a figure more variegated than his Black American counterpart, the struggle over Icek began much earlier. As we have seen, already by the turn of the century *Izraelita* was filled with protests. Such verbal outrage on the part of an established organ of public opinion was accompanied, as is usually the case, by the actions of 'hotheads'. In Warsaw in 1903 the young Noyekh Prilutski was arrested for organizing a demonstration protesting the performance of Stanisław Dobrzański's *Złoty cielec* (The Golden Calf), a comedy about Jewish stockmarket speculators.[92] Such actions were only one of many contemporary signs of a crucial awakening among Polish Jews. Inspired by a variety of political movements espousing one version or another of the slogan 'Self-emancipation', energized by the legalization of Yiddish theatre and press after the 1905 Revolution, a new generation of Jews embarked on the creation of an autonomous Jewish culture in Poland and, above all – the creation of a 'new' and 'proud' Jew. Be it Zionist pioneer, class-conscious proletarian or anguished Yiddish poet, the new images stood in absolute contradiction to the old. This new Jewish world would give no quarter either to Mr. Geldhab's apologias or Icek's comical antics. Indeed, the very word *majufes* was reappropriated by modern Yiddish (in the term *mayufesnik* and the expression *zingen mayufes* [to sing mayufes]) to denote a fawning, cringing Jew bereft of dignity – a Jewish Uncle Tom.

Change, of course, hardly spared the Poles. As Polish socialism and Polish nationalism, whose conflict was to define Polish politics until 1939, crystallized into mass movements in the first decade of this century, the New Folk began to split along class and especially national lines. What could have been a 'melting pot' began to look like a battlefield. Roman Dmowski's National Democrats (*Naródowa Demokracja, ND* or '*Endecja*'), which made strong gains among the lower middle class, espoused the slogan 'national egoism',[93] and developed a notion of nationalism which increasingly identified 'Polishness' with Polish ethnic stock and Roman Catholicism. Pointing to the lack of a native Polish middle class as the primary source of national weakness, the *Endecja*, amidst the fashionable currents of Western European antisemitism, identified Jews as an 'alien element' within the Polish 'organism', an element which was to be fought and ultimately expelled. By 1912 Dmowski had used the new mass-circulation tabloid press to launch the first anti-Jewish economic boycott in Polish history.[94] To which Y.L.Peretz, avatar of the new Jewish consciousness, writing in the pages of the new Yiddish press, responded: 'But if you don't want our cooperation, that's your business. You will *push us out*, and we will defend ourselves: defend ourselves with all the strength of our racial stubbornness.'[95] By the 1930s, Jews, beards and *kapotes* among them, fought pitched battles with their Endek attackers in the streets of Polish cities; in 1936 in Przytyk, besieged by an Endek mob, Szolem Lesko, 'not yet twenty years old, short and skinny, nearsighted, wearing glasses ... still in a long *kapote*, just a few years out of yeshiva ... a young man who had seen or heard of arms, shooting and rifles neither from his father nor his grandfather', shot and killed a Polish peasant.[96]

The appeal of Polish anti-semitism to masses of Poles, an appeal which gained strength continuously until 1939, was exploited by the *Endecja*, but hardly created by them. For this anti-semitism, as we can now better appreciate, was more than a question of economics or politics: it was linked to a crisis in the social identity of the Jew. So long as Icek dances, entertains with his drollery, all is well: he is that supremely familiar 'other' who provokes a healing laughter. Grudgingly, and assuming his finances are in order, he may be permitted to divest himself of *peyes* and *kapote* and attempt to become a Pole. But what if he rejects both 'roles'? Stripped of all familiarity, he is no longer Icek, nor even Geldhab, but simply 'other'. The rueful words, '*Niema już naszych żydków*' (Our *żydki* are gone) antedated the Holocaust, and provided the innocent psychological ground for the full fury of Polish anti-semitism.

From our perspective, at the very end of this difficult century, the crisis in Polish-Jewish relations which commenced at its beginning may therefore be seen as a 'crisis of representation', a crisis, that is, whose most perfect mirror is the stage.[97]

NOTES

I would like to thank the American Council of Learned Societies for its generous support during the writing of this article. I would also like to express my warmest thanks to my dear friend and mentor Professor Joshua Rothenberg: with the completion of this article I recognize, once again, what a debt my thinking owes to him.

1 *Yidishe tipn in der poylisher literature* (Warsaw, 1928), p. 7.
2 On the Jew in Western theatre, see for example: M.J. Landa, *The Jew in Drama* (New York, 1927); Edward D. Coleman, *The Jew in English Drama: An Annotated Bibliography* (New York, 1968), with an introductory essay by Edgar Rosenberg, 'The Jew in Western Drama', pp. 1-50 (separate pagination); Charlene A. Lea, *Emancipation and Stereotype: The Image of the Jew in German and Austrian Drama (1800-1850)* (Bonn, 1978); Ellen Schiff, *From Stereotype to Metaphor: The Jew in Contemporary Drama* (Albany, 1982). To my knowledge, the only study of the Jew in Polish drama is the work of the forgotten critic Ignacy Suesser (Süsser), 'Żydzi w poezji dramatycznej', first published in *Ojczyzna* (Lwów) and reprinted in *Izraelita* (Warsaw), nrs. 49-50, 21-29 December 1888; nrs. 1-2, 4-11 January 1889. Suesser (1870-1903), a Kraków attorney of Jewish origin, was also interested in Yiddish theatre. His sympathetic study of Yiddish theatre in Galicia, 'Kilka słów o żargonie i teatrze żydowskim', which contains much otherwise unobtainable documentation, was reprinted in *Izraelita*, nrs. 25-27, 27 June-11 July 1890. He also published one of the earliest Polish translations from the work of Y.L. Peretz-an excerpt from the ballad *Monish* in which the poet bewails the 'unsuitability' of Yiddish as a poetic instrument (entitled 'Mój język' and published in *Ojczyzna* in 1891) - as well as translations from medieval Hebrew poetry. Suesser, in addition, was one of the first translators of Ibsen, Strindberg and Hauptmann into Polish, and an early activist in the Galician socialist movement. See his obituary: 'Odgłosy', *Izraelita*, nr. 5, 30 January 1903; and Zalmen Reyzn, 'Ignacy Suesser - a fargesener fraynd fun yidish in Galitsye', *Literarishe bleter*, nr. 49, 8 December 1933. Several studies of the Jew in Polish literature also devote space to theatre: H. Viltshinski (cited in n.1 above); Jacob Shatzky, 'Referatn un retsenzyes: H. Viltshinski, *Yidishe tipn in der poylisher literatur*', *Yivo bleter*, v.4 (1932), pp. 60-67; Chone Shmeruk, *The Esterke Story in Yiddish and Polish Literature* (Jerusalem, 1985); Magdalena Opalski, *The Jewish Tavern-Keeper and his Tavern in Nineteenth Century Polish Literature* (Jerusalem, 1986). In this article, biographical and bibliographical information, unless otherwise noted, comes from the following sources: Ludwik Simon, *Bibliografia Dramatu Polskiego, 1765-1939*, 3 vols. (Warsaw, 1972); *Repertuar Teatrów Polskich*, 10 vols. (Warsaw, 1968-79); *Bibliografia Literatury Polskiej 'Nowy Korbut'*, 17 vols. (Warsaw, 1963-81).

3 Uneven developments within the various areas of partitioned Poland make it difficult to speak of a single 'society', let alone a single 'theatre'. During this period, while numerous Polish companies toured Polish communities in Russia, Austria and Germany, theatre was centred in three major cities: Warsaw, Kraków and Lwów. With varying traditions and shaped by varying political and social forces, theatre developed somewhat different physiognomies in each of these cities. For an excellent characterization of these differences, see Wilhelm Feldman, *Współczesna Literatura Polska, 1864–1923*, 7th ed. (Warsaw, n.d.), pp. 103–05. To simplify a complex situation, it seemed advisable to focus on Warsaw, which during the period of this study stood at the vanguard of key economic, social and cultural changes. Where relevant, I compare the situation in other parts of Poland to that in Warsaw.

4 The two State Theatres, located in the same building, were Teatr Wielki and Teatr Rozmaitości.

5 Zygmunt Szweykowski, 'Teatrzyki ogródkowe w Warszawie', *Pamiętnik Teatralny*, 1958, p. 414.

6 Antoni Zaleski, *Towarzystwo warszawskie. Listy do przyjaciółki przez Baronową XYZ* (Kraków, 1889; reprint Warsaw, 1971), p. 412. Theatre also attained powerful significance in German Poland amidst the anti-Polish *Kulturkampf*. For a marvellous description of the devotion to Polish theatre of petty gentry in rural German Poland, see Karol Estreicher, *Teatra w Polsce* (Kraków, 1876; reprint Warsaw, 1953), v.2, pp. 531–35.

7 I use the term 'bourgeois drama' [dramat mieszczański] as employed by theatre historian Tadeusz Sivert; see n. below.

8 For an excellent and highly relevant study of American vaudeville and its social context, see Albert F. McLean Jr., *American Vaudeville as Ritual* (University of Kentucky Press, 1965).

9 Henryk Sienkiewicz, *Gazeta Polska*, 1875, nr. 115; reprinted in *Chwila obecna* (Warsaw, 1950), p. 172.

10 For a more detailed discussion of the State Theatres, the garden theatres, and their Jewish audiences and performers, see my article, 'Jews and Polish Theatre in Nineteenth Century Warsaw', *The Polish Review*, v. 32 (1987), nr.4, pp. 439–58.

11 Plays which premiered in the State Theatres were sometimes revived in the 'gardens', as well as the reverse: a play might be 'tried out' on a garden theatre stage, and later 'merit' performance at Teatr Rozmaitości.

12 Korzeniowski (1797–1863) first published his play in Wilno in 1846; it premiered in Lwów in 1843, and in Kraków and at Teatr Wielki in Warsaw in 1844. Jacob Shatzky (in his review of H. Viltshinki's book cited in n.2) points out that Korzeniowski wrote the play in 1834, in the wake of the 1831 Polish insurrection, in which some Jews participated alongside Poles. Widespread expressions of Polish-Jewish 'brotherhood' in these years (comparable to those following the 1863 Uprising) doubtless influenced Korzeniowski's portrayal of Jews.

13 Act 4, Scene 2.

14 The play premiered in Lwów 'before throngs not seen in a long time'; see *Literatura polska od średniowiecza do pozytywizmu* (Warsaw, 1979), p. 529. In Kraków, in 1844, it opened to 'an extraordinary throng', see Jerzy Got (ed.), *Teatr Krakowski pod dyrekcją Hilarego Meciszewskiego, 1843–1845* (Wrocław, 1967), p. 69. On its first performances, see Bronisław Czarnik, *Korzeniowski i teatr lwowski* (Lwów, 1896), pp. 34–38; and 'Głos współczesny o pierwszem przedstawieniu *Żydów* Korzeniowskiego na scenie lwowskiej (1843)', *Pamiętnik Literacki* (Lwów), v.3 (1904), pp. 123–27. On its Jewish audience, see also '*Żydzi* J. Korzeniowskiego', *Gazeta Warszawska*, 1845, September 13, 1912.

15 Józef Szczublewski and Eugeniusz Szwankowski, *Alojzy Żółkowski-Syn* (Warsaw,

1959), pp. VII, 51, 102, 134. As late as 1912, the young Stefan Jaracz attempted the role in Warsaw; see J. W., 'Z teatru,' *Izraelita*, nr. 37, September 13, 1912.
16 'Żydzi w poezji dramatycznej', *Izraelita*, nr.49, December 21, 1888. On Suesser, see n. 2
17 Cor., 'Z powodu wznowienia *Żydów* Korzeniowskiego,' *Izraelita*, nr. 14, 10 April 1896. For other samples of Jewish press response, see the following articles in *Izraelita*: 'Kilka Uwag o dramacie pięcioaktowym *Żyd* p. Edwarda Lubowskiego', nr. 47, 26 November 1869; 'Pogadanki', nr. 22, 9 June 1876; Alf., 'Z życia', nr.40, 19 October 1888; H. Cohn, '*Żydzi*, Komedja Korzeniowskiego', nr.13, 27 March 1896; Alfred Lor, 'Z teatru', nr. 36, 14 September 1900.
18 This subject has understandably inspired a large literature; see, for example: N. M. Gelber, *Die Juden und der polnische Aufstand 1863* (Vienna-Leipzig, 1923); Artur Eisenbach, D. Fajnhauz and A. Wein (eds.), *Żydzi a powstanie styczniowe. Dokumenty i materiały* (Warsaw, 1963). On Meisels (1798-1870), there are two biographies: Efraym Kupfer, *Ber Meisels, zayn onteyl in di kamfn far der frayhayt fun poylishn folk un der glaykhbarekhtikung fun di yidn* (Warsaw, 1952) (published in Polish the following year); and Moshe Kamelhar, *Rabbi Dov Ber Meisels* (Jerusalem, 1970).
19 'Pamiętnik', *Nowiny*, nr. 134, 4 May 1880; reprinted in *Liberum Veto*, ed. Samuel Sandler (Warsaw, 1976), v. 1, p. 155. Świętochowski was reacting to a popular brochure entitled *Żydzi, Niemcy i My* by Jan Jeleński, who shortly after founded the weekly *Rola*, the first programmatically anti-semitic newspaper in Poland.
20 Wilhem Feldman, *Współczesna literatura polska, 1864- 1923*, p. 110. The most useful studies of the repertoire and social context of Warsaw theatre in this period are contained in Tadeusz Sivert (ed.), *Teatr warszawski drugiej połowy XIX wieku* (Wrocław, 1957). Of particular importance for this study is Sivert's 'Problematyka społeczna w dramacie mieszczańskim pozytywyzmu warszawskiego', pp. 133-91. See also his anthology of plays: *Dramat mieszczański epoki pozytywizmu warszawskiego* (Wrocław, 1953).
21 For further biographical information, see Sivert, *Dramat mieszczański epoki pozytywyzmu warszawskiego*, pp. XXII-LIV; Lubowski has also merited a full-length study: Ignacy Schreiber, *Twórczość dramatyczna Edwarda Lubowskiego* (Kraków, 1929). According to Jewish sources, both Lubowski and Zalewski were from converted Jewish families; see Ignacy Schiper, 'Żydzi polscy a sztuki piękne', in *Żydzi w Polsce odrodzonej* (Warsaw, 1932-33), v. 2, p. 122; Jacob Shatzky, 'In drang tsu totaler asimilatsye: der fal Aleksander Kraushar', *Yivo bleter*, v. 22 (1943), pp. 65-66. Among the predecessors of the Warsaw bourgeois dramatists were Jan Chęcinski, Wacław Szymanowski, and Józef Narzymski; their contemporaries, based in Kraków, were Michał Bałucki and Józef Bliziński. Moreover, nearly all the Positivist novelists at one time or another tried their hand at theatre. The discussion which follows is based on the following plays: Zygmunt Sarnecki, *Zemsta pani hrabiny: Komedia w 3 aktach* (Warsaw, 1870), reprinted in *Prace dramatyczne*, v. 1 (Warsaw, 1880), premiere Warsaw, 1869; *Febris aurea: Komedia w 5 aktach*, in *Prace dramatyczne*, v. 1 (Warsaw, 1880), premiere Poznań, 1871; *Słonecznik: Komedia w 4 aktach* (Kraków, 1883); premiere Kraków, 1882; Edward Lubowski, *Żyd: Dramat społeczny w 5 aktach*, in *Kłosy*, v. 9 (1869), nrs. 223-27, premiere Lwów, 1868, Warsaw, 1870; *Przesądy* (Warsaw, 1876), premiere Warsaw, Teatr Rozmaitości, 1876; *Jacuś: Komedia w 4 aktach* (Warsaw, 1884), premiere Warsaw, 1882; Kazimierz Zalewski, *Górą nasi: Komedia w 5 aktach* (Kraków, 1885), premiere Kraków, 1884; *Friebe: Komedia w 5 aktach*, in *Echo muzyczne, Teatralne i Artystyczne*, 1885, nrs. 75-83, premiere Warsaw, 1885; *Nasi zięciowie* (Warsaw, 1886), premiere Lwów, 1886; *Małżeństwo Apfel*, in *Echo muzyczne, Teatralne i Artystyczne*, 1887, nrs. 192-204, premiere Warsaw, 1887. *Febris aurea, Jacuś*, and *Friebe* have been reprinted in Sivert's *Dramat mieszczański epoki pozytywizmu warszawskiego*.

22 For example, Czesław Miłosz's influential *The History of Polish Literature* (Berkeley, 1983) entirely ignores the genre and its creators.
23 Solus, 'Przegląd teatralny', *Niwa*, v. 21 (1882), pp. 213 et seq.; cited in *Dramat mieszczański epoki pozytywizmu warszawskiego*, p. LV.
24 *Jacuś*, Act 4, Scene 2.
25 Act 1, Scene 2.
26 Zalewski, *Małżeństwo Apfel*, Act 3, Scene 1.
27 Bolesław Czerwieński, 'Pesymizm w naszej literaturze dramatycznej', *Echo Muzyczne i Teatralne*, 1883, p. 121; cited in *Dramat mieszczański epoki pozytywizmu warszawskiego*, pp. XII-XIII.
28 This play was popular enough to inspire imitations, for example, Feliks Kwaśniewski's *Zięć firmy L. M. Feinband i Spółka* [*The Son-in-Law of L. M. Feinband and Company*] which premiered in a Warsaw 'garden' in 1902.
29 Zalewski's play, *Friebe*, is an example of the less common emphasis on German-Polish intermarriage.
30 Act 4, Scene 4-5.
31 At the turn of the century, a new production of the play was praised chiefly because the actor playing the title role chose *not* to play a Jew; see M. Ar. [Mark Arnshteyn], 'Z teatru: Wznowienie *Pana Geldhaba*', *Izraelita*, nr. 42, 25 October 1901.
32 'Z notatnika pamiętniczego Juljana Bartoszewicza, 1842-1848', *Przeglad Historyczny*, v. 14 (1912), p. 132. Later Polish productions of the play were staged from a translation by Julian Ursyn Niemcewicz. The German original was Carl Borromäus Alexander Sessa's *Unser Verkehr* (1813). Some Polish theatre sources incorrectly identify the author as Iffland, a contemporary German actor and dramatist. The play, which premiered in Germany just prior to the notorious 'Hep-hep' riots, created a scandal; it was temporarily banned in Berlin in 1815; see Lea, *Emancipation and Stereotype* . . . , pp. 80-86.
33 Act 4, Scene 4.
34 Act 5, Scene 9.
35 Act 5, Scene 3. For a contemporary Jewish reaction, see 'Kilka uwag o dramacie pięcioaktowym *Żyd* p. Edwarda Lubowskiego', *Izraelita*, nr. 47, 26 November 1869.
36 Asnyk's play was produced at Teatr Wielki in 1870, published in 1875, and then revived at a Warsaw garden theatre in 1877. For some Jewish views of the play, see: Elkan, 'Z życia', *Izraelita*, nr. 28, 19 July 1889; Cor., '*Żyd* Asnyka', *Izraelita*, nr. 2, 8 January 1897.
37 Szymanowski's play was published in 1856, and first produced at Teatr Wielki in 1870. See the polemical review of *Salomon* in *Izraelita*: 'Recenzja - nie-recenzja. Słówko o dramacie *Salomon* p. Wacława Szymanowskiego', nr. 18, 6 May 1870.
38 *The Merchant of Venice*, translated into Polish by A. Jeske and with music by Stanisław Moniuszko, reached Warsaw in 1869. Another version premiered in Kraków in 1866; see Stanisława Dąbrowska and Ryszard Górski (eds.), *Wspomnienia aktorów 1800-1925*, (Warsaw, 1963), v. 2, p. 19. The renowned actor of Jewish origin Bogumił Dawison was particularly celebrated for his interpretation of Shylock.
39 *Około teatru: szkice, obrazki, wspomnienia* (Kraków, 1905), p. 257.
40 'Recenzja - nie-recenzja. Słówko o dramacie *Salomon* p. Wacława Szymanowskiego'. *Izraelita*'s editor, Samuel Peltyn, attached great importance to the representation of the Jew on the Polish stage, and often featured theatre reviews on the front page of his publication. In addition to the previously cited articles, see also: 'Pogadanki' [review of Lubowski's *Przesądy*], nr. 22, 9 June 1876; P. S., 'Z powodu wiersza p. Gomulickiego p. n. 'Szajlok' w *Kurierze Warszawskim*', nr. 47, 7

December 1888; 'Żyd polski o Szyloku', nr. 2, 11 January 1889; Alf., 'Z życia', nr. 6, 8 February 1889.
41 Act 2, Scene 4.
42 Act 5, Scene 1.
43 Act 4, Scene 4.
44 Act 5, Scene 8.
45 Jean-Christophe Agnew, *Worlds Apart: The Market and the Theatre in Anglo-American Thought, 1550-1750* (Cambridge, 1986), p. 112.
46 Ellen Schiff, *From Stereotype to Metaphor: The Jew in Contemporary Drama*, p. 7.
47 Schiff, p. 5.
48 See for example, Aleksander Hertz, *Żydzi w kulturze polskiej*. (Paris, 1961), p. 90. For general comments on the Jew in traditional Polish society, see also pp. 74-104 of Hertz's book. This important study has recently been translated into English as: *The Jews in Polish Culture* (Evanston, Il., 1988).
49 'The stereotype in yearly performance ceremonies: The image of the Jew in Polish yearly ceremonies', in *Actes du premier Congrès internationale d'Ethnologie européenne* (Paris, 1971), nr. 327, pp. 222-27; 'Changes in the Polish Village Wedding: The Introduction of a Jewish Figure into the Final Ceremony', in *Folklore Research Centre Studies* (Jerusalem), v. 4 (1974), pp. 133-40; 'The Figure of the Jew in Polish Folk Theatre', paper presented at the International Conference on Polish-Jewish Relations in Modern History, Oxford, England, September 17-21, 1984. And see also: Jolanta Czubek, 'Szopka warszawska w XIX wieku', *Pamiętnik Teatralny*, 1968, pp. 69-77; and the examples of Polish folk plays collected by Jędrzej Cierniak and edited by Antoni Olcha in *Źródła i nurty polskiego teatru ludowego* (Warsaw, 1963).
50 See for example: Ludwik Stomma, *Antropologia kultury wsi polskiej XIX w*, (Warsaw, 1986); Olga Goldberg-Mulkiewicz, 'Polish Folk Culture and the Jew', in Harold B. Segel (ed.), *Poles and Jews: Myth and Reality in the Historical Context*, photoduplicated by the Institute on East Central Europe, Columbia University (New York, 1986), pp. 479-90; Władysław Bartoszewski, 'Polish Folk Culture and the Jew', in *Poles and Jews: Myth and Reality in the Historical Context*, pp. 491-506; Alina Cała, *Wizerunek Żyda w polskiej kulturze ludowej*, (Warsaw, 1987).
51 Hertz, *Żydzi w kulturze polskiej*, p. 86.
52 On the image of the Jew in Polish folk art, see Olga Goldberg-Mulkiewicz, 'Kavim le-dmuto shel ha-yehudi be-yezirah ha-polanit ha-amamit', *Folklore Research Centre Studies*, v. 1 (1970), pp. 149-54; 'Postać żyda w polskiej rzeźbie ludowej', *Polska Sztuka Ludowa*, v. 34 (1980), nr. 3-4, pp. 219-27.
53 'Śmiech szlachecki w satyrycznych obrazach żydowskiego świata', in *Studenckie zeszyty naukowe Uniwersytetu Jagiellońskiego: Studenckie zeszyty polonistyczne* (Kraków), v. 7 (1988), nr. 3, *Ironja, parodia, satyra*, pp. 131-51.
54 Prokopówna, 'Śmiech szlachecki w satyrycznych obrazach żydowskiego świata', p. 132.
55 Prokopówna, p. 132.
56 Prokopówna, p. 133.
57 Such performances by Aloyzy Żółkowski Sr. in early nineteenth century Warsaw were apparently particularly well-received by Jews in the audience; see Jacob Shatzky, *Geshikhte fun yidn in Varshe*, v. 1 (New York, 1947), p. 295.
58 Generic Polish names for Jews, these are diminutives of Ber, Moyshe and Yitshok, respectively.
59 Prokopówna, 'Śmiech szlachecki w satyrycznych obrazach żydowskiego świata', p. 133.
60 'Raport Konstantego Benoe... 1844', in Jerzy Got (ed.), *Teatr krakowski pod dyrekcją Hilarego Meciszewskiego, 1843-1845* (Wrocław, 1967), p. 162; 'Raport Fryderyka Hechla... 1844', in the same volume, p. 204. On Ładnowski, see also p. 176 in

Got's volume; Karol Estreicher, *Teatra w Polsce*, v. 2 (Kraków, 1876; reprint Warsaw, 1953), pp. 51, 459, 531; Stanisław Dąbrowski, 'Antoni Gubarzewski i jego teatr wędrowny w latach 1857–1860', *Pamiętnik Teatralny*, v. 11 (1962), pp. 3–22; and the index in Stanisława Dąbrowska and Ryszard Górski (eds.), *Wspomniena aktorów (1800–1925)*, 2 vols. (Warsaw, 1963). Ładnowski's *Icek zapieczętowany* was one of the five most popular plays on Warsaw stages prior to 1870; see Szweykowski, 'Teatrzyki ogródkowe w Warszawie', *Pamiętnik Teatralny*, 1958 p. 415. It was reprinted six times between 1849 and 1927, and was translated into Russian and German. Other 'Jewish' skits by Ładnowski include: *Kimedia pod tytułem Żiwy i umarły czyli Powstanie na kuszer albo Psy wilka pożarły lub Tajfel Lorbe Fuszer* (approximate translation from the 'Polish-Jewish' jargon: A Komedy entitled Liveing and Dead, or Rising Up Kosher, or Dogs Devoured the Wolf, or Tajfel Lorbe Fuszer); reprinted in Jan Winczakiewicz (ed.), *Izrael w poezji polskiej: Antologja* (Paris, 1958), pp. 295–98]; *Życie i śmierć Jaśnie wielmożnego Święte Pamięciów Pana Rzegote Zajońćkowski gojm a grojsse inkwizytor* (The Life and Death of His Lordship of Blessed Memories Rzegote Zajońćkowski, A Grand Inquisitor of Gentiles); *Żyd w beczce* (Jew in a Barrel); and *Berek odpieczętowany* (Berek Unsealed); see Maria Brzezina, *Języki mniejszości narodowych w tekstach literackich i folklorystycznych: I Południowokresowa polszczyzna Żydów* (Warsaw, 1979), pp. 28–29. Ładnowski clearly merits further investigation.

61 The actor Konstanty Lewisohn wrote *Wesele Ojzerka i Ryfki* specifically for his benefit performance, that is, it was intended to be a crowd-pleaser; see Filler, *Melpomena i piwo*, p. 38.
62 Filler, *Melpomena i piwo*, p. 63.
63 Filler, p. 153.
64 On the terms *żydłaczenie*, *żydek* and related expressions, including a list of some eighty Polish words whose root is *żyd*, see Maria Brzezina, *Polszczyzna Żydów* (Warsaw, 1986), pp. 83–101 and 135.
65 Hieronim Cohn, '*Żydzi*, Komedja Korzeniowskiego', nr. 13, 27 March 1896; [Anon.], 'Ze scen ogródkowych', nr. 22, 10 June 1898.
66 M. Ar. [Mark Arnshteyn], 'Odgłosy: Z teatru: Wznowienie *Złotego Cielca*', nr. 4, 24 January 1902; 'Odgłosy: *Nocne ptaki* K. Krumiłowskiego', nr. 35, 29 August 1902.
67 Maria Brzezina's *Polszcyzna Żydów* is largely a study of these widespread genres.
68 M. Ar. [Mark Arnshteyn], 'Odgłosy: Z teatru', nr. 22, 7 June 1901. See also Arnshteyn's review: 'Odgłosy: Śmiech i satyra w Wodewilu czyli "Ni pies, ni wydra"', nr. 22, 30 May 1902. *Izraelita* during these years is filled with comparable descriptions and protests.
69 This for example was the case with Mark Arnshteyn's Polish productions of celebrated Yiddish plays in the 1920s; see my article, 'Mark Arnshteyn and Polish-Jewish Theatre', in Yisrael Gutman, Ezra Mendelsohn, Jehuda Reinharz and Chone Shmeruk (eds.), *The Jews of Poland Between Two World Wars* (Hanover and London, 1989).
70 Witold Filler describes the garden theatre composer Adolf Sonnenfeld (who was of Jewish origin) as having written 'ballets, vaudeville dances, polkas, quadrilles, mazurkas and *majufesy*'; see *Melpomena i piwo*, p. 148.
71 Alfred Lor, 'Z teatru', *Izraelita*, nr. 28, 20 July 1900; the play was Wilhelm Feldman's *Cudotwórca*. For similar complaints, see Hieronim Cohn, 'Z teatru', *Izraelita*, nr. 26, 7 July 1899, and nr. 32, 16 August 1901; Gabryel Kempner, 'Z scen letnich', *Przegląd Tygodniowy*, nr. 29, 21 July 1900; Alfred Lor, 'Z teatru', *Izraelita*, nr. 29, 27 July 1900.
72 Joseph Boskin, *Sambo: The Rise and Demise of an American Jester* (New York, 1986), pp. 10–11.

73 H. A. F., 'So Funny', *Chatterbox* (Boston), v. 2 (1877), p. 10, cited in Boskin, *Sambo* ..., p. 107.
74 Kenneth S. Lynn, *Mark Twain and Southwestern Humor* (Boston, 1959), p. 101; cited in Boskin, *Sambo* ..., p. 82.
75 Boskin, *Sambo* ..., p. 76
76 *Teatra w Polsce*, v. 2, p. 459.
77 See Constance Rourke, *American Humour: A Study of the National Character* (New York, 1931).
78 Witold Filler, *Melpomena i piwo*, pp. 125, 119, 122. On Szober [Schober], in addition to the reference works cited above, see pp. 121-28 in Filler, n. 2.
79 *Podróż po Warszawie: operetka w 7 obrazach* (Warsaw, 1878). Adolf Sonnenfeld wrote the music to this and Szober's other plays. In his *Geshikhte fun yidn in Varshe*, v. 3, p. 334, Jacob Shatzky incorrectly states that Gustav Makman's work *Di geheymniste fun yener velt oder der tkies-kaf* (Warsaw, 1865) was a Yiddish adaptation of Szober's play; elsewhere in the same volume (p. 266), he compounds the error by referring to Szober's '*Podróż do piekła*' (confounding Szober's plays *Podróż po Warszawie* and *Piekło*) as a 'strong influence' on Makman.
80 Although 'ox tail' in Polish is 'wołowy ogon', the deformation allows Szober an additional parody on such actual place names as 'Końska Wola'.
81 See the photograph of Ludwik Solski as Józio in Solski's *Wspomnienia, 1855-1893* (Kraków, 1955), p. 206. See also Adam Grzymała-Siedlecki, *Świat aktorski moich czasów* (Warsaw, 1957), pp. 246-47.
82 Filler, *Melpomena i piwo*, p. 128; *Kolce* (Warsaw), 23 September 1876, cited in Filler, p. 123.
83 *Barnaba Fafuła i Józio Grojseszyk na wystawie paryskiej: Śmiesznostka w 5 aktach* (Warsaw, 1878); according to Filler (p. 124), Szober wrote the play in two days.
84 Fafuła and Grojseszyk were so popular that they even materialized in the *szopki*, or puppet plays, performed in Warsaw homes at Christmas time; see Jolanta Czubek, 'Szopka warszawska w XIX wieku', *Pamiętnik Teatralny*, 1968, p. 76. And in 1924, the famed director Leon Schiller revived *Podróż po Warszawie* in one of the 'monumental' productions of his Teatr Bogusławskiego in Warsaw.
85 *Piekło, Operetka komiczno-fantastyczna w 5 aktach* (Warsaw, 1880); cited according to Filler, p. 127. Szober, like Ładnowski, will amply reward further attention.
86 Albert F. McLean, Jr., *American Vaudeville as Ritual* (University of Kentucky, 1965), pp. 1-6, 38-52, and *passim*.
87 See my article, 'Jews and Polish Theatre in Nineteenth Century Warsaw'.
88 *Wspólnota śmiechu: Studium socjologiczne komizmu* (Warsaw, 1976), pp. 80-81.
89 Alf. L., 'Odgłosy: Kalendarzyki humorystyczne', *Izraelita*, nr. 46, 1 December 1899.
90 Alf. L., 'Odgłosy: Kalendarzyki humorystyczne', *Izraelita*, nr. 49, 21 December 1900.
91 'Z teatru, *Izraelita*, nr. 44, 16 November 1900. The performance was by the new Teatr Ludowy (Folk Theatre), a government-supported institution which competed with the 'gardens'. The complex subject of Polish Jewish self-hatred warrants further study; certainly, neither Jewish attendance at anti-semitic plays nor the purchase of anti-semitic papers were in themselves necessarily signs of self-hatred.
92 *Leksikon fun der nayer yidisher literatur*, v. 7 (New York, 1968), col. 217. Prilutski (1882-1941) became a distinguished Yiddish linguist, ethnographer, theatre historian and political leader.
93 This is the title of a book published in 1903 by Zygmunt Balicki, an early Endek activist: *Egoizm narodowy wobec etyki* (National Egoism in Relation to Ethics).
94 *Gazeta Poranna Dwa Grosze* (Warsaw, 1912-18) specializing in high-pitched anti-semitic agitation, quickly attained a circulation of fifty thousand; on the boycott,

occasioned by Jewish support for a non-nationalist Polish candidate to the Russian Duma, see Frank Golczewski, *Polnische-Jüdische Beziehungen, 1881–1922* (Wiesbaden, 1981), pp. 90–120; and Steven Corrsin, 'Polish Political strategies and the Jewish Question during Elections in Warsaw to the Russian State Duma, 1906–12, forthcoming in *Gal-Ed: Studies on the History of the Jews in Poland*.

95 'Di frage', *Haynt*, May 28, 1912, reprinted in Y. L. Peretz, *Ale verk* (New York, 1947), v. 9, p. 273; the italicized words, emphasized in the original, were the *Endecja's* 'platform' with respect to Jews. Peretz's statement was addressed to Poles purely rhetorically, of course, since it was in Yiddish.

96 Joshua Rothenberg, 'The Przytyk Pogrom', *Soviet Jewish Affairs*, v. 16 (1986), pp. 36–37; the description of Lesko is by Jacob Leshtshinsky, who covered the events for the Yiddish press.

97 I will here suggest some directions for further research on the stage Jew in Polish theater in the period we have examined. First of all, the stage Jew must be investigated by genre, and in each case his relationship to the *żydek* defined. This includes the villainous Jew of 'folk plays' [sztuki ludowe], didactic works devoted to the 'peasant problem' of the stricken Polish countryside, such as Władysław Ludwik Anczyc's *Emigracja chłopska* (1877); the Jew as insurrectionist featured in historical dramas such as Aureli Urbański's *Pod kolumną Zygmunta* (1880); and the biblical heroes of plays such as Juljan Łętowski's *Izrael na puszczy* (1880). Secondly: the influence on theater of the numerous Jewish figures in contemporary Polish literature. Thirdly: the stage image of the Jewish woman. Although through long-established (and insufficiently understood) convention, the stage Jew was traditionally male, in our period the figure of the Jewish woman begin to appear on the Polish stage, both via Western Europe (the *femmes fatales* of Eugène Scribe's *La Juive* and S. H. Mosenthal's *Deborah*) and in indigenous versions: the converted Jewish heroine of Stanisław Graybner and Marian Prażmowski's bourgeois drama *Rothornówna* (prem. 1899), and most importantly, Esterka, the legendary Jewish mistress of King Kazimierz the Great. On Stanisław Gabriel Kozłowski's and Kazimierz Gliński's stage versions of this tradition, see Shmeruk, *The Esterke Story in Yiddish and Polish Literature*, pp. 28–36. Heroic Esterka found an exalted male counterpart in Karl Ferdinand Gutzkow's *Uriel Acosta* (1847, Polish premiere 1888), whose 'enlightened' Jewish hero, warring against the forces of Jewish 'darkness', recalled for Polish readers Orzeszkowa's Meir Ezofowicz. Translated into Yiddish in two different versions (Y. Y. Lerner and Avrom Morevski), *Uriel Acosta* was even more popular on the Yiddish stage (as were indeed *La Juive* and Deborah). Finally, a word about the interwar years. During the 1920s and 30s national tensions made the figure of the Jew on the Polish stage considerably less prevalent than in our period. The exception to this was cabaret, which developed the Jewish joke, monologue and sketch into a specific, extraordinarily popular, and often sophisticated genre known as *szmonces*, research into which will doubtless prove quite rewarding.

THE IMAGE OF THE *SHTETL* IN POLISH LITERATURE
Eugenia Prokopówna

The word *shtetl* in Yiddish is a diminutive of the word *shtot* or 'town'; its exact meaning is, therefore, 'small town'. Not every small town, however, can be called a *shtetl*. The name refers not only to a physical entity, but to a particular cultural entity: a *shtetl* represents the *modus vivendi* of Jews in Eastern Europe. It was a bastion of traditional Jewish culture, and the word thus became a synonym for, and symbol, of that culture.

Though many Yiddish words were assimilated into the Polish language, *shtetl* was not one of them.[1] It was usually translated as *miasteczko*, 'small town'. This was the translation used for the title of Sholem Asch's famous novella *Shtetl*.[2] Alternatively it was printed in italics, as an unassimilated foreign word, in order to convey a specific milieu. This linguistic fact seems to indicate that the Jewish *shtetl* was not perceived as a socio-cultural phenomenon by the Poles.

There remains the question of Polish literature. Did it recognize the *shtetl* as an entity? Did it record the fact of its existence?

'The *shtetl* – a Polish phenomenon, a very Polish product... The *shtetl*. A flower which has grown out of our soil. But the Poles were little concerned with it ... The *shtetl* was therefore not recorded by those writing in Polish.'[3] This judgement by Adolf Rudnicki is perhaps overly severe, for although it was understandably never as important a theme in Polish as in Jewish writing, the *shtetl*, as perceived in specific categories discussed below, did not go unremarked in Polish literature. The small Jewish, (or Polish-Jewish) towns scattered throughout the Polish province had already begun to appear in Polish fiction in the early eighteenth century and continue to do so to the present day: Andrzej Kuśniewicz's *Nawrócenie* (*The Return*); Waldemar Siemiński's *Kobieta z prowincji* (*A Woman from the Provinces*); Piotr Szewc's *Zagłada* (*Dissolution*) and Konwicki's *Bohiń*, are the most recent examples. In the eighteenth and nineteenth centuries, the theme of the *shtetl* was found predominantly in prose; in the twentieth century, and more specifically from the inter-war period, it also became a dominant theme in poetry.

How is one to explain Rudnicki's position? It is easily understood when one becomes familiar with his particular vision of the *shtetl* (*Krakowskie Przedmieście pełne deserów*, 1986 [*Krakowskie Przedmieście full of Desserts*]), which is presented in an idealized, romantic vein. This tone appeared in Jewish literature at the beginning of the century (the novel by Asch cited above is a prominent manifesto of this trend), and gained popularity after the Holocaust in a number of attempts undertaken at that time to present the phenomenon of the *shtetl*, whether in an anthropological way (E. Herzog, M. Zborowski, *Life is with People*, 1952) or in a more philosophical mode (A. J. Heschel, *The Earth is the Lord's*, 1950).

For Heschel – an outstanding philosophical 'norm-setter' in the idealization of East European Jewish culture and the forms created by it – the *shtetl* is neither a physical entity inhabited by Jews, nor a social organism, but the embodiment of a certain idea. His well-known essay *The Earth is the Lord's*, intended as a description of the everyday life of Jews in Eastern Europe – their rituals and traditions, values and aspirations – is in essence an attempt to capture its specific spirituality. The *shtetl*, where this way of life manifests itself, conceals a metaphysical purpose: *the place where the Scriptures are studied*, where in the synagogue and *beth hamidrash* the simple and learned, poor and rich discuss and deepen their knowledge of God's truth. Heschel informs us:

> Koretz, Karlin, Bratslav, Lubavich, Ger, Lublin – hundreds of little towns were like holy books. Each place was a pattern, an aspect, a way of Jewishness ... The little Jewish communities in Eastern Europe were like sacred texts opened before the eyes of God, so close were their houses of worship to Mount Sinai. In the humble wooden synagogues, looking as if they were deliberately closing themselves off from the world, the Jews purified the souls that God had given them and perfected their likeness to God ... Even plain men were like artists who knew how to fill weekday hours with mystic beauty.[4]

Like Heschel, Rudnicki does not acknowledge the description of Polish-Jewish towns that typically figures in Polish literature as part of the backcloth to the plot as being a true picture of the *shtetl*. In such descriptions, it should be added, the *shtetl* is almost always portrayed as rather ugly. Another reason might be the fact that the Polish image of the *shtetl* is usually of a Polish-Jewish, provincial 'miserable backwater' in which the Jewish world – shown in a fragmentary and episodic way – appears marginally in the background. This perspective is also common in contemporary historical works, for example in *Życie codzienne małego miasteczka w XVII i XVIII wieku* (*The Daily Life of a Small Town in the Seventeenth and Eighteenth*

Centuries) by Bohdan Baranowski (1975). In discussing various aspects of the everyday life of the Jewish inhabitants of these little towns, Baranowski says not a single world about the *shtetl* as a phenomenon.

But before the small town becomes part of a literary landscape, it is first of all part of the burning social question of towns and the middle class,[5] both in novels produced during the reign of Stanisław Augustus (the 'Stanisławowski novel') and then in the moralizing prose of enlightenment journalism in the first decade of the nineteenth century.

In Ignacy Krasicki's *Pan Podstoli* (*Mr Pantler*) (1778-98), or Michał Krajewski's *Podolanka w stanie natury wychowana* (*A Girl from Podole raised in a State of Nature*) (1784), 'the descriptions of the provincial towns are limited to ... a picture of destitution, neglect and decline, supposedly caused primarily ... by the Jewish population.'[6]

This socio-economic perspective, characteristic of an Enlightenment novel, is present, if variously stressed, in the image of the *shtetl* throughout the nineteenth century. It is particularly distinct in the novels of Stanisław Kostka Potocki, E.T. Massalski, and Jan Chodźko, who in the first half of the nineteenth century continue to debate the didactic problems of reform.[7] Linking the civic question[8] with the Jewish question meant, for Potocki or Massalski, that the most fundamental feature of an ideal town is its lack of Jews: 'We will not allow Jewish stallkeepers, for I am convinced that, without reform, any trade at all in their hands brings more harm than benefit to the country' – thus does Massalski's Podstolic express his reformatory *credo*.[9] Similar ideas reappear almost half a century later in the articles and prose of Klemens Junosza.

Independent of social tendencies or didactic aims, however, the use of the narrative device of a journey or peregrination that was employed so enthusiastically in the 'Stanisławowski' novel and early prose of the nineteenth century created a suitable and convenient opportunity to describe the provincial towns along the way. It was these frequently sketchy and stereotyped representations that gave rise to the cliché of the ugly scenery of the small town, the dirty 'miserable backwater', as Kraszewski was often to refer to it. 'Muddy, unpaved streets, covered with boards here and there, low houses, only a tenth part of them bricked, Jews and beggars everywhere', 'ill-built muddy towns, full of monasteries and Jews' – that is the view confronting the traveller's carriage journeying through Potocki's Ciemnogród.[10] This stereotype of the Jewish town must have been firmly entrenched in social consciousness, as in the 1840s a writer could introduce the scene of action in his novel as follows: 'I do not need to give a detailed description of Stanisławów for whoever has seen one Polish town has seen them all and knows that the Jewish element is predominant there'.[11]

Nor do we meet different portrayals in the work of Walery Przyborowski, *Hinda* (1869); Eliza Orzeszkowa, *Meir Ezofowicz* (1878); or Klemens

Junosza, *Czarnebłoto* (1895). Nor in Żeromski, whose hero Czaruś Baryka, in *Przedwiośnie* (*Before the Spring*) (1925)) is struck, on crossing the Polish-Russian border, by a sight which completely destroys his utopian vision of a Poland of glass houses:

> (spring) tried to shroud in its faint colours this *disgusting sight* [my italics, E.P.] which people had spread against its background, full of perpetually immortal beauty: a Polish-Jewish town. Cezary looked with gloomy eyes at the quagmire of muddy little streets, at the houses, all of various shapes, sizes colours and degree of filthiness, at the pigsties and puddles, at the farm buildings and burnt rubble. He returned to the market-place surrounded by Jewish shops, their doors and windows splashed with months-old mud, and unwashed beneath that for many quarters.[12]

Thus the small town of eighteenth-, nineteenth- and, very often, twentieth-century prose is a dark and ugly place. It is a very particular *locus obscurus*, a gloomy backcloth. Towns named or anonymous, real or fictional – Tenczyn, Berdyczów, Stanisławów, Brody, Radziwiłłów, Ostropol, Kazimierz, Szybów, Czarnebłoto, Kurzełapki, Cisy, Niemrawice – all are usually ruined, neglected, and wretchedly poor, greeting their visitors with the obligatory muddy puddle in the centre of the town square. Before the inter-war period the *shtetl* was not at all aesthetically ennobled. An attractive town was a striking exception, as was a clean town; so that when Julian Łętowski wants to give his pastoral tale of life in the *shtetl* ('Konkurencja' ['Competition'] 1890) an appropriate setting, he regards it as necessary to provide an appearance of verisimilitude: 'A small town, but clean and pretty. True, this first attribute is thanks to the river flowing through, its regular flooding and subsiding'.[13] Even in the twentieth century, the legend of Kazimierz on the Vistula, which Józef Czechowicz enthused about as a 'little town of paradise', was exposed as a harmful poetization of ugliness, wretchedness, and ruin. In Maria Kuncewiczowa's *Dwa księżyce* (*Two Moons*) (1933), Kazimierz, stripped of the idealizing veils in which the imagination of travellers, demanding the exotic and picturesque, had wrapped it, reveals the old, gloomy face of the *shtetl*.

Ugly and dilapidated it may have been, yet the provincial Polish-Jewish town was a typical element of the Polish landscape. Particularly in nineteenth-century prose – viewed from the noble's manor, from the windows of a traveller's carriage, through the eyes of a landowner going about his affairs via intermediaries from the town, or the eyes of a boy pausing on his way to school in the city – it can even constitute an important symbol of the familiar. In his novel *Latarnia czarnoksięska* (*The Magic Lantern*) (1844), Józef Ignacy Kraszewski asks: 'And do you know what makes every town Polish? The Jews. When there are no more Jews, we enter an alien country and feel, accustomed as we are to their good sense and services, as if something were not quite right.'[14] This sense of homeliness was still felt during the inter-war years when Ksawery Pruszyński, writing about two types of Polish town – the western Piast and eastern Jagiellonian, stresses that the towns on the Eastern borders were built by the nobleman and Jew.[15]

This last motif alluded to by Pruszyński seems to be fundamental. It appears that in the eyes of the *szlachta*, whose viewpoint was shared by Kraszewski and Pruszyński and is also the contemporary viewpoint of Kuśniewicz, the world of the *shtetl* is placed within the sphere of a specific understanding of familiarity, in which there is room for a paternalistic approach to 'our Jews in towns and villages'. I do not wish to suggest that for writers and story-tellers from the gentry the Jewish world was not an alien world. Indeed, it was exotic in its culture, but at the same time that exotic element perfectly harmonized with the Polish landscape, the landscape of 'our land', just as the Polish manor and Jewish town together harmoniously constructed a social landscape.

In as much as town scenes were common in eighteenth- and nineteenth-century prose, the *shtetl* as a cultural phenomenon was a rare theme. Polish literature usually portrayed individual Jewish types, characters removed from their native social context;[16] descriptions of the Jewish community and its specific organization and culture were rare. However, the proto-realistic prose[17] which arose during the period between the uprisings – travel reports such as J.I. Kraszewski's *Wspomnienia Wołynia, Polesia i Litwy* (*Recollections of Wołyń, Polesie and Lithuania*) (1840), and ethnographic works such as Ludwik Jucewicz's *Wspomnienia Żmudzi* (*Recollections of Żmudź*) (1842) – contained many generic images of life in Polish-Jewish towns. These were usually descriptions of market-fairs: short scenes recording what was then called 'Jewish trade', or characterisations of small-town merchants and tradeswomen. As a kind of documentary prose, these 'journeys' and 'memoirs' written between the uprisings give a certain outline of the history of the *shtetl*: in the towns of Kraszewski's Polesie and Wołyń, the memory of the massacre of Jewish communes, of the burning of towns at the mercy of the fire and sword of Chmielnicki's men during the Uprising is still alive.

The *shtetl* appears not to have been seen as a collective Jewish *modus vivendi* until the 1860s. It was then that Kraszewski, through his hero Jakub Hamon, the son of a tavern-keeper born in a village, who later comes to experience life in both small and greater towns, states his conviction that the experience of life in a Jewish community played an important role in recognizing, understanding and experiencing Jewish identity. Very characteristically, he regards the patriarchal elders of the *shtetl* as positive heroes, truly noble and ethical, embodying Jewish values and dedicated to a Jewish God, and contrasts them with semi-assimilated types, whom he regards as sceptics devoid of faith in anything.

The *shtetl* appears as a structure specific to Jewish life in the prose of the 1870s, in Eliza Orzeszkowa's *Meir Ezofowicz* (1878), described by the author as 'the short history of a small town';[18] and in subsequent decades in Wilhelm Feldman's *Żydziak* (*Jewboy*) (1889) and Klemens Junosza's *Czarnebłoto* (1895) and 'Słup' ('The Post') (1899). These were supplemented in the inter-war period by Kazimiera Alberti's novel *Ghetto potępione. Powieść o duszy żydowskiej* (*The Ghetto Condemned. A Novel of a Jewish Soul*) (1931). The title of Alberti's novel is extremely indicative. For writers adhering to Enlightenment-positivist ideals, the *shtetl* is identified with the ghetto, which they judge according to the standards prescribed by their own ideologies and obviously condemn. They see the *shtetl* as a community subjecting itself to the tyranny of completely inert laws which isolate it from the world. They consider it to be sunk in superstition, an anachronism and, indeed, a relic of barbarity in a Europe treading the road of progress. For them it represents the home of paupers and the Jewish question. The walls of the ghetto-town, they say, should be demolished, its inhabitants should be 'civilized', social and cultural reform should be carried out. They see no room for the approbation of traditional Jewish Eastern European culture, which they consider infinitely inferior to European culture even in its Polish version. For them, the *shtetl* was the subject of either serious arguments or satirical laughter. The latter attitude, less common, was an echo, interestingly enough, of the Jewish literature of the *Haskala*. The satirical portrayals of Czarnebłoto or Kurzełapki in Junosza – Mendele's translator – are clearly inspired by Mendele's incomparable Głupsk in *Przygody Beniamina Trzeciego* (*The Adventures of Benjamin the Third*).

The enlightenment-positivist criticism of the *shtetl*, outlined above in its standard variant, does acquire specific characteristics in the work of certain authors. These are undoubtedly most evident in the popular 'Jewish' novels of Klemens Junosza whose portrayals of small towns show the tangle of components constituting the author's outlook: Enlightenment ideals and a socio-economic perspective that sees the *shtetl* as an integral part of the Polish economic context, and finally, a satirical passion in which one hears the resounding note of the *szlachta*'s laughter.[19] Junosza also displays much interest in and understanding of the daily life of the *shtetl* and its structure, which demands that 'shopkeepers doze in their booths, Jewish women, settled on their thresholds, make stockings, and the learned rock over their tomes from morning till night.'[20]

The *shtetl* as it appears in the prose of the second half of the nineteenth century is in fact, as Orzeszkowa assures us, a place lying 'in one of the most secluded corners that can possibly exist in Europe today',[21] but these are corners which snippets of news and *Haskala* slogans can still penetrate, where emancipated, assimilated Jews still appear. Even in Szybów, far from the railway, arrivals from the provincial capital begin to settle – 'civilization's exiles', whose daughters amaze the local inhabitants with their boarding-school education and piano and French lessons; this, it is claimed, is a *shtetl* preparing for change, open to outside influences. In 'Słup', a story published by Junosza in 1899, the narrator, stylized as a naïve *shtetl* bard, allows the town's patriarchs to voice their complaints about the demise of the old ways: 'There *was* [my italics, E.P.] everything here: a quiet life, happiness, piety, wisdom, a little trade . . . Nothing was lacking. There was a school, a *mikva*, a *shokhet*, a rabbi'.[22] A sign of this decline is the slowly rotting post that marks the borders of 'the pious town of Kurzełapki', which finally falls over.

The *shtetl* motif undergoes a change in the inter-war years of the twentieth century with the appearance of a larger group of writers of Jewish descent who differ from their older brothers (e.g. Wilhelm Feldman) in their treatment of traditional Jewish culture. They no longer support the assimilationist ideology which demanded the rejection of traditional Jewish culture as the price for becoming European. On the contrary, for many Polish-Jewish writers (as they called themselves),[23] the heritage of the *shtetl* was something valuable which they did not wish to reject, which they were attached to and proud of, and which gave them roots in the world. They were the ones who made the *shtetl* a central theme in their writing. Thanks to Polish-Jewish poets, the *shtetl* also began to appear in poetry.

For Polish-Jewish writers, the *shtetl* was a physical entity, but above all an entity to which the first-person narrator is emotionally attached; therefore, although its physical appearance is still seen as ugly, it is evaluated in a different manner. It is a familiar and sympathetic entity, a happy and secure place, despite its aesthetic shortcomings. The *shtetl* now becomes, above all, the domain of childhood. It is not surprising, then, that it should be the affectionate abode of memory and imagination, an intimate entity. It is impossible to overlook or underestimate the importance of biographical experience in the construction of this image. This biographical element makes the *shtetl* a familiar and private domain, an area suffused with personal experiences and memories. Narratives of Polish-Jewish writers – Maurycy Szymel, Stefan Pomer, Czesława Rosenblattowa – about the *shtetl* are variations of the same story of having to leave the town in which they were born. Their creative writing is the memory reliving the places of childhood.

From these memories the *shtetl* emerges as a universal landscape, as it were, of Jewish biography. Its topography is characterized by its permanent features: the market-square, the synagogue, the inn, the spice shop, the crooked street, the Jewish cemetery. The synagogue, which is the true heart of the *shtetl*, is usually old and crumbling. Perceived with nostalgia, the whole landscape of the *shtetl* is the domain of the old and the ruined. The houses, synagogue, and cemetery are all dilapidated. The moss-covered walls crumble. Night can a throw a veil over this scene of decay, adding a layer of fantasy or other-worldliness to its dimensions.

This motif of decay, undoubtedly dominant in the description of the *shtetl* in Polish literature, was an undeniable reflection of the actual state of the Jewish provinces in the eighteenth, nineteenth and twentieth centuries. But while the *shtetl*'s dilapidation led writers who had rejected their links with the Jewish world to support demands for the reform of Jewish life, for Polish-Jewish writers the ruin of the *shtetl* was a symbol of the patriarchal world disappearing into the past. The native landscape infused with death became for them an elegiac theme. The first elegy on the Jewish town appears at the end of the 1920s, preceding Antoni Słonimski's *Elegia miasteczek żydowskich* (*Elegy on Jewish Towns*) by two decades. It was written by Stefan Pomer, whose volume *Elegie podolskie* (*Podolian Elegies*) (1931) was described in the inter-war years as 'a lyrical geography of Jewish settlements'.

It is a striking fact that in the work of writers from Jewish circles one looks in vain for the traditional Polish 'small town stories' that look at the Jewish world from the perspective of nineteenth-century Polish clichés (e.g. Kazimiera Alberti's *Ghetto potępione*). Seen from the inside, the *shtetl* does not appear as the compact social structure of old; the links once unifying its collectivity have weakened. The culture of the *shtetl* is no longer presented as a vital phenomenon worthy of ethnographic description (as Feldman saw it, for example). Usually, only fragments of this culture are mentioned, scenes of rituals fundamental to Judaism: the Sabbath, Yom Kippur, the Passover. Brief threads of folklore tradition, themes drawn from Jewish ballads, proverbs, and hasidic anecdotes appear in a stylized form. A whole gallery of small-town types are woven into the cast of characters: rabbis, beggars, tailors, salesmen, porters, and others. However, these, to use the title of one of the novels to emerge from the new Jewish circles are 'people who are still living' (C. Halicz [C. Rosenblattowa], 'Ludzie, którzy jeszcze żyją', 1934). This title effectively conveys the vision of the *shtetl* as a form which continued to exist, but which in essence already belonged to the past.

In any case, the literary hero and lyrical 'I' in the work of Polish-Jewish writers was also the inhabitant of the *shtetl*, 'the simple, believing Jew', as the authors claim. Though given a (Polish) voice, the town now clearly bears the mark of its times: one can meet a tragi-comic Charlie Chaplin in its streets, and, hovering above the *shtetl*, an aura of sadness, nostalgia, and melancholy, resounding in the music of the violin, the sentimental laughter that comes through tears.

Nor can one overlook the image of the *shtetl* in the work of two other writers of the inter-war period: Bruno Schulz and Adolf Rudnicki. In their work, too, the town becomes the intimate domain of childhood. For Schulz the town is a refuge for a hero worn out by the chaos of the world. The aura of the place emerges dimly from the sea of Schulzian metaphor, but in such a way that one cannot fail to see the market-square empty on the Sabbath like a biblical desert, houses fragrant with Sabbath smells while their inhabitants – Shlomo son of Tobias, Joseph son of Jacob – await the Messiah. In Rudnicki's *Szczury* (*Rats*) (1932), it is impossible not to identify in the depiction of the small town of Raj – the shops of Buch and Perlman, Groman's house – a particular leitmotif characterizing the hero's native milieu.

In post-war literature the *shtetl* inevitably becomes a historical theme, but it nevertheless persists as a theme. Who remembers it? Above all, Jewish writers born in a *shtetl* at the beginning of the century or in independent Poland, survivors, looking at the Jewish world from the other shore of the Holocaust, as it were. It is also remembered by their Polish contemporaries, those men and women from the provinces who, like Tadeusz Konwicki, grew up together with Jewish children in some

> provincial town, the quintessential small town on the outskirts of Wilno. This was a town among a vast archipelago of such towns, which produced the founder of Metro-Goldwin-Meyer and Józef Piłsudski, famous, miracle-working rabbis and the arch-traitor and tsarist spy Bałaszewicz, the leader of the Warsaw Ghetto Uprising, Wilner, and myself ... All that was best in Europe and America came from there and pushed old Europe and young America forward ...
>
> I remember Bujwidze better all the time. I dream of Bujwidze constantly. This microscopic town, this most typical of towns, in actual fact the name of the town alone without the town was something so characteristic and somehow formed types like myself, like Romain Gary, Soutine, David Halberstam and three-quarters of American directors, writers, actors and politicians.[24]

The Lithuanian Bujwidze, Galician Drohobycz (A. Chciuk, *Atlantyda. Opowieść o wielkim księstwie bałaku*, 1969) (*Atlantis. Tales of the Princedom of Lwów Argot*), or borderland towns are remembered by writers of the Galician or Lithuanian schools, to whom the Habsburg and Jagiellonian myths, offering a vision of open, multinational cultures, are dear. But the domain of childhood can equally be Kazimierz on the Vistula, disguised under the name of Laźmierz (W. Siemiński, *Kobieta z prowincji*, 1987). The vision of these provincial backwaters becomes so attractive that writers born in the 1940s, 1950s, and even the 1960s express a desire to inhabit them via their protagonists.

But the Holocaust stamps its seal on the memory and imagination of them all. A slaughtered town is, after all, something entirely different from a town gradually falling into decay. It is the term used by Kalman Segal in the title for his stories – *Tales from a Slaughtered Town* (*Opowiadania z zabitego miasteczka*, 1956). This death is also recorded by others – in an avant-garde style by Leopold Buczkowski (*Czarny potok* [*The Black Torrent*], 1954), realistically by Józef Wroniszewski (*Różdżka Jessego*, [*Jesse's Wand*] 1982). Szagalewo, the hero of Arnold Słucki's poetry, is indeed a surreal, Chagallian place with violins flying through the air, but it is also a place of suffering and death, bursting into ominous flames:

> There is a motionless world on the edge of the moving world,
>   huts of clay and fire – strange towns.
> Orthodox chapels standing on the heads of burnt synagogues,
>   drying like blind arks on their Ararats.[25]

The novels about inter-war Polish-Jewish towns by Artur Sandauer (*Zapiski z martwego miasta* [*Notes from a Dead Town*], 1963) and Andrzej Kuśniewicz (*Nawrócenie* [*The Return*], 1987) end on a chord of wartime fate; no turning back of memory, as Kuśniewicz would have it, can be a return to that world in a gesture of innocent ignorance.

Even Stryjkowski, concentrating on Jewish life with despair, clearly looks at that life as after a deluge; his gaze, made acute by the Holocaust, is sensitive to all portents of death. In his four-volume sequence begun in the 1940s (*Głosy w ciemności* [*Voices in Darkness*], 1946 [published 1956]; *Austeria* [*The Inn*], 1966; *Sen Azrila* [*Azril's Dream*], 1975; *Echo*, 1988), he gives us an account of the destruction of the internal structure of the town from the beginning of the century, a history of the breakdown of the codex of laws and hierarchy of values that united the Jewish community for a hundred years. The collective value of the *shtetl* cannot defend itself before the assimilationist, Zionist and socialist tendencies appearing among the Jews of Galicia. The patriarchal world perishes under the pressure of destructive contemporary forces. Stryjkowski does not depict the idyll of a *shtetl* dancing before the Lord. Instead, he tells the story of the family of a certain *melamed*, a teacher who is himself charmed by the 'wicked books' of the *Haskala*, but whose children betray their Jewishness: his daughter runs away with a *goy*, his older son joins the socialists, and the younger, who does not yet understand Polish well, finds himself in a Polish school. He tells the story of Tag and Azril, in whom desire for holiness and sinful desires do battle, and who, full of anxiety and guilt, cannot keep pace with the exigencies of loyalty to the ethical code of the community. True, for Stryjkowski the *shtetl* is marked by death, but it induced that death itself. The writer's heroes are unable to tread in the footsteps of their fathers (were their fathers really able to tread that path?); they betray their Jewishness or abandon it. The chain binding Jewish fathers and Jewish sons, a chain formed over a thousand years, breaks and falls apart; the chain of the covenant with the Lord suddenly snaps. The model given in traditional culture for forging the links of that chain proves impossible to repeat. Stryjkowski's hero, weak and easily fallible, is unable to fulfil his heavy ethical reponsibilities. The culture of the *shtetl* cannot survive as a particular form of existence, and this constitutes the nucleus of its death.

The inter-war *shtetl* that appears in prose from the 1950s on is always strongly invaded by waves of Polonization and secularization. In his *Zapiski z martwego miasta*, Artur Sandauer records its symbolic topography by causing his hero to wander between three spheres: the Jewish backwoods, the borderlands, and the centre of Polishness. He makes him a witness to a melodious dispute, conducted one Sabbath afternoon, by a family whose various members hum the Sabbath *zmirot*, Bialik's hymn 'Tehezakna', and the 'Red Flag' – a symbol of the dispute between traditional faith, Zionism, and socialism.

Similarly, in Kalman Segal's work, *The Town* (which remains anonymous, but is written with a capital) attempts to carry on its life according to the eternal rhythm in the valley of the San, but cannot isolate itself from the conflicts tearing inter-war reality apart. Though it clings to tradition, the latter is not the mainstay it once was. 'The old town was once a fortified castle with walls of granite and full of the wisdom of God and good customs like an ivory tower. This was a fortress and God was its foundations. What remains of the fortress? The shopkeepers and harlots shatter the Lord's holy temple. Fractious sons offend God and his prophets. Where is Isaiah, who will foretell their ruin?',[26] ask Segal's grey and bearded patriarchs.

The tone idealizing the *shtetl*, which in Segal's works rang out only in the voices of those literary heroes attached to traditional ways of life (Segal himself had a critical view, as expressed for example in the story 'Josełe' from *Opowiadania z zabitego miasteczka*), took on a different and more insistent character in the literature of the 1980s. The growing interest in the lost world of Polish Jews meant that the *shtetl* motif was now taken up by younger writers who had no memories of that world. Their towns, 'lying on the furthest reaches of the imagination',[27] can only (and this is no accusation) be visions constructed from inherited images. However, the choice made by Włodzimierz Paźniewski or Piotr Szewc, for example, from among the available clichés put forward by tradition, is extremely telling. Kuśniewicz's followers present the Polish-Jewish provinces of independent Poland in all their diversity, Kuśniewicz portrayed them as a gallery of types, amongst whom there were grey-beareded talmudists, lawyers' wives reading *Wiadomości Literackie* (what else), and communist tailors. But – and this is of great importance – Paźniewski and Szewc also write occasional prose elegies on the *shtetl*. Like Słonimski, a severe critic of traditional Jewish culture before the war,[28] who after the war lamented that never again would words of longing for Jerusalem be heard in Polish cherry-orchards, they too wish to see the picturesque and moving side of Jewishness, and also the exotic side: the warmth of spice shops, not to mention cinammon shops, and haberdasheries, the whirl of dancing *Hassidim*, the stillness of men poring over their sacred books.

This tone of nostalgic idealization, which can also be found in the writings of Holocaust survivors, is interpreted with psychological insight by Bogdan Wojdowski. His heroes in *Pascha*, living in contemporary Warsaw, watch the mystery-play of spirits in Perec's *Noc na starym rynku* (*Night in the Old Square*) at the Jewish theatre, resurrecting the *shtetl* in all its glory, but in all its conventionality also: 'The synagogue, the *heder* and the church stood on the market square together, and in the very middle, by the prompter's niche, was the well.'[29] Spiritually wounded and terribly sensitive, they long for a life among their own kind. As one character says:

> My whole youth. Among my own kind. And these walls? Let them collapse . . . I will exchange all I have, for such a small, the smallest of lives. So close to God. And God too in His place. And every sin and every good deed also in its place. The merchant behind his counter. The coachmen by their horses. Everything so small, so good and necessary.[30]

To him, the idyll of the *shtetl* means intimacy and imperturbable order in the world, certainty and security.

The idea of the spiritual beauty of the world of East European Jews and of Jewish traditional culture is proclaimed most fully in the voice of Rudnicki, who sensitively observes religious rituals and the spiritual truth still permeating them before the war (e.g. 'Lato', 1938):

> The *shtetl*. A complete triumph of the idea of a theocratic town, a theocratic state. The butcher, the writer, the rabbi – these are the ideological guardians of its life. Precise regulations speak of what is allowed and what is not allowed . . . A spiritual leader guides this life, is responsible for everything that happens. In the town one wakes with a prayer on one's lips, one falls asleep with a prayer. God is in every curve of the walls, everywhere. His shadow spreads over every meal, every word, over all work and rest. It might appear from the outside that the people were in the depths, that only a miracle could save them, but the miracle – in its own way – was their very life, their inner life.[31]

Clearly, Rudnicki does not attempt to paint an idyllic landscape of the town, but to show the depth and beauty of the Jewish tradition existing in the *shtetl*, a tradition which ordered the cosmos and everyday life. From ugly surroundings to a cultural terrain full of spiritual light, this statement could serve as a description of 'the Polish history' of the *shtetl*. A hidden light at first, but, as Heschel wrote, one whose brilliance would eventually penetrate all screens.

NOTES

1 See M. Brzezina, *Polszczyzna Żydów* (Warsaw, 1986), pp. 52-83.
2 S. Asch, *Miasteczko* (Warsaw, 1911).
3 A. Rudnicki, *Krakowskie Przedmieście pełne deserów* (Warsaw, 1986), pp. 39, 42, 43.
4 A. J. H. Heschel, *The Earth is the Lord's: The Inner World of the Jew in East Europe* (New York, 1950), pp. 89, 92, 93.
5 See Z. Leśniodorski, 'Miasta i mieszczanie w powieści stanisławowskiej', *Pamiętnik Literacki* 1-2 (1935); W. Wołk- Gumplowiczowa, 'Chłopi, mieszczaństwo i szlachta w powieści polskiej w pierwszej połowie XIX wieku', *Przegląd Socjologiczny* 1-2 (1939).
6 Z. Leśniodorski, 'Miasta i mieszczanie . . .', p. 188.
7 S.K. Potocki, *Podróż do Ciemnogrodu* (1820); J. Chodźko, *Jan ze Świłoczy, kramarz wędrujący* (1824), *Podróż do Pani Kasztelanowej* (1837); E. T. Massalski, *Pan Podstolic albo czem jesteśmy, czem być możemy. Romans administracyjny* (1831-3).
8 Similarly linked with the Jewish question was the so-called peasant question, which had a significant influence on the motif of the Jewish innkeeper and his inn in Polish literature. See M. Opalski, *The Jewish Tavern Keeper and His Tavern in Nineteenth-Century Polish Literature* (Jerusalem, 1986), pp. 21-2.
9 E. T. Massalski, *Pan Podstolic albo czem jesteśmy, czem być możemy. Romans administracyjny* (Petersburg, 1833), vol. ii, p. 55.
10 S. Potocki, *Podróż do Ciemnogrodu* (Warsaw, 1820), vol. 1, pp. 29, 146.
11 J. Brincken, *Józef Frank. Powieść historyczna z drugiej połowy XVIII wieku.* (Warsaw, 1845), vol. iii, p. 99.
12 S. Żeromski, *Przedwiośnie* (Warsaw, 1948), p. 109.
13 J. Łętowski, 'Konkurencja', in *Józefa Ungra Kalendarz Ilustrowany na rok 1890* (Warsaw, 1890), p. 18.
14 J. I. Kraszewski, *Latarnia czarnoksięska* (Kraków, 1977), series I, p. 271.
15 K. Pruszyński, *Podróż po Polsce* (Warsaw, 1937), p. 177.
16 See A. Hertz, *Żydzi w kulturze polskiej* (Paris, 1961), pp. 240, 241, 248, 254.
17 H. Markiewicz calls proto-realism an 'inter-uprising anti-romantic movement': see 'Próba periodyzacji nowożytnej literatury polskiej', in *Przekroje i zbliżenia. Rozprawy i szkice historycznoliterackie* (Warsaw, 1967).
18 E. Orzeszkowa, *Meir Ezofowicz* (Warsaw, 1988), p. 9.
19 See E. Prokopówna, 'Śmiech szlachecki w satyrycznych obrazach żydowskiego świata' (Studenckie Zeszyty Naukowe Uniwersytetu Jagiellońskiego), series VII, vol. 3; *Ironia. Parodia. Satyra* (Kraków, 1988).
20 K. Junosza, 'Froim', in *Łaciarz. Froim* (Warsaw, 1926), p. 34.
21 Orzeszkowa, op. cit., p. 9.
22 K. Junosza, 'Słup', in *Nowele i obrazki* (Warsaw, 1899), p. 12.
23 See E. Prokopówna, 'In Quest of Cultural Identity: Polish- Jewish Literature in the Interwar Period', *The Polish Review* 4 (1987).
24 T. Konwicki, *Wschody i zachody księżyca* (Warsaw, 1982), p. 86.
25 A. Słucki, 'Nieruchomy świat', in *Promienie czasu* (Warsaw, 1959), p. 51.
26 K. Segal, *Kochankowie w Sodomie* (Katowice, 1966), p.
27 K. Holzman, 'Truciciele publicznych studni', in *Krajobraz rodzinny i inne opowiadania* (Warsaw, 1981), p. 82.

28 See M. Opalski, 'Wiadomości Literackie 1924–1939: Polemics on the Jewish Question', typescript, p. 4. Paper given at the conference 'The Jews of Poland between the Two World Wars', Brandeis University, April 1986.
29 B. Wojdowski, 'Pascha', in *Krzywe drogi* (Warsaw, 1987), p. 19.
30 Ibid., pp. 29–30.
31 A. Rudnicki, *Krakowskie Przedmieście pełne deserów* (Warsaw, 1986), pp. 40–1.

ETHNIC DIVERSITY IN TWENTIETH CENTURY POLAND
Norman Davies

This essay aims to outline some of the main features of Poland's pre-war society, and to relate them to the study of Polish-Jewish relations. It is not a research paper, and does not present any facts that are not widely known. What it does is to stress the multinational character of old Poland, and to place the bilateral problems of Poles and Jews within the multilateral complexities of ethnic relations as a whole. It warns against the tendency of some modern historians to view the past anachronistically, or to reduce the complex realities to a simple confrontation between Poles and Jews.

Nowadays, the ethnic make-up of modern Polish society is remarkably, and artificially homogenous. Contemporary Poland is overwhelmingly Polish. As a result of the mass murders, mass deportations and comprehensive frontier changes of the Second World War and its aftermath, young Poles can grow up without ever hearing their neighbours speak a different language or practise a different religion. Very few Poles under the age of 45 or 50 – i.e. the great majority of the population – can ever remember having a German or a Jewish or a Ukrainian classmate or neighbour, or can remember seeing a recognisable 'resident foreigner' in their midst. Although they know, of course, that pre-war Poland contained many so-called 'minorities', the present state of affairs has inevitably strengthened traditional nationalist mythology linking the Polish 'land' exclusively with the Polish 'nation'. Government propaganda has undoubtedly played its part: but it was perhaps inevitable that an uprooted post-war generation of Poles should yearn for a national past in which their own antecedents held pride of place and where the 'minorities' played only a marginal role. Post-war historiography has certainly reflected this feeling.

Similarly, it is entirely natural that post-war Jewish opinion, traumatised by the Holocaust and properly impressed by the creation of the Jewish state of Israel, should be dominated by the Zionist perspective. Zionism (in the sense of modern Jewish nationalism) naturally stresses not only the existence but the distinctness of the Jewish nation in the past, as in the present. The thousand-year sojourn of the Jews in Poland is viewed less as an integral part of Polish history; but rather as a lengthy stage of the Jewish nation's Long March through the world's wildernesses, begun in Zion and ending in Zion.

The starting point of this discourse must obviously lie with the extremely complex kaleidoscope of ethnic settlement which developed in the Polish lands over a thousand years and more. Contrary to the picture painted by the Polish nationalist 'Autochtonous School', it is doubtful whether one can fairly talk at any period of history of a broad Polish heartland inhabited exclusively by Poles and overlapping with areas of non-Polish settlement merely on the outer fringes. In reality, the areas of mixed settlement both in West and East formed by far the largest part of the whole. By the late nineteenth century the cradle of historic Poland in Posnania (Wielkopolska) contained a large and growing German element. The *Kresy* or Borderlands in the East, with their mixed populations of Poles, Lithuanians, Byelorussians and Ukrainians were more extensive than the provinces which form the 'centre' of modern Poland today. The whole country, from Silesia in the west to deepest Ukraine in the east, was overlaid by what elsewhere I have called 'the Jewish Archipelago'. Jewish settlement was naturally very thin in the rural countryside. But it was concentrated in the small towns, the *shtetlach*, in the provincial centres, and in the growing cities, where, as often as not, the Jews would form an absolute majority in their particular ward or locality. In addition, the imperial régimes of the nineteenth century imported large numbers of foreign bureaucrats – Prussian Germans from Berlin, Austrian Germans from Bohemia or Vienna and Russians from St Petersburg – to administer their Polish provinces.

Given these complex patterns, I often think that it is misleading to describe Poland's multinational society in terms of the statistical 'Polish majority' on the one hand, and of the so-called 'national minorities' on the other. In a very real sense, most people in early twentieth century Poland lived in conditions which nourished their perception of being an exposed minority, surrounded by potentially hostile foreigners, and wearied by the universal feelings of insecurity. In particular, it would be wrong to identify automatically the majority population as the social oppressors, and the national minorities as the oppressed. Both the Polish and the Jewish communities displayed a wide range of social and economic standing, and in various times and locations different groups of Poles and Jews could sometimes be regarded as advantaged, sometimes as disadvantaged, elements of society. The lines between rich and poor, or between privilege and underprivilege, did not follow the ethnic divide.

If one examines the distribution of the Polish 'majority', for example, – say in 1921 at the first independent census – it soon becomes clear that there were not many provinces or towns of the reborn Republic which ethnic Poles could feel were exclusively 'theirs'. Having passed the entire nineteenth century as a minority group within Russia, Prussia or Austria, and having developed all the complexes to match, the nationalistic element within the Polish community now realised with no small sense of frustration that the new Poland did not measure up to their dreams. All too often, from their point of view, the Poles were still a minority, or at best an embattled and marginal majority, within their own land. In many of the former Prussian districts, the German element still maintained an economic, if not always a numerical supremacy. In the east, although the Polish landowners still dominated the social scene, the Poles were heavily outnumberd by Byelorussians and Ukrainians. In the urban centres, the Jewish presence was strong, and sometimes dominant. In Warsaw, the capital of Poland, the Jewish element, which was set to decline in relative terms, nonetheless stood only slightly below the 50 per cent mark.

For Jewish readers, especially in America, the picture of an isolated Polish minority living in a predominantly Jewish town and feeling uneasy at their predicament, may seem to be standing history on its head. And, of course, it wasn't the norm; but it was common enough in the eastern provinces. Memoirs and personal reminiscences of life in the former East Galicia, for example, in towns such as Buczacz, or Brody, or Podhajce in the late 1930s, recall Polish apprehension as the *Betar* movement marched its young people round the market square to chants of 'We will conquer Palestine' or 'We're not scared of Arabs'. In this case, Polish-Jewish tensions were tempered by the shared fears of local Ukrainian activists who tended to view both Poles and Jews as fair game for harassment. After all, there was a long history in those parts dating back to Chmielnicki's Revolt (1648) and the Massacre of Human (1768), when vengeful peasants on the rampage had slaughtered both Poles and Jews indiscriminately.

On the other hand, one needs to remember that the interests of the Polish community were supported by the full panoply of state power: whilst the interests of the 'minorities' were not. The reigning mood of Poland's state authorities in the inter-war period was 'unremittingly nationalist'. The prevailing convention, especially among the lower levels of the bureaucracy, was to view the Second Republic as a Polish state. As a result, the dealings of the Polish community with the other nationalities could not be conducted on the basis of equality. In terms of attitudes, the imbalance could only increase the embitterment of the 'minorities', which in turn fuelled the fears and suspicions of the Poles. In terms of political power and action, however, it gave the Polish community a commanding position. In the 1930s, there was no way that Polish Jewry could have properly defended itself against discriminatory legislation or against petty harassment by officialdom: no way that Poland's Ukrainians could have matched the firepower and resources of the army and the state police in their murderous campaigns of 'pacification'.

In my view, it was these specific conditions, where each of the ethnic communities had reason to feel insecure, that fostered the rise of rival nationalisms on all sides, and the growing threat of intercommunal violence. Nationalism – with its mission for strengthening the separate identity of each community, and its later stage of demanding a separate homeland for each nationality – fed on the tensions and flourished in proportion to people's anxiety. Regrettably, it also diminished the chances for maintaining mutual toleration and intercommunal harmony. Yet one glimpse at the maps shows that the nationalists' hopes for creating national homelands for each of the nationalities of the region could never have been achieved by natural evolution. To create a Poland exclusively for the Poles, a Ukraine for the Ukrainians, a Lithuania for the Lithuanians, or an Israel for the Jews required the unscrambling of a thousand years of social development, together with a degree of brute force and political compulsion which no one in pre-war Poland possessed, or even imagined.

During the Second World War, of course, the situation changed radically. The arrival of the Nazis and the Soviets, both of whom possessed the political will and the logistical capacity for social engineering on a mass scale, sounded the knell for Poland's multinational society. The Nazis with their plans for German *Lebensraum* and their predilection for mass murder, the Soviets with their practice of mass deportation, and the Allied Governments with their acquiescence in wholesale territorial and demographic changes, combined to bring Poland's traditional society to an end. The ethnic conflicts of pre-war Poland were not so much solved as destroyed (together with millions of people whose existence or address had not suited the plans of the Nazi and Soviet social engineers).

In the meantime, and especially in the rising tensions of the 1930s, each of Poland's ethnic communities increasingly felt itself to be caught in a trap from which there was no obvious escape. The Poles, inflamed by nationalistic elements with growing influence, felt that all the 'minorities' were ever more 'anti-Polish'. The Germans of Poland, won over by Nazi propaganda, felt that they were under attack by 'anti-German' oppressors. The Ukrainians, whose nationalist movement had sprouted an active terrorist wing, increasingly felt that their Polish, Jewish (and Russian) neighbours were 'anti-Ukrainian'. The Polish Jews, who in their scattered settlements were least able to defend themselves increasingly felt that all other groups in Poland – Poles, Germans, Lithuanians, Byelorussians, Ukrainians – were 'anti-semitic'. It is no simple matter to determine how far these mutual fears and hatreds were subjective, and how far they were based on cold, rational analysis. Yet it is impossible to deny that they were on the increase on all sides.

In the 1930s, each of the communities spawned activist groups who in their different ways were all beginning to think of radical solutions to (what they considered) an intolerable dilemma. The Polish National Democrats, and even more their radical and illegal offshoot, the *ONR-Falanga*, began to talk not merely of compulsory Polonisation of the minorities, but also of assisted emigration, even of expulsion. The Nazi 'Fifth Column' began to plan, and to arm, for a German invasion. The Ukrainian *O.U.N.*, apart from its terrorist campaign against the Polish authorities, aimed to attach themselves to the Nazis' bandwagon. The Polish Zionists were training young Jews in agriculture, with emigration to Palestine in view; and the Zionist-Revisionists were organising Jewish self-defence units. None of these radical groups had the means to put their wider schemes into operation.

Not everyone in Poland, however regarded the ethnic mix as a recipe for disaster. The entourage of Piłsudski, a native of the Wilno region whose inhabitants were familiar with particularly complicated patterns of ethnic settlement, had no sympathy for ethnic nationalism, tending instead to look for a revival of the multinational traditions of the old, pre-Partition Commonwealth. Piłsudski's outlook prevailed in the upper echelons of the Polish Government until his death in 1935. Similarly, each of the 'minority' communities contained groups and individuals resolutely opposed to the nationalist trend amongst them, dreaming instead of turning Poland into a 'Switzerland of the East'. Within Polish Jewry, for instance, the Zionist movement met stalwart opposition both from conservative, religious groups and, on the Left, from the *Bund*.

The *Bund*, though it was actively nationalist in the cultural sphere – especially in the promotion of Yiddish education and literature – would have nothing of the Zionist plans for a separate Jewish homeland. The vision of the *Bund*, as of Polish socialists in general, was of a multinational Poland, where each ethnic community could preserve its identity, but live with its neighbours in harmony and justice. Later apologists for the *Bund* have claimed that by the late 1930s it had assumed 'the leadership of Polish Jewry'.[1]

As things worked out, Poland's ethnic cauldron was knocked over by the Second World War before it ever reached spontaneous boiling point, and it is difficult to say whether, if left to itself, the situation would have developed into a generalised ethnic conflagration of the sort which has erupted elsewhere in the world – say in partitioned India, or in the Lebanon. All one can say is that the prospects were not favourable. As it was, Polish-German antagonisms led to terrible local blood-lettings and mutual reprisals that did not end until Poland's Germans were forcibly expelled in 1946–7. Polish-Ukrainian antagonisms led during and after the war to genocidal massacres on both sides, with thousands of Ukrainian civilians being killed in central Poland and tens of thousands of Poles killed in Volhynia and Podolia. In that context, where existing ethnic hatreds had been further inflamed by the overt racism of the Nazi Occupation, it is doubtful whether Polish-Jewish relations could have escaped unscathed. But, as it was, by constructing hermetic Jewish ghettoes at the start of the occupation, the Nazis forcibly separated Poland's Jews from the general population at an early stage, and proceeded to murder them from 1942 onwards in isolation. By that particular arrangement, the attitudes of Poles to Jews and of Jews to Poles, were for practical purposes rendered largely irrelevant.

After 1945, Polish society was transformed. Polish Jewry had been literally decimated by the Holocaust and most of the survivors were intent on leaving for western Europe, America or, when possible, Palestine. Individuals apart, the only Jewish groups who chose to stay were those who for one reason or another felt committed to the new communist-led régime.

It is ironic that it was in this phase of Polish-Jewish disengagement that the Kielce Pogrom of July 1946 produced an act of more flagrant and shameful anti-semitism than anything which had occurred in the critical years preceding the outbreak of war. Poland's Germans had either fled, or in 1945-7, were forcibly expelled. Poland's Ukrainians were either incorporated into the USSR by frontier changes, or forcibly deported or dispersed following the civil war of 1945-7. Moreover, throughout the war, the Soviet authorities had observed a narrow definition of Polish nationality – which excluded all non-Catholics, and/or non-Polish citizens before 1939. As a result, large numbers of non-Poles who might otherwise have take up residence in Poland were prevented from leaving the Soviet Union, even during the post-war 'repatriation' campaigns. The outcome was the ethnically 'Polish Poland' which we know today.

The implications of this multinational context for the study of Polish-Jewish relations are considerable. I wouldn't claim that the following observations are completely original but they may help to throw some new light on the subject, and to keep it away from the confrontational posture, which can still be encountered in some quarters.

I

Before the Second World War, Polish-Jewish relations formed but one aspect of a much more complicated ethnic mix, and cannot be judged in isolation, or simply as a bilateral issue.

As often as not, Polish-Jewish relations formed one axis of a trilateral ethnic framework. In Silesia, for example, where the Jews were assimilating fast into German culture, Poles, Jews, and Germans all contributed to the ethnic pattern. In Wilno, or in Lwów, the Jewish community held the middle ground in the complicated relations of Poles and Lithuanians, or of

Poles and Ukrainians. In Łódź, the Polish-Jewish-German triangle – so eloquently reconstructed in the main protagonists of Reymont's novel, *Ziemia obiecana* (The Promised Land) – requires that consideration be paid to all three sides of the problem.

The events in Lwów (Lemberg) in November 1918 provide a concrete example of the odd conclusions that can be reached if the Polish-Jewish relationship is artificially extracted from the wider, multi-ethnic context. At the end of a week-long battle for the city between Polish and Ukrainian forces, elements of the victorious Polish soldiery went back into certain streets, where they claimed to have been fired at by civilians, and massacred the inhabitants. An estimated 340 innocent persons were killed. Some two-thirds of the victims were Ukrainians. The remaining seventy or so were Jews. Many history books refer to these events as the 'Lemberg Pogrom', and cite it as one of the worst instances of Polish anti-semitism in action. Yet one has to wonder whether a massacre in which the majority of victims were Christians can fairly be described as a 'pogrom'. It is conceivable, of course, that two distinct atrocities occurred – one a pogrom of Jews inspired by Polish anti-semitism; the other a military massacre, four times as large, inspired by Polish anti-Ukrainianism. Or perhaps, a gang of embittered soldiers, brutalised by a vicious local war, simply went on the rampage, and killed every 'foreigner' they could find. Some clarification is necessary.[2]

II

The condition of any one of Poland's numerous ethnic communities can only be fairly described in relation to other elements within Polish society. Comparisons with western Europe, or with North America, are not very relevant.

For example, it is very understandable for present-day Americans to study the condition of their forebears in Poland, and to feel indignant at the poverty and oppression which they had to endure. Polish Americans, American Jews and others are all apt to undertake the same exercise, and to reach the same conclusions with respect to *their* own particular forebears. The greatest wave of emigration from Poland to North America took hundreds of thousands of starving people of various nationalities from Galicia – Poles, Jews, Ukrainians – in the decade or so before the First World War; and it is a sobering thought for their descendants living comfortably in the suburbs of Chicago, New York, or Toronto to compare their grandparents' life with their own. However, if the aim is to understand the realities of early twentieth-century Polish society, as opposed to the consequences of migration, one should be studying, above all, the interdependence and mutual hardships of all elements of Galician society, where the Jewish masses no less than the Polish and Ukrainian peasantry, were forced to live on the hunger line. In this way, one might learn that the various ethnic communities, despite their differences, had much in common. What is not in order, I think, is for a historian to take the misfortunes of his own group in isolation and to pretend that their misfortunes were somehow unique or isolated.[3]

III

Regional variations were very marked. Polish-Jewish relations in western districts, where Germans often predominated, could not be the same as in certain eastern districts, where the Poles formed a small but powerful landed élite surrounded by a largely Lithuanian or Ruthenian peasantry.

The same might be said of the Jewish community which in the western provinces was largely associated with the prosperous 'modernised' German bourgeoisie, but in the east consisted largely of an impoverished, traditionalist society. Arguably, in cultural no less than in economic terms, the Jews of Posnania or Silesia were separated from the *Ostjuden* of Lithuania or East Galicia by a gulf even wider than the barriers which separated them from their Polish and German neighbours. Ethnic divisions alone cannot begin to explain these variations.

IV

In so far as the ethnic divisions were correlated, at least in part, with social structures, it is essential to identify the socio-economic interests which underlie many of the traditional attitudes of the various communities to each other. Polish Jewry was the one major group which had never been subjected to serfdom, and comparisons between the lot of Polish Jews with that of black slaves in America are misconceived.

In the feudal society of the Old Polish Commonwealth, the Jews had formed a separate social and legal estate, but one which, through the *arenda* system, worked closely with the nobility. Attitudes deriving from former centuries often persisted long after the destruction of the Commonwealth in 1795, or the final abolition of serfdom in 1864. The Jews continued to fulfil many of the same social and economic functions which they had carried out in feudal times – being very strongly represented in the professions, as doctors and lawyers, in urban services and in trade and commerce. Of course, from the Jewish perspective, the changes wrought by a modernising society which saw the rise of an aggressive, and frequently anti-semitic Polish bourgeoisie, and in the inter-war period, the establishment of an expansive Polish state bureaucracy, were often seen in a negative light – even as a concerted 'anti-semitic' attack on the Jewish community. From the perspective of the peasants, however, and especially of the Byelorussians and Ukrainians of 'Polska B', who saw little escape route from their life of illiteracy and provincial backwardness, the Jewish community could easily be seen as a continuing agency of their former servitude, and as an obstacle to progress. None of these 'perspectives' is necessarily impartial, or scientifically accurate; and all viewpoints need to be weighed in the balance. But for anyone familiar with Polish social history, the fashionable transatlantic perspective which tries to liken the position of the Jews in Poland to that of the descendants of black slavery in the USA must surely be the least convincing.[4]

V

Nationalism is a force which has afflicted every ethnic community in Eastern Europe, and Zionism, with its goal of building a separate Jewish homeland in Palestine, should probably be seen as a variant of the other nationalisms prevalent in the area, rather than a phenomenon *sui generis*. The divisions and conflicts which the rise of Zionism provoked within Polish Jewry, as well as with their neighbours, could be profitably explored in the light of similar developments provoked by the rise of ethnic nationalism in each of the other communities of the Polish lands.

At this point, I should probably declare my own interest. In my studies of Polish history, I have always felt that 'Nationalism', though all-pervasive, is a phenomenon which on balance has done more harm than good. One of the minor upsets of my early career occurred when *Myśl Polska*, the organ of the Polish National Democrats in London denounced me as a communist agent. Later, having written one of the first non-nationalist histories of Poland, which pays due attention to all the non-Polish elements of the story, I received the applause of all sections of Polish opinion, except the Nationalist one. Before falling foul of certain distinguished and undistinguished commentators in the USA, I had the honour to be attacked as 'anti-Polish' in that fount of wisdom, the *Tydzień Polski*.[5]

With this background, I tend to look at Zionism in the light of my understanding of the parallel Polish experience. I see Zionism (meaning Jewish Nationalism in the broad sense) as encompassing both the national independence movement of the Jews, on the one hand, as well as the narrower or 'integral' ethnic Nationalist element on the other. In this line of reasoning, the broad and tolerant concept of Zionism, as practised by the founding fathers of Israel, strikes me as a cousin of the Polish Independence Movement of the early twentieth century; and David Ben-Gurion as a fellow-spirit to Józef Piłsudski. By the same token, the narrower, militant and nationalistic concept of Zionism, as practised by say the Zionist Revisionists and others, I take to be a relative of the Polish National Democrats. In this connection I was encouraged to read a recent comment along these lines by my colleague, Neal Ascherson, an author well versed in the history of Poland in the twentieth century: 'Perhaps, to be really pessimistic, the lasting legacy of pre-war Jewish politics in Europe is not democracy, but the blind 'national egoism' which some Zionists in Poland learned from the Nationalism preached by Roman Dmowski.'[6] Further to the Right, on both the Polish and the Jewish spectrum, I see further similarities between the extreme *fascisants* of both sides. In the continuing debates between the advocates of Piłsudski and Dmowski – as between those of Ben-Gurion and Begin, (though I know much less about it) – I do not conceal my critical but committed adherence to the cause of the non-Nationalists.

Of course, despite the accusations of careless critics, I have never advocated any exact equivalence between the characteristics of Polish and Jewish Nationalism: but I do maintain that it is a fruitful line of enquiry. I do not believe that the intense antipathy which Polish and Jewish Nationalists have tended to feel towards each other should blind us to the common mentality and philosophy which underlies each of their positions. The same would apply, in my view, to the relationship of Polish and German, or Polish and Ukrainian Nationalists. Just because Roman Dmowski saw German nationalism as Poland's prime enemy and campaigned against it throughout his career as the principal threat to Poland's survival, we are not entitled to conclude that Dmowski did not borrow many of his ideas from Germany, before transposing them for his own intensely Polish purposes. One of the themes of my writings which has won least approbation from the admirers of Dmowski, is that where I suspected Pan Roman of 'wanting to build a new Poland in the image of Prussia'.[7] This is not the place to explore the phenomenon in detail but I have long ruminated on the truth of a half-remembered aphorism by Oscar Wilde to the effect that 'excessive hostility is often the mask of secret affinity'.

VI

Xenophobia – the hatred of foreigners – is one of the deplorable features of all nationalist movements, which, in their eagerness to strengthen the separate identity of their own group, inevitably weaken the sense of solidarity with other groups. All nationalities complain of persecution and oppression by their neighbours; and it would be pertinent to enquire how far the antipathies, which undoubtedly increased between Poles and Jews, reflected the painful, but predictable tensions of an impoverished multinational society beset on all sides by Nationalist fervour.

In its extreme form, I suppose, the question being asked is: can anti-semitism be regarded as a variant of other forms of xenophobia, with essentially similar well-springs and characteristics, or is it something of an entirely specific and unique nature? In the context of Polish-Jewish relations, one has equally to ask whether the 'anti-semitism' which Jews often see among Poles is the same sort of phenomenon as the 'anti-Polonism' which Poles often see among Jews? Or perhaps, are not *all* the dialectical 'anti-Usisms' a reflection of the insecurity which all ethnic groups experience in turbulent, multinational societies and which strengthen the distinction between 'us' and 'them'.

Obviously, one of the difficulties lies in the elastic definition of the term anti-semitism, which in modern usage has been turned, especially in America, to all sorts of inappropriate uses. Along with others, I am one of the people who has tended to restrict my use of the term, not because 'an irrational hatred of Jews' is not a very real and deplorable fact of modern history but because it has been confused with all sorts of non-pathological positions, from 'a dislike of bagels' to well-intended criticism of Israeli Government policy.[8]

I would also count it essential to distinguish between attitudes which are the product of real political, cultural and socio-economic rivalry between nationalities (and in that case, however deformed and exaggerated, possess some sort of genuine rationale) and other attitudes which derive from thorough-going racist ideology. For example, I thought it distasteful to listen the other day to a BBC interviewer asking the Israeli Ambassador whether the attitude of the Israeli Government towards the Palestinian Arabs was not reminiscent of the Nazis' attitude towards the Jews. The answer, obviously, is that there is no comparison. It follows, however, that the tensions between Jews and Poles in pre-war Poland, emanating from the long-standing rivalry of two communities inhabiting the same country, also bear little resemblance to the relationship of the Jews and the Nazis during the Holocaust. The two relationships are different in kind, and not simply in degree.

Incidentally, one of the most paradoxical aspects of Polish-Jewish relations during the war concerns the parallel efforts of Poles and Jews to win the support of the British. It so happened that in 1942-3, at the height of Britain's life and death struggle with Nazi Germany, the British forces in

Palestine found themselves under attack from militant Zionists. As a result, when Zionist delegations in London were trying to persuade HMG that the Jews were a member of the Allied nations, the British were not disposed to agree.[9] At that same juncture, the Polish Army of General Anders made its appearance in Palestine, en route from Persia and the Soviet Union, and immediately found itself embroiled in the British-Jewish contest. Several thousand Jewish soldiers from Anders's Army deserted the Polish ranks and promptly took up arms against their erstwhile British patrons. To the Poles, such events can only have strengthened their claim to be Britain's first and most loyal ally. Yet they were not repaid in kind for their loyalty. When the chips were down at the end of the war, the British did not speak out for Poland's independence, in whose defence the War had originally been declared. Instead, in line with the USA, they conceded Poland's interests to the demands of the most recent, and their most powerful ally, the Soviet Union.

Naturally, one cannot deny that some sort of link exists between Nazi ideology and the ethnic conflicts surrounding the Jews in Central and Eastern Europe. In order to spin their hideous, pagan fantasies, the Nazis had first to draw on the existing body of German and especially Austrian anti-semitism, and on earlier conflicts between Jews and Christians, as well as on other hatreds born of the German nationalists' contempt for Germany's neighbours. On this score, one might only add that Nazi ideology did not consist merely of a monstrous, inflated version of anti-semitism. It was a theory of Master Racism, which was directed not only against the Jews but in different degrees against many other groups as well.[10] Nazi policies against the Poles, for example, were no less genocidal for the fact that they aimed to eliminate particular political and cultural classes rather than the Polish nation as a whole.

VII

> Although the goals of Nationalism have been achieved in Poland, and the Nationalities separated out into their respective homelands, a balanced view of history requires an equal appreciation of those individuals and movements who opposed Nationalism in all its forms, striving instead for the multinational harmony which was destined not to be.

It is one of the ironies of modern Polish history that the Nationalists' goal of an ethnically 'Polish Poland' was achieved not by Dmowski's right-wing National Democrats but by the allegedly left-wing Communists. Since 1945, in order to legitimise Poland's new territorial arrangements, the ruling Party has propagated an ideology where old-fashioned Polish

Nationalism has been mingled with 'revolutionary' Marxism-Leninism.[11] The whole post-war generation has been schooled in an ultra-nationalist, intellectual framework where the eternal Polish nation and the eternal Polish *macierz* (homeland) between the Oder and the Bug have been taken for granted. In such a system, an awareness of Poland's links with the various non-Polish peoples of Poland was not necessary. The memory of Poland's multinational heritage, when not actively suppressed, was ignored. Yet one of the features of the Polish 'Revolution' of 1980-1, when respect for the official ideology was cast to the winds, was the marked resurgence of interest in ethnic matters, including Polish-Jewish history. Since then, the authorities have not cared to reverse the trend and, as recent conferences have testified, Polish-Jewish studies have become a subject of widespread, and serious concern in Poland. Even more heartening to my mind is the newfound readiness of Polish scholars to re-examine some of the moral implications of Polish Nationalism and not to flinch before a discussion of even the most shameful episodes and attitudes. It is in this context, in my personal view, that the initiative of Professor Jan Błoński in *Tygodnik Powszechny* at the beginning of last year, must be most warmly applauded. Błoński's compatriots need not agree with every detail of his argument; but they must recognize the fine mixture of courage, modesty and self-criticism which raised the debate onto a higher plane. In my view, Błoński has set an example which all parties to the Polish-Jewish debate could profitably follow.[12]

On the Jewish side it is also clear that Zionism triumphed at the end of the war, and that in the last twenty years or so, the more nationalistic elements within Zionism have risen to prominence. (This in itself is an interesting parallel with the shift of political attitudes within independent Poland between the wars – a marked shift to the right occasioned by continuing tensions at home, and unresolved threats from abroad.) Certainly, the political atmosphere is bound to affect the conduct and direction of academic studies and debates, in the Diaspora no less than in Israel. In which case, one might conclude that in prevailing circumstances, if we are to understand the rich variety and achievements of pre-war Polish Jewry, there may be a special need to emphasize the non-Zionist and non-nationalist elements of the story and to explore in greater depth, and with greater sympathy, the aims and aspirations of those numerous Jews who were committed to life in Poland and who strove to improve the lot of all nationalities in the land of their birth. I am well aware that interventions of this sort may not meet with universal approval. Having myself made a minor foray in that direction, I know only too well that one can be rewarded with a nasty bout of earache.[13] But the outcry only convinces me all the more that the attempt is worth the making.

One positive aspect of the present situation, which enables us to take an optimistic stance in the wake of former tragedies, is the fact that Polish-

Jewish relations are very largely the concern of historians. For better or for worse, Poles and Jews no longer inhabit the same multinational society where their various aspirations were constantly interrupted by everyday fears and alarms. As a result, Polish and Jewish scholars, and rash interlopers like myself, have a real opportunity to study the past in relative tranquillity, and to recreate that international harmony of purpose which many people in former Poland longed for, but few enjoyed.

NOTES

1 See Bernard Johnpoll, *The Politics of Futility: the General Jewish Workers' Bund of Poland. 1917–43*, (Ithaca, 1967), p. 195.
2 One of the first reports to reach the west described the events in Lemberg as 'one of the worst pogroms in Polish history' *Manchester Guardian*, 30 Nov. 1918. Later, in 1919 in a series of articles written by Israel Cohen and entitled 'Pogroms in Poland', the *Times* followed the same line. See Israel Cohen, *Travels in Jewry* (London, 1952). Independent investigations by British and American missions, however, could not establish any clear conclusions. The British Embassy in Warsaw in particular thought that press reports had been inaccurate. In his covering letter to the Samuel Report in June 1920, Sir Horace Rumbold wrote: 'It is giving the Jews very little real assistance to single out . . . for reprobation and protest the country where they have perhaps suffered least.' Norman Davies, 'Great Britain and the Polish Jews. 1918–20', *Journal of Contemporary History* vol. 8, no. 2, 1973, pp. 119–42.
3 A persistent offender in this regard is Martin Gilbert, whose *Jewish History Atlas* (London, 1976), is one of the most popular introductions to the subject. Gilbert would argue no doubt that his atlas is limited by definition to the Jewish experience. But that does not save it from numerous misleading statements. For example, when, on his map of 'The Chmielnicki Massacres' (p. 530) he writes, '. . . his followers joined with the Polish peasants in attacking the Jews . . . Over 100,000 Jews were killed; many more were tortured or ill-treated; others fled . . .', the reader might easily get the erroneous impression that the Chmielnicki massacres were directed mainly, if not exclusively at the Jews. In fact, there were virtually no Polish peasants at that period in the areas marked on Gilbert's map, and the attacks on the Jews were but one part of the terrible vengeance wreaked by the Cossacks and their associates on everyone whom they regarded as the agents of feudal oppression. Similarly, on his map of 'The Jews of Austria-Hungary, 1867–1914' (p. 73), Gilbert marks a wide area of Galicia 'in which 5,000 Jews died each year through starvation, 1880–1914'. Again, the unsuspecting reader might be led to assume that the Jews of Galicia were the main or even the only victims of starvation. There is nothing in the text to indicate that the Polish and Ukrainian peasants of Galicia were starving in even larger numbers. Indeed, it was the desperate condition of the peasantry, on whom most of the Jews depended for their livelihood, which drove up to a quarter of the surviving population of the province to emigrate to the United States in those last two decades before the First World War.
4 Even Ezra Mendelsohn, whose brilliant article 'Interwar Poland: good or bad for the Jews?' avoids any direct equation between American racism and Polish anti-semitism, cannot entirely resist the analogy. 'Few, if any American intellectuals,' he claims, 'would deny that America was (and still is) an anti-black country. Possibly one reason why Polish scholars are reluctant to state that Poland was an anti-Jewish country is that they are accustomed to regard Poland as a victim and victims are

extremely reluctant to admit that they have victimised others. But such things are possible.' (In *The Jews in Poland*, ed. C. Abramsky *et al*, Oxford 1986, p. 138). To which, Amen. This is the heart of the matter. The study of Polish-Jewish relations is constantly bedevilled by the fact that both sides have had good reason to think of themselves as victims and underdogs. Both sides are reluctant to admit that they have victimised others; and it is only the exceptional scholar who can rise above the recriminations and admit that attitudes among his own people have sometimes been less than charitable. (See Note 12.)

5 See *Tydzień Polski*, (London) 6 September 1986, p. 6 and references.
6 Neal Ascherson, 'Peace Now and Israel's Nemesis', *The Observer* (London) 3 January 1988.

In their common opposition to Nationalism, both Polish and Jewish, the pre-war Bundists made no bones about what their opponents had in common. 'Zionism has become an ally of anti-semitism,' wrote Henryk Erlich in a polemic against the historian, Szymon Dubnow, in 1938. 'The worsening situation of the Jews throughout the world is exploited by the Zionists. The Zionists regard themselves as second-class citizens in Poland. Their aim is to be first-class citizens in Palestine, and to make the Arabs second-class citizens ...' (Quoted by Antony Polonsky, 'The Bund in Polish Political Life, 1935-39', draft paper for the Jerusalem Conference, January 1988.) Fifty years later, Ehrlich's words sound almost uncannily prophetic.

7 On Dmowski's ambivalent attitude to Germany, see Norman Davies, *Heart of Europe: a Short History of Poland*, (Oxford, 1984), pp. 138-9. 'Although Dmowski would have been the last to admit it, his model for this ideal [Poland] derived from the earlier German nationalists of the Blut und Boden school, the original purveyors of the mystical link between 'the blood and the soil'. By the same token, one might fairly suspect Dmowski of subconsciously wishing Poland to resemble that powerful, prosperous, ethnically cohesive and reunited imperial Germany, which consciously, he so much feared and hated ...'
8 For a summary of my views on the uses and abuses of the term 'anti-semitism', see 'Poles and Jews: an Exchange', in *New York Review of Books*, 9 April 1987.
9 When a Zionist delegation headed by Lewis Namier approached the Colonial Office in London in 1943 with a plea to admit Jewish children to Palestine, and 'to regard the Jews as an Allied people suffering more than any others at the hands of the oppressor,' a British official minuted: 'This is a major fallacy'. Martin Gilbert, *Auschwitz and the Allies*, (London, 1981), p. 98.
10 See, for example, Max Dimont, *Jews, God, and History*, (New York, 1978), p. 389. 'We must realise the fact that Nazism was not just anti-semitic, but anti-human.... If the Christian reader dismisses what happened in Germany as something which affected a few million Jews only, he ... has betrayed his Christian heritage ... And if the Jewish reader forgets the 7 million Christians murdered by the Nazis, then he has not merely let 5 million Jews die in vain but has betrayed his Jewish heritage of compassion and justice.'
11 On the post-war marriage of Polish Nationalism with Marxism- Leninism within the ideology of the ruling Party, see *Heart of Europe*, op cit. pp. 149–151; also *God's Playground*, op.cit., Vol.II, p. 551: 'The exclusive, intolerant approach to the problem of national identity, which among other things had distinguished the *PPR* and the *PZPR* from the pre- war *KPP*, marks the ultimate victory of the basic ideas of Dmowski's National Democracy.'
12 Jan Błoński, 'Biedni Polacy patrzą na Getto', *Tygodnik powszechny*, (Kraków), 11 January 1987.
13 Norman Davies, 'The Survivor's Voice', being a review of Hanna Krall, *Shielding the Flame: an Intimate Conversation with Marek Edelman, the Last Surviving Leader of the*

Warsaw Ghetto Uprising. (Translated by Joanna Stasińska and Lawrence Weschler. Preface by Timothy Garton Ash. New York, 1986), in *New York Review of Books*, 20 November 1986. This review, which expressed a positive view of Edelman, of the Bund, and of Hanna Krall's book, has inspired three lengthy, and less than positive responses: from Abraham Brumberg, in *New York Review of Books*, 9 April 1987; from Lucy S. Dawidowicz, 'The Curious Case of Marek Edelman', in *Commentary*, vol. 83, no. 3, March 1987; and from Jon Wiener, 'When Historians Judge Their Own', in *The Nation*, 21 November 1987. Each response has in turn provoked extensive correspondence, notably in the *New York Review of Books*, 9 April 1987; in *Commentary*, vol. 84, no. 2, August 1987; and in *The Nation* (5 March 1988).

THE JEWISH QUESTION IN THE WORK OF THE *INSTYTUT BADAŃ SPRAW NARODOWOŚCIOWYCH* IN WARSAW

Andrzej Chojnowski

A group of Polish politicians, journalists, and scholars known for their interest in the question of the national minorities in the reborn Polish state gathered in Warsaw in December 1921. Sharing the conviction that the solution to this important and delicate issue must derive from thorough knowledge of the situation of the particular nationalities, they decided to found an independent institution for research into nationality questions, or, in Polish *Instytut Badań Spraw Narodowościowych* (IBSN).

The founders of the IBSN were divided as to its scope and mode of operation. Some, like Ludwik Krzywicki, Stanisław Posner, and Stanisław Stempowski were apolitical in their approach, maintaining that the Institute should be a scientific centre which would gather material and provide inspiration for scholarly inquiries. Others, including Marceli Handelsman and Szymon Aszkenazy, had more far-reaching ambitions. They argued that, in the face of considerable ignorance in Polish society as regards the life and problems of its nationalities, the IBSN should strive to influence public opinion by breaking down myths and stereotyped preconceptions, while also offering services to the government in preparing the background for legal solutions, or acting as a mediator in contacts with representatives of minority groups. The debate was won by the supporters of an apolitical role, and the constitution accepted did not envisage the possibility of presenting requests and petitions to the government.[1]

The political atmosphere in Poland prior to 1926 did not favour the development of an initiative such as the IBSN. For this reason, its activities were originally confined to organizing a few discussions, while in the years 1924-5 it ceased to exist altogether. After the May *coup d'état*, however, new opportunities emerged. The entire country expected that the Piłsudski-ites, with their renowned pro-federation past, would inaugurate a new stage in the nationalities policy. During the first months following the coup, the authorities did indeed try to show willing by undertaking a number of measures that appeared to satisfy the hopes of national minorities. The existence of the IBSN was convenient for the government in this respect since it made it easier, both at home and abroad, to demonstrate their interest in the nationalities question. Another essential factor in the improved status of the IBSN at this time was the presence among its founders of persons who were closely connected with the country's new leadership.

The institute thus reactivated remained formally independent, but it in fact submitted reports to the Praesidium of the Council of Ministers. In return, it enjoyed the political and financial support of the government. The general secretary was Stanisław Paprocki, and the board included Leon Wasilewski, Stanisław Thugutt, Marceli Handelsman, and Jerzy Osmołowski. The Jewish question was dealt with by the Jewish Commission, which was composed of Wiktor Alter, Majer Bałaban, Zygmunt Dreszer, Apolinary Hartglas, Aleksander Haftka, Ignacy Schiper, and Mojżesz Schorr.

The activities of the IBSN took various forms. It inspired scientific investigations in statistics, demography, economy, sociology, history, and law. To this end it collected archive and library material and organized discussion. Publishing was another important domain: up to the outbreak of war in 1939 the IBSN issued scores of books and brochures, and from 1927 it published a bi-monthly entitled *Sprawy narodowściowe* (from 1928 also a French version, *Questions minoritaires*). From the beginning of the 1930s the IBSN also organized 'nationality seminars' for Warsaw students, which were seen as a way of training specialists for administrative positions in the state. In all these activities, attempts were made to involve scholars and political figures from among the non-Polish population. The IBSN avoided direct involvement in political activity, but none the less, as we shall see, it is possible to perceive connections between its own undertakings and the government campaigns.

The accession of the Piłsudski camp to power in May 1926 seemed to augur a new era in the national minorities policy. Public opinion expected immediate government decisions, particularly as regards the Jewish question, which was not quite as controversial as the Ukrainian or German issues, since the Jews did not threaten the state's territorial integrity.

The programme prepared by the Ministry of Foreign Affairs did foresee *inter alia* the alleviation of regulations concerning compulsory rest on Sundays, accelerated election to the Jewish *kahals*, and equality for Jewish schools within the state system. In the *Sejm*, Prime Minister Kazimierz Bartel condemned manifestations of economic anti-semitism and guaranteed that in the sphere of tax and credit policies the government would follow exclusively non-national criteria.[2]

Beyond these declarations of intent, the government also demonstrated its stand on minorities in more practical ways. At the end of 1926, the

Commission of Experts[3] held several conferences, with the participation of Jewish politicians, to deal with the project for amendment of the Sunday rest law, and also presented proposals for granting private Jewish schools (with Yiddish or Hebrew as the language of instruction) the same rights as public schools. The Jewish Commission of the IBSN announced a prize for work on the history of Jewish political movements as well as an enquiry into the *kahals*.[4] The latter was probably instigated by the government, which wished to become more closely acquainted with the party line-up among the Jewish population in the provinces. In April 1928 the government issued a presidential decree concerning the principles of organizing religious *kahals* (outside the Silesian voivodeship), which made it possible to hold *kahal* elections in the north-eastern voivodeships and in Galicia in the summer and autumn, which considerably stimulated Jewish political life in these areas.

The government failed to amend the law concerning compulsory rest on Sundays. It also rejected the proposals made by the IBSN and the Commission of Experts on granting public school status to Jewish schools. The latter received no financial aid from the state, and with few exceptions, existed only on private donations, fees, appeals and subsidies made by *kahals* and Jewish magistrates. At a meeting organised by the IBSN in February 1931, attention was drawn to the fact that, regardless of any material motives, the government's attitude was inspired by the hope of attracting Jewish youth to Polish schools. Meanwhile, Arieh Tartakower, a docent of the Judaistic Institute (*Instytut Judaistyczny*) in Warsaw, claimed that 'Jewish assimilation today belongs to the irretrievable past, and no one in Poland dreams about assimilation or supposes that the Jewish community would become Polonized ... The purpose of the state school policy should be a profound understanding for the Jewish school system, and an adaptation to its needs at every step of the way.'[5] But the government did not accept this type of argument, and the situation of the Jewish schools did not alter until 1939.

One of the most important demands made by the Jewish community was to rescind the legal limitations imposed at the time of the Partitions. The Polish authorities initially declared that this came under the Constitution of 17 March 1921, but in the light of opinions expressed by IBSN experts, they decided to enact a law that would dispel any doubts still harboured at the lower levels of the apparatus of power. In April 1931, the *Sejm* finally passed a law eliminating 'exceptional decrees connected with descent, nationality, race and religion'.

From the very beginning, the IBSN concentrated mainly on economic issues. Between 1927 and 1930 it published studies by Jerzy Gliksman and Izaak Bornstein on the professional structure and material situation of the Jewish population, based on the census of 1921.[6] Having ascertained significant concentrations of Jews in certain professions, the authors explained the historical reasons for this. They also took issue with the myths then current regarding the superior material conditions of the Jewish community, showing, for example, how the concentration of Jewish workers in some branches of the economy and in small industrial enterprises had a negative impact on their living conditions. A certain optimism in some of the statements made by the authors stemmed from a conviction about the inter-dependence between the Jews' economic interests and Poland's. Awareness of this was supposed to encourage the Jewish community to increase its efforts so as to improve the country's economic position, as this would in turn favour the attainment of a superior political *modus vivendi* and facilitate the Jews' assimilation. A reassuring development in this context was a certain stimulation of the Polish economy following the May *coup d'état*.

This proved to be only a passing phenomenon, however. From 1929, Jewish activists and politicians tried on a number of occasions to diagnose the reasons for the economic depression in Poland. Treating it as the result of a world-wide breakdown in the economic system, they nevertheless drew attention to those elements of the domestic situation which increased the dimensions of the Polish crisis, including the focus on grain production rather than animal husbandry, and the official fiscal policy. In the latter context, the Jewish community regarded the pro-nationalisation tendencies of the post-May camp with anxiety, and supported the idea of a free market economy. It attributed the deterioration of the economic situation to the tax system, which not only weakened the payment abilities of economically active groups but also decreased their capacity to perform. Jewish spokesmen therefore called for amendments to the industrial tax law, the alleviation of urban taxes, a moratorium on unpaid taxes owed by impoverished payers, and the complete exemption of the lower strata of merchants and petty craftsmen from taxation. It also called for an increase in state financial assistance for the Jewish co-operatives.

These demands compelled the authorities to consider a more general question: whether the decline in the material situation of the Jewish population was the effect of government policy or whether the causes for their pauperization lay beyond state influence.

A Committee for Research into the Economic Needs of the Jewish Population in Poland was set up by the Jewish Commission of the IBSN in June 1931 to deal with the problem. It comprised some twenty Polish and Jewish scholars, members of parliament, and higher state officials. The committee also incorporated a number of expert subgroups: on small industry and the crafts, trade, labour, credit and vocational schools. The committee presented its first demands to Prime Minister Prystor in November. These included elimination of all obstacles to the acceptance of Jewish youth to state vocational schools, and the liberalization of principles for licensing concessions to open vocational schools and other forms of vocational training. The committee likewise proposed a state subsidy of 532 million złotys for Jewish vocational schools and asked for a subsidy for Non-Interest Loan Banks, including a one-time donation of 1 million złotys.[7]

The anti-crisis proposals prepared by the Prystor government, however, ignored the proposals made by the committee. This caused considerable anxiety in the IBSN, on the grounds that rejection of the demands presented by the committee meant that its work was regarded as unproductive, which could jeopardize its further existence. This fear was increased by the growing disappointment in the government's nationalities policy. Between 1926 and 1930 the IBSN members believed in the sincerity of the Piłsudski camp's liberal declaration, but by the early 1930s the mood was changing. The IBSN's reports usually avoided direct comment, but the very listing of facts evidenced negligence and inertia on the part of the government.

The committee's fate was decided by the general secretary of the institute, Stanisław Paprocki, who insisted that it be retained. However, it abandoned its ambitions of directly influencing government policies and concentrated instead on research. The latter included a number of interesting statistical profiles of Jewish co-operatives, trade, and crafts, a survey of Jewish participation in supplementary vocational schools, and a survey on unemployment among Jewish artisans.[8] None of these studies provided a clear answer as to the causes of pauperization among the Jews, although there were many indications that the problem had its origins in the traditionalism of Jewish life. The author of a work about Jewish *kahals* emphasized *inter alia* that in the face of the thoroughly religious budgets of those communities 'only a slight part of the millions provided by direct and indirect taxes ... paid by the poor, is earmarked for combating hunger, productive assistance for the impoverished and unemployed, social hygiene, cultural purposes etc.'[9]

The participants in the discussion organized by the IBSN in 1931 and 1932 praised the government for its energetic reaction to the anti-semitic campaigns of the National Democracy. At the same time, they noted the systematic ousting of Jews from economic life and their relegation to the very depths of poverty. It was estimated that about 20 per cent of the Jewish population was devoid of all sources of sustenance, while 55–60 per cent lived below the poverty line, yet, at the same time, Jews paid 40 per cent of the indirect taxes. The reasons for this were sought in the general features of the economic structure, the attitudes of the Jewish industrialists who treated their own employees rather badly and the government's tax policy. The spokesmen of various Jewish political groups took the diagnosis a step further and charged the authorities with conducting a policy of economic discrimination; the government, in response, attributed the Jews' critical situation to 'their excessive number in Poland in general, and in certain branches of the economy in particular', and emphasized that ousting of Jews from economic life was a 'natural phenomenon, caused by structural transformations . . . and a world-wide economic depression'.[10]

By 1936, the state estimated that over a million Jews in Poland were threatened with total economic ruin. The government undoubtedly expected help from Jewish agencies abroad, not so much in the form of credits as of winning a market for exports, but negotiations undertaken on a number of occasions did not produce any results.

Other ideas varied from different forms of charity to a programme for restructuring of the Jewish community. Particularly popular was the idea of creating a network of non-interest loan banks with the financial support of such organizations as the American Joint Distribution Committee and the Board of Deputies of British Jews. One of the versions of such an undertaking was put forward by the IBSN.

At the beginning of 1934, the committee and the Central Society for Non-interest Loan Banks (*Cekabe*) proposed the creation of a 5-million złoty fund to set up some 20,000 new workshops in 666 small- and medium-sized communities (up to 15,000 inhabitants). The new workshops were to provide 'additional wage-paying work for the impoverished population who can only partially subsist on their existing professions'.[11] The endowment for the fund was to come from sums alloted by the directors of the Labour Fund (2.7 million złotys), compulsory contributions by the *kahals*, donations by more prosperous Jews, and aid from foreign organizations.

In May 1935, a delegation of the committee received by the Minister of the Interior, Marian Kościałkowski, was promised support for the project, but subsequently the authorities reneged on their promises. The initiators of the project were nevertheless able to collect money from the wealthier Jewish population and to obtain long-term credit from the Joint, which made it possible to expand the *Cekabe* network by 310 new posts. The idea of increasing the number of economic centres, however, was never realized.

The change in government policy was due in part to financial reasons, but may also be attributed to a new attitude to the Jewish question among the country's leadership. Prior to 1935, government policy did not follow a deliberate programme and was unable to eliminate the sources of recurring conflicts and tension; now a new approach to solving the Jewish question began to emerge in the Consular Department of the Ministry of Foreign Affairs. Its proponents abandoned the idea of the assimilation of Jews on the grounds that there 'exists an essential divergence between the interest of Poland and the Jewish interests' and that the two communities were in 'a state of war, without a formal declaration of war. This war is conducted by the Jews both offensively and defensively';[12] in particular, the authors of the report claimed, the nationalization of state policy and economy were regarded by the Jews as a threat to their interests. The only solution to this situation, the report maintained, was the mass emigration of Jews to Palestine, to the classical countries of immigration, and to additional destinations.

Following the formulation of the general principles of the emigration programme, the authorities launched a propaganda campaign both at home and in the international arena. This campaign pursued several courses, including the systematic dissemination of information to foreign governments, parliaments, and the press about the Jewish problem in Poland, in which emigration was promoted as the sole chance for its solution. Polish diplomatic posts were instructed to collect data on the possibility of Jewish emigration.

These new ideas were reflected in the work of the IBSN. The Committee for Research into the Economic Needs of the Jewish Population in Poland established an emigration commission at the beginning of 1936 and by the end of the year it had issued publications on the history of Jewish emigration from Poland and on the possibilities of emigration to countries other than Palestine.[13] These studies pointed out that Poland was overpopulated and 'no longer had land for unlimited settlement, while competition among the Jewish population is growing daily . . . the concentration of Jews in towns is rising, and the opportunities for a suitable scattering throughout Poland continue to decrease'. In this situation even part of the Polish population faced the prospect of emigration, and the solution of the Jewish question in any manner other than emigration could not be countenanced. The Jewish question was nowhere as urgent as in Poland, the authors went on, which had 'at least a million Jews too many'.[14]

Countering the opposition of certain Jewish politicians, authors from the IBSN maintained that 'for centuries the Jews have been known as a migratory nation', and that despite their diaspora throughout the world 'they are organized and cultivate national consciousness'.[15] The migration to Palestine and to a lesser extent to Argentina were cited as proof of the colonization abilities of the Jewish community.

The optimal level for Jewish emigration from Poland was estimated at 75–80,000 annually (taking into consideration an annual birth rate in the 1930s of about 30,000). The countries cited as targets for settlement included, apart from Palestine, the United States and Canada; Argentina, Paraguay, Brazil and Uruguay; and in Africa – Angola and Madagascar. This programme was promoted not only through the IBSN's publications but also through meetings and discussions to which Jewish politicans known for their active support of the Palestine idea, such as Vladimir Jabotinsky, were invited.

The establishment of the IBSN filled a gap which existed in Polish research into the national minorities. Despite the existence of several universities and a number of scientific institutions pursuing similar studies, until 1939 the IBSN remained the only centre conducting such investigations in a systematic and planned manner. During the eighteen years of its existence, it provided a framework for specialists drawn from all the national minorities of Poland; it published dozens of studies, initiated and conducted a number of sociological surveys. collected sizeable amounts of archive and library material, carried out complex cartographic work, and initiated co-operation with many similar institutes abroad.

The institute also performed services for the government. It produced a partial analysis of the results of the general censuses of 1921 and 1931, issued several monographs on the agrarian-economic situation in the eastern voivodeships, and gathered and prepared material on linguistic legislation in Europe.

The founders of the IBSN intended it to contribute to seeking effective ways of assimilating the ethnic minorities. The fate of those projects is a reflection of the dilemmas and inconsistencies of the nationalities policy pursued by the post-1926 Polish governments.

Despite the hopes of Jews, Ukrainians and Byelorussians that the accession of the Piłsudski camp, the former pro-federation group, would put an end to the period of idle 'examinations' of the national question, the new government did not follow a path of reform. Many historians attribute this to Piłsudski himself, claiming that he played down the significance of the nationalities and postponed real measures to the distant future. In fact, Piłsudski did not so much play down the importance of the problem as believe that Poland could not afford any experiments in this domain: to succumb to the demands of minorities could have intensified separatist tendencies.

Piłsudski strove to strengthen the authority of the government and achieve domestic stability by subjecting all citizens to what he perceived as the supreme interests of the state, which only the government was entitled to interpret. He was far from nationalistic phobias, but he remained convinced that the state would find enough strength to force its point of view upon the national minorities. Sources available today demonstrate that this was also the spirit of the instructions he issued to his colleagues. Piłsudski also emphasized the need to guarantee the superiority of the Polish language and to establish a compulsory Polish school system throughout the whole country. At the same time, the authorities did not refrain from calling for state assimilation, which formed the basis of their policy toward the minorities.

In this atmosphere, the IBSN was able to conduct and publish its research undisturbed, but chances for influencing government policy to meet the expectations of the non-Polish population remained slight. The original founders of the IBSN included many well-known men of letters, scholars, and politicians of democratic and socialist convictions. They represented that part of the Polish intelligentsia which cultivated a vision of the multi-language culture of the Jagiellonian commonwealth.

The attitude of this particular group on the question of national minorities was also affected by geo-political considerations. Russia was regarded as Poland's chief enemy, and at the beginning of the post-war period support was offered to the federation programme and the independence-oriented aspirations of the nations of the former Russian Empire. It was hoped to turn the non-Polish nationalities living in Poland into allies in a struggle against Russian imperialism. These views contained, none the less, an overtone of paternalism: the reborn Poland was to take care of her younger brothers in the east and to protect their freedom against Moscow. The republic was to play the role of a natural leader in a union of 'equal partners'. In accordance with this geo-political orientation, the founders of the IBSN regarded the Slav minorities as the most important. Their stand on the Jewish question was mainly one of an uncompromising condemnation of all forms of anti-semitism. They opposed those Polish nationalists who claimed that Jews constituted an element hostile to the Polish state and nation, and cited many examples in order to emphasize the assimilated Jews' great contribution to Polish culture. The institute did not consider national assimilation as a solution to all the problems of the Jewish minority, however, but merely wished to achieve state assimilation; hence the attempts to popularize the Polish language, and to awaken the Jewish community to a feeling of responsibility for the fate of the state.

These tasks were to be fulfilled by the Jews themselves, but only by those who remained Jews not in the name of the Talmud but in the name of their attachment to their own nation. Those Polish democrats who gathered around the institute anticipated profound social and cultural transformations within the Jewish community, and its liberation from the influence of rabbis and *tsaddiks*. This is why they gave moderate support to the Zionist movement as well as to the folkists and Jewish socialists, in whom they perceived the only force capable of making the walls of the ghetto crumble, and of facilitating cultural and political contacts between the Jewish and Polish communities.

At the same time, they rejected the demands of the Jewish nationalists who called for the recognition by the state of the distinct rights of the Jewish *kahals*, and especially of the right to use Yiddish in dealings with state authorities.

The IBSN attracted a group of people who attached great hopes to the rise to power of the Piłsudski camp, regardless of differing opinions on a number of issues. In later years some of these people did not hide their disappointment, but others, such as Hołówko and Paprocki, became members of the power structure and accepted the post-May *coup d'état* reality. Former courageous visionaries became careful and pragmatic politicans in whose statements *raison d'état* became a term of increasing significance and in whose name they abandoned all bolder ideas and experiments in national policies.

All told, the IBSN did not play an important political role. It did not prepare a comprehensive programme for resolving the national question, nor did it become a mediatory factor in relations between the governments and the representatives of the ethnic minorities. But it did leave behind a durable heritage, in the form of scientific studies and materials presenting various aspects of the lives of national minorities both in Poland and in Europe as a whole.

NOTES

1 Protocols of founding sessions of the IBSN, Stanisław Stempowski collection, Warsaw University Library, MS 1562.
2 Protocol of a session held by the Council of Ministers on 18 Aug. 1926, *Archiwum Akt Nowych w Warszawie (AAN)*, material of the Praesidium of the Council of Ministers; K. Bartel, *Mowy parlamentarne*, Warsaw 1928, p. 22.
3 From June 1926 it included Tadeusz Hołówko, Leon Wasilewski, and Henryk Loewenherz.
4 I. Bornstein, 'Budżety gmin wyznaniowych żydowskich w Polsce', *Kwartalnik Statystyczny*, 6: 1929.
5 *Sprawy Narodowościowe*, 5/2–3: (1931).
6 J. Gliksman, *Struktura zawodowa i społeczna ludności żydowskiej w Polsce* (Warsaw, 1930); I. Bornstein, 'Żydowskie organizacje gospodarcze w Polsce', *Sprawy Narodowościowe* 3/6 (1929).
7 Conclusions of the Commission, *Sprawy Narodowościowe*, 5/6 (1931).
8 A report on the activity of the IBSN for the period March 1932–March 1933, *Sprawy Narodowościowe*, 7/2–3 (1933).
9 I. Bornstein, 'Struktura budżetów żydowskich gmin wyznaniowych w Polsce', *Sprawy Narodowściowe*, 8/5–6 (1934).
10 Speech by Bernard Hauser, Ministry of Industry and Trade, at a meeting at the IBSN 3 June 1932; AAN, PRM, 64–5.
11 'The Committee for research into the Economic Needs of the Jewish Population in Poland', *Sprawy Narodowściowe*, 8/4 (1934).
12 Consular Department of the Ministry of Foreign Affairs, *Sprawa żydowska w roku 1938*, AAN, MSZ 10004.
13 N. Rejf, 'Rozwój i warunki emigracji żydowskiej z Polski', *Sprawy Narodowściowe*, 10/1–2 (1936); W. Ormicki, 'Warunki i możliwości emigracji żydowskiej', *Sprawy Narodowościowe*, 11/3 (1937).
14 Ormicki, op.cit.
15 Ibid.

THE UBIQUITOUS ENEMY. THE JEW IN THE POLITICAL THOUGHT OF RADICAL RIGHT-WING NATIONALISTS IN POLAND, 1926-39

Anna Landau-Czajka

INTRODUCTION

Defining the term 'radical right-wing nationalist' is not an easy task. Neither 'right-wing' nor 'nationalism' is unequivocal, and what, for one researcher, is a radical or extreme standpoint, may be, for another, a moderate, middle-of-the-road position. Thus, each writer may start out with a different definition, often one devised by himself and possibly completely at odds with those accepted before.

It is difficult to find any precise definition of the term 'right wing'. Each author finds himself like Winnie the Pooh when he looked at his paws: 'He knew that one of them was his right paw, and he also knew that when he had decided which of them was right, the other must be left, but he was never sure where to begin.' S. Kieniewicz writes: 'The one indisputably precise application of "right-wing" is to those political parties whose members sat in Parliament on the right-hand side of the chairman.'[1] Defining the term 'nationalism' presents similar problems. And here, as with the term 'right-wing', the fact that the concept of nationalism is to a large extent value-laden, is also significant. B.S. Schafer argues that '[arriving at] a precise definition which embraces all that is contained within nationalism and eliminates elements directly linked with it, is, in all likelihood, impossible.'[2]

In spite of these limitations, however, many scholars continue to study the nationalist right. It seems to me that one sure method of arriving at a definition of what is understood by the term 'radical right-wing nationalism' is to give a few of the conditions essential if a party or grouping is to be included under this heading. These criteria would include:

1 placing the good of the nation (e.g. the Polish) paramount among the hierarchy of aims and goals;
2 denying that the individual has any importance outside the national group;
3 wanting to create a new social structure in pyramidal form;
4 denying the importance, and even the existence, of internal conflict (especially that of class) within the nation;
5 opposing all manifestations of parliamentary democracy and the party system;
6 glorifying strength, and planning to use force to achieve the new order.

In inter-war Poland, then, there were groupings which we can unhesitatingly assign to the extreme nationalist right. We should bear in mind, though, that, despite the relatively large number of such groupings, the programme of these radical nationalists never found a mass public response. Such organisations were few in number and they usually split up after a relatively short period of activity. The activities of these nationalists – publication of numerous journals, pamphlets, leaflets, forming fighting squads – created the impression that support for the movement was much more widespread throughout the country than it was.

There were around twenty-five factions or groupings of the extreme nationalist movement. It is impossible to give an exact number because they continually merged and split. It must be quite clear then that to present, even in summary form, an account of the activities and the basic programmes of so many parties would be beyond the scope of this article. I shall restrict myself therefore to listing the parties, the dates they were formed, their main journals and their most important and active figures.[3]

I have not included the largest and most heavily-supported nationalist party – the original National Democrats. Although there is no doubt that they belonged to the grouping of nationalist parties, use of the term 'radical' in their case would be an exaggeration. The National Democrats accepted parliamentary methods and did not assume that force would be needed to achieve power. However, I did decide to include, after some doubts, the parties of the National Monarchists. These had a slightly different character from the other groups, but it was just as firmly nationalist. Furthermore, although they do not meet all the criteria (especially the fourth in the list), I have included below all those groups which described themselves as either fascist or national-socialist.

Youth Movement of the Camp of Greater Poland – RM-OWP. Broke away in April 1927 from the *OWP* (Camp of Greater Poland) formed on 4 December 1926 by Roman Dmowski. In October 1927 the government dissolved the *OWP* in Małopolska Wschodnia (Eastern Galicia) and then in other regions. In 1929 activity was limited to youth and workers' centres. In 1931 the autonomous Youth Movement was abolished and this meant that the whole *OWP* took on the character of its Youth Movement. It was finally made completely illegal on 29 March 1933. Periodicals: *Szczerbiec, Awangarda, Młodzi*. Activists: Z. Stahl, T. Bielecki, J. Zdzitowiecki, K. Hrabyk, J. Jodzewicz, J. Rembieliński.

Union of Young Nationalists - ZMN. Formed on 2 October 1932. Local organisations in the *provinces* of Pomorze and Poznań replaced the illegal *OWP*. Periodicals: *Akcja Narodowa, Awangarda Państwa Narodowego*. Activists: Z. Stahl, E. Hrabyk, J. Zdzitowiecki, R. Piestrzyński.

New National Movement - NRN. Formed in October 1934. Chief ideologue – A. Malatyński. After two months merged with the *ZMN*. Periodical: *Reduta*.

National Radical Camp - ONR. Formed on 14 April 1934 following the secession of younger activists from the Nationalist Party. Remained overtly active for only two months. The following signed its declaration: W. Dowbór, T. Gluziński, J. Jodzewicz, J. Mosdorf, M. Prószyński, T. Todtleben, W. Zaleski, J. Czerwiński. After the movement was declared illegal, it split into two factions; the *ONR-ABC* (Periodicals: *ABC, Nowy Ład, Sztafeta*; activists: H. Rossman, W. Zaleski, S. Piasecki, T. Gluziński) and the *ONR-Falanga* which was considerably more radical (Periodicals: *Falanga, Ruch Młodych, Przełom*; activists: B. Piasecki, W. Wasiutyński, W. Kwasieborski, A. Reutt, M. Reutt, W. Staniszkis, O. Szpakowski, S. Ciewzyński). *Wielka Polska* was a journal published by a group of people, from the *ONR* who left the organisation in 1938. Those invited to collaborate included T. Bielecki, Al. Bocheński, A. Bocheński, J. Dobraczyński, F. Goetel, K. Hałaburda, B.O. Kopczyński, J. Korolec, W. Kwasieborski, J. Mosdorf, S. Rymar.

Union of Young Poland - ZMP. Formed through an agreement between the *ONR-Falanga* and the *Sanacja* in 1937. The *ZMP* was in a sense an attempt to legalise the *ONR-Falanga*. Its leader was J. Rutkowski. Periodicals: *Młoda Polska, Akademik, Szturmowiec Pracy, Szturm Pracy, Bojownik Pracy, Żołnierz Pracy*.

Nationalist Socialist Party - PNS. Formed on 20 June 1933. Its programme was made public on 15 July of the same year. Periodicals: *Narodowy Socjalista, Front Narodowego Socjalisty, Polska Błyskawica*. Activists: F. Fijalkiewicz, M. Tomczak, A. Dec.

Union of National Socialist Youth - ZMNS. Youth organisation of the *PNS*. Polish National Socialist Workers' Party. Date of formation not known. Shortly after it was founded it was merged with the *PNS*. Journal: *Świt*.

Party of Polish Fascists – *SFP*. Formed in July 1926 (its journal began to appear in April of the same year). Ceased activity in September 1926. Journal: *Faszysta Polski*. Activists: S. Starodworski, W. de Vitt, W. Zaremba, R. Boguta-Starzyński.

National Socialist Workers' Party – *NSPR*. Its origins lay in the Independent Socialist Party (*NPS*) formed in April 1930. Its activities centred around two periodicals: *Jedna Karta*, and *Błyskawica*. The party was dissolved on 13 June 1934. Activists: W. Kozielski, J. Gralla, K. Macek.

Union of Polish Fascists (I) – *ZFP (I)*. Formed in 1926, a month later changed its name to the Union of Lechite-Fascists of the Polish Republic with its base in Poznań. Its activities most probably ceased in September after two issues of its journal, *Płomienie Odrodzenia. Dzwon Faszystów Polskich*, had appeared.

Union of Polish Fascists (II) – *ZFP (II)*. Formed in 1926. In June 1929 the party's journal reduced its scope drastically, and in all probability *Głos Faszystów* ceased to appear by the end of that year.

Polish National Socialist Party – *PPNS*. Precise date of formation unknown. Active during 1934. Journal: *Front Narodowo-Socjalistyczny*.

Radical Camp of Sarmatians – *ROS*. Formed in 1936. Its ideological manifesto appeared in July of that year, but its activities ceased most probably before January 1937. Journal: *Sarmata*.

Sword of Steel – *SM*. A group centred on the journal of the same name, *Stalowy Miecz*. Its first issue appeared in March 1936. The group was active until 1937.

Union of Polish Nationalists – *ZNP*. Formed in 1926 and ceased activity in the same year. Periodicals: *Nacjonalista Polski, Nacjonalista Mazowiecki, Nacjonalista Łódzki, Nacjonalista Radomski*. Founder: J. Raabe.

Radical Movement for Restoration – *RRU*. Formed prior to 1935. Activities suspended in May 1935, but in February 1937 the party renewed its activity under the name National Radical Movement for Restoration. From April 1938 collaborated with the *ZMN*. Journal: *Front Polski Zbudzonej*. Leader and ideologue – J. Kowal-Lipiński.

Zadruga. I have not been able to discover precisely when it was formed. The first issue of its journal appeared in November 1937. Its first programme appeared in the work by its chief ideologue- J. Stachniuk: *Heroiczna wspólnota narodu*. The *ONR-Falanga* were considered its closest allies. Journal: *Zadruga*.

Party of Monarchists of All Classes – *MOW*. Active from January 1926, initially under the name Peasant Monarchist Party. Journal: *Głos*

Monarchisty. Leader: A. Ćwiakowski. The Monarchist Organisation was formed in May 1925 and merged with the Organisation of Polish Monarchists in February 1926 to form the Federation of Polish Monarchists. This was dissolved in August 1926 when the Monarchist Organisation was reactivated. Journal: *Polak Monarchista*. Activists: M. Obiezierski, W. Dobiecki.

Party of National Monarchists – SNM. Founded in 1938. In July 1938 published its programme: *Program Narodowych Monarchistów (Bóg, Naród, Król)*. Journal: *Monarchia Narodowa*. Activists: W. Tyszkiewicz, J. Kamiński, B. Kwella, W. Korab Lamparski, E. Krzywda-Łoziński, E. Saryusz-Stokowski.

I have based what follows on the periodicals and pamphlets of the parties listed above. I have treated all the articles printed in a party's journal, irrespective of their authorship, as representing the views of that party (unless it is made clear that they were not). However, it was difficult to establish the authorship of some articles (many were unsigned) and there was a continuous movement of individual nationalists from one party to another.

Apart from problems of definition, another matter needs clarifying. This article is not 'historical' in the strict sense, although it is based on historical materials. It is an attempt rather to present elements of right-wing nationalist thought as though they were an entity, in the way that some monographs treat fascism. I am concerned here to present a certain type of thinking in a static form, and ignoring basic divisions, just as some historians and sociologists in creating a conceptual model of fascism, stress the similarities between the national varieties of fascism, rather than the differences.

JEWS

To exist, the ideology of the radical right-wing nationalists[4] needed to create the idea of an omnipresent foe (an internal as well as an external one), an enemy with almost unlimited possibilities of action, sufficiently concealed so as not to be too easily identified, and yet sufficiently well-known so as to convince the Polish community at large of his presence and evil intentions. The Jews provided the nationalists with that enemy.

It is probably a mistake to investigate nationalist attitudes towards the Jewish problem on the same level as those towards the other national minorities. For right-wing nationalists they were two completely different problems. They treated those of the national minorities as an important problem, but one of the second rank. Nationalists adopted the same attitude as other political parties – they talked in terms of assimilation,

Polonisation, education, territory, and so on. The Jewish question, however, was a central plank in their programme. The Jews were treated not as a typical national minority, but as an internal enemy, on the same level as communists and masons, international capital and other international organisations. The struggle with their enemy at home was regarded as the most important factor in the nation's survival.

This idea was crucial, since the concept of an enemy could be used to mobilise the Polish population. For the nationalists, who wanted to create a disciplined community on military lines, an opponent with whom they could wage war was indispensable. The nation had to understand the need for self-denial, to be ready for armed struggle, and to subordinate the individual to the interests of the state. This was possible only in an artificially-created atmosphere of permanent domestic conflict, a conflict which the Polish nation had to wage with its enemy, with what were called the fourth partitioners, the Jews.

Moreover, the idea of confrontation and struggle helped to conceal from their supporters certain shortcomings in the nationalists' programme of reform. They argued that the first task was to crush the enemy and only then would conditions be ripe for concrete systemic changes.

In many cases (for example in the fields of science and culture) expulsion of Jews was regarded as the only solution. By attributing any and every fault to the enemies of Poland, complicated political, economic and social problems were simplified at a stroke. Moreover, Jews were an enemy who, in practical terms, could not be destroyed. The Jewish menace could thus be used as an argument to rally the Polish nation for many years.

Distaste, and simply hostility towards Jews, proposals to limit their influence within the state, or even their physical expulsion, were ideas held without exception by all wings of the extreme nationalist right. Of course there were also some groups outside the nationalist fold which had anti-semitic views. But nowhere else did the question appear so clearly, nowhere else was there repeated reference to the Jewish question whatever the basic problem being considered.

The central tenet of nationalist thought was the assertion that Jews were the main enemies of Poland. It appears repeatedly on the pages of the nationalist press. 'Our greatest enemies are the Jews,' claimed a writer in the journal *Młody Rozwojowiec*.[5] In *Wielka Polska* a bold headline running across two pages read, 'Supporting the Jews or collaborating with them is treason'.[6] The author of articles in *Front Narodowego Socjalisty* wrote, '. . . we regard the Jewish element in Poland as an alien, harmful and hostile factor in the life of the nation'.[7] A. Wierny, in an article dedicated to Roman Dmowski warned that 'The independence of Poland is not complete, as long as we fail to achieve domestic independence: from Jews.'[8]

Nationalists believed it was totally impossible for Poles and Jews to live together in the same country. Some authors argued that Jews as a distinct race could not live in harmony with any people on the territory of the latter. Those who used the concept of race were most vocal in insisting that Jews should be segregated from the Polish community. It was claimed that unless this separation took place there would be a dangerous mixing of races, which might lead to the extinction of the Aryan one. A journalist writing in the periodical *Stalowy Miecz* put it this way: 'Like everything else in nature, the Aryan race also has a natural enemy, and that enemy is the Jewish race, the most materialistic and worthless of all the world's races. The Jewish race, like the most dangerous contagious bacteria, works unceasingly to destroy the Aryan race. This is its natural task, which it has to continue or to die. Destruction of the Aryan race – that is the aim of Jewry.'[9]

If one accepted this point of view, then harmony between Poles and Jews was impossible. The two communities had to be separated. Nationalists believed no-one born into a Jewish family could ever become a full member of another community, even though he absorbed its language, customs, or religion. The blood tie would make itself felt sooner or later. The periodical *Front Polski Zbudzonej* expressed it concisely: 'The Nazis are quite correct to investigate whether a prospective member of the party might have some Jewish blood in him. For . . . a pup will never become a foal, even if born in a stable.'[10] Anti-semitism therefore ought to be based not so much on religious, social or economic grounds, but on racial ones. 'We see then how correct the young nationalists are in demanding a resolution of the Jewish question, not on the basis of change of nationality or religion, but on the racial level' – we read in the journal *Awangarda*.[11]

The Jews, then, should be opposed as an alien and hostile race. There arose the problem, however, of who should be regarded racially as a Jew. In some cases the issue was clear. All those who professed the Hebraic faith and declared Jewish nationality were Jews. Nationalists also had no hesitation in regarding as Jews those who claimed Polish nationality, but professed the Hebraic faith and came from Jewish families. Problems arose, however, with men and women of Jewish origin who had been baptised themselves (or had baptised parents or grandparents) or else were the descendants of mixed marriages.

Those nationalists who maintained that there was a separate Jewish race agreed with the argument that baptism did not change the status of a Jew. In the *Głos Monarchisty* a contributor wrote: 'Conversion of Jews is meaningless from the national and political point of view. Infiltration of Jews into the Aryan community – even those with the most sincere desire to be assimilated – should be condemned, since Jews, and the converted ones most of all, are and will always remain, the catalyst for poison and upheaval.'[12] *Monarchia Narodowa* contained similar warnings: 'Conversion does not change a Jew's nationality. A baptised Jew . . . remains a Jew who has become a Christian; religion does not create nationality or race but the Polish community will treat the blood ... of a baptised Jew as that of a normal Jew, for it judges Jews on racial criteria and not on those of faith.'[13] A contributor to *Zadruga* wrote:

> A biological mass as a living organism cannot tolerate any foreign bodies within it. The organism cannot differentiate between a converted or actual Jew, or one that is neither; there is only semitic blood and a type cosmopolitan in spirit. This and only this is important and shows the value of anti-semitism in the national, nationalistic sense.[14]

Those from mixed marriages provided the most difficult problem. They were to be treated, according to right-wing nationalists, rather cautiously, and investigations should be made to establish whether or not they maintained contact with Jews of pure descent. The issue of heredity was greatly emphasised. People spoke out against mixing races, arguing on occasions that the Jewish race, being older, might choke the roots put down by such younger races as the Slavs. A writer in *Wielka Polska* explained the phenomenon thus:

> Jews, irrespective of their faith, remain Jews in their physical and spiritual features. The influence of heredity is exceedingly strong; for example, while the descendants of an Aryan race can be quickly and thoroughly assimilated in a given national setting, even a small addition of Jewish blood exercises an extraordinary influence on the physical appearance and character of the descendants, often over several generations. This fact can be explained by the ancient roots of the Jewish race and by the exclusiveness of Jews over many centuries, which has caused the elements of heredity in their blood to become unusually strong and to be able to prolong their existence in their descendants.[15]

It was considered that even the least addition of Jewish blood meant that the individual would have the defects of that nation. Jewish ancestors would influence the behaviour and mentality of several generations. Father J. Prądzyński recommended in *Wielka Polska*: 'Let those Polish families unfortunately already contaminated by the addition of Jewish blood, take steps to prevent further inflows, remembering that it takes a dozen or more generations before the admixture is fully purged.'[16] And T. Dworak pointed out in *Szczerbiec*: 'A Pole contaminated with a few drops of blood from a Jew or Jewess, very frequently goes to pieces morally and is an example of depravity.'[17]

Using these assumptions, some nationalist writers investigated the background and origins of well-known figures in political and cultural life. Those people who were discovered to have had forebears of Jewish origin should be prevented from influencing the life of the Polish community. On occasions their conclusions were very far-reaching indeed. For example one of the writers in the periodical *Zadruga* proved that the entire romantic and messianic tradition was the work of Jews.

> What kind of ideal could the poet Adam Myckiewicz (sic!) have had, this Polish-Jewish hybrid who said of himself: 'I am half Lechite, half Jew – and I am proud of it.' Now it is becoming clear why the *Księgi Pielgrzymstwa* are so reminiscent of the work of the prophet Jeremiah, weeping over the destruction of Jerusalem. What else, apart from martyrdom, the philosophy of lamentation, was the 'great national poet' from Nowogródek capable of, seeing that his spiritual temperament was inherited from his blood, thickened in the atmosphere of contemporary 'Polishness', which led via Rome straight from Judaea.[18]

However, even among the radical nationalist right, arguments based on the racial distinctiveness of Jews were not very common. Much more widespread were the assertions that Jews were distinctive not so much in racial terms, as in terms of their psyche – their mental characteristics. They represented, in the opinion of nationalists, a different branch of humanity, considerably inferior to the rest. The nationalists did not treat Jews as equals, or as superiors, but considered them inferior, as they put it, to 'settled' peoples. The periodical *Front Polski Zbudzonej* consequently declared: 'We do not hate the Jews, since one can only hate someone equal to or stronger than oneself. We feel only disgust for Jews, the same disgust that we would feel for rats and vermin.'[19]

The Jews, it was argued, were a community guided by an unacceptable ethic, one which called for hatred of everything except their fellow-Jews. The nationalists attributed this failing to the Talmud. Only by eradicating the Talmud from Jewish thinking could the Jewish ethic be transformed into one acceptable to Christians. It would allow the Jewish race to achieve a modicum of dignity and worth. As things stood, however, the nationalists considered the Jews an alien and repugnant group. 'Jews, that alien, detestable race, that hostile ethic and morality of the Talmud, requiring them to harm and injure the "goy" by any means they think fit. The ethics of the Talmud are the most hypocritical duplicity: one standard for one's own people, another for the rest.' This was how W. Fusek described Jews in *Wielka Polska*.[20]

> The question arises, why are Jews so universally detested by all peoples ... ? The answer lies in their very mentality, in the

corruption bequeathed to them by the Talmud, a work which one can safely call a collection of superstitions, instilling into the Jewish spirit hatred for everything non-Jewish, and which calls for them to live dishonestly towards non-Jews,' wrote a contributor to *Młody Rozwojowiec*.[21]

Jews also deserved to be hated because their ancestors had crucified Christ: no Christian could trust them or have confidence in them. Jews were, after all

Those, who seeing with the eyes of their forebears Christ's greatest miracle, the victory of life over death, did not cry out 'Alleluyah', but joined together with evil, ugliness and death and embarked on their diaspora with this poison, to conquer the historic roads of mankind which lead towards goodness and perfection,

as a contributor to *Narodowiec* emphasised.[22] Jews were therefore not only an immediate foe, but a permanent one, and this was an immutable state of affairs.

As inferior humans, Jews deserved the kind of treatment which matched their value. Some nationalists accepted this inferiority as something obvious, but others tried in various ways to prove it. Z. Łuczycki asserted that Jews were not even a nation, but only a 'monument to God's anger'.[23] S. Szukalski wrote, 'Jews are indeed a chosen people, a perfectly degenerate growth from the whole swarm of parasitic Negro-semites.'[24]

Apart from statements appealing to the reader's emotions and aimed, not to convince him by argument, but to create an automatic, reflex dislike for Jews, there were also attempts to provide justifications. The nationalist right assembled a whole array of charges against Jews, relating to various areas of Jewish life and aiming to prove how completely impossible it was to coexist with them in a single state. One of the most serious accusations was that of their antipathy or indifference towards the Polish state, or even of trying to harm it. It was claimed that Jews were attempting to achieve the maximum possible influence over the fate of Poland so as to use the country for their own purposes. The struggle with the Jews would therefore be a struggle with a foreign force: it would mean Poles conquering the state for themselves.[25]

The Jews were said to be appropriating Polish territory as their main base or centre, 'a second Palestine'. They were attempting to achieve their objective by demoralising the Polish people and turning them into a tool in Jewish hands. This situation called for a reaction to be rid of the 'internal occupants'. Anti-semitism was raised to the level of a national virtue. In an article 'Why I am an anti-semite', the author of *Przełom* answers in this way: 'I am an anti-semite because, as a legal heir of the Great Poland of the

Chrobrys, Żółkiewskis and Sobieskis, I cannot allow the parasitic Jew to destroy the organism of state from the inside, to shatter the nation's solidarity and to pollute the holiest feelings of Poles – I am an anti-semite because I cannot allow the parasitic Jew to grow fat on Polish soil, while the real landlord, transformed into a slave, starves. The struggle with Jewry must be the holy duty of us young people, united in the nationalist camp, and may our enthusiasm, energy and continuing work rid Poland of Jews and correct the errors of our forefathers.'[26]

The Jews themselves were accused of bringing anti-semitism on themselves, because everywhere they settled they tried to achieve supremacy and to extract the maximum material benefit. J. Bartoszewicz wrote in *Młody Narodowiec*:

> The anti-Jewish movement has its origins in the nation and community, not in racial confrontation nor in the political intolerance of a certain state, but in the character of the Jewish nation itself, in its clear refusal to be assimilated and in its organisation, aiming at ruling the world after demoralising and weakening the economies and fragmenting the societies of non-Jewish nations and states. Anti-semitism is therefore a natural reaction of a living community concerned with its own welfare and development against the destructive influences of a Jewish clique, which more and more is seen to be running the show.'[27]

Other writers felt, however, that nobody could be blamed for the past influxes of Jews, which were so dangerous for Poland. It was self-evident that all people, the Jews included, strove to achieve the best possible living conditions. The problem then lay not in attributing blame, but in the real conflict of interests of two peoples inhabiting the same territory. To achieve their aims the Poles had to defeat the Jewish people.[28] The fact that the instincts of the Jewish people were diametrically opposed to those of the Polish people, had to be instilled into children at school, from their earliest years.[29] No compromise could exist between the aims of the Polish and Jewish peoples, nor would such a compromise be possible in the future. 'The racial character of Jews, their traditions and the way they live among settled peoples are such that they can only be either alien nomads in a particular country, or its tyrants,' claimed Z. Wojciechowski.[30]

The very existence of the Jewish horde prevented the organisation of the Polish nation on its own territory.[31] Jews had in their very nature an anti-state mentality, as their whole history of wandering through various countries proved.[32]

In addition to these extremely general charges levelled at Jews, there were more specific accusations of activity against the Polish state. All parties concerned were agreed that 'Jewification' had contributed to the collapse of the Commonwealth and had led to the partitions of Poland. The weakening of the Polish state, after all, was in the interest of Jews and consequently they were opposed to its achieving independence. During the struggle for independence they not only failed to help the Polish cause, but helped the occupying powers. At the Versailles Conference they had made considerable efforts to deny Poland Silesia, Pomerania and Gdańsk. They had slandered Poland abroad.[33] Some considered that Jews had played a disreputable role during the Polish-Soviet War. According to the nationalists the Jews had sided with Russia, acting as spies and Bolshevik agents. Jews living in Soviet territory were the real cause of Soviet aggression against Poland:[34] the nationalists maintained that Jews had come to an agreement to wage war on Poland in order to achieve the maximum possible rights for the Jewish community. The Jews had agreed to libel Poland, so that power would fall to those people most favourable towards them; they had used all manner of influences to ensure that Polish currency lost its value in world markets and that communism would spread at home.[35] Jews were also accused of weakening Poland's military strength; the main evidence for this was apparently that they had contributed little to the Fund for Anti-aircraft Defence. This was not difficult to understand, added nationalists, since hitherto Jews had profited from each defeat suffered by Polish insurgents to occupy the positions vacated by Poles.[36]

From these few examples it is clear that the accusations levelled at Jews in the political arena centred on their trying to transform Poland into a state completely subordinate to themselves, a 'Judopolonia'.

All the same, in the view of the extreme right, the progressive economic conquest of the country was the really fundamental problem. It was most frequently and most strongly emphasised by the nationalists, since it touched on an aspect of life most familiar to the population at large. While, to the man in the street, the influence of Jews on the political system went unnoticed and therefore had to be documented, any Pole could notice the existence of factories, shops and kiosks belonging to Jews. A confrontation with politicians might be beyond the scope of most Poles, but an economic struggle was considerably easier.

In the writings of the nationalists, evidence of the economic harm done to Poles by Jews took up relatively little space; the authors regarded it as self-evident. They concentrated instead on how to remedy the situation.[37]

A great deal of space was taken up by the simple assertion that Jews controlled industry and trade and that this led to a situation disadvantageous to the Poles. It was generally acknowledged that without the removal of Jews from the economy there could be no real talk of complete independence. 'I believe that my Nation will achieve full economic self-determination, that it will free itself from the Jewish clutches, will conduct its own affairs, that Poland will be only for Poles,' wrote J. Grabowska in

Falanga.[38] 'Material possessions, Polish property, all the values which make up the economic substructure of the Polish state are passing into alien, hostile, Jewish hands,' exclaimed the *Deklaracja ideowa Młodzieży Rozwojowej*.[39]

The passing of economic power into Jewish hands was considered deliberate. Some nationalists accused the Jews of purchasing Polish property by duplicity.[40] Others claimed that Jews in Poland were merchants and usurers, because these were occupations which had always been regarded as disreputable. Usury made Jews rich at the expense of the Polish population. It was also claimed that all Jewish artisans were terrible bunglers.[41] Jewish machinations and fraud had led to Jewish per capita income being ten times that of the average Pole.[42]

The nationalist right emphasised that the social and demographic consequences of the Jewish presence in Poland could be especially dangerous. Jewish seizure of jobs was causing unemployment among native Poles. The situation was apparently made worse because Jews, by virtue of their occupations, lived mostly in the towns. One of the most dangerous effects was considered to be the 'uneven' spread of the Polish population brought about by the replacement of the Polish middle class by the Jewish.[43] This gradual Jewish takeover of the cities had begun in the 17th century. Those Poles unable to find employment in the towns had to seek work as domestic servants with Jewish families. In this way the latter influenced Polish customs and public life.[44]

There were even nationalist factions which attacked the Jews not so much for becoming the dominant force in trade, but simply for involvement in it. The evil did not lie in the fact that the merchants were not Poles, but in the very idea of trade for profit. 'The trader and financial middleman are the enemies of labour. We aim at the union of the forces of production or productive capital and labour in one united whole; to achieve our aim we are opposed to the financier, bankers, stockbrokers and merchants. This whole world of middlemen can be dispensed with. It is alien to the spirit of us settled people. We do not believe in the Polonisation of trade since trade by its very nature is a Jewish phenomenon.'[45]

Besides political and economic life, the third area where Jews threatened the Polish nation, according to the nationalists, was that of culture and education: 'Because the laws currently in force make a Jew the equal of a Pole, a citizen of the Polish state, and because we encounter him in all areas of life and it is currently considered that he has a rightful place and is admitted, as to a home, into our literature and art, into academic, economic and other areas of life, this has produced a certain slovenliness, especially as Jews are a race which brings with it nothing but decay. The situation is not yet lost, since Polish Aryan racial elements are too strong to submit quickly to the corrupting activity of the oriental Jewish race; but a degree of contamination must have occurred, if there are those who can regard a baptised, or even unbaptised, Jewish versifier as a Polish poet,' complained J. Gralewski in *Akademik Polski*.[46] Some writers even admitted that it was not in the political or economic spheres, but rather in cultural life that Jews posed the greatest threat to the nation.[47] It was feared that the older Jewish cultural and literary traditions might destroy or absorb the Polish, depriving the Polish nation of one of the fundamental sources of its identity.[48] 'The contact of a completely different civilisation, the alien and incomprehensible culture of the Jews, contaminates the Polish spirit, destroying its idealism and capacity for romantic achievements,' one writer stressed in *Młoda Polska*.[49] Even those well-intentioned Jews could not, according to the nationalists, be the creators of real Polish culture. Only a true-born son of the Polish fatherland could write in its beautiful language. They considered that Jews were unable to express their thoughts in Polish. Jews ought to write in their own language, a language suited to their way of thinking. Jews had always been distant from the Polish mentality.[50]

As important as the struggle against Jewish cultural influences, was, in the eyes of the nationalists, the infiltration of Jews into the Polish intelligentsia. This problem was aired frequently and bitterly in many journals produced by nationalist students, probably because the nationalist writers themselves felt threatened: they were in most cases young people, students or recent graduates of the universities.

It was claimed that Poland was the only country to allow a quarter of the resources allocated to higher education to be diverted for the formation of a new and foreign growth.[51] It was suggested that the percentage of people of Jewish background among the professions should be reduced. Appeals were made to avoid the situation existing in certain professions (such as law or medicine), where more Jews than Poles completed their studies and began to practise. Jews who were already studying should be isolated as completely as possible from their non-Jewish fellow students, so that the latter would not be endangered by their influence. 'A ghetto in each university is only the first victorious step of the younger generation in the struggle with Jewry . . . we are working towards the situation where landed property as well as trade will be only in Polish hands, and there will be no Jews in Polish universities,' wrote an anonymous author in *Akademik*.[52] Jews should in any case be completely excluded from academic life. Referring to the inaugural ceremony at the start of the academic year, *Akademik Polski* lamented: 'In this beautiful and interesting ceremony there was only one jarring element: members of a Jewish students' society were among the escort accompanying the banner. This amazed and dismayed the shocked Polish students who, because of the gravity of the occasion, could not react appropriately. In future, however, no Jews will enter the hall with the banner.'[53] Jews should also be expelled from student clubs and associations. 'The Lawyers' Circle of the Stefan Batory University in Wilno voted at a general meeting not to admit Jewish students to its ranks, irrespective of their faith. This resolution aroused an extremely strong reaction in Jewish circles and among the left-wing and *Sanacja* parties, but the majority of nationalist youth clearly approved of it,' reported the *Akademik Polski* with satisfaction.[54]

In the eyes of the nationalists, Jews were a threat in other areas as well. Their morality was at odds with that upon which a Christian state and a Catholic nation should be founded. 'One of the reasons we maintain that it is essential to eradicate Jewish influences from Poland is the irrefutable fact that Jewry is the personification of moral reprobation and gangrene' we read in *Młody Rozwojowiec*.[55] Even those aspects of current fashion disapproved of by the writer were seen as irrefutable evidence of Jewish influences. 'A young woman, showing parts of her naked body in the street, hair cut short, rouged face, dancing the Charleston – this is a victim of Jewish influences. The young man – drinking vodka, frequenting dancing clubs, ashamed to doff his hat in front of the church, cursing to left and right, lazy, exerting himself only to have a good time – this again is another victim of Jewish influence etc. etc.'[56] Readers were told that Jews had once traded in people and were engaged in a white-slave trade, conveying women to houses of ill repute.[57]

Opponents of agricultural reform accused the Jews of being the prime movers behind it.[58] In other words, all those aspects of community life which a writer felt to be harmful from the point of view of national development, were put down to Jewish influences. Besides spreading the influence of freemasonry, communism, liberalism and protestantism, the Jews were also accused of creating contemporary capitalism, of membership of the 'deceitful' Union of Esperantists, of breaking up the family, and of supporting class warfare. It is important here to bear in mind that, according to the nationalists' way of thinking, Jewish influences extended almost everywhere because of the international Jewish conspiracy. This line of thought is best illustrated by a quotation from *Polska Narodowa*: 'Polish Youth! Remember: the Jew is your enemy! Even that small poor figure behind the counter in his miserable shop, the person you know, and who you know has done nothing wrong and is himself starving, he too is the enemy of your Country. For behind him stands the whole of world Jewry – a growth sucking the blood of your people. That poor little Jew is one of millions of tentacles of the growth.'[59]

THE CALL TO RID POLAND OF JEWS

The demand that Poland should be freed from Jews was a major rallying cry for the majority of nationalists. Only a very few criticised the excessive attention paid to the Jewish question, given the size of the actual problem. Z. Stahl argued that the Jewish issue had become a psychosis, since the nationalists considered every problem from the anti-Jewish viewpoint, rather than from the Polish. They had made an important issue into the only issue. The Jewish question ought not to be the central ideological base for nationalist teaching, since it was merely negative.[60] Similarly F. Goetel wrote that despite his personal dislike of Jews, he could not accept that the Jewish race was completely incapable of adapting and coexisting with other peoples: this would merely reinforce the myth that Jews were the chosen people. In rejecting one superstition, one should not believe in another. There were good Europeans and good Poles of Jewish origin.[61] J. Drobnik warned that the Jewish question, although a pressing one for Poles, should not be coupled with contempt for the enemy.[62]

Generally, however, it was accepted that the struggle with the Jews in all spheres of life should be ruthless and lead to the reduction of their rôle in the state or even their complete removal from Poland.

The demands of the right-wing nationalists over the Jewish question aimed, in the first instance, at the complete separation of the Polish and Jewish communities. Under no circumstances should Jews mix with Poles in political or economic life, nor should there be any family liaisons. Generally, their ultimate goal was the complete expulsion of Jews from Poland. The majority of writers realised, however, that this would be extremely difficult to achieve, if not impossible. They therefore presented a partial or temporary solution until complete expulsion could take place.

The first stage on that road was to deprive Jews of their citizenship and the rights enjoyed by Polish citizens. The slogan that in Poland only a Pole could be a citizen, was used more frequently.[63] A similar opinion was expressed by those who demanded the withdrawal of political rights from Jews, either by legislation or by excluding them from the political life of the nation.[64]

Jews should also have a separate legal system. Some nationalists demanded the introduction of anti-Jewish legislation,[65] but others, working on the assumption that each nation should develop separately, proposed the introduction of new legislation for Jews. 'Laws designed for them should be neither better nor worse, but different, through being adapted to the Jewish mentality,' demanded a contributor to *Falanga*.[66]

In addition to being deprived of political rights, Jews should also be excluded from occupying high office within the state apparatus; they would be removed from offices, schools, local government and the army.'[67] Jews should also be prevented from taking part in national ceremonies, since their presence profaned these solemn occasions.[68] 'We know that the *Mazurek Dąbrowskiego* (Polish national anthem), when played by Jews, arouses distaste and disgust. We feel spontaneously a need to protest that Jews are not worthy to sing the national anthem with us – an anthem which for us is a sacred piece of music (but for them is mere humbug) – and to take part in state ceremonies,' wrote Z. Wasilewski in *Wielka Polska*.[69]

Excluding Jews from political life and the administration was only a small part of a whole programme of segregating the Jewish community. Polish and Jewish children were to be prevented from influencing each other by the creation of single-faith schools. In the universities, where such a division was impossible, the nationalist right campaigned in the first instance for the introduction of a *numerus clausus* (and less often for a *numerus nullus*) and for the introduction of a system of separate seating – the ghetto benches.

Jews were also to be excluded from social clubs and organisations frequented by Poles, particularly because they might 'infect or corrupt' members of the Polish population who became friendly with them. There was a further hidden danger in social relations between Jews and Poles, that of mixed marriages, which were thoroughly undesirable from the Polish point of view. Some writers – usually from those groups which acknowledged the racial distinctiveness of Jews – demanded that mixed marriages should be illegal under the new system, or else that the non-Jewish marriage partner should be treated as one who had been born a Jew (with the withdrawal of rights of citizenship, removal from state posts, and so on). 'Mixed marriages should not be valid in law, and sexual relations with non-Aryans should result in very heavy criminal sentences for both sides,' S. Kopeć suggested in *Polska Narodowa*.[70] Another draft proposal included the suggestion that a Pole who contracted a mixed marriage should lose his or her citizenship.[71]

Jews were to be segregated in all existing organisations and unions. It would also be most desirable for a separation to be effected at the workplace (Poles should not work in Jewish firms; Jewish lawyers should deal only with Jewish clients and their affairs; Poles should not work in the Jewish press, or Jews in the Polish press), although these demands were so unrealistic that they surfaced relatively infrequently. One writer even proposed that Jews should be prevented from spending time in the mountains. 'The Tatra mountains are under Jewish occupation ... A nationalist programme will have to take into account one more demand: there are to be no Jews in the National Parks!'[72] Another writer objected to professional sports in which Jews took part alongside Poles: 'Young Poles must be aware, must understand, that an encounter with a Jew, meeting him as an equal on the same field, degrades a Pole, but elevates a Jew. Is it possible to compete equally with an opponent lacking all honour, worth and respect?'[73]

Segregating Jews, according to the nationalist right, would have great benefits, politically, economically and morally. It was felt that the younger generation was already in a better position than its elders through having been brought up separate from Jews.[74]

A logical consequence of calls for the complete segregation of the Jewish community was the demand for a ghetto.[75] It was to be a transitional stage between the existing position and the complete expulsion of Jews from Poland. Projects of this kind were already in evidence by 1933. T. Dworak, writing in *Szczerbiec* in 1931, made the following demand: 'The chivalrous traditions of the bravest period in our history [i.e. the Middle Ages] appeal to us, at the very least, to force the Jews into a ghetto.'[76] Most of these statements came from the late 1930s and were clearly inspired by Nazi ideology. Here are a few examples taken from the publications of various parties: 'Jews should be thrown out of Poland! And until they cross the Polish frontiers we must shut them in the ghetto and not allow them to come out – we will not let them rob Poland of everything and swindle us. Jews to the ghetto!' wrote the *Narodowiec*.[77] 'We will continue to tolerate Jews for a while, but let us shut them in a ghetto, and prevent any further Jewish influence on the fate of Greater Poland,' suggested W.G. Jurczak in *Bojownik Pracy*.[78]

> 'Our epoch will be called a new Middle Ages: the Middle Ages were barbaric only for the Jews, for they were forced into the ghetto. The chosen people were not allowed to enjoy an everlasting happy life in the diaspora and to be a parasite on the organisms of settled peoples ... The contemporary doctrine of militant nationalism, "Jews to the ghetto!", is a thoroughly progressive slogan, because it grows out of the spirit of our age,' contended A. Niebieszczuński in *Narodowiec*.[79]

J. Białasiewicz in *Młoda Polska* gave the assurance: 'the demand for all Jews to be deprived of rights, and to be forced into the ghetto, was shaped by the sense of justice of the true inheritors of this land and will be carried through.'[80] 'At last Jews will not be allowed to live, trade or possess property in the towns, except in certain districts,' wrote S. Kopeć in *Polska Narodowa*.[81]

Once the Jewish ghettos had been created, the final stage in resolving the Jewish question would follow: complete, or almost complete, removal of them from the territory of the Polish state. Nationalists were aware that it would be difficult to carry through such a plan. For this reason they never designated any particular point when emigration would begin, nor did they reveal a detailed plan for carrying it out. Realising that the desire alone to expel Jews would not be sufficient, they agreed that resolving the Jewish question should become an international issue. Those states with fewest Jews should accept the surplus from Poland. Another solution would be to obtain colonies or to create a territory where Jews from all over the world could settle.[82] The cry – 'Jews to Madagascar!' – was even heard. Jews could also emigrate to Palestine. It was in the interest of all peoples to deprive Jews of their international character and settle them in one place which would become their own country.[83] The attempt to solve the Jewish question within one state would require impossible concessions from the Jews – changes in their whole mentality and way of life, the abandoning of all pan-Jewish concepts, agreement to the *numerus clausus* and many others.[84] Emigration was therefore a necessity in the eyes of the nationalists.

The first stage was to prevent the number of Jews increasing in Poland. *Falanga* called for 'The closing of our frontiers to those Jews wishing to enter, even if they are "Polish citizens", and the removal of those who settled here after 11 November 1918!'[85]

Although the planned emigration of Jews was never worked out in detail and planning remained limited to repeated calls for emigration, it is possible to distinguish two separate schools of thought. The first supported 'voluntary' emigration. Life for Jews in Poland should be made so difficult by the enactment of anti-Jewish legislation that they would decide themselves to leave Poland. The second view held that because one could not count on voluntary emigration, it would have to be brought about by force.

In many cases nationalist statements were so general that one cannot determine which of these two viewpoints they supported. An example is a sentence from the *Ideological-political declaration of the ZMP*: 'The Jewish question should be resolved by the emigration of Jews from Poland.'[86]

Those who argued that emigration of Jews was to be more or less voluntary had to consider which repressive measures might be most effective in inducing Jews to emigrate. There was almost general agreement on economic measures – barring Jews from trade and industry, or a complete boycott.[87] The majority, however, also supported more effective methods – removal of Jews from Poland by legislation. The National Monarchists among others demanded 'the resolution of the Jewish question by legislative means, involving the emigration of a certain percentage of Jews from Poland.'[88]

It was often emphasised in this context that such legislation would be in keeping with the Poles' right to decide on all matters relating to their national territory. 'Jews are an immigrant element with no links with Poland. Consequently we have the right to adopt the necessary political measures to remove the problem,' wrote J. Morawski in an article in *Młoda Polska*.[89] E. Basiński, writing in *Jutro Polski*, voiced a similar opinion: 'demands of state call for the complete elimination of the Jewish presence'.[90]

Emigration provided for by legislative means was to be paid for entirely by the Jews themselves. They would be deported from Poland and their property wholly or partially confiscated. One plan, which appeared in *Wielka Polska*, foresaw legislation to forbid Jews to remain in Poland and to leave the country with no more than ten thousand złotys. The rest of their wealth was to remain, as compensation for the damage which Jews had caused in Poland.[91] The question of finding a place to emigrate to was to be entirely a problem for Jewish organisations.[92] Writers linked with the Union of Young Poland (*ZMP*) were particularly enthusiastic about the emigration plan, and they were the nationalist group with the closest contacts with the *Sanacja*. It was all part of their vision of a Greater Poland.

In considering how to induce the Jewish population to emigrate, a group of nationalists, mainly, although not only, the *Falanga*, were inclined to use physical force. They cited on occasions the German example. A sentence taken from an article by O. Szpakowski in *Ruch Młodych* might serve as the slogan of the adherents of force: 'If humanitarianism delivers us into Jewish captivity, let us forget that the Jew is a human being.'[93] If the Jews resisted emigration or attempts to segregate them, force was to be used. Their forcible removal following the confiscation of their goods and wealth should be effected without humanitarian feelings or mercy, since these would be inappropriate.[94] Poles were to wage an uncompromising struggle against Jews on all fronts, using every opportunity. B. Kwella in *Stalowy Miecz* described what they should do:

> Battle stations are being drawn up and soon victory will be achieved, the fruits of which should be used totally and uncompromisingly. We must aim at the complete liquidation of the Jewish question on Polish soil and throughout the world in the most advantageous way for the Aryan race. All the means at our disposal must be mobilised. All the Aryan religious, political, economic and cultural organisations should be exploited in our coming struggle with the Semites. Aryan organisations must serve only the interests of Aryans. In this matter there is no room for any principles: for the time being these must be cast aside ... Membership of organisations linked in any way with Jewry should be grounds for the most severe punishments.[95]

Some did point to the drawbacks of employing force, but excused it. Breaking up market stalls and similar actions were not a suitable way to settle the Jewish question, although it was difficult not to agree that mass demonstrations and anti-Jewish disturbances showed the Polish community's concern. While disturbing public order might be inappropriate, it did indicate a basically sound defensive reaction by the Polish nation. For as long as the population was not legally protected from this Jewish flood, it would try itself to throw off the Jewish yoke.[96]

The future Greater Poland could not be endangered by playing with humanitarianism and such sentiments. The basic need was to rid Poland of Jews and all else must take second place.

> Jews, as a nation inclined to business and commerce, will always find suitable areas for their parasitism. We must not allow ourselves to become sentimental about their 'tragic fate': we must declare war relentlessly against romantic altruism, because our aim – a Great and Powerful Polish Nation – forces us to override such burning issues,

wrote J.G. Jurczak in *Bojownik Pracy*.[97] Father J. Prądzyński warned against misunderstanding the Christian theory of loving one's neighbour. The struggle against the Jews should be waged ruthlessly, ignoring whether or not it was consistent with Christian teaching,

> ... because Jewish-Masonic movements, while waging venomous and incessant struggle against Catholic and Christian thought, are trying to confuse the Christian conscience, by making it believe it was agreeing to something wicked in trying to remove Jewish dominance. Loving one's neighbour according to moral philosophers is a matter of degree, one in proportion to bonds of faith, blood or similar signs of community.[98]

The *ONR* and some of the fascist groups were most open in supporting using force against the Jews, while other organisations were less so. Even some of the fascists drew the line at such methods. Many writers, even those most hostile towards the Jews, warned against active persecution. They emphasised above all that anti-Jewish atrocities would do little to advance the moment when the Jews left Poland. They argued that if the Jewish question had to be considered at an international level, then this kind of activity would not help to achieve their objectives.[99] Atrocities also placed the Polish Government in a difficult situation, since it had to act within the framework of the existing law and side with the Jews, whatever its own real convictions.[100]

The Jewish question was too complicated to be settled on an *ad hoc* basis by breaking windows.[101] Jews had to be isolated, but without introducing repressive measures.[102]

> The anti-semitism of the streets, based upon breaking the windows of Jewish shops and similar activities is the product of mere racial hatred; 'cultural' anti-semitism, however, is distinct from the street variety not only in how it is carried out, but also, as it comes from, and is inspired by, love for Poland, it is really *Philopolonism* [underlined in the text]. Hatred is an agent of evil and as such can never be a creative force,

wrote J. Chrostowski in the journal *Ku Polsce Jutrzejszej*, which claimed to be fascist.[103]

Only one group of Jews enjoyed widespread nationalist support. These were the Zionists. Their aims to create a Jewish state were supported by the nationalist right for several reasons, especially as the Zionists' aim of emigration to Palestine matched perfectly the wishes of the nationalists. This apart, nationalist ideology was based on the principle that each people should tread its own path and achieve its own predestined mission. Nationalists were inclined to accept that, while Jews were a parasitic and harmful people in Poland, when settled on their own territory, they could develop into a true and useful nation. 'Jews, as an element alien to the Polish way of life, must leave. Poles will help them in emigrating to Palestine. This unhappy people will be able to fulfil its mission there,' wrote R. Dębicki in the fascist periodical *Świt*.[104] The headline of one article in *Narodowy Socjalista* ran: 'Sincere greetings from all Poles go to the Zionists' Congress.'[105] The following, expressed in an article in *Zadruga*, was typical of this way of thinking: those Jews one could like, respect and even feel a certain racial brotherhood for (in the light of ancient mixing of blood) were those who had gone to Palestine. Those who remained, however, were detested because they did not want their own homeland, but placed material interests above it.[106] Some nationalists, though, like K. Hrabyk, pointed out that, as the Zionists not only wanted their own state, but also sought to retain an influence over Polish affairs, they could not expect nationalist support.[107]

It is clear, therefore, that the nationalists tried to use various methods to attack the enemy threatening them, and that they regarded all Jews as the enemy. However, they also believed that there were other dangers besides the Jews menacing the Polish people.

COMMUNISTS, CAPITALISTS, MASONS: THE INTERNATIONAL CONSPIRACY

The real threat to Poland was seen as coming from the combination of the Jews with those forces who supported them (or were supported by them according to some versions), communism, capitalism, and secret organisations on a world-wide scale. In this form, the enemy was both domestic, Polish Jews, and external, international finance, communists, freemasons; it also had its agents within the country, Polish communists, the big capitalists, Polish members of masonic lodges. The enemy could manipulate large funds and they confused and misled the working class. Nationalists suggested to the Polish community that it was a fortress under siege, which could only emerge victorious or be destroyed.

Extending the concept of 'enemy' beyond the Jew had an additional advantage for the nationalists: scepticism about nationalist ideals could be attributed to membership of the enemy camp. Even if an opponent of nationalism did not have a Jewish grandmother, he could always be accused of communist sympathies, of being a wealthy property owner, of belonging to the masons or of supporting Esperantists. It was absolutely impossible to deny such accusations.

Of course, this choice of enemies had perfectly rational, socio-economic grounds. The economic programme of the nationalists and their basis of support in the community could not be reconciled with either contemporary capitalism or a socialist economic programme.[108] Nevertheless, although this explains why the nationalists challenged ideologically adherents of both programmes, it does not make clear why they treated them as enemies, as being, like the Jews, a threat to the Polish people.[109]

The nationalists stressed interminably the links existing between all the enemies of Poland. A few examples can be given. 'The child of merciless capitalism is Jewish socialism, and the child of socialism is atheistic communism,' wrote J. Kowal-Lipiński.[110] 'We must remember one thing above all else: capitalism and communism work to the detriment of the nation and are obsolete systems,' a contributor to *Sztafeta* maintained.[111] J. Sznarbachowski warned: 'Communism, socialism and capitalism are the way for the Jews to achieve control world-wide.'[112] 'The enemy, in the shape of the freemason and the communist, threatens Poland in the single shape of the Jew,' J. Diżyński stated in *Młody Rozwojowiec*.[113] In *Młody Narodowiec* P. Pychlik explained: '... the evil we see in liberated Poland today should not be blamed entirely on the poor system of government or other factors, even though these may play some part. The main evil is created by Jews through their capital, or through their allies-masonic and other – which they use to exercise control.'[114] In the *Nacjonalista Radomski* we read: 'The whole nation is divided into two factions – the supporters of capitalism and the adherents of socialism. Both are led by Jews disguised as either the defenders of the proletariat, or as "patriots" making use of the name of Poland to exploit labour with impunity.'[115] 'I want to help fight the Jews and their instruments, the overt and covert international ones – the communist system, socialism, freemasonry, with all their corruption and foreign poison – all the political, economic and cultural influences exercised by Jews, until there are no Jews, communists or masons left in Poland,' J. Grabowski declared in *Falanga*.[116] '*Szczerbiec* is opposed to the destructive masonic-Jewish influences (communism and socialism).'[117]

Of particular interest was how communism and capitalism were linked as two aspects of the same phenomenon. Nationalists emphasised that they were compatible, since both were contemporary manifestations of the materialistic idea.[118] Behind both capitalism and communism stood the Jews. They were therefore the most serious obstacle to transforming the current world economic, social and political system. Jews succeeded in the capitalist system and they directed each change within it. Because of this, socialism was even more successfully adapted to Jewish needs.[119] The system created by the rotation of big capital worked against the interests of settled nations, reduced them to the same spiritual level and robbed them of their national character. As a result of the rise of the capitalist ethic, international factors – gold and socialism – ruled the world. Both represented nomadic elements, which had no links with the soil or with the instincts of settled peoples, and had emerged through masonic influence.[120] The nationalists emphasised that the era of capitalism was coming to an end and had to be replaced with something different from the unsuccessful experiments of alien racial elements, since communism and marxism had failed in Russia.[121]

Of the three enemies – communism, capitalism and freemasonry – communism aroused most emotion. It was, apart from the Jews, most frequently mentioned as the chief reason for the misfortunes and crises of the country, and the reader was warned of its danger for the future. Writers expounded at length on why communism could not play any part in the future of such a great and strong country as Poland.

One of the most frequent accusations against the communists was that they represented the interests of the Jews, and just as often the most serious accusation levelled at the Jews was their membership of communist organisations and their spreading of communist ideas. In practical terms, nationalists did not differentiate between communists and Jews, working on the assumption that even if all Jews were not communists, all communists were Jews or at least their dupes or paid agents. Thus there arose the popular expression *żydokomuna* or *folksfront*. It is difficult to judge whether this standpoint came from real convictions or was just a propaganda device to encourage Polish distaste for Jews and communists alike.

The nationalists believed communist ideology was exclusively a Jewish product – both directly, in the sense that Jewish thinkers had spawned it, and indirectly, as a product of the 'Jewish soul' and 'vindictive Judaism'. 'The genius of the Jew, Marx, lies in that he managed to cloak his programme in scientific dress – when it was just a system for expropriating peoples for Jewish gain and profit,' wrote *Faszysta Polski*.[122] An article in *Nowy Ład* reminded its readers that Marx, the first promoter and propagator of communism, was the descendant of a rabbi.[123] When one looked more closely at this man, claimed the author, one could see the features, inherited from his race, of a vindictive and subtle being, a talmudic intellect and the personification of an oriental fanatic, hating everything that was not Jewish. Other founding fathers of socialist thought, such as Lassalle, were assessed in a similar manner. Nationalists claimed that they were only using communism as a way to achieve Jewish world supremacy.[124] All the founders of communism were Jews, even if they had converted to Christianity in order to secure greater privileges.[125] Marx, in spite of having been baptised, was always a Jew.[126]

The nationalists tried to convince their readers that marxism suited only the Jewish mentality, just as the Jewish religion was concerned only with temporal matters and world supremacy.[127] A writer in *Głos Faszystów* warned that communism was trying to destroy European culture:

> Communism, the offspring of the constant Jewish revolt against Roman culture, is trying to destroy all manifestations of the Roman spirit in the life of contemporary nations and, at the same time, to destroy the Catholic Church which is based on Roman principles. Like the embryo of the materialised Jewish spirit, communism emphasises material things, to the consequent detriment of spiritual factors, which it cannot understand.'[128]

Marxist doctrine and practice were a kind of barbarism, the elements of which were not susceptible to rigour and discipline and originated in Jewish tradition.[129] Jews and communists had introduced the alien element of semitic vindictiveness into the life of the Polish nation. Communism, according to the nationalists, could not be adopted by people raised in western culture. 'The Aryan world, founded on Greco-Roman culture, is far removed from oriental, Jewish hatred, which stones people to death just because they possess something,' wrote M. Reutt.[130]

The nationalists argued that the Jews, in creating the communist system, wanted to achieve world domination. They claimed that spreading ideas about the class struggle, which originated with Marx, benefited the Jews. Non-Jews were led astray and confused by this theory, which apparently led them into becoming the slaves of Jewish capitalists.[131] They insisted that organised, established and powerful Jewish economic forces existed, which aimed chiefly at maintaining communist organisations to prevent the unification – both mentally and culturally – of the Polish nation.[132] One of the writers in *Narodowy Socjalista* enumerated the following aims of the communist parties: to abolish all religions, except the Jewish; to demolish all places of worship, except the Jewish; to ensure that all the top positions in the communist state would be occupied by Jews; to murder the priests and the intelligentsia of the nation concerned; to abolish national frontiers and create one large communist state, which Jews would control; to turn other peoples into the slaves of the Jewish communist system.[133]

The struggle with communism and the struggle with the Jews were thus one and the same. Elimination of the Jewish element from the community was the only way to defeat communism.[134] 'We must chop off the tentacles by which the Jews are infiltrating this communist plague into the spirit of Polish youth,' appealed *Narodowiec*.[135] Poles should also be aware that the coming battle would be fought between the nationalist movement and the anti-nationalist movement under Jewish and communist leadership.[136]

The aim of the struggle was to free Poland from the influences of alien international agencies, communism and the Jewish-masonic network.[137]

Communism, however, was not only evil because of its links with Poland's age-old enemy, the Jews. Even without that element it threatened the existence of the nationalist spirit, and of Poland itself. The nationalists emphasised that communist organisations were the agencies of a foreign power, the Soviet Union. Communist parties were wholly subservient to the International, which pursued the foreign policy objectives of the USSR. Individual national parties served its ends, even where these went against the interests of their own states.[138] Consequently each state should treat communists as if they were in the pay of a foreign power.[139] A. Dębiec in *Narodowy Socjalista* even stated that communism was not a socio-political movement or an ideology, but a common spy ring.[140]

Marxism, being in harmony with the Jewish mentality, was claimed to be incompatible, therefore, with the Polish national spirit. Marxism must be odious to the Polish spirit since it was based on materialist foundations, and denied the existence of God and free will. The Polish spirit was based on the belief that human beings made their own history, rather than that they were its end-product, and that salvation was a stronger motive for action than the struggle for existence.[141] Communist ideas were unacceptable to a Catholic nation and if marxist principles were ever adopted on Polish territory, they would destroy the Polish nation. Communism would mean death for a Poland shaped on the principles of Roman and Catholic culture.[142] 'In communist totalitarianism, whose ideology denies the natural right to freedom, to family life, property, etc., everything tends towards destruction,' wrote J. Chróścielewski.[143] 'The young should not concern themselves with abstractions and false ideas about internationalism, since these could ruin people and deny them what set Man apart from animals.'[144] They should remain firm in the conviction that both communist activity and communist views were criminal. This alone would protect Poland from the advancing waves of communism. Poles had to defend themselves actively if they wished to maintain their culture and not lose it to the hell of communist barbarism.[145]

Nationalists accused marxism of defending the interests of only one social class.[146] It destroyed national unity and therefore from the viewpoint of nationalist ideology threatened the common good. Some of the nationalists denounced communism without bothering to analyse it, rejecting it completely. There was nothing to consider as far as bolshevism was concerned, they wrote: the only solution was complete rejection.[147] They emphasised that communism brought with it lamentable economic results, and the best example of the bankruptcy of the 'socialist paradise' was 'Soviet Russia'. Poland would not submit to experimental changes in its political system and, as could be seen, socialism had become a synonym for poverty.[148] The social consequences, too, would be disastrous.

'Banditry in Poland is politically organised and is one of the signs that the *KPP* has been active,' claimed M. Reutt in *Falanga*.[149] There were warnings that: 'Every government of the Republic must be respected and esteemed, except communist and socialist governments.'[150]

Although they attacked communism, some nationalists recognised that certain aspects of it were in keeping with the spirit of 20th-century nationalist movements. It was precisely for this reason, they insisted, that it was the most dangerous, indeed the only significant, opponent of nationalism. Although socialist ideology was atheistic, anachronistic, materialistic and rationalistic, nevertheless certain elements – such as its opposition to democracy, parliamentarianism, liberalism, and society based on discipline and hierarchy – could allow it great success.[151] J. Stachniuk, ideologist for the journal *Zadruga*, pointed out that communism was a struggle to introduce a new type of culture: it was an 'attitude to life which was fascinated with size. Communism is, apart from nationalism, the only "Philistine" force.'[152]

The next enemy – international capital – occurred far less often in the writings of the nationalists. Less emphasis was given, too, to the coincidence of the capitalist threat with the Jewish menace. Only a few writers saw the two as identical, unlike the widespread identification of communism with the Jews. Nonetheless, the common origins of capitalism and the Jewish danger were pointed out.

> We are the enemies of the capitalist system, although we fight it without spitting class hatred. We see the effective development of Polish national strength encumbered by it ... We do not want to settle accounts with the mercenaries of the Red Tsarist Régime and with international Jewish capital as well, merely in order to protect the old social system,

declared *Młoda Polska*.[153] Consequently it was the upper classes of society which were least aware of the Jewish question, because profit and capital had become a pagan god.[154] Capitalism, in the same way as communism, led to Jewish domination over indigenous peoples. Under capitalism money ruled and Jews could become rich more quickly than others, thanks to their deceitful machinations. Their craving for power over non-Jews found full satisfaction in the capitalist system. In reality the capitalist was no different from the director of the Soviet state enterprise or the commissar.[155]

In general, however, the question of capitalism was kept separate from the Jewish issue. The criticisms directed at the capitalist system were extremely varied. Nationalists writing about capitalism found themselves in a peculiar situation. Their economic programme was based on maintaining the principle of private property. Attacks on capitalism therefore could not touch on this cornerstone of the future order, but at the same time they had to demonstrate why the property-based capitalist order was the enemy of nationalism.

One basic point of attack was capitalism's international character.[156] To augment their wealth, people increasingly ignored the national frontiers which had previously restricted them. As international trade expanded there were increasing calls for the removal of frontiers so that financiers could more freely exploit all nations. Pacifism was being promoted enthusiastically, so that national interests did not threaten those of business.[157] International capital should therefore be swept away. In future, it should be broken up into the national groups, from which it had originated. In this way there would be a return to the proper, original system of capitalism.[158] The present anonymous, archaic and speculative capitalist system would be replaced by one based upon private capital, derived from labour and savings.[159]

Capitalism destroyed national unity. It divided the nation into opposing classes, led to domestic strife, and restricted the vitality of the nation.[160] In short, capitalism prevented the nation developing.[161]

Capitalism was also charged with being immoral and incompatible with Christian ideals. It was atheistic and anti-Christian. It ruined the moral order, the family (through forcing women to work), ownership (with joint share ownership it was impossible to point to one single owner), and most of all, the economic independence of the nation.[162] It worked against the moral order of civilised Europe and the idea of the family, stifled noble impulses, and reduced the level of intellectual life.[163] Because of the great Jewish fraud of contemporary capitalism, individual responsibility had disappeared.[164] According to the nationalists, capitalism was spoiling everything that was to be the foundation of the new, national order – God and nation, supported by the family, morality and private workshops.

W. Wasiutyński put forward a further argument for the incompatibility of capitalism with the proposed new order. He claimed that in capitalism the old feudal-state hierarchy no longer existed and the new one – the national hierarchy – had not yet been created. A clandestine hierarchy ruled, selected on the basis of wealth and regulated by the wealth of education.[165]

Some nationalists also tried to demonstrate not merely that capitalism was unsuited to the nationalist order, but that it was in general unjust, unprofitable and bound to become extinct. While it certainly achieved the maximum production, it assured neither a just division of goods nor a tolerable existence for the workers.[166] The struggle with capitalism was not a struggle against property,[167] but liberation of the individual from his Jewish-capitalist captivity.[168] A free and unrestrained play of individual egoisms had brought the world to its present catastrophe.[169] One writer even argued that capitalism, through the mechanisation of industry was leading the community to ruin. 'Machinery and rational methods, serving the dark forces of the bourgeoisie and Jewish finance, have kept the hands and minds of our young people from job opportunities.'[170]

Nationalism also regarded all international organisations as its enemy, and the chief of these was freemasonry. The freemasons were portrayed, like all the recognised enemies of nationalism, as allies of the Jews in the struggle for supremacy over nations. Nationalists insisted that international Jewry, with the support of the masons, was working to weaken Poland, and backed those movements wanting the break-up of the state.[171] A particularly harmful role was played by the Jewish-masonic movement of stateless sectarianism.[172] Freemasonry was now attempting to weaken the Polish state by overthrowing democracy.[173] Nationalist revolutions were anti-masonic revolutions, while the struggle with freemasonry was one struggle to prevent the demoralisation of public life which had spread during the democratic period. The entire history of democracy was the history of masonic lodges. Freemasonry threatened the life of the nation, because it was international in character and worked for agents hostile to the nation.[174] Freemasonry was the cause of the demoralisation, and it was furthered by the loss of morality, lack of ethical values and the pursuit of wealth.[175] Jews and freemasons were cooperating to destroy religion.[176] Freemasonry was also, according to some writers, an internal threat: organised, international Jewry, or freemasonry, with German help, was working to seize control of Poland.[177]

There should, therefore, be no place in Poland for people connected with freemasonry.[178] 'Anti-semitism and anti-masonic ideals are not why we exist, but they are essential to achieve our ultimate goals. We did not make Jews and masons our enemies: they did that themselves,' wrote *Głos Monarchisty*.[179]

Many other organisations besides freemasonry were regarded as enemies. One of the parties' programmes declared that they were fighting 'demi-liberalism', Marxism, freemasonry, cosmopolitanism and all secret international organisations.[180] A spokesman of another party wrote that they were attacking freemasonry and working for a unitary national state, where international influences would be eliminated.[181]

An example of one such 'hostile' organisation was the Esperantists. They had been created, according to the nationalists, by Jews for their own use. Their role was to poison young people by using slogans against anti-semitism and in favour of the 'progressive', 'tolerant', 'democratic', and 'peaceful' collaboration of all nations.[182] The enemy might change but the accusations remained the same. The weaker the right-wing nationalist party concerned, the more often it tried to frighten its followers with threats coming from within and outside the country.

It should be remembered that the parties of the extreme nationalist right, although vocal, were very small and had very few supporters. They were only active on the fringes of Polish political life during the inter-war period. Yet even fifty years later, the deep-rooted nature of their anti-Jewish psychosis remains shocking.

NOTES

1 Letter from Professor Stefan Kieniewicz to the author, 4 December 1982.
2 B.S. Schafer, *Le nationalisme, mythe et réalité* (Paris, 1964), p. 9.
3 Several works have appeared dealing with the history of the radical nationalist parties, including: J. Majchrowski, *Szkice z historii polskiej prawicy politycznej lat Drugiej Rzeczypospolitej* (Kraków, 1986); Sz. Rudnicki, *Obóz Narodowo-Radykalny* (Warsaw, 1985); R. Stanko, 'Społeczno-ekonomiczna doktryna Obozu Narodowo-Radykalnego' (a doctoral thesis at SGPiS – the Warsaw School of Planning and Statistics) (Warsaw, 1973); S. Potrzebowski, *Zadruga – Eine Völkische Bewegung* (Bonn, 1982). The reader can also find material on this topic in the following works: R. Wapiński, *Narodowa Demokracja 1893–1939* (Warsaw, 1980); J. Holzer, *Mozaika polityczna Drugiej Rzeczypospolitej* (Warsaw, 1974); J.J. Terej, *Rzeczywistość i polityka* (Warsaw, 1979); E.D. Wynot Jr., *Polish Politics in Transition* (Athens, 1974); J. Majchrowski, *Silni, Zwarci, Gotowi. Myśl polityczna ugrupowań katolickich* (Paris, 1984); W. Władyka, *Działalność polityczna polskich stronnictw konserwatywnych w latach 1926–1935* (Wrocław, 1977).
4 Because the expression 'radical right-wing nationalist' is rather unwieldy, I will now use the terms 'nationalist' or 'nationalist right' in referring to these groups.
5 J.Z., 'Idziemy do Ciebie – Młodzieży!', *Młody Rozwojowiec* (April, 1928), no.2, p. 6.
6 *Wielka Polska* no.3 (12 March 1934), p. 2.
7 W. Nałęcz, 'Ani hitleryzm – ani faszyzm', *Front Narodowego Socjalisty*, no.1 (8–15 January 1934).
8 A. Wierny, *Na szlakach dziejowych Romana Dmowskiego* (Piotrków Trybunalski, 1939), p. 130.
9 'Odnowa rasy. Opierajmy się wpływom żydowskim', *Stalowy Miecz*, no.3 (15 April 1936), p. 5.
10 'Ciekawe przejście na judaizm', *Front Polski Zbudzonej*, no.3 (20 January 1935), p. 1.
11 'Przyczynki do problemu "asymilacji"', *Awangarda*, no.1 (March 1928), p. 17.
12 'Żyd pisze historię', *Głos Monarchisty*, no.5 (August 1936), p. 7.
13 Wiking, 'O chrztach Żydów', *Monarchia Narodowa*, no.2 (15 February 1939), p. 5.
14 L. Zasada, 'O Żydach', *Zadruga*, no.6–7 (June-July 1938), p. 6.
15 'Jak rozwiązać kwestię żydowską w Polsce', *Wielka Polska*, no.4 (27 January 1935), p. 2.
16 J. Prądzyński, 'Wysiedlenie Żydów twardą koniecznością', *Wielka Polska*, no.42 (20 January 1935), p. 1.
17 T. Dworak, 'Tradycje rycerskie i żydowskie', *Szczerbiec*, no.30 (10 December 1931), p. 5.
18 M. Nowica, 'O przełom w literaturze', *Zadruga*, no.1 (January 1939), p. 11.
19 'Czym jest faszyzm', *Front Polski Zbudzonej*, no.12 (16–30 April 1934), p. 2.
20 W. Fusek, 'Na żydowskim chlebie', *Wielka Polska*, no.3 (26 January 1939), p. 3.
21 J.Z., 'Dusza żydowska', *Młody Rozwojowiec*, no.3 (May 1928), p. 16.
22 'Na Zmartwychstanie', *Narodowiec*, no.16 (17 April 1938), p. 1.
23 Z. Łuczycki, *Dwa ważne czyny w dziele odżydzania Polski* (no place of publication).
24 Stach z Warty Szukalski, 'Sławinizm Sjonizmu a nasze Żydzieje', *Zadruga*, no.4 (April 1934), p. 6.
25 W. Rościszewski, 'Kwestia żydowska', *Falanga*, no.1 (15 July 1936), p. 3.
26 'Dlaczego jestem antysemitą, *Przełom-jednodniówka* (November 1937), p. 4.

27 J. Bartoszewicz, 'Słownik polityczny. Antysemityzm', *Młody Narodowiec* no.7 (July 1931), p. 13.
28 S. Kopeć, 'Zagadnienie żydowskie', *Polska Narodowa*, no.9 (12 July 1936), p. 1.
29 Z. Wojciechowski, 'Z zagadnień polityki szkolnej. Wychowanie światopoglądowe młodzieży w szkole średniej', *Awangarda Państwa Narodowego*, no.6 (June 1937), pp. 189-207.
30 'Sprawa żydowska', *Szczerbiec*, no.1 (10 January 1930), p. 5.
31 Z. Dembiński, 'Sprawa żydowska', *Czuwamy*, no.29 (29 July 1934), p. 1.
32 'Co mówią czasy minione', *Błyskawica*, no.4 (3-10 September 1933), p. 2.
33 'Dlaczego przeciw Żydom', *Czuwamy*, no.4 (27 January 1935), p. 2.
34 W. Studnicki, *Sprawa polsko-żydowska* (Wilno, undated).
35 'Co mówią czasy minione', *passim*.
36 'Właściwe oblicze żydowstwa w Polsce', *Jutro Polski*, no.19 (7 May 1939), p. 6.
37 For how the struggle against the Jews was to be waged, see below.
38 J. Grabowska, 'Wyznanie wiary', *Falanga*, no.1 (15 July 1936), p. 2.
39 'Deklaracja ideowa Młodzieży Rozwojowej', *Młody Rozwojowiec*, no.5-6 (August 1928), p. 25.
40 Amongst others, in the article 'Dlaczego przeciw żydom' already cited, the author wrote that Jews hung about outside the bailiffs and bought up what was left of Polish property for a trifle.
41 'Historia i powody powstania Narodowego Socjalizmu i jego istotne cele', *Ilustrowany Tygodnik Narodowiec*, no.2 (26 November 1933), p. 2.
42 'Właściwe oblicze żydowstwa w Polsce', *Jutro Polski*, no.14 (7 May 1939), p. 6.
43 R. Dmowski, *Myśli nowoczesnego Polaka* (Warsaw, 1933).
44 T. Gluziński, *Odrodzenie idealizmu politycznego* (Warsaw, 1935).
45 K-icz, 'Bracia szubrawcy', *Nacjonista Polski*, no.9 (12 November 1926), p. 2.
46 J. Gralewski, 'Przyczyny kryzysu polskiej sztuki', *Akademik Polski*, no.9 (November 1931), p. 7.
47 Among others K. Hrabyk, *Nowe drogi w polityce narodowej* (Lwów, 1934).
48 J. Mosdorf, *Akademik i polityka* (Warsaw, 1926).
49 'Rozwiązanie kwestii żydowskiej w Polsce', *Młoda Polska*, no.2 (2 September 1937), p. 15.
50 'O przyszłość naszej twórczości duchowej', *Awangarda*, no.9 (September 1929), pp. 147-177.
51 W.J. Wasiutyński, 'Ćwierć', *Akademik Polski*, no.5 (October 1925), p. 4.
52 'Ghetto- to tylko pierwszy etap', *Akademik*, no.2 (16 January 1938), p. 4.
53 'Niemiły zgrzyt', *Akademik Polski* (20 March 1928), p. 1.
54 'O polskość kół naukowych', *Akademik Polski* (20 March 1928), p. 1.
55 'Siedemnastoletni "szajgec" wytrawnym szantażystą', *Młody Rozwojowiec*, no.1 (March 1928), p. 3.
56 'Walka z żydowstwem', Ibidem, no.4-5 (August 1928), p. 26.
57 Kraksa, 'Kwestia żydowska', *Front Polski Zbudzonej*, no.5 (1-14 March 1934), p. 2.
58 K. Stojanowski, *Chłop a państwo narodowe* (Poznań, 1937). The author attempts to prove that agricultural reform benefited Jews by delaying the drift of peasants to the towns. Reform was being supported by groups dependent upon Jewish backing and was being carried out in eastern Europe because there were more Jews there than elsewhere.
59 'Młodzieży Polska!', *Polska Narodowa*, no.32 (12 September 1937), p. 1.
60 Z. Stahl, *Idea i walka* (Lwów, undated).
61 F. Goetel, *Pod znakiem faszyzmu* (Warsaw, 1939).
62 J. Drobnik, *Przed startem* (Poznań, 1937).
63 E.g. 'Żaden żyd nie może być obywatelem' (No Jew should become a Polish citizen) - St. Kopeć in 'Ustrój polityczny państwa narodowego', *Ruch Młodych*, no.3

(December 1935), pp. 22-9; 'Only a fellow-Pole can become a citizen, and indeed only a fellow-Pole of pure Aryan-Slavic blood. A Jew cannot be a citizen.' - National-Socialist Workers' party, *Błyskawica*, no.1 (13-19 August 1933), p. 2; 'Jews who are prevented by their faith from accepting Christian citizenship are not citizens and can only live in Poland on the same basis as foreigners.' *Program Monarchistów Polskich. Nasze Tezy Polityczne* (no place or date of publication).

64 This kind of opinion is expressed in *Zasady Programu Narodowo-Radykalnego* (Warsaw, 1937) and in articles such as: 'Pozbawić Żydów praw politycznych', *Narodowiec*, no.2 (9 May 1937), p. 5; J. Korolec, 'Trzeba usunąć największą przeszkodę!', *Nowy Ład*, no.4 (December 1935), p. 5.

65 Introduction of anti-Jewish legislation was linked on the whole with the passage of similar laws in Nazi Germany. See, for example, J. Białasiewicz, 'O ustawy antyżydowskie', *Młoda Polska*, no.15 (November-December 1938), pp. 17-19.

66 'Kiedyś się wstydzili, dzisiaj mówią śmiało', *Falanga*, no.5 (10 February 1937), p. 3.

67 See, for example, the article by J. Korolec cited above; 'Pozbawić Żydów praw politycznych', *Narodowiec*, no.2 (9 May 1937), p. 5; 'Zasady programu narodoworadykalnego'; K. Wierczak, *O co walczą narodowcy* (Warsaw, 1935); M. Rzętkowska, 'Konsekwentne rozwiązanie sprawy żydowskiej', *Ruch Młodych*, no.8 (March 1936), pp. 20-5).

68 St. Kopeć, 'Zagadnienie żydowskie', *Polska Narodowa*, no.9 (12 July 1936), p. 1.

69 Z. Wasilewski, 'Żyd i szabla . . .', *Wielka Polska*, no.33 (7 May 1934), p. 3.

70 St. Kopeć, op.cit.

71 M. Rzętkowska, op.cit.

72 J. B., 'W górach polskich nie ma Polaków, *Wielka Polska*, no.24a (August 1934), p. 3.

73 K.B., 'Precz z zawodami sportowymi z żydowstwem', *Młody Rozwojowiec*, no.4-5 (August 1928), p. 34.

74 J. Mosdorf, 'Point de réveries. Precz z żydowskimi marzeniami', *Sztafeta*, no.3 (4 November 1934), p. 1.

75 This problem was closely linked with the relations some nationalist parties had with the German fascist movement. However, this is an issue beyond the scope of the present article.

76 T. Dworak, 'Tradycje rycerskie i żydowskie', *Szczerbiec*, no.30 (10 December 1931), p. 5.

77 Example of a leaflet in *Narodowiec*, no.33 (12 December 1937), p. 6.

78 W.G. Jurczak, 'Kolonie otrzymać musimy!', *Bojownik Pracy*, no.3 (1-15 March 1938), p. 2.

79 A. Niebieszczuński, 'Postęp czy zacofanie', *Narodowiec*, no.4 (23 May 1937), p. 3.

80 J. Białasiewicz, op.cit., p. 18.

81 St. Kopeć, op.cit.

82 E.g. 'Rezolucja Partii Narodowych Socjalistów', *Polska Błyskawica*, no.2 (3 December 1933).

83 J. Zdz. 'Dwie drogi sprawy żydowskiej', *Jutro Polski*, no.4 (15 January 1939), pp. 4, 6.

84 'Miłość i prawda w kwestii polsko-żydowskiej', *Front Polski Zbudzonej*, no.11 (1-15 June 1934), p. 2.

85 'Zamknąć granicę', *Falanga*, no.10 (8 March 1938), p. 5.

86 J. Rutkowski, 'Deklaracja ideowo-polityczna Związku Młodej Polski', *Młoda Polska*, no.1 (July 1937), p. 5. For similar views see also *Monarchia Narodowa. Zarys programowy Ruchu Monarchistyczno-Narodowego* (Warsaw, 1937); 'W co wierzymy i co walczymy', *Szturm Pracy*, no.4 (15 June 1938), p. 1.

87 'Partia narodowo-socjalistyczna do wszystkich pracujących Polaków', *Narodowy Socjalista*, no.5-8 (May-August 1933), pp. 1-5; R. Brzeziński, 'Kwestia żydowska',

Narodowy Socjalista, no.6 (December 1933), pp. 9–11; Mieszko z Koleb, 'Żyd pasożyt', *Wielka Polska*, no.13 (December 1937), p. 6.
88 'Program Narodowych Monarchistów – Bóg, Naród, Ojczyzna', *Głos Monarchistów*, no.13 (December 1937), p. 6.
89 J. Morawski, 'Problem ukraiński', *Młoda Polska*, no.6–8 (January-February 1938), p. 19.
90 E. Basiński, 'Polski imperializm', *Jutro Polski*, no.3 (8 January 1935), p. 3.
91 J. Wyganowski 'Przytyk, a kwestia żydowska', *Wielka Polska*, no.27 (19 August 1936), p. 1.
92 'Rozwiązanie kwestii żydowskiej w Polsce', *Młoda Polska*, no.2 (September 1937), p. 15.
93 O. Szpakowski, 'Trzeba będzie szargać świętości', *Ruch Młodych*, no.2 (November 1935), p. 39.
94 Among those sharing this opinion was A. Sendlikowski, 'Sprawa żydowska', *Sztafeta*, no.5 (18 February 1934), p. 2.
95 B. Kwella, 'Front Aryjski', *Stalowy Miecz*, no.12 (1 September 1936), p. 3.
96 'Żydów nie trzeba się bać', *Czuwamy*, no.10 (18 December 1934), p. 1.
97 W.G. Jurczak, op.cit.
98 J. Prądzyński, 'Wysiedlenie Żydów twardą koniecznością', *Wielka Polska*, no.42 (20 October 1935), p. 1.
99 We come across this point of view, for example, in articles by R. Brzeziński, 'Filosemityzm grozi z prawej strony', *Narodowy Socjalista*, no.1 (July 1932), p. 7; and 'Kwestia żydowska', ibid., no.6 (December 1932), pp. 9–11.
100 This was emphasised by J. Drobnik, op.cit.
101 R. Piestryżyński, 'O co chodzi', *Awangarda Państwa Narodowego*, no.9–10 (September-October 1934), pp. 112–7.
102 'Nasze postulaty konstytucyjne', *Głos Monarchisty*, no.7–8 (August 1933), pp. 6–12.
103 J. Chrostowski, 'Nie Antysemityzm, lecz Filopolonizm', *Ku Polsce Jutrzejszej*, no.6 (27 May – 2 June 1934), p. 2.
104 R. Dębicki, 'O ideologię narodowego socjalizmu', *Świt*, no.3 (20 October 1933), p. 1.
105 *Narodowy Socjalista*, April 1935.
106 Stach z Warty Szukalski, op.cit., pp. 4–6.
107 K. Hrabyk, *Kwestia żydowska* (Lwów, 1934); ibidem, *Nowe drogi w polityce narodowej*.
108 A. Doboszyński, *Gospodarka Narodowa*.
109 I am considering here only those views which treat communism, capitalism and the internationals as a great conspiracy, which threatened the Polish people. I have not analysed those views which judge these phenomena from an exclusively economic point of view, for example, criticising the very mode of production. Similarly I am not concerned with statements in which communism is identified with the Soviet Union and treated only as an external threat, since this takes us into the sphere of foreign affairs.
110 J. Kowal-Lipiński, 'Upadek kapitalizmu socjalizmu i komunizmu', *Front Polski Zbudzonej*, no.21 (26 July 1934), p. 1.
111 Tell, 'Drogi wyjścia z nędzy i bezrobocia mas', *Sztafeta*, no.2 (5 November 1933), p. 1.
112 W. Sznarbachowski, 'Zmierzch komunizmu, socjalizmu i kapitalizmu', *Sztafeta*, no.1 (22 October 1933), p. 2.
113 J. Diżyński, 'Uderzamy w dzwon', *Młody Rozwojowiec*, no.2 (April 1928), p. 5.
114 F. Pychlik, 'Zastanówcie się', *Młody Narodowiec*, no.6 (June 1929), p. 15.
115 'Od Redakcji', *Nacjonalista Radomski*, no.1 (14 September 1926), p. 15.
116 J. Grabowski, 'Wyznanie wiary', *Falanga*, no.1 (15 July 1936), p. 2.
117 'Pismo nasze "Szczerbiec"', *Szczerbiec*, no.6 (9 February 1927), p. 95.

118 Amongst others holding this opinion was M.Z. in the article 'Uwłaszczenie mas to naczelny postulat zdrowej organizacji społeczeństwa', *Polska Narodowa*, no.47 (12 December 1937), p. 1.
119 J. Korolec, 'Trzeba pogłębić', *Nowy Ład*, no.6 (June 1937), p. 1.
120 This thesis was put forward by T. Gluziński in his book *Odrodzenie idealizmu politycznego* (Warsaw, 1935).
121 'Rodacy! Narodowi Socjaliści!', *Błyskawica*, no.1 (13-19 August 1933), p. 1.
122 S.K. 'Socjalizm w świetle prawdy', *Faszysta Wielkopolski*, no.1 (June 1926), p. 4.
123 'Żydzi - przywódcy robotników', *Nowy Ład*, no.1 (January 1935).
124 Ibid., p. 1.
125 'Kto walczy o odrodzenie społeczne i narodowe', *Narodowy Socjalista*, no.14 (15 November 1936), p. 3.
126 M. Reutt, 'Intelektualizm nacjonalizmu', *Akademik Polski*, no.7 (April 1935), p. 4.
127 O. Szpakowski, *Polska przeciw marksizmowi* (Warsaw, 1936).
128 'Walka dwóch światów', *Głos Faszystów*, no.7 (15 March 1927), p. 4.
129 A. Giertych, *O wyjście z kryzysu* (Warsaw, 1938).
130 M. Reutt, 'Intelektualizm nacjonalizmu'.
131 Rem, 'Nie ma walki klas', *Wielka Polska*, no.10 (29 April 1934), p. 2.
132 B. Piasecki, *Przełom narodowy* (Warsaw, 1937).
133 'Kto walczy o odrodzenie społeczne i narodowe', *Narodowy Socjalista*, no.14 (15 December 1936), p. 3.
134 'Pozbawić Żydów praw politycznych', *Narodowiec*, no.2 (9 May 1937), p. 5.
135 'Ghetta w szkołach warunkiem narodowego wychowania młodzieży', *Narodowiec*, no.34 (19 June 1937), p. 1.
136 A. Grzelak, 'Nowa droga polskiego robotnika i chłopa', *Falanga*, no.4 (2 February 1937), p. 1.
137 'Walka młodego pokolenia', *Młoda Polska*, no. 1 (August 1937), p. 2.
138 A. Dec. *Narodowy socjalizm wobec komunizmu* (Warsaw, 1933).
139 J. Barka, 'Komunistyczna Partia Polski', *Nacjonalista Łodzki*, no.1 (14 November 1926), p. 5.
140 A. Dębiec, *Narodowy socjalizm* (Pabianice, undated).
141 O. Szpakowski, *Polska przeciw marksizmowi*.
142 J. Korolec, 'Szukanie własnych dróg', *Nowy Ład*, no.1 (August 1935), p. 1.
143 J. Chróścielewski, 'Katolicki totalizm narodowy konsekwencją katolicyzmu', *Akademik* (16 January 1938), p. 1.
144 S. Czarnecki, 'O narodowe wychowanie młodzieży', *Młody Narodowiec*, no.6 (June 1929), p. 5.
145 'Walka z komunizmem', *Akademik Polski*, no.3-4 (21 March 1927).
146 Amongst others, in the 'Deklaracja Ideowa Związku Faszystów Polskich z siedzibą w Poznaniu', *Głos Faszystów*, no.1 (5 December 1926), p. 2.
147 L. Gembarzewski, *Monarchia Narodowa jako hasło XX-go wieku* (Warsaw, 1934).
148 'Od redakcji', *Faszysta Wielkopolski*, no.1 (June 1926), p. 3.
149 This is the title of an article by M. Reutt which appeared in *Falanga*, no.11 (15 March 1938), p. 2.
150 K. Ksoll, 'Prawda zwycięży', *Front Polski Zbudzonej*, no.35 (30 November 1934), p. 2.
151 R. Piesztrzyński, *Naród w Państwie* (Poznań, 1934).
152 J. Stachniuk, *Heroiczna wspólnota Narodu (Kapitalizm epoki imperializmu a Polska)* (Poznań, 1935).
153 'Nasz radykalizm', *Młoda Polska*, no.2 (September 1937), pp. 1-3.
154 J. Rus, 'W ludzie przyszłość', *Wielka Polska*, no.12 (29 March 1936), p. 1.
155 J. Jeziorański, 'Ani komunizm, ani kapitalizm', *Polska Narodowa*, no.17 (30 August 1936).

156 I am ignoring here the question of foreign capital, which was disapproved of for reasons that were economic rather than ideological.
157 B. Muszyński, 'Bankructwo materializmu', *Polska Narodowa*, no.32 (12 September 1937), p. 1.
158 R. Fengler, 'Kapitał użyteczny czy pasożytniczy', *Awangarda*, no.11-12 (November-December 1932), p. 137.
159 L. Gembarczewski, op.cit.
160 *Katechizm Narodowy Polskiej Klasy Pracującej* (Warsaw, 1936).
161 M. Reutt expressed such a view in the article 'Zasady narodowego ustroju gospodarczego pt.1', *Akademik Polski*, no.8 (4 January 1934), p. 4.
162 *Kapitalizm, komunizm i gospodarka narodowa* (Warsaw, undated).
163 R. Dmowski, *Kwestia robotnicza wczoraj i dziś* (Warsaw, 1926).
164. W. Zaleski, *Polska bez proletariatu* (Warsaw, 1937).
165 W. Wasiutyński, 'Epoka kapitalizmu', *Ruch Młodych*, no.1 (October 1935).
166 M. Reutt, 'Kryzys chwili obecnej a nacjonalizm', *Akademik Polski*, no.1 (23 January 1933), p. 3.
167 *Zasady programu narodowo-radykalnego*.
168 W. Rościszewski, 'Kto nie pracuje ... ten nie je', *Falanga*, no.2 (22 July 1936).
169 K.P. Pomorze, 'Przebudowa ustrojów społecznych', *Front Polski Zbudzonej*, no.5 (1-15 December 1933), p. 3.
170 M. Zawada, 'Idźcie - a walczcie', *Zwycięstwo*, no.6 (15-31 March 1934), p. 3.
171 S. Wielkopolski, *Co to są narodowcy (ich cele i dążenia)* (Cieszyn, 1931).
172 M. Piszczkowski, *Przyczyny upadku Polski a chwila bieżąca* (Lwów, 1934).
173 It was the National Monarchists who most frequently accused the freemasons of attempts to overthrow democracy.
174 K. Hrabyk, *Nowe drogi w polityce międzynarodowej* (Lwów, 1934).
175 Joter, 'U źródeł zła', *Nacjonalista Łódzki*, no.3 (12 December 1926), p. 4.
176 'Z Bogiem - czy bez Boga?', *Zwycięstwo*, no.4 (16 February 1934), p. 4.
177 Z. Łuczycki, *Tabliczki czyli odznaki "Czujni Polskiej" celem oddzielenia polskiego chrześcijańskiego przemysłu, handlu, rzemiosł i wolnych zawodów od żydowskiego* (Lublin, 1926).
178 Z. Wojciechowski, *O nowoczesny polski obóz państwowo-narodowy* (Poznań, 1934).
179 'Dwa lata', *Głos Monarchisty*, no.3 (March 1933).
180 'W co wierzymy i o co walczymy', *Akademik*, no.11-12 (1-15 June 1938), p. 1.
181 'Zwyciężymy', *Awangarda*, no.4 (April 1933), p. 37.
182 'Międzynarodowa banda obraduje w Warszawie', *Falanga*, no.33 (17 August 1937), p. 5.

JEWS AND POLES UNDER SOVIET OCCUPATION (1939–1941): CONFLICTING INTERESTS

Paweł Korzec and Jean-Charles Szurek

INTRODUCTION

The attitude of a considerable number of Jews to Soviet power between 17 September 1939 and 21 June 1941 in the Polish territories annexed by the USSR has still not been adequately studied and the issue causes mutual resentment. One of the most commonly accepted points of view charges the 'Jews' with betraying the Polish state and 'collaborating' with the enemy, on the basis of the favourable welcome they gave the Soviet troops, for example, or the prominent position they held in the new administration.[1]

What is important, in the framework of the Jewish perception of twentieth-century Polish national history, is to establish whether available sources confirm the 'collaboration' of Polish Jews with the Soviet invader as an actual fact and, if so, how to characterize it, and to understand what place it occupies in Polish history.

Curiously enough the accusation of collaboration is rare in Polish historical works published in the West.[2] It appeared for the first time at the outbreak of war in reports on the situation in occupied Poland drawn up by the delegates of the government in London. These reports are a sort of synthesis in which underground observers mix on-the-spot information with their own political analyses. They note Jewish collaboration with the 'reds' but rarely supply precise facts, probably because of the difficulties in collecting them, presenting them, and conveying information from inside the area of Soviet occupation to the outside world. These observers were by no means independent investigators and they were also expressing the varying sympathies of the Polish government.

One of the earliest reports was written by Jan Karski, key witness in Claude Lanzmann's film *Shoah*. Karski's evidence is interesting on more than one count. First, he was the first courier to go to the Soviet zone at the end of 1939 and, as early as February 1940, to be able personally to inform the Polish government in exile, still at Angers, of the facts of the German and Soviet occupations. Secondly, although his report on the Soviet occupation is relatively vague compared with information which got through later, it expresses, in our view, the real complexity of the situation: a complexity based on the 'dialectic' of the two occupations. Karski was neither a typical witness nor hostile to the Jews, as his unique evidence on the Warsaw ghetto shows. His testimony reveals much of the spirit of the times. Thirdly, the fate which befell this text is also a reflection of the times, since two versions exist which have only been discovered recently. There were two versions because the author, at the request of the Polish government, modified passages which emphasized the growth amongst the population of an anti-semitism encouraged by the Nazi occupation. Government leaders, frightened by the negative image which emerged from it, asked Karski to soften and even reverse the import of this statement. But though it was harsh on the Jews, they did not ask him to change his description of their co-operation with the Bolshevik power.

The following are some of the significant points from the initial version of this report:[3]

The Situation of the Jews in the Territories Annexed by the Third Reich
The situation of the Jews in these territories is clear, uncomplicated, easy to understand.
They are outside of the law ... Officially they are intended, through the use of force, law, and propaganda, for destruction or removal.
Jews are being thrown out of these territories, their goods are being confiscated, the 'guilty' are being imprisoned – the intent is toward the complete cleansing of this area of the Jewish element.
Jews are deprived there of practically all possibilities of living – if they live, they do so surreptitiously, in fear, with no rights ...
All wear stars or patches (the same as in the Generalgouvernement), which indicate that they are Jews. Those who shun this obligation are threatened with severe repression ...
In several cases (also in the Generalgouvernement) the restrictions, ordinances and moral atmosphere surrounding the Jews pertain also to the Polish people. This, of course, occasions a quiet satisfaction among the Jews and all the more rancour, disappointment, and consciousness of humiliation among the Polish people.

Relations in the Generalgouvernement[4]

The tendency is towards a resettlement of all Jews from the annexed territories to the Generalgouvernement. The assumption of the Germans is that these territories, 'essentially German but disgracefully Judaized by the Poles,' should be returned re-Germanized without Jews.

In the Generalgouvernement, the Jews who are resettled from the annexed territories are housed in the preponderant number of cases in Lublin and its environs. This creates the impression that the Germans would like to create there something along the lines of a *Jewish reservation* . . .

In the territory of the Generalgouvernement the situation of the Jews is similar (as above), but it is mitigated by all of the consequences stemming from the facts that: 1) there are more Jews here; 2) Jews cannot be sent farther away from there; 3) the German population on these territories is quite small – and the Polish population does not yet at any rate reveal a disposition toward relations with the Jews along the lines of the methods and atmosphere being established by the Germans.

No less, however, do the Jews here have stars or patches, and the same injunctions as in the annexed territories apply to them here . . .[5]

The Jews – the Invaders – the Poles

(a) Under German Annexation (Occupation)

Usually one gets the sense that it would be advisable were there to prevail in the attitude of the Poles toward them the understanding that, in essence, both peoples are being unjustly persecuted by the same enemy. Such an understanding does not exist among the broad mass of the Polish populace.

Their attitude toward the Jews is overwhelmingly severe, often without pity. A large percentage of them are benefiting from the rights that the new situation gives them. They frequently exploit those rights and often abuse them.

This brings them, to a certain extent, nearer to the Germans . . .[6]

(b) Under Bolshevik Annexation (Occupation)

The situation of the Jews in these territories is fundamentally different. After all 'there are no distinctions made here among nationalities or religious groups.' 'Everyone finds conditions for work, and the protection of the law.'

The Jews are at home here, not only because they do not experience humiliation or persecutions, but [also because] they possess, thanks to their quick-wittedness and ability to adapt to every new situation, a certain power of both a political and an economic nature.

They are entering the political cells; in many of them they have taken over the most critical political-administrative positions. They play quite a large rôle in the factory unions, in higher education, and most of all in commerce; but, above and beyond even all this, they are involved in loansharking and profiteering, in illegal trade, contraband, foreign currency exchange, liquor, immoral interests, pimping, and procurement.

In these territories, in the vast majority of cases, their situation is better both economically and politically than it was before the war.

This applies first of all to the classes of petty merchants, artisans, proletarians, and the half-educated. The wealthiest and more educated circles [owners of homes, larger plants, factories, stores, as well as lawyers, doctors, engineers, etc.] are subject in principle to the same restrictions and pressures, and also to liquidation as a social group, as are other nationalities within the Soviet system.[7]

The attitude of the Jews towards the Bolsheviks is regarded among the Polish populace as quite positive. It is generally believed that the Jews betrayed Poland and the Poles, that they are basically communists, that they crossed over to the Bolsheviks with flags unfurled.

In fact, in most cities the Jews greeted the Bolsheviks with baskets of red roses, with submissive declarations and speeches, etc., etc.

However, one needs to insert here certain reservations.

Certainly it is true that Jewish communists regardless of the social class from which they came adopted an enthusiastic stance towards the Bolsheviks. The Jewish proletariat, small merchants, artisans, and all those whose position has at present been improved *structurally*, and who had formerly been exposed primarily to oppression, indignities, excesses, etc., from the Polish element – all of these responded positively, if not enthusiastically, to the new régime.

Their attitude seems to me quite understandable.

However, there are worse cases, where they [the Jews] denounce the Poles, Polish nationalist students, and Polish political figures, when they direct the work of the Bolshevik police force from behind their desks or are members of the police force, when they falsely defame the relations [between Poles and Jews] in former Poland. Unfortunately it is necessary to state that such incidents are quite common, more common than incidents which reveal loyalty towards Poles or sentiment toward Poland. In contrast, I have the impression that the intelligentsia, the wealthiest Jews and those of the highest level of culture [with, of course, certain exceptions, and not counting the pretenders], rather think of Poland often with a certain fondness and would happily greet a change in the present situation [leading to] the independence of Poland . . .

I am familiar, for example, with an authentic incident in which a Jew, the well-known attorney from Lwów, Mr. 48, warns Poles about the danger from the GPU, about threats of legal action against them, and about communist lawyers . . .[8]

The Jewish Problem as an Element of Internal German Policy in the Polish Territories

The attitude of the Jews toward the Poles and vice versa under German occupation is an extremely important and extremely complicated problem, much more important and much more consequential than their attitude under the Bolshevik conquest . . .[9]

'The solution of the Jewish Question' by the Germans – I must state this

with a full sense of responsibility for what I am saying – is a serious and quite dangerous tool in the hands of the Germans, leading toward the 'moral pacification' of broad sections of Polish society.
It would certainly be erroneous to suppose that this issue alone will be effective in gaining for them the acceptance of the populace.
However, although the nation loathes them mortally, this question is creating something akin to a narrow bridge upon which the Germans and a large portion of Polish society are finding agreement.'[10]

Hundreds of other reports followed Karski's and interpreted the Jews' role under the Soviet occupation in accordance with the information conveyed and the sympathies of their authors.

Jan Karski's text is, in our view, interesting in that, from the start, he emphasizes the specific features of each occupation. Thus he shows that, from the beginning, with the Polish army barely defeated, the German occupation was already imposing unparalleled war and living conditions on the Jews. The process of extermination was not yet in train, but segregation, the concentration of the mass of Jews – Karski visited the camp at Bełżec in December 1939 and said 'that he never saw anything so horrible'[11] – and arbitrary rule, had brutally erupted. This arbitrariness was calculated, and was specifically intended to draw the Polish population into the destruction of moral norms. The special *anomie* which set the Jewish population apart and which appealed to the Poles, constituted for Karski the most serious moral danger. During the first weeks of the war, a wave of 300,000 to 400,000 refugees flowed eastwards, fleeing the German threat,[12] and gave the Soviet troops a euphoric welcome because their presence meant that their lives were saved. Almost all these refugees were Jews.[13] In addition, the evidence indicates that they were mainly young and from politically conscious families.[14] Thus 15 to 20 per cent of all Jews from the German-occupied zone left. It is clear that the German danger and the Soviet presence did not weigh on Jews and Poles to the same degree.

Equally clearly the two populations could not view the Soviet occupation in the same light. Moreover, in order to live, this mass of refugees had to seek work, and found it notably in administration, that same administration which until a few months before had been closed to them by the Polish state. The effect of 'collaboration' would thenceforth be visible, physical, and would naturally feed witnesses' reports and memoirs. There was also active ideological collaboration – we will return to this. Here, we want to emphasize two aspects of this complex situation which Karski reveals: first, despite the inter-ethnic clashes, there was not *one* Jewish community with homogeneous attitudes, but social and political groups with interests which diverged and converged at different times. Under the German occupation, the Jewish community formed an objective entity, while on the other side of the Bug (the river which separated the two zones) national differences were subordinated to Sovietization and therefore *in principle* there was equality before the law. When discrimination reached the Poles, it was not in the name of hostile ethnicity *per se* but in the name of a social and political programme. Secondly, it follows from this that, because of the different nature of the two occupations, certain words have differing meanings. Thus ideas of collaboration, or betrayal – even if they are expressed in this vocabulary – have different connotations. Karski, patriot that he was, clearly stated right from the start that there was no possible parallel between the two zones, between the Jews' 'betrayal' and the demoralization to which the Germans subjected the Poles.

Better to understand what was involved here, we must now approach the specific character of eastern Poland (the *kresy* or borderlands) and the nature of the Soviet occupation.

THE SPECIFIC CHARACTER OF EASTERN POLAND

On the morrow of World War I, the frontiers of the Second Polish Republic, especially its eastern frontiers, were discussed at length. What territorial shape should Poland take after 123 years of eclipse as a state? Should it return to its boundaries of 1772, which included a considerable number of nationalities, or to a more limited but ethnically more homogeneous territory? France, in favour of a Poland strong enough to resist the Bolsheviks, supported the first option, Britain the second. The principal Polish political leaders (Dmowski, Piłsudski), certainly followed by the majority of public opinion, fiercely defended the idea of a state extended eastwards, even if they had different policies on ethnic minorities.[15] Military conflicts, which finally settled the matter, were favourable to Poland (the Polish-Soviet war of 1920, and the struggles with the Ukrainians and Lithuanians). Poland thus found itself ruling over a large area where national minorities represented about 35 per cent of the population and where Poles were not in the majority in more than half of it.

This situation was most marked in eastern Poland, that is to say in the territories situated east of the Curzon line – which the USSR invaded on 17 September 1939. Polish identity, traditionally preserved by a minor nobility and a not very large peasantry, had weakened in the nineteenth century, whereas nationalism had increased amongst the Ukrainians, Lithuanians and Byelorussians.[16] Frequently surrounded by hostile ethnic groups, the Poles were only in the majority – and at times only slightly so – in a few regions: Białystok, Wilno, Nowogródek, Lwów. If Poland had consisted solely of the eastern territories, it would only have been represented by a third of its nationals.[17] And it is clear that the majority of Byelorussians, Ukrainians, Lithuanians and Germans found themselves, involuntarily, in a state they rejected.

Relations between the Second Republic and the Jews were equally difficult, and characterized by mutual mistrust. Here too a certain sociological and political heterogeneity must be noted within the Jewish minority. There was a world of difference between assimilated Jews, such as those who had fought for Polish independence in Piłsudski's legions, and the 'Litvaks' from the Wilno or Polesie regions, who spoke Russian or Yiddish better than Polish. Generally, if the Jews on the eastern borders of the Polish state spoke Yiddish amongst themselves, they used their respective languages with the ethnic majorities. The language of the Jewish intelligentsia was Russian in Lithuania, and Polish and German in eastern Galicia. This linguistic imbroglio best symbolizes the tangle of national, religious and social identities which the new state inherited. In towns such as Białystok or Wilno, the Jews bordered on 50 per cent of the population.[18] At the political level, a common characteristic of all the main units was opposition to the nation-state which Dmowski stood for. Whether they were Zionists, Bundists, socialists or communists – all, in their own way, saw a solution to Jewish identity elsewhere than in the increasingly hostile framework of the Second Republic. From this point of view the Jews were scarcely distinguishable from the other national minorities. But they never displayed irredentist and independent tendencies – unlike the other minorities, especially the Ukrainians, who did not hesitate, despite everything, to ally themselves with Germany. On the contrary, by and large they advocated a policy of status quo, peace, integrity and the security of the Polish state. The Jewish demand, as politically and publicly expressed, complied with a legal requirement, namely that the Jewish *national* minority be integrated into the Polish state. The 'national' claim therefore necessarily covered a variety of forms.

The problem of nationalities undermined this state from its birth. The power holding élites as well as most of the social body adhered to the nationalistic ideology of the National Democrats which looked forward to the Polonization of the Ukrainians and Byelorussians and the emigration of the Jews. This policy was applied in regions where Ukrainians predominated; for example, the government introduced Polish as the main language in the administration and education, arousing a wave of manifest discontent amongst the Ukrainians.[19] This discontent lasted throughout the inter-war period.

The policy was also applied to the Jews. As early as 1935, 'Jewish questions' were handled by an emigration department of the Ministry for Foreign Affairs. According to this department, there was 'an essential contradiction between the interests of Poland and the Jewish interest', and 'a state of war existed, without war being formally declared', between the two populations. 'The Jews waged the war both defensively and offensively.'[20] The Polish government of the day put forward a policy of emigration, even making contact with Zionist organizations, notably that led by Jabotinsky, envisaging the transfer of the Jewish population to Palestine, Uganda or Madagascar. The expulsion of the Jews was also sought through economic methods: the government supported the boycott of Jewish enterprises, especially businesses, carried out by militant nationalists in 1938-9. This was, indeed, one of their main goals. 'The economic struggle, certainly,' exclaimed Prime Minister Sławoj-Składkowski in open parliament, in a phrase which has remained famous. General Skwarczyński, the principal leader of the government group, for his part, stated that 'the assimilation of the Jews cannot be the aim of a policy on nationalities,' pointing his finger beyond the frontiers of Poland.[21] A draft law at that time even foresaw stripping all Jews of their citizenship, another only the Jews in the east, and it is a well-known fact that numerous Polish leaders followed the measures adopted in Germany attentively.[22] The place the 'Jewish question' occupied on the eve of war is best symbolized by the Camp Zbąszyn affair, which took its name from the Polish-German frontier post where thousands of Polish Jews crowded for several months during the winter of 1938-9. They had been expelled by Germany, and the Polish government refused to allow them to set foot on the national soil. It is therefore no exaggeration to say that a sort of obsession surrounded the 'Jewish problem', and this was shared by an increasing number of organizations, and fed by the economic difficulties of the country and an outbreak of violence.

The difficulty of resolving social and national conflicts *at the same time* was particularly clear-cut where they were intermingled: east of the Bug. The weakness of the Polish presence in the eastern territories even led the State authorities to develop a colonization programme in the twenties and a programme to re-polonize the minor nobility in the thirties. The colonization programme exacerbated social and national tensions in a quite exceptional manner. We will pause for a moment to study this question because it makes it easier to understand Soviet policy in 1939.

Colonization was at first military; then, from 1923, civil. In the east, colonists could obtain free land formerly belonging to Russian landowners. Often it was also the land of former Polish nobles which had been confiscated (because of participation in uprisings) and entrusted to Russian dignitaries. The colonists could enjoy preferential loans, and free buildings and means of production. The local populations - Byelorussian peasants, for example (predominant in the north-east of the country) - were opposed to this, all the more so as the agrarian structure there was polarized. Vast landed properties in the hands of the Polish landowners, who were often nobles, side by side with a mass of small Byelorussian farmsteads, made for a deep-seated hunger for land. The colonization had a strategic character: the colonists had weapons and constituted military associations, a sort of reserve army which also watched over the frontiers for smugglers. They were the object of particular hatred, noted an observer from the government camp.[23] The land taken over for colonization exceeded the land assigned for agrarian reform in the Polesie and Nowogródek regions, and, according to one of the best-known Polish historians, 'most of the colonists left the land derelict'.[24] Part of this land was sometimes even sold to merchants, or rented out.

Some Polish historians today do not hesitate to describe the policy pursued towards eastern Poland as colonial.[25] Colonization was not only ethno-military, it also took the form of the export of raw materials (particularly wood), the absence of investment and consumption which represented only a quarter of the national total, whereas population was almost equally divided between Poland A (west) and Poland B (east), according to a Polish administrative formula of the day.

> In every administrative region, every town hall, commune, not to mention the police, even the post office, even in the streets of towns and villages of the eastern region, the atmosphere, the social order, was different from that in the rest of the country. Likewise the laws, which apparently had nothing to do with the nationalities policy, became instruments to oppress the local population.[26]

Repression struck equally at the Orthodox population forced by the authorities to embrace Catholicism,[27] and at Catholic Byelorussians who had not wished to abandon their nationality.[28] As for the programme to re-polonize the *'szlachta zagrodowa'*, (peasant-nobles) a product of the minor nobility of the pauperized and largely peasant-dominated borders, it aimed in a very concrete fashion to recall Poland's historic roots in these territories. The authorities organized ceremonies for this minor nobility, manifestations of national cohesion. Genealogies were researched. They sought to convince the peasants that they were former nobles and to make them join associations. The peasants frequently declined this offer so as not to become estranged from their Byelorussian or Ukrainian neighbours. These peasants also enjoyed different privileges, especially in the area of education. It was primarily the military authorities who encouraged this quest for identity in the borders, but this *szlachta zagrodowa* movement – a final attempt to give substance to a historic right denied in practice – remained of slight extent.[29]

In short, it would seem that the borders and the territories to which, sometimes ephemerally, they gave access elude established 'attempts at classification',[30] to use the formula of Czesław Miłosz, who was born there. Criss-crossed by ethnic groups and nationalisms, the borders symbolized a frame of reference, a foundation myth for the Ukrainians and the Poles, the Byelorussians and the Lithuanians. Similarly, the Jews who were driven by poverty or anti-semitic oppression to leave them for America, Palestine or Western Europe, retained an equally idyllic image of the 'old country'. A town like Wilno, so important for Polish culture or history, was also a cultural capital for the Jewish world. This was something the Polish élite knew nothing about. Miłosz described, long after the war, with candour as nostalgic as it was profound, in a work which is more evocative than any scholarly treatise of that 'Commonwealth' that the *Kresy* were:

> The Jewish religious literature, born in this part of Europe and translated into many languages, has become famous throughout the world: you merely have to open an anthology of religious thought to alight on Hasidic parables and learn to revere those sages who were natives of the lost villages, the Baal Shem Tov, Rabbi Nachman of Braclaw, Rabbi Itsik of Lublin, Rabbi Pinkas of Korzec, men who on all evidence reached the heights of evangelical love. Here too were born secular Yiddish prose and poetry, full of both tragedy and incomparable humour. On the spot in Wilno where these books were printed for the international market, we knew absolutely nothing about it. I was able to learn about a few elements of it much later, when I bought books in New York: in other words one had to learn English to reach what one had on one's doorstep.[31]

Partial heir to the breakup of empires, Poland also inherited ethnic conflicts for which the Polish nation-state, represented by the Second Republic, was certainly not prepared. The question of its 'betrayal', especially in the east, when the Polish presence there was in the minority, and enforced, cannot convey the entanglement of conflicting interests. Which is far from meaning that Poland had no legitimate rights there. On the contrary, the *Kresy*, a geographical, historical and literary area, constituted one of the symbolic landmarks in Polish culture, a legendary territory from where the greatest Polish writers came. But these were precisely those writers for whom the spirit of liberty opposed the ethnic cult: writers such as Mickiewicz or Miłosz. Again it is Miłosz who best expresses the spirit of an area which, because of its multicultural composition, abolished frontiers – until the policy of the Second Republic forced all the protagonists to erect new ones:

> I myself must confess that it is precisely the strangeness of the region from which I come and the impossibility of communicating anything of its past to strangers which has been my obsession since the beginning of my life as an émigré. Because when I am asked about my country of origin, I cannot reply 'Poland', even if that is what is expected of someone who writes in the Polish language. I have to add

that my years at school and university were spent in a town which changed hands thirteen times in the course of this century, thirteen, I have counted them. Having said that, I have worked assiduously and with a persistence which is a proverbial Lithuanian virtue to bring my native region to life in all my writings.[32]

If the rise of Polish nationalism had the effect of broadening the irredentism of national minorities other than the Jews, it also provoked 'centrifugal' tendencies amongst the Jews. The Zionist organizations accelerated plans for departure; the *Bund*, in its struggle against the authorities' anti-Jewish intrigues, found it increasingly difficult to propose 'cultural autonomy' and drew closer to the communists. As for the Jewish communists, they campaigned actively within the Communist Party (KPP), in which they formed an energetic and conspicuous minority, particularly in the eastern territories,[33]. The relationship between the Jews and communism cannot be summarized here in a few words, any more than the orientations of all the Jewish parties, especially the predominant religious parties. It is certain, none the less, that communist messianism attracted the Jews, particularly the Jewish youth, all the more so because the Polish nation state denied them assimilation and a place as citizens. The communist ideal suited the Jews even more because it reduced the 'national question' to a perspective in which all ethnic programmes could be absorbed. Even if communism was supported only by a minority of Jews in Poland, it none the less played a notable part in the left/right cleavage. Communism radically opposed the fascism which was in its turn based on the Catholic national tradition. It authorized the Jews to abandon their traditional social links (religion, family, community) and embrace the ideals of Progress, Reason and Modernity inherited from the Enlightenment. Was there no place, one might ask, to maintain these ideals within the nation-state? Perhaps, but in inter-war Poland, where the Jewish minority saw its areas of identification reduced, the Jews' national hope, when it existed, could most easily adopt either Zionism or, by 'disguised inversion', communism. The latter, by its abstract internationalism and its social teleology, also constituted a method – or rather, a hope – for assimilation into the nation-state. From this point of view, the Soviet Union, perceived as stripped of national impediments, and as the 'homeland of the workers', also constituted a homeland for the Jews. It was not a nation-state like the others, nor an empire like those before 1914. The Jews who wanted to stay in Poland, and claimed the status of a national minority, did not have territorial claims. They did not identify territories with 'homelands', above all in eastern Poland where all the minorities fought for power and where the Jews themselves, particularly those who spoke the Russian language, saw their destiny closer to revolutionary Russia than to the Poland 'of the colonels'.

REFLECTIONS ON THE NATURE OF THE SOVIET OCCUPATION

The Sources

Although no overall work exists on Polish-Jewish relations under the Soviet occupation, there are a considerable number of archives, memoirs and testimonies dispersed in different collections (the Hoover Institution at Stanford, the Sikorski Institute at London, the Institute of Jewish History in Warsaw, the Yad Vashem archives, etc.), as well as numerous literary sources, which make it possible to approach this question. Much of what follows will be based on the testimonies published by the sociologist Jan T. Gross. They come primarily from Polish sources and illuminate some essential aspects of this period.[34] However, what is lacking, as far as we know, are syntheses built on Soviet, Byelorussian, Ukrainian, Lithuanian and Jewish sources. It goes without saying that we cannot here – it would need a book – do more than sketch out the arguments necessary to our thesis.

The Sovietization of the Western Ukraine and Western White Byelorussia

The Soviet seizure of eastern Poland was carried out under this heading. In fact, since the twenties the Soviet Union maintained that Byelorussia and the Ukraine should be reunified.[35] In attacking the 'Polish landlords', Soviet propaganda justified the Red Army's invasion by a double liberation, social and national.

The testimonies of the first days of the occupation emphasize the form that the Soviets intended it to take and that it took – or did not take. A short analysis of these first days also makes it possible to highlight the interests at stake.

Right from the start, the Soviets tried to raise the Ukrainians, the Byelorussians and the Jews against the representatives of the Polish state, even trying to convince the Polish soldiers to turn their arms against their officers.[36] It is certain that all the nationalities, except the Poles of course, welcomed the Soviets' arrival, often with open demonstrations of joy. It was primarily the end of Polish rule that was fêted, noted Jan T. Gross, rather than adherence to the new régime.[37] Of course, the Ukrainians hoped to see the question of their national independence resolved, the Byelorussians – particularly the peasants – their social and national struggle, while the Jewish proletariat hoped for equal rights.

Accumulated hatred provoked the settling of local accounts, and blood flowed 'without Bolshevik participation'.[38] During those first days,

> the principal victims were the Poles: the military colonists, the minor nobility of the borders, the landowners, the police, the forest guards, as well as small groups of soldiers and officers from units of the Polish

army broken up by the German offensive. In the course of a few days in September, the Ukrainians, the White Russians and the 'locals' had made those who had been the instruments of the Polonization of the provinces of the south-east for the past twenty years pay for it. What aggravated the confrontation was that the Soviet occupation excluded certain categories of the population from rights, people in the service of the Polish state as well as 'class enemies' - that is to say landowners and rich peasants - and that it simultaneously subjected them to 'official' terror. Nevertheless, there too the local population (rapidly regrouped into sections of the militia, including not only the Ruthenian national minorities but also numerous Jews) committed acts of direct violence.[39]

Sovietization did not aim at the destruction of the Polish nation but at the subjection of purported interests in the local populations - social and national - to the Kremlin's aims. That is why the Soviet authorities essentially attacked the representatives of the state and the 'propertied classes': police, army, colonists, forest guards, landowners, rich peasants. In short, they attacked all the bureaucratic-economic caste abhorred by the Byelorussian and Ukrainian peasantry, who thus saw their social and national hopes become a reality. The Polish witnesses often believed that they were the object of repression on account of their national origin, whereas it was actually their social role which was the target. The terror of the first days, particularly that practised by the peasants, was tolerated by the Soviets as 'rightful anger of the masses'. Then the political organs (including the NKVD and the army) organized the occupation.

In the militias and revolutionary committees which were spontaneously created or initiated by the Soviet authorities, the Jews certainly played a role, which was important although not exclusive, since they also contained the newly 'dominant' nationalities as well as common-law prisoners freed by the Soviets in the name of the class-struggle. But there too, the Jews did not form a homogeneous entity: it was primarily the Jewish youth and the poverty-stricken masses who were a real mainstay of the new power.[40] This qualified aspect of the Soviet occupation is confirmed by Jewish evidence: 'The Russians relied primarily on the Jewish element when allocating positions, naturally distinguishing between the bourgeoisie and the proletariat.'[41]

The 'class struggle' remained the basic motive of pro-Soviet Jews, and they applied it with revolutionary intransigence in respect of the whole bourgeoisie, including the Jewish bourgeoisie, as noted by Max Wolfshaut-Dinkes:

> ... I must confess that I found the conduct of the Jewish communists during the Soviet occupation terribly repugnant: they had a far too

brutal attitude towards their employers. The Polish and Ukrainian employees did not denounce their employers as exploiters so that their undertaking would be nationalized and they themselves sent to Siberia; unfortunately, the Jewish communists had no hesitation in doing this.[42]

The social/national conflict thus recurs: the Jewish communists, supported by a radicalized youth, reckoned that an essential revolution, with themselves as the heroes, was coming about thanks to their support. The Ukrainians and Byelorussians, during the first weeks at least, believed that the Soviet presence would settle the question of their national independence. Note that, according to the testimonies in Gross's book, the bloodshed which the Polish populations complained of during the beginning of the occupation came much more from inter-ethnic conflicts than from the 'class struggle'. Revolutionary intransigence proved less sanguinary than the quest for national frontiers. This detail is frequently forgotten when 'Jewish collaboration' is discussed, as if the 'betrayal' of the Byelorussians and Ukrainians must naturally be self-evident and naturally cause blood to flow.

The social programme which Sovietization embodied brought the Jews equal rights with *others*. That is what the Jewish testimonies indicate, as reported by Gross: 'The changes which began to occur in the village after the Russians' arrival were a total surprise ... To the Jews, they could only consider it a dream, as if the Messiah had come. The Russians raised their status, they gave them something – a status that they had never had in their lives'.[43] Gross mentions the case of a rich millowner who, although he did not like the Bolsheviks 'because they valued a thief or a murderer more highly than us and he had more chance of living than us', nevertheless added, 'There was no racial or national persecution and, for the first time, the Jew was not a second-class citizen'.[44]

If Sovietization meant the destruction of Jewish community structures (liquidation of political parties, prohibition of the teaching of Hebrew, closure of religious schools), it did, on the other hand, permit Jews to occupy the symbolic places of employment which were inaccessible to them previously: administration, university, a variety of jobs.

The 'Judaeo-Bolshevik' alliance and the equality of nationalities, apparently in effect, were actually subject to the logic of Sovietization. In the politico-administrative hierarchy which was set up, it was the *vostochniks*, that is to say, the people from the east (officials, factory managers, trusted Soviet agents intended to make the occupation secure) who occupied the key positions. They included Russians and Ukrainians, Byelorussians and Jews from the east. Then came the local Ukrainians and Byelorussians whose 'homelands' were to be joined to the Soviet Union by a semblance of elections. Then the Jews, whom the Soviets called on for help and who, for the reasons indicated, would not fail them. The Jewish presence was all the more conspicuous because the Byelorussian and Ukrainian populations, uneducated and consisting to a vast extent of peasants, could not occupy the administrative machinery which was created under the Soviet umbrella.[45] Henceforth, every Pole who lost his job applied to an official, a teacher, an examining magistrate – many of whom were Jews. And yet there too the attitude of the 'Jews' cannot be reduced solely to acceptance of Sovietization.

JEWISH ATTITUDES UNDER THE SOVIET OCCUPATION

For many, the arrival of the Red Army meant relief in comparison to the advance of the Germans, whose crimes against the Jews were already known: at Przemyśl, for example, the Germans shot 640 communal notables as soon as they entered the town.[46] 'With the Soviet entry into the town,' Max Wolfshaut-Dinkes recounts, 'the people calmed down a little. They were no longer afraid of massacres'.[47]

During the first fifteen days of September, between the German advance and the disbanding of the Polish army – and before the Russian army intervened – the Jews were most afraid of pillage and seizures. 'With the arrival of the Germans [Lwów region], pillage and persecution of the Jews began, not only at the hands of the Germans; the Ukrainian-Polish underworld also utilized this period against the Jews'.[48]

It was therefore *spontaneously*, in the absence of any authorities, that urban militias formed, composed of numerous Jews and with a primarily *civil* role. In the town of Dubno, for example:

> Because of the progress of the German army, the local Polish authorities decided to leave the town ... The police also left the town and a militia ... was created in its place. Note ... that numerous young Jews were to be found in this militia, they were armed and guarded the bridges and military stores, abandoned by the Polish army. The town was disturbed and the Jews were afraid of the Polish and Ukrainian anti-semites.[49]

The joy with which the Jews, including the bourgeoisie – who were to lose their fortunes and often their liberty from contact with the Bolshevik 'revolution' – welcomed the Russian troops was born of the guarantee of *order* they assured. This joy already expressed the anguish of a minority race who, in the years of the war, would suffer the German hordes, the Ukrainian peasants, the Polish 'indifference'. Note that Poles and even Ukrainians were fleeing westwards,[50] though to a much smaller degree than the Jewish exodus eastwards. It is in the light of this 'exchange of ethnic groups', to use Max Wolfshaut-Dinkes's phrase, that the upheaval in the borders under the double Soviet-German impact can be understood: the choices open to the Jews and the collaboration by some of them.

Consequently, the Jews' pro-Soviet attitude cannot solely be explained, even superficially, by their adherence to communism. Moreover, this attitude was qualified: the assimilated bourgeoisie of Lwów, for example, although it was protected by the Soviet presence, was offended by this 'fourth partition of Poland'. It is also well known that a section of the Jewish communists were troubled by the pact and by the transport of Soviet merchandise to Germany. And the numerous refugees from western Poland expressed particularly ambivalent attitudes towards the USSR.

As time went on, this mass of refugees posed problems for the Soviet authorities, not only because it was difficult to house them and to find them work, but particularly because their critical and sometimes slightly mistrustful attitude to the new power made Sovietization more difficult. The authority decided to deport them to the interior of the USSR, as it had already done with 'enemy' categories (there were four large deportations: in February 1940, peasants and colonists were deported; in April 1940, their families; in June 1940, the refugees from central Poland, therefore primarily Jews; in June 1941, a mixture of these categories – in all, over a million people).

The deportation of June 1940 is of especial interest here. In fact, there is a certain degree of coherence about Soviet policy even if all the testimonies concur in indicating that arrest and deportation could fall indiscriminately on anyone. The aim of the first deportation was in principle the eradication of all the categories which symbolized the Polish state (colonists, police forces, minor nobility, reputedly rich peasants, forest guards). How could the deportation of a mass of reputedly friendly Polish Jews logically be included here?

Once the attachment of western Byelorussia and the western Ukraine to the Soviet Union had been proclaimed, the authorities instituted a compulsory census of refugees. The questions asked were simple: (1) Do you wish to adopt Soviet citizenship? (2) Do you wish to return to your country of origin [therefore, as it might happen, to Germany]? There was considerable disarray amongst the refugees who did not know the rules of the Soviet game in weighing up what was at stake. They were given no explanation and communal institutions had been closed since the beginning of the occupation. The census was conducted by 'committees of aid for the refugees', in actuality auxiliary organs of the NKVD. A majority registered for return: fear of Soviet citizenship and of simultaneously losing Polish citizenship partly accounted for this decision.[51] Some people considered this measure unrealistic and did not imagine that the Soviets could surrender them into German hands, particularly not such a massive number of individuals. Others thought that they could escape the problem under the German occupation.

The aim of the census was revealed when people who had declared themselves Polish were arrested and deported in June 1940. Note that – a cruel and paradoxical irony of history-deportation saved the lives of several hundred thousand Jews, while the minority who became Russian and who remained in this territory were exterminated during the German occupation.

Another aspect of Sovietization and 'collaboration' was the search for jobs. The destruction of trade, crafts and the liberal professions – predominantly Jewish sectors – meant that the Jews had to look for a place in the new structure:

> People tried to find work in the administration because their origin was unfortunate ... Some of the craftsmen joined the *artels*, others thought that the time was ripe for possible social advancement ... some even went into the militia ... Most of the people reckoned that collaboration with the Soviets was an obligation, but deep down inside they opposed it ... Everyone thought that the Jews served the Soviet power with enthusiasm and joy because it was in their interest for the Bolsheviks to remain. The Jews were afraid of explosions from other minorities, victimized by the Soviets.[52]

This account, written by an inhabitant of Volhynia and not by a refugee, shows the reasoning which governed the conduct of numerous Jews: more than 'collaboration', it was participation, even passive participation, which the régime wanted of them. They had no other solution, either because of economic uprooting or as a result of inter-racial conflicts. This was the same reasoning which led all citizens, including the Poles – except those at the bottom of the social scale – to participate in the semblance of elections intended to legitimize the annexation. There was never any question, as Jan T. Gross says, of convincing the local populations, but of making them accomplices,[53] through successive losses of personal autonomy. Fear, brainwashing, the search for well-being in a wretched environment remained determinant elements of Sovietization for all.[54]

The word 'Jews' therefore covers a varied spectrum. What was the common factor between the Jewish communists who participated actively in Sovietization and those who, although communist, rejected it; between the refugees who, although grateful to the Red Army for having saved them, refused Soviet citizenship, and those who, pauperized, accepted administrative jobs willy-nilly; between those who accepted the Soviet order with relief so as not to be engulfed in the ethnic-social conflicts, and those who saw an unprecedented equality of rights being achieved?

Is it really possible to talk of 'collaboration' in all these cases, and particularly in the case of Jews, who were not assimilated and not identified with the Polish state and who welcomed the change of régime? The word has too many echoes of the 'other' collaboration and does not seem to convey a complex reality, a reality which was in no way comparable with the German occupation, even for the Poles.

The Soviet occupation of 1939–41 embraced a heterogenous Jewish population, in the grip of a historic involvement with other peoples, where the resentments of the inter-war period, the exodus, adherence to Bolshevism and many other factors interacted. Finally, it is not irrelevant to recall that the 'Jewish' price in deportations to the Soviet camps was not negligible: 30 per cent of the deportees were Jews, 52 per cent Poles, 18 per cent Ukrainians and White Russians.

CONCLUSION

There are at least two ways of talking about betrayal. One is positivist: it is steeped in the aims of nation states, of their dominant forces, and to some extent espouses them, defending their frontiers with greater or lesser conviction, and acknowledging that different or conflicting national schemes can lead to betrayal. Thus the positivist approach can express any national scheme: for example, the Ukrainians would set out the reasons for their betrayal and their rapprochement with Poland's enemies; the Jews would suggest that it was the Polish state which betrayed them and not vice versa.

The positivist categories do not, in our opinion, take Polish-Jewish relations under the 1939–41 Soviet occupation sufficiently into account, whether methodologically or epistemologically. The imbroglio of ethnic groups and nationalisms, the Second Republic's policy on nationalities, the Soviet-German impact on the borders, the presence of communism amongst the Jews – all these factors require a multi-dimensional reading of the objectives discussed, capable of surmounting any frontier. 'Betrayal', if this term is appropriate to the ethnic clashes and still means anything, then takes on a completely relative sense. This second, somewhat analytical approach, in our view, makes it possible to assess the conflicting arguments.

If, as we hope we have shown, ideas of 'betrayal' and 'collaboration' are inapplicable to the situation described here, how has their use in this context become so widespread? It was primarily spread in the clandestine press during the occupation and in reports by correspondents of the Home Army (*AK*). Moreover, close reading of these reports shows that the information they contain is much less exact than the sources used here, which were often, of course, drawn up after the 1939–41 period, or hedged about with caveats.[55] Let us advance the hypothesis – which is after all quite commonplace — that the use of 'betrayal' was conveniently integrated into the political strategies of the different underground parties, extending, in radicalized terminology, to the 'Jewish question' debated before the outbreak of war: did not some Polish leaders for example, make every effort to propose a transfer of Jews to the Odessa region during the winter of 1940?[56] The charge of betrayal also made it possible to justify and put in relative terms the unbridled anti-semitism of the population which Karski talks about. This anti-semitism was therefore widely developed well before the fusion of the two zones of occupation under German control, which made it possible to become familiar with the 'behaviour' of the Jews in the east.

And what should we think of the use of these words today? Do they make it possible to combat the negative stereotypes which overcome the Poles as soon as the Jewish question is broached? Is it rather a question of showing that it was communism, and therefore the Judaeo-Bolshevik alliance, which fundamentally increased an anti-semitism which was scarcely more excessive — and perhaps even less — than before? This hardly makes sense. Destiny ordained that the murder of the Jews of Poland, the largest Jewish community of Europe, took place on Polish soil, in the greatest of isolation. The mechanisms are often still incomprehensible, but it does not seem to us sensible to explain them by arguments which seem to be of a political nature.

'Betrayal' belongs to the classical anti-semitic vocabulary, as much moreover as it does to the vocabulary of a Jewish literature which loves to dwell on fantasy.[57] Its use seems to us best treated with reserve.

NOTES

1 This question has been raised recently in several works, particularly in Aleksander Smolar, 'Les Juifs dans la mémoire polonaise', *Esprit*, 127 (June 1987), pp. 2–8; Krystyna Kersten, *Narodziny systemu władzy 1943–1948* (Paris, 1986), 172.
2 The taboo which surrounded Polish-Jewish relations, particularly in a Soviet dimension, not to mention the Soviet occupation, made publication inconceivable in Poland. However, the vast amount of underground published material is beginning to broach both aspects equally.
3 The English translation is taken from David Engel, 'An Early Account of Polish Jewry under Nazi and Soviet Occupation Presented to the Polish Government-in-Exile, February 1940', *Jewish Social Studies* 45:1 (1983), 2–16.
4 The western part of the Polish territories had been annexed to the German Reich; another part, situated in the south-east, with Kraków as its centre, had been transformed by the occupying forces into a sort of protectorate called the 'General-Government'.
5 Engel, 'Early Account', 1–2.
6 Ibid.
7 Ibid.
8 Ibid.

9 Ibid.
10 Ibid.
11 In fact Karski was to revisit Bełżec, which later became a death camp.
12 The estimate generally put forward. Cf. Franz Beranek, 'Das Judentum in Polen', in Werner Markert (ed.), *Osteuropa Handbuch Polen*, (1959), 124.
13 Cf. the memoirs of Gina Mehr, Yad Vashem, 3042/170-N, or those of Reiss Walter, an inhabitant of Lwów, who writes: 'In September, 1939, the Russian army came to Lwów, and the Germans, who were already in the suburbs, withdrew behind the San. This fact was welcomed very joyfully by the Jews of Lwów, although nothing very good was expected from Soviet power,' Yad Vashem, 03-2241.
14 Personal memory of Paweł Korzec, who was one of the refugees in 1939.
15 Dmowski's nationalist camp put forward a theory, known as incorporationist, which aimed at incorporating the non-Polish ethnic groups into the nation state; Piłsudski's was a federalist solution: both collapsed quite quickly.
16 Cf. Andrzej Chojnowski, 'Problem narodowościowy na ziemiach polskich w początkach XX w. oraz w II Rzeczypospolitej', in *Z dziejów Drugiej Rzeczypospolitej*, a collective work edited by A. Garlicki (Warsaw, 1986), 177-94. See particularly p. 177, where the author writes that 'on the other side of the Bug, the phenomenon of obliteration of national identity brought about the regrouping of Polish peasants and minor nobility'; and 'If the assimilationist effect of Polish culture on the native population there was limited, this was the result of the Russifying action of the Tsarist government and the national activation of the Lithuanians, Ukrainians and Byelorussians.'
17 In the Polesia region (*województwo*), they only formed 14.5 per cent of the population; in Volhynia, not much more than 16 per cent.
18 Chojnowski 'Problem narodowościowy', 180.
19 Whereas the number of Polish schools was unchanged, the number of Ukrainian schools in eastern Galicia decreased in five years (1924-8) from 2,151 to 716. In their place and during the same period, the number of schools described as bilingual had increased from 9 to 1,793. The bilingualism, which introduced Polish as the first language, was only a screen for Polonization.
20 Quoted by A. Chojnowski, *Koncepcje polityki narodowościowej rządów polskich w latach 1921-1939* (Kraków, 1979), 222.
21 Quoted by Chojnowski, ibid, 226.
22 At the time of the discussions between Ribbentrop and Lipski (Polish ambassador to Berlin) on 24 October 1938, a real *Gesamtlösung* was envisaged in respect of Jewish emigration, cf. Artur Eisenbach, *Hitlerowska polityka zagłady Żydów* (Warsaw, 1961), 123.
23 K. Srokowski, *Sprawa narodowościowa na kresach wschodnich* (Kraków, 1924), 19.
24 W. Pobog-Malinowski, *Najnowsza historia polityczna Polski* vol. 2 (London, 1956), 441.
25 Aleksandra Bergman, *Sprawy białoruskie w II Rzeczpospolitej* (Warsaw, 1984), 101.
26 Ibid.
27 Cf. Chojnowski, *Koncepcje*, 193.
28 Cf. Bergman, *Sprawy białoruskie*, 102.
29 Cf. Chojnowski, *Koncepcje* A contemporary military report indicated that the 'nobility factor ... has remained ... as the sole link between this group of the population and Polishness.' Quoted by Chojnowski, p. 228.
30 Daniel Beauvois (ed.), *Les confins de l'ancienne Pologne, Ukraine, Lituanie, Bielorussie*, Preface by C. Miłosz (Lille, 1988), 11.
31 Czeslaw Milosz, *Une autre Europe* (Paris, 1964), 100.
32 Beauvois, *Les confins*, 9.
33 There is a copious literature on the relationship between the Jews and communism.

Localized descriptions are thinner on the ground: 'In our town, May 1 was described as a Jewish holiday. In fact, Jewish youth occupied a leading place in the processions with flags and posters bringing together all shades of the Left.' Miłosz, *Une autre Europe*, 97. 'In our town I never knew a non-Jewish communist,' says Max Wolfshaut-Dinkes, a native of Przemyśl; cf. Max Wolfshaut-Dinkes, *Echec et mat. Recit d'un survivant de Przemyśl en Galicie*, published by Association des fils et filles des deportés juifs de France, (Paris, 1983), 21.

34 Jan Tomasz Gross and Irena Grudzińska-Gross, 'W czterdziestym nas matko na Sybir zesIali' in '*Polska a Rosja 1939-42*' (London, 1983). This book, with a preface by Jan Gross, brings together a sample of testimonies from adults who left the USSR with the Anders army, and from children evacuated by the Polish authorities. These documents, which describe their perception and experience of the Soviet occupation, were drawn up at the request of the Polish government. They can be found at the Hoover Institution, Stanford. Cf. also Jan T. Gross, 'Wybory', *Aneks*, 45 (1984), 129-60, 46/47 (1988), 171-210. These articles are the theme of his book, *Revolution from Abroad: Sovietization of Western Ukraine and Western Bielorussia, 1939-1941* (Princeton, 1988).

35 The existence in Poland of distinct communist parties (Communist Party of Western Byelorussia, Communist Party of Western Ukraine), although subordinate to the Polish Communist Party, constitute one of the symptoms of this.

36 Cf. Jan T. Gross, 'W czterdziestym' 16.
37 Ibid., 20.
38 Ibid., 17.
39 Ibid., 18.
40 Ibid., 28.
41 Ibid., testimony 033/666 at Yad Vashem.
42 Wolfshaut-Dinkes, *Echec et mat*, 22. Or again: 'The Jews lived in fear, haunted by the prospect of expropriation and deportation to Siberia. They mistrusted one another and, above all, they feared the Jewish communists. These latter were fanatical supporters of the régime, zealous servants of the authorities. Faithful to their "duty", they fought unscrupulously against the "terrible" class enemy, composed of shopkeepers and craftsmen,' Ibid., 36.
43 Gross, 'W czterdziestym', 30, quoting Testimony 03/2821 at Yad Vashem.
44 Ibid., quoting Testimony 03/3381 at Yad Vashem.
45 Testimony of Fela Schnek, drawn up on 10 December 1947 at Yad Vashem (E/664, p. 1), indicates that in the Lwów region, 'From the start the Jews occupied most of the positions in the Soviet administration, although the key posts were always in the hands of Soviet officials.'
46 Cf. Wolfshaut-Dinkes, *Echec et mat*, 30.
47 Ibid., 31.
48 Account by Gina Mehr, Yad Vashem 03/3381, pp. 2-3. She adds (p. 3) that it was fortunate that she was separated from her husband because a great danger would then have threatened him: 'With the help of the local Ukrainian intellectuals, headed by Dr. Birecki, a list of 70 people to be eliminated had been drawn up and my husband and his brother figured on it. Fortunately this sentence was not carried out because the Germans, as a result of the agreement with the Soviets, were to withdraw behind the San, and after an agonizing 14 days, we were freed by the Soviets.'
49 Moshe Kahan, 'Two years of Soviet rule in Dubno', in the *Yizkor-buch* of Dubno, ed. Yaazov Arimi, (Tel Aviv, 1966).
50 'Many Polish and Ukrainian families left the side of the village occupied by the Soviets and went into the German-occupied region. This was, as it were, an exchange of ethnic groups.' Wolfshaut-Dinkes, *Echec et mat*, 31.

51 Cf. Kahan, 'Two years'; personal memory of Pawel Korzec, who opted for Soviet citizenship.
52 Pat Yacov (general editor), *Fun noentn over*, 3 vols., published by Congress for Jewish Culture (New York, 1957), testimony of Beti Ajzensztajn-Kesher, 'The Jews in Volhynia, 1939–41', pp. 3–30. The author adds that 'it was the Jewish communists who abolished the teaching of Hebrew and the Hebrew schools, in two months. The non-Jewish *politruks* (political commissars) did not even know that Hebrew was taught.'
53 Gross, 'Wybory' (see above, n. 34), p. 204.
54 Soviet 'discipline' even reached the Polish partisans, who were the most zealous supporters of the Soviet régime: thus Wanda Wasilewska, the communist writer who gave great support to the Kremlin's policy, was present in Lwów in 1940 at the assassination by unknown persons of her husband, a worker who did not refrain from criticizing the system. Cf. Ola Watowa, *Wszystko co najwazniejsze* (London, 1983) 30–1.
55 We have a certain number of these 'situation' reports in our possession, but their analysis goes beyond the scope of this article.
56 This suggestion was made by Roman Knoll, former ambassador to Berlin and leading government personality, in a report sent from Warsaw in March 1940 to the authorities in exile in Angers. The suggestion was taken up by the Minister of the Interior, Stanisław Kot. Knoll added that the Polish people would not tolerate a return to the pre-1939 situation and that only the territorial solution that the Zionists envisaged would prevent the use of violent methods. The choice, he wrote, was between 'Zionism and extermination' (for him a Zionist solution might well have been carried out on the coast of the Black Sea). Cf. David Engel, *In the shadow of Auschwitz: The Polish Government-in-Exile and the Jews, 1939–1942* (Chapel Hill, North Carolina, 1987) p. 65.
57 In his book, *Bruno Schulz* (1989), Henri Lewi brings up the idea of betrayal as essential to salvation present in Schulz's work, and derived from a mystical tradition which goes back to the seventeenth century.

POLISH-JEWISH RELATIONS AND THE HOLOCAUST

Antony Polonsky

> 'And which of you, still living, has not seen death without feeling guilt.'
>
> Tadeusz Borowski

The difficult problems raised by the Nazi Holocaust in Poland, and, above all, the vexed question of the Polish response to the mass-murder of the Jews have long been a sore point in Polish-Jewish relations. Far from healing the divisions between Poles and Jews, the Nazi Holocaust, carried out as it was largely on Polish soil, considerably strengthened those barriers of suspicion, fear and even hatred between the two communities which had already begun to grow alarmingly in the last years before the outbreak of the war. To the small group of Jews who survived in Poland or who returned from the USSR, Polish behaviour during the war seemed to have confirmed their worst suspicions. It was clear to them that they were not wanted on Polish soil and that it was even dangerous for them to remain in Poland. In their eyes, the Poles had stood aside while the Nazis had implemented their murderous plans. The small amount of assistance provided was, in their eyes, outweighed by the activities of the denouncers and blackmailers, while the attitude of the majority was, at best, indifferent. This feeling of alienation was only strengthened by the post-war insecurity and the anti-Jewish outbreaks which culminated in the Kielce pogrom of July 1946 in which at least 40 Jews were murdered. It would probably not be going too far to say that the scarring effects of the Holocaust were so traumatic that they made the establishment of a sizeable Jewish community on Polish soil in the post-war years impossible.

The impact of the Holocaust on the Poles was no less traumatic. It has been well described by the Polish-Jewish sociologist, Zygmunt Bauman:

> But the Poles were scarred, too, and scared – by the crime committed on their soil before their eyes. Reactions to the harrowing experience

were as if drawn from the psychology textbook. Some tried to talk themselves into believing that the Jews, after all, deserved what they got, brought the hatred upon themselves and hence no-one ought to be castigated for not helping them. Some others tried to shift all the guilt on to the murderers. The odds were overwhelming and nothing we could possibly have done would have balanced them out. Some sought consolation in remembering that they also were on the receiving end of the crime: we all suffered, we all have our dead to commemorate and the Jewish claim that their victims should be treated differently is just another insidious attempt to cast aspersions on their Polish hosts ... However different the reactions, they were all responses to an unresolved moral problem of suppressed guilt.[1]

Indeed, the divisive effects of the Holocaust greatly complicated any rational discussion of Polish-Jewish relations during World War II, as well as making much more difficult any genuine Polish-Jewish reconciliation. The two sides argued not so much with, as past, each other, exchanging mutual recriminations in a tragic dialogue of the deaf. As Bauman has observed: 'Equality in suffering unites and heals; "singling out" part of the sufferers for special treatment leaves hatred and moral terror in its wake. Far from dispersing the clouds of mutual suspicion and antipathy which hung over Polish-Jewish collaboration, the Holocaust made reconciliation more difficult than ever before.'[2]

There were also other factors which inhibited a proper consideration of the implications of the Holocaust in Poland, as well as the wider question of the reasons for the development there in the 1930s of a climate of pervasive anti-semitism and the extent to which this facilitated the Nazis' murderous plans. In the immediate post-war period, before the imposition of a rigidly Stalinist and Soviet-dominated regime, there were a number of efforts to come to terms with these issues. It was at this time that Michał Borwicz and his colleagues at the newly-established Jewish Historical Commission initiated a very valuable attempt to document the events of the *Shoah* and to preserve the testimony of the survivors. Several courageous Polish voices including Jerzy Andrzejewski and Stanisław Ossowski also castigated the evil of anti-semitism.[3] But already the political climate was exercising a baleful effect on these attempts to 'overcome the past', as the similar process in Germany has been described. In the period 1944–47, Poland was the scene of a sort of civil war, which resulted in the imposition of an unrepresentative communist régime, closely linked with and effectively controlled by the Soviet Union. This régime saw anti-semitism as a useful brush with which to tar its opponents. It was certainly true that this period was disfigured by a number of anti-Jewish excesses (Lucjan Dobroszycki has calculated that these led to the deaths of nearly 1500 people),[4] which were provoked partly by fears that returning Jews would seek to regain their property and partly by the feeling that the régime, in which there were a number of prominent Jewish communists, was the realization of pre-war fears of Judeo-communism ('Żydo-Komuna'). The communists were determined to deny to their opponents any political virtues and to claim that they were the only political force in Poland which had repudiated anti-semitism and its associated fascist doctrines. Thus in the years immediately after liberation, although an 'All-Polish Anti-Racist League' was set up, its activities were soon restricted to protesting about the oppression of Blacks in the southern United States.[5] Similarly the role of non-communists in helping the Jews during the war was belittled. This applied particularly to the Council for providing Aid to the Jews (cryptonim *Żegota*) which was created by the main non-communist underground body, the Home Army, (*Armia Krajowa* - AK) in 1942 and which was a unique body in Europe.

Under these circumstances, a dispassionate analysis of the roots of Polish anti-semitism proved impossible. In the rest of Europe, those right-wing groups which had espoused anti-semitism had been discredited by their collaboration with the Nazis. In Poland, their anti-Nazi record was, for the most part, impeccable, and, now, in addition, they were being persecuted by the communists. They thus retained a degree of legitimacy and respectability which was not to be found elsewhere in Europe.

The situation became still worse when a fully Stalinist régime was established after 1948. The war-time non-communist resistance, and above all the Home Army, was bitterly reviled, and many of its members, including those who had set up *Żegota*, like Władysław Bartoszewski, were imprisoned. Anti-semitism, like fascism, was seen as the inevitable consequence of monopoly capitalism and, according to the official ideology, it would only disappear with the abolition of capitalism. The Communist Party of Poland was the only force which had opposed the rising pre-war anti-Jewish tide, and the whole of the Polish non-communist camp was hopelessly tainted by anti-semitism and other reactionary vices. At the same time, from about 1952, coinciding with Stalin's growing anti-Jewish paranoia, the number of Jews holding important positions within the régime was considerably reduced. This process went still further after October 1956 when Władysław Gomułka succeeded in establishing a national communist régime as a consequence of the de-Stalinization process within the Soviet Empire.

The Gomułka régime found the Jewish issue an embarrassment. It was determined to establish its national credentials in the eyes of Polish society. It permitted the re-emergence of a number of national symbols and also, partially at least, recognized the role of the Home Army (AK) in the anti-Nazi resistance. Any serious discussion of the Jewish question could only raise difficult problems and could prove destabilizing, both because of the sensitive issue of the role of Jews in the party, and, above all, the security apparatus, between 1945 and 1953, and because of the presence within it still of a fair number of Jewish cadres. The Jewish issue thus became taboo, emerging only in the period 1967-8, when a younger group of party activists sought to take advantage of the hysterical climate engendered by the Israeli victory in the six-day war to advance their position by attacking their opponents in the party for 'Zionism' (a Soviet-bloc code-word for Jews). This bid for power by General Moczar and his supporters was unsuccessful, but it did lead to a major anti-Jewish purge within the administration and to the emigration of the bulk of Poland's remaining Jews.

In the 1970s this situation began to change and a new willingness to look again at the thorny and difficult problem of Polish-Jewish relations during the Second World War began to develop. This was, indeed, an inevitable consequence of the growth of interest in the Polish-Jewish past which was a feature of these years. The importance of the development of the Jewish community in Poland, which had for nearly 1,000 years been one of the main centres of Jewish life, was increasingly recognised. Departments of Jewish history were set up at the Jagiellonian University, the University of Warsaw and the Catholic University of Lublin. Indeed, interest in the Jewish past became surprisingly widespread.

This interest was partly nostalgic in character. Poland, today, is practically mono-ethnic and mono-religious and there is a genuine sense of loss at the disappearance of the more colourful Poland of the past, with its mixture of religions and nationalities. It did, however, have a deeper character. The experiences of the Solidarity years gave Poles a greater sense of self-esteem. In sharp contrast with the traditional outside view of the Poles as quixotic and impractical political dreamers, in these years Poland astonished the world by its political maturity. A non-violent movement challenged the might of the Soviet Empire for nearly a year and a half, and, though it was finally crushed, it won a great moral victory. Under these conditions, there was a greater willingness to look at the more controversial aspects of the Polish past and to consider again more critically how the Poles had treated the other peoples alongside whom they had lived, above all the Jews and the Ukrainians. A reckoning with the less admirable aspects of the Polish past was, indeed, seen by important sections of the opposition as a necessary part of the creation of the plural society for which they aimed.

In the words of a younger historian, Andrzej Bryk:

> The recent Polish search for the lost history of Polish-Jewish relations is not an abstract intellectual exercise. It is morally legitimate and necessary and long overdue. At stake is Poles choosing between freedom, which requires as full a recognition as possible of history,

and imprisonment as a people desperately committed to historical myths.[6]

His sentiments were echoed by Jerzy Turowicz, the editor of the principal Catholic weekly *Tygodnik Powszechny*:

> ... the dispute about Polish anti-semitism ... is a subject much larger [than the mere question of rooting out the remnants of this ideology] ... It is a dispute ... over the choice of a model for Polish culture, what kind of culture it is, changing, as does any culture, over the ages, and what form it ought to have.[7]

Increasingly, too, particularly among the younger generation, there has been a growing feeling of shame over the events of 1968. At the time, the prevailing mood was that this was merely a settling of accounts among the communist élite and that all the factions fighting for power were equally tainted. By the late 1970s however, the realisation that one of the consequences of those years had been to deprive Poland of most of what remained of its Jewish intelligentsia and that the society had allowed itself to be manipulated by the crude use of anti-semitic slogans led to an increasing feeling of anger. The role of the 1968 crisis in depriving the régime of political legitimacy has, in general, been greatly underestimated.

Another factor stimulating a more critical look at the Polish-Jewish past and, in particular, at Polish-Jewish relations during the Holocaust, was the series of Polish-Jewish historical conferences which began in Columbia in Spring 1983 and culminated in the conference in Jerusalem in February 1988. All points at issue between Poles and Jews were extensively aired and the discussions were often acrimonious, painful and difficult. Perhaps equally important in provoking discussion of these thorny issues was Claude Lanzmann's film *Shoah*. When it was first shown in Paris, it was bitterly attacked by the official press as an anti-Polish provocation, and the Polish government even delivered a note of protest to the French government, which had provided part of the finance for the film. When *Shoah* was finally shown in Poland, as a result of a change of heart by the authorities, reactions were more complex. Most Poles rejected Lanzmann's division of European society during the Holocaust (particularly in Poland) into the murderers, their victims and bystanders, largely unsympathetic to the fate of the Jews. Yet many were shocked by his interviews with Polish peasants living in the vicinity of the death camps, which revealed the persistence in the Polish countryside of crude anti-semitic stereotypes. For Catholics, which, of course, meant the overwhelming majority of Poles, Lanzmann's argument that Nazi anti-semitism was the logical culmination of Christian anti-semitism was also unacceptable. But it, too, forced the re-examination of many strongly-held attitudes.[8]

It was in this climate that Jan Błoński wrote in *Tygodnik Powszechny* on 11 January 1988 his article 'The Poor Poles look at the Ghetto', (reprinted in POLIN, vol. II, pp. 321-36), which sparked off what has certainly been the most profound debate on the implications of the Holocaust in Poland since the Second World War. Błoński's argument is by now well-known. Poles, he claimed, had to accept a degree of responsibility for the mass murder of the Jews. They had not participated in the murder, which had to a considerable extent taken place on Polish soil, but their attitude to it had been characterised by a 'holding back', 'an insufficient effort to resist' and an indifference to Jewish suffering. The failure to act in what were, after all, very difficult conditions was not, however, the central issue. More important was the more distant history:

> If only in the past we had behaved more humanely, had been wiser, more generous, genocide would perhaps have been less imaginable, would probably have been considerably more difficult to carry out, and almost certainly would have met with greater resistance than it did. To put it differently, it would not have met with the indifference and moral turpitude of the society in whose full view it took place.[9]

Błoński employed a powerful analogy:

> We did take the Jews into our home, but we made them live in the cellar. When they wanted to come into the drawing-room, our response was - Yes, but only after you cease to be Jews, when you become 'civilized'. This was the thinking of our most enlightened minds, such as Orzeszkowa and Prus. There were those among the Jews who were ready to adhere to this advice. No sooner did they do this, than we started, in turn, talking of an invasion of Jews, of the danger of their infiltration of Polish society. Then we started to put down conditions, like that stated *expressis verbis* by Dmowski, that we shall accept as Poles only those Jews who are willing to cooperate in the attempts to stem Jewish influence in our society. To put it bluntly, those who are willing to turn against their kith and kin.
>
> Eventually, when we lost our home, and when in its premises the invaders set to murdering Jews, did we show solidarity towards them? How many of us decided that it was none of our business? There were also those (and I leave out of account common criminals) who were secretly pleased that Hitler had solved for us 'the Jewish problem'. We could not even welcome and honour the survivors, even if they were embittered, disorientated and perhaps somewhat tiresome. I repeat: Instead of haggling and justifying ourselves, we should first consider our own faults and weaknesses. This is the moral revolution that is imperative when considering the Polish-

Jewish past. It is only this that can gradually cleanse our desecrated soil.[10]

He concluded with an appeal to the Poles to imitate the way the Catholic Church has repudiated its anti-Jewish past, whose central feature, he argued, was just such a refusal to excuse past wrongs.

> We are familiar with the Church documents in which – already at the time of Pope John XXIII – the relationship between Christians and Jews, or rather, between Christianity and Judaism, was redefined, hopefully for all time. In the Pope's speech as well as in these documents, one aspect is immediately clear. They do not concern themselves with attributing blame, nor with the consideration of reasons (social, economic, intellectual or whatever) that made Christians look upon Jews as enemies and intruders. One thing is stated loud and clear: The Christians of the past and the Church itself were wrong. They had no reason to consider the Jews as a 'damned' nation – the nation responsible for the death of Jesus Christ, and therefore as a nation which should be excluded from the community of nations.[11]

These were strong words and, not surprisingly, they provoked strong reactions, both positive and negative. Indeed perhaps the most typical response was in an article by Janina Walewska, in which she simultaneously agreed and disagreed with Błoński. One of the ironic features of the whole debate is that it was among Catholics, whose Church had been a major factor in the development of pre-war anti-semitism, that the strongest calls for a rethinking of Polish attitudes have been heard, whereas representatives of the communist establishment have indulged in traditional Polish apologetics, which have verged on the anti-semitic. This development is the consequence both of the imperatives of an unpopular régime seeking to justify itself as the defender of the 'national interest' in the eyes of its subjects, and of the change in Catholic thinking on the Jews and Judaism since World War II and, in particular, since the papal encyclical *Nostra aetate*.[12]

The general points of division in the debate are very clear and were, indeed, already sketched out by Błoński in his article. Those who agree with Błoński are at one with him in considering that Polish responsibility consists, above all, of an insufficient concern for the fate of the Jews. As a result, the Jews were not included in what Helen Fein has called the 'universe of obligation', 'that circle of persons towards whom obligations are owed, to whom rules apply and whose injuries call for expiation by the community'.[13] This is regarded as a cause for shame. The Poles, as a group, could not have done much to help the Jews, but by their indifference they condemned them to much lonelier and more solitary deaths than they would otherwise have suffered. This indifference is seen as a direct consequence of pre-war anti-semitism, which is admitted to have been widespread in Poland. Błoński's supporters also stress, like him, the unique character of Jewish suffering during the war, something which has been difficult for the Poles to accept.

One statement of Błoński's from which even his supporters demurred was his claim that the Poles only failed to participate in the mass-murder of the Jews because 'God held back our hand. Yes I do mean God, because if we did not take part in that crime it was because we were still Christian and at the last moment we came to realise what a satanic enterprise it was.'[14] According to Jerzy Turowicz, this 'grave accusation is incorrect and unjust'. 'I strongly contend that – despite everything – the likelihood of our participation in the crime of genocide did not exist. But this is not to say that the problem of a shared guilt does not arise.'[15]

Błoński's protagonists also go less far than some Jewish observers who, bitterly and probably unfairly, accuse the Poles of active collaboration in the Holocaust. At a discussion in Jerusalem on 'Ethical Problems of the Holocaust', one of the questions posed from the floor asked whether the Poles' responsibility lies not 'in their indifference but in the prevalence of religious, national and popular hate. Many people considered the Nazi policies to be an opportunity to remove a national minority which was very embarrassing.'[16]

This question was discussed by one of Błoński's supporters, Teresa Prekerowa. She argued that there were indeed many cases when Jews were denounced to the Nazis by Poles. These 'crimes' she claimed, 'did not, as is sometimes suggested, stem from anti-semitism. Greed was the motive, and anybody sufficiently defenceless could have fallen victim. Nevertheless, the lack of sympathetic interest in the fate of the Jews on the part of the surrounding population facilitated the commission of the crime.'(p. 56) She continued: 'There is similar discredit to Polish society in the existence of the blackmailers and "smalcownicy" (criminal Poles who blackmailed Jews). They lived at the expense of the Jews in hiding, whom they would accost in the vicinity of ghettos and on the streets of towns.'[9]

Responding to the opposition lawyer Władysław Siła-Nowicki who had strongly attacked Błoński and who wrote, 'Those who denounced the Jews to the German authorities were sentenced to death and those sentences were carried out by us while running the risk of death ourselves,' she observed:

That's right, but from when? From September 1943, whereas they started their profitable under-hand dealings the moment ghettos were closed, and that meant in Warsaw from the autumn of 1940. For three years therefore they could continue to operate undeterred. In the last year, 1943–4, in all five blackmailers were put to death in

Warsaw and a few in Kraków and its environs. There is no doubt that fighting them, and in particular spotting and identifying them, was difficult, but, and I repeat the question, could we really 'not do much more?'[17]

Błoński's critics followed the apologetic line already set out and criticized by Błoński in his article. They are concerned that he has blackened the reputation of the Poles. The Poles did all they could to aid the Jews during the war and therefore have no cause to feel guilt or shame. In Siła-Nowicki's words:

> I am proud of my nation's stance in every respect during the period of occupation and in this I include the attitude towards the tragedy of the Jewish nation. Obviously, the attitudes towards the Jews during that period do not give us a particular reason to be proud, but neither are they any grounds for shame, and even less for ignominy. Simply we could have done little more than we actually did.[18]

Polish society was itself in danger of total destruction, or as Siła-Nowicki put it 'both the Jewish and Polish communities were faced with the threat of biological extinction'. The Jewish failure to resist further reduced the opportunities for providing assistance. According to Siła-Nowicki, 'Passive behaviour – seeking security by accepting German orders – was the first and principal obstacle to the possibility of extending help to the Jews.'[19]

This accusation of passivity – important in Poland where the tradition of active resistance to tyranny is highly valued and actively cultivated – was rejected with some heat by Błoński's supporters. Turowicz was at his most magisterial:

> Several million innocent people, including women, children and the old, people who were our neighbours, were murdered before our eyes, on our soil and we were helpless witnesses, unable for the most part to do anything about it. This fact is so horrifying that we cannot ever forget it, nor can we fail to ask ourselves whether this does not still present a moral challenge to us. And may I suggest that it is at least insensitive – to avoid a stronger term – to accuse the Jews of being passive when we consider their fate.[20]

Teresa Prekerowa pointed out that the underground functioning of political parties, a clandestine press, education and cultural activities were large-scale phenomena in the ghettos and can only be seen as a form of resistance. She also points out that most of Polish society was also 'passive' and that flight to the 'Aryan' side was fraught with danger for Jews.[21]

In the eyes of Błoński's critics, the responsibility of the Western allies and of Jews in the west for failing to prevent the mass murder of the Jews was much greater than that of the Poles, a view rejected by his adherents as irrelevant to Polish moral responsibility. In addition, the Jews had been a privileged group in Poland before the war. Thus talk of anti-semitism at that time is greatly exaggerated.[22]

What is really at issue in this debate is what Zygmunt Bauman has called the problem of the 'rationality of evil'. The process of mass murder rested on persuading all involved, both victims or bystanders, that it was more sensible to cooperate than to resist, whether by false claims that what was involved was merely resettlement, by holding out the hope that some would survive and by stressing the penalties for non-cooperation.

> By and large, the rulers can count on rationality being on their side. The Nazi rulers twisted the stakes of the game so that the rationality of survival would render all other motives of human action irrational. Inside the Nazi-made, unreal and inhuman world, reason was the enemy of morality. Logic required consent to crime. Rational defence of one's survival called for non-resistance to the other's destruction. This rationality pitched the sufferers against each other and obliterated their joint humanity. This rationality absolved them from immorality. Having reduced human life to the calculus of survival, this rationality robbed human life of humanity.[23]

This is why, as Jerzy Turowicz has observed, the argument between the two sides is conducted on 'different planes'.[24] In Bauman's words:

> Siła-Nowicki and Błoński do not argue with, but past, each other. Błoński wrote of the moral significance of the Holocaust, Siła-Nowicki responded with an investigation of the rationality of self-preservation. What he failed to notice was the ethical meaning of the very form such rationality took (or, rather, was forced to assume): the very fact that the Nazi régime set the logic of survival against the moral duty (as a value superior to ethics) was simultaneously the secret of the technical success of the mass murder, one of the most sinister horrors of the event called the 'Holocaust', and the most venomous of its consequences . . .
>
> As far as the substantive argument goes, Siła-Nowicki argues past Błoński's point. Błoński speaks of *moral* shame, not of the shame which in our rational world we use to associate with a botched job or inefficient work. No one calls in question the earnestness and industry of Polish resistance; no one doubts that not much more could *practically* have been done without incalculable cost. This does not mean, however, that moral qualms can be put to sleep. Neither does it mean that a moral person's feeling of shame is unfounded

(even if, as could be claimed, it is 'irrational'). To this feeling of shame – our ultimate victory over the pernicious legacy of the Holocaust – the most scrupulous and historically accurate computations of the numbers of those who 'could' and those who 'could not' help, of those who 'could' and those who 'could not' be helped, are irrelevant.[26]

In fact, as Bauman correctly states, the issue is not

whether the Poles should feel ashamed or whether they should feel proud of themselves. The issue is that only the liberating feeling of shame – the recovery of the moral significance of the joint historical experience – may once and for all exorcise the spectre of the Holocaust, which continues to haunt not only Polish-Jewish relations, but also the ethical self-identity of the Poles and the Jews alike, to this very day. The choice is not between shame and pride. The choice is between the pride of morally purifying shame, and the shame of morally devastating pride.

What perhaps stops Wladyslaw Siła-Nowicki (for all I know of him, a person of the highest ethical standards) from admitting the moral need of shame, is his conviction that shame, rather than ennobling and purifying, is equivalent to an admission of a 'material guilt' of sorts. That it means confessing to a sinful deed, or worse still – to a base aspect, or a wicked streak in the national character. I do not agree. It was the inhuman world created by a homicidal tyranny which dehumanised its victims, pressing them to use the logic of self-preservation as absolution for moral insensitivity and inaction. No one can be proclaimed guilty for the sheer fact of breaking down under such pressure. Yet no one can be excused from moral self-deprecation for such surrender. And only when feeling ashamed for one's weakness, can one finally shatter the mental prison which has outlived its builders and guards until today.[27]

It is this, too, which gives to the whole controversy a larger dimension. It is not primarily about Polish-Jewish relations, the behaviour of the Poles during the war or even the type of society which one should aim to create in Poland. It is about how and in what conditions resistance can be offered to an all-powerful tyranny. It is too early to speak in any meaningful way of a 'Jewish response' to Błoński's article and the ensuing controversy. Yet certainly among those Jews involved in Polish-Jewish dialogue the article has been seen as embodying a fundamental change in Polish attitudes. This was clearly reflected in the discussions in Jerusalem:

According to Rafael Scharf:

I read Błoński's article, for the first time, with growing excitement and quickened pulse. At one point he makes reference to one of the speakers at the Conference in Oxford in 1984, whose words, he said, inspired him to ponder these matters. From the words quoted by him it was clear that he was referring to me. I was startled and also moved to see how one word, a sentence, a thought can strike another man's mind, can germinate there and bear fruit beyond expectation.

I was talking then, at least that is how Błoński understood it, to the effect that we Jews no longer expected anything from the Poles but the admission that they have been, in some way, at fault. For many years we listened, waited for a sign – but voice came there none. In the end, I had thought, we would be straining our ears in vain. But now, at last – we hear the voice of Błoński...

More than a year has passed since Błoński's voice sounded. I would like to assure all those who feared that it would have a harmful effect on Poland, that quite the opposite has occurred. His article is seen, in itself, as a rehabilitation of sorts. I myself, in many instances, when, paradoxically and undeservedly, I am put in the role of an 'advocatus Poloniae', recall this article and some of those which followed. I maintain that one can no longer speak loosely about the Poles' opinion on the subject without taking into consideration these new voices, which save the reputation of Poland.[28]

Viktor Erlich, son of the Bundist leader Henryk Erlich, murdered by Stalin in 1941, observed:

Today, in the twentieth century, Polish-Jewish relations have taken on the character of a vicious circle. Amongst many Jews, a feeling of distrust was born in relation to the Poles as a result of official or pogrom Polish anti-semitism. This was the cause of behaviour which could be described as anti-Polish, in conditions of a national catastrophe. Those acts, in turn, added oil to the fire, and fanned deeply-rooted and virulent prejudices. The historical significance of the discussion which was initiated by Jan Błoński's article, a discussion which we are continuing today, is dependent precisely on the fact that remarks such as those made by Jan Błoński, Ewa Berberiusz, and Jerzy Turowicz help us to find a way out of that vicious circle. They help us to find the conditions for a Polish-Jewish dialogue devoid of prejudice and misunderstandings, of irresponsible generalities and self-defensive denials, for a dialogue characterised by its mutual respect and, what is more, respect for what are at times painful facts. We have started that dialogue late, and the path is a long one. Perhaps, however, by a joint effort we will succeed in fulfilling our common duty – and once again I quote Jan Błoński – to look at our past in truth.[29]

In addition, partly in response to the belief that Polish attitudes now recognise more sensitively the nature of the Jewish tragedy during World War II, and partly, too, as the trauma of the Holocaust diminishes slightly with the passage of time, there has emerged a more balanced attitude on the Jewish side to the awful moral dilemmas of those years.

It was Yisrael Gutman who stated:

> Sometimes I hear Jews accusing the Poles of deliberately not helping them even though they could have done so. Such observations are expressions of pain, which eclipse a sensible attitude. More could certainly have been done to save Jews, but the Poles in the conditions of the occupation could not have fundamentally changed the fate of the Jews. The Allies could have perhaps done so, but even that is not certain in the final phases of the murderers' insanity. I shall permit myself to say more – there is no moral imperative which demands that a normal mortal should risk his life and that of his family to save his neighbour. Are we capable of imagining the agony of fear of an individual, a family, which selflessly and voluntarily, only due to an inner human impulse, bring into their home someone threatened with death. Are we capable of understanding the pressure of those fears when a fugitive had to be kept out of sight of neighbours and relations, when a cough of a sick person dared not be heard outside and those hiding the fugitive lived in an unending fear, when all that was needed was one house-search for both the hider and the hidden to have an end put to their lives? The Poles should be proud that they had so many just lights, of whom Ringelblum spoke, who are the real heroes of the deluge. And we can never do enough to thank these rare people. But by force of events, such a willingness to sacrifice could have been only a marginal phenomenon.[30]

He further observed poignantly: 'Once as a young Zionist, I believed that we Jews would never harm another nation, others who lived amongst us, that the lesson of history which the Diaspora taught us would suffice. Today I know I was naïve and that explains and teaches much.'[31]

Similarly, a recent issue of the Jewish Anti-Defamation League's quarterly journal *Dimensions* was entitled 'Was there "Another Europe"?' and was devoted to the people who willingly risked death during the Holocaust to rescue nearly 200,000 Jews. According to Dr Dennis Klein, Director of the ADL's International Center for Holocaust Studies, in an implicit rejection of Claude Lanzmann's views:

> A desire is growing to understand how and why some people defied anti-semitic mandates or resisted the social pressures to conform to them ... [There is] impatience with dividing Europe eternally into

perpetrators, victims and bystanders . . . Even if resisters and rescuers were numerically marginal, don't their actions bear a historical and moral significance beyond their numbers?[32]

There has also been an increasing realisation, similar to that on the Polish side, that what is involved in this discussion is not primarily a Polish-Jewish argument, but something much more fundamental. In Rafael Scharf's words:

> With the passage of time it will become clear that the agenda is not about us alone; that our debate and controversy is merely incidental to something bigger and more comprehensive. What is at issue here is a great, common cause of universal significance. The extermination of the Jews on Polish territory was a crucial event in history, marking the crisis of Christianity and the crisis of our civilisation (some people regard these concepts as synonymous, but fortunately this is not so). Those events cannot be forgotten or ignored, they will weigh upon the future generations for all time.
> What lesson man will draw from this, how will he face up to it, conscious of the enormity of evil which he is capable of perpetrating; how will he renew his faith in the basic moral values in a world of which, in Adorno's words, 'we cannot be too much afraid' and where there exist instruments of destruction which put even the gas-chambers in shadow. On answers to these questions hang all our tomorrows.[33]

Voices have also been raised criticising what has been seen as the excessive Jewish preoccupation with the Holocaust. At the international Holocaust conference 'Remembering for the Future' the Chief Rabbi of the United Kingdom, Lord Jakobovits, remarked:

> I have some doubts about the sanctification of the Holocaust as a cardinal doctrine in contemporary Jewish thought and teaching. I respect the widely-held view to the contrary, but I still wonder whether it can be accepted as authentically Jewish, or even as conducive to healing the wounds inflicted on the morale and spirit of our people . . .
> The Holocaust and its victims, together with their historic legacy, must of course be remembered for ever with supreme reverence. I also recognise that the Holocaust will remain a major factor both haunting and galvanising Jewish life for a long time to come. Indeed – I believe, contrary to the opinion of Ben Gurion and others – that the State of Israel would never have emerged when it did, were it

not for the desperate pressures and superhuman Jewish energies generated by the Holocaust.

But at the same time we must beware against nurturing and breeding a Holocaust mentality of morose despondency among our people, especially our youth . . .[34]

In Jerusalem, Błoński correctly pointed out that the controversy was not primarily about facts. 'There may have been differences over the facts, but this divergence [between Polish attitudes and those outside Poland] was too great to be explained on this basis. It was rather in the understanding of the facts that the differences lay . . .'[35] Yet paradoxically, the articulation of the moral problems at the centre of the controversy has made possible a much more effective analysis of the factual problems involved. The study of the subject of Polish-Jewish relations during the Second World War can thus become less the field for emotional exchanges and be advanced by the application of the traditional skills and techniques of the historian. This was the approach of Mrs Prekerowa, who, in an important article, manages to shed considerable light on the vexed questions of how many Jews were saved in Poland during the war (40–60,000 according to her) and how many Poles were involved in hiding and aiding Jews (1-2.5 per cent of the adult population).[36] One may dispute the figures, but her approach is certainly one of the paths we need to follow. A similar set of scholarly imperatives was suggested at Jerusalem by a younger historian, Jan Tomasz Gross.

The articulation of the central moral problems also enables us to move on to another plane in our examination of the Holocaust in Poland and elsewhere. One does not have to share the Chief Rabbi's theological predilections to agree with him that too much attention has perhaps been devoted to the process of mass murder and not enough to what was destroyed. What was at issue here was not only the terrible crime of the cold-blooded murder of 6 million innocent men, women and children but the destruction of a whole civilisation, the civilisation of East European Jewry. At the Jerusalem conference, Professor Gierowski observed that 'what we are undertaking at the moment is an attempt to save what can still be saved'. This attempt to preserve the memory and values of the 'murdered Jewish nation' to use the phrase of the poet Yitshak Katzenelson, who himself died in Auschwitz, unites both Poles and Jews. It is an investigation of our common Polish-Jewish past, with all its good and bad sides. Its recovery will not be an easy task – the last words should perhaps be left to the poet Jerzy Ficowski:

> I did not manage to save
> a single life
> I did not know how to stop

> a single bullet
> and I wander round cemeteries
> which are not there
> I look for words
> which are not there
> I run
>
> to help where no one called
> to rescue after the event
>
> I want to be on time
> even if I am too late
>
> The first poem in his
'A Reading of Ashes'

NOTES

1 Review of Irena Hurwic-Nowakowska, *A Social Analysis of Postwar Polish Jewry*, in *POLIN. A Journal of Polish-Jewish Studies*, vol.III, pp. 440–1.
2 Ibid, p. 441.
3 See, for instance, Andrzejewski's contribution to *Martwa Fala* (Warsaw, 1947) or Ossowski's response to the Kielce pogrom.
4 L. Dobroszycki, 'Restoring Jewish Life in Post-war Poland', *Soviet Jewish Affairs* 2 (1973), p. 59.
5 On this see W. Bartoszewski's essay in this issue, pp. 243–54.
6 A. Bryk, 'Polish-Jewish Relations during the Holocaust: The Hidden Complex of the Polish Mind', Paper presented at the International Conference on the History and Culture of Polish Jews, Jerusalem, February 1988.
7 'Ethical Problems of the Holocaust in Poland. Discussion held at the International Conference on the History and Culture of Polish Jewry in Jerusalem on Monday 2 February 1988', Reprinted in ed. A. Polonsky, '"My Brother's Keeper?" Recent Polish debates about the Holocaust,' to be published London, 1989, p. 240. Henceforth this discussion is cited as 'Ethical Problems of the Holocaust in Poland . . .'
8 On the debate about *Shoah*, see Władysław T. Bartoszewski, 'Jews as a Polish Problem,' *POLIN*, vol. II, pp. 391–403.
9 *POLIN*, vol. II, p. 331.
10 Ibid., pp. 330–1.
11 Ibid., p. 329.
12 The best account of the debate is given by W.T. Bartoszewski in *Polish-Jewish Relations: A Current Debate among Polish Catholics*, Institute of Jewish Affairs Research Report no.7, October 1987. It is also sensitively discussed by Zygmunt Bauman in 'On immoral reason and illogical morality', *POLIN*, vol. III, pp. 294–30. Janina Walewska's article 'W jakimś sensie jestem antysemitką' was printed in *Tygodnik Powszechny*, 5 April 1987.
13 Helen Fein, *Accounting for Genocide. National Responses and Jewish Victimization during the Holocaust* (Chicago, 1984), 33,
14 Błoński, p. 332.
15 'Ethical problems of the Holocaust', p. 114.
16 Ibid., pp.244–5.

17 T. Prekorowa, '"Sprawiedliwi" i "bierni",' *Tygodnik Powszechny*, 29 March 1987.
18 W. Siła-Nowicki, 'Janowi Błońskiemu w odpowiedzi,' *Tygodnik Powszechny*, 1987.
19 Ibid.
20 J. Turowicz, 'Racje polskie i racje żydowskie,' *Tygodnik Powszechny*, 5 April 1987.
21 T. Prekerowa, '"Sprawiedliwi" i "bierni".'
22 This point was strongly made by Siła-Nowicki.
23 Z. Bauman, 'On immoral reason and illogical morality', p. 296.
24 'Ethical problems of the Holocaust', p. 112.
25 Z. Bauman, 'On immoral reason and illogical morality', p. 296-8.
26 Ibid.
27 'Ethical problems of the Holocaust . . .', pp. 204-5.
28 Ibid., pp. 212-13.
29 Ibid., p. 216.
30 Ibid., p. 220.
31 *Dimensions. A Journal of Holocaust Studies*, vol. 3, no.3, Summer 1988.
32 'Ethical problems of the Holocaust . . .' p. 202.
33 I. Jakobovits, 'Some personal, theological and religious responses to the Holocaust' in 'Remembering for the Future'. Papers presented at an International Scholars' Conference held in Oxford, 10-13 July 1988, supplementary vol. , pp. 175-6.
34 'Ethical problems of the Holocaust . . .', p. 190.
35 '"Sprawiedliwi" i "bierni".'

THE FOUNDING OF THE ALL-POLISH ANTI-RACIST LEAGUE IN 1946

Władysław Bartoszewski

There are no accounts in histories of Poland after the Second World War of the All-Polish Anti-Racist League, founded in 1946. There are also few accounts of Jewish society in Poland after the Second World War. To date, it is a waste of time to search scholarly works for even a brief mention of the League, its origins and public activities, or the contents of the League's publication *Prawo Człowieka* [The Right of Man]. The terrible experience of the war years and the dreadful crime committed against Polish Jews – and against Jews from other European countries in Nazi extermination centres on Polish soil – have rather pushed actions and phenomena which were, in a sense, marginal to the whole picture, to one side. In fact, brief references and occasional reports did appear as early as 1945 and 1946–47 in the Polish and Jewish press about the activities of the Council for Aid to the Jews (its code name was *Żegota*) during the recent German occupation.[1] There were assessments of both the practical and moral significance of this area of close wartime co-operation between Poles and Jews of various political outlooks to help people in mortal danger, and also of its importance in influencing public opinion in Poland. Although the All-Polish Anti-Racist League was *sui generis* an ideological continuation of the council's work, so far scholars have not been interested in its existence, and this is despite the significance, even dramatic significance of the time when the League was established – ten months after the end of the Second World War and three and a half months before the Kielce atrocity! – for people whose consciousness had been shaped by the experience of the Holocaust period.

Even before the start of the Soviet Army's January offensive in 1945, the Central Committee of Polish Jews (established in Lublin on 4 November 1944) had begun since July 1944, to register those Jews who had survived in territories freed from the Germans which were now part of the Polish state. This registration, continued in 1945–46 throughout the whole of People's Poland, could not provide a full and accurate picture. Registration was voluntary; some of the people to whom the Nazi Nuremberg

Laws had applied did not feel Jewish enough to want to register with Jewish institutions; furthermore, mass migration made it difficult to discover exactly how many Jews were on Polish soil at a specific time between 1944 and 1946. Professor Krystyna Kersten, the leading expert on the problems of migration during this period, accepts the Central Committee of Polish Jews' estimate for January 1946 of about 100,000 Jews.[2] This refers, however, to the period before the mass migration of Polish citizens, including Polish Jews, from the old and new territories of the USSR. At the same time as these were arriving in Poland from the East and also from the West, other Jews were leaving Poland for the West or Palestine. We know that in 1945 and 1946 tens of thousands of Jews left Poland. In July 1946, after the formal completion of the resettlement programme from the USSR, the number of Jews in Poland was 245,000.[3] However, they were still leaving the country throughout this period. An official Jewish Agency Emigration Bureau continued to function in Poland until autumn 1948, organising emigration to Palestine and then to the new state of Israel.

The acute political tension in Poland from 1944–48 is well-known, and was characterised by incidents commonly found in a state of civil war. Acts of repression, violence and terror, mass arrests, deportations (until summer 1945), bloody confrontations claiming thousands of dead and injured, were an everyday occurrence, particularly in the first year. Through ruthless political and police methods, a new political order and system was introduced, which was rejected by a significant part of society. The problem of whether to resist the new system – actively or passively – or to adapt to it was undoubtedly the major political issue facing many Poles. Generally speaking, the political result of the Second World War came as a great shock not only to active participants in the struggle for independence and the social groups most closely associated with them, but also to millions of others of all generations.

The post-war period should have begun a new epoch in Polish-Jewish relations. The antagonism which had undoubtedly existed before 1939, the anti-semitism fanned from 1934 especially by political groups with fascist tendencies (especially by the illegal National Radical Camp – *ONR*), ought – as one might have imagined – to have been largely eliminated. The tragedy of the genocide of the Jews was, after all, a great psychological shock for many Poles. The Nazis were a common enemy and their administration and police forces were universally hated. The experiences of the German occupation had demonstrated that in Poland, as everywhere in occupied Europe, people ready to risk their lives to save others were only a minority. However, those Jews who did manage to survive on Polish territory usually did so with the help of Poles, even when, at the same time, other Poles who were prepared to cooperate criminally with the occupier represented a grave threat to them.

Apart from this ethical reason, from a practical view the few Jews in Poland, survivors of a previously large society, ought not to have led to any significant hostile attitudes, ideas and certainly not actions. Unfortunately, this is exactly what did happen. After the Second World War, the stereotype of the communist Jew – advanced by the pre-war parties and right-wing political groups, and also to a certain extent by Church circles – was unexpectedly and spectacularly reinforced by the public activity of those Jewish communists who played an important role in the security and propaganda apparatus, at a time when the majority of Polish society was inclined to see this activity as pursued in the direct interests of the USSR. There was a dangerous, and morally absolutely unacceptable tendency to blame the Jews in Poland *en masse* for the complete suppression of human rights by the new authorities and for the misfortune of the nation which felt it had lost its independence, despite nominally winning the war against Germany as one of the Allies. It should be added that similar generalisations regarding members of the security apparatus who were *not* Jewish were notable for their absence.

Almost 40 years after the war, an outstanding Polish political commentator wrote as follows under the pseudonym Abel Kainer in his essay 'The Jews and Communism', in the independent quarterly *Krytyka*, no.15 (Warsaw, 1983):

> In the public mind the Jewish member of the Security Forces symbolizes the rôle of the Jews in the first decade of the Polish People's Republic. Several directors in the Ministry of Public Security (*MBP*) under Bierut and Gomułka were actually Jews or of Jewish extraction. This is an inescapable fact, which is little-known in the West, and readily admitted by Jews in Poland ... Both parties are more willing to talk about Stalin's anti-semitism (the doctors' plot etc). The apparatus of terror in Poland functioned in a similar way to that of other communist countries in Europe and beyond. Instead of looking for evidence to prove that Jews organised this dreadful terror, what needs to be clarified is why Jews, or Poles of Jewish extraction, were employed. The obvious answer is ... the political police needed people they could depend on most and this meant they preferred pre-war communists, which included many Jews and people of Jewish extraction. But in addition, as there were not very many old and trusted comrades around, anyone who could be counted on to display one hundred per cent loyalty was considered suitable. Someone, therefore, who was largely on his own, without the support of family or neighbours: someone attracted by socialism who wanted to make the party his home.

And further:

> The Jews had therefore something to fear. But their behaviour only served to confirm for those anti-semites in organised groups how right they had been in their conflict with the Jews, and to convince who knows how many others of the same. This, in turn, made the Jews even more dependent on the communists.

Professor Krystyna Kersten believes the following:

> In the conditions prevailing in Poland after the war, Polish-Jewish antagonism changed its character and gave way to an intensification of the mutual sense of a strong and growing threat. The Jews' lack of security grew psychologically as well as physically. This had some foundation and it is not really important to what extent awareness of hostility or even downright hatred by Polish society was commensurable with actual aggression. The figures recorded in Western literature of thousands of victims of murder and pogroms in their thousands are exaggerated, unless one applies the criteria of Nuremberg – that of descent – and includes all those who perished not because they were Jews but as defenders of the new order who had Jewish ancestors. But even if they are reduced by a half, or by two-thirds, the phenomenon of feeling threatened because one was a Jew remains and every event which left a deep impression on the minds of those who survived the Holocaust was liable to be generalised, contributing towards an image of Polish society as a whole. In the source material and in people's memoirs one finds descriptions of hostile behaviour, to which an anti-semitic character is not always deservedly ascribed. There were several motives contributing to this behaviour and the fact that the victim was a Jew or recognised as a Jew was one, but often not the only, cause of aggression.[4]

According to the figures of the Central Committee of Polish Jews, 150 Jews perished at the hands of Poles during the first quarter of 1945, and 81 during the next four to five months. During spring and summer 1945, minor anti-Jewish excesses and incidents were noted in Radom, Miechów, Chrzanów and Rabka, and on a larger scale, though also without actual injuries, in Kraków on 11 August 1945. These incidents were raised publicly by the Central Committee of Polish Jews. Its president, Emil Sommerstein, spoke, among other things, about the repeated murder of Jews at the so-called National Council for the Homeland (*KRN*), the institution acting as an interim parliament at the time, to which he was a deputy.

Both in the Polish press and on the radio at that time there was no lack of voices to oppose these tragic incidents, and the recent suffering and extermination of Jewish society in Poland were also mentioned. Articles, memoirs and references to the subject can be found in the first post-war dailies *Robotnik, Dziennik Ludowy, Gazeta Ludowa, Kurier Codzienny*, in the weeklies *Nowa Epoka, Odrodzenie*, and particularly in the Kraków *Tygodnik Powszechny*. The active Jewish Central Historical Commission, as well as some Provincial Jewish Historical Commissions, produced a series of valuable pamphlets and books as early as 1946. Particularly worth mentioning is the publication 'On the third anniversary of the destruction of the Kraków ghetto (13.III.1943–13.III.1946)', published in Kraków in the first half of 1946. This included Tadeusz Seweryn's then unique account of aid to Jews in Kraków during the occupation, organised and led by the parties and organisations of the 'London' underground which were indiscriminately condemned after the war.

It was then that an initiative was taken during the first weeks of 1946 by former members of the occupation Council for Aid to the Jews. This was to establish a loosely structured, all-Polish society to discuss the problem of the moral and political danger for Poland and the Poles of actions dictated by anti-semitic views and anti-Jewish prejudices, whatever their causes. The participants in these private discussions (Ferdynand Marek Arczyński, Adolf Berman, Tadeusz Rek, Władysław Bartoszewski) were well aware of the complexities of the political situation in Poland. Many worthy participants in the struggle for independence during the occupation, as well as people with a clear democratic past, were being denied the chance to enter public life. On the other hand, many people taking the lead in the official political hierarchy had little public prestige or were even complete strangers to the general public. The communist Polish Workers' Party, as well as the active section of the Polish Socialist Party and Peasants' Movement (*Stronnictwo Ludowe*), were waging an intense political struggle against the Polish Peasant Party (*Polskie Stronnictwo Ludowe*) and Labour Movement, which were then undoubtedly supported by most Poles.

Former members of the Council for Aid to the Jews held different political views and filled various positions in Polish public life. They were, however, unanimous in recognising the importance of using their own authority and enlisting the public support of others of importance in the struggle against the degrading chauvinism in Poland, against manifestations of national, religious and racial hatred, and, above all, against all unsympathetic or hostile attitudes towards Jews who had survived. After a few weeks' preparation a quite representative group met in Warsaw on 30 March 1946. Its members included intellectuals with no political affiliations, as well as members of the *PPS*, the Democratic Movement, the *PSL*, the Labour Movement and Dr Adolf Berman – vice-president of the Central Committee of Polish Jews and Jan Wesołowski, a member of the

PPR. At the beginning of April 1946 a pamphlet was published and appeals appeared in many national and local dailies, calling for the establishment of an Organisation Committee for the All-Polish Anti-Racist League:

> On 30 March 1946 a group of social and political activists, representing all circles of Polish social and political thought, prompted by deep moral feelings and sharing the conviction that the interests of the Polish nation required nationwide action in the struggle against racism, have established an Organisational Committee for the All-Polish Anti-Racist League, based in Warsaw.
>
> The Committee unanimously appointed an Interim Presidium for the League on 2 April 1946 consisting of the following members:
>
> President – Deputy Mgr Juliusz Górecki
> 1st Vice-President – the lawyer Tadeusz Rek
> 2nd Vice-President – Deputy Dr Adolf Berman
> General Secretary – Deputy Marek Arczyński
> Deputy – Deputy Mgr Stanisław Dobrowolski – also director of the League's Regional-Organisational Section
> Treasurer – Irena Sendlerowa
> Members of the Presidium:
> Deputy Prof. Dr Kazimierz Kumaniecki – also director of the League's Educational Section
> Editor Władysław Bartoszewski – director of the League's Press-propaganda section
> Jan Wesołowski – director of the League's Youth Section
> The director of the League's Foreign Section is Józef Gójski.

The majority (i.e. six) of the presidium of the League was made up of people who belonged during the occupation to the organisers or most energetic members of the Council for Aid to the Jews in Warsaw and Kraków (in alphabetical order: Arczyński, Bartoszewski, Berman, Dobrowolski, Rek, Sendlerowa). The President of the League, Mgr Juliusz Górecki, a socialist of the older generation, was a journalist and man of letters, who had spent the occupation in Warsaw. Prof. Kazimierz Kumaniecki, then a deputy for the Labour Movement to the National Council for the Homeland, a well-known classical philologist and a professor at the University of Warsaw, had been active during the occupation in the independent underground, was an officer of the *AK*, and a participant in the anti-Nazi psychological diversion action known as Action 'N'. Jan Wesołowski was a cultural worker in Warsaw's amateur theatre, whose views brought him close to the communist movement;

during the occupation he had taken part in Warsaw in actions on behalf of the Jews. Finally, Józef Gójski, a member of the Union of Rural Youth (*Wici*) and *PSL* activist, had spent the Second World War in Switzerland.

The following were soon co-opted onto the above directing body: *KRN* deputy Henryk Wyrzykowski of the People's Movement; Prof. Dr Olgierd Górka from the Democratic Movement and the editor Michał Pankiewicz of the *PPS*.

The activities of the All-Polish Anti-Racist League were to be based on the following programme (quoted also in a condensed report of the League's proposed activities in the *PPS* paper *Robotnik* on 14 April 1946):

> The whole of the evil and barbarity of Nazism can be summed up in the slogan: racism, anti-semitism, pogrom. Here, writ large, was all that is worst in man, everything expressing crime and darkness and depriving human society of its right to live, simply because it is alive.
>
> Under this banner, man's lowest instincts take precedence over a thousand years of Christian spiritual civilization. The degradation of humanity, the numbing of man's sensitivity to the pain and suffering of his neighbour, the corrupting of human conscience – this is the work and sin of racism. The fight against this evil in Poland is not only the concern of a handful of our Jewish fellow-citizens: the fight against evil is the concern of man, of every man, and is a question of the nation's moral honour.
>
> Racism and anti-semitism cast a shadow over Poland and on her good name in the eyes of the world.
>
> The most important task now in Poland is the reconstruction of social and economic life, destroyed by the Germans. No less crucial is the need to rebuild the spirit of the nation, to educate the people in the future in the spirit of brotherhood. In this momentous work we should follow the ideas of Kościuszko and Mickiewicz, Czacki and Lelewel, Orzeszkowa and Konopnicka, Żeromski and Strug. We shall follow the great truths of humanism and humanity. An example to us should be the all-Polish action of the Council for Aid to the Jews which led the way in helping the victims of racism and anti-semitism during the occupation, when responsible people from all sections of society, the intelligentsia, workers and peasants, whatever their political affiliations, socialists and populists, members of the *PPR* and *SD*, Catholics and free thinkers, rushed to help the victims of racism. In the name of human conscience, in the name of Polish culture and the vital interests of the state, this work is being continued by the All-Polish Anti-Racist League.

On 11 and 12 April 1946, the official representatives of the state authorities in Poland at the time, the President of the *KRN* and the premier, received a delegation of members from 'the all-Polish Council for Aid to the Jews active during the occupation and of members of the presidium of the recently founded Anti-Racist League' (*Robotnik* 1946, no. 102, 12 April) and publicly expressed their support for the League's programme of action.

The establishment of the Anti-Racist League was noted sympathetically in the American, British and French press. An article appeared on 2 May 1946 in the Paris weekly *Fraternité*, the journal of the 'Mouvement National Contre Racisme', entitled 'The Polish battle against racism'.

In Polish domestic politics the newly-founded League was one of very few organisations in which members and activists of the *PSL* (Mikołajczyk's party) were represented, alongside members of political parties to which the *PSL* were decidedly opposed. The first public meeting organised by the League in summer 1946, in Warsaw's largest hall, 'Roma', was also attended by representatives of all political parties then operating legally in Poland. The lawyer Stefan Korboński, the president of the Warsaw Committee of the *PSL*, spoke on behalf of his party. He saw the aims of the League as a continuation of the idea of the pre-war League for the Defence of the Rights of Man and the Citizen, and stressed the need for comprehensive action against hatred and discrimination on the basis of nationalism, race, ideology or politics.

The newly-founded League aroused some interest in intellectual circles in Łódź and Kraków, two important metropolitan academic centres. In Łódź, a local branch of the League was immediately established and led by Henryk Wyrzykowski, an *SL* (People's Movement) deputy.

In late spring and summer 1946, the League's Press and Propaganda Section began work on a journal for the League which was intended to be a monthly. It was called *Prawo Człowieka*, linking it to the recent tradition of defending human rights. The Editor-in-Chief was Prof. Olgierd Górka, a journalist, political activist and historian, before the war at the Jan Kazimierz University in Lwów, a specialist in 17th-century Polish history. Professor Górka (b.1887) had been general secretary of the Institute of Eastern Affairs and director of the School of East European Affairs from 1931 until the outbreak of the Second World War. During the war he was a senior official in the Polish government in London, the head of the Nationalities section in the Ministry of Internal Affairs and, after his return to Poland (1946–47), Director of the Bureau of Jewish Affairs in the Warsaw Ministry of Foreign Affairs.[5]

Even before the first issue of *Prawo Człowieka*, dated 15 September 1946 appeared, public opinion was shocked to hear of the brutal murder of over forty Jews, including women and children, at Kielce. The crowd included a number of armed officials of the communist Civil Militia and other state organs (e.g. prison guards and the Railway Guard Service), who played a significant rôle in the murder. Some people outside Kielce – in Piekuszowo, Herby, Koniecpol and Chmielnik – were also murdered the same day, so that the number of dead later turned out to be greater. This crime, unprecedented on Polish soil, besides protests from intellectuals and others in society, brought an immediate public reaction from the All-Polish Anti-Racist League. The League's protest of July 1946 was distributed in the shape of leaflets and posters – original copies have been preserved in some public archives in Poland – and was published in some newspapers. It was also reproduced and displayed prominently in the first issue of the monthly *Prawo Człowieka*:

POLES!
There has been a terrible incident in Poland, an atrocity!
A pogrom in Kielce!
A bestial crowd, incited by defamatory propaganda, in mad racial hatred has murdered and tortured 40 innocent people. This pogrom, UNPRECEDENTED IN OUR HISTORY, shames us all, every Pole and Christian, the whole of Poland! At a time when even the greatest German criminals are trying to explain away the murder of the Jews by their obedience to Hitler and Himmler, here in our midst indigenous executors of their will continue to act.

Despicable, ridiculous and slanderous lies concerning the abduction of Christian children are now being spread by the enemies of Poland in our cities and towns to incite people to murder and plunder.

To our shame, Poles also are involved and are repeating the abominable crimes of the tsarist 'black hundreds', Nazi Gestapo and SS cut-throats. Their followers are the most ignorant mob, the most despicable scum.

TO THE POLISH NATION!
Are you going to allow the forces of darkness and barbarity to prevail?!

Are you going to allow the minds of Poles and Christians, the minds of Polish youth and Polish children, to be poisoned by Nazism, racism, and anti-semitism?!

Are you going to consent to the name of Poland being put to shame before the world by pogroms, murders, robbery and the violence of criminals murdering Jews?!

POLES! Workers! Peasants!
      Polish Intelligentsia!
In the name of Christian ideals,
In the name of human conscience,

In the name of national honour,

we appeal to you to take action and fight these crimes! Take action to oppose despicable lies, slander and incitement to murder and robbery!

Remember that saying and doing nothing are acquiescence in crime!

To destroy the Nazi anti-semitic disease, we must declare the RIGHT of every man to a FREE LIFE, we must declare the eternal IDEALS OF MORALITY AND HUMANITY!

Let us all struggle for the THE GOOD OF THE POLISH SPIRIT, for the vital INTERESTS OF OUR NATION!

WE APPEAL TO ALL THAT IS GOOD, NOBLE AND JUST IN EVERY POLE!

The All-Polish Anti-Racist League

General Secretary   President of the League Central Council
Deputy MAREK ARCZYŃSKI   Deputy JULIUSZ GÓRECKI
Ed. Wł. BARTOSZEWSKI, Minister BOBROWSKI, Helena BOGUSZEWSKA, Prof. CZARTKOWSKI, Pro-dean Pharm. Dept. Univ. of Łódź, Deputy Mgr St. DOBROWOLSKI, Dr R. FLESZAROWA, Prof. Dr W. GOETEL, Prof. Dr. O. GÓRKA, Eng. Deputy E. HIŻOWA, Zofia HRYNIEWICZOWA, Jerzy KORNACKI, Prof. K. KUMANIECKI, Prof. Dr M. MICHAŁOWICZ, Ed. M. PANKIEWICZ, League Vice-pres. in Łódź Fr. PATYNOWSKI, T. REK, Dir. Town Council of Social Welfare, I. SENDLEROWA, Deputy H. WYRZYKOWSKI, League Pres. in Łódź J. ŻUKOWSKI, Prof. Łódź University.

WARSAW – KRAKÓW – ŁÓDŹ
July 1946

Among the 22 people who signed this appeal, besides those connected in the past with the conspiratorial Council for Aid to the Jews (Ferdynand Marek Arczyński, Władysław Bartoszewski, Stanisław Wincenty Dobrowolski, Emilia Hiżowa, Tadeusz Rek, Irena Sendlerowa), other signatories include professors from institutes of higher education (Professors Cz. Bobrowski, Czartkowski, W. Goetel, K. Kumaniecki, M. Michałowicz, J. Żukowski), journalists and writers (Helena Boguszewska, Juliusz Górecki, Jerzy Kornacki, Michał Pankiewicz), librarians (Dr R. Fleszarowa, Z. Hryniewiczowa), parliamentary deputies (deputies to the *KRN* from the *PPS*, *SD SL* and *SP*) and a Catholic priest.

In the second half of May 1946, a few weeks therefore before the Kielce incidents, the Council of the Anti-Racist League had already drafted a letter to the head of the Catholic church in Poland, Cardinal August Hlond, appealing to the episcopate to condemn the various forms of anti-Jewish activity occurring in the country. It was not until after the Kielce atrocity, however, that a special three-man delegation from the League's governing council went specially from Warsaw to Poznań on 19 July 1946. These representatives were Kazimierz Kumaniecki, Professor of classical philology at Warsaw University, a well-known Catholic activist and parliamentary deputy for the Christian Democrats; Tadeusz Rek, a lawyer active in the peasant movement and Michał Pankiewicz, a journalist, associated politically with the Social Democrats. As Cardinal Hlond was not in Poznań, the delegation was received by Archbishop Walenty Dymek. After delivering a letter, its contents were discussed in detail. The delegation appealed for the Jewish murders to be discussed at the episcopal conference. However, this address by the Anti-Racist League to the Church authorities in Poland was unanswered.

The tragic events in Kielce showed clearly the basic need to establish the Anti-Racist League. The full range of the organization's activities are beyond the scope of this preliminary communication and deserve a separate study. During 1946, three issues of the monthly *Prawo Człowieka* were produced. But in 1947 the journal failed to appear. Some of the founders and creators of the League voluntarily resigned from further public activities, and the director of the League's Propaganda and Press section and co-organiser of its monthly publication was falsely accused and imprisoned by the communist security authorities in November 1946. Soon afterwards, one of the League's vice-presidents, Dr Adolf Berman, emigrated to Israel. Due to pressure from the Polish Workers Party (from December 1948 the Polish United Workers' Party) and state propaganda organisations, both the Anti-Racist League and its journal *Prawo Człowieka* were to be forced in a later period – beyond the scope of this article – fundamentally to change their character and direction.[6] Texts on Jewish themes did continue to appear sporadically in the journal, but the further activity of the League was basically concentrated against ... 'American and British imperialists' persecuting Negroes and other coloured peoples.

This later development in no way alters the moral or political value of the establishment of the Anti-Racist League in Warsaw in 1946 and then in Kraków and Łódź. The extremely rich contents of the monthly *Prawo Człowieka* in its first year, as well as several valuable pamphlets published during 1947 (M. Borwicz, *Organizacja wściekłości*, foreword by Z. Nałkowska; T. Zaderecki, *Legenda krwi. Historyczna i krytyczna analiza tzw. mordu rytualnego*, the collective work *Martwa fala* with contributions by J. Andrzejewski, S. Flukowski, J. Zawieyski and Maria Kann among others), are permanent achievements of the Polish intelligentsia in the struggle against hatred and prejudice.

At a time of increased interest in the theme of Polish-Jewish relations and of various organisational and institutional projects in this field, it is worth remembering the decision to set up the All-Polish Anti-Racist League in 1946, and the first steps taken to realise that ambition in very difficult circumstances, when great willpower and civic courage were required.

NOTES

1 For example: on the history of the Council for Aid to the Jews – Mr Marek, a member of the *Żegota* presidium, *Dziennik Ludowy* (Warsaw, 1945), no.8; Marek Arczyński, 'W obliczu wspólnej tragedii', *Nowa Epoka* (Warsaw, 1945, no.17; Władysław Bartoszewski, 'Prawdziwe oblicze akcji *Żegoty*. Jak Polska Podziemna ratowała Żydów', *Gazeta Ludowa* (Warsaw, 1946), no.97; Benedykt Hertz, '*Żegota*. Organizacja za mało znana', *Robotnik*, (1947), no.268.
2 Krystyna Kersten, *Narodziny systemu władzy. Polska 1943–1948* (Paris, 1987), p. 169.
3 Ibid.
4 Ibid., p. 170.
5 O. Górka was later Polish consul in Jerusalem from 1947–52. He died in Poland in 1955.
6 In 1948 numbers 1–10 of the journal appeared under a new editorial board. Numbers 1–12 appeared in 1949 and 1950. In 1951 the publication was closed after one issue.

THE CONTEXTS OF SO-CALLED JEWISH QUESTION IN POLAND AFTER WORLD WAR II

Krystyna Kersten and Jerzy Szapiro

Any historian seeking a better insight into the nature and dynamics of Polish-Jewish relations after World War II, must force his way through areas which have been distorted for many years by two types of falsehood: lies of silence and lies of word and deed. Both have their causes – great fear and petty cowardice, deep defeatism and everyday opportunism, occasionally feelings of shame, but, all too frequently, purely tactical considerations. When the lie of silence persists too long and its failure to hide the truth becomes evident, the authorities try to prevent their further discrediting in world and national opinion, while the nation, even more sensitive to world opinion, strives also to drown out the voice of its conscience. At this point the silence is shattered. As this change does not usually stem from a love of the truth, but is rather an unwilling concession to avoid opprobium and condemnation, the areas passed over in silence are then deliberately filled with bogus models which project a mystified reality in order to mask the genuine situation. These facades are in fact half-truths based on conveniently selected facts, some unauthenticated and some genuine, manipulated to convey false messages. So that these constructs can perform their camouflaging function effectively, they are set within carefully chosen contexts which permit the clearly pejorative character of even universally condemned views and actions to be concealed, thus making them appear as elements of a higher order.

This mechanism, likely to be a universal one, has been widely applied in the game of appearances played in Poland over the last 40 years, and has allowed the masking of anti-semitism to gain dangerous popularity. Given the thorough discrediting of anti-semitism, negative attitudes towards Jews were forced to seek out contexts that could legitimize and even ennoble existing prejudices, antipathy, hostility, and discrimination. Consequently, cunning collages known to influence public opinion were created; in order to cloak the shameful nakedness of anti-semitism, they had to present themselves as apparently cleansed of racial criteria. Thus, both among the rulers and the ruled, the depiction of Jews exclusively as 'emanations of Jewishness' became, as it were, a taboo subject. Instead, depending on the needs of the moment and on specific opinion-moulding groups, the image of the Jew was linked with other factors conveying something alien or hostile – with communism or anti-communism, with the régime in power or its opponents, with cosmopolitanism, freemasonry or Zionist nationalism. In one way or another, the myth of the Jew – never sufficiently Polish – remained in force.

Another method of diverting attention from the significant presence of anti-semitism has been the institutionalization of official rites designed to furnish proof that sympathy for the memory of the Holocaust victims is still alive. These ceremonies were clearly mere façades, however, for their contents were quite obviously biased, and demonstrated disregard for historical truth. These alibi-creating manoeuvres were orchestrated to convey the message that Polish society's attitudes towards Jews were, on the whole, positive, and that helping Jews and heroic attempts to save them during the Nazi occupation were typical responses. In fact, the propagation of this touched-up image led world opinion to swing to the opposite extreme. Both of these half-truths employed a hackneyed technique: *pars pro toto*, for they focused on the actions of a decided minority, while consigning to oblivion the dominant attitudes of society, in all their complexity.

On the part of the régime, manipulation, both through the use of such contexts and the construction of façades, was, for the most part, a conscious operation, reflecting current political trends. For society, however, these were exercises in self-deception – defensive reactions aroused by a strong feeling that the nation's existence was threatened, consequently promoting an even stronger need for national self-affirmation. The label 'Polish anti-semites' was incompatible with the cliché 'Poland – inspiration of the world'.

We touch here on one of the most important factors in the vicious circle of Polish-Jewish relations. For historical reasons, a feeling of threat has been so thoroughly encoded in each of these peoples that the sensation of being threatened remains even when real danger begins to vanish. This, in turn, arouses psychologically understandable defensive reactions, the evolution and consequences of which could prove to be even more sinister than their initial sources: there is less and less room for any rational appraisal of the situation, and more and more for irrational thinking, dominated by aggressive tendencies, which perceive evil or hostility in all that hinders the fulfilment of the psychological needs of the individual, group or nation. History shows that in unfavourable circumstances, populations sharing the same homeland – especially populations so battered by fate as the Jewish and Polish – almost inevitably fall into insidious traps which direct defensive reactions against one another rather than against the threat itself. The intensity and near fatalism of these reactions, so often aggressive, are clearly displayed in the interaction of old and new aspects of the Jewish question in Poland over the last four decades. These arose through the overlapping and mutual reinforcement of several causes of conflict: first the burden of archetypes in how Poles and Jews looked at each other, still functioning in the realms of both the sacred and the profane; second, the direct and indirect consequences of the German occupation; and finally Poland's situation after the Second World War.

Let us review the expectations of Poles and Jews at the end of the war in the face of the tragic and antagonistic roles allotted them by history. Poland emerged from the war subjugated, with a régime imposed on her, and one which the majority of society considered to be alien and threatening to the nation's spiritual existence. What is more, even with their glorious record of resistance against the Germans, the nation's sons now found themselves persecuted by a new régime. Fratricidal struggle was the hallmark of the era, claiming new victims. Thus victory over the Germans did not bring Polish misery to an end; liberation from the nightmare of Nazi occupation did not lead to the anticipated sovereignty. The programme of rebuilding the country after the ravages of war did not eliminate an almost universal frustration which was deepened by a feeling of isolation, already familiar to the participants in the Warsaw Uprising, accompanied by disillusionment with the Western allies, a feeling growing since Yalta. Finally, there was anxiety, even fear, in the face of everything that came from the East, because of a series of painful experiences stretching back to 1939. It is not surprising, then, that the imperative of biological and spiritual survival and of the defence of national identity were instilled into the behaviour of Poles, and that the call for resistance, variously conceived, remained alive, and was directed against everything seen as subjugation and, consequently, against those perceived as its perpetrators.

The expectations of Polish Jews, who owed their salvation largely to the Soviet Union where they had spent the war, or who had survived in Poland – hidden by Poles or with the help of so-called Aryan papers – to be later liberated by the Soviet army, could not possibly have been the same. Nor were different expectations held only by those who decided relatively early to emigrate. Of those Jews wishing to remain in Poland, many maintained the belief, dating from before the war or from during it, that a system proclaiming social justice would finally end racial and ethnic discrimination.

Others, at first far from being communists – and there were many – maintained the belief that the introduction of a communist régime in Poland would eradicate anti-semitism and bring real, not merely formal, equality, and they therefore pushed ideological and political reservations about the new order aside. The memory of bitter and inhuman past experiences and, above all, the shocking discovery that anti-semitism had survived the Holocaust, inclined many of those unwilling or unable to emigrate towards acceptance of the new reality. Some of the slogans propounded by the new régime were welcomed: the cliché of 'reaction' was already functioning, linking all opposition to the authorities with the right, nationalism and anti-semitism. This mystification, which was achieved by including many who approved neither of the new order nor of anti-semitism within the category of so-called 'reaction', proved effective, though not as effective as the stereotype of the 'communist Jew'. Ultimately, these were two, almost contradictory, distortions reflecting the functioning of the same process – namely constructing in the mind a concocted, synthetic image of the enemy. Mystical thinking came into play here, seeking to rationalise the negative feelings produced – of hostility, enmity, aggression – and born of a sense of helplessness in the face of threats towards established values and even towards the security of individuals and society as a whole. The road to making minds captive to the logic of higher reasons lay wide open, reasons meant to justify hostile archetypes and contemporary prejudices and, furthermore, to absolve them of their ominous consequences. Neither the adherents, nor the opponents of the new system managed to avoid this road. Mutual Polish-Jewish relations also failed to avoid it, and, paradoxically, became even more sensitive than hitherto. This worried those Jews who at that time were not susceptible to any propaganda, and who had decided to rebuild their lives in Poland despite the painful conviction that their feelings towards the country were not reciprocated. All they could hope was that the mutual resentments sustaining anti-semitism and feelings of alienation would gradually fade.

Thus the expectations of the majority of Polish Jews did indeed differ from those of the majority of Poles, even given the heterogeneity of the group classed as Jewish. After all, these were people of diverse beliefs, whose ethnic, religious, and cultural links with the Jewish world were at times strong, at times weak, and often extremely tenuous; at times they were awakened only as a manifestation of normal human dignity, or as a community spirit among victims of discrimination. When reference is made to Jews in this essay, we have in mind all Jews: from those Poles of Jewish descent so closely fused with Polishness that the word assimilation understates the strength of this tie, to Jews who tried to preserve a separate ethnic, religious, or cultural identity in Poland, their homeland.

What, then, were the hopes of the Jews who had survived? They believed, desired to believe, and, indeed, had to believe, that after the inhuman experiences of Nazism, endured by Poles and Jews together, they would live normally, as Poles or as Polish Jews, without the imposed, or at times adopted, handicap of Jewishness, without ostracism, of whatever kind. The death-knell of anti-semitism – this was to be the posthumous triumph of Polish Jewry. Too often the opposite was the case:

despite these natural human expectations, the few who escaped annihilation met less with rejoicing and welcome from their surroundings than with indifference, antipathy and even hostility. This hostility was on occasion vented in atrocities, not only in the infamous Kielce pogrom. Of course, it would be simplest to attribute such acts of violence exclusively to the barbarity bequeathed by the war, to the kindling of provocation or to civil war. But it must not be forgotten that at this time it was not rare for Jews to be killed by Poles just because they were Jews.

This atmosphere, in which Poles and Jews harboured different hopes, produced the scenario for the future drama. The régime, perceived by Poles as a hostile one, seemed to Jews to safeguard their lives and to offer the chance for equal rights. Past and present meshed to produce a situation boding ill for Polish-Jewish relations. Logically, this would seem absurd. The virtual total annihilation of Polish Jews removed from the Polish scene a numerically significant community which had expressed its distinctiveness through its separate religion, speech, dress and behaviour. Generally speaking, then, the previous bases for antagonism and antipathy – even the economic ones – that existed before 1939, had disappeared. While it is true that Nazi methods evoked condemnation, these persecutors of Poles and Jews alike had practically fulfilled the programme or dreams of Polish anti-semites – Poland was well-nigh free of Jews. Attempts to revive the Jewish community in 1945–48 failed. Most of the survivors left Poland during the first five years after the war.

But, as the old saying goes: when reason sleeps, ghosts walk. Millions of Polish Jews had perished, yet the Jewish question in Poland persisted. New post-war antagonisms, reinforced by different experiences during the war, overlapped with everlasting irrational prejudices and phobias. The common martyrdom of Jews and Poles proved to be less significant than the difference in fates assigned to them in the occupier's policies. These had shown a different intention, scale, and timetable in persecuting Poles and Jews. The argument over which side had suffered the most victims and martyrs was a new, tragic component in the Polish-Jewish entanglements, clouding mutual perceptions and affecting mutual relations. Furthermore, the stereotype imposed by the Nazi racist selection criteria was absorbed into the consciousness of all living through the day-to-day realities of occupation. Even with full awareness of the criminality of these criteria and with their complete rejecting in theory, it was difficult to ignore them, since they defined the fate of individuals: they divided society into those who were condemned to immediate execution and those for whom this sentence was suspended, allowing them to live for a while. Their different fates left deep, traumatic scars in the consciousness of both Poles and Jews. Jewish survivors not only remembered that some Poles had maintained contact with them, helped them and rescued them, at a risk to their own lives, while others had blackmailed them or betrayed them to the

Germans. They also remembered their fear, not only of the Germans but also of their 'Aryan' fellow citizens. But what persisted above all was the consciousness of the indifference during the war of most of those around them, sometimes coloured with sympathy, but often with antipathy. The position of the Jews was too dreadful for them to afford the luxury of objective reasoning which would enable them to see that these embittering attitudes and disillusioning behaviour did not stem entirely from anti-semitism, but also from the intensification of terror, which was far greater in Poland than in the occupied western countries. Feelings of abandonment and isolation dominated everything, together with the perception that the dying Jewish population was separated from the Polish population by a wall built of more than just bricks.

The memory of this isolation was to persist for years, decreasing and increasing its impact, depending on circumstances. These feelings were a reminder that in conditions of terror, both the awareness of fellow victims and solidarity with them can awaken and grow, but that they can also fail to be awakened and may even die out. The consciousness will also grow, that in those inhuman times, moral norms and codes of behaviour were affected not only by reprehensible motives – prejudices and hostility, indifference or callousness – but simply because fate forced a person to choose between alternatives all of which involved a decision or action which was both human and inhuman and did not fit into the natural realms of human imagination. Keeping faith with these norms and codes, a readiness to provide concrete aid to save a life, sometimes had to be limited – in the face of cruel reality – to the symbolic sphere, to showing feelings of brotherhood and solidarity. Such a position cannot, of course, replace attempts to save lives, but it can protect the condemned from feelings of isolation and apathy, and those to whom they look so desperately for help, from the accusation of indifference, callousness and passivity. Moreover, it may create an atmosphere mobilising both the victims and the potential rescuers to overcome the fatalistic approach of which the practical consequences cannot be underestimated. But even this position was far from universal. And so the 'sin of abstention' became one of the stigmas of that time, although – later on – this designation happened to be unjustly extended to all acts of abstention, some of them unavoidable. The truths of these times are thus complicated and multi-dimensional: they explain much, allow much to be understood, but they do not absolve everything. They indicate that human lack of imagination does not make it easier to understand the dilemmas of the human fate of others, that it does not enable one to overcome mutual misunderstanding. Once again it appears that one's own hell and that of others, like one's own truth and that of others, are weighed on different scales.

The memory of Poles after the war was dominated by the consciousness of their own martyrdom and of the dramatic history of the resistance movement. Reminders of the awkward role played by mostly passive witnesses to the Holocaust were an unwelcome disturbance to this image. This troubling awareness was not uncommonly relieved by evoking a myth portraying Jews as the bearers of evil, a myth rooted in the Christian tradition, which was later adopted by the ideology of extreme nationalism. Even during the war this myth fed on every convenient argument, whether valid or deceptive; for example, reports on the pro-Soviet behaviour of national minorities, including Jews, to the east of the Bug in 1939–41. After the war, this myth was nurtured by the highly visible presence of Jews in the ruling apparatus, especially in the security services, and even by those supporting or acceding to the new order proclaimed by the communists.

The image of Jews as internal enemies was thus strengthened in society, this time by attributing to them the role of communist oppressors of the Polish nation – all the more for being concealed in Polish national costume. With the passage of time, the authorities cynically accepted this argument in their attempt to direct the authentic aspirations of society into the course of anti-semitic resentment to suit one of the subsequent tactical twists of the régime. It was used against persons of Jewish origin, first to settle scores within the establishment, and later, for many years, in the struggle with the opposition. Knowing that the fundamental contexts for the Jewish question and its dynamics since 1945 have been determined by the inimical relationship between the régime and society puts the problem of anti-semitism into concrete historic perspective and reminds us that the so-called Jewish question in Poland, is after all, also a Polish question. It is this political context that caused the widening vicious circle of mutual Polish-Jewish resentments, a rationalisation of mutual prejudices which many Poles and Polish Jews were unable to free themselves from completely.

Let us survey the complicated dynamics of these contexts over the past four decades.

In the first decade after the war, the régime, following its doctrinal premises, declared war against anti-semitism and employed accusations of anti-semitism to discredit its ideological and political opponents. As a matter of fact, this policy unintentionally served to strengthen in public opinion the linking of Jews and the authorities as a threat against Polishness. Things got even worse as a consequence of the authorities' attempts to camouflage the background of people of Jewish descent who occupied responsible positions at various levels of the administration.

The world of façades constructed with great care in this first decade according to doctrinal and political demands, and meant to mask reality, collapsed with the system's first crisis in 1956. Tendencies surfaced which expressed differences in views among both the ruling élite and in society. These were to become a permanent element in Polish life for some time to come. The Jewish question did not escape this process. Part of society was aware of frequent anti-semitic occurrences in Poland, but always saw this as a reprehensible phenomenon; others, also condemning anti-semitism, denied its existence as a social phenomenon, especially as in many strata of society and among some generations it was not at all noticeable. Another, quite notable, sector of society still displayed vital, though repressed, resentment and prejudices. The more they had previously been suppressed, the more actively they erupted at a moment of crisis for the régime. This was helped by the fact that many Jews held important political positions, which *eo ipso* made them jointly responsible for the actions which society demanded should be called to account. Simultaneously, among the ruling élite, which was divided over how to react to threats to its authority, there emerged a group propagating nationalistic and populistic slogans. At first timidly, and then more and more blatantly, this group gave these slogans anti-semitic overtones. Proposals to eliminate Jews from government were advanced to prove the authorities' national character and divert attention from fundamental problems, and to saddle Jews with the blame for all past evils, thereby freeing the communist party from responsibility.

In 1956 such tendencies were not allowed to be voiced openly, but they were observed by society, in which a new movement to defend sovereignty, truth, and freedom began to take shape. This was composed partly of workers, but at its heart was an important section of the political, intellectual, and cultural élite, which included many Jews, who had diverse reactions to the deep ideological and political crisis. For various reasons, some Jews acknowledged this crisis as a sign of the bankruptcy of the idea that Poland could have a future for them, and they emigrated; around 40,000 people left Poland at that time. Others continued to identify in a general sense with the order introduced in Poland in 1945, or saw in the Polish October either a reflection of the proper direction of change, or a necessary, but palliative cosmetic operation. Still others, aligning themselves with the aspirations of society, opted to merge even more with it; and even if some of them had until then maintained close ties with the régime, they sooner or later broke them and gradually moved to definite opposition. As a result, a new cliché appeared in the 60s: Jews as enemies of the Polish People's Republic, opponents of socialism, sowers of discord. Alongside this cliché a renovated stereotype was propagated of Jews as national nihilists, alien to Polishness and the mainstays of Stalinism.

In 1968 these new and revived make-believe constructs which had served to mask xenophobic and basically racist attitudes, employing descent criteria instead of self-identification, and which were propagated with some success by one of the factions in power in the mid-1960s, revealed their spiritual kinship to the Nuremberg laws. The authorities, disturbed by processes under way in society undermining their authority, welcomed an option to appeal to anti-Jewish resentment. This time the strategy was immediately successful: Jews were attacked and the framework of society was disturbed. Society was disoriented, intimidated and divided, and remained unaware – with the exception of a few groups – that one of the most important aims of this action was to disarm the nation both morally, and, as later became clear, intellectually. The instigators of this operation anticipated that the attack on Jews would be met in part with passivity, and in part with society's approval, thus helping to divert attention from the real causes of increasing dissatisfaction. And in fact, the resurgence of anti-semitic slogans, coupled with populistic and anti-intellectual appeals, did not disappoint these expectations. This campaign, which did not hesitate to adopt old *ONR* models, reactivated old stereotypes: Jews as Jew-Communists, the Jewish mafia, Jewish freemasons. In addition, a new phantom appeared: the Jew as Zionist. In creating this, the evident and, not only Jewish, welcoming of Israel's success in the Six Day War, had to be suppressed by raising an artificial furore about a supposed fifth column, which had allegedly revealed itself, and was meant to show that Polish Jews considered Israel to be their true homeland.

This hate campaign revived among Jews the seemingly extinct fear felt during the war or even before it. The subsequent purge not only deprived people of their positions or even of the possibility to practise their professions: it also attempted to strip them of their dignity. This led to an exodus of almost 20,000 Jews from Poland who were ultimately reproached merely with being Jewish – the racist key behind this purge could not be hidden, despite attempts at ideological camouflage. The authorities did not hesitate to link the pretence of voluntary emigration with the supposed repudiation of the Polish homeland, although it was clear that many of the departing Jews would continue to live culturally as Poles, even as *émigrés*. It is difficult to describe the deep grief, outrage and shame of those Poles who fully realised that this was, in fact, expulsion provoked by the authorities; but also that this banishment could never have attained the scale it did, had quite a few social groups not allowed fear, indifference or silent consent to overshadow condemnation of the methods employed.

The emigration following the events of March 1968 virtually completed the removal of Jews from Polish land. In a perverse historical paradox, the Jewish question did not die out, but instead began in subsequent years to acquire a new dimension. March 1968 proved to be a deep-seated, traumatic experience. It was deeply imprinted on the consciousness and subconsciousness of the victims of this ignoble witch-hunt; it affected the consciences of the thousands and the thoughts of the millions who had witnessed it. What is more, in the long run, it took its toll among the hunters and their aides themselves, who later experienced more than one disappointment. It also affected those who were linked with them in various power-relationships and who opportunistically did not oppose but sometimes even helped them in March, not sensing that the odium from their shameful silent cooperation would cling to them for good. The policy of anti-semitism was taught an unequivocal lesson: the Jews departed, but the plagues remained.

The March inheritance accelerated the polarisation of already differentiated positions, expressing not only the mutual antagonism between the authorities and society, but also the divisions within these structures. For these positions to crystallize, a new, historically significant factor had to find its voice: the attempt by society to organize itself, an attempt which emerged increasingly openly for the first time in many years. This process – combined with the need to consider critical world opinion – forced the authorities to shatter the lie of silence, although not immediately.

New contexts for the Jewish question began to function against this background. The façades meant to hide the existence of anti-semitism were constructed with greater and greater calculation, but authentic tendencies of renewal also began to appear more strongly in society, which had had its fill of both the lie of silence and the lie of speech or 'Newspeak'. As far as the régime in general is concerned, the hunters and their aides maintained and continue to maintain the sinister equation created in the 1960s of Jews as eternal enemies of socialist Poland. But at the same time, within the establishment itself, among people who were perhaps genuinely ashamed, but who knew that to maintain their cowardly silence confirmed their joint responsibility for the régime's shameful and unforgettable actions in 1968, aspirations emerged to remove the stigma with which the régime was stamped. This tactical approach won out among the authorities shortly after the crushing of Solidarity, but the measures undertaken were far from truly cathartic. As was true for the authorities' general strategy towards society, actions towards the 'Jewish question' were, and still are, incomplete, inconsistent, and timid. Still fearing open and unequivocal condemnation of the actions of 1968, and still permitting the undisturbed continuation of March discriminatory practices in certain areas, the authorities balance between truth and falsehood.

This policy was expressed in the sudden, almost ostentatious interest shown in the topic of Jews. It is now essential for Poland's rulers that there be much discussion of Jews. They are adopting this policy (not so much *glasnost* as *głośność* [vociferousness]) on an unprecedented scale and a scope that probably astonishes even them. In the new domestic and international situation, the authorities felt forced to present society with truthful and valuable information long denied to it. Thus in the media, in publishing houses and in theatres, products of Jewish culture, both old and contemporary, began to appear more frequently; the viewer, listener, and reader were given the opportunity to get to know the literature, art, and religious and secular customs of a community that for centuries had been a part of the multi-national Republic.

Alongside these actions, delayed for an entire generation, the old deceptive stereotypes continue to exist. The sudden zealous observance and publicizing of anniversaries to honour Holocaust victims are the most evident façades. Activities designed to show only one side – the praiseworthy and heroic one – of Poles' relations to Jews during the war – also jar, with their half-truths. The illusion is thus created that it is the authorities who represent moral values which were in fact upheld by the opposition movement developing in the last ten years as an expression of the independence regained by society. This is not the first appropriation committed by the authorities.

It is undeniable that emancipation movements before Solidarity – in particular the most powerful of these, the Committee for Social Self-Defence, KOR, together with the sectors of society coperating with it – not only unequivocally condemned anti-semitism, but also exposed the façades which concealed it. Among the ideals of this movement was the need for authentic – and not illusory and alibi-creating – absolution for the sin of indifference towards anti-Jewish actions and for their silent concealment especially when they were undertaken by Poles. This was thus an expression of the need for a genuine catharsis with respect to such actions, those of the distant past, and those more recent, both those resulting from the régime's policies – that is from the adversaries – and those from society itself. It was painfully clear that, although the Jewish community had almost vanished from the Polish scene, the ghost of the Jew still wandered through Poland, and, unfortunately, for a large part of society, it still has symbolic meaning: that of the outsider, someone not to be trusted, someone to be guarded against, to be blamed for every failure, even for the disasters of fate.

The supernatural strength of this symbol was felt during Solidarity's sixteen-month existence. This was surely an indirect consequence of society revelling in pluralism, or more concretely, of its willingness to listen to all viewpoints provided they claimed the legitimacy of opposition to the authorities. Now, however, these basically anti-semitic tendencies, whether directed against the authorities or against persons or groups within the opposition, found determined resistance. A significant majority had no doubt that this was an inadmissible contamination of the emancipatory, democratic, and humanistic ideals on which Solidarity was based. This majority included people of different generations and outlooks, with different past histories: those involved in the resistance movement during the war and who had been harassed or imprisoned after it, but who had never tolerated witch-hunts or the search for scape-goats; and those fascinated in their youth by the imported New Faith, who, finally grasping the connection between the capture of consciousness by the logic of higher goals and the dehumanization of the human condition and that of the nation, recognized they had to demystify reality, a reality which courageously challenged the authorities but was not always popular with society; and those among believing Catholics who found in Christianity an *imprimatur* for their support of the harsh régime's opponents who were not always admirers of religion; and those believers and non-believers for whom the Church had become a buttress and an ally in the difficult struggle to save the internal sovereignty of the nation; and finally, those who in the brutal lesson of 1968 discovered the link between the anti-semitism peering out from behind ideological masks and the shattering of society through its moral and, at times, intellectual disarmament.

This link not only laid bare the cynicism with which these false stereotypes of Jews as Zionists, cosmopolitans, national nihilists, and trouble-makers were created, but also demonstrated that opposing anti-semitism – everywhere, in all its forms and masks – is an inseparable part, but only one part, of the struggle to heal social life threatened by deprivation. It also showed that this goal cannot be attained exclusively by attacking the authorities; it is necessary in addition, to find the strength and courage to identify and demonstrate the negative phenomena rooted in society itself. And the nation – or indeed any nation – does not like this at all.

Condemnation of anti-semitism was therefore part and parcel of this moral renewal of society from the start. It was important, especially in Poland, a country of such deep-rooted Catholic traditions, that the Church hierarchy after Vatican II joined in secular efforts to break down ancient unfavourable stereotypes of the Jews. In the religious sphere these measures removed the centuries-old anathema on Jews and Jewry, and, moreover, created a propitious climate for Christianity and Judaism to meet on the basis of philosophical discourse and mutual respect for existing differences.

The suppression of Solidarity – the movement which confronted the lie of silence and persistently exposed spoken lies for the first time on such a scale – did not deter the nation's real determination to end the shameful failure to recognize the history of the Jewish community on Polish lands, and the practice – by no means limited to Poles - of distorting the picture of Polish-Jewish relations. True, one still meets attitudes that almost automatically continue the traditional embellishment of the Polish nation's past, thus avoiding unpalatable truths about Polish-Jewish issues among others. But a new spirit is in the air, leading to greater hope because it is developing especially among the younger generation. It is still embryonic and takes many forms. It includes believers and non-believers, Poles and Jews alike. Its central aim – in this case not directed at the construction of façades – is to find out about the history of Polish Jews, to restore the Jewish culture of these lands to its place in the treasury of Polish culture, so impoverished and distorted by the long practice of the cult of the single-nation state, and, what is most difficult but also most important, to reveal the whole truth, even in its most unpalatable form, about Polish-Jewish relations. In spite of psychological inhibitions, fears of misunderstanding, semantic difficulties, a gradual, courageous and genuinely purifying removal of masks and exposure of pathologies and prejudices has begun; not in order to accuse others or to accuse oneself, not to admit one's sins and beg for forgiveness, not in the name of philosemitism, but to satisfy the real need to comprehend the dramatic entanglements of human relations. For the truth about Poles and Jews, living side by side and subjected in the last half-century to various forms of totalitarianism, is a part of the universal truth about man's fate.

Though human fate obviously and naturally varies according to the histories of particular individuals, groups, nations, in different times and places, it is none the less similar in general. This should be remembered in any discussion of the causes, nature and consequences of Polish antisemitism, as well as of the contexts in which it is manifested. Although there is no doubt as to its specific character, it is at the same time an illustration of a much more widespread phenomenon, namely the origin and maintenance of stereotypes which perceive with animosity those who are different, labelling them as alien or hostile. These stereotypes tend always to become generalisations, within which feelings of hostility are transferred from the individual to the group and from the group to the nation.

This phenomenon arises from unsatisfied needs, from disappointments, from dissatisfaction with oneself or one's life, or in the face of opinions – one's own, those of one's surroundings or of the world – about oneself, one's group, one's nation. It emerges from the desire to compensate for feelings of inferiority, from the unsatisfied need to affirm one's worth. It is born under the pressure of experience and emotions arising most often from fear, out of the feeling that the individual, a group, or a national, religious, or ideological community is under threat, whether real or imagined. This process is characterised by exaggerated defensive reactions directed against real or imagined rivals or adversaries; as a rule it evolves toward views which, often helped by irrational thinking, serve to rationalise and justify negative emotions and aggressive defensive reactions. These can – but do not have to – lead to the sort of vicious and even criminal attitudes and acts often seen in the past; and they are all the more threatening because they claim the legitimacy of high aims: *ad maiorem Dei aut nationis gloriam*.

In this century, in which both crimes have been perpetrated, and scientific progress achieved, on an unprecedented scale, all beliefs, doctrines, systems, and revolutions – whether political, social, religious, scientific or technological – have proved helpless in the face of this pathology which appears as various anti-isms all over the world. History knows no successful prescription for the ailment. Experience none the less shows that a major role in the development of such phenomena is played by conflict between the truth, that is reality, perceived variously in the recent past or present, and the hierarchy of values recognised by the individual, group, nation or any specific community, often dominated by immoderate egocentrism or individual or collective egoism. The historian's duty is thus to tell the truth so that the often vulnerable individual and collective psyche can learn to accept often unpalatable conclusions. The proliferation of facts will not suffice to achieve this. What might help would be to reveal the role of mechanisms – both those imposed from without and those which facilitate self-deception and sustain professed notions, even in defiance of the facts. Becoming aware that our truths are only partial truths, and that even praiseworthy notions reach disproportionate dimensions under the influence of egocentric and egoistic attitudes, often distancing us, step by step, from the claims of humanism, helps us to endure less painfully the cruel test of time. The ancient historian understands this: the great distance of time assists him. For the modern historian, it is different: he must assist time, he must stir up truth so that it does not become barren; he must stir up, agitate, the hierarchy of values so that it does not become inhuman.

CHANGING IDENTITY AMONG YOUNGER POLISH JEWS IN SWEDEN AFTER 1968
Julian Ilicki

In the years 1968–1972, some 2,500 Polish Jews immigrated to Sweden. This immigrant group, like post-war Polish Jewry as a whole, was made up of two major components: 1) those brought up before the war, and 2) those born or at least brought up in post-war Poland. In other words a 'generation of parents' and a 'generation of children'. Because of the Holocaust, the number of persons belonging to the generation 'between' these two major groups was much smaller.

From the Jewish point of view, these two generational groups had been brought up in two different Polish situations. Persons belonging to the 'generation of parents' experienced, at least during their early childhood, contacts with traditional Jewish life. On the other hand, persons belonging to the 'generation of children' were in most cases brought up with a very weak or, indeed, no contact at all with Jewish traditions and were either on the way to total assimilation or were already 'Polonised' to the degree of complete or almost complete assimilation. A small number of them did not even know of their Jewish origin.

After a number of years in Sweden, a growing interest in 'Jewishness' among the Polish-Jewish immigrants could be observed. In the case of the 'generation of parents' in most cases, this could be considered as a 'return' to a Jewish consciousness – a phenomenon not totally unknown in the Jewish history. However, similar tendencies could also be observed among the younger generation, that was brought up without Jewish traditions, and, therefore, did not have anything to 'return' to. This younger generation of Polish Jews immigrating to Sweden in 1968–1972 is the object of my study, of which a summary is provided in this article.

The central point of interest in my study is the change in the self-perceived national 'ethnic-cultural' identity observed among the younger generation of Polish-Jewish immigrants to Sweden. The main empirical tool was a questionnaire sent in spring 1984 to all members of the group studied, that is persons who immigrated to Sweden in 1968–1972 in the framework of the emigration of the Jews from Poland, and who were born between 1935 and 1962. In this article, I outline some of the empirical results of this study.

IN POLAND

As I have mentioned, members of the group studied were born between 1935 and 1962. Their age structure reflects very clearly the conditions during World War II. The number of persons born increases remarkably directly after the war with a peak in 1946. From 1951 on, a steady decrease of the number of persons born each year can be observed.

37% of the respondents were brought up in 'mixed marriages', where one of the parents was a non-Jew. The great majority had a non-Jewish mother and a Jewish father.

Nearly half of the respondents resided in Warsaw. Other big concentrations were Lower Silesia and Łódź. Interestingly, there are significant differences between respondents from Warsaw and respondents from Lower Silesia with regard to the professions of their parents and the social status connected with these professions. In Warsaw, social categories with a quite high social status, such as higher officials, professionals and intelligentsia dominated, while in Lower Silesia, social categories like craftsmen and lower officials were more frequent.

In the context, it is also interesting to note that similarly significant differences between Warsaw and Lower Silesia existed with regard to the degree of Jewish and Polish identification of the families of the respondents. Practically speaking, all variables measuring this aspect show very clearly that the degree of 'Polishness' was much higher in Warsaw than in Lower Silesia and the degree of 'Jewishness' was higher in Lower Silesia than in Warsaw.

Another interesting observation pertains to the question of whether respondents' families celebrated Christmas, that is a holiday totally alien to the Jewish tradition. Regarding the 'extrinsic' aspects of adopting the cultural tradition of the surround milieu, such as putting up Christmas trees and sharing Christmas gifts, the process of acculturation went so far that as many as nearly three quarters of the respondents' families integrated, at least periodically, these traditions in their family lives. These aspects can be easily imitated from the surrounding non-Jewish milieu without taking over all elements of that culture.

But as soon as the questions in the questionnaire pertained to the more 'intrinsic' aspects of Christmas celebration, such as singing traditional Polish Christmas carols (in Polish *kolędy*) and 'breaking and sharing the sacramental wafer' (in Polish *dzielenie się opłatkiem*; a Catholic Polish Christmas eve tradition showing some similarities to Eucharist), in other words, aspects indicating assimilation to Polish society, the percentage of those respondents observing these details in their family home drops to one third. These more 'intrinsic' aspects of Christmas celebration require, obviously, that in order to be able to pass these traditions on to their children, the parents themselves must have been brought up with these traditions, or that the family indeed keeps Polish Catholic traditions and does not only imitate the more 'extrinsic' aspects of them.

The ethnic origin of the parents is, interestingly enough, not significant for the observance of the 'extrinsic' aspects of Christmas, though, naturally, it plays some part. However, the family's social status seems to play a significant role in this context. Those with higher social status and those who lived in Warsaw show a higher degree of adoption of the 'extrinsic' aspects of Christmas than those with lower status and those who resided in Lower Silesia.

With regard to more 'intrinsic' aspects of Christmas, family social status and geographical location do not play any role. However, naturally enough, the ethnic origin of the parents does: respondents who came from mixed marriages show a higher degree of observance of the 'intrinsic' aspects of Christmas celebration than respondents both of whose parents were Jews.

Another interesting observation was that the group studied was very secular. 72% report that they were atheists in Poland and 14% that they were agnostics. The degree of Christian religiousness (that is in the mixed marriages) seems not to be dependent on the social status of the family. However, the degree of Jewish religiousness decreases very clearly with the increasing social status of the family. Yet for respondents both of whose parents are Jewish the percentage of non-religious is even higher.

IN SWEDEN

In order to make some of the arguments in the following presentation and discussion understandable, it is necessary to start this section with a very short review of some aspects of the historical and social development of the Swedish Jewry.

The history of the Swedish Jewry began in 1774. During the 19th century, Swedish Jewry was primarily influenced by the *haskala* tradition and by the then new reform ideas which came in its wake. The Jewish congregations thus considered themselves to be only religious associations, a state of affairs described by the historian of the Swedish Jewry, the late professor Hugo Valentin, as 'a fiction inherited from the period of emancipation'. This was reflected in the names the congregations adopted: *Mosaiska Församlingar* (Mosaic Congregations). Thus, Swedish Jews did not consider themselves as Jews, rather as 'Swedes of the Mosaic faith'. As in other countries in Western Europe, this development resulted in strong secularisation and assimilation tendencies among the Swedish Jews. These reformed trends were particularly strong in Stockholm and in Gothenburg on the west coast of Sweden. However, in Malmö in southern Sweden, which is the third major centre of the Swedish Jewry, the development of Jewish life was different.

At the end of the 19th and beginning of the 20th centuries the Swedish Jewry was strengthened by an influx of the East European Orthodox Jews, who settled primarily in the south of the country. For this reason, the Jewish congregation in Malmö, established in 1871, that is a century later than those in Stockholm and in Gothenburg, became an Orthodox one. A second big wave of Jewish immigration to Sweden, mostly from Eastern Europe, occurred during and directly after World War II. Some 4,000 of a total of some 12,000 Jews who arrived in Sweden at this time remained in the country. A significant part settled in the south, and the Orthodox character of the Jewish congregation in Malmö became even stronger.

The number of Jews in present-day Sweden is estimated as approximately 16,000 persons, served by three congregations: one in Stockholm, one in Gothenburg and one in Malmö. All three are 'unity congregations', that is, they serve all Jews, from the orthodox to those who are completely secular. Nevertheless, the Stockholm and Gothenburg congregations can be described as basically Conservative, while that in Malmö is basically Orthodox. At the end of the 1970s and beginning of the 1980s, the congregations changed their names to *Judiska Församlingar* (*Jewish Congregations*).

The degree of the urbanisation of the group studied is very high. 41% reside in the Greater Stockholm area, 18% in the Malmö area, 16% in the Gothenburg area, 12% in the university town of Lund just outside Malmö, 4% in the university town of Uppsala, some 70 kilometres north from Stockholm and 1% in the industrial town of Västerås in central Sweden. In addition, 6% reside in other big towns and 2% in smaller places. This high degree of urbanisation is hardly surprising. However, it is interesting that differences are also evident between the four biggest geographical concentrations of the respondents as regards their family's social status in Poland. In Stockholm, the percentage of respondents from families with higher social status is visibly higher than in the other three cities. In Malmö, the percentage of respondents from families of lower social status is significantly higher than in other cities. This can, in all probability, be explained by the fact that Malmö does not have a university. The fact that most of the respondents were of secondary school or university age at the time of their immigration was possibly a decisive factor in the choice of residence.

The level of education among the respondents is very high. Only one respondent has only a grammar school education. As many as 86% have post-secondary education: 64% have university degrees and 22% have non-university post-secondary education. Medical doctors (including some dentists) are the single largest professional group among the respondents, namely 12%. Other major professional categories are computer specialists (9%), graduate engineers and architects (8%), research scientists and university teachers (7%) and other teachers (7%). Students constitute 10%. Here also there are differences between Malmö and the other three cities. In general, the respondents from Malmö have a lower level of education and occupy lower status positions than those from Stockholm, Gothenburg and Lund. Also, the Malmö respondents are younger than those from other cities.

17% of the respondents report that now they consider themselves 'Poles', 'Swedish Poles' or 'Poles of Jewish origin'. 4% report that they now consider themselves to be 'Swedes', and 68% report that they now consider themselves to be 'Jews', 'Polish Jews' or 'Swedish Jews'.

The degree of 'Jewishness' is higher in Malmö than in the other three cities. Naturally, this has to do with the fact that the Malmö respondents were, generally speaking, brought up in the lower status families residing in Lower Silesia, that is those social strata which had a higher degree of 'Jewishness' in Poland, to a higher degree than respondents residing in other cities in Sweden.

19% of the respondents belong to one of the three Jewish congregations in Sweden. The percentage of respondents who belong to some other Jewish or Israel oriented organisation is significantly higher than the percentage of those who belong to some Polish exile organisation.

80% report that they are not affiliated with any Jewish congregation. There are two major reasons for their non-affiliation: 44% report that the congregations are religious organisations, while they themselves are non-religious Jews, and 25% report that the membership fees are too high. Those who gave these reasons for their non-affiliation were asked if they would become members, should the character of the congregations become less religious and more 'generally Jewish' (i.e. more secular and cultural) or if the membership fees were reduced significantly. Among those respondents who gave the religious character of the congregation as the reason for their non-affiliation, 39% report that they 'probably' or 'certainly' would affiliate with the local congregation should it undertake more secular activities. Among those who reported high membership fees as the reason for non-affiliation, 66% report that they 'probably' or 'certainly' would affiliate with the local congregation should the membership fees be reduced significantly.

In this context, too, interesting differences between the different geographical locations can be observed. The percentage of respondents who were willing to affiliate with the local congregation should it carry out more secular activities is greatest in Malmö and in Lund, that is in the area of the Malmö congregation. Other data also show very clearly that respondents who reside in the area of the Malmö congregation feel more alienated from the established Jewish communal life than respondents in other cities. This finding is even more striking in view of the fact that the Malmö respondents, generally speaking, experienced significantly higher degrees of 'Jewishness' in their family homes in Poland than respondents residing in Stockholm, Gothenburg and Lund.

Practically speaking, all of the variables that measure the emotional attachment of the group studied to the 'Polishness', 'Jewishness' and 'Swedishness' demonstrate clearly that Jewish attachment is strongest and Polish is weakest. Swedish attachment is weaker than Jewish but stronger than Polish. Considering, generally speaking, the low level of 'Jewishness' and the high level of 'Polishness' in the group studied before their emigration from Poland, this finding is very remarkable. Also the emotional attachment to the state of Israel is very strong, much stronger than to Poland.

Another very interesting finding is that the group studied shows a somewhat higher degree of emotional attachment to Jews outside Sweden than to Swedish Jewry. Presumably, this can be explained by the hypothesis that the process of changing identity now in progress takes place on the 'abstract' level, that is the respondents develop a 'theoretical' attachment to Jews who they do not meet on the everyday basis. This can be a stage in the process of changing identity. The first step in this process could be, thus, a 'theoretical' feeling of fellowship with the more 'abstract' representatives of the group with which the identification is growing. This 'theoretical' projection is transferred afterwards onto a more practical level, that is, 'the degree of idealising' of the 'abstract' group decreases and one begins to identify himself or herself with the 'ordinary people' who belong to this group, who one meets in everyday interaction. Other findings also seem to support this hypothesis. However, this hypothesis is not proved by these findings.

CHANGES OF IDENTITY

One of the central issues in this study pertains to possible changes in the self-perceived ethnic-national identity. Therefore, one of the questions was about the self-perceived definition: who (in ethnic-national terms) the respondents considered they were during the years before 1967/68, after 1967/68 but before the emigration, shortly after arrival in Sweden, and now. The following alternatives were given in the questionnaire: *Pole, Pole of Jewish origin, Polish Jew, Jew, Swede, Swedish Pole, Swedish Jew, of other nationality*.

Merging the alternatives 'Pole', 'Pole of Jewish origin' and 'Swedish

Pole' into a common category of 'Pole', and in a similar way, the alternatives 'Jew', 'Polish Jew' and 'Swedish Jew' into a common category of 'Jew', we get figures showing very clearly the changes that have taken place. These figures are presented in Table I.

However, these very dramatic changes do not reflect changes in religious affiliation. The percentage of non-religious dropped slightly from 86% to 82%. The only significant change that could be observed in this context is that the percentage of atheists decreased and of agnostics increased. Also interesting are changes in the attendance at Jewish religious services by the respondents: the percentage of those who attend, occasionally or regularly, has increased from 19% in Poland to 38% in Sweden. The highest increase was noted in the alternative 'occasionally', which was exemplified by 'for example, on *Yom Kippur*' – from 11% in Poland to 26% in Sweden. However, as shown above, the variable 'religious affiliation' changed very insignificantly.

These findings can be interpreted in the following way: the group studied was brought up in Poland not only in a secular but also, frequently, in an anti-religious atmosphere, that is with some contempt for all religious observance. Now they are undergoing a process of changing identity in the direction of a Jewish identity. After years in Sweden, their anti-religious attitudes have softened somewhat, and, even if they have not become significantly more religious, their respect for the religious, and –

TABLE 1

'JEW' OR 'POLE' AT DIFFERENT TIMES

percentages

Identity	Before 1967/68	After 1967/68, Before Emigration	Shortly after Arrival In Sweden	Now (1984)
'Pole'[1]	58	42	31	17
'Jew'[2]	39	55	65	68
Other[3]	3	3	4	15[4]

n=441

[1] 'Pole' means here one of the alternatives 'Pole', 'Pole of Jewish origin' and 'Swedish Pole'.
[2] 'Jew' means here one of the alternatives 'Jew', 'Polish Jew' and 'Swedish Jew'.
[3] 'Other' means here the alternative 'Swede', some other answer and no answer.
[4] Including 4% who answered 'Swede'.

perhaps even to a higher degree – national, Jewish traditions, has increased. Participation in Jewish religious services on the most important Jewish holidays, is thus one of the ways of expressing their still secular but growing feeling of belonging to the Jewish people.

Changes of identity can take place on different levels: national-cultural atmosphere at home, national-ethnic self-identification and religious affiliation. Moreover, the changes in the two first levels can take three different directions: Polish, Jewish and Swedish. All these types of changes do not necessarily follow each other.

Regarding changes in *Jewish religiousness*, 39% of the respondents became more religious (most of them slightly more), 9% became less religious and the degree of Jewish religiousness remains unchanged for 52%. It is important to keep in mind, in this context, that the phenomenon being studied is the *change* in Jewish religiousness and not religiousness itself. Thus, a respondent reporting a high degree of Jewish religiousness in Poland, and a similarly high degree of Jewish religiousness in Sweden, is considered to have experienced no change in Jewish religiousness. The same is also valid for the other types of changes, that is changes in the national-cultural atmosphere at home or in the national-ethnic self-identification.

Regarding changes in *feelings of belonging to the Jewish people*, 63% feel more Jewish than in Poland, 8% feel less Jewish and for 28% these feelings remain unchanged. Regarding changes in *feelings of belonging to the Polish people*, the situation is in principle the reverse: 63% feel less Polish than in Poland, 5% feel more Polish and for 30% these feelings remain unchanged. Regarding *feelings of belonging to the Swedish people*, 48% feel more Swedish, 4% feel less Swedish and for 19% these feelings remain unchanged.

Growing *Jewish religiousness* is characteristic mainly of persons married to or cohabiting with Swedish Jews, who reside in Stockholm, who have higher levels of education and who come from families of middle and higher social status in Poland. The percentage of respondents showing decreasing Jewish religiousness is considerably higher in Malmö than in the other three cities: 20% of Malmö respondents belong to this category as compared with 6%-8% in Stockholm, Gothenburg and Lund. Also other variables show that place of residence in Sweden plays a very important role in this context. It is, then, clear that among the respondents residing in Malmö, who experienced a higher degree of 'Jewishness' in their family homes in Poland, the tendency to move away from Jewish religiousness is significantly higher than among those residing in Stockholm, Gothenburg and Lund, and that the move towards growing Jewish religiousness is also weakest. Another significant variable, although to a considerably lower degree than place of residence, is age. The changes in Jewish religiousness are more common among the younger respondents than among the older ones.

Generally speaking, the same categories whose degree of Jewish religiousness increased also show a higher degree of growing *feeling of belonging to the Jewish people*. However, the process of change is now broader. The background variables which played a very important role in the case of changes in Jewish religiousness, such as the religious affiliation or national-ethnic origin of wife/husband/cohabitant or place of residence in Sweden, now play a much less important role. This means that the changes studied are now less dependent on those particular background variables, and that there are broader categories of respondents who show an increasing feeling of belonging to the Jewish people than those who show an increasing degree of Jewish religiousness. Even in this case, the situation in Malmö differs from the situation in other cities. Jewish life seems to be less attractive for respondents residing in Malmö than for the rest of the group studied.

What is immediately apparent when analysing the changes in the *feeling of belonging to the Polish people* is that the process is the opposite to that of the changes in feeling of belonging to the Jewish people, that is the categories in which the Jewish national identification increased also show decreasing Polish national identification. The independent variables which played an important role in the changes in Jewish national identification here play a less important role, which means that the process is broader than in the case of changes in the Jewish identification. The independent variables 'place of residence' and 'national origin of wife/husband/cohabitant' here play as little role as other independent variables. The broad character of these changes can be illustrated by the fact that even among those respondents who are married to or cohabiting with non-Jewish Poles, that is where the Polish stimulus would be thought to be the strongest, as many as 56% now feel less Polish. Another variable playing an important role in changing feelings of belonging to the Polish people is age: the younger the respondents were when they left Poland, the greater are these changes in the direction of 'feeling less Polish'.

The most important role among the independent variables studied with regard to changes in the *feeling of belonging to the Swedish people* is played, hardly surprisingly, by the national-ethnic origin of wife/husband/cohabitant. Such variables as age or place of residence play a minor role in this context. Also, it is interesting that those persons who were more 'Polonised' in Poland now feel somewhat more Swedish than the others.

Changes in Swedish identification do not lie in the same plane which is described by the scale 'less Polish – more Jewish'. In other words, the 'Swedish' changes take place independently of the 'Polish-Jewish' changes and depend to a high degree on the opportunities for integration into the Swedish society.

The national-ethnic origin of wife/husband/cohabitant plays the most important role of all independent variables studied with regard to changes in the *national-cultural atmosphere at home*, especially when studying changes in the *Swedish* character of the home. Some role is also played by social status of respondents' homes in Poland, but only with regard to changes in the *Jewish* and *Polish* characters of homes in Sweden, and not in the Swedish one. Place of residence is also important, but its importance decreases when studying the Polish character of the homes and is still weaker when studying the Swedish character.

SOME COMMENTS ON THE SPECIAL SITUATION IN MALMÖ

As we have already noted a number of times, the situation in Malmö, and to some degree also in Lund, differs significantly from the situation in other towns. These differences merit special attention. On what do they depend?

Partly, they can be explained by the fact that the main objects of the study are changes in the self-perceived identity and not the identity itself. This means that if a respondent shows a high degree of Jewish self-identification in Poland, and a similarly high degree of Jewish self-identification in Sweden, he or she is considered to have experienced no change in his or her Jewish self-identification. Since the Malmö respondents had a higher degree of 'Jewishness' in their family homes in Poland, they also had 'something' to move away from, as compared with the respondents from other towns in Sweden who, generally speaking, did not have anything to move away from. However, this explanation provides a kind of 'social entropy', that is a tendency towards a uniform social equability with regard to certain social phenomena within a population, in our case the degree of self-perceived Jewish identity among members of the group studied. It is possible that the phenomenon of 'social entropy' partly explains the differences observed between the situation in Malmö and in the other three towns. However, I consider this explanation to be a minor one and one of the reasons for this is the situation in Lund: if social entropy is to be considered as a main reason, the changes of identity among the respondents residing in Lund ought to be of a similar character to those among those from Stockholm and Gothenburg, which is not the case.

Therefore, I suggest that the most important explanation is to be found in the fact that organised Jewish communal life in Malmö differs, in many respects, from Jewish communal life in Stockholm and Gothenburg. The empirical findings show that contacts of the group studied with organised Jewish life in Poland were very limited and in many cases simply non-existent. Thus, the picture that the respondents have today of what Jewish life, Jewish traditions and the Jewish bond is about have been formed after their arrival in Sweden and in contact with organised Jewish communal life in their new places of residence. And since the Jewish congregations in Sweden present different pictures of Jewish life, the respondents in different towns have been influenced by these pictures in different ways.

Two general tendencies support this hypothesis. The first is the situation in Lund. Despite the fact that the background variables of the respondents living in Lund resemble those of respondents living in Stockholm and Gothenburg, the process of the changes studied is similar to the situation in Malmö. The second tendency is the role played by the variable 'place of residence' in the changes studied. The role of this variable is the strongest when analysing the *Jewish* dimension of changes and has a much weaker effect on the Polish and Swedish dimensions.

Both the empirical data collected and my own knowledge of Jewish life in Sweden leads me to the same conclusion, namely that the Jewish congregation in Malmö creates a more repellent picture of Jewish life among persons belonging to the group studied than pictures created by the congregations in Stockholm and Gothenburg. This is so not only because of the Orthodox character of the Malmö congregation, but also because of the very special background of the group studied.

As has been stated above, the group studied was very secular in Poland and it has not become more religious in Sweden. What has changed is the feeling of identification with the Jewish people and not religious affiliation. Therefore, it is quite natural that a more Orthodox congregation is perceived as more alien by members of the group than a less Orthodox congregation, where they can get not only religious but also more secular Jewish and general intellectual stimuli. As far as I know, no research has been done on the social structure of the Jewish congregations in Sweden. Nevertheless, it can be said that there are not only religious but also social differences between the congregation in Malmö and those in Stockholm and Gothenburg. It appears, namely, that among members of the Malmö congregation there is a higher percentage of persons belonging to lower social strata and lower percentage of persons belonging to the intelligentsia, than in the cases of the Stockholm and Gothenburg congregations.

All this taken together leads me to the conclusion that, generally speaking, the very highly educated Polish Jews who belong to the group studied, who were brought up in very weakly Jewish or non-Jewish milieux, who were very secular and who now undergo a process of changing identity towards Jewish identity; that this very special group feel that they have much less in common with an Orthodox congregation of Malmö type, than with non-Orthodox congregations of Stockholm or Gothenburg type. And since their view of what being Jewish is about, has been strongly influenced by the congregations in Sweden and their characters, the process of changing identity takes different patterns in different towns. As far as I can see, this explanation is the most important one. Another contributing factor is the fact that in Lund, which is located just outside Malmö, there are two organisations that attract the younger generation of Polish Jews and, therefore, function as a kind of alternative to organised Jewish communal life as institutionalised by the Jewish congregation in Malmö.

The conclusion is, then, that the picture of what Jewish life and Jewish identity is about that one gets from the Jewish milieu around one's own social environment, is of great importance if such a Jewish identity is to be perceived as attractive by Jews who are not brought up in a significantly Jewish milieu and who now search themselves to their 'Jewishness'. Obviously, if one is looking for a way 'back to one's roots', these roots must be perceived as interesting and not repellent.

NOTES

PROBLEMATIZING THE 'JEWISH PROBLEM'
Iwona Irwin-Zarecka

The growing interest, academic and otherwise, in Polish-Jewish history heightens our sense of what actually happened in the seventeenth century, during the 1930s or in 1968. More and more, we are beginning to understand what went right and what went wrong at different points. Conceptual shorthand – terms such as 'tolerance', 'anti-semitism', 'conflict' – now appear to trap us in all-inclusive abstractions that hide rather than reveal the realities behind them. That we take the meaning of those notions for granted is the key problem, not the terms themselves. Naming, so important a process for any culture, must not be the sole, or even the main goal of inquiry. Little can be gained, especially in a domain as complex as Polish-Jewish relations, from working with categories which 'everyone understands'. The categories do matter, but not as tools; instead, they should become *objects* for critical scrutiny.

What I am calling for here is not simply a refinement of definitions; as useful as it might be, an abstract concern with precision will not suffice. Rather, we need a great deal more reconstructing, layer by layer, of the texture, social as well as symbolic, of the Polish-Jewish encounter. (David Engel's work [1983, 1987] presents the best example of just such an approach.) Only *after* we gather all the pieces does it make sense to define and categorize.

As a cultural sociologist, I did not learn this lesson from theoreticians. I learned it when trying to make sense of the recent upsurge of interest in things Jewish in Poland (see: Irwin-Zarecka, forthcoming). From early 1982, when I began working on my project, it was clear that all the 'noise' increasingly surrounding the Jew was significant both for those who talked and for those who listened. What was much less clear – indeed, what has taken several years of research to assess – was the meaning of these new developments. Now that Jewish history and Jewish culture were being discussed, at least in part, on their own terms, what was changing? Now that Poles were beginning to talk more openly than ever about the legacies of anti-semitism, what was not changing? Was the new discourse a way of coming to terms with a difficult past? Or was its function morally to neutralize much of that past?

To answer these questions meant sifting through a rapidly growing pile of books and articles; it also meant talking to those people in Warsaw who were the most active in rediscovering Poland's Jewish heritage. Furthermore, it meant connecting what I now read and heard to my own memories of growing up Polish and Jewish in Warsaw in the sixties as well as to the ideas about Jewishness I absorbed later, in North America and France.

In juxtaposing notions I once shared with what we would call the '1968 generation', and the ways of seeing I learned from Jews living in large communities, I first began to question the extent of change in the perception of the Jew in Poland today. Later, recognizing that the new talk about the Jew had at least the potential to change the Poles' perception of themselves as well, I began to question the *relation* between certain persistent ideas about Jewishness and the continuing inability to see, let alone examine, the moral demands of the past for Polish self-definition. There was a strong intellectual and emotional link, I discovered, between defining the Jew as a 'problem' and finding Polish-Jewish history morally comfortable. Moreover, there was an even stronger one between taking the 'Jewish problem' as a given and the absence of self-critical reflection on the role of Catholicism in that history.

Considering how frequently anti-semitism is condemned in Poland today, considering how warmly and respectfully most things Jewish are discussed, considering the appeals to study the whole of the Polish-Jewish past objectively, the scarcity of voices challenging Polish conscience cannot be ascribed to the lack of good will. Nor, I feel, can it be explained by reference to the mysterious qualities of 'Polish national character', leaving Poles incapable of self-criticism. No one likes to ponder the 'dark chapters' of the past, especially when the present is so bleak, but Poland's historical consciousness is in no way an exclusively comforting reservoir of heroic deeds; the debates still surrounding the 1944 Warsaw Uprising – to take the most obvious of examples – certainly offer little solace.

That Poles are so ready to dismiss questions about the moral reponsibility for the fate of the Jews as a non-issue (especially evident during the debates surrounding Lanzmann's *Shoah*) is not merely the product of psychological defence mechanisms either. Voices like Lanzmann's – and others coming from the West – naturally force people to defend their good name. Even allowing for that, the absence until very recently of hard and self-critical reflection on the past is rooted in something well beyond the requirements of national image. When the concern with image does translate into an inquiry rather than a defence, as it did in Błoński's article 'The Poor Poles look at the Ghetto' (*Tygodnik Powszechny*, 11 Jan. 1987), the acceptance of responsibility does *not* leave the realm of immediate cause-and-effect relationships. In other words, whether in self-defence or in self-critique, 'Polish-Jewish relations' in general, and during the Holocaust in particular, remain coloured by *action*, the facts and figures of history. And within such an 'action frame', one can indeed forever debate the relative importance of good deeds and bad deeds, of good individuals and bad individuals, without addressing the morally and intellectually tough questions of how, in a civilized *world*, the 'Final Solution' could happen.[1]

I stress the global dimension, for the Holocaust is clearly *not* a 'Polish problem', but a challenge to the whole of Western culture, to Christianity, to our ideas about 'humanity' and 'civilization'. Forty years after, scholars, theologians, artists and survivors are still grappling with the task of understanding *what* happened, while the question of *why* – the one which implicates all Western civilization – remains at the core of their work.[2] It may seem obvious, but it clearly is not in Poland, that Poles too must share in this broad sense of moral responsibility, responsibility for *defining* the Jew as a 'problem' to be solved.

That even the most vicious among anti-semites in Poland never advocated mass extermination as a 'solution' is historically important. But the Western critique 'after Auschwitz' is not limited to people who did. It is, rather, concerned with a much larger myth, in which the Jew is seen as a threat. Asking 'why the Jews?' does not mean simply asking why the Jews were killed; it means probing into what made the Jew a 'legitimate' target (see, esp. Steiner, 1971, 1987; Arendt, 1973; Lifton, 1986). The question has in no way been settled; it may never be. Yet without an attempt to answer it, we *are* in danger of allowing history to repeat itself.

In the West, inquiries into the mythic structure of anti-semitism lead in many different directions: some focus on the role of Christian theology (e.g. Trachtenberg, 1943/1983; Isaac, 1964), some on the dislocations produced by modernity (e.g. Wilson, 1982), some on the manipulation of fear (e.g. Cohn, 1967). Whatever the area, these analyses share the basic premise that it takes *work* to define Jews, Jewishness or Judaism as 'problems'. The complexity of historical legacies notwithstanding, nowhere is anti-Jewishness perceived as 'natural'. At times, circumstances make the Jew an easier target for hostility than others; at times, the degree of hostility bears little relation to any 'objective factors' – the case, in fact, with Nazi Germany. At times, the Jews' acceptance of their society's vision of their condition lends legitimacy to 'progressive solutions' aiming to make the Jew less Jewish – the case of France, until fairly recently. At times, the Jews see their condition as a 'problem' indeed, but on terms radically different from most – the case in Poland during the inter-war period.

In short, neither the process of defining the Jew as a 'problem', nor the Jews' own contribution to it, are constant. Historically, there are no obvious connections, for example, between the extent of Jewish presence and the extent of 'Jewish threat'.³ In the contemporary context as well, the size and position of a Jewish community is a poor measure of the depth of anti-Jewish feelings among the populace (see: Lewis, 1987; Sachar, 1986).

Definitions change, especially in this century. In Canada, where Jewish refugees from Hitler were not admitted for fear of 'contamination' (Abella and Troper, 1983) and where quotas for Jewish students persisted into the 1950s, the well-organized Jewish community today serves as a model of multi-cultural accommodation to other ethnic groups. Canadian Jews may still hotly debate the wisdom of publicly speaking up against anti-semitism (see: Weimann and Winn, 1986), but when they do, they enjoy overwhelming popular support. And Jewish businessmen wearing skull-caps to the Toronto stock exchange are no longer even objects of curiosity.

Jews have never been a homogeneous people. Even before moderniza-tion, which so greatly transformed the definition of 'proper' Jewishness, Jews could hardly be called uniform in their ways of life or their relations with others. And historical record prohibits generalizations by which a *type* of Jewish identity could be associated with the *burden* it represented. For example, very traditional Jews who lived in the Arab world before de-colonization began enjoyed far greater acceptance than their modern brethren in nineteenth-century Paris. Islam did not define being Jewish as a 'problem' (see: Lewis, 1987); the ethos of 'liberté, égalité, fraternité' did. Even today, that legacy is still 'operational', as the young Sephardim in France (whose parents or grandparents immigrated from North Africa) appear much more at ease with the new, self-assertive Jewishness, than do the descendants of the old French Jewry (see: Schnapper, 1980).

The case of France is particularly instructive when one seeks to understand the *persistence*, in Poland, of identifying Jewishness with a 'problem'. Put quite simply, it is in France that we find the roots of the humanistic ethos shared by many Polish social reformers of the past and the democratic opposition of the present. The basic notion of 'equality', as applied to the Jews in post-revolutionary France, was very explicitly aimed at *individuals*. With no provisions for Jews as a people, 'emancipation' allowed only for individual entry into society (see, esp. Philippe, 1979). Jews were not asked to convert (though it obviously helped when some did), but they were expected to become like everyone else and to restrict their Judaism to the private sphere. The ideal of citizenship, together with the strongly anti-clerical thrust of 'progress', denied religion as a basis for group solidarity. Culturally, French Jews were to become French, leaving their faith at home, so to speak.

This they did, though without sundering community ties (see: Cohen, 1977). When large numbers of Eastern Europeans emigrated to France in the late nineteenth century, French Jews 'de vieille souche' responded with a combination of loyalty and embarrassment, fear of consequences and energetic efforts to 'solve the problem' (see: Kriegel, 1977). The very appearance of all those 'caftan Jews' was an offence to propriety; the sooner they could be 'civilized' the better.

This perception of Jews as a backward people (a people who could become useful citizens only after being properly groomed in modern ways),[4] coupled with an optimistic belief in the value of education, was at the heart of progressive thinking on the 'Jewish question' in Poland as well (see, esp.: Cała, 1984). The aim of reform, directed at peasants even more than at Jews, was to bring all social strata into the national community, at the very time that the existence of Poland as a European nation was threatened. For a while, the ideal of assimilation appeared to gain ground. Polish Jews – especially those in large cities – were modernizing and adopting much of Polish culture as their own. There seemed only a small step to social integration.

That integration did not happen; Polonized Jews remained largely outside the 'purely Polish' social circles.[5] Yet the *appeal* of integration (via assimilation), however challenged by practice, remained strong among a minority of Jews and a majority of Polish progressive intelligentsia (see: Hertz, 1979). Ideally, a person's being Jewish was to become *irrelevant* in social intercourse, where everyone would be treated equally. Even to mention that someone was Jewish became an offence to etiquette, gradually to be considered anti-semitism par excellence.

During the inter-war period, the ideal of the Jews' polonization represented only one among many options for Jews – and for Poles. Twenty years later, in the 1950s, it would become the predominant, if not the sole, prescription for Polish-Jewish coexistence. And what happened in the interim – the Holocaust – was greatly to strengthen both its desirability and its pragmatic inevitability, as it were.

The few Jews who survived, and the even fewer Jews who remained in Poland after 1947, were no longer considered an 'economic problem'. If not all of them could *yet* be categorized as 'Poles of Jewish origin', they could – with the help of the Polish majority – render their Jewishness altogether invisible. Already 'properly Polish' in their outward appearance, already declared patriots, these 'nominal Jews' were now to be fully accepted as Poles. What was unrealized before the war now seemed possible, as long as everyone could agree that being Jewish was not to matter.

Once again, a good deal of inspiration for this view came from France. In 1947, the Polish translation of J.-P. Sartre's reflections on the 'Jewish question' rapidly became standard reference for discussions of anti-semitism. Sartre argued, essentially, that Jewishness was a creation of the hostile environment, that if only Jews were not constantly 'reminded' of their origins, they could and would become like everyone else. Coming only a few years after the Nazi 'reminders' had sentenced even converts to death, Sartre's analysis chimed in very well indeed with the legacy of horror. To single out all people of Jewish ancestry as Jews became inseparable from the memory of the 'Final Solution'. If history was not to repeat itself, the Jew had to be welcomed to 'blend in', never to stand apart again.

The anti-Jewish violence which marred the first years after the liberation (see: Bauer, 1970; Dobroszycki, 1973; Hillel, 1985), and the July 1946 pogrom in Kielce in particular, added a local component to this general lesson on conflict management. For the Jews who resolved to stay, those strongly committed to the future of Poland (and to their own future there), becoming invisible offered protection and some hope. The psychological discomfort inherent in 'passing' was often counterbalanced by the energy and optimism of participating in the reconstruction of the war-ravaged country, *their* country. Those who survived the Holocaust by 'passing' were the last to question the value of being like everyone else.[6]

Polish democrats, recognizing that the Holocaust did not bring an end to anti-semitism, now had another frighteningly solid reason for advocating the Jews' integration. For anti-semitism to disappear, education would not be enough. To avoid provoking hostility, the Jews themselves needed symbolically to 'disappear'.

The model of 'silent Jewishness' which resulted from the combined Polish *and* Jewish effort at peaceful coexistence received very strong support from Poland's new régime, both ideological and practical. (Indeed, if there was one group of Polish Jews which adopted this model with nearly unanimous fervour, it was the Communists.) Long-held beliefs in the principle of 'internationalism', mixed with pragmatic concern over the popularity of a clearly unpopular party (see: Polonsky and Drukier, 1980), produced a complex strategy of public attack and silence – 'attack', since (at least in the early post-war years), public expressions of anti-semitism were actively fought, while public remembrance of the Holocaust became prominent in the official view of history; 'silence', as the last traces of Jewish culture gradually disappeared not only from the homes of Jewish Party activists (see: Blumsztajn, 1985), but from the public sphere as well.

Not only was the strategy complex, but, to a large extent, it was self-contradictory and self-defeating. The emphasis on Jewish martyrdom, exemplified by the construction of the Warsaw monument to the ghetto fighters in 1948, *before* any of the Polish resisters were honoured, could not but produce popular resentment (see also: Smolar, 1986). Condemnation of anti-semitism, when framed within the propaganda effort to extol the Soviet 'liberators' of Poland, backfired as well. Most importantly, the high Jewish presence within the ranks of the régime – and especially within the sensitive areas of economic planning, cultural policy and security – was recognized by Poles both despite and because of the 'invisibility tactics'.[7]

The point here, however, is not that the official strategy failed. It is, rather, that the implicit message of *both* the Communists and the much more authoritative democratic forces was practically the same: the Jews needed to assimilate if the 'Jewish problem' was to be solved.

Apart from the clearly political interests, which had little to do with ethics, the intentions behind the 'silence imperative' were quite benevolent. The *results*, however, were not. However successfully or unsuccessfully the Jews' integration proceeded, the identification of Jewish presence as a 'problem' was almost guaranteed to remain unchallenged. When being pro-Jewish came to mean respecting a person without regard for his background, Jewishness had little hope of being recognized as worthy of respect in and of itself.

The distinction between 'equality' for individuals and 'equality' for *collectivities* has more than a theoretical significance here. As long as being Polish is the standard of 'normality', and being Jewish is perceived as a deviation best politely ignored, the Jews remain inferior by tacit definition.[8] As long as the statement 'he is a Jew' implies that 'something is not quite right ...', true acceptance of the Other is impossible (see also: Mrożek, 1984, 1985).

In the course of my research, I was twice strongly reminded of just how pervasive is this idea that being Polish is somehow *better* than being Jewish; on both occasions, the reminding was done by Polish Jews who did not leave the country until some years after 1968. At issue was something seemingly simple – my insistence on talking about 'Poles' and 'Jews'. The criticism focused, quite naturally, on the inappropriateness of calling a 'Pole of Jewish origin' a 'Jew', whatever his feelings on the matter. Not to respect the person's right to Polishness, I was told, was to play into the hands of anti-semitic propagandists (at the time still prominent in Polish officialdom).

While I agreed that the single category of 'Jews' downplays the psychological complexity, I also argued that Jewishness, self-declared or not, did matter *sociologically*. Only later, after a similar query from my American thesis advisers, one pointing out the absurdity of saying, for example, 'Americans *and* Jews' (when referring to American Jews), did I realize what lay behind the definitional disputes. My granting Poles and Jews separate-but-equal status as *peoples* not only ran counter to the deeply cherished notion that Jews *could* become Poles, but also defied the tacit assumptions about the problematic qualities of Jewishness itself. I sensed, in short, that the very choice of words was making the statement, one I clearly wished to make, that Jews are *not* a 'problem'.

That words make a difference can be seen by tracing the language shifts which have occurred in France. During the nineteenth and early twentieth centuries, French Jews were named 'Israélites', largely to avoid the traditionally negative connotations of the term 'Juifs'. Today, 'Israélites' is perceived as an archaic description, or worse, as a symbol of effacing one's Jewishness at the demands of the French establishment. The word 'juif', however, while now widely used to describe French Jews, also met with disfavour as a more self-assertive collective identity began to emerge some twenty years ago. Why? Because 'juif', an adjective, parallels the adjective 'catholique', thus projecting a restrictively religious distinction. On the other hand, the noun 'Juif', which has gained most ground, parallels 'Français', a clear sign to French Jews and to their country that Jews are indeed a people (see: Irwin-Zarecka, 1984). French Jews, one should add, have not become any less French in the process; rather, they have been moving away from the idea that being Jewish is 'gênant' (meaning a mixture of shame and embarrassment), the idea still in force in the late 1970s (see: Harris and Sédouy, 1979). As their country begins to acknowledge that it is *not* ethnically homogeneous, French Jews become ever more adamant about their *collective* rights to equality. In the new pluralistic vision of their society, the old 'aspirations' to be French have given way to efforts to grow culturally *as* Jews.[9]

For a number of French Jewish intellectuals, this new and assertive cultural agenda has necessitated first settling some accounts with France. This did not just mean bringing to public attention the crimes of Vichy, though the discussion of the part played by the French in the 'Final Solution' was obviously important. Less known in the English-speaking world, but equally significant for re-defining French Jewishness, were the scathing critiques of the ideological premises, both Rightist and Leftist, which turned the Jew into a 'problem' (see: Lévy, 1981; Trigano, 1982; Sternhell, 1983). The whole mythic structure of anti-semitism was opened to analytical scrutiny, without much regard for political preferences. And what has emerged so far is a complex picture indeed of hard ideological *work* behind this little adjective 'gênant'.

The process of coming to terms with the legacies of the French-Jewish past is a difficult one for French Jews perhaps even more than for their non-Jewish compatriots (see: Harris and Sédouy, 1979). Precisely because to be French was for so long considered superior to being Jewish, it takes a great deal of time and effort to establish one's identity in non-problematic terms.[10]

For most Polish Jews, such an issue does not exist. Theirs was indeed a problem-ridden existence in Poland, but they did not define themselves as inferior. I. B. Singer, to take the best known example, never 'aspired' to be Polish; he loved his country, his city, his people, but did not want to blend in with the majority (see: Singer and Burgin, 1985). The more traditional religious Jews had no use at all for the Catholic-inspired view of the world; they too felt at home without any desire to 'advance' to Polishness. When they and their secular brethren discussed the 'Jewish problem' in the 1920s or 1930s, they did not perceive *themselves* as a problem; at issue were economic hardships, job discrimination, political powerlessness and violence (see: Korzec, 1980). However divided, as they very much were, most Polish Jews had a strong sense of their identity as a people, a sense they retained when leaving for America or Palestine.

In North America in particular, Jewish immigrants from Poland parted ways with the Poles who came at the same time.[11] Their attachment to Poland, much like Singer's, is an attachment to 'Jewish Poland', especially strong after this world had been destroyed (see: Kugelmass and Boyarin, 1983). And if they have any problem coming to terms with the past, it is that of recognizing the *positives* of Poland's treatment of the Jews (see, esp.: Mendelsohn, 1986).

The people for whom 'Jewishness as a problem' is an issue – or should be – are both the Polish Jews who worked hard to become Polish and the Poles themselves. For the Jews, what is at stake is primarily a certain peace of mind, a way of reckoning with one's own biography, an often difficult choice of personal loyalties and commitments. (Although an individual journey, such reckoning can have public impact as well, especially when it takes place *in* Poland.)[12]

For the Poles, the stakes are in many ways much higher. Though from a purely pragmatic point of view re-defining the terms of Polish-Jewish relations is much less urgent than changes in perceptions of Ukrainians or Lithuanians or Czechs, the 'theoretical' significance of the Jew is a different matter altogether. Such a significance has been recognized by many Polish intellectuals, especially those of the younger generation (see, esp.: Redakcja *Arki*, 1987). The great interest (not to say fascination) generated by things Jewish in the last ten years is both explicitly and implicitly linked to a desire for a more *pluralistic* sense of Polishness. Deprived of their 'natural' Other, Poles now appear eager to re-invent him, as it were, by welcoming him into their memory. Polish culture can only gain, after all, from being enriched by the centuries-old Jewish heritage. And, perhaps most importantly, the Poles' understanding of themselves can also only gain from a better appreciation of Polish-Jewish experience.

Once again, despite the vast differences between the political implications that this new welcome to the Jew represents for the régime and the democratic forces (within both the Catholic milieu and the opposition), the overall message is essentially the same: the Jew now becomes worth knowing, respecting and remembering; there is no 'Jewish problem' in a country with only a few thousand Jews remaining. And once again, the *intentions* behind this 'memory invitation' are by no means malevolent (even allowing for the purely instrumental uses to which it is often put by the régime).

To assess the *results* of this new approach to things Jewish, especially at a time when it is still being shaped and re-shaped, has been difficult. As in any analysis, much here has depended on the questions asked of what I term a 'Jewish memory project' – the intensive effort to recognize Polish Jewish history as Poland's own. For if one is interested solely in Polish attitudes towards Jews, current developments clearly spell *change*. But if one is concerned, as I was, with the deeply-held assumptions about the Jew – or with the Poles' understanding of the past – the 'Jewish memory project' still has considerable progress to make before any significant transformation.

As I have said, these two concerns are very much connected. What connects them is precisely the idea that the Jewish presence is problematic by definition, at the individual as well as societal level. In other words, until Jews, as people and as a people, are perceived as 'normal' (thus equal to Poles), there is little chance for Poland truly to reckon with the legacy of the past. As long as it is taken for granted that the very presence of Jews (*their* position in society, *their* separateness, *their* actions) naturally, and inevitably, leads to anti-semitism, a huge, morally challenging area of Polish-Jewish history remains beyond the reach of questions.[13]

With all the best intentions, and all the animus against anti-semitism in the current discourse, the key obstacle to a self-critical re-evaluation of the past is primarily of cognitive order. However, it is *not* ignorance which is at issue here, but the sense that one already knows all there is to know about Polish-Jewish experience just by looking at what *kind* of problems the Jews posed; the question of *why* the Jew was considered a problem to begin with has thus been excluded from the intellectual agenda.

To remove this 'cognitive block' from the inquiry into Polish-Jewish history would mean much more, however, than an intellectual shift of perspectives. It means also, or rather primarily, acceptance of a share of *moral* responsibility for what happened to the Jews. Their being defined as a problem was not simply a symbolic matter; it had very real consequences – in 1930, in 1943 or in 1946. The question of what made it possible for the Jews to be a target of murderous wrath *after* the Holocaust cannot be answered, morally or intellectually, without first addressing the history of the Jew's definition as a problem.[14] Nor can questions about Polish-Jewish relations during the Holocaust. In essence, no question about recent history in particular can bypass the issue, not if one aims for a fair picture of the past.[15]

The serious moral implications notwithstanding, I think that change in this area need not necessarily come from increased moral sensitivity. For better or for worse, a willingness to search one's conscience does not automatically produce a departure from the 'problem approach';[16] the unwillingness to do so, on the other hand, does not automatically preclude it. What can – and to some extent already does – make the difference is exposure to the Jew on his own terms.

In that respect, three aspects of the 'Jewish memory project' allow for a moderate degree of optimism, for hope that among the younger generations, in particular, the perception of the Jew will be freed of the 'problem approach'. First, the very appeal of Jewish culture (in its traditional forms as well as the modern ones), so evident in the popularity of artistic productions, however coloured it may be by a certain exoticism, does bring to the public an increasing variety of the Jews' perceptions of themselves. In the process, the Jew begins to 'normalize', to exhibit all the usual human strengths and weaknesses, to gain respectability *as* a Jew.

The symbolic shift towards 'normality' cannot be accomplished without some actual human contact. It is then very important for Poles today to see and hear a growing number of Jewish scholars, artists or simply 'unashamed' Jews from the West, including the Israelis. For a person whose view of the Jew is predicated on the 'problem approach', such contacts may, of course, only reinforce the notion. But for many young people who are only now making sense of what 'Jewish' is, listening to Leonard Cohen may be a first step towards recognizing that Jewishness is *not* a problem.

Finally, the 'Jewish memory project', for all the heated debate on Poles and the Holocaust, has brought the *Jewish* experience during the Holocaust into a new, much closer focus. Although by no means displacing the popular vision of Poles on a par with Jews as victims of Nazi genocide,[17] the rapidly augmenting array of historical source-materials and high-standard analyses begins to set the background for a serious reflection on the Holocaust, a reflection which would take the question beyond the area of Polish-Jewish relations. All this is important for Polish perceptions of the Jew, because it is with the reflection on the uniqueness of the Holocaust that the full recognition of the *mythic* structure of anti-semitism emerged. In other words, the realization of *what* can happen once the Jew is defined as a legitimate target has led to the concerted effort to understand *how* such a definition came to be. And this, the inquiry into the development of the 'problem approach', is what is most lacking from the discussions of things Jewish in Poland today.

At issue here, I should re-emphasize, is not the need for more studies of 'anti-semitism in Poland'. Indeed, if there is a proper starting point for inquiries into the problematization of Jewishness, it lies with the ideas and actions of people who were *not* anti-semites by any reasonable stretch of the definition. (Cała's work on the problematics of assimilation [1984] exemplifies the value of such an approach.) On the contemporary front as well, it is the well-meaning and polite silence vis-à-vis the Jew which demands attention, rather than loud proclamations by the Association Grunwald. It is only with the shift of critical focus *away* from unabashedly anti-Jewish views that we may arrive at a better understanding of the texture of Polish-Jewish experience (see, e.g.: Kuroń, 1981/1983; Mrożek, 1984).

Such a shift of perspectives requires work – emotionally, intellectually, morally. It demands, most importantly, a recognition that the 'Jewish problem' was *not* an inevitable product of history (and human nature).

Making it possible – today – for Poles to think of Jews as their equals is clearly a positive step. But if the 'Jewish memory project' is to fulfil its obligations to the past as well as to the future, it must also make it possible for Poles to see what is behind the frequently heard assertion that their country no longer has a 'Jewish problem'.

NOTES

1 The urge to bring universal concerns back into the realm of 'objectively accessible' deeds is clear in the recent discussion on the Holocaust in *Więź* ('Między . . .', 1986). Indeed, among Polish writers, only Lem, in one of his 'reviews of imaginary books' (1984) addresses the Holocaust without simultaneously speaking of Poles.

2 Questions about *direct* responsibility are not absent; indeed, these questions have been gradually applied to the ever-widening spectrum of collective actors – from Western governments (see: Morse, 1983; Abella and Troper, 1983; Laqueur, 1980; Marrus and Paxton, 1981) to the American media (Lipstadt, 1986) to Jewish organizations (Nurenberger, 1985). The freer historians feel to analyse a field long considered too imposing (see: Marrus, 1987), the more this trend will continue.

3 A study of England (Glassma, 1975) is most instructive in this respect; it was during the fifteenth and sixteenth centuries, when no Jews lived there, that English literature became filled with anti-Jewish stereotypes.

4 Cuddihy (1987), though himself *not* questioning this perception, offers a challenging analysis of its impact on modern Jewish intellectuals.

5 Indeed, many Polonized Jews would join Jewish national movements – Zionism or Bund, for example (Mendelsohn, 1981, Ertel, 1982).

6 The very direct, life-saving value of assimilation may explain why the *principle* retained such popularity in Poland. In the West, in contrast, the Holocaust became a lesson on the failure of assimilation; in North America especially, memory of the Holocaust gradually evolved into a strong basis for Jewish identity (see, e.g. Fackenheim, 1978).

7 The Jews' *political* prominence replaced their economic 'domination' as a basis for their being defined as a problem. The politicization of the 'Jewish problem', in turn, provided an all-too-convenient explanation of the post-war anti-Jewish violence (see, esp. Kersten, 1986).

8 The argument here closely parallels the feminist critique of the 'man's world'. As long as masculine traits remain the standard to be aspired to by women, equality is a delusion.

9 The cultural 'renaissance' of French Jewry takes many forms, from the growing popularity of Jewish studies to tremendous literary and artistic activity, to political consolidation of the community. (Return to full religious observance is an option adopted by relatively few.)

10 The best account of shifts in Jewish identity – with emphasis on the new interest in the past – may be found in Finkielkraut's aptly titled *Le Juif imaginaire* (1980).

11 Exceptions to this general rule may be found among the Jews who left in the aftermath of 1968; with a high number of mixed marriages, however, and often strong prior identification with Polishness, this emigration is quite different from the earlier ones (see: Bauman, 1969).

12 The small group of young Polish Jews who returned to a culturally self-assertive form of Jewishness – and who make their concern with the Jewish heritage very public indeed – is a *symbolically* important challenge to the older, silent Polish-Jewish identity

(see also Wieviorka, 1984; Niezabitowska, 1986: 77–111). Their views on the 'Jewish problem', however, are not altogether different from those of most Poles.

13 Kieniewicz (*Polityka*, 15 Dec. 1984) and Tazbir (*Polityka*, 21–7 Dec. 1985), both prominent historians and both writing for a popular audience, best exemplify this 'inevitability principle' in explaining anti-semitism. Cała's work on the problematics of assimilation (1984, 1986) offers a still- too-rare instance of an analysis *not* operating on this premise, as does the study by Eisenbach (1983).

14 For this reason, when explanations are couched in purely political terms, as they are in the case of the Kielce pogrom, they essentially neutralize the past. Removed from consideration is precisely the origin of 'Jew = Communist = problem' (see e.g.: Kersten, 1986).

15 I stress 'recent history' here, for while the process of problematizing the Jewish presence began centuries ago, it was not until the collapse of the feudal system that the 'Jewish problem' acquired its full mythic structure.

16 For example, the widely debated statement by Lipski (1983), while raising many a morally tough question, ultimately leaves the 'problem approach' intact. It defines anti-semitism as a tool used by Poland's enemies, but does not raise questions about what made such a tool viable.

17 Both in 1983 and in 1988, on the occasion of commemorating the Warsaw Ghetto Uprising, the emphasis on Jewish victimization existed side-by-side with an emphasis on *shared* fate.

REFERENCES

Abella, Irving and Troper, Harold 1983: *None is Too Many: Canada and the Jews of Europe 1933–1948*. Toronto: Lester & Orpen Dennys.

Arendt, Hannah 1973: *The Origins of Totalitarianism*. New York: Harcourt Brace Jovanovich.

Bauer, Yehuda 1970: *Flight and Rescue: BRICHAH*. New York: Random House.

Bauman, Zygmunt 1969: 'The End of Polish Jewry. A Sociological Review'. *Bulletin on Soviet and East European Jewish Affairs*, 3 (Jan.): 3–9.

Blumsztajn, Seweryn 1985: *Je rentre au pays. Polonais, juif, membre du KOR et de Solidarité*. Paris: Calmann-Lévy.

Błoński, Jan 1987: 'Biedni Polacy patrzą na getto'. *Tygodnik Powszechny*, (11 Jan.).

Cała, Alina 1984: 'Kwestia asymilacji Żydów w Królestwie Polskim (1864–1897): Pozycje, konflikty, stereotypy'. Warsaw: Instytut Historii PAN. (Ph.D. dissertation).

—— 1986: 'Kwestia asymilacji Żydów w Królestwie Polskim (1864–1897): Refleksje i dygresje'. *Znak*, nos. 377–8 (4–5) (Apr./May): 64–92.

Cohen, Phyllis Albert 1977: *The Modernization of French Jewry: Consistory and Community in the Nineteenth Century*. Hanover, N. H.: Brandeis University Press.

Cohn, Norman 1967: *Warrant for Genocide: The Myth of the Jewish World-Conspiracy and the 'Protocols of the Elders of Zion'*. New York: Harper & Row.

Cuddihy, John Murray 1987: *The Ordeal of Civility. Freud, Marx, Lévi-Strauss, and the Jewish Struggle with Modernity*. Boston: Beacon Press.

Dobroszycki, Lucjan 1973: 'Restoring Jewish Life in Post-War Poland'. *Soviet Jewish Affairs* 2: 58–72.

Eisenbach, Artur 1983: *Z dziejów ludności żydowskiej w Polsce w XVIII i XIX wieku*. Warsaw: Państwowy Instytut Wydawniczy.

Engel, David 1983: 'An Early Account of Polish Jewry under Nazi and Soviet Occupation Presented to the Polish Government-in-Exile, February 1940'. *Jewish Social Studies*, 45 (1): 1–17.

—— 1987: *In the Shadow of Auschwitz. The Polish Government- in-Exile and the Jews*. Chapel Hill: University of North Carolina Press.
Ertel, Rachel 1982: *Le Shtetl. La bourgade juive de Pologne. De la tradition à modernité*. Paris: Payot.
Fackenheim, Emil L. 1978: *The Jewish Return into History. Reflections in the Age of Auschwitz and a New Jerusalem*. New York: Schocken Books.
Finkielkraut, Alain 1980: *Le Juif imaginaire*. Paris: Seuil.
Glassma, Bernard 1975: *Anti-Semitic Stereotypes without Jews: Images of the Jews in England 1290-1700*. Detroit: Wayne State University Press.
Harris, André and Alain de Sédouy 1979: *Juifs et Français*. Paris: Grasset.
Hertz, Aleksander 1979: *Wyznania starego człowieka*. London: Oficyna Poetów i Malarzy.
Hillel, Marc 1985: *Le massacre des survivants. En Pologne après l'holocauste 1945-1947*. Paris: Plon.
Irwin-Zarecka, Iwona 1984: '"Jewish Rennaissance" in France'. Paper presented at the ASA Meetings, San Antonio, Texas.
—— 1989: *Neutralizing Memory: The Jew in Contemporary Poland*. New Brunswick, NJ: Transaction Books.
Isaac, Jules 1964: *The Teaching of Contempt: Christian Roots of Anti-Semitism*. New York: Holt, Rinehart and Winston.
Kersten, Krystyna 1986: *Narodziny systemu władzy. Polska 1943-1948*. Paris: Libella.
Kieniewicz, Stefan 1984: 'Polacy i Żydzi w XIX wieku'. *Polityka* (15 Dec.).
Korzec, Paweł 1980: *Juifs en Pologne. La question juive pendant l'entre-deux-guerres*. Paris: Presses de la Fondation Nationale des Sciences Politiques.
Kriegel, Annie 1977: *Les Juifs et le monde moderne*. Paris: Seuil.
Kugelmass, Jack and Jonathan Boyarin (eds. and tr.) 1983: *From a Ruined Garden: The Memorial Books of Polish Jewry*. New York: Schocken Books.
Kuroń, Jacek 1983: 'Między październikiem 56 a marcem 68'. *Zeszyty Edukacji Narodowej* (1), (edited presentation at Warsaw University, 1981).
Laqueur, Walter 1980: *The Terrible Secret: An Investigation in the Suppression of Information about Hitler's 'Final Solution'*. London: Weidenfeld and Nicolson.
Lem, Stanisław 1984: *Prowokacja*. Kraków/Wrocław: Wydawnictwo Literackie.
Lévy, Bernard-Henri 1981: *L'idéologie française*. Paris: Bernard Grasset.
Lewis, Bernard 1987: *Semites and Anti-Semites: An Inquiry into Conflict and Prejudice*. New York: W. W. Norton.
Lifton, Robert Jay 1986: *The Nazi Doctors: Medical Killing and Psychology of Genocide*. New York: Basic Books.
Lipski, Jan Józef 1983: 'Polscy Żydzi'. *Kultura* 6/429 (June): 3-9.
Lipstadt, Deborah E. 1986: *Beyond Belief: The American Press and the Coming of the Holocaust 1933-1945*. New York: The Free Press.
Marrus, Michael R. 1987: *The Holocaust in History*. Toronto: Lester & Orpen Dennys.
Marrus, Michael R. and Robert O, Paxton 1981: *Vichy France and the Jews*. New York: Basic Books.
Mendelsohn, Ezra 1981: *Zionism in Poland: The Formative Years, 1915-1926*. New Haven/London: Yale University Press.
—— 1986: 'Interwar Poland: Good for the Jews or Bad for the Jews?', in Abramsky et al., eds, *The Jews in Poland*. Oxford: Basil Blackwell.
Morse, Arthur D. 1983: *While Six Million Died: A Chronicle of American Apathy*. Woodstock, NY: The Overlook Press.
Mrożek, Sławomir 1984: 'Nos'. *Kultura* 442 (July); 443 (Aug.): 37-45.
—— 1985: 'Podejrzenie'. *Kultura* 458 (Nov.): 42-4.
Niezabitowska, Małgorzata 1986: *Remnants: The Last Jews of Poland*. New York: Friendly Press.

Nurenburger, M.J. 1985: *The Scared and the Doomed: The Jewish Establishment vs. The Six Million*. Oakville, Ont.: Mosaic Press.
Philippe, Béatrice 1979: *Être juif dans la societé française*. Paris: Editions Montalba.
Polonsky, Antony and Bolesław Drukier 1980: *The Beginnings of Communist Rule in Poland*. London: Routledge & Kegan Paul.
Redakcja 'Arki' 1987: 'Filolodzy kontra komunizm'. *Kultura* 472 (Jan.); 473 (Feb.): 173–91.
Sachar, Howard M. 1986: *Diaspora: An Inquiry into the Contemporary Jewish World*. New York: Harper & Row.
Schnapper, Dominique 1980: *Juifs et israélites*. Paris: Gallimard.
Singer, Isaac Bashevis and Richard Burgin 1985: *Conversations with Isaac Bashevis Singer*. Garden City, NY: Doubleday.
Smolar, Aleksander 1986: 'Tabu i niewinność'. *Aneks* 41-2: 89–134.
Steiner, George 1971: *In Bluebeard's Castle. Some Notes Towards the Re-definition of Culture*. London: Faber & Faber.
—— 'The Long Life of Metaphor: An Approach to "the Shoah"'. *Encounter* (Feb.): 55–62.
Sternhell, Zeev 1983: *Ni droite ni gauche. L'idéologie fasciste en France*. Paris: Seuil.
Tazbir, Janusz 1985: 'Staropolski obraz Żyda'. *Polityka* 21-7 Dec.
Trachtenberg, Joshua 1983: *The Devil and the Jews: The Medieval Conception of the Jew and its Relation to Modern Anti-Semitism*. Philadelphia: The Jewish Publication Society of America) (first edn.: 1943, Yale University Press).
Trigano, Shmuel 1982: *La République et les Juifs après Copernic*. Paris: Les presses d'aujourd'hui.
Weimann, Gabriel and Conrad Winn 1986: *Hate on Trial: The Zundel Affair, the Media and Public Opinion in Canada*. Oakville, Ont.: Mosaic Press.
Wieviorka, Michel 1984: *Les Juifs, la Pologne et Solidarność*. Paris: Denoël.
Wilson, Stephen 1982: *Ideology and Experience. Anti-semitism in France at the time of the Dreyfus Affair*. East Brunswick, NJ: Associated University Presses.

OF HELP, UNDERSTANDING AND HOPE: RIGHTEOUS RESCUERS AND POLISH JEWS

Nechama Tec

On 17 September 1984, nearly forty years after the surrender of Nazi Germany, the Holocaust Memorial Council convened its first international conference on Christians who during World War II endangered their lives to save Jews. This conference was titled 'Faith in Humankind (Rescuers of Jews During the Holocaust)'. This gathering was to honour these selfless heroes, to exchange ideas among scholars, and to promote good will and interfaith harmony.

What had prompted the organizers, Harry Cargas, Carol Rittner and Elie Wiesel, to convene this important event?

Harry Cargas told me that by concentrating on heroism, compassion and goodness, they had hoped to reduce the pain and despair that inevitably came with the examination of the Holocaust. These expectations made sense. But why did their special interest, and the very recently evident interest of others, come so late? After all, the destruction of European Jewry and the acts of selfless protection happened at the same time, more than forty years ago. Why only now have we become involved in learning about and celebrating this rare and special kind of goodness?

Perhaps the answer lies in the very nature of the Holocaust, its extreme cruelty and devastation? For in those tragic times compassion and self-sacrifice were rare, hence easily overshadowed by the enormity of the Nazi crimes. Not surprisingly, therefore, only after we became acquainted with the main features of that period could we even begin to notice these rare and selfless heroes. Once noticed, however, their presence inevitably led to a desire to understand, to learn and to honour.

Not unexpectedly, then, on that sunny September day more than a thousand people showed up. Seventy-five of them had risked their lives for Jews. They were but a fraction of all righteous Christians, a title bestowed upon them by Yad Vashem, the Jerusalem Memorial for Martyrs and Heroes of the Holocaust.

As for the rest of the arrivals, they fit into a variety of overlapping categories; Jewish Holocaust survivors who did and did not benefit from Christian aid, scholars, politicians, diplomats from different countries and representatives of the mass media. In addition to their past and occupation the differences between these participants extended to nationality, religion, age and no doubt much more. Both the size and diversity of this turnout only underlined the appeal and need for such a gathering.

Reflecting this wide range of interests, the printed programme was subdivided into three broad parts: plenary sessions, sessions devoted to special European regions or countries, and sessions that concentrated on special issues: research, education, psychology and others.

Heading the list of distinguished speakers were the writer, educator and Chairman of the Holocaust Memorial Council, Elie Wiesel, and Barttlett Gamatti, President of Yale University. Among the dignitaries from abroad was the Israeli supreme court judge Moshe Bejski, Chairman of the Committee of the Righteous in Yad Vashem, Jerusalem. Originally from Poland, Bejski was saved by the famous German industrialist Oskar Schindler. Another easily-recognized name was that of Jan Karski, Professor of Government at Georgetown University. During the war, Karski, a member of the Polish diplomatic corps, became a courier travelling between occupied Poland and the free West. In Poland, Karski met with Jewish leaders in the Warsaw ghetto. He also risked his life by smuggling himself into the death camp, Bełżec, because he wanted to observe directly what was being done to the Jews. When he reached the West he conveyed his impressions to the Allies, to Jewish leaders, and to the Polish government in exile in London. This happened in 1942. What the Allies did with this information belongs to history.

Participation in this Washington conference was not limited to holders of famous names and scholars. On the contrary, many of the speakers were simply Christians who had saved Jews, and survivors who had benefited from their aid. Most of them were invited because of their wartime experiences, experiences they were asked to share. The rich and diversified programme made it clear that the main purpose of this gathering was to listen to and honour those who selflessly risked their lives for Jews.

Indeed, when the conference opened with an air of festive anticipation, this handful of heroes received a warm welcome. After all, we had come to celebrate human goodness! Besides, with the official endorsement of the government, with the John F. Kennedy Center and the State Department building as the setting, and with Secretary of State George Shultz as a guest speaker, this gathering promised to fulfil its goals. The first day ended with a congenial cocktail party and an air of eager expectation.

Only the next day did the section on Poland convene, the one I was to participate in. Unlike most other countries that shared a time and place with one or more others, Poland was by itself, alone. Before the specified time my fellow panellists and I arrived at the large auditorium. This was a carefully planned meeting with each of us assigned to a special seat on the podium, in order of appearance. The moderator, the Reverend John T. Pawlikowski, a professor of ethics, was to make the announcements and introductions.

My professional qualifications brought me here, rather than my personal experiences as a Polish Jew who survived the war by passing for a Christian. Since 1977 I have been conducting research on Jewish rescue during World War II with special emphasis on Poland. Though the title of my presentation was 'Christian-Jewish Cooperation in Poland during the Holocaust', much of what I said had to do with Polish-Jewish history, particularly with conditions that had bearing on Polish rescue of Jews. First, I reminded the audience about the ten centuries of Polish-Jewish history and how stormy and uneven they had been. Dominated first by religious anti-semitism, Polish-Jewish relationships improved during the fourteenth century when Poland became a haven for Jews. At that point a few heads nodded approval, while others showed displeasure when I mentioned that Jewish privileges did not extend to land ownership, and that, eventually, these measures were followed by anti-semitism.

When I began to talk about the rebirth of Poland in 1918 and its accompanying virulent anti-semitism, I could sense an uneasy tension. At the mention of Marshal Piłsudski's reign, 1926–1935, which brought a halt to anti-semitic excesses, some listeners, probably Poles, became more relaxed. Then again as I described the many anti-semitic measures in the economic, educational and political spheres and how in 1938 the Polish government went so far as to send a delegation to the island of Madagascar, to explore the possibility of settling Jews there, I could feel the tension mount.

I tried to emphasize what a serious impediment to Jewish rescue this strong and traditional anti-semitism had been. I continued by describing the large pre-war Jewish population in Poland and its lack of assimilation, and how this was reflected in all aspects of Jewish life, including speech. I detected glimmers of recognition, a nod here and there, particularly at my mention of the Polish pre-war census in which only twelve per cent of the Jews identified Polish as their native tongue. Examples of specific Jewish expressions translated into Polish brought out a few smiles. These reactions seemed to be coming from both Poles and Jews. In the back of the auditorium a green sign went up signalling that I had two minutes to wind up my talk. Sitting down I wondered how I had done. The audience had been attentive but not necessarily approving. My feeling was that reactions were divided along Polish-Jewish lines. Was I right or was I simply appraising the situation in terms of my own personal prejudices? I was sure about mounting tensions, but not about much else.

Except for the moderator and myself, the rest of the panellists were asked to talk about their personal experiences as rescuers and rescued. We proved to be a disciplined group who scrupulously followed instructions. We stopped on time and began at the appropriate cue. The audience was attentive as story after story began to unfold about extraordinary danger, heroism and compassion.

The panellists shared their experiences in a matter-of-fact, even apologetic way. It seemed that they were deliberately trying to play down the events. Perhaps they wanted to control their emotions, emotions that were on the verge of breaking out of control. Told in simple yet moving ways these accounts moved onto an exceptional and unusual plane.

And so I listened to the story of soft-spoken Irena Opdyke, who at the age of nineteen saved twelve Jews by hiding them in a cellar, in the house of the German officer for whom she worked. I also heard Ludmila Svinka Zielinski, whose parents saved Jews, denounce anti-semitism. Then I became absorbed in Emanuel Tanay's fascinating description of the complex relationship of victim and saviour. A prominent psychiatrist, Tanay spent part of the war in a convent where he passed as a Christian.

One of the other panellists, my friend Dr Joseph Kutrzeba, came with his saviour Reverend Falkowski, who had arrived from Poland only a few days before. Inseparable, these two men gave the unmistakable impression that they were tied by mutual bonds of strong affection, an affection that defied verbal description. I knew that Falkowski, a parish priest in a Polish village, took the fifteen-year-old Joseph into his single room when he came to him from nowhere, without papers, penniless, friendless and starved. I also knew that for the remainder of the war the priest's protection continued.

My mind was drifting in and out of the conference when Kutrzeba's words reached me: 'You told me that Jews were murdered because they crucified Christ. They were being punished for their sins.' This was not an accusation, just a statement of fact. A part of the audience gasped, while others adjusted their posture to a more erect position. Did I hear correctly? I did. Right away, taken aback and in disbelief the priest asked: 'Did I really say that? Are you sure I told you that?' Reverend Falkowski sounded surprised. It crossed my mind that if he had said it then, he must now have changed his mind. I was glad.

Again without a trace of resentment, quietly and in a flat voice, Kutrzeba answered: 'Yes, you said it. This is how you justified the Jewish tragedy.' With the presentations coming to an end I sat motionless, trying to sort out my own strong and mixed reactions. A brief and tentative silence was followed by the subdued voice of the moderator, the Reverend John T. Pawlikowski. He reminded the audience that the time had come for their participation.

He had barely finished when hell broke loose. It was as if a powerful explosion had just taken place.

Emotionally charged accusations, shouts and insults burst into the open. 'Why', one Jewish man wanted to know, 'were the Jews in Poland slaughtered in such large numbers?' He himself supplied the answer: 'Because the anti-semitic Poles were helping the Germans, they were only too happy to see the Jews destroyed.' Others picked up his arguments. Then someone yelled: 'Why didn't your American Jews help you?'

Of the panellists, Reverend Falkowski tried to give answers, insisting that many Poles saved Jews. In fact, he made the mistake of claiming that most did. His comments were met with jeers. 'How could we do more with the Nazi terror?' someone asked. This was answered by a description of how the Danes managed to save all their Jews. 'Why', someone shouted, 'did the Germans build all the concentration camps in Poland. Why? The Germans knew that the Poles would not mind.' This implied that there was a direct connection between Polish anti-semitism and the building of concentration camps. I heard no direct reaction to this. But then someone wanted to know why the Catholic Church was so indifferent to the Jewish plight. Reverend Falkowski, by now carried away by strong emotions, stood up for the Vatican, not very convincingly. No doubt to help him someone yelled: 'For propaganda purposes you Jews distort the facts!' 'We, too, were helpless, how could we oppose Hitler's terror?' Falkowski's defence of the Vatican did not pass unnoticed. It was followed by a personal attack against him. With more anger and loud volume, the arguments were becoming less coherent. Then Dr Kutrzeba, the man saved by Reverend Falkowski, red-faced, pounded the table. 'This conference is to honour those who helped . . . I would not be here if it were not for my friend, my saviour, my brother . . . this saintly man who risked his life . . . He shouldn't have to defend the role of the entire church in World War II.' Strong applause followed, only to be interrupted by rude cries.

I wanted to calm the atmosphere: 'Poles and Jews had so much in common, if we would only . . .' No one was in a moderating mood, at least not those whose screams took over the meeting. My sense of disappointment was mixed with anger. Soon both of these feelings turned towards myself. I had failed. I blamed myself for a failure to soften the two extreme and rigid positions. Perhaps the content of my presentation should have been different? On balance what I had said was negative. I had concentrated on Polish-Jewish differences, prejudices, estrangement and hostility. Why, at a conference that aimed at promoting brotherly love and harmony, did I choose this down-beat path? Why did I focus on this largely unpleasant negative history? Was I concerned with historical accuracy? Hardly. What, then, had I tried to accomplish? I certainly had no intention of reviving Polish-Jewish antipathies. Nor did I want to point an accusing finger at anyone. I had hoped to achieve the opposite and more. I knew that this conflict-ridden past was a stumbling block for Polish-Jewish cooperation. I also knew that here in that audience there would be some extremists; Poles who refuse to concede that Poland has been an anti-semitic country and Jews who deny that Poles, any Poles, had risked their lives to save Jews, and some who blame the Poles for part of the Holocaust. I had hoped that by facing up to the long and painful past, by airing what kept the Poles and Jews apart, I might succeed in narrowing the gap.

More importantly, I felt that after hearing about the traditionally strong Polish anti-semitism and about other serious impediments to Jewish rescue, the audience would appreciate how difficult it was in this kind of a setting to save Jews. I wanted to impress upon these listeners that Polish anti-semitism, the large number of Jews, their low level of assimilation – each and all interfered in the rescuing of Jews. In short, I wanted them to know that these conditions together with the Nazi terror made the protection of Jews next to impossible.

I might have reached some members of the audience, because, despite the chaotic mixture of voices, a large part of the audience said nothing. Some watched in bewilderment. Others seemed at a loss. Here and there among these speechless onlookers one could see a silent tear. Some tears were wiped absent-mindedly, others were simply left to fall. What did these lonely tears mean? Were they shed for the past? The present? Perhaps even the future? Was it the hostile and conflicting interpretations of what had happened in wartime Poland that caused these tears to appear? Still, within this sea of Polish-Jewish misunderstanding there are some basic facts on which the two sides agree. What are these areas of agreement?

Most concede that the Nazi master plan of Jewish extermination was especially successful in Poland. The estimates for Jewish survivors range from 50 to 100 thousand, compared to the pre-war population of three-and-a-half million. These figures refer only to Polish Jews who during the war remained in the country. Another 200 to 250 thousand left for Russia. Most of them returned after 1945. Of those who remained in Poland and survived some did so in concentration camps, some by staying in the forests fighting as partisans, and by passing or hiding in the forbidden Christian world. No exact figures exist for the different modes of survival, and the estimates for each vary greatly. For the Jews who survived on the Christian side the more realistic figures range from 40 to 60 thousand.

Similarly, most agree that the German preoccupation with Jews did not prevent them from persecuting Poles. In one of their first repressive moves the Germans turned on the Polish élites: the intellectuals and professionals, the clergy and army officers. Many of them were murdered. Others were sent to German concentration camps, and, a little later, to the newly completed concentration camp, Auschwitz. Initially, in Auschwitz, most inmates were members of the Polish élite.

Nor did the Germans limit their persecution to the society's upper echelons. After they had annexed western parts of Poland to the Reich they began to Germanize the region. This was done by a removal of large segments of the native population. Such transfers were performed forcibly and without regard to human cost. As a result many Poles lost their lives. In addition, guided by their economic needs, throughout the war the Germans continued to deport Poles to work in the Reich. An estimated 2.5 million were moved this way. Some of them were worked to death, while others returned in deplorable condition.

Finally, too, throughout the long years of occupation the Germans responded swiftly and brutally to all signs of political opposition. Over time, Nazi abuses created an atmosphere of terror and led to many deaths. Some claim that the Germans succeeded in virtually eliminating the Polish intelligentsia. Others estimate that out of more than thirty million, over two million civilian Poles fell victim to Nazi terror. More precise figures are elusive.

Apart from such agreed facts, much of what transpired between the Poles and Jews during the war is still being disputed. What did actually happen? What role, if any, did the Poles play in the annihilation of Jews? To what extent did the Poles hinder the Germans, and to what extent did they aid them? Finally, who of the Poles and who of the Jews is best qualified to give the answers?

Of the different kinds of Holocaust survivors, concentration camp inmates suffered the worst. According to the Nazi scheme those who moved to concentration camps had entered the final stage of annihilation. Humiliated, starved, deprived of all rights, most of these concentration camp inmates faced death. Miraculously, a few survived. As a rule, moving from the ghettoes to concentration camps meant that, for most of the war, these Jews were isolated from the rest of society. In the camps their isolation was total. And while they can tell us much about the ultimate in human degradation and about the ultimate struggle for life, they are less knowledgeable about Polish-Jewish relationships during the war.

Limited also must be the experiences of those who found refuge in Russia. Such moves usually took place before the outbreak of the Russian-German war, before June 1941. The systematic annihilation of Jews began later.

Of the Poles, too, most can tell us nothing or very little. Those who were sent to Germany have only limited information. The same must be true for those who were personally uninvolved, the indifferent bystanders. As for the Nazi collaborators, even though they have important information, it is doubtful if any of them would admit to their wartime activities. This kind of information is lost.

Only those few who were directly involved in the rescuer-rescued relationship know what happened. Each was exposed to dangers that came from a variety of sources. The personal experiences, then, of those who

OF HELP, UNDERSTANDING AND HOPE: 303

were directly involved, Jews and Poles, ought to throw some light on these tragic events.

On the day of the conference, before I even entered my hotel room, the phone rang. An anxious voice of one of the organizers, wanting to know, presumably from an objective person, what had happened. His questions told me that distortions had already begun. As I responded to his inquiries, I minimized the conflict, trying to smooth over the rough edges as if in a family quarrel.

When I hung up, my thoughts turned to a meeting I had had with Mordechai Paldiel, Director of the Department for the Righteous at Yad Vashem in Jerusalem. At one point my host noted that European Jews who lived illegally on the Christian side tend to describe their contacts with Christians in moderate terms, claiming neither exceptionally good nor exceptionally bad experiences. One exception to this pattern was Poland.

At the mention of Poland my attention sharpened and I urged him to explain. Unlike others, he said, Polish Jews who lived in the forbidden Christian world describe their contacts with Poles either in extremely glowing or extremely horrible terms, leaving no room for moderate views. These comments reminded me of a book by a Polish underground figure, Wacław Zagórski. Echoing Paldiel's observations, Zagórski points out that even the Nazis were aware of Polish extremism. Thus, tipped off by a Pole, an SS man remarked: 'You Poles are a strange people. Nowhere in the world is there another nation which has so many heroes and so many denouncers.' Knowing this, should I have been prepared for what happened? Did my emotions interfere with a more realistic assessment of facts?

That evening we attended a special dinner. I was approached by an older woman, a righteous Christian from Poland. She wanted to know why I called her an anti-semite. After all, she had risked her life for Jews: how could I do that? I tried to tell her that she misunderstood. I tried to explain that, historically, Poland was a country with a traditionally strong anti-semitism. I was being unfair, she insisted, unfair to her personally and to all the Poles who only wanted to help. The more I tried to explain the less she was able or willing to accept. I gave up by turning to the man next to me, a Jewish survivor from Poland.

His question was different: 'Why do you bother studying righteous Christians in Poland? There were hardly any such Poles!' Without giving me even a chance to say something he informed me that my speech was biased and that I absolved the Poles from all responsibility. I whitewashed them by distorting the facts. Too tired, I made no effort to answer. Then, I remembered how much care I had taken to make my presentation balanced, how much I had wanted to be fair and show both the Polish and Jewish side. Clearly my speech did not smooth matters. I was depressed. I was disappointed that in Washington more than forty years later the suffering and compassion that were a part of the rescuer-rescued relationship were expressed only in quiet and subdued tones. In contrast, the long-standing hostility between the Poles and Jews received a resounding hearing. In the past the Jews would not have dared to voice their objections as aggressively. Here, this place and time gave to both sides the freedom to express themselves openly. Each took advantage of this opportunity.

Next day in his closing remarks, Elie Wiesel referred to the Polish section as the most controversial part of the programme. Also next day, with good reason, the *Washington Post* described these exchanges as 'spattered venom'.

To what extent are these extreme positions justified? What did actually happen in Poland? What do the rescuers and the rescued tell? What can be said about the many concentration camps in Poland? Were the Poles responsible for the existence of these concentration camps on Polish soil, as some have suggested?

We know that, quite early on, the Nazis designated Poland as the centre for Jewish destruction. Whether in so doing they were prompted by the country's concentration of Jews or whether they counted, if not on actual support, at least on the indifference of Poles, or on the absolute subjugation of the Poles, we shall never know. For this decision the Germans left no records, no explanation. What they left were records of unprecedented human destruction. I am aware of no evidence that would directly link the Poles to the responsibility for building or maintaining these concentration camps. Nor, in fact, do I know of any Polish concentration camp guards.

But did the Poles aid the Germans in other ways? What do those who survived in the forbidden Christian world say?

One of the profound ironies of the Holocaust was that Hitler's success in stoking virulent anti-semitic feelings was based on the emotional argument that the Jews of Europe were not simply another ethnic minority, but rather a separate race, with separate and readily distinguishable values and, in particular, physical characteristics. Yet belying this myth was the fact that the Germans occupying Poland could not, by employing their own distinctions, separate Jew from Christian. There were some Polish Jews who looked and acted like Poles, and many more who, though dark-haired and dark-eyed, by no means fitted the German stereotype. Unfamiliar with Polish culture, the Germans enlisted the aid of those Poles who were willing to help them ferret out passing Jews.

Who were these Poles who volunteered to find Jews for the Nazis? Polish patriotism, which was strong throughout the country, should have worked against any collaborations with the Germans. To an extent it did: there is no evidence, for example, that any Polish leaders collaborated with the Nazis, either in the rounding up of Jews or in any other way. There was not, for example, on the political level, a Polish Quisling.

The situation for most Poles might well have been described as purposeful uninvolvement. Struggling themselves, they neither aided the Germans nor hindered them. However, there were Poles who did help the Germans, often with a perverse degree of enthusiasm, particularly in turning in Jews, and they often showed these Polish Jews the same lack of mercy that the Germans showed. Some collaborated for the monetary rewards the Nazis made available, others because that was the law and they obeyed it. But for some the traditionally strong Polish anti-semitism was the key factor. Well aware of this anti-semitism, the Germans invested much time and effort in promoting it. Even as late as 1943, in a letter to a high-ranking Nazi official, Heinrich Himmler urged the wide circulation in Poland of stories about Jewish ritual slaughter of Christians. This came after the Nazis had already widely distributed posters and movies depicting the Jew as evil, ugly, dangerous, dirty and disease-ridden. Not only had the Jews been characterized as subhuman, as vermin to be exterminated, they had also been blamed for every conceivable ill, including the war and Communism.

Toward the end of 1941 the Germans passed a law that made any unauthorized move outside the ghetto a crime punishable by death. The same death sentence applied to Poles who helped a Jew make such a move. This law was widely publicized and rigidly enforced. In their public announcements the Nazis urged Christians to denounce the fugitives. The many pressures to apprehend Jews created a virtual witchhunt. Suspicion was rife. Anyone who lived alone, had no relatives, no friends, received no mail, was automatically suspect.

The Nazis were efficient. As an additional way of enlisting the necessary cooperation, the Germans offered special rewards to anyone who would denounce a Jewish fugitive. The nature of these rewards varied with the locality and the demand for certain goods; they might include sugar, vodka, cigarettes or clothing, and in some instances, half the property of the apprehended Jew.

Some Poles responded. Some were lured by the rewards while others became affected by Nazi propaganda and seemed to be taking over the definition of Jews as subhuman. Ashamed of his countrymen's treatment of the Jews a prominent Polish doctor, Zygmunt Klukowski, observed:

> In general towards Jews there exists some wild animal-like response. A certain psychosis took hold of the Polish people, who by following the example of the Germans, do not see a human being in the Jews. Instead, they perceive the Jews as dangerous and threatening animals. Creatures which ought to be exterminated in any way possible just like one needs to exterminate rats with rat poison.

Some of the impediments, then, that Jews encountered in the Christian world could be traced to Polish-German cooperation. Ironically the more obstacles and barriers the Jews encountered as they were trying to survive among Poles, the greater was their dependence on Polish help. In a real sense, then, such Jews were caught in the middle between two extremes: the good and the evil. As they were trying to stay alive they had to learn how to keep away from prospective Polish denouncers and learn how to recognize potential Polish rescuers. What did they have to face as they tried to differentiate between friend and foe?

In time, as the pace of Jewish extermination intensified, so did the search for runaway Jews. All those who tried to blend with the Polish population faced continual suspicion and danger. Not surprisingly, suspicion and danger gave rise to fear. Fear became a constant companion of passing Jews, making their situation even more hazardous. For it was fear that made them lose their self-assurance and behave in cautious ways. Caution, hesitance and movements expressing a desire and need to make oneself invisible, each and all could and did have disastrous effects. They made the Jews not less but more visible. Eventually caution, hesitancy, lack of self-assurance, became associated with Jewishness. They made the Jews not less, but more visible.

Tragedy and fear, so much a part of Jewish life, had a depressing effect. Depression was often reflected in the sadness of the eyes. Eventually, in the lives of Jews, the possibility of sad eyes became an ever-present threat, a threat most were aware of. Jews were known for their sad eyes. They could be recognized just by the sadness of their eyes. Many were.

Thus, for example, Pola Stein, not yet ten years old, and her father, were hidden by an exceptionally kind peasant. For a short while, however, because of impending danger, she had to live with another family. In this new place, instead of hiding, Pola moved around freely pretending to be a relative who had come for a visit. All seemed to be going well until one of the neighbours said: 'Whom are you kidding, that this is your cousin? This is a Jewish child frightened as hell, one can see it in her sad eyes!' Right away she had to be sent back. It was too dangerous to stay. One never knew.

Frida Nordau, a survivor I interviewed in New York, was exposed to Poles who were avid anti-semites determined to destroy Jews, and others who were exceptionally noble and ready to help. At one stage after a few futile attempts to find shelter, Frida and her family built a special bunker in the forest. This hiding place consisted of a hole camouflaged by branches and another hole leading into it. The second hole was their actual hiding place. They thought that if those searching for Jews came across an empty hole they would conclude that its occupants had run away and not look further. They made their home in this second hole and at night a few of them would venture into the village for food. They always came back with some provisions donated by local peasants. Frida remembered:

One night those who left returned with a warning that the Germans were preparing to raid the forest. Early next morning my father insisted that I and my sister leave. He wanted at least some of us to survive. He felt that here in the forest only death awaited us. He himself was afraid to leave; he had a beard and he knew that he could not pass for a Pole. Actually neither could we, we could be recognized through our speech and partly by our looks ... The moment we moved out of our hiding place Poles caught us. They were armed with axes and rakes. We begged them to let us go but they would not listen, all they said was: 'You are Jewish and you have no right to live.' They took us to a village where they left us with the Germans. Maybe these were the Germans who were supposed to make the raid, I don't know. But after we were left there the Germans started to kid us on how pretty we were, they seemed so relaxed. I was fourteen, my sister was nine. I said to her: 'Come let us walk away, let them kill us from the back. I don't want to be shot at from the front.' I took my sister by the hand and we started walking away. As we did I waited for the bullets. I walked and walked and nothing happened. Then I began to think that maybe this was death. I was afraid to look back, I just walked. Later, curious, I slowly turned my head. The Germans were far away. They did not kill us ... I had an address my father had given me of some peasants. I decided to go there, maybe they would take us. Father always used to help these peasants, lending them money, doing favours for them. Now we told them our story and how we saved ourselves. The peasant said to us: 'You go into the barn and I will know nothing.' It was cold, and snow was falling. We were glad, we hid in the straw. Then we heard shooting, we saw that the forest was on fire. They were looking for Jews. I cried all day long. My mother, father, brothers were there. We had no food but we were thankful to have a roof over our head.

The raid was conducted by Germans and Poles. The place where Frida's family hid had not been discovered, because after seeing the first empty hole the raiders assumed that the Jews had left. That night the entire family was reunited. But this was one close call of many. Eventually, only Frida and one of her brothers survived.

What about the Polish rescuers? How did they cope with their own lives and with the protection of Jews? No doubt Poles who tried to save Jews were surrounded by a variety of perils, some of which were unrelated to Jewish rescue. But were they helpless, as some have claimed? Could they have done more? What price did they, in fact, pay for aiding Jews?

While individual experiences of each rescuer varied in most unusual ways, together they point to two broad impediments: the Nazi implementation of the 'Final Solution' and Polish anti-semitism. Each was well expressed in the actual experiences of rescuers. One such illustration is offered by Stefania Dawidzuk, a poor working class woman who defied the Nazis by saving a life. Into her one-room apartment Stefa accepted a Jewish fugitive, Irena, whose semitic features spelled danger.

Initially, this stranger came for one week only. Soon it became clear that Irena could not find other shelter. When the weeks stretched into months Stefania's husband, an avid anti-semite, began to object, claiming that he was unwilling to die, especially for a Jewess. Though under pressure and aware of the dangers, Stefania could not dismiss this uninvited guest. A violent scene ensued that ended with Stefania's husband storming out of the house. He never came back. Pregnant at the time, poor, faced with continuous threats, Stefania never wavered in her determination to rescue.

As the war was nearing the end, Stefania made one more supreme sacrifice. In 1944, during the Polish uprising in Warsaw, it was too dangerous to stay in the apartment. To avoid recognition, Irena bandaged her face. In the cellar, Stefania introduced her to the rest of the neighbours as a cousin who had just arrived. Eventually the Poles lost the battle, incurring terrible losses, and the victorious Germans began to evacuate the civilian population.

Stefania heard that mothers with young children would be allowed to stay. In Irena's case evacuation would have meant exposure to many people, danger and possible death. After all, she could not keep her face bandaged forever and the bandage itself could arouse suspicion. Recognizing the danger, Stefania had no intention of abandoning the woman.

She explained: 'When we were about to be evacuated I told Irena to take my baby. I told her: "I will try to stay with you; in case I get lost take care of him, like of your own child.".... When the German saw her with the child he told her to return to the apartment. Somehow I too was allowed to go with her.'

Stefania cried as she told the story. But I began to doubt the truthfulness of what I heard. I could not imagine giving my child away! I asked for more information. I wondered how Stefania could risk losing her baby. Surprised, she shrugged and then answered: 'Irena would not have harmed him. She would have taken good care of him. Besides no one knew what might have become of me. I could have died too.'

Stefania continued to cry and I continued to doubt. My doubts lingered on until I came across a testimony Irena gave before a historical commission in Warsaw. In this official document she spoke about Stefania in the most glowing terms, listing Stefania's many sacrifices and exceptional treatment. The testimony also contained Irena's version of the incident with the baby:

Before the end of the war there was a tragic moment ... We learned that the Germans were about to evacuate all civilians. My appearance on the streets even with my bandaged face could end tragically. Stefania decided to take a bold step which I will remember as long as I live. She gave me her baby to protect. As she was leaving me with her child she told me that the child would save me and that after the war I should give him back to her. But in case of her death she was convinced that I would take good care of him ... Eventually we both stayed.

Inevitably, all Poles knew that by helping Jews they were risking their lives. Frequently, however, more than their own lives was at stake. The Nazis adhered to the principle of collective responsibility. This meant that punishment applied not only to the 'transgressors' but to their families as well. In fact, children of all ages, including infants, were subjected to the same fate as the 'guilty' adults. Frequently Nazi interpretations of collective responsibility came to include neighbourhoods, communities and Poles in general. Equally chilling was the Nazi practice of public executions. The Germans wanted other Poles to see the consequences of such activity and they understood that official notices of those punished were not a substitute for eye-witness accounts.

How many Poles defied the Nazis and rescued Jews we shall never know. By the end of 1986, the Yad Vashem committee had bestowed the title of 'righteous Christians' on almost 7000 individuals. Of these, more than 2000 were Poles. More cases are pending before the committee. But a requirement that the rescued Jew and not the rescuer apply for this title deprives many deserving people of ever receiving it. Some Jewish survivors are dead, others have lost touch with their protectors, others simply refuse to apply and still others are not even aware that such a distinction exists.

Many of those who will be recognized are dead. Some had lost their lives because they were protecting Jews. Usually they died together with their charges and the Yad Vashem distinction will not be offered to them. I have tried to count some of those who lost their lives while saving Jews and who were identified by name. I came up with 668 individuals. At times, the Germans would surround entire villages that were accused of harbouring Jews and burn them with all their inhabitants. Neither the names nor the numbers of those who died this way are known. For the reasons mentioned, and no doubt others, most of the Polish righteous will never be recognized and honoured.

Looking back, what do the experiences of the rescuer and the rescued tell? To what extent are the Polish-Jewish accusations and counter-accusations justified? On balance, these experiences deny the validity of the two extreme positions. Clearly, the responsibility for the Holocaust and the concentration camps belongs to the Germans. On the other hand it is true that some Poles, an unknown number, did abet the Germans. But it is equally true that some Poles risked their lives for Jews and some lost their lives in the process. Precisely because Poles faced the formidable barriers to Jewish rescue the few that did overcome these impossible impediments deserve special recognition. They are the true altruistic heroes.

Reality refutes the existing Polish-Jewish gap, and denies validity to many of the hostile accusations. Personally I am convinced that vehement denials, and the unbalanced presentation of facts, only enhance and perpetuate Polish-Jewish tensions. What we need instead is a healthy respect for each other's differences, frailties and shortcomings. Moreover as a people, Poles and Jews have much in common: our tragic history that deprived each of us of a country, our excessive individualism, our divisiveness and ties that extend for a thousand years. I believe that all these could become the basis for our mutual understanding, an understanding from which we both could benefit.

Still, perhaps one could argue that to those familiar with Polish-Jewish history, such heated exchanges should not have come as a surprise. After all, Poles and Jews have had a long and stormy history, a history filled with strong conflicts and powerful contradictory loyalties. During the war and into the present these complex forces have continued to work at cross purposes.

Perhaps those of us who were saddened and disappointed by these emotional outbursts ought to have been satisfied with the absence of physical violence. Perhaps we should have been gratified that soon the heated arguments criss-crossed the Polish-Jewish lines, as Jews began to object to statements made by Jews, and Poles to remarks coming from other Poles. Could it be that despite this lingering historical hostility, we have taken a step toward reconciliation?

Illustrations to Jews in Jarmolińce
Stefan Kieniewicz

Figure 1

Figure 2

Figure 3

Figure 4

Figure 5

Figure 6

Figure 7

Figure 8

Figure 9

Figure 10

JEWS IN JARMOLIŃCE
Stefan Kieniewicz

Jarmolińce is a little town in the former province of Podolia, Płoskirów (Proskuriv) district. It lies on the Uszyca river, an affluent of the Dniestr, about 50 km to the east of the former Austro-Russian frontier. On the eve of our century it counted some 3000 inhabitants, mostly Jews. Apart from the synagogue, it had two parish churches, an Orthodox and a Roman Catholic one, a stately manor, the residence of the Counts Orłowski, and the remains of a small castle built in the 16th century as a defence against Tatar raids.

The place stood out, before World War I, mainly on account of its annual fairs, held on St Peter and Paul's day, that is from June 15 to July 1. It was a big affair, with a turnover of 1.5 mln roubles, specializing in petty goods, furs, farming implements, but above all in horses bred locally, searched by purchasers from all parts of the Russian Empire. Up to 2000 horses were sold each year in Jarmolińce. Most of this trade remained in Jewish hands.

The Geographical Dictionary (1882) describes Jarmolińce as: 'A town built mostly in wood, and muddy, like all Podolian settlements'. Up to 1914, it had neither highway, nor railway connections, but smart horse-races were held there during the Fair.

Tadeusz Dachowski, a squire of the neighbourhood, a great horse-lover and excellent rider, attended these races and the horse-show regularly; he also took photographs of the site. A set of these amateur snapshots, taken presumably between 1905 and 1914, was happily preserved in the hands of his son, Mr Kazimierz Dachowski in Warsaw. It seems that the photographer was not interested exclusively in horses, but also in the people around them. Mostly, of course, Jewish people: salesmen, brokers, money-lenders, drivers, porters, or simple onlookers, caught unawares in their trading activity. Eighty years ago, such scenes were a common enough sight for Eastern European country dwellers. Today they represent a rare document, a vivid image of a civilization which has disappeared for ever.

CAPTIONS TO ILLUSTRATIONS

1. A general view of the Jarmolińce Fair, giving a notion of its size and set-up.
2. An Orthodox clergyman inspects a team of horses driven by two Jews. A porter to the left. Big poster of a circus. The white- blue-red Russian flag, adopted in the Empire after the 1905 Revolution, allows an approximate dating of the photos.
3. The shopping centre. The largest Russian signboard runs: 'Pivnaia zala Zinkov[skogo] pivovarennago zavoda V. Divisheka' (Beer Hall of V. Divishek's brewery in Zinkovtsi). To the left: 'Shorno-siedletskie galerii Berka Vainshellboima' (Berek Weinschellbäum's Harness and Saddle Galleries). Still more to the left, another saddler's: F. M. Salomonov. The other signs are difficult to make out. Two Orthodox priests in the foreground. To the left, a Jew hauling a carriage.
4. Groups of Christian and Jewish dealers near a muddy pool. Some of the Jews in European dress and bowler hats. Umbrellas in use because of the sun.
5. Old and middle-aged Jews among horses.
6. An old Jew with a stick, two others with whips. They are all wearing big caps with peaks, not skullcaps.
7. A Jewish dealer recommending a horse.
8. A Polish squire in a 'britzka', approached by some distinguished-looking Jewish middlemen.
9. The same moustached squire in conference. To the left, some Jews at a stand, presumably with soda water.
10. Dogs were also occasionally sold at the Fair. Young Christian and Jewish onlookers in various attire. Among them, a peasant in linen shirt and pants. In the foreground, a university student.

PERSONAL VIEW

WORMWOOD AND ASHES (DO POLES AND JEWS HATE EACH OTHER?)

Roman Zimand

> 'The real enemy of man is generalization'
> Czesław Miłosz

> 'I don't believe in running away from problems'
> Justine Wise Polier

For a long time I have been troubled by the question: why do I write? Not why other people write, that is their affair. But why do I write, I, who believe that the world is innundated by a muddy flood of printed paper, I who love forests and dislike cellulose, who consider writing a shameless activity, almost always sterile and usually devoid of sense.

We live in excess. Even in poor countries like Poland or completely destitute ones such as Bangladesh or Mali, we live in an excess of words, and I am adding to that excess. Why? I am unable to answer the question. Even if I write little (which is a fact) and strive to be succinct (at which I hope I succeed) these are still only half-measures, and it is obvious what one should think of half-measures. It would be a poor defence, then, if I were to say that every sentence of this essay and certainly every paragraph could be developed, sprinkled with metaphors, examples, exclamations and every manner of rhetorical ornament. This would mean only that I had relinquished all stylistic extremes. Which is true, since I am searching for a compromise, a compromise between silence and speech, as if it were at all possible for them to meet halfway.

There is, perhaps, one justification for the activity of writing: that one has something important to say comprehensibly. But only written texts can convey this, and only after publication. Thus writing is, at best, a risk undertaken alone.

I

The majority of people throughout the world who switched on the radio in June 1986 and heard the words 'The Argentinians are really splendid' would have known immediately that eleven men were in question and not, as the grammar of the sentence might have indicated, 31 million individuals of different ages and both sexes. If these listeners were questioned as to what these eleven Argentinian men might have to do with their remaining 30,999,89 fellow citizens, who make up the actual life of the Argentinian nation, they would probably not understand the question which is, as a matter of fact, a vague one. It is doubtful, however, whether they understood it or not, that they would agree to acknowledge the eleven men running around the football field as the personification of all the remaining Argentinians, or at least of their merits.

However, when the same radio listeners learned in spring 1982 from the radio news-reader or journalist-commentator that the Argentinians had lost a war, then they surely subconsciously realized that in some way all the Argentinians were involved, independent of age or sex. These included the few who might be of the opinion that since not a single inhabitant of the Falklands wanted to be an Argentinian citizen and that all of them wished to be the subjects of Her Majesty Queen Elizabeth, then perhaps they should not be forced to become Argentinian.

So much for the Argentinians, news of whom via the radio reaches – at times such as the above – the Spaniards, the Dutch, the Haitians and the inhabitants of Darjeeling, Drohiczyn, Dunkirk or Des Moines. To the Argentinians themselves, things might look a little different in this particular case. One can assume that they would acknowledge that not only had they lost the war (thanks to which they rid themselves of quite unpleasant leaders, their uniforms dotted with medals), but furthermore that the sentence noted here at the beginning: 'The Argentinians are really splendid' refers in some way to all of them, that each of them participates in Diego Maradona's successes, or that this concrete and individual Diego represents a part of them all.

So much for certain opinions about Argentinians.

However, when we hear the sentence: 'Poles are anti-semites', or: 'The Jews act against the interest of Poland', we know that all Poles are implied (with the exception, perhaps of Władysław Bartoszewski) and all Jews (with the exception, perhaps, of Artur Rubinstein). It would appear from the above, that the sentences cited about the Argentinians are occasional; that is, their sense depends on the context within which we hear them, whereas those about Jews and Poles are analytical statements, or maybe even synthetic *a priori*. In this second case we would be dealing with a fairly specific addition of common convictions – held by some Poles and by some

Jews – to phenomenology and the philosophy of Kant. This is no joke, or if it is, it is a particularly bloody and dismaying one. Let us take two statements: 'During the Nazi occupation the Poles handed Jews over to the Gestapo', or: 'Jews occupied high positions in the leadership of the communist party and Ministry of Public Security'. The number of Jews who consider the first statement to apply to *all* Poles, and the number of Poles understanding the second to apply to *all* Jews is dangerously high.

The examples above are not meant to develop competence in the area of logic, but to make the reader aware that a number of pitfalls lurk in the way of the attempt to express the main problem of the subject and in calling things by their true name. They could easily be removed by banning the use of the great quantifier and allowing only statements along the lines of : 'There were and are Poles who . . .' or: 'Some Jews . . .'. But, however true statements thus formulated might be, I know of no one who would believe in such a linguistically prescriptive way of solving and appeasing Polish-Jewish relations. I do know people, however, who are certainly not stupid, who are of the opinion that it is better not to discuss Polish-Jewish affairs at all. Whatever is said, they argue, will be wrong; these old relics should be left to lie in the cupboard, or rather in a safety deposit box of silence. And as proof they cite numerous examples of manipulation when dealing with problems . . . ('painful problems?' – we hear from both one side and the other – 'we don't have a problem, they're the ones with the problem . . .' A fine prospect for dialogue.) The manipulation was employed solely by communists and anti-semites (the two need not be mutually exclusive), or Jewish chauvinists. However, the problem with old skeletons in the cupboard is that not all of them agree obediently to dry up and crumble into dust. Even the best safety-deposit box has cracks and, goodness me, the things that can slip through. Thus, looking at it pragmatically, the hope that several million people will swear a vow of silence regarding a theme of vital concern to many of them seems quite hopeless. Elementary ethics suggest, then, that if anti-semitism and polonophobia deserve condemnation (or praise according to some), how is one to condemn or praise in silence?

But to speak means to confront the pitfalls presented by words, or rather the reefs hidden under the surface of words. It would seem that these can be avoided in two ways. Either one assumes that everyone understands the question perfectly, or one undertakes to be specific. Experience teaches us that the first alternative leads too often to obvious misunderstanding, whereas the other, after the examination of all possible meanings, leaves us suffering a paralysis of precision, or simply incapable of remembering the meaning of what has been settled.

Are these all the navigational pitfalls of the exploration proposed here? They are not even the most important ones. I probably do not realize just how many traps lie in wait, but I would like to say something about two of them.

The first is the danger of primitive empiricism. It is expressed in the following statements: 'My grandmother was tortured by a Jewish *ubek* (secret policeman). All Jews are scoundrels, communists and hate Poles'. And from the other side: 'When my grandmother returned to Kraków from the camp she heard in the street on the very first day "What, haven't they got that Rifka yet?" All Poles are worse anti-semites than the Nazis.' I call such reasoning primitive empiricism because I assume that in both cases the first part is true: the grandmother of Mr X was tortured by an *ubek* who was a Jew and the grandmother of Mrs Y did hear these words in the spring of 1945 when she returned to Kraków. We preserve the stories of such experiences within our family histories; approached primitively, they become the support for a demagogy of unusual emotional intensity. And no wonder – it is sustained by the two most terrible phenomena experienced by twentieth-century Europe: nazism and communism. In this direct way all Jews, not excluding those born the day before yesterday in California, are considered guilty of cooperating in the criminal activities of a handful of lunatics who dedicated themselves to materealize an ideological utopia and for whom communism was an *escape* from Jewishness. All Poles, on the other hand, are identified with *szmalcownicy* (blackmailers).

Four-fifths of discussion on the theme of Polish attitudes to Jews during the Nazi occupation is completely fruitless, though very passionate, because it is made up of just such real (though sometimes fabricated) examples. One individual was betrayed to the Gestapo by a house keeper, another was saved by a member of a landowning family. Thus formulated, one forgets as a rule that in all nations, 3 per cent will be scoundrels and 3 per cent heroes, whereas any talk of Polish attitudes to the 'final solution' should be concerned with the remaining 94 per cent, who neither betrayed, nor did they save. Many and different witnesses – whose testimonies include literary accounts and the reports of the Commander-in-Chief of the *AK*, General Grot-Rowecki – attest to the complete indifference of Polish society towards the extermination of the Jews. This in itself constitutes a sufficiently bitter truth without bringing up the subject of *szmalcownicy* who made money out of it, and those neighbour-informers who were prompted neither by fear nor even cupidity. This, in the end, is but a part of the whole dismaying truth about the indifference of the world toward the mass murder of the Jews. A truth of which, after the experience of Biafra, Cambodia or Ethiopia, we should all be aware.

My own life has been such that if I were to sum up all the statements full of hatred I have come across in the course of the last 20 years made by Poles about Jews and by Jews about Poles – that is since obtaining my passport and travelling in the West – then there would probably be more of the latter than the former. This does not prove anything, first because it could just as easily have been the other way around, and secondly, with all due respect to empiricism, I cannot bear those versions of the latter which abuse the rules of correct reasoning. I hope, therefore, that traces of what I call primitive empiricism will not be in evidence in this essay.

Neither will there be any high-mindedness here which demands that one should close one's eyes to the nature of life and treat what is dear to one's heart as the real. I think that there are situations in which pure high-mindedness can constitute a trap into which one falls all the more willingly because it protects us from that which is unpleasant and spiritually uncomfortable.

So this will not be an essay about the magnificent Poles who joyfully welcomed the victory of Israel in the Six Day War. Or about the emotional Jews who enquire with tears in their eyes about Gęsia Street or Ciechocinek. Both of these types truly exist, but they are not the subject of this discussion. Nor will it sketch how good it is already and, when it gets still better, then it will be so good that the trees in Eden will turn green with envy.

This essay maintains that things are bad, and if they are to be at all better, if the mutual relations of Jews and Poles are to achieve at least a level of decency – and that is no small thing – then those for whom this really is important must know not only what they are aiming for, but also what their point of departure is. And that place is not the good-will of those among us who wish to ameliorate something, but the fact that a notable number of Poles (all over the world) and Jews (all over the world but, paradoxically, perhaps least in Israel) nurture towards each other a daily latent, but occasionally erupting, hatred. No one knows or is in a position to ascertain how notable a number, or what percentage. For many reasons. Not least because Polish non-anti-semites or Jewish non-Pole-haters are very often silent when confronted with the chauvinism of their countrymen. For hatred very often also paralyses decent people, because they are prone to underestimate openly primitive statements and paralogisms calling for vengeance; because in at least some situations they think that solidarity with their compatriots is more binding than the imperative to condemn evil; and, finally, because it is easier that way – silence does not demand effort. An additional point with regard to the Polish People's Republic (PPR) is that there is no such thing as public opinion, freedom of speech, or opportunity for debate in the official media. The communists ruling Poland have an instrumental attitude towards anti-semitism of which the career of Tadeusz Walichnowski, once known as 'the Dr Globke of the PPR' provides an excellent example. In general, they behave as if they considered anti-semitism to be an innate Polish characteristic. They expressed this conviction in 1967–69 by introducing an 'anti-Zionist' campaign and it was clearly discernible more recently in 1985, in a *Sejm* speech by Czesław Kiszczak, a member of the Politburo, or in the particular manoeuvres organised around the film *Shoah*.

On the other hand, they take pleasure in suggesting to the West – including various Jewish activists – that only they are capable of restraining this anti-semitism. Another aspect of this juggling with the 'Jewish' argument is the persistent offer of a 'shield' to Polish society which is meant to protect them against virulent anti-Polish Jews (on an international level, naturally). Meanwhile, however badly Polish-Jewish relations are going, all actions aimed at alleviating this situation must take place outside the communist arena. For communism is the common enemy of Poles and Jews, independently of what the two may feel towards each other.

The only answer, then, that I am able to give to the question – what number of Poles are possessed by the paranoic obsession called anti-semitism or what percentage of Jews by an equally paranoid polonophobia is: a number sufficiently large to be recognized as dangerous from a social point of view. Morally speaking, every individual incident deserves condemnation, but as I have said, this essay is not going to be high-minded.

Another negative element characterizing this point of departure is complete ignorance. I do not consider myself a naïve epigone of *Aufklärung*, who thinks it is enough to enlighten people to make them virtuous. But it is a fact that ignorance gives rise to evil rather than good, and certainly makes understanding more difficult. Meanwhile, the mutual ignorance of Jews and Poles remains simply immeasurable, and one of its consequences is that they are not in any position to foresee most of the reactions of the other side.

There is something bound up in this ignorance which could be called unconscious polonophobia and unconscious anti-semitism. One area in which this manifests itself is in linguistic fossils which may not be meant to offend but which nevertheless express deeply-rooted presumptions. Classic examples of this are statements: 'He's a Jew, but a decent person'; 'A Pole, but intelligent'.

And all this is overgrown with resentments, complexes, suspicions.

And if we try to convince ourselves that things are different, if we cite the examples of Józef Lichten, Władysław Bartoszewski, Jan Józef Lipski, Simon Wiesenthal and many others – then we will achieve nothing. For it is not they, despite their merits, who are representative. If the majority of Poles thought and acted like Fr Jacek Salij, or the majority of Jews like Simon Wiesenthal, then I could with a clear conscience take up an easier task than the writing of this essay. A correct exposition of the thought of Heraclitus, for example, an interpretation of Blake's poetry or an attempt to discover the meaning of *Samuel Zborowski* (a particularly obscure, mystic tragedy of the Polish poet Juliusz Słowacki).

II

Contemporary Polish-Jewish relations consist of emotions in their purest form. 95 per cent of Poles have never once laid eyes on a living Jew, and the reverse is equally true.

III

I wrote that this was not going to be a high-minded essay. What I mean by this should emerge clearly throughout the text as a whole. But I would like to state three things directly.

I am not going to try to prove here that hatred is an impoverishing, stupefying emotion and as a result always destroys the one who hates. It is evil even when it does not destroy the one who is hated. Nor am I going to explain why this premise has any sense when, and only when, we recognise its absolute nature. If someone does not know this, or knows but does not acknowledge it, then he can calmly forego reading this text any further, for I do not explain why hatred of anyone or particularly of other nations is immoral and stupid.

The other omission in the high-mindedness of which I want to speak directly does not belong to the order of *sollen*, but to the order of *sein*. It is sometimes the case that noble-minded people cannot imagine evil, so that when they are confronted with manifestations of it, in their consciousness they push it aside as marginal to the world. I mentioned paranoid obsessions, complexes, resentments, suspicions. But it is not the case that I regard anti-semites or polonophobes as mentally unbalanced. On the contrary, they are – with a few exceptions – normal people, not distinguished by anything in particular, and if something distinguishes them, separates them from the whole, which we habitually call European culture, then it is not their hostility towards, or even hatred of Jews. For in European culture the mixture of hostility, fear, and contempt towards the Jews, has been a constant element for two thousand years, and this very mixture has provoked every so often an explosion of active hatred. Similarly, when including Jewish culture in Europe within the above whole – and there is no way to do otherwise – we have to say that an element of European culture as a *totum* is the Jewish fear and mistrust of Christians and contempt for them. He who wishes to work for the improvement of Jewish-Polish relations and is not conscious of the weight of the heritage of negative elements contained within the whole of European culture, will come across astounding obstacles, on both sides, on more than one occasion.

When an outstanding French neurologist, coming from a family of

Polish Jews, states that John Paul II is an anti-semite and that he will prove it, it can be seen as an example of individual aberration. When in 1946 the bishop of the Lublin diocese states that the trial of Beilis did not definitively decide the question of the blood libel one can only be petrified. However, I am not concerned with emotional reactions, but with informing the reader that both statements arise, unfortunately, as a result of a long heritage that goes back centuries.

I do not think that people are the slaves of their own history. Historiolatry is deeply depraving – not only in its communist version. Furthermore, it is so vague that it practically begs for intellectual and political card-sharping. But it would be equally foolish completely to negate the essential influence on our behaviour of both heritage, that is of something unconscious, and of tradition, that is of something that we choose in some way or other.

Banalities? Obviously. But if I did not spell them out here then God knows what *horrenda* would be ascribed to me, which I do not espouse at all. I am prepared to defend what I declare, but it bores me to be assailed for something which I have not written.

Finally, the third ignoble thought which I would like to mention directly concerns the problem of collective responsibility. The question is a very complicated one, and I will therefore present my theses here without packaging, illustration, or arguments for or against. All this one can imagine for oneself, of course... The whole viewpoint presented here can also be rejected, as indeed can the whole essay.

In the eyes of the law, a person should be held responsible only for that which he has committed himself, or which he renounced. This is quite clear. However, when it comes to morality, things become immeasurably more complicated, in the case of two communities at least: the religious and the national. (I have in mind discretionary religion and discretionary nationality.) In the case of religion I will make no statement, taking advantage of the fact that it is not the subject of this essay. I think, however, that in the moral sphere nations are responsible for their own history, and first of all for the negative side of it. This is a banality, or rather a self-evident fact which has by necessity to be recorded here. It is too often the case that when conversation turns to the bad, unpleasant chapters or sub-chapters of the history of a given nation, it then emerges that others are responsible for it. And only others.

I admit that this is a complicated situation and one bristling with difficulties. And one of these is the process of passing from general theses to concrete human behaviour. Let us limit ourselves to excluding two extremes, leaving the rest to common sense and tact. Thus this responsibility cannot be raised when people do not take into consideration facts they find unpleasant. It should also not be realized by constant complaining along the lines of: how base we were. And we should perhaps add that, despite what the so-called Left likes to do in the West, this should not be a 'fashionable' responsibility; in the West it is commendable to acknowledge responsibility for nineteenth-century colonialism, but not for Yalta, which leads to a particular type of moral blindness. Morality cannot be a question of fashion.

An extreme conclusion: the nation, which does not wish to be morally responsible for its own past does not deserve to have a history.

IV

What exactly do I want, what do I hope to achieve by writing this hopeless text? That Poles and Jews, in a confusion of mutual prejudice, separated by mutual ignorance as deep as an abyss, should suddenly come to love each other? I am neither so demanding nor so naïve. I would like them to desire to get to know something about each other, so that instead of repeating nonsense they should begin to think, to behave decently instead of convulsively cutting capers.

And if this is the case, then why do I write about emotions and not facts, about something which is neither measurable, nor which can be rationally described, and which thus runs counter to my positivist nature? For I am deeply convinced that for centuries emotions have dominated facts in this issue; they illuminate them and often actually create them. One has only to pick up practically any account of the attitude of Christians to Jews (and vice versa) to see that the description of events is not clear, but that the level of emotions is, as a rule, high.

Oh, one argument exists in favour of decent behaviour, and it is a strong one, addressing itself equally to the emotions and to the intellect – it is the common threat which communism constitutes for both Jews and Poles. In the face of this threat which is fatal to both cultures – to both spiritualities as some call it – all guilt, both real and imaginary, should at least be suspended. This is true, and the idea could be further developed. It would, of course, be an argument from an essay about gains and losses which is surely worth writing. However, this essay is not concerned with that which is advantageous, but with that which is decent. And it is on this point that I am almost a maximalist. I think that decency should be maintained in mutual Polish-Jewish relations, even without the existence of communism.

To return to the questions. If I am right, if it is not facts, or, to be precise, not events but emotions, which constitute the essence of Jewish-Polish relations, then why am I writing about history, having in mind both recent history and that going back centuries and embracing the whole history of relations between Christians and Jews in Europe? In part it is obviously because these are emotions passed down for centuries from generation to generation, usually in the form of tales, and not as bare statements. But, above all, because contemporary mutual relations between Poles and Jews are usually presented (by both sides) as completely independent of a European base. In the eyes of contemporary Polish anti-semites, the Jews conspired exclusively to bring about Poland's downfall, but, strangely enough, without harming the Scandinavian countries or France, for example. In the eyes of contemporary Jewish polonophobes, only Poles are anti-semites in today's Europe. The absurdity of this situation can be at least partly explained against the background of the history preceding it. A long and astounding history.

I will now discuss a few of these historical curiosities.

V

The one truly immutable accusation the Jews could make against Christians goes as follows: how could you believe in the false Messiah, reject the Law, forget that 'the Lord is one'?

The one truly immutable accusation that the Christians could make against the Jews goes as follows: how could you fail to recognise Jesus as the living God; how could you reject His teaching?

From these two immutable accusations one can reason – which does not mean logically deduce – the possible scope of Jewish-Christian or Christian-Jewish relations, which range from a mixture of bitterness, compassion and hostility, from the need for complete separation to a hatred of varying degrees of intensity. *In nuce* an awareness of community is also inherent in these accusations; without it the feeling of being torn asunder would make no sense and could not arise. But this does not become audible until the second half of the twentieth century. And this voice is – at the moment – very weak. I write: in the second half of the twentieth century, and it is necessary to be more precise – more or less in the quarter-century following the extermination of the European Jews – and this is a significant fact. It means at the very least that the lesson of the Final Solution is a difficult one to assimilate.

It would seem, looking at things *ex post*, that taking the experience of two thousand years, one ought to be able to discover some permanently applicable rules in the history of these mutual relations. Meanwhile these rules either fail to appear, or they are so confused that they are beyond the analytical capacities of the author of this essay. Strictly speaking, I detect two, one of which appears to be evident, and the other rather surprising. The evident rule dictates that the side availing itself of force will have greater opportunity to give its emotions material form. This means that throughout the far greater part of the last two thousand years, the active side which could most effectively realize its emotions was the Christian one. A certain convergence of aims appeared only when it was a question of realizing the need for separation. It should be added, however, that in the early Middle Ages neither side felt such a need, or at any rate both behaved as if the difference existing between the two faiths co-existing peaceably side by side constituted a sufficient guarantee of separation. Some of the clergy looked on this with a hostile eye, which was a result, among other things, of an amazingly enduring and rather mistaken, or at least certainly exaggerated, conviction about Jewish proselytizing and the particular attraction of the Mosaic faith.

The rule which may appear surprising, says that the intensification of repression directed against Jews can be the result either of religious fanaticism or of a tendency to move away from the religious aspects of the conflict. In the first case, forces can be found within Christianity which mitigate this fanaticism. The fact that these forces quite often stemmed from the Apostolic See is explained, apart from purely religious reasons, by the fact that repression is usually stronger in the 'provinces' than in the 'centre'. In the second case, the more un-religious the nature of hatred towards Jews, the more it becomes virulent and unrestrained until eventually it ends in the 'final solution'. In the complicated transition from religious, Christian anti-Judaism to modern, secular and ideological anti-semitism, a particularly sad role was played by those representatives of the clergy who not only supported anti-semitism but actually incited it. A phenomenon, let us not mince words, which was not uncommon in the first half of the twentieth century in Poland.

I have said – and will add (despite many authors) – that I cannot specify the rules which, it would seem, should govern these relations. Furthermore, I am of the opinion that one can observe phenomena here which contradict reasonable suppositions. This only serves to testify to the limited explanatory capacities of common sense to which I nevertheless remain attached.

It might therefore appear that the closer what I have called 'immutable accusations' are in the historical and 'logical' order of things, the stronger mutual hatred should be. However, from the perspective of two thousand years, things look exactly the opposite. One is even tempted to say, bearing in mind the memory of rare examples from that time, that the further removed hatred is from 'immutable accusations', the more lethal it, and its results, become. And especially that which is further removed in 'the order of logic'. The greater moves were made at the height of, or during, the late Middle Ages – not to speak of during modern times – to impose legal limits on Jews and enact physical repression, the rarer it was to hear about the fact that they did not believe – which is a fact – and the more frequently do theological accusations appear *ex cathedra* which are today recognised as false or plainly fantastic: the spreading of disease, poisoning of wells, and finally the blood libel – an accusation still levelled in Poland in the 1960s by the security police spreading rumours about the murder of Bohdan

Piasecki. It was in the Middle Ages that a mélange of anti-Judaic accusations appearing to be religious appeared alongside completely 'secular' accusations. This mixture in which the second type of accusation begins to predominate led, with the passing of time, in the nineteenth century, to the appearance of a completely non-religious and purely ideological anti-semitism.

Historically, a transition was achieved within two thousand years from 'the immutable theological accusation', whose lethalness was in the end limited and not at all necessary, to an immutable racial-ideological accusation, whose lethal nature was unavoidable and unlimited. Also in the sense that ideological anti-semitism produces Jews according to its own requirements. And so assurances that inherent Polish chivalry, typical even of ideological and racist anti-semites, would have stopped them from anything, can be seen as self-deception. This is not exclusive or specific to the Poles. The remark about the lethal character of ideological chauvinism applies to all nations. One should also say that, where manifested, the hatred of Jews towards Poles carries marked signs of racism. According to these Pole-hating statements, the Poles are anti-semites in an intrinsic and irredeemable way.

The distinction appearing in some underground publications between 'political' and 'pathological' anti-semitism is a dubious one. We are dealing with the dubious procedure of rationalisation of emotion, that is something which is an irrational element – so the borderline between 'politics' and 'pathology' cannot be identified here. It is a fact that it is the irrational that constitutes the essential material of anti-Judaism and anti-semitism; it means that despite the statements of many historians, it is difficult to say why here and not there, why at this time and not another. Among the many wounds in Jewish consciousness, two are linked with countries – Spain and Poland – where a religious anti-Judaism was unswervingly put into practice by the Inquisition, or ideological anti-semitism appeared after centuries of peaceful coexistence.

It seems that the roads travelled by human hatred are as inscrutable as the roads of Providence, except that neither historians nor sociologists need, nor should investigate the latter.

VI

The above discussion about the transition from religious anti-Judaism to ideological anti-semitism demands further development.

Raul Hilberg maintains that, basically, as far as making Jews repugnant is concerned, Nazism did not come up with anything original, and only repeated what had been voiced by various Christian theologians throughout the ages, by preachers, authors of pamphlets, and politicians. He also draws attention to the fact that hundreds or even thousands of anonymous Third Reich officials, without whom the mobilization of the great machinery of the *Endlösung* would have been impossible, considered themselves good Christians, that they undoubtedly attended churches and chapels regularly and did not consider their bureaucratic-executionary work as something that contradicted their Christian conscience in any way.

I think that this second observation is undoubtedly true. It should be included in a future history of the attitude of the Christian churches to Nazism. Perhaps one day some great two-volume work will be written: Vol.I – Individual Conscience and Totalitarianism; Vol. II – Institutionalized Religions and Totalitarianism. Perhaps they will even be read.

As far as Hilberg's first thesis is concerned, this excellent historian appears to have overlooked one practical detail and one major theoretical problem.

The practical detail is the fact that throughout centuries of religious anti-Judaic campaigning, European Jewry lived, developed and experienced periods of magnificent blossoming of religious and philosophical thought, and authentic folk culture. Thus even if the Nazis adopted part of their anti-Judaic arguments from Christian religious writers, they clearly augmented them with the idea known as the 'final solution'. And, to a large extent, they managed to realize this idea.

The theoretical problem can be formulated in the following way: Christianity had what we shall call two in-built 'mechanisms'. The first of these was an ambivalent attitude to Judaism and its adherents, which is probably most succinctly conveyed by the fifteenth-century theological formula according to which being Jewish is an unpunishable crime. The second mechanism is made up of a series of prohibitions and commandments which, in theory at least, make the very idea of mass slaughter impossible, not to speak of its realisation. Its links with the basic tenets of Christianity are obvious. But the first mechanism, that is the dual attitude to the Mosaic faith, seems to be equally linked not only with the 'genesis', but also with the 'structure' of Christianity.

The functioning of both these elements, here referred to as mechanisms, can be seen clearly in the example of the concept of Jewish 'impure blood'. This concept arose in the sixteenth century in the milieu of the Spanish Inquisition, that is amongst the clergy, in an attempt to validate their practices; namely, to justify the necessity of constant and detailed supervision of the Marranos (i.e. those Jews who had been forcibly converted) observation of whom extended to the third, and sometimes fourth generation, which was deemed necessary, since this Jewish blood, so to speak, did not accept Christianity. It was, then, an attempt to create religious racism. Thus, though having numerous and powerful supporters, the concept was in the end rejected for doctrinal reasons.

No one in his right mind will maintain that these 'mechanisms' worked automatically or faultlessly; even an average knowledge of European history provides many examples of their deceptiveness. But it is a fact that they did function, and that their sometimes peculiar effectiveness can be grasped within the framework of the history of 'long endurance', that without them there would simply be no Jews in Europe. For Christians were always physically, and quite often emotionally, capable of extermination (cf. the Prussians and Sudovians), and of the Carolingian method of conversion (cf. the Saxons). With regard to the Jews this last method was twice attempted on a national scale – both times (in the seventh and sixteenth centuries) on the Iberian peninsula.

So, returning to this section's point of departure, that is the polemic with an American historian, one should say, that ideological anti-semitism has no inbuilt braking-mechanism of the kind mentioned, which is characteristic of medieval religious anti-Judaism and of the beginning of modern times. Exactly the contrary, as we know.

However, the tragic ease of the transition from religious anti-Judaism to ideological anti-semitism (with the agreement, and often the assent, of Christian ecclesiastics . . .), is worth reflection and analysis.

One should add that for a long time Jews also were unaware of the difference between these two phenomena and treated twentieth-century anti-semitism as a successive wave of persecution not differing at all from previous ones.

This failure to understand the peculiarity of ideological anti-semitism can be seen as part of a quite universal misunderstanding of the essence, and of the completely different nature of totalitarianism. There would be much truth and little comfort in this.

VII

Should I really explain what my attitude is to the religious anti-Judaism of Christians (and at the same time to the anti-Christian elements contained in the religion of my ancestors)?

VIII

So much thus far about Jews and Christians. For, without this part of the European heritage, that which happened and continues to happen between Poles and Jews is reduced to the theses voiced by Polish anti-semites and Jewish polonophobes. Namely that Poles simply are that way – they hate Jews, or that Jews simply are that way, all they want to do is cause trouble for Poland. For that is the way of the world.

Let us begin with an essential characteristic of Jewish polonophobia. (The whole business is so painful that one can equally unsuccesfully begin at any point, for searching for a 'beginning' is really meaningless).

If Jews (I have in mind the many among them whom I have met in France, England, Belgium and West Germany) maintained that in the twentieth century anti-semitism was particularly strong in East or Central Europe, the thesis would quite simply be true. But they do not refer to the Slovaks, Ukrainians, Lithuanians, Russians or Austrians – but exclusively to the Poles ('all of them', of course). I have called this an essential feature, for it fundamentally differentiates the Pole-hatred appearing among Jews from that general aversion of Jews towards Christians which has a religious basis. The latter was linked with the whole world of values inscribed in the Talmud, in the rabbinical commentaries, in the whole of culture, and restricted or limited by this whole. For centuries it also served to maintain Jewish separateness. Polonophobia is a-religious and serves no purpose other than the cause of communism, which makes it additionally harmful for Jews themselves.

The reciprocity of hatred in Polish-Jewish relations is truly astounding. A contemporary Polish anti-semite does not maintain that Jews act against the interests of the United States or Sweden, that they have vowed to bring about the downfall of Romania, Hungary or Georgia. No. Just as in the eyes of the Jewish polonophobe, Poles alone are anti-semites, so in the historiosophic phantasmagoria of the Polish anti-semite the sole object of treacherous Jewish plotting is Poland.

I will not enter into a polemic with these visions of the world. Instead, I would like to draw attention to a certain peculiarity connected with them. Thus, if we can basically say that hostility towards Judaism or to Jews is something 'normal' in European culture (in the statistical sense, i.e. the frequency of its appearance over long periods), then when we talk with a concrete Jew-hater we come away with the irresistible impression that we are dealing with a paranoiac. An anti-semite behaves like an individual in a state of manic depression, convinced that 'they' want to destroy him. That is, he is in a state in which he is prepared to absorb all arguments and to adapt them to his own vision of the world. A convinced Jewish Pole-hater behaves in a similar way. (Note that this is a stance characteristic of all adherents of any ideology with distinct totalitarian aspects. The so-called ideological communist, if he wants to maintain relative homeostasis, must behave like a paranoiac, and since he is not a paranoiac, he must then repeatedly blind himself.)

Let me turn sharply at this point to an individual case which, I hope, will not cause me to digress too far from my course.

I am concerned here with reactions to Claude Lanzmann's film *Shoah*. I will not discuss either the communist machinations which accompanied the appearance of this film or the *ex post* statements of Lanzmann himself;

the work of documentary art which *Shoah* is, stands despite these. However, since I have taken up this line of argument, I cannot by-pass one particular individual reaction. I am thinking here of Jerzy Turowicz's article entitled 'Shoah and the Poles'. If a man of such intelligence and uprightness can fail to understand the film to such a degree, it proves that Polish-Jewish relations are painful in a truly alarming fashion.

Shoah is a film about the extermination of the Jews and the indifference of the world in the face of it. Objections that Lanzmann does not speak of attempts to save or to help the Jews are as significant as resentment against *reveille* because it does not lull one to sleep. The Poles in this film are not the substance of the problem, but its attribute. *Shoah* is undoubtedly the work of a possessed man, in the sense that Dostoevsky was possessed, or Mickiewicz at certain periods. For me, this moving film lacks one question and one answer: 'During your time in the ghetto (in Treblinka, in Terezin) did you hear anything about Babi Yar?' The response would have to be in the negative, but that is unimportant. What is important is that the name Babi Yar does not occur once in the film. So I believe that an artist is permitted to be a possessed person. But a possessed person is not permitted to be a deceitful one.

IX

The *pièce de résistance* of Polish anti-semitism: the Jews have long been communists and hated the Poles – hence their mass participation in the communist government forced on the Poles and their eager participation in directing the communist apparatus of repression. One should also mention that this argument was employed by all who happened to want to turn the attention of Polish society in just this direction. 'All' refers in this case to 'classic' anti-semites as well as to communists, and also to those members of the clergy who did not want to condemn the Kielce pogrom (and other similar incidents, for example, in Rzeszów).

The *pièce de résistance* of Jewish polonophobia: the Poles – as inborn anti-semites – took part *en masse* in the Nazi extermination of Jews, which would have been impossible without Polish cooperation, which is proved by the well-known fact that Jews in hiding with 'Aryan papers' were far more afraid of Poles than of Germans.

To put it briefly, in a single sentence: both sides accuse the other of collaboration – to the detriment of the other side – either with nazism or with communism (in its Stalinist phase), that is, of collaboration with the most criminal régimes in the history of the world.

At this point one could say: so what is the point of all this? Many European governments worked with the Third Reich, not only those which are today universally seen as guilty of treason against their own nations (France, Slovakia, Hungary and so on), but also the British government during the Munich Conference – not to speak of the Ribbentrop-Molotov pact. The number of completely voluntary supporters, helpers and glorifiers of communism was, and has been, so numerous over the last 70 years that one can easily think in terms of eight figures. Should one not then say: so what is the problem? If others have done the same, then why not drop it and leave it at that; no one has to be either better or more vindictive.

One could take that view, but I am unable to do so. And that is not because practical considerations argue against such a formulation of the question. It simply would not be effective. I cannot suitably articulate my reluctance to pseudo-absolution based on the argument; 'but others also . . .'. I am not talking about an obvious issue: 'Others too' is an argument from the sphere of statistics, and not decency. For beyond that, some limitation stirs in me that commands me to say: others, even markedly happier Lotophagi, do not concern me at all; I want to get, if not to the very bottom of this issue, then at least as far as I am able.

I will begin, then, by stating that some particle of truth is contained in both these crazy generalizations. And the one way of combatting these generalizations, with their unprecedented strength of persuasion, must be through the extraction of this truth, that is separating it from falsehood.

But with this aim in mind do I not commit a mistake based on the attempt to convince those who cannot be convinced? I hope this is not the case, and that is because I am not addressing them. From the outset I hold that in normal decent relations between nations there are groups of 'incorruptibles' who will always believe that 'others' are the source of all evil. For some Georgians these are obviously the Armenians, and vice versa; in Poland, in the sphere of unofficial culture, this type of 'intransigent' anti-semitism is presented in the publications of the Union of Contemporary Humanism. It may reflect badly on me, but I do not care about these 'incorruptibles' or the irredeemably sick; let them find their own salvation – they are, after all, human beings possessing free will. Writing this essay I have in mind those who, when they come across anti-semitism or virulent polonophobia, say: well, X is obviously exaggerating, but something about them (Jews, Poles) is not right. And those who on hearing Pole-hating or anti-semitic statements think: if there were a Pole (Jew) here then I'd protest, for one should not offend others, but as we are amongst our own kind, then, what the hell! In other words, I am concerned with those to whom it does not occur that anti-semitism does not shame Jews but Poles, and that Pole-hatred does not reflect badly on Poles, but on Jews.

X

This is more an attempt to describe and explain than duly to mete out justice. Hence the appearance of aiming for symmetry: maybe in this way something can be done with this sick confusion. But, on the other hand, I do not think that justice depends on symmetry. Rather I think that one can say – paraphrasing Tuwim – that symmetry is the ethics of fools.

XI

How did it come to pass, that in some countries (Russia, Poland, Hungary) the participation of Jews in the communist movement was so notable? Furthermore, this participation was high as a percentage in relation not to the number of Jews residing in a particular country (in Poland not more than ten thousand out of three million), but in relation to the size of the communist party. The usual reply is: this is due to the extent of anti-semitism in these countries. I think this is a wrong answer, but more of that in a moment. For the time being I will state my case more mildly and say that it is unsatisfactory both on the factual level and the moral one. So far as facts are concerned, this explanation appears not the least sufficient. For if it is true that during periods when communism was fashionable in the United States there were, relatively speaking, many Jews both in the communist party and around it, it is also true that anti-semitism in the States, in comparison with Hungary, Poland or Russia, was chicken-feed. On the other hand, in the fatherland of ideological anti-semitism, France, the participation of Jews in the communist movement was small, and practically non-existent within the party leadership. So much for the factual side. If one were to treat this explanation as a *justification* – and it is sometimes taken as such – then it sounds as if somebody had said: because I was attacked by syphilitics, I have become a leper. (I apologise to syphilitics and lepers.)

I have said that in the issue under analysis, anti-semitism is an explanation that is at least insufficient. I will add: for anti-semitism to act as a stimulus inclining the Jews towards communism other contingencies would also have to play a part. Above all those which cause the Japanese, Poles, Egyptians and Italians to join the communist party. When someone says that anti-semitism inclined Jews (perhaps one should add: some Jews) towards communism, he is also saying that apart from generally functioning elements, something also appeared in a given case which pushed Jews in this direction as Jews. Thus, I am of the opinion that there are elements in the culture of every nation that are skilfully manipulated by communists. These can be characteristics which appear perfectly neutral or at most slightly irritating – as in the case of the French penchant for empty rhetoric.

I think that in Jewish culture there were three elements making some of them more susceptible to communism simply by virtue of being Jewish. First, this culture's pervasive legalism, often tinged with a liking for casuistry; secondly, the particular status of so-called assimilated Jews; and thirdly, the widespread conviction (not only among Jews), that the so-called left could not in essence be anti-semitic. (The distinction between 'left' and 'right' is, I think, surely inaccurate for the twentieth century, and quite often misleading in the analysis of the nineteenth-century situation. I would thus ask readers to regard further use of 'left' and 'right' as if in inverted commas.)

I will develop the above hypotheses in another order than that presented above, and I will begin with the simplest question. The conviction that the left cannot in substance be anti-semitic (more broadly speaking: that it cannot declare hatred towards other nations) is false. Proudhon, – a committed socialist and anarchist, therefore a man of the left – was an anti-semite. Fourier was an anti-semite. Some members of the Russian *People's Will* were anti-semitic. Marx was in private life an anti-semite. Voltaire and Holbach were anti-semites *avant la lettre* and fierce ones at that, and undoubtedly men of the left *avant la lettre*. With the exception of the private anti-semitism of Marx, with which those who have come across the biography of his youngest daughter, Eleanor, will be particularly familiar, these facts are quite easily discovered, but simply shamefully hidden. The French historian, Leon Poliakov, an author influenced more by Voegelin and Besançon than, for example, Sartre, seems to feel embarrassed by the anti-semitism of Voltaire and goes into digressions on the theme of the unhappy childhood of the 'patriarch from Ferney' and his castration complex. Good Lord, and what do we know of the childhood of Julius Streicher and what he did or did not want cut off! On this subject of anti-semitism there is no substantiality either of the left or the right. There exists only the probability that ... And that is not so very great as one might imagine. For one might have thought that good Catholics should not acquiesce to ideological anti-semitism, but in the nineteenth and twentieth centuries – beginning, for example, with the mayor of Vienna, Karl Lueger – history teemed with Christian, ideological and party anti-semites.

Where, too, did the false truism stem that people of the left, and therefore socialists, and also communists, could not be anti-semites? I suspect that this is due to a number of coincidences, that is, to the so-called caprice of history. At the turn of this century a few issues coincided which were not all necessarily simultaneous : the crystallization of modern anti-semitism, the birth of Zionism, the Dreyfus affair, the Dreyfusites' enlistment of Jaurès' support (though he had to be persuaded) and finally the fact that Bebel and Wilhelm Liebknecht were opponents of anti-semitism, which gave the German social-democrats, then the strongest socialist party, a sense of direction.

The mistake which arose at the turn of the century, that is the acceptance of a contingency as a truth, was strengthened by what I have called the legalism of Jewish culture. The mosaic faith is the faith of the Covenant, that is an agreement between the Lord and his people (and not only his own people, for the first Covenant, entered upon with Noah, concerns all mankind). One of the two basic aspects of rabbinical thought is called *Halakha*, which can be translated as Law and is made up of an exposition and commentary on the Law. (Even an educated Christian is astounded when he learns that the Talmud contains an unambiguous and absolute ban on the death sentence.) The responses of the rabbis are also to a great extent legal texts. Law is a basic concept in Judaism, whereas the Christian equivalent is Grace (or Love). This view that Law in its more extreme forms (like Marcionism) is clearly incompatabile with the text of the Hebrew Bible and the New Testament, and is, as a result, unacceptable to practising Jews and Christians, for religious reasons. However, I think that one can state the problem in the following way: in Jewish culture the concept of the Law is dominant, and in that of Christianity the concept of Mercy. Thus the conviction held by some Jews which emerged from the cult of law (not *the* Law), that the problem of anti-semitism could be solved with the help of certain prohibitions, and that communism would do this. Two tragic misunderstandings. First, there is no law in communism, and secondly even if there were, it would not be capable of solving any national conflict. The law can ban certain activities, but it has no power to order emotions.

Thus if some Jews believed that communism was a remedy for anti-semitism, then they were being above all foolish; they had many opportunities to realize that it was not only a deceptive remedy, but also one that contributed brilliantly to the spread of that which it was supposed to liquidate. And if they did not realize this, then they were such hopeless fools that they were practically asking for all they met.

But, really, I think that in the case of the majority of Jews who acceded to communism, they were not so much concerned with anti-semitism as with an attempt to escape their own Jewishness. And here we come to what I have called the particular status of so-called assimilated Jews.

XII

Let us agree to use the term emancipation to describe the transitional process of European Jewish society from a status that was feudal, and more religious than national, to the cultural status or civilization of an industrial society. Let us also immediately stipulate that in this particular case, despite its etymology, emancipation did not at all signify an unambiguous move from a state of slavery to one of freedom. That which is universally portrayed as a straightforward lack of freedom, was a state which involved a certain level of freedom which varied from country to country and even from town to town, and which was in some cases very important for Jews. That which is presented as unambiguous liberation also involved various disadvantages which were crucial for pious Jews. Let us take two examples: general election and compulsory military service. The fact that the latter was linked to the inevitable transgressions of Mosaic law – violation of the Sabbath, violence and manslaughter (both condemned by traditional Jewish culture) – was absolutely clear to Jewish believers. Moreover, the advantages accompanying participation in the election of deputies to parliament were not necessarily evident with Cartesian clarity. Even the most promising versions of emancipation – and realistic versions were by no means idyllic – always had the character of a conflict; it always took place on the basis of 'something for something'. In its particulars, the process was 'foredoomed' in as much as it resulted from the mechanism within which civil societies emerged, processes of industrialisation and also secularisation. In Europe as a whole, these processes have not been completed within the sphere of consciousness to this day, as the work of such outstanding writers as Isaac Bashevis Singer or Henryk Grynberg demonstrates. In the spheres of law and customs this process lasted from around the end of the eighteenth century until the 'final solution'. (The emancipation of the Russian Jews is a separate question, in that it took place outside the framework of the civil society which did not exist, nor was it meant to, in Russia – and especially not in the country of Triumphant Socialism.)

Let us posit for the sake of simplicity that the process of emancipation went on for just under two centuries. On a global scale, the first half of this period took place under the patronage of the Enlightenment in the broader sense of the term. And like the majority of valuable ideas of the *Aufklärung*, it was excessively optimistic in its assumptions and not entirely clear as to its ultimate aims. For example, the postulate of equality before the law, directed at legislators, was often accompanied by a postulate addressed towards the Jews, calling on them to abandon their 'superstitions'. The first was more or less clear, but the second was not.

More will be said of the particular circumstances in which the emancipation of Jews developed in Poland in a separate section. Generally speaking, this process can be compared to a caravan of wagons which set off on a journey in an unknown direction by an untrodden road. Along this road particular vehicles stop in different places, turn off, meet and part again. In the sphere of culture, emancipation had to involve the inclusion of growing areas of lay and 'non-Jewish' knowledge into traditional Jewish education and in practice, in the third or fourth generation, pushing it onto the margins. This was most often, though not always the case. In the political sphere, a whole range of emancipatory possibilities appeared at the turn of the nineteenth and twentieth centuries, together with the establishment of Jewish political parties (the Zionists, the *Bund*, and the so-called religious parties).

The above concerned the realization of an emancipation which would, above all, maintain Jewish autonomy. There were also versions whose ultimate aim was to be the liquidation of any differences between Jews and non-Jews, the maximalist reduction of that which was regarded as 'Jewishness'. In this case one talked of assimilation, that is *imitation*. And I would like here to take up one particular aspect of assimilation.

There is no doubt whatsoever, that assimilated Jews have made a great contribution to the European civilization. One could fill whole pages with surnames, which I will spare both the reader and myself, as this aspect of assimilation has been researched *ad nauseam* and to the point of being ridiculous. It is more rarely that attention is drawn to the attitude of assimilated Jews to their remaining countrymen. Both Hannah Arendt and Isaiah Berlin have written that assimilated Jews – as if recognizing that their privileged position is linked, among other things, with the fact that they are relatively few in number – were not at all interested in the wholesale emancipation of the Jewish population *en masse*. What is worse: many of them despised this 'rabble' and were afraid of it. When, in *Lingua Tertii Imperii* one reads fragments full of disgust about poor Jews from Eastern Europe, and one realizes *when* it was written, one is overcome with a feeling of horror.

Klemperer alone is responsible for what he wrote, and no one else. It does seem, however, that the above sections of *Lingua Tertii Imperii* can be treated as an extreme expression of a certain more generally-held stance.

We are speaking here of assimilated Jews, that is those whose native tongue was Polish, German, French and so on, who lived and worked in the culture of a certain nation; the believers amongst them very often described themselves as Poles (Frenchmen, Italians etc.) of the Mosaic persuasion. From the end of the nineteenth century to the rise of Nazism, this group was also most exposed to various types of anti-semitic action, and notably more susceptible on this score than the devout inhabitants of provincial towns or of districts like Nalewki in Warsaw. Thus *some* of these assimilated Jews had an extremely ambiguous attitude to their own Jewishness. Though they did not deny it, they nevertheless regarded each mention of the fact that they were Jews as a manifestation of anti-semitism. Their behaviour said: but we have made the effort not to be Jews and here is someone trying to remind us that we are. The conviction that to be a Jew was something worse constituted the silent background of this type of reaction. It could be said that these people had *likened* themselves not to the Poles, Dutch, Austrians and so on, but to Polish, Dutch or Austrian anti-semites. Generally speaking, people of this type wanted Jews to both exist and yet not exist at the same time, that is they dreamt about the philosopher's stone. And it was this that propelled them in the direction of communism. For communism appeared to them as a noble escape from their own Jewishness, a paradise in which nations both exist and do not exist.

I could be accused of writing about assimilated Jews (let us add again – of some of them) and of omitting to mention those famous Jewish tailors of which communist poets wrote with such fervour. And indeed they were showered in abundance. Unfortunately, the poets have forgotten that the majority of these tailors were very pious and that, in their eyes, Bolshevism was above all an atheist disease; others in their turn belonged to the *Bund*, which in Poland from 1921 was evidently anti-communist. Furthermore, among the leading Polish communists of Jewish extraction like Finder, Lampe, Berman, Minc, Zambrowski or Borejsza there was, curiously enough, not a single tailor from the *shtetl*. They came from wealthy and usually assimilated families; they served a criminal ideology and committed terrible acts, in part because they wished to escape their own Jewishness. They must always have lived in fear: first they were afraid of being Jews, then they lived in fear of Moscow and of the fact that they were still Jews. The poet says: 'Who recognises the perfection of acts/ let him die a defenceless death'.

XIII

I do not know if I should have cited precisely those names. Among them only Finder died at the hands of the Gestapo, and the story of how he came to be there belongs, it seems, to one of the secret pages of the history of communism in Poland. But not only has the grass grown over all of them, but Tartars too have walked across it. Maybe I should have added: Lobman (a leading and very dogmatic communist journalist). That would really cause a scandal. But is it worth causing scandals over someone so wretched?

XIV

The process of the emancipation of the Jews took place in time and was also a particular aspect of the appearance of modern nations in Europe. Emancipation was not simply the transition from being Jewish, that is a member of a religious community, to being a Jew, that is a member of a nation. Zionism as a political expression of the will to be a nation like others appeared over 100 years after the beginning of the emancipatory process, if the beginning of this process is taken as Moses Mendelsohn's translation of the Hebrew Bible into German. A conventional and probably very debatable periodisation. In the eighteenth and nineteenth centuries emancipation was naturally an entry into another, non-Jewish culture. The process was generally very difficult and in Poland, partitioned between three invaders, full of further complications.

Let us begin our demonstration of these complications with an extreme simplification, a certain pseudo-quantification. The process 'should' have occurred relatively peacefully where there were few Jews and where the number of 'feudal' freedoms they enjoyed were few. In the above thesis the simplification rests on the fact that the influence of quantitative elements on the course of processes connected with assimilation was limited. Ideological anti-semitism was born, as I have mentioned, in France, where there were few Jews, and, furthermore, in that part where there were hardly any Jews at all. It was brought to a murderous paroxysm in Germany which was for decades considered to be a particular 'paradise' of emancipation. So far, however, as the above quantitative element which played a role within certain limits is concerned, Poland was a 'bad' country. That was because there were many Jews there and they enjoyed quite a range of 'feudal' freedoms. So much for the extreme simplification.

And now a question which is not simplified but merely simple. Leaving the ghetto demanded effort and sacrifice. It was coming out into the unknown, abandoning the 'familiar' for the 'alien'. Let us not deceive ourselves: this alien element was rarely sympathetic; it was rather indifferent and derisive, or actually hostile.

In France, in England, even in fragmented Germany, this departure was naturally to lead towards French, English or German culture. For Jews it was also in accordance with the basic prescriptions regulating behaviour in the Diaspora. These state that in so far as no contradiction is present between the fundamental tenets of the mosaic faith and the laws of a particular country then, as the formula goes, 'the law of the country (in which you live) – is the law'.

In partitioned Poland everything looked different. Coming out of the ghetto and into Polish culture did not happen 'naturally' at all and was not obvious. The law which had to be acknowledged was not Polish law. We should add that for ages the basic link between the Jews and a certain country in the Diaspora was loyalty to the monarch. This state of affairs was also recognised by the Christians. Aquinas expressed it in the following way: Jews are the slaves of princes, but this is an exclusively civic slavery and does not concern either divine laws or natural laws. Thus in nineteenth-century Poland the principle of loyalty towards the monarch had to apply to the tsar, emperor of Austria or Prussian king.

Due to the circumstances described above and many others besides, the emancipation had the following results: throughout two-thirds of the nineteenth century it progressed very slowly, and the more slowly the further east one went. Traditional Jewish culture continued and developed in part, whether in its Orthodox, Hasidic, or to some extent enlightened versions. Towards the end of the century a sudden acceleration of the process occurred, which, in a process such as emancipation, does not give exclusively good results. This acceleration more or less coincided with the appearance of modern Jewish political movements (Zionism, the *Bund*, religious parties), which was seen by a notable section of Polish authors and so-called assimilators as a negative phenomenon. I do not share this view. The acceleration was a fact, and the appearance of modern Jewish political movements did in sum soften the cultural shock of such an acceleration.

Until the moment when Jewish political movements began to appear, the process looked, in very general terms, as follows.

In the Prussian partition it was almost exclusively a move towards German culture. In ancient Lithuania simply incorporated to Russia, it was primarily a move towards Russian culture. In the so-called Congress Kingdom – in particular before the influx of Russian Jews following the wave of pogroms in the 1880s – it was a move towards Polish culture. In Galicia there was a move towards both Polish and Austrian culture, but never towards the Ukrainian. If then, in such complicated circumstances, the emancipation of a notable part of Jews went in the direction of Polish culture this bears witness to the amazing attraction of the latter. For apart from mentioning the freedoms which Jews enjoyed before the fall of the Polish-Lithuanian Commonwealth everything spoke against such a choice.

The 'natural' Polish view according to which all Jews *should* move towards Polish culture is based on a manifold misunderstanding. First, the Jews regarded Poland – like Hungary, France or Austria – not as their fatherland, but as a country of the Diaspora. An exceptional country throughout many ages, true, and the Jews were well aware of it (there are many records testifying to this) but nevertheless a country of the Dispersal. The concept of a fatherland could not then be present at the beginning of emancipation – it could only be a result of it. If this outrages anyone, then he should realize that during about two thirds of the nineteenth century, Polish peasants, that is Polish speaking Christians, did not understand the concept of fatherland in the way that we do today or in the way it was used by writers of the Enlightenment, Romantics or conspirators. Secondly, moving towards Polish culture, at least in the Russian or Prussian partitions, meant moving towards more or less severe repressions for that very reason. Instead of directing accusations at Jews because some of them chose a road to emancipation other than the Polish one, one should instead be surprised that so many moved towards the culture of a defeated and oppressed country.

XV

Checking something in the third volume of Poliakov's *Histoire de l'antisémitisme*, I came across a fragment by Zalkind-Hurwitz. He was a Polish Jew, a Talmud scholar who after many vicissitudes became the keeper of the oriental section of the library of Louis XVI. He was also the author of the *Apologie des Juifs*... written in 1775 in which he explains his 'French-Sarmatian style'. In the painful confusion, into which I have here tried to introduce some order, this 18th-century Jew-Sarmatian, a Talmud scholar and royal librarian provided the only moment – if I can put it thus – at which I smiled.

XVI

I cannot abide the term 'Holocaust'. It means exactly 'burnt offering' or a sacrifice made to God (the gods). Among the Hebrews before the destruction of the Temple, and for the Greeks, except for the poor Iphigenia it was exclusively an animal sacrifice. I am unable to understand how it could have entered someone's head that to force a few million Jews through a chimney was in any way an offering to any kind of god. The moment that we consider the semantics of *sacrifice* we automatically raise the murderer to the honour of a priest, or the indifferent witness of the murder to the honour of a participant in a ritual.

Yes indeed: indifference. At least a quarter of a century ago a certain historian collected extracts from the Polish underground press from the time of the occupation concerning the 'final solution'. I have read them myself. The historian decided against publishing the anthology, believing that it could harm Poland. I do not think he was right. I think that such an anthology will sooner or later see the light and it would truly be better if someone published it who does not wish to harm Poland, otherwise someone who does will take advantage of the opportunity. And these texts cannot be burned in any Ministry of Truth.

We say – and I have written this myself at the beginning of this essay – that the indifference of a notable number of Poles in the face of the extermination of the Jews is a particular aspect of the indifference of the world towards the mass murder. We add, or should add, also, that this indifference is something evil. There is, however, a kind of helplessness in such statements. For we know that today, in the summer of 1986, many peoples are being exterminated on a mass scale, the Afghans, Ethiopians, Khmers, and that the Kurds and the inhabitants of Biafra suffered similarly not so long ago. Organised extermination has become something so frequent in the twentieth century that it exceeds our capacity for compassion and empathy. In the democratic countries those who are at all moved by this undertake a variety of roles; some try to help the Afghans, others the tribes of Ethiopia deliberately condemned to death by starvation, others the Christians of southern Sudan.

When we speak of Polish-Jewish relations we usually employ a mode of reasoning which stems from a particular incident to the general which declares: the world is indifferent towards mass murder. Let us try, however, to put the argument the other way round. Let us say: evil in the world resides, among other things, in the fact that people are indifferent in the face of the extermination of others; the Poles, or, more accurately, a notable portion of them, were indifferent in the face of the extermination of the Jews, for such is the nature of evil in the world.

But evil in the world rarely appears in its unqualified, pure shape. There is normally some here and now involved. And let us add that in the case of not so few Poles it was not only a question of indifference, but also of the expression of statements which testified to the feeling of a specific relief: here is someone who has done something essential for us, something which we ourselves could not perhaps be able to do.

How did it come about that normal and quite decent people, felt, thought, and spoke in this fashion?

From the death of Piłsudski in 1935, the majority of Polish circles moulding public opinion claimed that Jews should be got rid of and a notable number of these spokesmen said and wrote that Jews as Jews constituted a very grave threat to Poland. For example: a completely objective, purely quantitative lexical analysis of the *Mały Dziennik* [a Catholic newspaper published under the direction of Fr Maximilian Kolbe] shows that it was not a question of communism (although the paper was anticommunist), but that the Jews were bad as Jews. The reader of the *Mały Dziennik* was repeatedly told that the Jews wanted to conquer Poland. This would, incidentally, have proved the Jews' foolishness rather than the wisdom often ascribed to them, but let us not be petty about details.

So, for the good of Poles and Poland, the Jews must be removed ...

XVII

In 1941, General Grot-Rowecki, Commander-in-Chief of the Home Army, felt it necessary to send a dispatch to London (mentioned recently by Krystyna Kersten and other authors in *Aneks* 41/42) in which we read:

> Please accept as a fact that an overwhelming majority in the country is anti-semitically oriented. Even the socialists are no exception here. The differences lie only in tactics. There is practically no one who would recommend following German methods. Even secret organ-

isations who remain under the influence of pre-war activists of the Democratic Clubs or the Polish Socialist Party accept the postulate of emigration as a solution to the Jewish problem. This is as obvious to everyone as, for example, the need to remove the Germans from the country ... Anti-semitism is presently a widespread attitude.

The description given here in a few sentences of prevailing moods meant in practice that Jews in ghettos died at the hands of Germans and feared Germans, whereas Jews living with 'Aryan papers' or hiding in cellars, cupboards and forests perished at the hands of Germans but feared the Poles.

I am not dealing with history here as a sequence of events in time. I agree with Walter Laqueur. He wrote that, contrary to the widespread opinion, it was not because of Polish anti-semitism that few Jews were saved in Poland; taking into account the widespread anti-semitism in Poland (particularly in the 1930s) one should state that an exceptionally large number of Jews were saved. For myself I would like to make two points. First the Polish government in London was the *only* Allied government that demanded *practical* measures of the main partners of the coalition aimed at stopping the extermination of the Jews. Unsuccessfully, as we know. And it is not true – here is my second point – that any military or financial considerations spoke against such measures.

Let us stay with the question which I formulated at the end of the previous section: was the indifference of the Poles towards the 'final solution' prompted by something else, not only by the 'general evil in the world'?

I shall try to answer this question with reference not to historical, but to logical order. As my point of departure I shall take a 'group portrait' of statements of a certain type currently appearing in the underground press expressing convictions which I do not believe to be universal, but which are certainly not inspired by the communists. These are, as a rule, the statements of people declaring themselves to be the critical continuators of *Endecja* thought, or at any rate expressing admiration for Roman Dmowski. I am not arguing with specific authors here for two reasons. First, because I am discussing a way of thinking and not the text of some Mr Ajacki or Bajacki. Secondly, I am certain as far as some authors are concerned, and I presume about others, that they are not anti-semites. Consequently I accept that both concrete authors as well as my collective author *de facto* do not realize what it is they are writing.

And they write the following.

First, the question of Polish anti-semitism belongs unambiguously to the past, as there are no Jews in Poland.

Secondly, it is difficult to say what constituted anti-semitism in independent Poland and what was an understandable reaction to the improper behaviour of Jews, and what was a political conception for solving the Jewish question.

Thirdly, in Poland between the wars the Jewish question depended on the fact that there existed an over three-million-strong national minority, politically passive on the whole, non-Polish in its traditions, and economically and culturally active, which hampered the development of the Polish economy, barred the Poles' access to the free professions and introduced foreign elements into Polish culture.

Fourthly, in this context the propositions of the *Endecja* aimed towards the protection and promotion of the Polish state of possession both in the economy and in the sphere of education and culture. It was a question then of placing certain limits on the activity of Jews in the above spheres and encouraging them to emigrate; the latter initiative was also supported by the Zionists.

Fifthly, in politics Jewish parties were not concerned about the good of Poland, but about defending the rights of the Jewish minority. A part of this minority strengthened the ranks of the communist party which denied Poland's right to an independent existence.

In the sixth place, it should perhaps be acknowledged that the Jews could not behave in any other way, but neither by the same token could the Poles. Since the emigration of Jews was impossible, a situation with no solution arose.

This kind of reasoning is characterized by two very important oversights and a few assumptions hidden so deeply that – perhaps – people thinking in this way do not themselves realize their existence, although I believe, on the whole, that people say what they think.

The first oversight concerns the following question: among all the minorities of inter-war Poland, the Jews were the *only* ones, in contrast with the Ukrainians, Germans or Lithuanians, who did not have any territorial demands and recognized the Treaty of Versailles without any reservations. (I am not, of course, speaking of the communists here, but they were supporters of the Soviet solution independent of nationality). *In potentia*, the Jews were therefore the only minority interested in the existence of an independent Poland. At the same time that successive cabinets, beginning from 1918, needed a rallying concept of ruling a multinational state, which, as we know, none of these governments possessed. After 1935 the policies of Rydz-Śmigły's groups regarding the Jews antagonised Jewish society as a whole. A few months before the outbreak of the Second World War a notable section of the clergy and the group directly ruling the country saw the prohibition of Jewish ritual slaughter (*shekhita*) as one of the most important political problems! This had nothing to do with fighting communism – for it was well-known that communism liquidates ritual slaughter along with meat.

Post-*endecja* thought presented here as a group portrait contains four hidden assumptions without which this whole mode of reasoning could not have appeared at all. First, that Poland should be a mono-ethnic society. Secondly, that the Jews, by virtue of definition, are more intelligent than the Poles both in the economic sphere and in so-called spiritual culture. Thirdly, that the economy and, for example, medical care, should not be assessed by categories such as efficiency, professionalism, the raising of the well-being of the country, the health of its inhabitants etc., but divided according to whether functions in them are carried out by the 'familiar' and the 'alien'. Fourthly, in this situation a short-term solution was to place *legal* restrictions on these alien and more intelligent people and in the long-term to remove them from the country. For this one needs not some decaying democracy, but strong state intervention heading in the direction of apartheid.

And finally, the second of the oversights mentioned.

Not only the collective author I have constructed, but real authors, do not allow the thought to occur to them that if Poland had at its disposal not two but several decades of independent existence, then perhaps Polish-Jewish relations might have fallen into the pattern of those in Italy or France, not to speak of the United States.

In fact, I did not have to present the post-*endecja* argument here in its entirety. Point six and the second oversight are in fact enough. For if it were meant to be that in the year 1939 Polish-Jewish relations found themselves at a point without any solution, then the Nazis proved that this was not the case. They found a solution. And suddenly it becomes understandable how someone could say: this is truly deplorable, but the fact is that Hitler settled one problem for us.

It must be added here that this post-*endecja* collective author writing for the underground press *never* actually says this. On the contrary – he vehemently condemns the Nazi murders. But at the same time, despite his own intentions he shows how it came about that there were Poles who did say this in 1943, in 1946, in 1949.

XVIII

Two theses often accompany each other in underground publications: that the political analyses of Roman Dmowski can serve as a model of clear assessment and precise cold political calculation, and that he was not a 'pathological' anti-semite. Let us pass over *Przewrót*, the twice-issued collection of articles by the sage of the *Endecja* before the war, in silence, and let us say that the political works of Roman Dmowski taught a certain style of thought, and that someone brought up on these texts could behave in a number of ways during the occupation, whereas someone brought up on Kazimierz Wybranowski's novel *Dziedzictwo* was much more likely to inform the Gestapo that the neighbours were hiding a little girl with suspicious features, and do it without looking for any profit. And everything would be OK if not for the fact that Kazimierz Wybranowski and Roman Dmowski are one and the same person. (A bibliographical note here: *Dziedzictwo* was reprinted at least twice before the war; furthermore it appeared in 1942 in London and in 1944 in Kraków straight – so to speak – out of the oven.)

I do not personally think that the attitude of a notable number of Poles to the 'final solution' during the occupation was the result of reading the *Gazeta Warszawska* or even *Falanga* or *Prosto z mostu*. Whatever I might think of these publications, they were in their own way élitist and concerned mainly with politics, albeit understood in a particular way. And only a small section of society is interested in politics on a day-to-day basis. On the scale of mass hostility, dislike and hatred towards Jews was incited by various publications such as *Samoobrona Narodu* or *Mały Dziennik* or books such as *Królestwo Szatana*.

It was the author of *Królestwo Szatana* (a Catholic priest), who wrote in March 1939, conducting a polemic on the pages of *Samoobrona Narodu* with the 'scandalous', in his opinion, theses of Maria Winowska that one cannot be a Catholic and an anti-semite at the same time:

> Woe is me if this is true! Not only have I been practising anti-semitism for many decades but not long ago in articles written marking Christmas Eve . . . I developed the thesis that the First Anti-Semite was born in the person of the Child of Bethlehem, who established the bases of the Church's anti-semitism. And I have not met with any criticism either on the part of the church or the public for this.

The fact that both the spiritual guardian of the *Mały Dziennik* and the author of the words cited above perished in Hitler's concentration camps can prompt various types of reflection. But none of them will change the views, and above all the emotions which the readers educated by them directed towards Jews in, say, 1942.

XIX

I am curious to know if the cretin is still alive who raised an outcry in the spring of 1968 in the Israeli Knesset because of Roman Zambrowski's removal from the government of the Polish People's Republic. This is what he chose as a crowning proof of anti-semitism! If he was so worried about Jews then he should instead have thanked Gomułka and Moczar. Zambrowski was not only an arch-communist: in the forties as the chairman of the Extraordinary Commission in the Fight against Speculation he was responsible for the destruction of the only vital sector of the Polish economy and for imprisoning thousands of innocent people in camps and prisons (he did not care whether they were circumcised or baptized; he was in this respect a true egalitarian).

This deputy to the Israeli parliament whose name I do not know provides an excellent example of the ethnocentric idiocy which leads to moral abomination.

XX

A further note on symmetry.

The counting of crimes is an absurd occupation.

In the years 1939–1940 on the part of Poland taken over by the Soviets, a certain number of Polish officers were handed over to the *NKVD* by Jewish informers. During the Nazi occupation Jews in hiding were quite disinterestedly turned over to the Gestapo by Polish denunciators. Are we to say that while the number of denounced, that is those given over to death, was equal on 'both sides', Jews and Poles were morally speaking on a par?

People, come to your senses.

XXI

A further note on principles.

One is tempted to say that the longer and more peaceful the time between the extinguishing of religious anti-Judaism and the birth and blossoming of ideological anti-semitism, the greater the chance that a part of the Christian clergy will not become involved in extinguishing fires with oil. And vice versa.

XXII

Spring 1986. Paris. Dinner. At the table: the master of the house – a lawyer, the lady of the house – a professor of biology, a film director, a young sociology professor, the muse of the latter.

I arrived towards the end of dinner in the middle of a heated discussion on the theme of. . . . anti-semitism in the films of Wajda. It was the sociologist who was holding forth with the help of the muse. As I sat down he was saying something more or less along the lines of: 'Well, how does he portray that Jew – thin, pale with a hooked nose and side-locks, it's just a caricature!' This obviously took more than one sentence and I did not realise immediately that he was talking about *Brzezina*. I hesitated to join the argument mainly because the sociologist was himself pale, thin, had a hook nose, and his side-locks had been replaced by an afro hair-style. I had an urge to bring a mirror from the hall; I glanced at my hosts and at the director and discovered that, like myself, they were trying to control their laughter. Meanwhile the sociologist, quite carried away, went on: 'And those rich Jews in *Promised Land*. There were no rich Jews in Poland!'

'You know,' I said smiling, 'our host is the grandson of a wealthy Polish Jew and I am the son of a positively rich one'. (The grandfather of this Parisian lawyer who lived in Złoczów was the oldest of my father's brothers whom I can remember. He visited us sometimes; my mother gave him only tea, for our house was not kosher enough for him). 'Well,' said the sociologist, 'maybe there were a few rich ones, but they were exceptions.' I tried to carry on talking normally: 'You're mistaken, the wealth of Polish Jews varied enormously, and there were several rich ones. In fact, a notable part of the wood and textile industry belonged to them.' But the Parisian sociologist knew better of course. 'Polish Jews,' he maintained, 'were wretchedly poor with a few exceptions.'

I wanted to refer him to Joseph Marcus's book, but he had angered me. I looked at him for a moment and then in a quiet voice, taken straight from the freezer, I said: 'Gentlemen don't quarrel about facts'.

My Parisian cousin was as entertained by this as a child and repeated it several times, savouring the English saying.

When I come across fanatical chauvinism, whomsoever it concerns, my first reaction is: but this is a sick person. But I know that this isn't true. It is not so simple. This Parisian sociologist, and millions like him of various nationalities, are perfectly normal. Nothing can cure him because he isn't sick. He will wander the world and rave about Wajda being an anti-semite. The more magnificently his Smorgon [an academy for training bears] or Sorbonne career develops the more will his resistance to argument strengthen.

Does this mean that I regard the Parisian sociologist mentioned here as a fossil of Jewish chauvinism? He is certainly a chauvinist. However no one should be denied the right to change his views, in the hope that he will change worse for better ones. I suspect, however, that so far as chauvinism, Leninism and so on are concerned, people change their views not because something has happened around them, but because something has happened inside them. This does not, of course, include the opportunists who exist in notable measure in every nation.

XXIII

One could say that the tragic nature of Polish-Jewish relations is linked with particular temporal shifts of some ideas proper to European culture, first of all the idea of *Judenreinheit*. For whole centuries from the Middle Ages to the end of the eighteenth century, the Jews were moved on from various countries of Europe, or did not have the right to settle. Examples are England, France, Spain, Muscovy. It is in the eighteenth and nineteenth centuries that Jews gain the right to settle all over Europe with the exception of Spain, Portugal and the Russian Empire in which there was the so-called Pale of Settlement, mainly on the lands of the former Polish-Lithuanian Commonwealth. In Poland from the time of the Piasts to the loss of independence the privilege *de non tolerandis Judaeis* was relatively rarely put into practice by specific towns and generally not maintained for long. The idea of resettling all the Jews does not appear until the Congress Kingdom, and throughout the nineteenth century remains on the margins of Polish political thought. It can be said that its shift from the margins into the centre of concern for notable sections of the political and religious élite of the country in the years directly preceding the Second World War contradicted the whole tradition of Polish political culture. And the more vociferously the intrinsic Polishness of this idea was proclaimed, the further it was from that tradition. None the less 'it came about' that when a fatal threat hung over the fragile independence of the Polish state, the idea was proclaimed that a basic condition for happiness and power was to rid Poland of all its Jews. And it was promoted by people who enjoyed the respect of many Poles. These people put a lot of effort into propagating the idea of *Judenreinheit*, an effort which – who knows? who knows? – might have been better employed in a worthier cause and with greater benefit for the Poles. Not only political benefit.

We speak with respect of those who rescued Jews during the war, risking their own lives in the process. But we do not say everything even in this case. For in answer to the question: did Poles fear other Poles during the Nazi occupation, the correct response goes: not at all ... providing they did not help Jews. (This last does not apply to convents in which Jewish children were hidden; as far as I know, there is not a single case of a convent being betrayed.)

In 1938 the dream of a Poland without Jews might have seemed utopian. Tadeusz Hollender even wrote a cheerful and amusing novel *Polska bez Żydów* (*Poland without Jews*) which ends with an account of the exiles' moving return to the country. And yet this utopia was realised. It could be said that the dream which was presented as arch-Polish and truly Catholic became a reality.

And so ... ? Well exactly.

XXIV

After 1945, the Jewish question was absorbed into the web of official lies enveloping Poland, as it was in every society ruled by communists. Or more precisely, it was transferred from reality to a pseudo-reality created by Newspeak. And however difficult the question may really be, in communist pseudo-reality it becomes completely insoluble. It has to be retrieved from there and also from out of the cocoon of pious silence; it has to be discussed again in normal language, with no regard to the ashes of deeds and the wormwood of words.

Out of this darkness of lies I would like to extract onto white paper an incident of which, so far as I know, nothing has been written to date.

The communists realized the desire of assimilated Jews, or, at any rate, of a notable number of them. They created a situation in which Jews both existed and did not exist. They existed in as much as various façades existed such as the Social Committee of Polish Jews, in as much as appropriate celebrations were held at appropriate times, and some completely surrealistic pieces appeared in the press from time to time. There were, however, no actual Jews. To say of someone that he was a Jew was at best tactless and could be seen as a manifestation of anti-semitism.

Assimilated Jews took part voluntarily in this dance of masks which was accompanied by the orchestra of the Main Bureau of Control of the Press, Publications and Public Spectacles. They agreed with alacrity that it was alright to be called Jabłecznikowski, but bad to be called Apfelbaum, that the name Maria was beautiful but that Miriam was repellent, and as for the name Abraham – it was enough to make one split one's sides with laughter. They constructed new biographies for themselves, thus unconsciously proving that in this aspect there was some similarity between the Nazi occupation and the communist régime. As these were 'All-Polish' biographies they had a false note, for no 'All-Polish' – or, for example, 'All-Japanese' – biography exists, nor can it. They denied their grandparents and parents regardless of whether the sun of Treblinka shone indifferently on their fate or that of Karaganda. They raised their children in falsehood, carefully concealing from them what is an element of every childhood and adolescence – the passing on of authentic family myths in the form of stories. In both totalitarian systems, people had to remove various 'faults' from their biographies in order to save their lives. But that is not the case in the examples quoted in this, and the following section.

I knew so-called old communists whose children did not know who they were or the names of their grandparents. I knew some in whose houses it was forbidden to say the word 'Jew' in front of the children and grandchildren. I knew a man who was so far gone in his camouflage that he would recount how he was in the openly fascist and racist *ONR* before the war. The only thing he could not explain was how it was that in the Polish Army organised by the Soviet Union he was immediately directed to work in communist Intelligence. I also knew a woman who, when she discovered after the death of her mother that the latter was a Jewess, beat the table with her fists and cried repeatedly: why have I been told, why have I been told ...

An unintentional service on the part of the people called 'national communists' (there were national socialists, why shouldn't there be national communists?) was that from the years 1967 to 1969 they revealed the whole fragility of these lies. It is not out of the question that the Jews should put up a monument to Moczar. Well, maybe a small one. For it seems to me that in certain circumstances one can honourably wear a yellow star. I do not think one can honourably wear a false biography.

XXV

Somebody born in either 1938 or 1939 told me recently: 'For Polish Jews just after the war the only option they could possibly accept was *de facto* that of communism'.

A mistake. Above all a factual mistake. Jews left Poland for a number of reasons. In general let us say – for rather sad reasons. But also because they did not wish to accept the communist option. It is assumed – with a wide margin for error – that after the war in Poland there were never more than 200,000 Jews at any one time. Some portion of them managed to survive within the country, the majority probably in the USSR (300,000 were arrested and deported mainly in 1940, not counting those who managed to escape from the Nazis just after the outbreak of the Soviet-German war). So in 1967 according to very detailed officially collected data there were 30,000 of them left. This would appear to be a somewhat small number, given the Jews' supposed attachment to communism. And why indeed should it be otherwise? I do not think that the Jews differed in this respect from the Poles, Lithuanians or Hungarians.

XXVI

There is an English word 'expendable' which means, among other things 'fated to be a victim', 'doomed'.

For centuries a permanent element of European culture was the conviction that the Jews were expendable, they were meant, or rather could be seen to be meant, to be doomed. I will disregard the theological bases according to which this was concurrent with the divine economic plan, for this interpretation was never universally accepted in Christianity, and today, I think, has been completely rejected. One way or another, the conviction of which I speak became autonomous and began to function as such. Thus if any kind of difficult situation could be resolved by 'writing off' Jews who happened to be at hand, then one should take advantage of such an opportunity. There were commendable exceptions to the rule, for example the refusal to hand over the Jews of Lwów to Chmielnicki's army, for which price he had been willing to refrain from besieging the city. Generally speaking the principle worked like a Swiss watch. Its 'autonomy' depended on the fact that it was simply convenient, and someone who acted in this way could even lament it, but he nevertheless recognised it as normal practice.

In the mid-twentieth century.

I think that one of the basic reasons why the Roosevelt administration granted the Nazis silent permission to murder European Jews was the conviction held by that American President that they were expendable. FDR was in the end consistent after a particular fashion. He did not impede Hitler in his murder of the Jews – he actively helped Stalin to fill Soviet camps. Just to think that many progressive American intellectuals to this day maintain a cult for the co-author of Teheran and Yalta! Congratulations...

But let us not trouble ourselves with American affairs.

No. 21/22 of the Lublin journal *Spotkania* (Spring-Summer 1983) contains Antoni Pilch's paper dated September 1944 entitled 'The emergence and activities of the Polish partisan division in the Stolpecki district'. I see this as an extremely valuable initiative. I believe that the text itself, the editor's commentary, and the wide range of questions associated with it will some day become the subject of analysis and discussion. I hope that at least some of the resulting analyses will call things by their name. I would like to quote only five sentences here, pointing out that the first sentence I quote is found in Pilch's report some five pages after the section from which the following four sentences are taken.

First the later sentence: 'I do not know how our authorities imagined we could live and dress without requisitioning...'

Now the other four: 'On 17 November [1943] an unpleasant incident occurred: the squadron in the area met a group of Jewish partisan-looters who were indiscriminately robbing the village of Sobkowszczyzna. The leader of the squadron decided to go there – took the Jews, disarmed them, tied them up and ordered that they be led to a camp 25 kilometres away. The Jews tried to escape along the way and were shot and discreetly buried. But the blunder was that two of the Jews fled and informed the Soviet headquarters of it.'

Let us put aside our emotional reactions; with regard to the art of words this would be all too easy. I shall point out instead what struck me in my reading of 'The emergence and activities of the Polish partisan division in the Stolpecki district'. Throughout more or less forty pages of normal typescript, there is in Pilch's report not a trace of hostility towards the Jews. An impression of cool calculation comes across, the resolution of an unpleasant technical problem with the help of a few statistics. In the Nalibocki forest the following military formations are operating: that of the Wehrmacht, the divisions of the *AK*, loosely attached to the Nowogródek command, Soviet partisans and some small squads of Jews who survived the liquidation actions — it is doubtful if any of these consisted of more than twenty people. (The author of the afterword to Pilch's article used the phrase 'Jews who had escaped from the surrounding towns and townships'. This would seem to indicate a masterly grasp of the art of euphemism.) There is little food available and it can be obtained only by requisitioning, that is by using threat or force which does not on the whole awaken much enthusiasm among the peasants; Pilch includes the Byelorussians, that is the local peasants, among the enemy. The Jewish squads were the weakest of these contenders for potatoes, calves and pigs. What is more, they were the only one who had no base which meant that they could be liquidated without risking any losses or any ultimate unpleasant difficulties. Therefore Pilch completely approves the behaviour of his subordinate, together with the stereotypical formula 'shot while trying to escape' and the discreet burial, or hiding of the traces. Not so difficult in the great forest.

I emphasise once again: not one word in Pilch's report hints at the fact that he might feel any hostility towards the Jews whatsoever. Neither does anything suggest that he has any scruples. The Jews are simply 'expendable' — written off.

Let us assume that the readers of this text know that no one should be 'expendable' and this is not about to be proved here. I would like, on the other hand, to draw attention to a certain detail of modern Polish history.

European politics has for the last two hundred years accepted the concept that Poland and its independence is 'expendable', written off. (Reminding people of this is one of the favourite persuasive devices of Polish communists, but that is another question which we will not discuss here.) Of the three treaties regulating the relationship of power in Europe over the last 170 years — Vienna, Versailles, Teheran-Yalta — only the Treaty of Versailles, despite all its shortcomings, recognized both the independence and sovereignty of Poland. Since the people in Poland are rather attached to both independence and sovereignty, they are aware not only of the principle of which I spoke above, but also have their own experience of it; they can therefore imagine that others do not like to be written off.

XXVII

It would seem, that since I have written so much, probably over 10,000 words, that the remark at the beginning of this essay concerning succinctness sounds like an empty boast. Yet I do not lose hope that, considering the theme undertaken, I have been laconic, though no doubt my thoughts could have been expressed much more briefly.

In the autumn of 1984 I was to take part in a conference held in Oxford on the subject of Polish-Jewish relations. Preparations were undertaken by letter between myself and the passport office and by telephone between myself and the Oxford organisers. No arrangement was concluded with the first of these: this time the gnome in the passport office pulled the lottery ticket with the answer 'declined'. As to the second, we talked a little – and we talked a little more. In the course of one of these calls (when was a cable put under the Channel? Probably earlier than the bug in my house) I was asked to give the title of my paper. This amused me since there is a rule in my book: until I have a passport in my hand I will not write any paper for any overseas symposium. However I did not want to explain to the person in Oxford how I came to have this principle or why it has saved me much effort. I decided that it would be simpler to think up a title there and then. This I did, saying clearly: 'Do Jews and Poles hate each other?' Putting down the receiver I thought up the first and last sentence of this non-existent paper: 'A lot of them, yes.'

And this really ought to suffice for thinking people of good will. But thinking and good will do not often go hand in hand. And so I tried to unite them.

XXVIII

At one point I called this text a hopeless one. For many reasons. For example because, if I am right, if the issue is rooted in emotions, in prejudices, then I am facing something that will not be persuaded. I also have the unpleasant conviction that the theme of this essay cannot be dealt with the means I have at my disposal, and so I have written something which has to be unconvincing and cannot be good.

Yet, probably because I was born where I happened to be born and at this and not another time, and since I am a person whose profession is writing, then I had to write this text at some point.

XXIX

Oh, to wake up one morning with the feeling that I could say like Rhett to Scarlett: My dear, I don't give a damn.

June-October, 1986.

To the Editor of *Próby*

Herewith the article which you ordered 'blind', that is without suggesting a specific subject many months ago. I have managed to hit the very middle of what some call 'the never-ending Jewish festival' in all areas of the press – both official and underground, and the émigré press also. In a word, I have taken up a fashionable theme. This does not bother me, because the unconditional rule of deliberately not writing about that which is fashionable consists in itself of a particular dependence on fashion. Furthermore, I flatter myself that my way of writing is decidedly out of fashion.

People have varying attitudes to the appearance of the Jewish theme in the underground, Catholic, and émigré press. Apart from those who think it better late than never, there are also those who declare that they will take no part in this because of the times – it would have been different ten years ago. Finally, there are also those who claim that all this is the work of Jewish-Masonry which hopes in this way to draw the attention of society – pardon me, of the nation – away from the really important issues. We will not concern ourselves with them.

An interesting fact from the field of social psychology demands an explanation: why 'now' and why 'so much all at once'. That 'so much all at once' arises from the fact of 'now'. In other words: the subject is obvious and only failed to be undertaken for certain reasons; and also the breaking of the dam caused a flood (let us not exaggerate) of publications on Polish-Jewish themes. One question remains: why now? Whosoever attempts a response should remember that a certain, though not fundamental rôle, was played by chance here. In 1979 the editors of the then underground *Res publica* planned a 'Jewish' issue and even began to commission articles. After August 1980 the idea was laid aside. Another example: as far as I know, the Lublin journal *Spotkania* had already conceived their 'Polish-Jewish' issue before December 1981. The issue itself (29–30) bearing the date 1985 appeared in fact in 1986 and reached me literally a few days ago.

It is not for me to give an opinion on the articles appearing in *Puls*, *Znak*, *Spotkania* or *Aneks*. I do this indirectly, by writing my paper in the way I have written it. From the point of view of somebody who will read all these papers, the question whether I had read the above journals before, during or after writing 'Piołun i popiół' (Wormwood and Ashes) is irrelevant.

One more point: language.

I think that we have no language in which we can speak normally of Jewish-Polish affairs. I do not think my essay has discovered such a language. This is not mathematics nor is it poetry – there is no way of discovering something in a moment of illumination. This language will emerge in the course of discussion. If 'Wormwood and Ashes' contributes just a little towards establishing normal speech about Judaica or Polish-Jewish relations, then we can tell each other that we have done something useful. And that is no mean thing . . .

Sincerely,
Roman Zimand
7 December, 1986

EXCHANGE

POLEMIC AS HISTORY: SHMUEL KRAKOWSKI, THE WAR OF THE DOOMED. JEWISH ARMED RESISTANCE IN POLAND, 1942–1944

Stanislaus A. Blejwas

In recent years books, memoirs, teachers' guides, and media productions devoted to the Holocaust, have flooded the popular and scholarly market. Nearly all of these materials focus on the unique and tragic wartime suffering of the Jews, and most broaden our understanding of the Holocaust. Nevertheless, it has been argued that the exclusive focus upon the Jewish wartime experience results in an asymmetrical understanding of World War II. This distorted perspective is especially noteworthy in relation to the question of Polish-Jewish relations during the war. The historian Richard Lukas writes: 'By failing to broaden the scope of research on the Holocaust, we have allowed our perspective on it to become distorted, and this has led to simplistic and false conclusions about the subject ... writers have perpetuated the stereotypical view of the anti-semitic Pole as the primary or even the sole explanation for Polish attitudes and behaviour towards Jews during World War II'.[1] The recently published work by Shmuel Krakowski on Jewish armed resistance in Poland between 1942 and 1944 illustrates Lukas' point.[2]

Krakowski's purpose is to 'determine the basic facts and clarify the extent of the Jewish armed resistance movement in the *General Gouvernement* and to analyze its character, its uniqueness, and its results' (ix). He discusses Jewish resistance in the forests, Jews in Polish partisan and commando units, the Warsaw Ghetto Uprising (1943), armed resistance in other ghettos and in the camps, and Jews in the Warsaw Uprising of 1944. Jewish resistance is divided into isolated elements (ghettos, camps and partisan units) and those integrated into the Polish (communist and non-communist) underground. Krakowski argues that the isolated elements were of greater significance for Jewish resistance in terms of both numbers and morale. Overall, he concludes that Jewish armed resistance was unique among all the resistance movements in Nazi-occupied Europe because of the special situation of the Jewish population during the Nazi occupation, the lack of any support from the allies or from influential groups in the allied camp, and because of 'the discriminatory stand of the Polish government-in-exile and the majority of the Polish underground' (p.301).

Although the work draws together and recounts various strands of Jewish resistance, thoughtfully arguing for its distinct treatment, there are, however, extraordinary problems with methodology, sources and their use, and interpretation. The result raises the question of whether this is a polemic under the guise of a work of dispassionate scholarship.

Jewish armed resistance emerged late, only in 1942 and 1943, after the 1941 Nazi invasion of the USSR and when the Nazis had already initiated the extermination of Polish Jewry. Krakowski does not adequately examine the reasons, political or otherwise, for the late emergence of a Jewish armed resistance, a delay significant in view of the existence of an organized Polish resistance since the Fall of 1939. Nevertheless, a Jewish armed resistance did begin to emerge in extraordinary and desperate circumstances. Krakowski argues that those who could escape from the ghettoes or transports to the death camps gravitated to immediate and active armed resistance, but encountered hostility among Polish partisans, especially the Home Army (*Armia Krajowa*), not to mention the local civilian population. By and large, Krakowski attributes such tensions and conflicts to anti-semitism. While not questioning the existence of anti-semitism, the reader would have expected to find a more sophisticated analysis of developments in occupied Poland. There are no statistics to indicate the extent of anti-semitism, or whether or not it increased or decreased as Poles, also victims of Nazi persecution, witnessed the tragedy of Polish Jewry. Furthermore, political and military developments are viewed out of context.

Krakowski suggests that the *AK* was dominated by anti-semitic political groupings. He writes, for example:

> The political make-up of the Home Army is very significant. The largest group of registered members put under the command of the Home Army by various political groups was the National Armed Forces (*NSZ*) – extreme fascists and anti-Semites – who numbered 70,000. (p.7)

While the numbers cited are from the Commander-in-Chief of *AK*, General Bór-Komorowski,[3] Krakowski's terminology is inaccurate and misleading. Krakowski asserts that the virulently anti-semitic *NSZ*, the radical right, belonged to the *AK*, constituting 'the largest group of registered members' (70,000). In fact, it was the moderate right-wing National Military Organization, the military wing of the National Party, which was subordinated to the Union for Armed Struggle (later renamed the Home Army). The radical right rejected this unification, split from *NOW*, and formed the *NSZ*, the vehemently anti-semitic wing of the nationalist movement. It was not until March 7, 1944, that the *NSZ* subordinated itself to the *AK*, a move which provoked another split within its ranks. In actual fact, the *NSZ* never finally merged with the *AK*. It remained an unmerged military formation, membership of which the Polish Government-in-Exile did not recognize as service in the Polish Armed Forces.[4]

This complicated political history of the Polish underground suggests that assertions about the *AK* being dominated by anti-semitic political groups must be very carefully examined and distinctions made. Such assertions overlook the Polish underground's role in transmitting information to the Allies about the extermination of the Jews as, for example, the well-known mission of underground courier Jan Karski.[5] They also overlook the well-documented and widely-recognized role of the underground's Council for Assistance to Jews (*Żegota*) as well as other official and unofficial initiatives to help Polish Jews.[6] This is not to say that anti-semitism did not exist nor to deny the existence of those marginal elements of Polish society who denounced Jews to the Nazis, but to stress that information in what purports to be a historical manuscript should be precise and accurate.

The historical framework erected by Krakowski as the background for his particular topic is asymmetrical. The author, for example, is critical of the low level of *AK* partisan activity in 1942 and 1943, expressing an opinion often voiced by Marxist historians in the postwar Polish People's Republic. Such opinions, by and large tendentious, do not adequately appreciate the nature of the Polish underground state, which was both political and military in character, and whose ultimate goal was the preservation of the population and the regaining of independence. Unlike the communist underground, which only appeared after June 22, 1941, and which favoured immediate sabotage actions to relieve pressure on the beleaguered Red Army, the patriotic underground, aware that the Eastern Front was still deep in the USSR and far from Poland, favoured carefully planned and selectively targeted military operations, focusing much of its efforts on intelligence and organization. The immediate objective was to limit the Nazi application of the principle of collective responsibility against the civilian population. The ultimate objective, and an understandable one, was to preserve the population in preparation not only for coordinated nationwide uprisings as the Nazis retreated and the front advanced, but for the reconstruction of an independent postwar government and society.[7] Given this broader context, one asks whether clashes between Jewish partisans and other units resulted from conflicting political allegiances and military strategies; from Jewish partisans being perceived as communists or allies of Soviet or Polish communist partisans (who themselves were disliked because of their pro-Soviet stance); from anti-semitism; or were they localized engagements over supplies or individual confrontations in the forests? The dramatic complexity of wartime conditions in the East suggests that the answers require a thorough examination of each individual encounter rather than simplified generalizations.

Krakowski claims that a certain 'Order nr. 116' (September 15, 1943) issued by General Bór-Komorowski served as 'official permission' for attacks on Jewish partisan units, arguing that local *AK* partisan commanders understood the specific reference to Jewish women in the order as meaning Jewish partisan units in general, which, supposedly, Bór-Komorowski was equating with bandits, whose numbers were, as even Krakowski concedes, large. The order cited by Krakowski was not nr. 116, but Bór-Komorowski's *Organizational Report nr. 220* (31 August 1943), which he dispatched *to the Government-in-Exile in London*, which *inter alia*, discusses the problem of uncontrolled bandit and partisan activity which provoked Nazi retaliation against the local civilian population. Krakowski not only misidentifies the order, which was not the text sent to local commanders, but summarizes Bór-Komorowski's report in a manner which could lead the reader to misunderstand its intent.

Krakowski version:

Well-armed gangs ramble endlessly in cities and villages, attack estates, banks, commercial and industrial companies, houses and large farms. The plunder is often accompanied by acts of murder, which are carried out by Soviet partisan units hiding in the forests or by ordinary gangs of robbers. Men and women, especially Jewish women, participate in the assaults ... I have issued an order to the region for area commanders to go out with arms, when necessary, against these plunderers or revolutionary robbers.(p.14)

Original:

Well-armed gangs ramble endlessly in cities and villages, attack estates, banks, commercial and industrial companies, houses and apartments, and larger peasant farms. The plunder is often accompanied by acts of murder, which are carried out by Soviet partisan units hiding in the forest or ordinary gangs of robbers. The latter recruit from all kinds of criminal subversive elements.

Men and women, especially Jewish women, participate in the assaults. This infamous action of demoralized individuals contributes in a considerable degree to the complete destruction of many citizens, who have already been tormented with the four year struggle against the enemy.

The occupier has not basically opposed the existing state of affairs. When German security organs are sometimes called in, in the more serious instances, they refuse to help, avoiding the bandits. Often the reverse occurs – the greater act of banditism calls down repression upon the innocent population.

In order to give some help and shelter to the defenceless population, I have issued an order –with the understanding of the Chief Delegate of the Government – to the commanders of regions and districts regarding local security. I have ordered the commanders of regions and districts, when necessary, to move with arms against these plundering or subversive bandit elements. I emphasized the need to liquidate the leaders of bands and not efforts to destroy entire bands. I recommend to the local commanders assuring the cooperation of the local population and of the representative of the Government's Delegate in organizing self-defence and of a warning system.[8]

A reading of the full text of this part of the Report in its correct context suggests that it is very debatable, at the least, to describe it as 'official permission' for *AK* commanders to attack Jewish partisan units, even if this was the text of an order (which it was not) sent to the local *AK* partisan commanders. Bór-Komorowski's Report nr. 220 addresses the serious problem of uncontrolled partisan activity which provoked Nazi retaliation directed against the local population. The local commander would have to make the final decision as to whether a unit was a group of partisans or bandits, and it is significant that the order focuses on the elimination of *leaders*, and not of the entire group, which creates a different impression to that given by Krakowski.

A copy or version of the actual Order nr. 116 (15 September 1943) sent to local commanders is reportedly available in the *Archiwum Zakładu Historii Partii* (The Archive of the Institute for Party History in Warsaw). It reads:

Instructions: 1. Security and public order do not exist in some districts or exist to an insufficient degree. The local population is exposed to plunder of property, hardships, assaults and often to the loss of life at the hands of bandits of different origin. The occupier has not basically opposed this existing state of affairs. As a rule repression is applied against the innocent population tormented by the bandits. This state of affairs strikes at our interests and plans. The Armed Forces in the country must take steps with the aim of public security in local areas. 2. I recommend to the commanders of sub-districts and districts to step in where necessary against plundering or subversive bandit elements. 3. Every action must be decisive and must have as an objective the suppressing of lawlessness. Action ought to take place only against groups especially troublesome for the local population and for the Armed Forces in the country, above all against those who murder, rape, or plunder. 4. One ought to act with the intention of liquidating the leaders and agitators in the bands, not concentrating on the liquidation of the entire band. Every action must be organized and conducted with full application of the conditions of conspiracy. It is not permitted to start to liquidate without the certainty of the complete achievement of success. 5. Sub-district and district commanders will assure themselves of the goodwill and cooperation of the population in the fight with banditism. The district representatives of the Government are to cooperate in the organization of self-defence and of a warning service. In many instances band members are recruited from among the local population and constitute an element which accidentally found itself in the band or was forced by the occupier to leave the family homestead. One ought to influence this accidental element through the local population to leave the band. . . .[9]

This version of the order does not specifically mention Jews, and it is difficult, therefore, to see how Krakowski could write that Order nr. 116 was 'official permission' for *AK* commanders to attack Jewish partisan units. However, the Soviets and the Polish communists immediately charged (as have their historians) that the phrasing of point 2 – 'I recommend to the commanders of sub-districts and districts to step in where necessary against plundering and subversive bandit elements' – was so general as to permit its being interpreted as recommending the liquidation of groups or partisans not subordinated to the Polish Government-in-Exile, especially of Soviet partisans and of the Soviet-supported partisans of the Polish communist People's Army (*Armia Ludowa*). While some local commanders may have thus interpreted Order nr. 116 because of the chaotic situation in Eastern Poland where *AK*, Soviet, Polish communist, Ukrainian, and Jewish elements contested for space in the forests,[10] this was not Bór-Komorowski's intent.[11]

The tendentiousness which appears in Krakowski's work is also illustrated in his treatment of the 1944 Warsaw Uprising. The author writes: 'most historians believe that this revolt was the result of faulty calculations', and of insufficient military preparation and inadequate execution, but cites only one author in support of this overdrawn assertion about an indeed controversial topic.[12] Furthermore, the Soviet role, particularly the halt of the Red Army on the other side of the Vistula during the first week of August 1944, is not mentioned as a factor contributing to the Uprising's defeat! Such an omission results in a presentation of the Uprising which could be published by the present Polish Ministry of National Defence which, while praising the heroism of the insurgents, blames the anticommunist Polish Government-in-Exile for launching a politically motivated military action and excuses Soviet inaction.

Tendentiousness and questionable use of sources afflict other chapters, including the one on the Warsaw Ghetto Uprising of 1943. Krakowski is not only critical of the *AK* for supplying arms only to the *Żydowska Organizacja Bojowa* (Jewish Fighting Organization), but also for providing too little. Citing *AK* resources 'at the time' (i.e., 1942–1943) to justify his opinion that the *AK* provided only a 'minute' part of its resources to the Ghetto fighters, Krakowski omits several relevant factors. The pages cited by Krakowski from the basic documentary work, *Polskie Siły Zbrojne*, to illustrate *AK* supplies in Warsaw, refer actually to materials saved and hidden after the September 1939 campaign and under the control of the underground on 1 September 1941. While the supply of arms and ammunition increased by 1942 and 1943, Krakowski does not mention the conditions and availability of this equipment (pp.299–300). In the *AK*'s Organizational Report Nr. 190 for the period 1 September 1942 to 1 March 1943, the reader will find that much of the *AK*'s arms were held individually, while many items, after being buried for three years in the ground, were unusable. The *AK* estimated that only 30 per cent of its hidden arms were properly preserved.[13] Certainly such facts, as well as the Ghetto's physical isolation, the slow emergence of armed resistance there, the difficulty in transporting (i.e., smuggling) arms to the Ghetto, and the *AK*'s suspicions about the leftist political orientation of the Ghetto fighters, are also factors to be taken into account in any consideration of the materials supplied by the *AK*. Furthermore, considering the Nazi military and police presence in and around Warsaw and the fact that the Eastern Front was still deep in the USSR, the only thing that would have been accomplished if the *AK* had thrown its entire strength into the Ghetto Uprising would have been the complete destruction of both the Ghetto fighters and the *AK*. For the Ghetto Uprising to be something more than a tragic and heroic gesture of protest, there would have had to exist a realistic chance for victory, which the current military situation decisively precluded. This larger, and much more complex picture is, however, absent from Krakowski's book, which instead suggests simple Polish lack of concern, or animosity.

There are also questions about sources the author failed to utilize. With regard to Polish materials, Krakowski tends to rely more upon printed materials published in postwar communist Poland up to 1972 and the party archives. Such sources cannot be ignored, but neither can the relevant materials abroad. While claiming to have used 'reports from the archives of Polish historical institutes in Warsaw and London', (x.) unpublished materials from such fundamental repositories as the Sikorski Historical Institute and the Underground Poland Study Trust do not figure in either the footnotes or in bibliography, an absolutely unacceptable omission in view of the author's opinion about 'the discriminatory stand of the Polish government-in-exile and the majority of the Polish underground' (p.301). Equally unacceptable is the omission of the important multi-volume printed series, *Armia Krajowa w Dokumentach, 1939–1945*, issued by the Underground Poland Study Trust.[14] Furthermore, the recent, readily available works by Stefan Korboński, Jan Tomasz Gross, Walter Laqueur, and Jan Nowak do not figure in the bibliography, while Yisrael Gutman's 1982 monograph does. There is also no reference to the works, in either Polish or English, by Władysław Bartoszewski.[15] Additionally, erroneous citations and the failure to cite pages in some instances will also raise questions in the reader's mind as to whether or not to use the term scholarship to describe Krakowski's work. What appears to have been presented to the reader is an English version of an earlier, but not updated work. If this is the case, these facts should have been discussed in either the foreword or the preface.

The topic of Jewish armed resistance is important, and examined in its full historical context can add to our knowledge of Nazi-occupied Poland and of Jewish-Polish relations. This work brings together various strands of that resistance, but history is more than one person's or one group's view and interpretation of the past. The citations and assertions of this work will have to be re-checked to see whether history has been taken out of context. The failure to examine all sides of an issue and to utilize all available resources runs the grave risk of producing polemic and not scholarship.

NOTES

1 Richard Lukas, *The Forgotten Holocaust: The Poles under German Occupation, 1939–1945* (Lexington, Kentucky, 1986), p. 220.
2 Shmuel Krakowski, *The War of the Doomed: Jewish Armed Resistance in Poland, 1942–1944* (New York, 1984), xxi, p. 340.
3 Tadeusz Bór-Komorowski, *Armia Podziemna* (London, 1951), p. 91. Krakowski erroneously cites pp. 66–67.
4 Stefan Korboński, *The Polish Underground State. A Guide to the Underground, 1939–1945* (Boulder, Colorado, 1978), pp. 104–6; Zbigniew S. Siemaszko, *Narodowe Siły Zbrojne* (London, 1982), pp. 46–152; and *Polskie Siły Zbrojne w Drugiej Wojnie Światowej. III Armia Krajowa* (London, 1950), pp. 149–159.
5 Jan Karski, *Story of a Secret State* (Boston, 1944), pp. 320–54. Most recently, see Walter Laqueur, *The Terrible Secret: Suppression of the Truth about Hitler's 'Final Solution'* (Boston, 1980), pp. 101–22, 229–38.
6 See Władysław Bartoszewski and Zofia Lewin, *Righteous Among Nations. How Poles Helped the Jews, 1939–1945* (London, 1969), and Teresa Prekerowa, *Konspiracyjna Rada Pomocy Żydom w Warszawie 1942–1945* (Warsaw, 1982).
7 Jan Tomasz Gross, *Polish Society Under German Occupation: The Generalgouvernement, 1939–1944* (Princeton, New Jersey, 1979), pp. 283–91.
8 Krakowski, p. 14, & *PSZ*, III, pp. 531–32. Krakowski erroneously cites p. 431. The translation from *PSZ* is by the author of this review.
9 This document is printed in Ireneusz Caban and Zygmunt Mankowski, *Związek*

Walki Zbrojnej i Armia Krajowa w Okręgu Lubelskim, 1939-1944. Część Druga - Dokumenty (Lublin, 1971), pp. 517-8.
10 See R. Nazarewicz, 'Stosunki polityczne w podziemiu polskim w rejonie górnej Warty i Pilicy w latach 1943-1944', *Najnowsze Dzieje Polski 1929-1945*, VI (1962), pp. 115-120.
11 The reader should consult the full text of Bór-Komorowski's Organizational Report. See 'Gen. Komorowski do N.W.: Meldunek Półroczny o Sprawach *AK* i Położeniu w Kraju. 31/8/1943', in T. Pełczyński, et al., eds., *Armia Krajowa w Dokumentach, 1939-1945. III. 1943-1944* (London, 1976), pp. 63-133. For Bór-Komorowski's reaction to the Soviet and Polish communist charges see his report of 14 October 1943, *ibid.*, pp. 156-7.
12 Krakowski cites Władysław Pobóg-Malinowski, *Najnowsza Historia Polski, III (Część druga tomu drugiego). Okres 1939-1945* (London, 1981), pp. 627-8, but omits recent works, both criticisms and defences of the Uprising. See Jan M. Ciechanowski, *The Warsaw Rising of 1944* (Cambridge, 1974), and J.K. Zawodny, *Nothing but Honour: The Story of the Warsaw Uprising of 1944* (Stanford, California, 1978).
13 See 'Meldunek Organizacyjny dowódcy A.K., Nr. 190, 1/III/1943', excerpted in *PSZ, III*, pp. 325-6. The reliability of some of the historiography about the Warsaw Ghetto produced in postwar Poland is questionable. Concerning this point, see Adam Ciołkosz, 'Komunistyczne źródła antypolskiej kampanii', in Adam Ciołkosz, *Walka o prawdę. Wybór artykułów 1940-1978* (London, 1983), pp. 333-6. This article originally appeared in 1968, and could have been profitably consulted by Krakowski.
14 T. Pełczyński, et al., eds. *Armia Krajowa w Dokumentach, 1939-1945*. (London: Studium Polski Podziemnej, 1970-1981). Vols. I-V.
15 Works by Korboński, Gross, Laqueur, and Bartoszewski have been cited in previous footnotes. See also Jan Nowak, *Courier from Warsaw* (Detroit, 1982). This is a translation of a 1978 Polish language edition. While Krakowski cites Yisrael Gutman, *The Jews of Warsaw, 1939-1943. Ghetto, Underground, Revolt* (Bloomington, Indiana, 1982), it is unclear what he used from Gutman's extensive bibliography.

RESPONSE TO BLEJWAS
Shmuel Krakowski

There is no doubt that Professor Blejwas and I approach the problem of the Holocaust and the understanding of its essence differently. For me the Holocaust, probably best defined by the Polish word *Zagłada* (annihilation) or the Hebrew *Shoah*, is an unprecedented phenomenon in the history of mankind. The mass and total murder, planned by a state machine and carried out by using enormous forces and means with complete ruthlessness in relation to all those of a given nationality, from infants to the old on their death beds, regardless of any national consciousness, or degree of religious attachment, outlook, organisational or political involvement, profession or education, had never taken place anywhere else. It is a phenomenon not comparable to all the other forms of Nazi terror during the Second World War. It is also not comparable to all other events associated with the Jewish martyrdom of many centuries in the diaspora or to the martyrdom of the Polish nation under Nazi occupation.

Professor Blejwas certainly does not thus understand it if he quotes the book of Richard Lukas, *The Forgotten Holocaust*. Professor Blejwas supports – in my opinion incorrectly – the theses of Lukas, the title of whose book alone, *The Forgotten Holocaust*, misleads the reader. There is no denying that the Second World War was a most difficult period in the history of the Polish nation. Every tenth Pole fell victim to the cruel Nazi terror. There is, however, a fundamental difference, not only quantitative but also qualitative, between the Nazi terror meted out to Poles or other nations, and the policy of total annihilation applied to the Jews. Whilst fully appreciating the enormity of suffering and sacrifice on the part of the Polish nation, it has to be accepted that, in comparison to the Jews, the Polish nation was not the object of an 'annihilation' or Holocaust. The concepts introduced by Lukas, with which Blejwas identifies, are historically incorrect.

Professor Blejwas writes:

Krakowski does not adequately examine the reasons, political or otherwise, for the *late emergence* (my italics S.K.) of a Jewish armed resistance, a *delay* (my italics S.K.) significant in view of the existence of an organized Polish resistance since the Fall of 1939 . . .

I do not want to dwell on the fact as to whether my explanations of these events are sufficient or not. The reader himself will probably assess this best. However, I have to express my surprise at the second part of the statement by Professor Blejwas, where he speaks of the 'late' appearance of a Jewish resistance movement. In my opinion we are dealing here with a total lack of comprehension of the situation. The Jewish resistance movement appeared neither too early nor too late. It quite simply appeared at the time when there were specific, even if the most minimal, conditions for it. The imputation that this movement supposedly appeared too late suggests that its earlier formation might have somehow changed the situation. I believe that a historian, who investigates the problem in depth cannot share this opinion. To compare the Jewish to the Polish resistance movement, is, in my opinion, completely pointless, although – incidentally – the creation of organisational structures (from the autumn of 1939) should here be separated from real action (at a considerably later date).

I am also not able to agree with Professor Blejwas's interpretation of the Home Army (*AK*) Commander, General Bór-Komorowski's order on the 'fight with banditry'. I would not like to undertake here an exhaustive analysis of the various changes and differences in the contents of individual versions of the document – whether the contents of Order no. 116 are more reliable, or the Organisational Report no. 220. It would take up too much time and space to analyse in detail which archives house which copies of documents and in which publications they have been cited partially or in their entirety. It is important that in each version, including that cited by Professor Blejwas as reliable, the role of Jewish women was emphasised when the problem of banditry was discussed. The relevant quotation in the translation given by Professor Blejwas reads:

> Well armed bands ramble endlessly in cities and villages, attack estates, banks, commercial and industrial companies, houses and apartments, and larger peasant farms . . . Men and women, especially Jewish women, participate in the assaults . . .

And, thus, there is no doubt that in the Home Army Commander's document dealing with the plague of banditry in Poland, emphasis was placed on the role of Jewish women in brigand attacks. I am extremely sorry, that in my book, *The War of the Doomed*, a printer's error appeared and I am grateful that the mistake has been pointed out to me. The text of the cited document is in volume III of *Polskie Siły Zbrojne* on pages 531–532, and not as mistakenly given in my book on page 431. Let us return, however, to the fundamental issue, the contents of the document dealing with the participation of Jewish women in the gangs, which is not questioned by Professor Blejwas, and let us remember that the date is 1943.

Could there really have been a problem of Jewish women (or maybe Jews) in 1943 in gangs, which required intervention at the level of the Home Army Commander? As we know, in 1943 in occupied Poland there were various types of forest units operating: the Home Army, National Armed Forces (*NSZ*), the People's Guard (*GL*), Soviet partisans, armed Jewish units and armed units pretending to be partisans but devoting themselves to normal robbery. In the latter there were neither, nor could there have been, Jewish men nor women. (A King's ransom to anyone who can give but one name). However, it is true that a large percentage of the members of the Jewish units were women.

Was the emphasis placed on the participation of Jewish women in assault groups really unintentional? Is it not proof of an elementary lack of sensitivity and understanding on the part of the Home Army Commander to the enormous tragedy of the remnants of Jewish women in the forests, who had survived the waves of deportations to the extermination camps? And what were the consequences of that order or the organisational report?

In the telegram of the Home Army Commander sent to London on 14 October 1943 it is stated (text published in volume III of the collection of documents: *Armia Krajowa w Dokumentach 1939–1945*, published by the Polish Underground Study Trust, London, 1976, pp. 156–157):

> ... I ordered that all assault gangs which destroyed our people be fought irrespective of their nationality and insignia. I do not attack Soviet partisans as partisans ...

And, thus, extermination irrespective of nationality. Moreover it is stated, that the Soviet partisans were not included here. And what other nationality could have been taken into account in Poland if not that of the Jews?

All the partisan units were called bandits by the German occupier. Various armed formations also used the same terminology for formations which were politically antagonistic to them. This terminology was used, and very often, for Jewish armed units. And I would like in any case to find a document of the Commander of the Home Army, which speaks of the tragic situation of these units, and generally of groups of escapees from the camps and ghettos, who sought cover in the forests. Is there a document with a call by the Commander of the Home Army to give help to these people?

And how did these issues appear further afield? Scores of memoirs by members of Jewish groups who survived or other Jews who hid in the forests and villages speak of this. These recollections, housed mainly in the *Yad Vashem* Archives (and in many others) are available to anyone doing research, and it has to be regretted that Professor Blejwas up till now has not familiarised himself with them. The recollections do not present the one-sided rose-coloured picture, which we come across in many apologetic works. They certainly record a great deal about the help also given to Jews by the Home Army, but there is also no shortage of words of the greatest disappointment and bitterness about what was, after all, the largest Polish underground organisation.

I also differ with Professor Blejwas on the subject of the help given by the Home Army to the insurgents of the Warsaw Ghetto. I do not wish once again to present my interpretation here, which was set out in the book reviewed by Professor Blejwas. It strikes me, however, that Professor Blejwas, when giving the whole array of reasons as to why in his opinion the Home Army was not able to give more effective help to the fighting Ghetto, cited — I hope only as a result of normal modesty — the fear that those arms would end up in the possession of left-wing elements in the Ghetto. Professor Blejwas writes:

> ... the *AK*'s suspicions about the leftist political orientation of the Ghetto fighters, are also factors to be taken into account in any consideration of the materials supplied by the *AK*. (p. 360)

I believe we also have in this case an example of a ridiculous lack of understanding of, and elementary sensitivity for, the enormous human tragedy of the Holocaust. Speculation as to in whose hands a few score, or even if it was to be a few hundred, firearms might fall, in relation to a community which had been almost totally destroyed, provokes — at least in me — the strongest protest. After all, we are dealing here with a motivation which is only ostensibly political, but which is, in reality, deprived of any characteristics of normal human feeling.

Professor Blejwas raises only one of the problems discussed by myself, namely the problem of the Home Army's attitude to the Jewish armed resistance movement. I admit that the book, *The War of the Doomed*, has gone nowhere near exhausting that complex problem. The attitude of the Home Army, not only to the question of the Jewish resistance movement, but also to the Jews under German occupation in general, requires further intensive research. His general apologetic approach, avoiding a real analysis of the problem, certainly does not aid the understanding of this complicated subject, particularly in view of the very complex political structure of the Home Army. Alongside the help given to the Jews there was no shortage, after all, of attitudes of total indifference, and, what is more, of extreme enmity.

Research on this problem is unusually difficult as a result of the practice still in existence of not making available many archival documents. The records of the Home Army are basically housed in two archives: The Archives of the Central Committee of the Polish United Workers Party (formerly the Archives of the Department for the History of the Party) in Warsaw and in the Archives of the Polish Underground Study Trust in London. It is to be regretted that in both these archives there is still not open access for people undertaking research.

One final methodological remark. The collection of documents in the volumes *Armia Krajowa w Dokumentach 1939–1945*, published by the Polish Underground Study Trust is undoubtedly very valuable. It is, however, as is any collection, the result of a selection made by the editors. With the lack of a fully open access to the relevant archival collections, it is difficult for those doing research to judge to what extent the areas of interest to them are suitably presented in the selection made. I personally am concerned as to whether the Jewish problem has been presented adequately and in a balanced manner.

REPLY TO KRAKOWSKI
Stanislaus A. Blejwas

I fully agree with Professor Krakowski that the relationship of the *Armia Krajowa* to the Jewish resistance, and to the Jewish population under Nazi occupation demands further intense and precise research, and that all the relevant archives should be accessible to all scholars. Those parts of his book dealing with the *AK* should have been researched as precisely as those sections devoted to the Jewish partisan units, a justifiable criticism and expectation in view of Professor Krakowski's assessment of the Polish Government-in-Exile and of the majority of the Polish Underground. My review of his book was not, as he implies at the outset, about the meaning, use, or ownership of the term Holocaust, but about a thorough knowledge of events in occupied Poland so that we can arrive at as accurate an understanding as possible of Polish-Jewish relations during that tragic period.

Regarding Organizational Report 220 and Order Nr. 116, it is not clear whether Professor Krakowski has understood my criticism of his serious mis-citation. The order sent to local commanders did not specifically mention Jewish women, and was understood by others, such as the Polish communists, as being directed against them. Furthermore, how local commanders understood orders from headquarters has to be examined on an individual basis. Krakowski has not made an ironclad case, either from above or below, for Order Nr. 116 being 'official permission' for the *AK* to attack Jewish partisan units simply because they were Jewish. Even when Soviet partisans were not attacked (Doc. 491, *Armia Krajowa w Dokumentach, 1939–1945*, III), there were still other groups in the forests besides Jewish partisans, including Ukrainians in Eastern Poland. Finally, one expects scholars to be concerned about the mis-citation of documents and mis-attributions, both of which occur in Krakowski's book and which are more serious than simple typographical errors.

The question about the late emergence of a Jewish armed resistance is not raised to suggest a direct comparison with the *AK*, but to suggest that it may have influenced the thinking of some Poles about providing armed assistance to the Jews. The controversial question of *AK* assistance to the Warsaw Ghetto is raised to indicate that there are various factors which may have influenced *AK* actions, and not just the indifference or discrimination suggested by Professor Krakowski. Whether these factors are rationalizations is something that the individual reader will decide for himself. But the reader should know about them. Furthermore, the suggestion that someone who raises such issues is an apologist or lacks 'understanding and elementary sensitivity for the enormous human tragedy which was the Holocaust' is not the professional response that one expects to scholarly criticism. Such an attitude could be interpreted (and I do not do so) as suggesting that certain areas are beyond historical analysis.

Professor Krakowski responds to criticism of his failure to use *Armia Krajowa w Dokumentach 1939–1945* by saying that until there is complete access to the Studium Polski Podziemnej, it is difficult to judge the selection of documents. And yet he cites the work in his response. Scholarship is something more than polemical convenience. Professor Krakowski implies that he was denied access to the archives of the *SPP*. If that is so, why did he not mention that in the introduction to his book, where it could be implied that he had access?

If nothing else, Professor Krakowski's response confirms my contention that history is more than one person's or one group's interpretation of the past.

REVIEW ARTICLES

THE STRUGGLES FOR POLAND
Andrzej Bryk

The Struggles for Poland, television series co-produced by Channel 4, WNET, Norddeutscher Rundfunk, 1987.

Neal Ascherson, *The Struggles for Poland*, London:Michael Joseph, 1987, pp. xiv, 242.

'Once upon a time Poland was the largest and freest country in Europe. Once upon a time the Germans turned Poland into the land of death. This is the story of hope against all the odds'. Thus begins a nine-hour series devoted to the history of Poland in the 20th century, produced jointly by Channel 4 (UK), WNET (New York) and *Norddeutscher Rundfunk* (Hamburg). The series is an event without precedent – never before has the history of Poland been presented on this scale on the international scene in a form designed to appeal to a mass audience. If only for this reason, it merits our attention.

The film has been shown in Great Britain, the German Federal Republic and the United States. In all, twenty countries have bought it. A copy of the whole series has also been presented to Polish television in the hope that it will be shown in Poland. Most of the programmes were directed by Martin Smith, although Bolesław Sulik was responsible for three of them. Chief consultant was Neal Ascherson, who also wrote a book under the same title. The book was intended to complement the series. It stands on its own, however, and can be used as an introduction to modern Polish history independently of the film. The historians, Antony Polonsky and Lucjan Dobroszycki, played an important role in preparing the commentary. In the American version, Roger Mudd presented a brief introduction and some closing remarks.

The film was prepared by four production teams over a period of four years and cost over $16 million. The search for documents and witnesses of the events described took in seventeen countries, some two hundred archives were visited for documentary material, and the research turned up unique film footage from old newscasts. In a word, the makers devoted a great deal of energy and resources to the project, seeing in it the chance to explain the background and causes of Poland's current situation to a world viewing audience.

I would imagine, that if three large western television companies are prepared to invest huge sums of money (the amount contributed by Poles abroad came to less than $300,000) in filming a nine-hour series about Poland, then they must be motivated by other considerations than mere friendship. Poland is not a country with an important role in the modern world. It was once a powerful country and a uniquely tolerant one, but that was long ago and moreover during a period which lies outside the parameters of this series.

We might feel, of course, that the history of Poland in the twentieth century is so dramatic that just telling the story is not a bad idea for a film. But Poland's misfortunes during the twentieth century, tragic though they are, are not unique and the competition in this regard is fairly stiff. It is as well then, that the creators of the series have resisted the temptation to look at Poland's fate through the 'tragic' perspective, in a way that would have resulted in a bright reflection of the romantic, polono-centric myth of Poland as the 'Christ of Nations', taking on herself all the sins of the world, and by her suffering, bringing it salvation. They have not always succeeded in avoiding this sentiment, however, and, at times, the fascination with such a remote and exotic location, condemned to an appalling geopolitical position and celebrating its provincial myths and traditions in a colourful way, obscures another, deeper goal of the film's makers.

This other aim is the attempt to examine Poland as a country in which certain universal truths of European civilisation gather together and are crystallised; where the front line in the dispute between East and West is located (or, putting it another way, between two mutually exclusive philosophies of the human condition: freedom on the one hand and tyranny, particularly in its contemporary totalitarian variety, on the other). It is in this sense that I think we should understand the words of Martin Smith:

> For me the project was a personal adventure. I knew that I would be dealing with all the main problems of the twentieth century – fascism, communism, totalitarianism. In stories about Poland, as nowhere else, they form a persistent undercurrent. We also find issues such as nationalism, urbanisation, Catholicism and religious passion. It reflects in full the history of our epoch.[1]

In this light, one can only regret that the producers of the series concluded their history of twentieth century Poland with the emergence of 'Solidarity', barely mentioning its arrival on the scene.

The makers of the series have adopted a well-practised technique, based on three complementary elements: narration, comment and witnesses' statements. Into this have been interwoven photographs and rare old film footage. Smith has rejected the temptation to add background music to match the visual material, fearing that by doing so he would unduly manipulate the feelings of the audience. So the only musical accompaniment in each episode is a piece of old gramophone music. This has at times an astonishing effect. Some critics have drawn attention to tedious passages in the film, caused by – in their view – too many 'talking heads'; those interviewed often talk about details which are not entirely relevant from the point of view of general history, parts of their reminiscences are meaningless. In some cases this criticism is justified, but one can look at this problem from another point of view. The director has reached as far back into Polish history as human memory itself takes us, covering the period that its direct participants have lived, creating their version of Polish history as a family saga. What is being conveyed here is a certain collective truth about the course of recent Polish history, in which history consists of a single great family saga, a bastion beyond which no partitioning power or propagandist could penetrate.

The history of Poland is just such a mixture of private family histories, formed from fragmentary reminiscences of Nazi executions, Soviet labour camps, and the feverish excitement of the first underground resistance activity – recounted with the same fervour as though the speaker were telling of his first love. As Michael Kaufman has observed; 'Everything is described at top C, the listener is generally treated as a potential ally or indeed a conspirator recruited to the national crusade. Poles, when they are talking about themselves, often fall into a sentimentalism and a sense of presumption which borders on a polono-centric view of world history; they talk of themselves with such repulsive enthusiasm'.[2] However he adds that, paradoxically, it is in this same Poland that none other than the *babcia* (granny) has defeated Marxism, remaining at home with the children, when the parents went out to work and passing on the family saga of the age-long yearnings of Poles and all men for freedom.

Poles often maintain that their history is too complicated and too confusing to be presented to outsiders, their literature too difficult and exotic to translate. Consequently Polish attempts to impart to foreigners some idea of Polish history have been largely ineffective. As a result, there has been a temptation for Poles to shut themselves away in their own inner world. It is fortunate that lately a number of western historians have refused to be deterred by this myth of the 'exclusive club' and have written books about Poland which are fascinating and have astonished Poles themselves with their excellent analysis of the Polish *Weltanschauung*, locating them firmly in the real world.

The series begins with an episode entitled 'Once upon a time', which deals with the period 1900-1923. Emphasis has justifiably been given to the importance of the eighteenth century partitions of Poland in giving a specific, mystical quality to modern Polish patriotism. The revolution of 1905 is recognised as the first stage in the Polish struggle for independence. At the same time there is emphasis upon the particular character of Polish socialism which never, with the exception of certain small factions, allowed itself to be seduced by an illusory and empty internationalism. Conspiratorial activity and struggle is shown against the wider background of the European drama - the First World War, the revolution in Russia and the shaky Treaty of Versailles. The restored independence of the Polish State, without in any way diminishing Polish efforts to achieve this goal, is seen emphatically as a political miracle resulting more from the collapse of the partitioning powers than from any real efforts that Poles themselves may have made.

The director is guilty of a certain unevenness, however. The Polish-Soviet War of 1920 - undoubtedly one of the main events of that period of European history, and of no little importance for the West - is mentioned only in passing. This is a pity since it is one of the moments in European history which is at the same time both dramatic and a turning point - ideal material for a film 'story'. After all, until Afghanistan this was the first and only defeat the Red Army had suffered in wartime. So too the use of the term 'nationalism' in describing Polish strategy and activities during their struggles over the frontiers of the resurgent state in 1918, with no reference to the mythology of the multinational Republic of Nobles, is a simplification, notwithstanding the fairly full coverage of Józef Piłsudski's federal plan. It was interesting, however, to see the German viewpoint aired during the coverage of the Silesian Uprisings.

The second episode, 'A False Dawn', dealing with independent Poland during the years 1923-39, draws our attention to the many problems of the Republic, from its devastated economy, the unresolved, and in fact unresolvable, problems of the national minorities, the almost insuperable difficulties of merging three regions with differences resulting from the partition years and the poverty which prevailed in an overpopulated countryside. The central political conflict of modern Poland between Dmowski and Piłsudski is the hinge on which the narration turns. The whole dramatic story of Poland's foreign policy is also covered, with the desperate attempts to avoid a new partition at the hands of the totalitarian Germans and Soviets.

Some of the other issues have been treated rather schematically. The Catholic Church has unfortunately been presented - possibly in spite of the authors' intentions - as something out of folklore; a very traditional organisation, with masses of benighted peasants forming its main support and also openly anti-semitic. Although this picture of the Church has a certain validity, it seems to me that the basic social and political role of the

Church in strengthening the independent state has eluded the director.[3] Although it also had a negative role later in acting against the full pluralism of the state and community, the Polish Church's role during the tribulations brought about by Nazi occupation and also the fact that it rapidly became the defender of fundamental human values during the Stalinist period, cannot be understood without taking into account this side of its work.

These activities were the basic reason why Poles remained faithful to it. At a time when they were being sorely tested by the Nazis and by Stalinism, only the Church could take on such a role, precisely because it was prepared for it, was conscious of the need for it and did not flinch from the responsibility. The folkloristic or traditional aspect of the Catholic Church in Poland can be seen in this light, as only an ornament, a detail of minor importance which was never intrinsic, but which reflected the desires, or in fact the characteristics of the whole community. Without taking into account this aspect of the Church's role, by which the community followed the Church's lead only when that Church was faithful to the community, there is no way of understanding recent Polish history. This side of the Church's activity is better illustrated in the film during the postwar period, but it is a mistake to suggest, as the film tends to do, that this occurred only during the German occupation or the Stalinist period. The Polish Church would never have survived an attack on it after 1945 – just as the Church in Czechoslovakia did not survive – were it not for the fact that this constituted at the same time an attack on the identity of Polish society. Here too lie the roots of the sectarian view propounded by left-wingers in the west, the failure to understand the role of the Church in 'Solidarity' and even the basic nature of totalitarianism.[4]

The role of Witos and the Peasant Party, as well as the Polish Socialist Party, have been rather glossed over. Bereza Kartuska is referred to as a 'concentration camp', which is how it was originally described, but in the context of what is later understood by this term, its use is confusing here. Nor do the authors go into the doubtful theory that it was preparations by the National Democrats for a revolution which prompted Piłsudski to carry out his coup d'état. The Brześć court proceedings and the creating of *OZON* are also taken out of context.

This is nevertheless the most moving episode of the series, ending with a beautiful scene from the film 'Pan Tadeusz' in which an elegant procession of patriotic nobles dances in tune to the music of Ogiński's enchanting polonaise. This scene is then cut to film of the burning tower of the Royal Castle in Warsaw, bombed by the Germans, of the Polish cavalry charging into battle and the silent faces of well-known figures from the interwar period who appeared in the film: Czesław Miłosz, Wacław Jędrzejewicz, Lidia Ciołkosz. This is one of the moments when the director has succumbed to the mood of the Polish predicament, showing, through the faces of figures from varying political backgrounds, all the pain and despair of the loss of homeland in 1939.

Poetry, however, can be deceptive. Both the director of the film, and Ascherson in his book, cast doubts on the story that Polish cavalry attacked German tanks in 1939. Nevertheless the filmed image of charging cavalry was too powerful to be left out altogether, as a symbol of the fruitless Polish gesture. Ever since Wajda's film 'Lotna' in 1957, cavalry and suicidal charges have been, and will no doubt remain, part of the western image of Poland in 1939. This image, though, is false. Although unexpected encounters between cavalry and tanks did occur, on the whole they were avoided like the plague. Polish cavalry did not attack tanks. Horses only served to effect a speedy movement to the battlefield, where hussars then fought as infantry. What is more, in spite of the myths that have sprung up, Polish cavalry was particularly well supplied with anti-tank weapons and unusually effective in fighting battles with tanks on foot. This was borne out, for example, during the battle of Mokra when cavalry fought as infantry. It should be added that prewar cavalry manuals warned against attacking any enemy position that employed machine guns.

The third episode is entitled 'A Different World – The Plight of the Polish Jews 1919–43'. This means that in a film of twentieth century Poland a whole episode is devoted to the Jewish community. It is a good deal of space but a good thing that the makers of the film took this decision. Not only because Poland was one of the principal places where Yiddish culture flowered during the twentieth century and not because the later extermination of Polish Jews by the Germans has left Poles, in spite of themselves, bearing a collective stigma. And the programme is not only an epitaph for Jewish civilisation. This question can be looked at from another perspective. In the course of recent Polish history, it is difficult to find another issue which more accurately fits the description 'missed opportunity'. Perhaps relations with the Czechs during the interwar period, perhaps Ukrainians in 1918–19 – both events, though, without that burdening feeling of irreversibility, of the final closing of a historical chapter. Anyone who writes about Jewish culture in Poland during the years 1918–1939, cannot help thinking about its fate at the hands of the Germans during the war. The extermination of Polish Jews, for which Poles cannot in the least be held responsible, found them nevertheless unprepared in moral terms for such a catastrophe. This lack of preparedness resulted, among other things, from the atmosphere of cultural anti-semitism which prevailed in Poland during the prewar years.[5] It resulted in the feeling on the part of the majority of Jews, that, as the Holocaust was taking place, they stood completely alone. Nothing and nobody could have saved the Polish Jews, least of all the Poles who were themselves decimated and reduced to the status of slaves. But insofar as we are concerned with the 'missed opportunities', this is by the way. If anyone is to be accused of complicity or failure to make the most of practical measures to rescue the Jewish people, it cannot, of course, be the Poles. Polish culture, though, must answer the question of why Jews faced the Holocaust with such a dreadful feeling of isolation. So, too, in the film's treatment of that period, there comes through a dwelling on the moral abandonment, on the moral exclusion, beyond the pale, of people whose suffering should have been considered a part of our own suffering and whose fate should have been part of our own fate.

It is not surprising then that, working back from such a clearly defined problem as Polish-Jewish relations during the period of the Nazi inferno, the authors sought to trace and analyse the sources of this moral anaesthesia. As a result, we see many examples from the interwar period of anti-semitic behaviour, of the atmosphere of prejudice and bias, even hate, which killed off any sensitivity to the fate of a neighbouring group, destroying the organic links, frail for natural and historical reasons, of co-residence. The opportunity of educating for freedom and equality was lost. And since this opportunity was wasted, the shadow of the Holocaust in some ways touches the Polish spirit and weighs on the Polish ethos to this day. This pain of the lost opportunity is all the more shameful, in that Poles themselves waged a life and death struggle with the Germans and were themselves victims.[6]

It is not true that the makers of the film found nothing of a positive nature in Polish-Jewish relations during the inter-war years – as many critics have attempted to maintain.[7] They describe quite clearly that great and admirable Jewish civilisation which existed in Poland, with its political parties, its cultural and social life, with its mass of newspapers and periodicals, its representation in the Polish parliament. They describe too, in the words of the Polish Jews, how the links of cohabitation with non-Jewish Poles were, for the most part, entirely normal and natural. Only a biased or unintelligent person would fail to perceive that the makers of this film took as a starting point the 'normality' of Jewish life in Poland between the wars, that they maintain that such a rich civilisation could not have arisen in a hostile environment, or in opposition to it; to appreciate the fact that the Polish state – in spite of everything – created conditions for Polish Jews, and indeed gave them the chance, to develop their community and to pray to God unhindered. Anyone who has difficulty in understanding this should listen carefully to those Polish Jews in the film, should listen carefully to how they speak about Marshal Piłsudski and what he means to them; indeed to this day they sing songs about him. Jews mourned his death with the same feeling one normally reserves for a close family member.

Certainly it would have been better if the makers of the film had included more about the '*Żegota*' organisation and referred to the thousands of Jewish children rescued by Polish nuns and those shot for hiding Jews; if they had mentioned Father Kolbe, not only in the context of his anti-Jewish religious activity before the war, but had drawn attention to the fact that he concealed many Jews at Niepokolanów, or to his martyr's death in the bunker at Auschwitz when the struggle of ideas ceased and the period of final choices began. They could have shown more of the *AK* (Home Army), which passed sentences on those who betrayed Jewish fugitives to the Germans, and more of the *AK* soldiers fighting symbolically beneath the walls of the ghetto. Of course, the director would have smoothed Polish susceptibilities if he had mentioned the efforts of the Polish Government-in-Exile to bring news of the Holocaust to the world's attention, and the courier Jan Karski had been allowed to recount a little longer the details of his dramatic mission. All this is true. Except that this is to expect that the edifice of Polish history be constructed only of diamonds. And more. It is to expect the overt acknowledgement by others that Poles were part of the civilized world and not part of barbarism, part of Judeo-Christian civilization, that they defended its values and professed its faith in the face of the pagan world. It is an indication of hidden complexes and provincialism. After all, no-one in the film questions this. Is the history of Poland, even in this not very creditable chapter of Polish-Jewish relations, not treated as a part of that civilization and that ethos? Do the makers of this film not assume that the discussion is carried on, not between a gangster and his victim, but between equals, to whose face one has both the right and the duty to speak the truth? And that truth is one of missed opportunities of playing out Polish-Jewish co-residence to the end, not in an atmosphere of alienation and dislike, but in an atmosphere of tolerance. Indeed, let those who still fail to understand that the hostility did not even disappear despite the almost complete extermination of Polish Jews, try to explain how pogroms could take place in Poland in 1946, as a result of which that year is remembered by Polish Jews as a nightmare. What is more, before people start to bandy arguments about provocation on the part of the *UB* or the *NKWD* and 'żydokomuna' (Judaeo-Communism), let them listen to what witnesses of this event say, forty years after the Kielce pogrom, in Piotr Łozinski's film 'Świadkowie' (Witnesses). It becomes clear that the outburst was directed not at communists, but at Jews – the same Jews as over the centuries. It is true that communist manipulation of the slogan 'the struggle with anti-semitism' has left traces of blood on the history of that period; true also, that the role of Jewish communists in the apparatus of government after 1945 requires comprehensive analysis,[8] but to pretend that the problem of anti-semitism during the period was caused by this, amounts to a refusal to confront the truth of one's own past.

The Jewish episode is also a subtle, almost imperceptible reply to Lanzmann's *Shoah*, and especially in its Polish section. Ascherson touches on the problem only very lightly in his book, writing, 'There are some, like the film-maker Claude Lanzmann, director of *Shoah*, who charge Poles with direct complicity in the murder of the Jews, arguing that Hitler placed the gas chambers in Poland because he could rely on Polish anti-semitism to raise no protest'. Ascherson insists that this is not only slander, but also a misunderstanding of Polish attitudes. 'Polish anti-semitism was an archaic, principally religious distrust located in a mental world remote from the "scientific" systematic racism of the Nazis'. Ascherson does not develop this idea, yet it is worth taking to its conclusion on the basis of the example provided by one of the scenes from the film. This is an account of how a young Jewish girl and her whole family were hidden from the Germans by a Polish peasant. Today Professor at an American university, she speaks emotionally about the saintliness of the deed done by her benefactor, who risked death in the process. She adds at the same time that when the Germans transported the Jewish population from the neighbouring town, this same peasant went to watch the deportation, explaining to his charges that just as the Jews had led the Lord Jesus Christ to his death 2000 yeas ago, now he was going to watch them being taken away. The supposition, of course, was that it was payment for an act carried out centuries before. There was no joy or satisfaction in the peasant's words, only a certain fatalism in his perception of the catastrophe.

It is probably coincidence that a similar scene and similar argument appear in Lanzmann's film, aimed at showing Polish pleasure at Jewish suffering and cruelty. But Lanzmann is carried away here by the emotion of a Paris intellectual, which has very little in common with the truth of the human condition or with the mental processes of people who lived through that period; who has little awareness of a Truth which is presented in this series more deeply and without any false moralizing. For the average Polish peasant, Jews were an integral part of the landscape, like the things of nature, the sky above, and himself. He might not have liked them, might have maintained only the most superficial trading relations with them, but their disappearance was unimaginable. They were part of God's universe, even if an inferior part, viewed with suspicion. The complete extermination of his neighbours in a small town or village was for that peasant not only a crime in human terms but a fundamental violation of the universal order, of God's order. It was such a monstrous and absurd deed, that it could have been possible only through the will of God himself. Had he not, after all, been taught that Jews were guilty for the death of Jesus, the death of God? So, perhaps, this was the sentence for that deed? Hence the fatalism in perceiving the Holocaust, a certain self-defence through rationalisation against the madness of a deed equal only to the anger of God. Of a deed which must have been inspired by some hidden logic. The extermination was so terrible, surpassing human imagination to such an extent, that there had to be some hidden meaning in it.

It is true that there were peasants who were pleased by the smoke drifting from the chimneys, who made their way into the ghettos just after they had been cleared, in order to loot; there were those who hunted down Jews. There were also many who rescued Jews or else died along with their families for having tried. Probably the defence against losing one's sanity because of one's impotence, the impossibility of preventing the Jewish Holocaust did indeed take on the form described by the peasant.[9] So, the film conveys a certain important truth about the human condition of the time. A truth is rendered more completely perhaps when it is described by those who, exposed to full examination by Satan, seek rationality in the deepest absurdity. It is sad that they found rationalisations in anti-semitic stereotypes, dinned into them for centuries, but superstition, stupidity, moral error did not have to be, and for the most part were not – as with the heroic peasant from the film – joy or relief. It was a tragic, anti-semitic rationalisation, one painful for the Jews with the pain of centuries of rejection, which showed itself even at a time such as this, a sinful rationalisation which demanded atonement. But it was a rationalisation of a completely different order from that which Lanzmann puts forward.

In both the episode covering the Polish Republic during the years 1918–39 and in that dealing with Polish Jews, a striking feature is the dominating figure of Marshal Piłsudski. It is something of a shock to be made aware that one's own fascination is shared by foreigners. For the majority of Poles, their attitude towards Piłsudski is irrationally idolatrous and there can be no other. Piłsudski represented and still represents the myth of a Great Poland. He was the last link in recent Polish history between the greatness of the tolerant, powerful and multinational Republic of Nobles and the modest Poland of today. He was, and is, a continuing challenge to Polish pettiness, xenophobia and above all, despair and defeats. He is a reminder of the achievement of independence and the victories of 1920, and therefore a palliative to later subjection.[10] So, in the minds of the majority of Poles, there is a readiness to forgive him for almost everything which, in later years, did not reflect credit on him. This Polish fascination has, of course, its particular flavour and local colour. But the assumption behind the dispassionate 'Struggles for Poland' series is that the figure of Piłsudski dominates the history of the first decades; this becomes evident both in the commentaries and the memoirs, as well as in the moving archival film. Was he indeed such a giant peering beyond the narrow horizon at the unrealised hopes of Poles?

These two episodes provoked the protests of a number of Polish emigré organisations. In Great Britain, where the series was shown first, the protests took on more concrete form. A Committee for the Defence of the Good Name of Poland (*Komitet Obrony Dobrego Imienia Polskiego*) was formed, which received the right to a half-hour reply after the series had been screened on Channel 4. It also prepared an hour-long television film intended to present Polish history in its entirety in what the Committee felt was a more objective light. This film, directed by Witold Zadrowski, with script written by Józef Garlinski entitled 'Poland – a European Country' – emphasized not only its geographical position, but also its spiritual links to Europe.[11] Of most recent historical events, the Polish-Soviet War of 1920 was given greater emphasis and its significance for Europe, the Ukraine and for Poland was underlined. A considerable amount of time was devoted – especially in the comments of historians Antony Polonsky and Konstanty Zelenko – to the problem of the national minorities, especially the thorny problems of the Ukrainian and the Jews. Adam Zamoyski also spoke on the latter subject reminding his audience that during the 1920s and 1930s, anti-semitism could be detected in the political life of almost every European country. He observed quite correctly that there was nothing to distinguish anti-semitism in Poland from the traditional type of European anti-semitism, which had nothing in common with the racist anti-semitism of the Nazis. He pointed out that anti-semitism in Poland never became a major political question, as it did in the Axis states, and he explained that the reasons for this were to be found in Polish history and culture. He ended with the statement that 'Poles and Jews scattered throughout the world do not realise how much they owe to each other, much more certainly than they would want to admit'. There was discussion of the Jewish Holocaust during the war by Władysław Bartoszewski, a specialist in the period, former member of the *AK* and its associate body, '*Żegota*', and also for many years an inmate of Stalinist prisons for his *AK* activities.

What comes through strongly in this film is the hope for a united Europe, and linked with this the hope that Poland will achieve complete independence. It is hard to resist the impression that this film, skilfully made and containing much material complementary to the 'Struggles' series, is anticlimactic after the series. As for the protests and demonstrations against 'The Struggles for Poland', they are the result of a tendency which Boleslaw Wierzbiański, editor of the New York *Nowy Dziennik*, has described in the following words:

> As a nation we are still not able to swallow the truth, that we missed our historical opportunity; from the position of one of the most powerful states in Europe, we have declined to being a nonentity among nations. We would like to see ourselves as the foremost democracy (even though limited to the noble class) in Europe, as the victim of the partitions, as the bulwark of Christianity ... forgetting that as a nation we have always left behind us unfinished problems ... In this historical incompleteness and in an inborn tendency to factiousness and dissension lie the reasons for the Polish decline, yet

we seek to see ourselves as a nation without flaws, heroic, martyred and suffering.[12]

The majority of protests concentrated on three issues: (a) the charge that 'The Struggles for Poland' understated the achievements of the Second Republic; (b) overemphasis of the degree of anti-semitism during the interwar period, and the contention that Polish Jews, too, had something to answer Poles for (e.g. their welcoming of the Red Army units which came to partition Poland in 1939); (c) the treatment of the Ukrainian and Byelorussian minorities in the period 1918–39 was presented tendentiously. Jerzy Samborski answered these criticisms sharply;

> Poles ... as a nation have still not advanced beyond the narrowness of egotistic thinking ... ['The Struggles for Poland'] is an extraordinary event of historical importance ... it is not a superficial and banal glorification of Poland, its people and its history. On the contrary it often touches on the most secret, shameful, embarassing and painful truths ... But it does not change the fact that the series presents Polish reality, whether we like it or not. It shows the way others see us ... and this is what we are like, not any different ... A man and nation achieve their social definition only through perception and evaluation by another. We are not the way we think we are – we are only the way we appear to others ... 'The Struggles for Poland' and the reaction of Polish viewers provides emphatic evidence that the inertia in Polish thinking has not yet been overcome ... The current lesson is clearer ... because we can see our own image, though painted by strange hands, a revelation of where we are going and how we appear against the background of objective reality.[13]

Indeed, Leonard Neuger, reviewing 'Poland – a European Country' together with the film 'Świadkowie' (about the 1946 Kielce pogrom) added:

> 'Świadkowie' is an awful documentation of how the crime echoes in the minds of the witnesses even to this day. We saw and heard people who spoke of the events without emotion. In writing about the Kielce pogrom, [one of the critics] spoke of a bestiality after the war. During the Kielce pogrom, it was Poland which went wild. The second film ('Poland – a European Country') is a beautiful picture-postcard, a joyful picture free from conflict, emitting rays of childlike pride and self-contentment. In this picture-postcard Poland, of course, pogroms could not happen. Evil came from outside. I think that both these traditions – wildness and childishness – are also a part

of the Polish inheritance, although it may be that they should not be considered side by side ... No! they must be put alongside each other: breeds uninhibitedly bestiality when infantilism obscures the vision.[14]

It could be said that Polish protests had their psychological roots in an eternal non-fulfilment. The drama and at the same time the consolation of nations which have heavy experiences and losing ones, is not so much in analysing their history, but rather in playing it through again – just as today many American Southerners see themselves leading Pickett's charge on the decisive second day of the Battle of Gettysburg. The collective history of Poles, too, is a theatre of struggles to which we attempt to engage the attention of a world absorbed with itself, seeing ourselves still leading the armies of Piłsudski and Petliura to Kiev in 1920, when the scales of history trembled uncertainly. The Polish problem is also one of dealing with the fact of 'normality' as an ideal and a reason for pride, whilst for nations which have enjoyed success, 'normality' is something obvious, which no-one talks about. One speaks rather of how to win and in sitting down to play does not think of bankruptcy.

Other episodes in the series are devoted to the partition of Poland by the Germans and the Soviet Union in 1939, the Nazi terror, the front-line battles in which Poles fought the Germans at all the fronts during the Second World War, and the diplomatic manoeuvrings over the future of Poland. It is to the credit of the authors that they have gone out of their way to show in some detail the similarities in the genocidal policies of Hitler and Stalin, which created a death zone on Polish territory. Although the extermination of Poles by the Germans is fairly well known, the Soviet deportations to the Siberian labour camps, prisons, the killing at Katyn and other sites of almost the entire officer corps taken prisoner in 1939, are not on the whole known to a wider audience. The only false note is an error in the commentary where it is claimed that over 1.5 million people were deported to the interior of the Soviet Union, where 'thousands died'. Actually almost half of them died.[15] This makes a difference not only in mere numbers, but also in the nature of the deed. Failure to make it clear obscures the truth about the Stalinist genocide practised on the Poles until the Germans attacked the Soviet Union in 1941.

The battles which Poles fought on all fronts during the Second World War as units of Allied armies, although independent formations, is one of the more creditable examples of living up to the old Polish saying 'For Your Freedom and Ours' (At the end of the war Poles constituted the fourth largest military power in terms of manpower after the USSR, the USA and Great Britain). A considerable amount of space has been allocated to the largest urban insurrection in European history – the tragic Warsaw Rising in 1944. The presentation of the Polish problem as one of conflict between the great powers is objective and clearly illustrates that the Polish Government-in-Exile in London, continuing to insist upon full independence of the state, did not have any reasonable alternative, even such as Jan Karski outlined during the war – 'The alternative not of how to win, but how to lose the war'. So the Polish Government's stubbornness and insistence on this point proved to be the only real choice.[16] The depiction of the German occupation in Poland is interesting, emphasizing not only the impressive Polish Underground State, the society with no Quislings, its martyrology, but equally the realities of everyday life, the unceasing struggle for existence by illegal trade, or the alternative – starvation.

The episodes which take us up to the end of the Second World War are clear, have a good rhythm and good narrative. The later ones lose something of this dynamism, which may be a result of the authors' indecisiveness in knowing how to deal with the establishment of communist rule in Eastern Europe. A certain ambivalence of approach has always characterised those who have attempted to look at the problem objectively. Both the ideological right, as well as the left – and I use these terms in their fully conventional meaning – never experienced such difficulties; the one rejected, the other approved the establishment of a new political order and put forward its own version of events. And although the right was always nearer the truth, as Khrushchev's secret speech confirmed, a certain ambivalence in assessing the communist experience has remained. On the one hand, huge social changes, industrialization, a universal – although fairly primitive – welfare state, the conquering of illiteracy; on the other hand, crimes on a mass scale, the liquidation of all independent political and social groups, the abolition of private property, the elimination of independent culture, in other words, a totalitarian state based on the dictatorship of one party, whose existence even the communists who are interviewed in the film admit to.

The makers of the film have also failed to rid themselves of this ambivalence. It is true that Neal Ascherson has on this occasion avoided the naïveté in assessing and interpreting the first postwar years in Poland (1945–49) from which his earlier book was by no means free (in it he described this period as an epoch of almost authentic revolution),[17] but the uncertainty remains. We must attribute this no doubt to the decision of the film's makers not to engage in any deeper analysis of the establishment of communist rule in Poland, but to satisfy themselves with an interesting and correct chronological description of events. Because of this there is a failure to explain the key mechanism of seizing power (totalitarian control) as a process of successively breaking down the opposition. After all, the theory of 'modernization', to some degree perceptible in the film, that the communists introduced totalitarian power so as to carry through the modernization process (i.e. it was the price paid for modernization) is very dubious to say the least. Totalitarian power had to be employed because the community defended itself and sabotaged the new order. It was the dictatorship installed for political reasons which undertook the task of industrialising and modernizing (in a manner so large-scale as to be irrational), but it was not the task of modernization which blindly demanded the introduction of a dictatorship.

There is more interesting presentation of the major crises of postwar Poland, although the attack of the Party on Polish culture and the antisemitic campaign of 1968 are treated so colourfully and narratively as to be shallow. I feel that the political origins of the anti-semitic campaign as an inter-party struggle rooted in the existence of rival communist factions during the war period, should have been more clearly presented, although it is true that even today, owing to the lack of source material, we are reduced to speculating on the matter. Gierek's decade is rightly presented as a prelude to 'Solidarity'. It is a pity, though, that 'Solidarity' itself is barely introduced. We have the Gdańsk agreements and a quick review of the most important events of the first few months. And yet 'Solidarity' had a universal relevance unique in recent Polish history, in that all the problems of contemporary Europe which were reflected in Poland, and which formed the justification for the film, showed up with unusual clarity. The director let slip the chance to show how 'Solidarity' opened a new chapter in the history of Eastern Europe, with ramifications far beyond its geographical confines. The importance of the union's role did not lie in the fact that it propounded a particularly original programme, although many elements of it were certainly innovative.[18] The question of whether or not 'Solidarity' had a cohesive programme, of whether its leaders realised that the Gdańsk Agreements were not a social agreement between the authorities and the community (which many still believe to this day), but a *de facto* division of power with all the consequences for a totalitarian political system, is not important. 'Solidarity' destroyed the psychological basis of the totalitarian system of holding power and the psychological bases of acquiescence. What is more, it revealed the whole absurdity of the system and the crisis at its core. This is one fact which has registered itself clearly in Gorbachev's mind, irrespective of the conclusions which he attempts to draw from it. Indeed, one could argue that 'Solidarity' was too recent a phenomenon to attempt a deeper assessment of its significance, but this argument is unconvincing since at the time the film was being made the universal significance of 'Solidarity' was being recognised and chronicled.[19]

In one of the last episodes, a good deal of space is devoted to the Catholic Church and the significance which Cardinal Wojtyła's election as Pope had for the rise of 'Solidarity'. We are informed of how left-wing intellectuals moved closer to the Church during the 1970s in an alliance for the defence of human rights. It was perhaps worth emphasizing the fact that it was not the Church which changed its perception of reality, not at least in basic issues, rather the truth of its position was vindicated as ideological trends passed by and faded one by one.[20] In this sense the traditional and conservative ethos of the Polish Church in questions of social customs or of some problems, which so excites and fascinates left-wing intellectuals in the West, is, as a Catholic journalist on the weekly *Tygodnik Powszechny* put it, 'the kind of problem which reminds one of a discussion about various types of toothpaste taking place in a labour camp'.

If there is something missing from the series, it is, in my opinion, some clarification of the phenomenon of the Polish intelligentsia. The Polish intelligentsia was the inheritor of the ethos of the Republic of Nobles and its concept of honour, of the inalienable rights of the individual, of suspicion of all forms of authority which bordered on anarchy. It is a paradox that that intelligentsia, originating from the mass of impoverished nobility and absorbing its ethos during the 19th century, should transmit it to the majority of the modern Polish nation, which traces its own origins after all to the peasantry. It was this ethos which became the universal ethos in the country and the basis of national education. One cannot understand, for example, the Polish experience of communism and its distinctiveness without being aware of that individual feeling of independence which was the ideal, although very often not practised, of the collective consciousness of Poles. The fact is that the clash between the ethos of the Polish intelligentsia and communism resulted in all the quirks of postwar Polish development and, as the makers of the film themselves argue, its 'least intimidated position' in the socialist bloc. It is no accident moreover that both the Germans and the Soviets, after they had divided Poland between them in 1939, set about exterminating the Polish educated classes as a priority of their occupation policy. They all but achieved their goal, and this meant that Poland had to wait a whole generation for the gradual rebirth of independent élites which in the 1970s and 1980s laid *political* claim to the honour of the community.

An accompanying book to the series has been written by Neal Ascherson. It is a concise work, superbly written, and stands as a publication independent of the programme. It is perhaps the best introduction to Polish history currently available in any language. One cannot refrain from asking why it should be that the best books about Polish history for the general reader are being written by foreigners these days. Why do Polish authors not have that force and momentum, the ability to reshape the drama of the Polish situation in clear language, which is exciting stylistically, or have indeed that sense of synthesis in the best tradition of European historiography? There is in Ascherson's book an unmistakeable fascination with his subject. Ascherson does not merely recount the events of Polish history, he creates a drama. Nowhere does the author cross the boundary between myth and reality, and where the temptation overtakes him he is rescued by irony and the sense of paradox.

It is impossible to review this book as a purely academic work. It does not after all make claim to this label. It has to be seen as a key to Polish history, a canvas painted with broad strokes of the paintbrush. After the excellent 'Preface', which introduces the subject and makes clear why the author thinks it worth writing about, Ascherson manages to synthesize in 34 pages almost one thousand years of Polish history (966–1900). There follow chapters on Poland in the twentieth century which link up more or less with the chronology of the film series, although Ascherson finishes his account in 1986.

As happens in every work of this kind the aim to synthesize material effectively sometimes leads to mistakes or omissions. The Piast dynasty ruled until 1370, and not until 1138 (p. 16). The claim that 'Michał Kalecki was a pioneer of modern socialist economics' is imprecise (p. 87). If anyone fits this role it is Oskar Lange; indeed, Kalecki was a distinguished precursor of Keynesianism. It is a myth that the 3 year plan, (1947–50) was a rational and effective plan (p. 157). This is correct only if one compares it with the destructive mania for ever larger projects, which characterizes later 5 year plans. In the course of the 3 year plan, privately owned services and light industrial concerns were put out of business. Poland is still suffering the consequences. The claim that, 'The Soviet Union showed good will by imposing only light sentences on the kidnapped resistance leaders in Moscow' reveals a curious interpretation of words such as 'light' and 'good will' (p. 142). Writing of the Polish tendency to avoid extremes, Ascherson writes: 'Piłsudski had not put his enemies to death and Bierut had spared the nation the worst of Stalinist tyranny' (p. 229). The author's attempt to generalise has here taken precedence over his good taste and has led him to compare the dictatorial leader of a pluralist state with its independent courts, and a Stalinist leader, under whose presidency and with whose knowledge, more than ten thousand innocent people were sentenced to death.

The 1965 letter of Polish bishops (to their German counterparts) with its famous wording 'we forgive and we ask for forgiveness' aroused violent emotions, as Ascherson correctly points out. But from the historical perspective, its political and moral role was a good deal more far-reaching (resulting in the later accord with the Federal Republic of 1970) than the people with such emotions would like to admit. And certainly Khrushchev, in his speech to the 20th Party Congress, did not so much acknowledge and revile Stalinist crimes (p. 157) but – if one reads his words closely – only condemned crimes against innocent communists. And there is a great difference, as one can appreciate, if one observes what is currently happening in the USSR and how that magical Rubicon is being crossed. I am not too sure, either, what the author had in mind when he wrote, 'The real tragedy of the Polish-Soviet War lay deeper. The revolution of 1917 had raised the real and marvellous hope that with the fall of the Tsardom, the relationship between Russians and Poles might escape from its terrible past and be transformed into a lasting friendship'. If we are to understand from this that the great empire was breaking up and that self-determination for all its subject nations might have resulted, then I agree. Because neither in the policy of the Whites, nor that of the Bolsheviks – with the 'Decree on the Self-determination of Nations' which was skilful in propaganda terms, but never an honest expression of their policy – was that assumption taken seriously.[21] And so the war over the independence of Poland, as an overwhelming majority of the population understood it, lay on the cards. Perhaps the conflict with the Ukrainians over Lwów could have been avoided, with all its consequences. It was almost impossible to avoid conflict with the Russians in 1917. That friendship will have to await a further revolution.

The reservations expressed above relate to details rather than to any mistakes in overall concept or ideas. Of the latter I have uncovered only one. This is linked to the interpretation of the diplomatic game prior to the outbreak of World War II. There is no space here to go into this question in any detail. It does seem to me, however, that Ascherson greatly overestimates the freedom of manoeuvre in foreign affairs of the Polish government in the 1930s. In addition, his belief that Stalin could have been enlisted for the anti-Nazi coalition in 1939 does strike one as naive in the extreme. Stalin, in the late 1930s was faced with the choice of a risky alliance with the West and an understanding with Hitler which would satisfy his territorial aspirations in Eastern Europe and involve the Germans in a war with the west. Being a convinced believer in the principles of power politics, it is not surprising that he chose the latter. The strategy he devised, proved to be extremely effective and represents the bases of the present-day division of Europe, with certain modifications at Teheran and Yalta. Only that instead of the *Pax Germania*, we have the *Pax Americana*,[22] much more useful from the strategic point of view than the *Pax Germania*, since after all, one can always count on the Americans pulling out of Europe one day – especially if one directs persistent diplomatic efforts to that end.

It is a pity that Ascherson did not sketch in this aspect of the European conflict, since, in this scheme, the role of an independent Poland, and indeed of all the countries of east-central Europe, seemingly extends beyond the realm of the purely regional. Polish independence was a stabilizing factor in the European order, foiling, or at least complicating, the imperial plans of Germany and the USSR. What is more, this perspective adds a certain continuity to the value of the independence of Poland and the other states of east-central Europe in overcoming the dangerous division of Europe based upon an anachronistic political understanding. That division of Europe, brought about forcibly by the subjection of eastern Europe to the USSR, is not only a legacy of Yalta, but also of the Hitler-Stalin Pact, which Yalta only confirmed. So we have ideas such as the 'neutrality of east-central Europe', 'Finlandization' and other variants found in the midst of deliberations over the future of Europe and intended to ensure it stability.[23] Overcoming this division of Europe will be the last act in the burial of European Stalinism, the relics of which remain with us still.

The film and the book together, in spite of these shortcomings, are a great event. They run the gamut of nearly the whole Polish experience, locating it firmly in the European tradition. Michael Kaufmann is both right and wrong when he writes that 'the essence of Polishness has been captured [in the film] in the harmony of unfulfilled longings, of old romantic fetters and the temptations of martyrdom, and above all in the pervading feeling of the tragic'.[24] He is right in that Polish history cannot be understood without that element. But perhaps he is wrong when he assumes that it is a measure of an inescapable Polish fate. Perhaps entering the 21st century, when ragged ideologies have fallen apart and at a time when the last anachronistic, 19th century type empire and the very idea of empire seems so ineffective as to be funny to a democratic world, perhaps this film emphasizes that Poland is something more than just the helplessly sick, tragic man of Europe. Perhaps, if that Europe makes a sizeable film, it is not to be excited for the ever-fevered Poles, who have time after time undermined European order. Perhaps this series is proof that Poland is still seen as a legitimate and important part of a future, united Europe to which European standards must be applied. If so, the concept of Europe must be widened. And this is the point where Polish myths, at last, perhaps coincide with European expectations. Perhaps, then, this series is both a signal and a hope that there can be an end to the tragic nature of Polish fortunes, when surrounding empires collapse. Meanwhile, let us learn something from this film what is important for Europe in the picture it has painted of Poland. What values it holds dear and on what conditions, other than external, we should become a fully participant member of that Europe. The fact is that we will remain as one of those eternal Polish myths from which we cannot free ourselves, but of which, also we should not be ashamed. Let us pay attention carefully, meanwhile, to our provincialism, our pettiness, even our xenophobia, instead of being outraged that we have not been presented in our best clothes. It is for this reason that the film is important, very important and necessary – to Poles above all. To have such friends in today's world, when people are so often turned in upon themselves, is a thing of real value.

NOTES

1 Quoted in Michael Kaufman, 'Polska: Od Niepodległósci do Komunizmu'. *Nowy Dziennik – Przegląd Polski*, 21 July 1988, p. 2.

2 Ibid.
3 W. Lamentowicz, 'Katolicyzm w kulturze politycznej Polski'. *Kultura*, Paris (May 1988), 95–109.
4 See, for example, D. Singer, 'The Road to Gdańsk'. *Monthly Review Press* 1981.
5 For more on this, see; A. Bryk, 'Poles and Jews during the Holocaust – the Hidden Complex of the Polish Mind', in ed. A. Polonsky, '"My Brother's Keeper?" Recent Polish Debates on the Holocaust' (forthcoming).
6 The only reservation I have – although perhaps I am nitpicking – is to the title of this episode. If 'A Different World – The Plight of the Polish Jews 1918–43' is intended to indicate the distinctiveness of Jewish civilization in Poland and its distinctive course, then fine. It may, though, suggest a continuity, in the sense that the Holocaust carried out by the Germans was in some way a fulfilment and continuation of anti-semitism in interwar Poland; this is nonsense.
7 See. Z. Raciecki, 'Zmagania o Polskę', *Nowy Dziennik*, 25 August 1987.
8 Recently Jerry Muller has attempted this: 'Communism, Anti-semitism and the Jews', *Commentary*, August 1988. See also M. Chęciński, *Poland: Communism, Nationalism, Anti-semitism*, N.Y., 1982.
9 This subject has been discussed more fully by A. Smolar: 'Jews as a Polish Problem', *Daedalus*, Spring 1987.
10 A. Michnik has developed this in: 'Shadows of Forgotten Ancestors', in *Letters from Prison*, University of California Press, Berkeley, L.A., London 1985. 201–222.
11 T. Wyrwa, 'Dzieje Polski na ekranie', *Zeszyty Historyczne*, no. 2, 1988.
12 B. Wierzbiański, 'Telewizyjne Zmagania o Polskę', *Nowy Dziennik*, 15 July 1988.
13 J. Samborski, 'Lekcja historii' in *Słowo Ojczyste*, no. 1 (149), Autumn 1987. This periodical is published by the *Macierz Szkolna*, an institution which supervises Polish education in centres of Polish emigration. This issue was withdrawn at the suggestion of the Polish Ex-Combatants' Association from all Polish bookshops under its control. By way of answer, Neal Ascherson published the text in *Index on Censorship*, no. 1 (1988), from where I have drawn this quotation.
14 *Zeszyty Literackie*, no. 2 (Summer 1988), p. 144.
15 See J.T. Gross, *Revolution from Abroad*, Princeton University Press, Princeton, 1988.
16 See M. Król, 'Polskie Niedopełnienie', *Aneks*, no. 45, 1987.
17 Neal Ascherson, *The Polish August*, Penguin, London, 1981. The occupation undoubtedly radicalised Polish society, and this was reflected in the programmes of reform prepared by the Polish Government in London and the political parties. This radicalisation, though, had very little in common with the communist model of reform and methods of carrying it through.
18 For more on this see: A. Bryk, K. Dadak, 'The Self-Governing Republic: A Critical Review of the Major Reforms Proposed by Solidarity', *Review of Socialist Law*, no. 11 (1985), 309–331.
19 T.G. Ash, *The Polish Revolution. Solidarity 1980–82*, Jonathan Cape, London, 1983. Also, L. Tyrmand, 'Notes on the Polish Question', *Policy Review*, Summer 1982.
20 A. Michnik, *Kościół, Lewica, Dialog*, Instytut Literacki, Kultura, Paris 1977.
21 L. Kolakowski, *Main Currents of Marxism*, vol. 2, Oxford University Press, Oxford/ New York 1978, 398–405.
22 This concept is not understood, of course, as meaning the domination of the USA over Western Europe, but its presence as a stabilising element along with the nuclear umbrella and NATO.
23 See Z. Brzeziński, 'East-West Relations and Eastern Europe -Special Address', *Problems of Communism* May-August 1988, 67–70.
24 M. Kaufman, op cit.

UNCHANGING VIEW: POLISH JEWRY AS SEEN IN RECENT ONE-VOLUME HISTORIES OF THE JEWS

Gershon C. Bacon

The appearance of *POLIN*, along with the on-going series of international conferences on the history and culture of Polish Jewry, provide eloquent testimony to a growing interest in the topic in the scholarly community. Even before this recent spurt of activity, a growing, if still small, number of monographs have slowly refashioned and refined our understanding of this important Diaspora community. The question remains, though, if there has been any 'trickle-down' effect from the research field to more popular works on Jewish history. These for better or worse, reach larger audiences and provide those audiences with their basic knowledge and perspective on Jewish history. Even in an age of increasing specialization, the one-volume history has proved to be a comparatively durable medium, and can be found in the form of 'coffee-table books', high-school and undergraduate course textbooks, and introductions for the interested general reader. Do these works communicate to the reader the research findings of the last generation, or has Cecil Roth's synthesis in his frequently reprinted *History of the Jews* remained the dominant view of the Polish Jewish community?

This question concerns not only bibliographical completeness, but historiographical perspective as well. The fears, concerns, and interests of historians writing in a period when mass migration of East-European Jews to the west was a living reality, when Nazism was a growing threat, and when Polish Jewry numbered three million, differ considerably from the concerns two generations later, when Polish Jewish history is basically a finished chapter, and the scars of the era of destruction, if never healable, can begin to be integrated in a larger historical perspective on the development of Polish Jewry. Have the prejudices of some Jews of earlier generations toward East-European Jewry been overcome? Essentially, our examination of some recent surveys sought an answer to the basic question: has a new historical and historiographical agenda emerged regarding Polish Jewry? To answer the question, we have examined five recently-published one-volume general histories of the Jews to see how they portrayed Polish Jewry.*

As a starting point, we considered the *History of the Jews* by Cecil Roth, often reprinted and originally published in 1935 under the title *A Bird's-Eye View of Jewish History* and intended for the interested adult reader. One might assume that by the 1970s, the bird would need at least a stronger pair of glasses, but, in the section on Poland, Roth's text remains almost identical to that of the first edition. His approach to the subject combines the topics outlined by his distinguished pioneering predecessor, Nathan Neta Hannover, with the concerns of an Emancipation-era historian. Like Hannover in his *Yeven Metsula* (1653), Roth portrays Polish Jewry before the Chmielnicki uprising as the embodiment of the classical Jewish values of *Torah* learning, worship and benevolence, with its institutions based on truth, justice and peace. Its autonomous institutions were unparalleled in the long history of the Diaspora, and the *Vaad Arba Aratsot* (Council of the Four Lands) 'was virtually the Parliament of Polish Jewry, with authority nearly as absolute as any legislature' (p. 270). Following Hannover, Roth notes the almost universal spread of Jewish education in Poland, only criticising the *pilpul* method of study, which he describes as 'futile, wasteful, and from certain points of view, even pernicious' (p. 271), though it sharpened the minds of generations of pupils.

In many ways, though, Roth's treatment of Polish Jewry reflects the sensitivities and the historical consensus of the late-19th and early-20th centuries, as exemplified by such works as Dubnow's *History of the Jews in Russia and Poland*, with the addition of Roth's own views and emphases. This can be seen first in the amount of space allotted to Polish Jewry, 13 out of the 384 pages (3.4% of the total). These have to cover Poland and the rise of Hasidism; modern Poland and Hasidism after the first two generations receive hardly any mention. There is, then, the awkward way Polish Jewry is put into the general scheme of Jewish history, with the chapter 'Poland (to 1648)' sandwiched between 'Levantine Refuge' and 'Life in the Ghetto' in the larger section entitled 'The Break of Dawn 1492–1815'. This necessitated jumping back several centuries in order to mention ancient Greek inscriptions in the Black Sea region and the Khazar kingdom of the 8th and 9th centuries. With Roth and, as we shall

* Abba Eban, *My People* (new edition; New York: Behrman House and Random House, 1984); Chaim Potok, *Wanderings* (New York: Alfred A. Knopf, 1978); H. H. Ben-Sasson ed., *A History of the Jewish People* (Cambridge, Mass.: Harvard Univ. Press, 1976); Paul Johnson, *A History of the Jews* (New York: Harper and Row, 1987); Robert Seltzer, *Jewish People, Jewish Thought* (New York, Macmillan, 1980). Page references in the article are to these editions and to Cecil Roth, *A Bird's-Eye View of Jewish History* (Cincinnati: Union of American Hebrew Congregations, 1935).

see, with many of his successors also, there seems to be a problem of exactly how to fit Polish Jewry into the on-going stream of Jewish history; and one gets the feeling that they regard Polish Jews as almost a sideshow to Western Jewry, where the decisive events of Jewish history took place.

The following few examples are typical of Roth's approach on issues of historical judgement, and provide useful comparisons with more recent surveys:

1. the Khazar theory of Polish Jewish origins is not dismissed out of hand. Roth suggests that the original Jewish settlers were overwhelmed by the superior culture of the newcomers from Germany;
2. he accepts the authenticity of the Hasdai ibn Shaprut-Joseph correspondence;
3. he emphasizes the charters granted to Jews, notes the continued antipathy of clerics and non-Jewish merchants and occurrences of violence. All in all, however, Poland appears a more secure place for Jews;
4. Roth points out the demographic importance of Polish Jewry, from whom the majority of world Jewry are descended;
5. as a result of the Chmielnicki uprising and its aftermath (which Roth sees as the whole next century), there occurred 'the complete ruin of Polish Jewry'. Poland (at least its southern region) would cease being a centre of Jewish life as had been the case before 1648. Jewry began a migration westward;
6. Roth describes the rise of *Hasidism* in a simple, uncomplicated manner, with no hint of the complex factors involved in the birth and spread of the *Hasidic* movement.

On one specific point of interpretation, Roth follows Dubnow and others in seeing the Lithuanian Council (*Vaad Lita*) as a breakaway from the Council of the Four Lands, rather than as an institution which evolved around the same time as, if not before, its Polish counterpart. As mentioned before, the vibrant communal life of Polish Jewry in the interwar period rates no mention in Roth's narrative, except for a short note on government anti-semitism. While this oversight may have been understandable in 1935 (even then it seems strange), by the 1970s it surely cried out for revision.

ROTH'S SUCCESSORS: ANY CHANGE?

General observations

In the five recent surveys under review, there has been no radical revision or expansion of the historical or historiographic agenda concerning Polish Jewry. With a few exceptions to be noted, the major subject headings in Roth remain those of his successors. All of the authors in question deal with about the same limited number of topics. Blatant errors of fact are gratifyingly few, among which we might cite Eban's inclusion of Lithuania as one of the four lands which made up the Polish *Vaad*, and Johnson's claim that the the Vilna Gaon finished out his days in the Land of Israel. As to the amount of space allotted to Polish Jewry in the volumes, the approximate results are as follows:

Eban 11 out of 539 pages (2%)
Potok 18 out of 398 pages (4.5%)
Ben-Sasson 50 out of 1100 pages (4.5%)
Seltzer 20 out of 766 pages (2.6%)
Johnson 13 out of 587 pages (2.2%)

These figures count the number of pages devoted to extended discussion of Polish Jewry, not counting brief mentions of Poland or discussion of the Holocaust. Though these rough figures do not of themselves tell all, they do give some indication of the importance each author assigns to the topic of Polish Jewry within the admittedly difficult and limiting one-volume history format. The space allotted to different topics within the discussion of Polish Jewry differs markedly from author to author, although *Hasidism* stands out as a topic favoured by all the authors reviewed here. With the sole exception of that edited by Ben-Sasson, none of these histories devotes any extended discussion to Polish Jewry after the partitions, to Warsaw as a major Jewish centre (other than by citing its large Jewish population), to the development of Jewish party politics and their achievements, or to *Hasidism* after the first two generations.

To some extent, writing a concise history of the Jews involves 'name-dropping', that is, peppering the text with a certain number of names of individuals memorable or important enough, for whatever reason, to be included in a wide-ranging survey. Given the keen interest in the beginnings of *Hasidism* and the career and personality of its founder, it should not surprise us that the three Polish-Jewish personalities singled out by all the authors are Jacob Frank, the Baal Shem Tov, and the Vilna Gaon. Among non-Jewish figures, we find Casimir the Great and Bogdan Chmielnicki. Some characters who have decreased in popularity include

Bolesław of Kalisz and Esterka, whom some of our authors no longer believe crucial for a quick survey of Polish Jewish history. A more thorough reconsideration of Polish Jewry should produce a more complete list of names for inclusion in such brief histories: for example (in no particular order) Lewko, the Kotsker Rebbe, the first Gerrer Rebbe, Berek Joselowicz, Dov Berish Meisels, Yitshak Grunbaum, and Roman Dmowski are people who had a major impact on, or are illustrative of, one or another aspect of Polish Jewish life.

The problem of organising material does not lend itself to a totally satisfactory solution, and reflects the generally problematic nature of all periodization. As with Roth, the favoured approach remains siting the major discussion of Polish Jewry somewhere in the sixteenth-seventeenth century section of the general narrative, and at that point providing some introductory comments on the earlier beginnings of Polish Jewry. The general headings for this section vary, however, each one reflecting the author's attempt to fit all of Jewish history within a few catchy rubrics. Thus Eban includes Poland under 'New Centres of Jewish Settlement', while Potok incorporates Polish Jewry, for better or worse, in the section called 'Secularism: Messiahs for a Broken World', and Johnson places his narrative under 'Ghetto'. Seltzer takes the safest and best approach by calling his chapter 'Early-Modern Period: 16th to mid-18th centuries'.

Before we turn to each history in turn, one final note is in order. In the final analysis, the reader should expect from the author of a concise history of the Jews reliable information, and balanced, up-to-date historical interpretation. Within these limits, the authors under discussion acquit themselves at least adequately and, in most cases, quite well. The differences between them emerge more from subtle turns of phrase and from an occasional sentence which provides the reader with a more balanced view of the issue under discussion. This is possible even within the confines of a brief history.

Abba Eban's *My People*

Even if regarded as a 'coffee-table book', Eban's book proved the most disappointing of the ones under review. For the most part, it remains confined to the subjects and approach of Roth; it is also lacking in nuances and historical perspective, and could well mislead the reader on several key points. For example, he quotes the preamble from the *privilegium* of Bolesław of Kalisz as being 'noteworthy' (p. 207), without offering any explanation whether this *privilegium* or its preamble differed from those given to Jews in other countries. Nor does he mention that Bolesław's charter applied only to part of Poland. In discussing attempts by ecclesiastical officials to impose on Polish Jewry the restrictions in force in Central and Western Europe, Eban remarks that 'Jews were segregated from the Christian population and reduced to the position of a despised caste' (p. 208), an overstatement which does not necessarily reflect Polish reality, but more the wishful thinking of worried churchmen. Like many of the authors under discussion, Eban views the achievements of Polish Jewish autonomous institutions through the perspective of Nathan Hannover, with the Council of the Four Lands being described as the supreme legislative and executive body of Polish Jewry whose legal decisions and regulations were binding. But he gives no indication of the limitations on its authority and the lack of effective means to enforce it. Eban notes that the main communal expenditure of the local *kehilla* went for welfare, health and education, while omitting to say that most of the *kehilla* budget went on taxes and on bribes and gifts to various officials, rather than for internal Jewish needs. While discussing Jacob Frank, Eban summarises his important ideas, but neglects to mention the salient fact of the mass conversion of Frank and his followers to Christianity. He describes *Hasidism* as a revolt of the 'unlearned' against the strict rule of the rabbis, also linking it with the generally wretched conditions in Podolia, but the more complex factors in the rise of *Hasidism* are not covered. On inter-war Poland, only government anti-semitism rates a mention.

On the positive side, Eban takes pains to distinguish between Jewish status in Poland and in Lithuania, in favour of the latter, without, however, explaining why this was so. Though he stresses anti-Jewish disturbances and expulsions, Eban also does a creditable job in setting out the ways Jews managed to come to terms with and prosper in the Polish economy.

Chaim Potok's *Wanderings*

Certainly the most beautiful to look at of the five histories under review (more recently, an unillustrated, paperback edition has appeared), *Wanderings* also has something to offer the reader between sips of coffee at the coffee table. Potok's very personal history of the Jews is a well-written and sensitively drawn portrait, and his discussion of Polish Jewry in some places displays a balanced approach which shows awareness of scholarly debate. Thus Potok mentions that some Polish cities were granted the right *de non tolerandis judaeis*, but notes their limited number. Though he presents *Hasidism* in the context of the failed Messianism of Sabbatai Zevi, he describes *Hasidism* as neutralizing active Messianic hopes. Most significantly, while Potok gives some of the standard descriptions of the horrors of 1648–1649, his assessment of the long-term effects of this disastrous period demonstrates the complexities and historical controversy surrounding the issue. In dealing with Jewish colonization in Poland, Potok gives the reader a sense of the pioneering aspects of this venture, even to the point of characterizing the frontier atmosphere of the Polish eastern territories (the Wild East?), where 'like everyone else, Jews took easily to their weapons' (p. 336). Potok also tries to give at least a hint of the demographic growth and importance of Polish Jewry.

On the other hand, *Wanderings* does have its drawbacks over Polish Jewry. Like Roth, Potok is reluctant to abandon the Khazar theory of Polish Jewish origins, commenting that 'it cannot as yet be satisfactorily substantiated, though it is not to be entirely discounted' (p. 335). In a sort of overcorrective to his earlier emphasis on the legal status of Jews, Potok makes do with a too facile description of the Jews of Poland as 'the lubricant in an otherwise impossible economy of indolent nobles and enslaved serfs, their rights carefully protected by royal charters' (p. 336). There is a similar vagueness in his description of the Council of the Four Lands. The narrative is also not free of apologetics, as when Potok comments that it was 'an accident of history' that placed Jewish capital in the sensitive areas of large-scale *arenda* and tax-farming. The omission of any significant discussion of modern Poland is rather puzzling in Potok's case, in the light of his personal connection with the events of Poland's rebirth through his father's membership of Piłsudski's legion, an event which formed the basis for one of Potok's novels, and which he mentions in his introduction. Potok devotes by far the greatest part of his discussion of Polish Jewry to *Hasidism*, and here his narrative is both strong and gripping. His description of other topics is too sketchy.

Ben-Sasson and Ettinger's *A History of the Jewish People*

Though originally published in Hebrew as three separate volumes, with each section written by a different author, this massive *History* appeared in a one-volume English translation in 1976, and is consequently included in the present survey. Both Ben-Sasson and Ettinger have made important contributions to the field of East-European Jewish history, and their expertise makes its presence felt throughout the narrative. The authors impress the reader not only with their specialized knowledge of the field, but even more by their attempt to cut across geographical and political boundaries to present European Jewry as a whole, with East-European Jewry as one example of continent-wide phenomena. Thus the Bolesław of Kalisz *privilegium* of 1264 appears in the context of the expansion eastward of the legal arrangements for Jewish communal autonomy (p. 462), the disruption of prayers as a form of social protest found in several countries (pp. 506–507), and the institution of the chief rabbinate is considered as part of the relationship beween the Jews and their Gentile rulers in Poland and other countries (pp. 601–2).

In their discussions of Polish Jewry, Ben-Sasson and Ettinger excel in providing the balance, perspective and nuance in the historical narrative that, even within the confines of a short general history, can inform and guide the sensitive reader. They successfully communicate the complexities of how the Jews established themselves in Poland. Though paying due attention to the golden age of Polish Jewry, Ben-Sasson takes pains to note that the foundations of that relatively secure age had already been laid in the fourteenth and fifteenth centuries. He mentions expulsions and pressures on Polish Jewry, but spells out their failure to dampen Jewish economic activity. He notes the differences between the status of Jews in Poland and in Lithuania, and tries to account for them (p. 582). Especially noteworthy is Ben-Sasson's discussion of Jewish economic life in an expanding Poland, including the development of the *arenda*, and the accompanying social tensions (pp. 639–644). As in other surveys, the phenomenon of cities with the right *de non tolerandis judaeis* comes in for scrutiny, but only here are we given a more balanced picture which includes the development of the *jurydyki*, by which nobles aided Jews in evading these restrictions. In dealing with the 1648–1649 disaster, Ban-Sasson describes the losses, but also provides an account of the position of Polish Jewry after the deluge: the losses were certainly significant and some emigration to the west took place, but Jews remained a major urban class in Poland, and many Jews still prospered. Practically alone of the authors surveyed, Ben-Sasson makes an effort to note some important trends and events in general Polish history, such as the Reformation and Counter-Reformation, and their effects on the situation of Jews in the country. Finally, we should mention how he uses to good effect the results of his own research to present some aspects of social attitudes among Polish Jews, and the social background and social tensions inherent in rabbinic literature and legislation.

Ettinger, too, manages to present the reader with a well-balanced account of the modern period in Eastern Europe within a rather compact narrative, again using his expertise in the field to great advantage. He shows the differences between the economic life of Jews in Eastern and Western Europe, while making the reader aware of the way the Jews from the two regions of the continent co-operated economically. In his description of the eighteenth century, Ettinger goes beyond standard clichés about communal decline in that period and looks sensitively at the social institutions of Polish Jewry and contemporary social tensions. His presentation of *Hasidism* distinguishes between the lifetime of the Baal Shem Tov and the period of his successors. Only in the latter period, claims Ettinger, did *Hasidism* become a fully-fledged movement (p. 770). In this regard, Ettinger offers a well-rounded picture of *Hasidism's* following within scholarly and less scholarly circles, as well as varying developments in the leadership of the movement at different stages. Most notably, he provides the general reader with a perspective on the lesser and greater evils of the partitions and pre-partition eras, noting that with all its drawbacks, the Jews' situation in a decaying Polish state still had its advantages: '... the arbitrary whims of the magnates and the dangers embodied in the political anarchy were in some respects less harmful to the Jews than the rigid administrative measures legislated by the absolutist régimes' (p. 753). The partitions of Poland thus represented a worsening of the position of Polish Jewry. Lastly, we should remark that Ettinger is the only author in our survey who analyzes the crucial demographic developments of the 19th and 20th centuries of East-European and world Jewry, and who chronicles both the anti-Jewish discrimination and the political and cultural growth of the inter-war period. Those detailed sections on Eastern Europe in the *History* are of the highest quality, and the patient reader thumbing through further scattered references to Polish Jewry within more general discussion will find much food for thought in the authors' integrated approach to European Jewry.

Johnson's *A History of the Jews*

The newest entry in the list of general histories of the Jews, Paul Johnson's *A History of the Jews*, provides the perspective of a perceptive outsider, the author of numerous historical works on a similar grand scale. Other reviewers have commented amply on the achievements and drawbacks of Johnson's approach, and we shall limit ourselves to some remarks about his presentation of East-European Jewry within the general framework of his history. We have already called attention to the fact that Johnson's book does have an occasional factual error. In addition, certain turns of phrase could mislead the reader, such as his statement that *Hasidism* spread to Germany, and from there to the world (p. 298). One presumes he means by this Martin Buber's restatement and reformulations of *Hasidic* tales and doctrines, but it is not at all clear from the text. One wonders also at his statement that the Baal Shem Tov 'worked outside the synagogue system' (pp. 295-6), since the traditions concerning the Besht contain numerous stories about his actions, particularly leading the congregation in prayer, in various synagogues. Johnson too follows the view of *Hasidism* as a movement of the ordinary, humble Jews, without mentioning the important cadre of scholars and lower-level Jewish intelligentsia also attracted to the movement.

Despite these notes of caution, Johnson's *History*, probably because it was written by a newcomer to Jewish history, provides some interesting and thought-provoking insights into Polish Jewry. In his presentation of events, the balance has swung in an entirely new direction. Jewish legal status and *privilegia* rate scarcely a mention. Instead, he looks at the larger phenomenon of the eastward movement of the Jews, and the fact that they were needed in Poland. Even with periodic anti-Jewish riots and expulsions, Poland by 1500 had come to be regarded as the safest country in Europe for Jews. Benefiting from the insights of Ben-Sasson and Ettinger, whom he cites, Johnson devotes much of his discussion of Poland to communal and economic affairs, pointing out that the interests of both Jews and Polish rulers were served by the system that evolved. He describes the abuses inherent in the *arenda* system, but also the attempts by Jewish communal bodies to ameliorate matters. Here and there we find the sort of sweeping statements that have either irked or intrigued reviewers, for example Johnson's observation that 'in many settlements [Jews] constituted the majority of the inhabitants, so that for the first time outside Palestine they dominated the local culture' (p. 252). While exaggerated, this comment does raise some serious questions as to the long-term effects on Jews and Poles of the 'Jewish-street' phenomenon, by which Jews made up such a large percentage of the urban population of Poland. Almost in passing, Johnson compares the Baal Shem Tov and John Wesley, presumably to help the non-Jewish reader understand this Jewish holy man and charismatic leader. One wonders why Jewish historians have not made similar comparisons and contrasts between Hasidism and contemporary or later forms of charismatic leadership, rather than looking for influences (this has been done with mixed results) to understand Hasidism as a religious phenomenon. Like most of his fellow authors of one-volume histories, Johnson gives short shrift to Polish Jewry after the rise of Hasidism, noting post-Holocaust anti-semitism in Poland and some other scattered references, but providing no sustained narrative. All in all, Johnson's treatment of Polish Jewry is generally balanced, occasionally imaginative, but too brief for any overall picture of that community.

Seltzer's *Jewish People, Jewish Thought*

In its aim and scope, Seltzer's *Jewish People, Jewish Thought* possibly does not belong in our list of one-volume histories. The title of the work sums up its major aim, namely 'to address itself to one of the greatest puzzles facing the modern student: that Jewish history is at the same time an account of a people and a religion . . . (p. xi)'. This textbook-type volume probes both the body and mind of Judaism, with more emphasis on the latter. With all this, the section in Seltzer's book on Poland provides a good introduction to the topic for the serious reader, and shows repeatedly Seltzer's abilities as a teacher and expert on East-European Jewry. The parts of his work devoted to historical narrative are concise and economical, yet Seltzer manages in a small space to convey a sense of the historiographical issues at stake and the conflicting views of historians. On all the outstanding issues on the classic agenda of historians of East-European Jewry, we find in Seltzer's treatment a balanced presentation by a professional hand. Thus Seltzer manages in four or five sentences to describe the origins of Polish Jewry and of the charters governing Jewish status, while at the same time setting out the stages of Jewish settlement in Poland, the ethnic origins of Polish Jewry, and the move eastward of the *privilegia* into Poland and Lithuania (pp. 474-5). He relates the anti-Jewish actions of churchmen and Christian townspeople, but reminds the reader that 'these negative pressures were exceptions in a generally propitious environment' (p. 476). The period of the Deluge receives more than adequate treatment, and Seltzer takes pains to catalogue the variety of Jewish responses to the catastrophe. On *Hasidism*, one of the focuses of his narrative, he provides background information on Podolia, the birthplace of *Hasidism* and home of other sectarian movements, and notes the historiographical problems in using the *Shivhei Ha'Besht*, until very recently our only source on the life and career of the Baal Shem Tov (p. 487). The reader also learns that '*Hasidism* was not itself a movement of the uneducated . . .' (p. 493) and further gets at least a hint of the influence of the *Hasidic* movement after its first two generations (pp. 495-6). Seltzer's description of the classical age of Polish rabbinic culture stands in stark contrast to the gloomy views of Roth. Though noting contemporary critiques of the *pilpul* and *hilluk* methods of study and their frequent abuse, Seltzer reminds the reader that these same methods 'made possible a creative participation in rabbinic religious intellectuality, a tearing-down and building-up of subtle argumentation that kept the halakhic tradition alive and flourishing in East Europe' (p. 478). The demographic weight and importance of Polish Jewry is explained as well.

As with almost all the other works under review, the chief drawback to Seltzer's book lies in the chronological cut-off date of his discussion of Polish Jewry, limiting it to the early-modern period. Within its limits, however, *Jewish People, Jewish Thought* has much to recommend it to the general reader.

CONCLUSION

As we have seen, the historical agenda of general Jewish historians regarding Polish Jewry has changed little since the days of Nathan Hannover and Cecil Roth. Some glimmerings of a newer approach can be found here and there. While we realize that the intended audience of such one-volume histories is presumably most interested in Western Jewry, American Jewry, the Holocaust and the rise of Israel, we believe that even within the space available and limitations of subjects, a clearer and more balanced picture of Polish Jewry might deepen the reader's understanding of the other topics. If the Polish chapter of Jewish history is now over, that was not the case in 1800, 1880 or 1930, and any survey of modern Jewish history that treats Polish Jewry as merely a demographic reservoir or group of victims misses much that would inform the reader on the development of the modern Jewish identity. It is in this field that the one-volume history has some catching up to do, to assimilate pre-Holocaust Polish Jewry into the framework of the on-going sweep of Jewish history.

THE TEACHING OF THE HISTORY OF THE JEWS IN SECONDARY SCHOOLS IN THE POLISH PEOPLE'S REPUBLIC, 1949–88

Anna Radziwiłł

The aim of this article is to analyse the nature and extent of material about the history of the Jews taught in 'general secondary schools' from the end of the 1940s to the present day. The word 'taught' is perhaps not precise enough. Since the basic material being considered is curricula and textbooks, it would be more accurate to define the subject of analysis as the material that was 'meant' to be 'taught'. There is no way of knowing how individual teachers put this into practice, what additional information or commentaries were provided to supplement the curriculum and, furthermore, to what extent this information was conveyed to students and how it was received.

At the same time, one has to remember that education at school was not necessarily the only source of information. Facts could also be instilled at home, during catechism or by various publications. The discussion therefore concerns an area of educational policy rather than the actual extent of knowledge of Jewish history possessed by those who completed their secondary education after the war. What interests us is the activity of the 'addressor' rather than the 'addressee', although, of course, some conclusions about the general knowledge, or rather ignorance, of Jewish history should also emerge indirectly from this analysis. It would be very interesting for someone to investigate what the average Pole in 1988 with a secondary education knows about the history and culture of the Jews.

The basic source materials used are the curricula and set history textbooks for general secondary schools from 1949–88. The year 1949 has been taken as a starting point because a completely reformed curriculum was introduced then by the new government (previous programmes had merely modified pre-war curricula). These particular schools were chosen as they are the easiest in which to trace changes in the formulation of material relating to Jewish history during the last forty years and also because their curricula contained the widest material. The differences in material employed by other types of school were determined by educational criteria, and analysing them would therefore contribute little to the subject under discussion.

The Polish Language curriculum has also been considered, since literary texts are a potentially much richer source of information about Jews than history textbooks. Looking at Jewish issues as taught in schools exclusively on the basis of history lessons would not give a complete picture and might perhaps give a false one.

There are obviously great dangers of 'over-interpretation' in such a fragmentary, comparative analysis of set texts and curricula, looking at them on the basis of the treatment of this single issue. The texts concerned are usually very short and in the case of curricula often consist of single sentences. What is more, even differences in choice of information and formulation which appear very important do not necessarily represent the views of their actual authors about the Jews. There are a variety of reasons for this – political, ideological or educational – but all are influenced by general considerations about presenting a particular historical period and not just the Jewish question. One therefore has to be very careful not to fall into pitfalls of the 'elephant and the Polish question' type, or in this case 'the elephant and the Jewish question', and begin to look at everything from the basis of the treatment of the Jewish question.

Differences in formulation are also due to the shape of the curriculum as a whole. For example, the curriculum from 1950 was unusually broad, every theme being developed in enough detail to form the basis of an actual lesson. This is obviously because it was a period when the authorities wanted to maintain the fullest possible control over teaching methods. Constant vigilance was demanded to prevent possible independent action on the part of teachers and, at the same time, there was an almost magical belief in the sanctity of the word and any variation on what was set down was viewed with great suspicion. On the other hand, the curricula from 1956 onwards were more general and shorter, until 1981 when recent history was once again dealt with in more detail. This was a result both of lack of textbooks and because the curriculum was agreed through negotiations between the educational authorities and Solidarity, who hoped to ensure that various issues would be examined in a less biased way.

Limiting oneself to a straightforward description of what was written about Jews in curricula or in textbooks could provide excellent material for both pro-Jewish and anti-semitic propaganda pamphlets. But such an analysis would be thin on facts and would probably give a false picture. The picture would appear especially false to a foreign reader, someone unfamiliar with the nuances of Polish history after the Second World War, not to speak of the country's educational policies. It is, therefore, necessary to make a few additional comments for foreign readers. 'General secondary schools' were four-year schools which, as a result of the 1948 reform, were to be attended by pupils who had completed the seven-year elementary schools. In 1961 the elementary-school course was extended to eight years. Thus in the immediate post-war period secondary schools were attended by pupils from 15 to 18 and later from 16 to 19.

Around 20 per cent of the pupils of elementary schools went on to these secondary schools during the period in question. More or less the same number went on to secondary vocational schools where the history curriculum was similar, but less detailed. The history taught in Polish secondary schools throughout the period consisted both of a general historical overview from ancient times to the twentieth century and of the specific history of Poland (the date at which courses stopped differed). This was an expansion of material taught from the fifth class in elementary schools. The teaching of Polish Language included linguistic studies and the history of Polish literature from the Middle Ages to the present day, together with some aspects of foreign literature.

In the years between 1948 and 1988, the choice and form of material obviously underwent many changes. This began with a complete reform of teaching programmes, including the humanities, in 1949–50. When read today, the curricula drawn up and introduced in schools at that time seem almost surreal in content and language. They were compulsory and underwent no major changes (with the exception of a gradual reduction of material) until the academic year 1956–7. A basic change in content and style appeared after the 'Polish October', that is after 1956. 'Post-October' curricula were further modified in the 1960s in connection with the reform of the school system (the introduction of eight-year elementary schools) and because of ideological and political demands. Subsequent versions of the curricula appeared in 1964, 1967 and 1970 and are not very different. The next, quite fundamental, change did not occur until the beginning of the 1980s. As far as the humanities are concerned, this change was, above all, a result of Solidarity's activities, but was also linked with the general curriculum reform carried out by the education authorities for non-ideological or non-political reasons. History and Polish Language also underwent further changes after the introduction of martial law (13 December 1981), but these are not significant. The curricula presently in use were confirmed in 1986 and are a slightly modified version of those of 1981, with some corrections from the martial law period. Thus as far as the humanities are concerned, one can speak in general terms of 'Stalinist', 'Post-October', 'late-Gomułka', 'Solidarity' and finally the present 'post-Solidarity' curricula.

Changes in the curriculum should, theoretically, also have involved changes in textbooks. In practice, the situation was not so straightforward. Textbooks did not always keep up with the curriculum. Generally speaking, there were three 'waves' of textbooks over this forty-year period:

1950s textbooks (where all general history was taken from Soviet textbooks), the textbooks which appeared in the early 1960s and, finally, the textbooks from the beginning of the 1970s, which are only now being gradually replaced by new, 'fourth-wave' ones. As far as recent history is concerned, from 1981 schools have in fact been 'textbook-less' (with the exception of a book covering the 1939–45 period).

One should also note that textbooks are not necessarily authors' works. Obviously the author is responsible for a book in his name, but this responsibility is more often a 'seal of approval' for a particular interpretation than for its actual creation. This is a significant point, especially in evaluating textbooks, and this is why I have referred to textbook statements rather than those of authors.

To achieve a clearer picture of the history of Jews as taught in schools, the material has been divided into four parts: ancient history, the Middle Ages and early-modern history (to the eighteenth century), the nineteenth and twentieth centuries (to 1939), and finally the Second World War and the Holocaust.

ANCIENT HISTORY

Until the mid-1960s, pupils at general secondary schools were meant to have one lesson on the history of Palestine and ancient history. They were taught in greater or less detail the geographical position of Palestine, its socio-economic structure, the most important political events and its religion (with an explanation of the concepts of monotheism, messianism and the Bible). This information was presented in the same way as that for other ancient eastern civilizations: as something in the distant past that was now over. In the mid-1960s there was a general reduction in the amount of material about antiquity and the subject of Palestine or Judaism was not included. Of course one can speculate on how far this was for educational reasons (the need to reduce material) or non-educational ones (a pretext for removing information about the Bible). Information about the Jewish faith was re-introduced in 1981, but in a different context. The subject of 'Judaism and the Bible' was covered within the context of Catholicism and the origins of Christianity, and was, therefore, part of religious and cultural studies rather than of the history of the Israelites.

One should remember that the whole question of imparting information about ancient Israel is linked, particularly in the Polish situation, more with the attitudes of political decision-making to religion problems in education than with the issue of Jewish history itself. Similarly, in the Solidarity period, many teachers demanded that the 'Bible' should be included as a subject in the curriculum: they were more concerned about acknowledgement of the fact of Christianity's past than about any recognition of the role of Jewish culture. This is one reason to beware of strictly 'Judeo-centric' interpretations.

At present, only the textbook for secondary schools by E. Wipszycka and J. Tazbirowa includes a separate lesson on the history of ancient Palestine and a broad, elegantly-written, section on Judaism and an explanation of how it differed from other religions of the ancient East. Its links with Christianity are also clearly explained. On the other hand, the textbook by J. Dowiat, which was still compulsory in the academic year 1987–8, emphasizes in a chapter entitled 'The Beginnings of Christianity' the formalism and exclusiveness of the Jewish religion.

Of course, one could say that these differences are a result of the context. The description of Judaism in the context of the history of Israel will obviously differ from that in the context of late-Roman Imperialism and the birth of Christianity, that is the Judaism of the Diaspora, but there is surely more to it than this.

The question of presenting the links between Judaism and Christianity in schools is really quite complex. One can argue that discussing Judaism almost exclusively in the context of Christianity legitimises Judaism, and that, in particular, showing how Christianity grew out of Judaism helps, in a Catholic country, to break down certain anti-semitic stereotypes.

THE MIDDLE AGES AND EARLY-MODERN HISTORY (TO THE EIGHTEENTH CENTURY)

Pupils studying general Medieval and Early-Modern History as well as studying Polish History specifically, do not appear to learn anything about Jews at all, according to the various curricula: it is as if the Jews had ceased to exist. One gets the impression that this ancient civilization vanished like that of the Phoenicians. No version of the curriculum contains a single heading or reference to the Jewish population.

It is the same with textbooks in those sections dealing with general history. However, there are some references to Jews in the sections on Polish history. It should be noted here that throughout this whole forty-year period, there were only two versions of the Polish History textbook going up to the eighteenth century for secondary schools, ignoring the work of the early 1950s by G. Missalowa and J. Schoenbrenner, which was to 'serve' pupils from the fourth class of elementary school and then throughout their secondary school.

The first of these two textbooks is by H. Michnik and U. Mosler which was a set book from the late 1950s until 1979. The section on the organization of the Republic in the 16th century mentions that the Jews paid a separate tax and were subject to the authority of the *wojewoda*, and the section on the internal situation of the Republic in the eighteenth century states that they gave loans and took part in the organization of the manufacturing industry.

The Jewish question is discussed at greater length in the context of the Four Year *Sejm* (1788–92) (the activities of the Deputation over Jewish reform), and the speeches of Tadeusz Kościuszko, the leader of the Uprising in 1794, on the issue of treating the Jewish population as full citizens of the Republic.

From 1970, the set textbooks covered general and Polish history in a single volume. These textbooks, since slightly modified, by J. Dowiat, J. Gierowski and J. Leszczyński, are still compulsory today. Only Dowiat's textbook refers to the Jews in Poland, stating that under Casimir the Great in the fourteenth century, they lent money for interest – and that is all. Elementary school textbooks dealing with this period also ignore the Jews.

It might be worth considering the possible causes of this phenomenon, and the ultimate consequences for the pupils' knowledge. The simplest answer to the first question might be that limitations on the amount of material intended for secondary schools means that detailed issues of this sort cannot be included. But this seems an unsatisfactory answer, given that when discussing the ethnic make-up of the Republic in the sixteenth century, or national attitudes in towns in the fifteenth and sixteenth centuries, the textbook mentions Italians, Armenians and Tatars, but there is not a single word about the Jewish population.

It is interesting that there are no references to the Jewish population in Poland before the Partitions (with the exception of the references in Michnik and Mosler), regardless of changes in approach to the internal history of the Republic, including the question of national minorities. There was no mention of the Jewish question from the time of the Stalinist curricula, when there was an obligatory unambiguously negative view of Polish history, until the curricula of the 1980s, in which there is more and more emphasis, almost to the point of apotheosis, on the peaceful coexistence of many nationalities and faiths within the Republic and the state's tolerance. It appears that those who made the decisions thought it was unnecessary in the first, 'black', version to discuss, for example, the pogroms of Jews in the east of the Republic in the seventeenth century (this may have been because they certainly were not conducted by the *szlachta*), or to boast in the second, 'white', version of the exceptional privileges, in the context of Europe at the time, granted to Jews in the thirteenth and fourteenth centuries, or of the real tolerance shown Jews when they were being burned and resettled *en masse* in Spain.

It is worth noting, that in the 1964 and 1966 curricula the sub-heading 'The Republic as a multi-national state' appears under the overall heading 'The Question of Union with Lithuania', which was changed in 1970 to 'The Republic of both Nations'. While the first formulation enables the presentation of the complicated ethnic mosaic of the Noble Republic, the second suggests a political-legal approach.

This complete omission of even a few basic facts about the Jewish population is difficult to explain, but it is surely important for how the general picture of Jewish history in Poland was being formed in pupils' minds. The Jewish population would consequently not be seen as 'old', as an integral part of the Republic's historical landscape when the Republic was at the height of its strength and development. Jews appear only in the period of decline and partition. They are never seen as 'admirable', awarded privileges by the rulers, or having their own *sejms*. And this, inevitably, influences the general 'view' of Jewish history in Poland, although those responsible for the curriculum, not to speak of the pupils, do not realise this.

THE 19TH CENTURY AND INTER-WAR PERIOD

In the material covering the general history of the 19th century and the inter-war period, no version of the curriculum and no textbook mentions the history of the Jews, except for a brief reference in the section on the internal history of the Third Reich. Nothing is even said about decisions relating to the fate of Palestine after the First World War. However, the situation is a little different as far as the history of Poland itself is concerned.

I shall look first at the curricula themselves, bearing in mind the necessary methodological considerations when making comparisons of this sort. The omission of a point in the curriculum does not necessarily mean there is a parallel omission in the textbooks, although, of course, the inclusion of some formulation or phenomenon in the text of the curriculum emphasises its significance. Curricula headings on the history of Poland after the Partitions directly concerning the Jewish population appear only in the versions from the early 1950s. Here 'assimilationist tendencies among Jews and attempts at Polish-Jewish rapprochement' in Russian Poland in the period between the uprisings (mid-nineteenth century) are mentioned. And in the 1981 version, a separate lesson heading appears: 'National relations within the territory of the former Republic' (second half of the nineteenth century and beginning of the twentieth century). The curriculum advises teachers to explain the 'position of the Jews' alongside the development of the national consciousness of Ukrainians, Byelorussians and Lithuanians. In the 1986 version of the curriculum, this note is omitted, and the problem of national relations in the former Polish-Lithuanian Commonwealth is included (without further detail) under the theme 'The socio-economic and national situation in the Polish lands (at the turn of the century)'. Of course, one can again speculate whether it is simply a question of cutting material for educational reasons, or a conscious omission of these problems.

However, in both the 1981 and 1986 versions the curriculum advises that the activities of the *Bund* should be mentioned when discussing the revolution of 1905–7.

In the sections of the curricula listing compulsory material for the history of the Second Republic, no headings directly touch on the Jewish question. The 1981 curriculum which, as I have said, was a special case, having been drawn up after negotiations between the education authorities and Solidarity, is an exception here. The theme, 'The position of the Jewish minority, anti-semitism and its causes', is included under the heading 'The question of national minorities in the Second Republic' which was to form a separate lesson. This heading proved a short-lived one, and does not appear in the 1986 curriculum.

All versions of the curriculum obviously include the question of the national minorities in inter-war Poland. And it is worth comparing the different ways this issue was formulated for they seem to provide a good, if fragmentary, illustration of characteristic changes in attitude to the history of the Second Republic during different phases of educational policy.

In the period before 1956, the list of theme-headings about the history of the Second Republic (discussed until 1952 under the heading 'Education about Poland in the contemporary world'), had the overall title 'Poland in the twenty-year inter-war period (until the September catastrophe)'. The appropriate assessment suggested by this title is unambiguous: the period was to be shown as one leading to ruin. One of the themes included in this list reads 'Poland as an oppressive state and exploiter of national minorities', and in the more detailed development of this theme, the question of the Ukrainians and Byelorussians was given most attention.

From 1957, the formulation used was far more neutral: 'The question of the national minorities'; in 1964 it once again became: 'The intensification of political discrimination against the national minorities' (after 1926). The 1966 curriculum made no changes.

It is worth noting that these curricula included a heading mentioning the development of fascist tendencies in the Second Republic after 1926. Only in 1970 did this become merely 'elements of fascism in the constitution of 1935' and the term 'the authoritarian government of Piłsudski' was introduced. In the 1970 curriculum, instead of the theme on 'political discrimination against national minorities', we find: 'the multi-national character of the state as a source of weakness'. One point under the heading 'The Culture of Inter-war Poland' was 'the education of national minorities'.

As I have said, 1981 saw a return to the 'post-October' formulation. The heading 'The question of national minorities in the Second Republic' again indicated that, besides criticism of the state's policies towards nationalities, it was intended that the national minorities themselves and the attitude of Polish society to them should be studied.

The present curriculum has returned to the more limited heading of 'The Policies of the authorities towards national minorities' but also recommends that their political groupings should be discussed.

It is also worth mentioning that, from 1966, a point was introduced into the curriculum recommending inclusion of the National-Radical Camp (*ONR*) (removed from the present version).

Although teachers do not usually pay attention to such nuances, they show, nevertheless, the intentions of the creators of the curriculum, and so should also be reflected in the contents of textbooks. However, the textbooks have not kept pace with the curricula. In the period before 1956 there was a textbook, called 'Materials for teaching in the eleventh class' (ed. Ż. Kormanowa), only covering the period 1864–1945, whereas the textbook mentioned above by G. Missalowa and J. Schoenbrenner was used for the earlier period, although this was basically meant for the fourth class of elementary school, that is for 10–11 year olds.

From the end of the 1950s to the early 1970s the textbook edited by S. Kieniewicz (covering 1795–1864), and that by H. Sędziwy covering both general and Polish history (from the 1970s to 1945), were compulsory. Subsequent editions were adapted, with sections marked to be covered in specific classes, and partly re-edited (for a short period at the end of the 1960s a textbook was introduced for 1804–1917 on general and Polish history by H. Katz, T. Łepkowski and H. Sędziwy). At the beginning of the 1970s textbooks by A. Galos, J. Gierowski and J. Leszczyński (from 1815 to the 1870s) were issued, and are still set texts, with some changes, as well as R. Wapiński's textbook for the period from the end of the nineteenth century till after the Second World War. R. Wapiński's textbook was removed because of the events of 1981 (a decision taken by the education authorities together with the author) and a new one has not been produced (with the exception of the textbook for the period 1939–45).

In the textbook edited by Kormanowa pupils learn that anti-semitism was above all 'spread by reaction' (material on the pogroms organized by the Tsarist government in Siedlce and Białystok in 1905–6, the 'unleashing of an anti-semitic campaign' by the National Democracy, the anti-semitic demagogy of the *ONR*). At the same time, the textbook emphasizes that there was solidarity in the labour movement between Polish and Jewish workers. The *Bund* is described as 'petty bourgeois, nationalistic and conciliatory', but nothing is said about its activities. There is also a reference to the *PPS* activist S. Mendelsohn joining the 'Zionist' party – the term is not explained but from the context it appears to be something negative. The general narrative of this textbook is full of value judgments rather than information: the intention is to emphasize the darker side of the 'pre-revolutionary' period, and history appears as the history of class struggle and economic interests. None the less, it must be stressed that schoolchildren in the first half of the 1950s were taught about anti-semitism and anti-Jewish activities in Poland though in rather a strange context: for example the party which represented 'nationalism' was said to be the Polish Socialist Party.

In the period after October, subsequent textbook versions mention briefly, in the material covering Polish history from 1795 to 1864, the reform of A. Wielopolski which introduced equal rights for Jews. The textbook edited by Kieniewicz also mentions the number of Jews in the Polish Kingdom – and that is all. The Jewish issue appears, and then in a limited form, only when a later period is under discussion.

Of course, all the textbooks mention that the programme of the National-Democratic Movement contained anti-semitic slogans, but only R. Wapiński's textbook attempts to explain this phenomenon. He mentions the economic competition between the Polish and other, mainly Jewish, bourgeoisie and the rejection of assimilationist slogans, adding that relevant to this was 'the fact that most of the Jewish population maintained a very important cultural separation and were also indifferent to Polish national affairs' (p. 42). It is also maintained that the situation was made worse by 'the developing Jewish national movement, and particularly the growing nationalistic tendencies within it in the shape of Zionism' (p. 42). It should be noted that no further explanations are provided about this last term. It is also characteristic that only Sędziwy's textbook of 1961 contains anything about pogroms organized with the blessing of the authorities during the 1905–7 revolution (though much less detailed than in the textbook edited by Kolmanowa). Subsequent textbooks say nothing at all on the subject.

In discussing Poland in the inter-war period none of the editions of Sędziwy's textbook gives the number of Jews in the newly-established state. The first edition (1961) mentions the anti-semitic programme of the *Endecja* and the rapprochement between the *Sanacja* Camp of National Unity and the National Radical Camp over the 'racism and anti-semitism' propagated by the latter and its anti-semitic actions at institutions of higher education, claiming that most of the population were disgusted by them. The second edition (1967) contains no separate information about the *ONR*, and only mentions the demand for a *numerus clausus*, the economic boycott of the Jews and even pogroms incited by the National Democracy. It should be remembered that, in both versions, the internal history of the Second Republic is necessarily presented as a gradual 'growth of fascist tendencies', a term used to describe the activities of both the National Camp and the Piłsudski Camp.

Wapiński's textbook is slightly different in emphasis. Both anti-semitism and 'growth of fascism' are ignored. The anti-semitic slogans in the programme of the Camp of Great Poland and the 'anti-semitic' atrocities organized by the National Radical Camp are mentioned in a single sentence, together with the arrest of the leaders by the government. 'Fascisizing' tendencies are spoken of (instead of the earlier term 'fascist'), and these are linked more with the activities of the National Camp than the *Sanacja*. The structural tendencies in Poland in the 1930s are described by the term 'totalization'.

Given the present lack of a secondary-school textbook covering the period 1864–1939, it is worth checking what is said about the Jews in set textbooks for elementary schools, published in the mid-1980s. The textbook for the fifth class, by J. Skowronek, presents the role of the Jews in the ideology of Polish nationalism in some depth (in the glossary provided at the end the term 'anti-semitism' is explained: 'hostility, hatred to Jews, usually incited and fed in a conscious and organised way' p. 234). The author attempts to explain the origins of anti-semitism, mentioning the 'separate and large Jewish sector' in Poland and economic competition which might have caused anti-Jewish attitudes amongst part of Polish society. The account is accompanied by a reproduction of a Grotger sketch, showing characteristic 19th-century Jewish types.

The textbook for the eighth class, by A. L. Szcześniak, contains a sub-chapter on national minorities in the Second Republic, a large part of which concerns the Jewish population. The author explains, as if filling the gaps in textbooks for earlier periods, that the Jews had come to Poland centuries ago when they were 'persecuted in other countries'; he also writes about the resettlement of the Jewish population from central Russia in the eastern borderlands of the former Republic. Statistics are included illustrating the 'ethnic make-up' of the inhabitants of the larger border towns, showing the high percentage of Jews who significantly outnumbered the Poles. In general, the pupil is left with an impression of the relatively large number of Jews in Poland. However, the cultural and religious distinctiveness of the Jewish people and their relations with the Polish population are ignored completely.

In describing the political groupings in the Second Republic after 1926, the textbook has a strangely worded reference to the Camp for a Greater Poland (*OWP*), saying that it 'propagated anti-semitism and turned it into a struggle' (p. 98). Any pupil reading this would be unsure what was meant.

It is worth considering what were the intentions of the educational authorities expressed in subsequent versions of the curriculum and textbooks and how these affected the students' perception of the Jewish question. The information imparted to pupils can be divided into two kinds: 'quantitive' information and material about anti-semitism. On the whole, there seems to have been gradually less emphasis on the anti-semitism. This appears to have been the result of the process of the so-called recantation of the image of Poland's past, or rather its presentation in a more favourable light, especially in the period of the Second Republic.

All information about Jews is always seen in relative terms- within the context of Polish attitudes to them. The participation of the Jews (or people of Jewish extraction) in the political and cultural life of the Polish nation is completely omitted. Pupils are told nothing about the attitude of Jews to Poles and Poland; only Wapiński's textbook clearly places Jewish society outside the Polish one, emphasizing its separateness and indifference to Polish affairs. Other textbooks ignore the subject. However, pupils would learn about this by reading Polish literature, and this is certainly important for an understanding of many aspects of Polish culture.

The life and culture of the Jewish population nowhere merit even the briefest descriptions. Thus, metaphorically speaking, the Jews are silent and absent, while the Poles who are present are those who do not particularly like this mysterious people.

THE SECOND WORLD WAR

For obvious reasons the fate of Jews during the Second World War is dealt with in a similar fashion in all the textbooks. All versions include the annihilation of the Jewish people and the nature of Jewish resistance (the Warsaw Ghetto Uprising). However, the context for these themes changes and the textbooks describe them in different ways. The heading 'Education about Poland and the contemporary world' of 1950 (the Second World War period was included under this heading until 1952) contained the point: 'the extermination of the Jews' (this term sounded wrong and by 1951 had been replaced by 'the murder of the Jews') and advised that the 'poisoning of [Polish] consciousness by racist propaganda' should be discussed; it also included: 'the uprising in the Warsaw Ghetto', which was next to: 'the collaboration of the *AK* leadership with the Germans' – an interesting juxtaposition.

Instructions in the curriculum of 1957, under the theme 'The Occupation', advised discussion of 'the persecution and annihilation of the Jews'. The heading 'the resistance movement in Poland', which in any case contained a strange mixture of material, included the 'uprising in the Warsaw Ghetto' (in the following context: 'The most important military organizations: *AK*, *GL*, *BCh*, *AL*. Diversion and sabotage. The Partisans. *ZWM* 'Grey Ranks'. Secret education. The uprising in the Warsaw Ghetto. The Warsaw Uprising').

The 1964 curriculum also spoke of 'the annihilation of the Jews'. Under the heading 'The main resistance movements in Poland and their class structure', and especially in the section devoted to the 'left', we find 'the uprising in the Warsaw Ghetto' just after headings on the *PPR*, The

Union for Struggle of Youth (*ZWM*), People's Guard (*GL*) and Peasant Battalions (*BCh*) (this remained unchanged in the 1966 version).

In the 1970 curriculum, the theme: 'The resistance movement in Poland' was separate from headings concerning the political structure of the underground and consisted of a list of types of resistance. In this context appeared: 'Uprisings in the ghettos', and immediately after 'Aid to the Jews – *Żegota*', '*GL* actions'. But the approach to the Second World War period changed quite drastically in the 1981 curriculum. Among subjects of interest in the situation after September 1939 are noted 'The annihilation of the Jews. The annihilation of the gypsies'. And under the heading 'The resistance movement' appear: 'The resistance movement in the ghettos. The uprising in the Warsaw Ghetto. *ŻOB*, aid to the Jews – *Żegota*'.

The 1986 curriculum retains the reference to the annihilation of the Jews and Gypsies and, under the theme: 'Fighting Poland', includes the point: 'The uprising in the Warsaw Ghetto – aid to the fighting Jews'. It is probably not insignificant that the phrase regarding aid to all Jews, and not only to those 'fighting', has disappeared.

What about the contents of textbooks? As I have said, the differences here are greater. The textbook, edited by Kormanowa, from the early 1950s contains a lengthy description of the persecution and extermination of the Jewish population and states at the same time that 'Polish reactionaries' 'supported [Hitler's] barbaric racist policies' (p. 393). One should remember that in this textbook 'Polish reactionaries' include all groups except the *PPR*; as the text claims, the *émigré* government 'was preparing a return to fascism in Poland after the war' (p. 396). The textbook discusses the uprising in the Warsaw Ghetto in some detail, claiming that 'the *PPR* organized the resistance movement in the ghetto', and its activities 'brought about the establishment of *ŻOB*' (pp. 413–4). According to the textbook, the only organization aiding the uprising was the People's Guard (*GL*). The description of the uprising ends with the statement that it acted as a spur for the spread of armed struggle throughout the country, 'restrained in vain by the *Delegatura* and the *AK*' (p. 414).

I have looked at the textbook edited by Kormanowa separately because of its peculiarities. It is worth attempting, however, a detailed comparative analysis of four different versions of textbooks from the post-1956 period. These are those by H. Sędziwy (1961 and 1967 editions), R. Wapiński (1st edition, 1969), and finally T. Siergiejczyk (1st edition, 1986). To make the comparisons more straightforward one can identify three basic issues: the description of the persecution and annihilation of the Jews, the Jewish resistance movement and, finally, the question of Polish attitudes to the Jewish Holocaust. All the textbooks discuss these problems, but in quite different ways and on different scales.

The description of the growing persecution of the Jewish population, the situation in the ghettos and the gradual annihilation, is presented in three of the textbooks. Only Wapiński's textbook completely omits this issue (!), limiting itself to laconic remarks that around 6,028,000 Polish citizens perished 'including 2.7 to 3 million Jews and persons recognized as Jews by the Nazi authorities' (p. 73).

The first edition of Sędziwy's textbook names the concentration camps to which 'the Nazis brought the condemned from all over Europe' (p. 207). There is no indication that the latter were mainly Jews, but it is stressed elsewhere that mostly Jews were annihilated in camps such as Bełżec or Treblinka and that over 2 million Jews were killed in Oświęcim.

The second version of the textbook differentiates between 'concentration camps' and 'mass death camps'. This distinction disappears in R. Wapiński's textbook. In the present set textbook by Siergiejczyk the context suggests that all camps (including Birkenau, Chełmno, Bełżec, Sobibór, Treblinka) were meant mainly for Poles. The term 'concentration and death camp' is used or 'mass death camp'. At the end of the book it says, 'The physical losses of the Polish nation in 1939–45'-these came to 6.028 million (!). On the whole, there is a tendency, especially in the two later textbooks, to juxtapose facts so that the exceptional fate of the Jews is not apparent; for example the textbook used at present contains a chapter headed 'The extermination of the Polish, Jewish and Gypsy population'.

In presenting the problems of the Jewish resistance movement there are notable differences in the textbooks. These are determined to a large extent by differences in the general approach to the issue of the resistance movement. Sędziwy's textbooks of 1961 and 1967 discuss the *ŻOB* uprising in 1942, mentioning Anielewicz, then briefly describe the fighting in the ghetto, and at the end of a sub-chapter state 'the uprising in the Warsaw ghetto was the first mass armed action of the resistance movement in Poland against the Nazis' (p. 220, p. 258 in the 1967 edition). When compared with the pre-1956 textbooks, only the phrase about the *AK*'s attempts to restrain this resistance has been omitted.

To understand such an account of events, one must realise that the obligatory description of the Polish resistance movement made this type of generalisation necessary. Hardly any information is given about the struggle organized by the Polish underground, except for that by the communist underground. Various underground structures are said to have existed 'separately', but no clear picture is given of what they were doing, except that all these claimed there were 'two enemies' (that is Germany and the USSR), and that society was 'separate' from the underground and organized various forms of struggle against the occupier. Finally the *PPR*, *GL*, and *ŻWM* are also said to have existed 'separately' and conducted active organized struggle. Against this background the uprising in the ghetto, according to the textbook, is clearly part of the 'left'.

It should also be added that the 1967 edition of Sędziwy's textbook states that 'the blow' to the activities of the *GL* in 1943 forced the *AK* to be more active.

Wapiński's textbook unprecedentedly cuts short the description of the Ghetto Uprising. There is not a single word about *ŻOB* or Anielewicz. It merely says that an uprising was begun by 'the ghetto population' and then immediately goes on to describe help given by the Poles. There is therefore more on Polish aid than on the Jewish struggle. The present set textbook, by Siergiejczyk, mentions, for the first time, the difficult problem of the passivity of 'a significant number' of Jews, explaining it by the treacherous Nazi propaganda. The paragraph describing the ghetto uprising begins with the rather peculiar phrase 'a specific kind of fighting of the Polish underground was the undertaking in 1943 of battle with the occupier by Polish Jews enclosed in ghettos' (p. 199). The Jewish National Committee, the Jewish Army Union and *ŻOB* are mentioned but the subject of Polish aid is usually stressed rather than the description of the uprising. However, the attempts at resistance in the ghettos of Białystok, Wilno, Krzemieniec, and in Treblinka, are also mentioned.

Both Wapiński's and Siergiejczyk's textbooks ignore the exceptional role of the uprising. In the former, this appears to be because of the general tendency to limit what is said about the Jewish situation during the Second World War; in the latter, it would have appeared out of place against the background of the broad and detailed description of the Polish armed resistance's successes which precedes information about the ghetto uprising.

The amount written about Polish aid to Jews in subsequent textbooks gradually increases. Both versions of Sędziwy's textbooks limit themselves to saying that *ŻOB* made contact 'with Polish armed organisations outside the ghetto walls', with the addition in 1961 of 'particularly with the *GL*' (p. 219): this addition is omitted in the 1967 version.

Wapiński's textbook claims that the uprising 'met with the support of the whole democratic Polish underground, which from the beginning of the occupation gave the Jewish population all-round help' (p. 94). *Żegota* and its activities are also mentioned, as is an extract from the decree by the governor of the Warsaw district, L. Fischer, dated 10 November 1941, imposing the death sentence on Poles helping Jews.

The current textbook by Siergiejczyk mentions the existence of the Jewish police and the *Żagiew* organization formed by the Gestapo but also mentions the Polish *szmalcownicy*, claiming that the activities of the latter 'met with the general condemnation of the Polish people' (p. 158) and were punished by the Polish underground. Information is also included about aid to the Warsaw Ghetto rebels by the *GL* and the *AK* and the activities of *Żegota*: 'Of the 200,000 Jews saved by Polish society, the majority owe their survival to the activities of *Żegota*' (p. 205).

Again it is worth trying to make a few general points about the way Jewish problems during the Second World War are taught. The following points should be borne in mind: first, all curricula and textbooks tend not to let the extermination and martyrdom of the Jewish population overshadow the martyrdom of the Poles. It is not clear when and how this very harmful conviction arose, that to describe the exceptional nature of the Jewish Holocaust – which in no way lessens the terrible persecution of the Polish nation by the Germans – would detract from the memory of murdered Poles. However, this contest over martyrdom does seem to affect the content of textbooks. Problems also arise over describing the Jewish resistance movement. In the early 1950s, as I have said, the need to condemn totally the entire non-communist underground movement produced a strange paradox: the Jewish resistance movement was portrayed almost as an inspiration to the Polish resistance. This approach obviously disappeared later, but the difficult problem remained of showing how the Jewish resistance movement was an integral part of the Polish resistance.

There is also a difficulty of emphasis when describing the passivity of the majority of the Jewish population and the desperate heroism of the fighting groups. There are added complications when discussing the extent of Polish aid to the Jews on the one hand and phenomena such as *szmalcownicy* or the looting of former Jewish properties on the other.

When comparing subsequent textbooks, it is fair to state that a tendency can be identified, similar to that mentioned in the description of the Second Republic, which concentrates increasingly, for example, on Polish aid to Jews. At the same time it has to be admitted that there is also a movement towards simply providing a fuller picture of the Occupation and indicating at least its complicated problems when there were both collaborators and heroes. One could criticize Siergiejczyk's textbook for not providing information about Polish collaborators alongside that about the Jewish organisation *Żagiew* which collaborated with the Nazis. This is surely linked with the tendency to try to assess the Polish nation positively.

The strikingly little that is said about the Holocaust in Wapiński's textbook is a separate issue. The first edition of this textbook appeared in 1969, and the date provides a strong temptation to give this a political interpretation, but there is insufficient evidence to do so. One can assert, however, that the peculiar 'lack' of Jews in the picture of Poland before the Second World War presented to pupils makes it difficult for them to appreciate the exceptional nature of the Holocaust.

These are the main ways in which the issues of Jewish history are presented in history as taught in schools. On the whole, it seems clear that, apart from the well-known subject of the Jewish Holocaust, pupils are simply unaware of any other issues. If one asked a product of a secondary school, of whatever age, what he was taught in history lessons about the

Jews the reply would probably be: nothing. This does not mean that pupils do not come across Jewish history at all, or more precisely the history of Jews in Poland. They tend to do so in literature rather than the curriculum or textbook. In such works as *Pan Tadeusz* or *Lalka* (The Doll), *Przedwiośnie* (Before the Spring), or *Wesele* (The Wedding), which are part of the permanent literary canon in schools, pupils meet Jewish characters, simply because Jewish society existed in Poland for centuries and is obviously portrayed in Polish literature. The image of Jews in Polish literature is a completely different question, and beyond the scope of this article, but it is worth tracing how the issues of Jewish history and culture have been dealt with in Polish Language curricula during the periods under discussion. It appears that there have been similar tendencies to those found in the teaching of History.

The most important element of the Polish Language curriculum is the list of set works, and it would therefore be useful to compare works included and omitted during this forty-year period which directly mention the situation of Jews.

In the 1950s in the eighth class (when students have not yet begun literary history) – students were to familiarize themselves with journalistic articles and essays about 'the struggle for Jewish equality' conducted by Polish Positivists, then with sections from K. Brandys's novel *Samson* and Z. Nałkowska's *Medaliony* (Medallions) about the Jewish Holocaust; M. Konopnicka's novel *Mendel Gdański* (Mendel of Gdańsk), describing Polish-Jewish relations at the turn of the century and the birth of anti-semitism, were studied in elementary school.

The systematic course of literary history included the study of Norwid's poem 'Polish Jews', with an interpretative note that it was to be read as 'a protest against racial discrimination'. The list of supplementary texts included Mickiewicz's *Skład Zasad* with its beautiful invocation of the Jewish nation.

A compulsory work on the reading list for the Positivist period was E. Orzeszkowa's *Meir Ezofowicz* (the curriculum advised drawing attention to 'the portrayal of Jewish society indicating its social stratification; assimilationist tendencies'). In the eleventh class Wl. Broniewski's poem 'To Polish Jews' was compulsory.

The curriculum of 1957 greatly reduced the number of set texts: *Samson*, Norwid's poem and *Skład Zasad* (List of Principles) were omitted, and *Meir Ezofowicz* was transferred to the list of supplementary texts; A. Rudnicki's stories-literature directly about the Jews – were added to the latter. In the section on the Positivist period the curriculum advised discussing 'the struggle with anti-semitism and clericalism', which was quite an original juxtaposition.

In the new curriculum of 1964, there are no works until the tenth class dealing directly with the Jewish situation. Interestingly enough *Meir*

Ezofowicz has even been removed from the list of supplementary texts. Only in the eleventh class does Brandys's *Samson* return as a supplementary text and the remaining stories by Rudnicki (from the volume *Żywe i martwe morze* (Live and Dead Seas)). In the 1971 curriculum, so far as issues of interest are concerned, in the first class Z. Kosidowski's *Opowieści biblijne* (Biblical Texts) is introduced into the supplementary list (of course this was because of their anti-religious tone and not because of material on Jewish culture), while *Samson* was removed from the programme for the fourth class. However, T. Borowski's concentration camp tales have been added to the list of compulsory works.

From 1981 the curriculum was reworked, interpretative guidelines were considerably reduced, and the list of works to choose from was lengthened (e.g. the list of supplementary texts included *Skład Zasad*, *Meir Ezofowicz*, *Mendel Gdański*, *Sklepy cinamonowe* (Cinnamon Shops) by Bruno Schulz, J. Korczak's *Diary* describing the ghetto, J. Stryjkowski's *Austeria* (The Inn) and *Głosy w ciemności* (Voices in Darkness) about Jewish society on the eastern borderlands at the beginning of the 20th century, Rudnicki's stories and Hanna Krall's reportage on the ghetto uprisings.

In 1983 there were certain editorial changes, which were nevertheless quite symptomatic since they show how small quasi-editorial changes can conceal very basic intentional changes. It might be worth citing two examples: in the guidelines for 1981 one finds: 'E. Orzeszkowa – a choice of novel (e.g. *Nad Niemnem* (By the Niemen), *Meir Ezofowicz*, *Cham* (The Boor), *Dziurdziowie*)'; in 1983: 'E. Orzeszkowa – *Nad Niemnen* or another novel (e.g. *Meir Ezofowicz*, *Cham*, *Dziurdziowie*)'. Another example, in 1981: 'M. Konopnicka – a *novella* (e.g. *Mendel Gdansk*, *Miłosierdzie gminy* (The Mercy of the Commune))' and in 1983–'M. Konopnicka– a chosen *novella* (e.g. *Miłosierdzie gminy*, *Mendel Gdański*)'. In 1983 A. Rudnicki's stories and Stryjkowski's *Głosy w ciemności* were removed from the list of supplementary texts.

In the present curriculum, introduced in 1986, *Meir Ezofowicz* had been definitely transferred to the supplementary reading list, and the *novella Mendel Gdański* has been removed, as have Korczak's *Diary* and Krall's reportages.

Thus it is clear that in the Polish Language curriculum, like that for history, most of the literature dealing directly with the subject of Jews appeared in the early 1950s and then in the Solidarity period, although one should beware, as stated earlier, of over-interpretation when making these general statements. As far as twentieth-century literature is concerned, the removal of Hanna Krall's reportages, for example, in 1983 could be linked more with the author's political views than the theme of the actual reportages; again the introduction of Schulz's prose would have been impossible in the 1950s because it did not comply with the demands of 'realism'. There are numerous examples, but the point is to discover the many and complex causes for changes in the list of set texts. None the less, certain changes seem to show the intentions of the curriculum setters and are, in general, the same tendencies apparent in the teaching of history, especially in textbook content.

The material offered to show how the presentation of Jewish history appeared, and appears, in history teaching in secondary schools (the cursory analysis of the Polish Language programme was simply supplementary to the main theme) indicates that there are no sharply delineated stages between the different treatments of Jewish history. Such stages do appear clearly in the general concept of history courses in schools and also the interpretation of many concrete problems or whole periods, but changes in material concerning Jewish history are not so evident and are as a rule symptoms of wider tendencies, which have been indicated above.

Pupils were given most information about Jewish history, especially most recent history, during the period of the 'Stalinist' and 'Solidarity' curricula (no textbook appeared for the latter). The least information was provided in the curricula and textbooks of the 1970s.

Throughout the whole forty-year period the extent of information in school material about the history of the Jews was and is very limited. The picture of the Jews' fate is one-sided, but free of negative connotations – with one proviso (which I have mentioned already), that is the textbooks of Wapiński and Siergiejczyk.

In surveying the material presented here as a whole, it is worth considering three questions: the role of school education, the need to know about the history and culture of the Jews for those generations educated in Poland after the Second World War, and the importance of the problem of anti-semitism.

The minimal amount of information, amounting to mere references to the history of the Jews, which appears in the school history course (independently of prevailing political attitudes) might lead one to conclude that what is taught in schools bears no relation to what an average person with secondary education knows about the Jewish past. But this is surely not the case. Education tends to produce a body of facts which are not quickly forgotten; general 'views' of events, certain stereotypes and a series of automatic connections are produced in the minds of pupils in a way they often do not fully realize. Positive or negative connotations tend to be remembered rather than concrete examples. It is precisely through lack of information, or its selectivity, presenting events through the context in which these few details are given or through the language used, that the school history course forms a certain general 'view' of a given problem. The extent of material is identified with the way it is given. At the same time the introductory nature of school history courses makes any subtle evaluation or explanation of complicated or controversial problems almost impossible.

It is probable therefore that although, or perhaps because, the curriculum contains so little information about Jews, education influences the formation of the above view of the history of the Jews. This image, to put it very simply, would lead to a picture of a society that was persecuted and dying out. Jews 'appear' in Polish history in the 19th century, fulfilling a vague role (previously they had demonstrated a certain amount of economic activity); there are large numbers of them and they are persecuted for reasons which are not at all clear. This image remains throughout the Second Republic and it is not until the Second World War that something more is learnt about them. The aspect of their history covered in most detail is their annihilation. Although I have consciously overstated the whole problem, it seems that such a general 'view' does indeed persist as a result of teaching.

All this begs the question whether such an 'overview' is sufficient and whether the thesis about the need for wider knowledge of Jewish history in Poland can be justified. The specific issue is that of the history of Jews in Poland, for knowledge of Jewish history in other countries is linked with the separate issue of the role of general history in education and is beyond the scope of this article.

A basic and also very complicated problem arises here: how far the history of Jews in Poland is an integral part of Polish history (I will leave on one side the debate over whether the subject 'Polish history' concerns Poland, the Polish state, the Polish nation or Polish society). This problem is very difficult to solve, not least because neither the Jewish nor the Polish side seems to have a clear view about it.

Leaving on one side even this probably unanswerable question, it can be said that over a long period of time many rich centres of Jewish religious and cultural life developed in Poland, that a large part of the world's Jewish population resided there, that kinds of Jewish parliaments were established there and that hasidism was born there. For centuries Jews played a large (whether positive or negative) role in Polish society, although they maintained their separateness from it for the most part. Many people of Jewish descent took part in, and continue to contribute to, the Polish historical, cultural and spiritual achievement. Finally, Poland became the site of Jewish martyrdom. When one adds the fact that the problem of relations to Jews and 'the Jewish question' is still alive in Polish society, then all these phenomena can surely be seen as providing sufficient justification to state that, though the history of Jews may not be an integral part of Polish history, elementary knowledge about the history and culture of Jews should be an integral part of historical education in Polish schools. It is not only a question of extent of knowledge but of its content. Jewish history cannot be approached in a relative manner, that is by looking at their role exclusively in relation to Polish history, or – as in current curricula – the attitudes of Polish society to Jews. Jewish culture and traditions should be a separate theme, even if only covered very generally, and the history of Jews in Poland should be looked at, if only in certain parts of the material, from their point of view. This, of course, would significantly undermine the present model of Jews as passive victims of persecution.

This approach harms neither the autonomy of the history of the Jewish nation nor the character of Polish history. Describing Poland's past without the presence of the Jews is like describing the past of a completely different country. Not so very long ago, at the end of the 1960s, it was said by an official spokesman, that people should choose to be either a Jew or a Pole, and that there was no room for 'Polish Jews'. If there is no room for them, then there is no room for history itself. That there is a peculiar, though perhaps understandable, attitude on the part of many Poles of Jewish descent to their own genealogy is a separate issue.

No discussion of issues of Jewish history can avoid the problem of anti-semitism. It seems to me that the problem should be discussed in schools as thoroughly as possible, and should be above all explained. Of course the issue is a very difficult and delicate one. On the one hand there is the fear of 'offending' the Poles. It is no accident that Polish anti-semitism was most forcefully exposed during the early 1950s, when the dark side of Poland's past was concentrated on and everything could be blamed on unspecified 'reactionary' forces. On the other hand, attempts to explain the origins of Polish anti-semitism are often treated as actual manifestations of anti-semitism. Attempts to explain the causes of anti-semitic views are sometimes interpreted as attempts to justify them. According to these critics, anti-semitism should be the object not of explanation but only of condemnation. I think that one should move away from these very harmful approaches and begin to accustom pupils, that is young people still undergoing education, to rational thought rather than to making judgments.

This article is neither intended as an accusation of anyone nor to provoke old arguments or Polish-Jewish hostilities. But I think that they are unavoidable, for there are too many constitutive elements which have never been completely analyzed. However, they should be approached calmly, one should try to see that they do not impoverish or falsify what, roughly speaking, we like to call 'historical truth'. Finally, it seems to me, that a useful continuation of this article would be to trace how Jewish history in Poland has been drawn in the many syntheses of Polish history which have appeared in post-war Poland.

BIBLIOGRAPHY

Only those works directly referred to are listed below.

History curricula

Historia. Program nauki w 11–letniej szkole ogólnokształcącej. Projekt (History. Curriculum for the 11-year general school. Project), Warsaw: PZWS, 1950. Ministry of Education.

Nauka o Polsce i świecie współczesnym. Nauka o społeczeństwie. Program nauki w 11–letniej szkole ogólnokształcącej (The study of Poland and the contemporary world. Social Studies. Curriculum for the 11-year general school), Warsaw: PZWS, 1950. Ministry of Education.

Historia. Instrukcja programowa dla szkół ogólnokształcących na rok szkolny 1957/8–klasy VIII-XI (History. Curriculum notes for general schools for the academic year 1957/8-class VIII-XI), Warsaw: PZWS, 1957. Ministry of Education.

Historia. Program nauczania Liceum Ogólnokształcącego (klasy VIII-XI) (History. Curriculum for general secondary schools [class VIII-XI]). Warsaw: PZWS 1964. Ministry of Education.

Historia. Program nauczania Liceum Ogólnokształcącego. Klasy I-IV (Tymczasowy) (History. Curriculum for general secondary schools. Class I-IV [Temporary]), Warsaw: PZWS, 1966. Ministry of Education.

Historia. Program nauczania Liceum Ogólnokształcącego. Klasy I-IV (Tymczasowy) (History. Curriculum for general secondary schools. Class I-IV [Temporary]), Warsaw: PZWS, 1970. Ministry of Education and Higher Education.

Historia. Program nauczania Liceum Ogólnokształcącego. Klasy I-IV (History. Curriculum for general secondary schools. Class I-IV), Warsaw: WSiP, 1981. Ministry of Education. School Curriculum Institute.

Historia. Program Liceum Ogólnokształcącego oraz Liceum Zawodowego i Technikum (History. General secondary, vocational and technical school curricula), Warsaw: WSiP, 1986. Ministry of Education. School Curriculum Institute.

Polish Language curricula

Język Polski. Program nauki w 11–letniej ogólnokształcącej. Projekt (Polish Language. Curriculum for 11-year general schools. Project.) Warsaw: PZWS, 1961. Ministry of Education.

Język Polski. Instrukcja programowa dla Liceum Ogólnokształcącego. Kl. VIII-XI (Polish Language. Curriculum notes for general secondary schools. Class VIII-XI), Warsaw: PZWS, 1957. Ministry of Education.

Język Polski. Program nauczania Liceum Ogólnokształcącego (kl. VIII-XI) (Polish Language. Curriculum for general secondary schools [class VIII-XI]), Warsaw: PZWS, 1964. Ministry of Education.

Język Polski. Program nauczania Liceum Ogólnokształcącego (kl. I-IV) (Polish Language. Curriculum for general secondary schools [class I-IV]), Warsaw: PZWS, 1971. Ministry of Education and Higher Education.

Język Polski. Instrukcja programowa dla Liceum i Technikum (Polish Language. Curriculum notes for secondary and technical schools), Warsaw: WSiP, 1981. Ministry of Education. School Curriculum Institute.

Język Polski. Program Liceum Ogólnokształcącego, Technikum i Liceum Zawodowego (Polish

Language. General secondary, technical and secondary vocational school curricula), Warsaw: WSiP, 1983. Ministry of Education. School Curriculum Institute.

Język Polski. Program Liceum Ogólnokształcącego, Liceum Zawodowego i Technikum (Polish Language. General secondary, vocational and technical school curricula), Warsaw: WSiP, 1986. Ministry of Education. School Curriculum Institute.

Textbooks

G. Missalowa and J. Schoenbrenner, *Historia Polski* (Warsaw, 1951), 1st Edition.

Ż. Kormanowa, ed., *Historia Polski 1864–1945. Materiały do nauczania w kl.XI* (Warsaw, 1953), 3rd edition.

H. Michnik and L. Mosler, *Historia Polski do r. 1795* (Warsaw, 1961), 6th edition.

S. Kieniewicz, T. Łepkowski, W. Łukaszewicz, T. Mencel, *Historia Polski 1795–1864* (Warsaw, 1961), 6th edition.

H. Sędziwy, *Historia dla kl.XI. Cz.I. Od Komuny Paryskiej do końca I wojny światowej* (Warsaw, 1963), 4th edition.

H. Sędziwy, *Historia dla kl.XI, Cz.II. Od końca I wojny śiatowej do konferencji w Poczdamie* (Warsaw, 1964), 3rd edition.

H. Katz, T. Łepkowski, H. Sędziwy, *Historia 1804–1917* (Warsaw, 1967), 1st edition.

H. Sędziwy, *Historia dla kl.XI. Od Wielkiej Socjalistycznej Rewolucji Październikowej do końca II wojny światowej* (Warsaw, 1967), 1st edition.

J. Dowiat, *Historia dla kl.I liceum ogólnokształcącego* (Warsaw, 1985), 7th revised edition.

J. Gierowski and J. Leszczyński, *Historia dla kl.II liceum ogólnokształcącego* (Warsaw, 1984), 13th edition.

A. Galos, J. Gierowski, J. Leszczyński, *Historia dla kl.III liceum ogólnokształcącego. Cz.I* (Warsaw, 1977), 7th edition.

R. Wapiński, *Historia dla kl.III liceum ogólnokształcącego Cz.II* (Warsaw, 1977), 9th edition.

R. Wapiński, *Historia dla kl.IV liceum ogólnokształcącego* (Warsaw, 1977), 9th edition.

T. Siergiejczyk, *Dzieje najnowsze 1939–1945. Historia dla szkół średnich* (Warsaw, 1986), 1st edition. J. Skowronek, *Historia. Do Niepodległej. Podręcznik dla klasy siódmej szkoły podstawowej* (Warsaw, 1987), 2nd revised and supplemented edition.

A.L. Szcześniak, *Historia. Polska i świat naszego wieku lata 1918–1939. Książka pomocnicza dla klasy ósmej szkoły podstawowej* (Warsaw, 1986), 2nd revised edition.

WORKS IN HEBREW ON THE HISTORY OF THE JEWS IN INTER-WAR POLAND
David Engel

When Edward Wynot published his pioneering article in 1971 on the Jewish question in Polish politics during the post-Piłsudski years, he observed that 'there is surprisingly little reliable material' on the history of inter-war Polish Jewry.[1] In the sixteen years since then, this gap has been largely filled. Indeed, in the past decade alone, several serious books dealing entirely or in part with aspects of this history have appeared in Western languages or in Polish.[2] Happily these works have attracted widespread attention and have been discussed at some length in scholarly journals throughout the world.

There is, though, another group of works on the same subject, no less serious and no less important than any of these, that has received hardly any significant comment in international academic circles. This group consists of books by Israeli historians, written and published in Hebrew. Among the most important are studies by Shlomo Netzer,[3] Emanuel Melzer,[4] and Moshe Landau.[5] These three Hebrew monographs, alike in so many ways that they can reasonably be treated as a whole, have advanced our knowledge of inter-war Polish Jewry far beyond the level possible by scholars limited to Polish and Western languages. They are very rewarding for students of Polish-Jewish history willing to learn to read them.

The authors of these works come from remarkably similar backgrounds, and they have used the latter to good advantage in their work. All were educated in inter-war Poland, yet completed their university studies in Israel. As a result, all have a thorough command of Polish, Yiddish, and Hebrew, the three essential languages for the study of Polish Jewry. In addition, all possess an insider's familiarity with both the Polish and Polish-Jewish scenes, a familiarity that has generally stood them in good stead in choosing their source materials and in evaluating their significance. This familiarity has also helped them deal with the complexities of Polish-Jewish organisational life, often so bewildering to outsiders, with a minimum of confusion and error.

To be sure, the authors' past lives have led to some difficulties as well. For political reasons, none of them could consult archival sources in Poland while undertaking their research.[6] They have nevertheless managed partially to make up for this deficiency in various ways: all have combed through Polish printed sources and the Polish press; Melzer and Landau have made ample use of the archives of the Sikorski Institute in London; and Landau has managed to obtain materials indirectly from the Archive for Recent Documents (*Archiwum Akt Nowych*) in Warsaw through the assistance of colleagues. There is also no doubt that their personal backgrounds have made it rather difficult for them to be objective. However, all of them are trained professional historians, and although their emotional involvement with their subject is often evident, they have, for the most part, managed admirably to keep it from interfering with their scholarly responsibilities.

At the centre of all three studies is the conduct of the Jewish political leadership in independent Poland. Indeed, the large-scale involvement of Jews as Jews in Polish politics was one of the hallmarks of Polish Jewry, distinguishing it from Jewish communities elsewhere. Netzer pays particular attention to this distinction; in fact, he begins his study with a discussion of the origins of the policy of promoting individual and collective Jewish welfare through elected Jewish representatives participating directly in the political institutions of the society around them. He sees these origins primarily in a general politicising movement among many of the ethnic minorities of the multi-national Russian and Austro-Hungarian Empires in the second half of the nineteenth century. Suggesting that the social and economic distress suffered by large segments of society in both empires was attributed by many to defects in their political systems, Netzer notes the mounting demands for fundamental political reform. He points out that dissatisfaction with the structure of both governments included complaints by various minorities that they lacked a means of expressing their collective interests. Hence, he writes, 'the demands of the national minorities ... for civil and national rights became part and parcel of political demands for changes in the character of the regime (p. 9)'. He observes that this applied particularly to the Jews: 'Jewish political activity in the countries of Eastern Europe centred on looking for immediate ways to relieve the masses' distress; yet it assumed the form, *inter alia*, of national demands parallel to those of other national minorities (p. 15).'

Curiously, though, Netzer's analysis of the Jews as one of several minorities in Eastern Europe virtually ends at this point; except for one chapter devoted to the Minorities Treaty of 1919, and part of another to the early negotiations to establish a Minorities' Bloc before the elections for the first regularly constituted parliament in 1922, the rest of his book covers either exclusively Jewish or bilateral Polish-Jewish issues. These include the efforts of the various Jewish political parties to establish a single representative national body to speak for all Polish Jewry; Jewish strategies during the electoral campaign for the Constituent *Sejm* in 1919; the organisation of the Jewish caucus (*koło*) in the Constituent *Sejm* and the debates there on questions of parliamentary strategy and tactics; how the Jewish parliamentary representatives dealt with outbreaks of anti-Jewish violence during the first years of Polish independence; the Jewish representatives' efforts to have legislation passed favourable to Jewish interests and to defeat that unfavourable to them; and the extra-parliamentary negotiations between Jewish leaders and various Polish governments to improve relations between both sides. These issues are treated in great detail, far more than elsewhere, and from many different points of view. Indeed, the discussion often depends upon close analysis of specific pieces of legislation, parliamentary questions, reports issued by various Jewish and Polish bodies, and debates in the Polish and Yiddish-language press. For example, a full eight pages (pp. 168–75), including 36 footnotes, are devoted to a discussion of the implications of the Citizenship Law of 31 January 1920 for Polish Jewry and to an exposition of the efforts of the Jewish representatives in the Constituent *Sejm* both to modify it before and after its passage and to mitigate its adverse effects upon the Jewish population. In contrast, Pawel Korzec treats the same subject in less than a page, while Joseph Marcus and Frank Golczewski do not deal with it at all.[7] Similarly, eleven pages are devoted by Netzer to how various Jewish groups viewed the Sunday day of rest law, as against six by Golczewski, two by Korzec, and none by Marcus.[8]

Perhaps Netzer's primary concern with Jewish parliamentary activity caused him, relatively early in his discussion, to abandon attempting to analyse Jewish political behaviour against the background of wider movements among the various minorities, for until six ethnic German deputies joined the Constituent *Sejm* in 1920, Jews were the only minority group represented there. Landau, on the other hand, suggests that, during the early years of the Second Republic, Polish Jewry hoped to safeguard its group interests less through parliament than through international guarantees of its right to organise its internal communal affairs as it saw fit. Such guarantees were sought, however, according to Landau, within the framework of 'an all-inclusive rule benefiting the various minorities rather than a specific delimitation of Jewish interests', mainly because Jewish leaders feared the latter would arouse a hostile backlash among Poles (p. 9). Thus Landau, in his discussion of Jewish political behaviour, has to cast his net wider than Netzer, giving greater weight to issues concerning minorities in general, and particularly to the Minorities Treaty of 1919. He considers such topics as Polish public opinion over the Minorities Treaty, the debate about ratifying the Treaty, and how the Treaty's provisions were implemented or subverted by subsequent Polish legislation. His exposition of these matters will interest not only historians of Polish Jewry but also students of the minorities question in Poland in general.

However, Landau is primarily concerned with Jews; his principal theme is the effect of the Minorities Treaty both upon the development of Polish-Jewish relations and upon the political behaviour of Polish Jewry. He begins by noting that the acceptance of the idea of an international guarantee of minority rights by the Versailles Conference, largely because of pressure from Western Jewish organisations, made the Jews of Poland optimistic; they saw it as 'legitimising their representatives' political struggle for the trappings of national and cultural autonomy' (p. 9). He then observes, however, that the Jews seriously over-estimated the ability and willingness of the Western powers to enforce the Treaty, while at the same time under-estimating the profound sense of insult to Polish sovereignty and honour that the Treaty's adoption engendered in Poles of virtually all political persuasions. Thus, he contends, far from increasing Jewish security and advancing Jewish interests, the Minorities Treaty actually became a major cause of Polish-Jewish tension, while successive Polish governments systematically ignored its provisions.

Beginning with these observations, Landau tries to explain the Jews' misplaced optimism and the Poles' hostile reaction. He attributes the former to the success of the various Jewish national councils that sprang up alongside similar national councils formed by other subject minorities of the Austro-Hungarian and Russian Empires during the final stages of World War I. These councils managed to take practical control of Jewish affairs and gain access to the peace conference through appealing to the principle of national self-determination. According to Landau, these councils saw the peace conference as the proper forum for converting their *de facto* position to a *de jure* one based on international law. He suggests that when Jewish delegates at Versailles saw that a Polish National Committee had also been allowed there and was basing its claim to national sovereignty on the principle of self-determination, they came to believe that the Poles would agree to a political settlement based on applying this principle to all nationalities in Eastern Europe. Obviously they misread Polish intentions: Landau explains that, whereas Jewish leaders interpreted national self-determination as implying cultural pluralism, Polish spokesmen understood it as bestowing cultural hegemony upon the dominant national group. Thus, he notes, Poles tended to look upon Jewish demands for national cultural autonomy as an infringement of their sovereign rights; when Jews raised these demands in an international forum and helped create a situation in which Polish independence was in effect made conditional upon recognition of the collective rights of other national groups within the new state's borders, many Poles began to view Jews as enemies seeking to undermine their newly-won independence.

Such an argument reflects what might be called a subjectivist – as opposed to an objectivist – interpretation of the origins of Polish-Jewish tension in the Second Republic: it implies that tension stemmed primarily from conscious ideological and behavioural choices on both sides rather than from a clash of interests inherent in the economic and social structure of the new state. Indeed, Landau's chapter on 'The Foundations of the Confrontation between Poles and Jews' (pp. 43–66) deals exclusively with these political issues, ignoring completely the socio-economic background of Polish-Jewish relations. In this he parallels Netzer, who also has little to say about social and economic matters.[9] Yet even between these two subjectivists, there is an important difference of emphasis. Netzer suggests that continued Polish opposition to the idea of Jewish national autonomy was at bottom an inevitable outcome of the conception of Poland as a 'national state' (*państwo narodowe*) advanced by the majority of the Polish national movement, contrary to the notion of a 'state of nationalities' (*państwo narodowościowe*) put forward by Jewish spokesmen. Landau, on the other hand, while acknowledging the force of this view, also attributes major influence to a widespread Polish belief that Jews were implacably hostile to the national aspirations of the Polish people. Perhaps this is why, in analysing Jewish behaviour as awareness dawned that the Minorities Treaty would not satisfactorily guarantee Jewish interests, Landau is more sympathetic to the more conciliatory approach towards the Polish political leadership of such Jewish spokesmen as Leon Reich and Ozjasz Thon than to the strategy of 'principled opposition' advocated by Yitshak Grünbaum and others. For example, he sees the creation, largely on Grünbaum's initiative, of the National Minorities Bloc before the elections to the first proper parliament in 1922, as a red rag to the Polish people and believes it significant in heightening Polish-Jewish tension (pp. 150–56). On the other hand, Netzer believes that 'the organisation of the [Minorities] Bloc and the Jewish activity behind it clearly demonstrate accumulated parliamentary and organisational experience that enabled [the Jews] to confront a hostile governmental machine' (p. 318). However, Landau presents the *Ugoda* (Agreement) of 1925, which represented a victory for the proponents of conciliation, as a courageous effort by the Jewish leadership to strengthen the hand of those Polish spokesmen who believed it in Poland's interest to restrain open hostility towards Jews. If this attempt at Polish-Jewish co-operation failed, he argues, this was the fault of the determined opposition of extremists on both Polish and Jewish sides, who did not believe it possible or desirable to establish Polish-Jewish relations on a rational basis (p. 238).

Landau concludes his study with a lengthy discussion of the complex relations between the Jewish political leadership and the Piłsudski camp immediately before and immediately after the *coup d'état* of May 1926 (pp. 276–335). The years of the Piłsudski dictatorship itself, however, are beyond the scope of his work. Indeed, this period still lacks the sort of detailed systematic treatment that the three authors under discussion have provided for earlier and later times. Melzer, in the introductory chapter of his book (pp. 13–38), certainly offers a rather ambitious summary of the major political, economic, and social changes between 1929 and 1935 as they affected Polish Jewry, but the scope of this discussion hardly matches his analysis of the four years between Piłsudski's death in May 1935 and the outbreak of the Second World War. In fact, he subjects this difficult period in the history of Polish Jewry to even more minute scrutiny and provides an even greater wealth of detail than that offered by Netzer and Landau for the periods they consider.

Melzer sees Piłsudski's untimely death as a major turning point both for the history of Poland in general and for the history of Polish Jewry. He argues that it 'let loose forces that had been kept under control during his lifetime', forces that had crystallised 'against the background of the consolidation of the Nazi regime in Germany and its improved relations with Poland' (p. 58). Thus, he argues, the Marshal's death 'contributed to the worsening of the position of Polish Jewry as well as to the strengthening of anti-semitism in all its manifestations and organisational ramifications' (p. 39). He depicts the *Endecja* as moving from verbal hostility towards Jews to physical violence. He argues that the government, responding to popular pressure to act against the Jews and fearing that 'a petty Hitler' might seize power in a *putsch* from the right, found it politically advisable to adopt a highly visible anti-Jewish public posture. This trend, which, he maintains, represented a departure from Piłsudski's own étatist principles, became ever more pronounced with time; indeed, the break with the Piłsudski-ite heritage was symbolised in his view by the creation of *OZON* in February 1937 and its adoption of the Thirteen Theses on the Jewish Question in May 1938.

Much of Melzer's book is devoted to fleshing out this basic perception of the period. The author painstakingly reconstructs how the economic position of Polish Jewry was undermined through a combination of government and popular action. He chronicles the spread of anti-Jewish agitation, which resulted in a wave of violence during the years 1936–38. He describes the campaign to restrict Jewish access to institutions of higher learning and to segregate Jewish students within them. And he carefully follows the evolution of the government's policy of encouraging the mass emigration of Jews from Poland.

Throughout, Melzer is aware of the struggle of segments of Polish society against the growing anti-Jewish agitation. At the same time, however, he notes that the climate of mounting hostility towards Jews influenced parts of the centre and the left of Polish politics. He is concerned throughout with identifying the positions of the various Polish political parties over the specific issues treated and has combed through the newspapers of all Poland's major political groupings. In the end, though well aware of the differences among them, he concludes that virtually all sectors of organised Polish society were affected by antisemitism; even those groups that professed abhorrence of the way the country's attitudes towards Jews were evolving were prone at times to accommodate the prevailing trend.

In the face of such overwhelming enmity, as well as because opportunities for Jewish emigration were steadily diminishing at this time, many Polish Jews began to view their situation, as the title of Melzer's book suggests, as a blind alley. Indeed, Melzer makes clear his belief that there was virtually no way the hostility of so much of Polish society could have been appeased. On the other hand, though, he also argues that the Jewish leadership did not resist the attacks upon its followers as vigorously or as effectively as it might have. By carefully studying how various Jewish political organisations and social groups responded to discrimination, violence, and emigrationist pressures, he concludes that during the four years before the outbreak of World War II Polish Jewry suffered from a serious lack of responsible leadership. Their representatives in parliament, whom Netzer describes as being central to the Jews' struggle for their collective interests during the first four years of the Second Republic, now appear, according to Melzer, as a body of second-rate individuals incapable of arousing united Jewish resistance to oppression. The initiative for mobilising resistance thus passed, according to Melzer, either to the three major Jewish political groups – the Zionist parties, *Agudas Yisroel*, and the *Bund* – or to local Jewish bodies. These groups scored noteworthy successes in the field of physical self-defence, economic self-help, and the rescuing of Jewish honour, but these successes merely underscore the lack of a unified, co-ordinated, nationwide effort by Polish Jews to withstand the attack on their position. As Melzer shows, the Jewish parties were unable to overcome their ideological differences; nor were they prepared to endanger their own tactical positions in the political arena for the sake of Jewish unity. And although such divisiveness was not apparent at the local level, local organisations lacked the resources to lead more general resistance.

Despite this highly negative assessment of the Jewish leadership, Melzer does not suggest that greater resources and a greater spirit of unity would have given Jewish resistance efforts more than a palliative effect. Essentially, he, Netzer, and Landau, for all their differences of emphasis, believe the fate of Polish Jewry during the inter-war years rested more in the hands of the Polish community – primarily the Polish government – than in those of the Jews themselves. Likewise, all believe that the various Polish governments could, if they had wanted to, have acted to bring about significant improvement in the Jewish situation. Thus they present the history of Polish Jewry during the inter-war years primarily as a Jewish struggle against successive manifestations of hostility from the society around them.[10] In this way, they implicitly reject the approach to Polish-Jewish history during this period suggested by Jerzy Tomaszewski, among others. This approach suggests that much of the tension between Poles and Jews was rooted in the intractable economic and social problems of the new Polish state as a whole, which could not simply be solved by an exercise of will by the Polish governments. This approach therefore rejects descriptions of the Jewish situation as '"Jews *contra* Poles" or "Jews *contra* the Polish state"'.[11]

It must be remembered, however, that the 'Jews *contra* Poles' approach of the three authors under discussion was adopted as the result of extensive – in many cases exhaustive – disciplined academic research; it should not, therefore, be regarded in their case, as some seem to have implied, as primarily a reflection of their ideology or personal feelings.[12] Certainly there is room for historians to take issue with this approach. However, it seems reasonable to expect that those who do so ought at least to be thoroughly familiar with Netzer, Landau, and Melzer's arguments and evidence. Because of the scope of the three authors' research and the breadth of their ideas – unmatched by most writing on the subject today – their works deserve to be taken as a starting point for future scholarly debate on inter-war Polish-Jewish history. However it is highly unlikely that any of these books will appear in a more widely accessible language in the near future. This is, of course, unfortunate, but rather than decrying it, scholars seriously interested in studying inter-war Polish-Jewish relations should try to acquire a reading knowledge of Hebrew. Only then will historians outside Israel be able to discuss this subject with their Israeli colleagues on the level established by the three authors considered here.

NOTES

1 Edward D. Wynot, '"A Necessary Cruelty": The Emergence of Official Anti-Semitism in Poland, 1936–1939', *American Historical Review*, 76:4 (1971), pp. 1035–58.

2 Among the most noteworthy are Celia S. Heller, *On the Edge of Destruction: Jews of Poland Between the Two World Wars* (New York, 1977); Andrzej Chojnowski, *Koncepcje polityki narodowościowej rządów polskich w latach 1921–1939* (Wrocław, 1979); Paweł Korzec, *Juifs en Pologne: La question juive pendant l'entre-deux-guerres* (Paris, 1980); Frank Golczewski, *Polnisch-jüdische Beziehungen, 1181–1922: Eine Studie zur Geschichte des Antisemitismus in Osteuropa* (Wiesbaden, 1981); Ezra Mendelsohn, *Zionism in Poland: The Formative Years, 1915–1926* (New Haven, 1981); idem., *The Jews of East Central Europe Between the World Wars* (Bloomington, 1983); Joseph Marcus, *Social and Political History of the Jews in Poland, 1919–1939* (Berlin, 1983); Jerzy Tomaszewski, *Rzeczpospolita wielu narodów* (Warsaw, 1985). For a discussion of accounts of inter-war Polish Jewish history in recent Polish historical writing, see Andrzej Chojnowski, 'The Jewish Community of the Second Republic in Polish

Historiography of the 1980s', *Polin*, I (1986), pp. 288–99. For more general bibliographical information, see Gershon David Hundert and Gershon C. Bacon, *The Jews in Poland and Russia: Bibliographical Essays* (Bloomington, 1984), pp. 183–94.

3 Shlomo Netzer, *Ma'avak Yehudey Polin al Zehhuyoteyhem haezrahiyot Vehaleumiyot (1918–1922)* (The struggle of Polish Jewry for Civil and National Minority Rights, 1918–22) (Publications of the Diaspora Research Institute, Tel Aviv University, Book 33, Tel Aviv, 1980), pp. 338+X, with English summary.

4 Emanuel Melzer, *Ma'avak Medini bemalkodet: Yehudey Polin 1935–1939* (Political strife in a blind alley: The Jews of Poland 1935–1939) (Publications of the Diaspora Research Institute, Tel Aviv University, Book 35, Tel Aviv, 1982), pp. 384+XII, with English summary.

5 Moshe Landau, *Miut Leumi Lohem: Ma'avak Yehudey Polin 1918–1928* (The Jews as a National Minority in Poland, 1918–1928) (Monographs in Jewish History, Zalman Shazar Center for Jewish History, Jerusalem, 1986), pp. 397+VII, with English translation of Preface.

6 With the recent improvement in Polish-Israeli relations this problem no longer exists, and future work by these scholars should not be hampered by such political obstacles.

7 Cf. Korzec, *Juifs en Pologne*, p. 105. It should be pointed out that Hebrew texts tend to be relatively compact, and when translated into Western languages they often take up about 30–50 per cent more pages.

8 Cf. Golczewski, *Polnisch-jüdische Beziehungen*, pp. 275–80; Korzec, *Juifs en Pologne*, pp. 103–4.

9 This comment should not be taken as criticism, but merely as a statement of fact. A discussion of the relative merits of subjectivist and objectivist interpretations is beyond the scope of this essay.

10 Note the appearance of the word 'struggle' (*ma'avak*) in either the title or the subtitle of all three works.

11 Jerzy Tomaszewski, 'Some Methodological Problems of the Study of Jewish History in Poland between the Two World Wars', *POLIN*, I (1986), pp. 164ff.

12 Tomaszewski, 'Methodological Problems', p. 164; Norman Davies, 'Foreword', in Bruno Shatyn, *A Private War: Surviving in Poland on False Papers, 1941–1945* (Detroit, 1985), p. viii.

OSTJUDEN
Peter Pulzer

David Sorkin, *The Transformation of German Jewry, 1780–1840*. Oxford: Oxford University Press. 1987. Pp. 255.

Jack Wertheimer, *Unwelcome Strangers: East European Jews in Imperial Germany*. Oxford: Oxford University Press. 1987. Pp. ix, 275.

Trude Maurer, *Ostjuden in Deutschland 1918–1933*. Hamburg: Hans Christians Verlag. 1986. Pp. 972.

Ivar Oxaal, Michael Pollak and Gerhard Botz (eds.), *Jews, Anti-semitism and Culture in Vienna*. London: Routledge and Kegan Paul. 1987. Pp. xiv, 300.

The term *Ostjude* to describe the traditional Jew of East-Central and Eastern Europe did not become current until the beginning of this century, but the concept dates back at least another hundred years. Since we are talking about cultural categories rather than places of residence, and since one could have found 'Eastern Jews' in New York while 'Western Jews' predominated in Prague or Riga, it is best to adopt Ezra Mendelsohn's categorisation of two *types* of Jewish community in modern times. The first, 'Western', shows high acculturation, a strong desire to assimilate, low allegiance to religious orthodoxy, abandonment of Yiddish, high rates of intermarriage and rising social status. The second, 'Eastern', shows the opposite characteristics. Even where its members are acculturated, they are not assimilated: when politicised, they become Jewish Nationalists or Zionists rather than the Liberals or Social Democrats of their Western co-religionists.

Until the end of the eighteenth century almost all Ashkenazi Jews were 'Easterners', a low-status minority overwhelmingly engaged in marginal economic activities. It was with the coming of the Enlightenment that Jewry diverged culturally. The divergence was sharper in German-speaking Central Europe than anywhere else for two largely unconnected reasons. The first had to do with the physical proximity of the great majority of 'Eastern Jews', as a constant immigration threat. Indeed, after the partitions of Poland 'Eastern' and 'Western' Jews were to be found within the boundaries of the partitioning states, Prussia and Austria. The fact that in the course of time many of the most prominent 'Western' Jews, such as Eduard Lasker, Leo Baeck and Joseph Roth, were 'Easterners' in origin did little to diminish the prejudice against *Ostjuden*, one that was shared by many 'Western' Jews. Nor has this constant shifting of the boundaries between the two types affected the retrospective idealisation of the Eastern Jews as sentimentalised fiddlers on the roof, set firmly in a premodern time-warp.

The second reason had to do with the intellectual transformation of Germany in the second half of the eighteenth century. While the Jewish immigrant to relatively liberal, open societies like those of Britain, America or the Netherlands could justify himself by commercial success, in Germany the role-model became the *Bildungsbürger*, the cultivated member of the middle class. It is the impact of this on the Jewish community that is the subject of David Sorkin's book. It remains important for the present day, for this impact defined the relationship between 'the Germans' and 'the Jews'. Whereas in Western Europe the betterment of the Jews was a matter of individual achievement and emancipation was discussed in terms of natural rights, in Germany Jewish betterment was initially seen in collective terms. For Christian Wilhelm von Dohm and most of his successors among advocates of Jewish emancipation, moral regeneration was to take place within a political framework, as part of a contract. As a *quid pro quo* for being accepted in civilised society, Jews had to accept the norms of that society, in particular the norms of the cultivated, educated middle class. And indeed the first generation of Jewish advocates of emancipation accepted the terms of this deal: it is impossible to imagine a French or British David Friedländer or David Fränkel.

All of this had a number of important consequences for Jewish history. It explains why the *haskalah*, the Jewish enlightenment, was German in origin and also why it had limited impact outside the German sphere. It explains the peculiarly intense relationship that German Jews had with classical German literary and philosophical culture, a relationship that unkind historians have dismissed as an unrequited love-affair. It explains above all the neurosis about *Ostjuden*, all those Jews not embraced in the contract, Jews who were a threat not merely to the hard-won sense of nationality that Germans had acquired in the nineteenth century, but to all those German Jews who thought they could forget the world of pedlars, *schnorrers* and village tavern-keepers they had only recently left behind.

The transformation of German Jewry, its re-creation in a secular, bourgeois form as a sub-culture within urban Germany was, as Sorkin argues, defined by the 1840s and virtually complete by 1871. In this conclusion he does not differ from other scholars. What is original about his thesis is that, for reasons to be sought in the nature of the German enlightenment, the way German Jewry modernised marked a *Sonderweg*, a special path; it was not, as many historians have previously argued, the paradigm of Western Jewry.

Once the new German-Jewish sub-culture was in place, the *Ostjuden* became both a cliché and an anti-type. For anti-semites they were the 'real' Jews, whose undesirable characteristics emancipated Jews had only superficially abandoned. For official Germany, even liberal official Germany, they were a source of pressure, even blackmail. To prove that they were honouring the emancipation contract, German Jews had constantly to show that they had left 'Eastern' behavioural norms behind. What constantly amazes one about the German 'Jewish Question' is the small numbers involved. In the period of the Empire and the Weimar Republic they numbered little over 600,000 or about 1 per cent. *Ostjuden*, i.e. those born in the Russian or Habsburg Empires or in Romania, never exceeded 80,000 before the First World War or 100,000 thereafter. Indeed the Dutch, Belgian and even Swiss 'Eastern Jewish' communities were relatively larger. (It is one of the merits of both Wertheimer's and Maurer's books that they contain excellent statistical material.)

The salience of the 'Eastern Jewish' Question, even greater after the First World War than before, merely indicates the general sensitivity of German politics to this theme; moreover, as the tone of anti-*Ostjuden* propaganda quoted by Maurer shows, this was frequently no more than a stick with which to beat the Weimar Republic, and the sometimes illiberal measures of the Prussian authorities against Polish Jewish immigrants show how vulnerable the authorities were to this constant barrage of hate. Indeed, the devices and language with which they tried to limit immigration, to expel immigrants and to obstruct naturalisation showed that within the civil service, police and army anti-semitic attitudes that could no longer be used against native Jews were turned against *Ostjuden*.

Yet how separate a community were *Ostjuden*? Wertheimer makes it clear that though social barriers existed between Germans and Easterners, the two did not occupy watertight compartments. To some extent the German Jewish community depended on Easterners for a supply of rabbis and other community employees. Wertheimer stresses that up to 1914 Eastern Jews in Germany failed to build up the kind of organisational network that characterised them in Britain or America. In part this may be explained by small numbers and general insecurity; but it also suggests that an Eastern Jew in Imperial Germany occupied a transitional rather than a static status. Maurer's detailed evidence for the post-war period, in contrast, suggests that the barriers had increased, causing frequent tensions in communal life.

The East-West tensions in German-Jewish life had their equivalents in

Austria, though in different forms. They appeared above all in Vienna, where the Jewish population grew from a few thousand in the 1850s to nearly 200,000 by 1914. Ivar Oxaal and Steven Beller show in *Jews, Antisemitism and Culture in Vienna* that the Jews provided one of the most creative artistic and literary avant-gardes of our time, increasingly surrounded by a traditional and impoverished Eastern immigrant population. This meant that the *haskalah* had little impact: among the observant Orthodoxy prevailed, while the minority who adopted the enlightenment were overwhelmingly secular and assimilationist. There were, in fact, several compartmentalised Jewish communities in Vienna, relatively segregated residentially, with not much inter-marriage. The impact of these divisions on Jewish communal politics are well analysed by Walter Weitzmann.

Anyone wishing to pursue the separate and joint developments of 'Western' and 'Eastern' Jewries over the last two centuries will find much information and stimulus in these four books. The Oxaal, like many conference volumes, has its weak spots and Maurer's Teutonic thoroughness makes her book longer than the other three combined. But these are not serious defects.

ON ZWEIG
Sergiusz Michalski

Arnold Zweig, Hermann Struck, *Das Ostjüdische Antlitz*. Wiesbaden, Fourier Verlag, 1988.

This book, with a text by Arnold Zweig and pictures by Hermann Struck (52 drawings), was first published in Berlin in 1920. It is a literary and artistic document which details the profound changes in the appreciation of the Eastern Jews by their Western brethren. Zweig and Struck both served in the German Army in the East during World War I and both there discovered the fascinating world of the *Ostjuden*. Both were German Jews, whose sense of cultural and moral superiority did not survive this 'strange encounter' (Aschheim). In this respect, they were similar to many other German-Jewish intellectuals who served in the East. On a theoretical level, the tendency to re-evaluate the Eastern Jewish experience had become an even stronger strand of Jewish thought long before the fateful encounter of 1914. It is, however, in this book that the glorification of the *Ostjude* reached its absolute height.

In a hymnic, proto-expressionist style, tinged with sentimentalism, Zweig sings the praise of the poor Jews of the East, who in his eyes, represent the essence of Jewishness. Their poverty and traditionalism but also their attachment – in the face of manifold oppression – to traditional Jewish moral and ethical values have saved them from the crass and empty materialism of their Western brethren. Zweig is intent on creating a positive stereotype of the *Ostjude*, with the spiritually hollow assimilationist German and West-European Jew as the ever present negative reference. He brings out the inner justification of Eastern European Jewish tradition and its mainly ethical foundations: 'All the creative forces of this *Volk* reach out into the ethical sphere'. Zweig gives a lucid analysis of the inner coherence of the Jewish family; he praises the heroic endurance of the Jewish woman. One should note a very sympathetic description of Hasidism. Though Zweig shrinks before an outright apology for the *shtetl* – popular acceptance of it is, after all, a product of the post-1945 era, when it no longer existed – he does try to explain the reasons for its shoddy appearance and the peculiar character of the civilisation it embodied. These short remarks do not do justice to the literary, human and intellectual qualities of Zweig's text. It ranks as one of the great books on East European Jewish life before the Holocaust.

Zweig's text possesses also distinct political undertones. Through the whole book runs a streak of scepticism about Jewish revolutionary activities, a mistrust of Jewish participation in Bolshevism. At one point Zweig explicitly suggests the primacy of Zionism: '... colonising Palestinian socialism is surely a truer embodiment of this idea than the concept which postulates that the world must first be violently destroyed, so that it can be rebuilt.' I am not sure whether Zweig radically changed his views after 1948 – when after bitter disappointments in Palestine, he settled down in East Berlin for twenty increasingly lonely and melancholic years (despite outward success and official esteem). His decent stance in 1967, in the face of official anti-Zionist rumblings, goes back to the ideals and convictions of his youth. Hermann Struck (1876–1944), at that time a well-known draughtsman and illustrator (though now rather forgotten) was a life-long friend of Zweig. Since the editors of this handsomely produced reprint have not chosen to provide us with a normal editorial comment (I have a rather cynical theory about the reason but will keep it to myself), some information culled from a slightly out-of-the-way article by Zweig devoted to the memory of his friend – 'Herman Struck, ein Meister der Graphik. Zum 80 Geburtstag des Kunstlers', in *Bildende Kunst*, 1956, Nr.3, p. 148–150 – will follow. Zweig and Struck met in the rear of the Eastern front in 1917. Struck held – according to Zweig – a high position in the German military administration; he was, namely, in charge of the section 'Jewish population' in the famous 5 Department (*Politische Abteilung*). They stayed close friends till Struck's death in Palestine in 1944. For *Das Ostjüdische Antlitz*, they both chose 52 of more than one hundred extant sketches and drawings.

I must admit to some reservations about the artistic value of Struck's drawings. They are well-meaning and compassionate, but as regards their formal qualities, they constitute a somewhat bloodless amalgam of various strands of German realism. It seems to me that, from an artistic point of view, Struck was a much better illustrator of Jewish life in his youth (e.g. 'Polish Rabbi', 1901), when he made use of a very expressive *Art Nouveau* idiom.

I cannot, alas, review the book without taking up once more – please believe me that I do it really *contre coeur* – the everlasting and muddled 'Poles vs. Jews' controversy. In his preface to the first edition (dated summer 1919) and in some remarks contained in the text, Zweig paints a uniformly bleak, horrifying picture of a 'murderous' Polish anti-semitism.

Referring to the developments after November 1918 he states that '... Poland and the pogrom has engulfed the whole Eastern Jewish people ... gradually one hears about what happened there -murder and butchery, the rule of plunder, of the whip, executions and murders, disappearance without trace and death in prison'. At this time, Zweig was already back in Germany and he bases his statements on reports from newspapers and hearsay without checking their verisimilitude. He omits all the grave external circumstances (Polish-Soviet, Polish-Ukrainian war, the conflict with Lithuania) and is characteristically vague about concrete facts. One cannot escape the conclusion that the undeniable atrocities – albeit on a very limited scale – committed by Polish troops and civilians in Lwów, Wilno and above all Pińsk (for a balanced article about the Pińsk massacre see *POLIN* Nr.2) have been used as a pretext for creating a picture that reflects more certain of the apprehensions of Lithuanian Jews (despised by antisemitic Poles as 'Litvaks') than the reality of 1919. Zweig's statement that the Tsarist administration was better to the Jews than the new Polish one is, after all, rather mind-boggling.

In the preface to the second edition, Zweig strikes a new tone. He undertakes something very meritorious, though, unfortunately, too often absent from all the heated discussions about Polish anti-semitism: he makes comparisons. This will not satisfy staunch defenders of Polish honour, since Zweig does not retract any of his accusations. He simply states that, in the time which has elapsed between the two editions (1920-1922), the Ukrainians and the Hungarians have proved to be much worse. He is of course absolutely right, incidentally also as regards the (then) future. The evident dislike of Zweig for the Poles was based probably on a variety of factors. One of them was certainly the 'normal' Polish anti-semitism, the other that attitude towards life, which a German leftwinger could only interpret as gentry arrogance. Zweig had also a penchant for the Russian *Seelenmensch*, and from the height of his ideal looked down on the prosaic Poles. This is a manner of thinking sometimes met among German intellectuals fascinated by Eastern Europe. Leaving aside the question of Zweig's attitude towards the Poles, let us simply state that the real situation in the Eastern territories until 1921-22 did not justify the scale of the accusations levelled by a German against a reborn state.

The reprint of Zweig's book has already produced a resurgence of familiar clichés about Polish anti-semitism. In a review for the prestigious *Frankfurter Allgemeine Zeitung* (11 June 1988) the eminent, but somewhat biased German poet Gunter Kunert used Zweig's work as a pretext to claim once more that the choice of Auschwitz as the central death camp came about 'because the mass murderers knew very well the boundless anti-semitism of the Poles'. This drew a just rebuttal from Władysław Bartoszewski (FAZ, 7 July, 1988).

As it happens I have a soft spot for Arnold Zweig, because in the late fifties, he was our neighbour in East Berlin and displayed a kind attitude towards a somewhat precocious boy of nine (I got lovely postcards from him). I have a high esteem for the literary talent of Kunert, who is well versed in East European affairs. But what to think about a formulation of Zweig, taken up sarcastically by Kunert: 'Therefore we say to the Poles directly, that the Polish people itself will avenge our brothers through Polish socialism'. Great are, oh Lord, the sins of the Poles (including anti-semitism), but have we really deserved the subsequent course of events?

READING RINGELBLUM
Tomasz Gąsowski

The discussion on the Polish attitude towards the Holocaust, renewed several years ago, has recently been augmented by the publication in Poland in book form of Emanuel Ringelblum's essay, first published forty-five years ago.[1] Although this discussion has not bridged the fundamental differences between Polish and Jewish views, and is far from concluded, its more objective tone has enabled both sides to discover each other's standpoint. Consequently, the time spent waiting for this work to be published has not been totally wasted. We are now better prepared to read the text calmly and seriously, without prejudging it as extreme and biased or becoming angry at its attacks on the 'good name' of the Polish people.

Ringelblum wrote this extended essay while in hiding at 84 Grójecka Street at the turn of 1943 and 1944, and it was the last work of a scientist, social worker, and then conspirator and escapee from the camp at Trawniki. Soon after finishing it, his hiding-place was discovered by the Germans, and all its inhabitants and their protectors were killed. His name is also linked with the priceless collection of documents collected in the Warsaw ghetto by a group of his helpers. These describe the fate of the Jews in occupied Poland. This so-called *Ringelblum Archive*, part of which has survived, is the most important source for the history of the Holocaust.

The central idea of Ringelblum's work is contained in the following statement: 'The Polish nation, and the Polish government could not prevent the Nazis crushing their Jewish citizens. But we do have the right to ask, whether the response of the Polish nation was adequate, given the magnitude of the disaster which befell the Jews?' His answer came in the more detailed questions which followed in the introduction. 'Did the Jews' last sight of this God-created world, in "death trains" speeding from various parts of the country to Treblinka and other places of mass murder, have to be that of the unfeeling, or even satisfied, faces of their neighbours?' The author's final conclusion is clear and severe. 'As the sword of the pitiless Holocaust hung over the Jewish nation, except for a few who managed to flee, the state authorities did nothing to save even the Polish Jews who remained.' He adds further: 'The callousness of Polish anti-semites, who had learned nothing, is responsible for the death of hundreds of thousands of Jews, who, despite the Germans, could have been saved.' These very bitter words leave no doubt that Ringelblum's voice is that of a witness for the prosecution, even though he does admit that 'the statements of some Jewish circles, that all Poles welcomed the Holocaust of the Jews ... are far from true.' He believed the misbehaviour of the majority of the Polish people towards their fellow-citizens, friends, neighbours and relatives, who were threatened by death, was caused by their deep-rooted anti-semitism, which increased in the years just before the outbreak of war.

Although Ringelblum is not a neutral witness, his scientific honesty made him warn any future reader:

> The sources for this work are still very recent, and have not been subjected to the objective judgement of a historian ... The opinions stated here are those expressed in some progressive circles, among those who have survived the extermination of the whole nation. As such they are material for the future historian of the history of the Jews in Poland during the Second World War.

This statement is vital for a correct understanding of the whole work. As this has not always been considered, it is necessary to stress again, with the author, that this work is just a contribution, written in the belief that there would be further research in the future. This is confirmed by the simple subtitle of the essay – '*Uwagi i spostrzeżenia*' (Notes and observations).

Despite signs of scholarship and research, Ringelblum's study remains, above all, a personal account of someone who lived for several months through the death of his nation. No wonder, therefore, that dispassionate scientific analysis was combined with emotional descriptions of the fate of the Jews in occupied Poland. Based on personal observations and experiences, as well as wide, but fragmentary information, it is an important historical authority, if not free of subjective overtones. It cannot therefore be treated as a complete and neutral presentation of Polish-Jewish relations. The subjectivity of the account does not diminish its value, providing, however, that this is noticed by the reader, as the author wished. It is of course unfortunate that there was no similar contemporary account giving the Polish viewpoint of Polish-Jewish relations. It is not possible to fill this gap with material in the Archives of the Sikorski Institute in London, which only provides a picture of the development of Polish-Jewish relations in the years 1939–1941 in Poland's eastern territories occupied by the Soviets after 17 September 1939. This gap, probably accidental, can also be considered symptomatic.

Some of Ringelblum's statements are inevitably debatable and need appropriate comments. The editor of the text, Professor Artur Eisenbach, has provided these. His own contribution, consisting of an extensive introduction and almost 200 notes, is an integral part of the book. The statement of a scholar has to be considered in a different way from an emotional account and can be judged according to criteria applied to ordinary scholarly dissertations.

Eisenbach's sketch of Polish-Jewish relations in the years just before the outbreak of war, presented in the introduction, consists of only two colours – black and white. He says that the Jewish population was totally loyal towards the state, but was threatened by numerous anti-semitic manifestations from the Poles. But this is a dubious generalisation, as is inevitable when attempts are made to present developments by using generalisations. Both communities had deep social, political and ideological divisions, and there were differences in Polish attitudes to the Jews and Jewish loyalties to the Polish state. These problems still need proper investigation.[2] Although an extensive undertaking, it is a realistic one because sufficient sources have survived. One could begin by using such Zionist dailies, published in Polish, as the Warsaw *Nasz Przegląd*, the Lwów *Chwila*, or the Kraków *Nowy Dziennik*. Although their tone was often reserved, they did make some suggestions for co-operation. Which position was the real one must remain unresolved for the moment. On the other hand Polish anti-semitism was born, and developed, much earlier than fascism, which merely provided it with fresh momentum. But there were other tendencies within Polish political life, even in the late 1930s. The programme of encouraging Jewish emigration from Poland, treated by Eisenbach as a clear expression of Polish anti-semitism, was warmly approved of by the followers of Zionism, the strongest tendency in the Jewish community. The Zionists were determined opponents of anti-semitism, believing that the sole means of defending themselves against this was by creating their own state. But this did not prevent the most radical Zionists of the Jabotinsky faction from maintaining close contacts with the influential political-military circles in the Second Republic.[3] As to the pogroms of the 1930s, it would be useful to work out at least an estimate of the number of such incidents and the number of victims, rather than guessing at them.[4]

It is true that Eisenbach has tried to give some idea of the attitude of Poles towards Jews, but he has done so in a very schematic way. He presents an undefined, cohesive, right wing, both fascist and clerical, which, by definition was anti-semitic, and a democratic left, which had a proper, or even positive attitude towards Jews. The problem is, that such a division did not match the reality. For example, it is known that conservatives, who can hardly be counted as leftists, condemned unreservedly the anti-semitic incidents of the 1930s.[5] On the other hand, the most anti-semitic groups often had very radical social programmes. Eisenbach also tries to transfer this model to the war years, when attitudes towards Jews were more a matter of individual sensibility and moral choice rather than a function of ideological orientation or membership of a political party. After all it was Catholics, people who were hardly of the left, who initiated the action *Żegota*. This fact is overlooked by the author, and it is therefore no wonder that the names of Zofia Kossak-Szczucka, or Władysław Bartoszewski have been omitted. A somewhat similar approach is adopted in the case of the *Armia Krajowa* (The Home Army), considered, of course, to be rightist. When its activity on behalf of the Jewish population is discussed, such enigmatic names as *ruch oporu* (resistance) or *podziemie* (underground) are used to describe it, but when accusations are levelled against it, then its proper name always appears. A small, but symptomatic example is that of the man who helped Ringelblum escape from the camp in Trawniki, and to whom the author devoted a sympathetic fragment of his essay. He was a railway employee called Teodor Pajewski and it is only apparent in the last footnote, and then in passing, that he was an officer in the Home Army. The Catholic Church's activities during the occupation are no better presented: it would be hard to reconcile the clergy's efforts to save Jews with the general view that the church was the stronghold of anti-semitism. It should be noted also that Eisenbach mixes up Cardinal Aleksander Kakowski with the Kraków Archbishop (not yet a Cardinal) Adam Stefan Sapieha. The editors of the English translation made the same mistake.

Some of the material in the footnotes needs to be clarified or corrected. For example the attitude of the west European nations, especially that of the French and the Dutch, to the Holocaust was, as recent research has shown, much more varied, and certainly not as free from criticism as Eisenbach's account suggests.

The problem of the imprisonment of a group of Jewish soldiers in the camp in Jabłonna in July 1920, was once fiercely debated by M. Adus (not A. Adamus), A. Ciołkosz, M. Borwicz and W. Babiński.[6] Their controversy, however, did not succeed in explaining what actually happened and the subject still awaits its historian. In the so-called *Archiwum Belwederskie* (The Belweder Archive), in the Piłsudski Institute in New York, a separate portfolio about Jabłonna has survived. Some documents can also be found in the *Archiwum Akt Nowych* in Warsaw, and the whole controversial subject could be cleared up, if someone were to work on it. But it is possible, even today, to state that the claim that several thousand were killed in the camp is incorrect. It can also be added that the author of the decision to imprison the Jewish soldiers and officers, General Kazimierz Sosnkowski, was never the head of the General Staff.

Another controversial problem is how much help was given to the Warsaw ghetto, as it prepared to fight to the death. It is not a matter of debate that too few arms were supplied by the *AK*, but this does not mean that the *AK*'s magazines were packed with arms, as Eisenbach maintains, following Kermish and Krakowski.[7] Ringelblum's opinion should also be corrected, as the Jewish community could not have demanded arms several months before the July deportation, as it was then not organised for the struggle. Both Ringelblum and Eisenbach are convinced of the antisemitism of the *ŻWŻ/AK*. But the basis for their conviction needs to be questioned: has there been any thorough research on the *AK*'s attitude towards the Jews?[8] This problem is not as clear cut as it appears, and as Eisenbach seems to think. One of the main arguments in support of this belief is General Bor's order no 116 of 15th September 1943, about fighting banditry. Yet neither in the order itself, nor in the instruction attached to it, is there any mention of the Jews.[9] The implementation of the order could have affected those who escaped from the transport trains, since they, as Ringelblum himself explained, had to rob and live like bandits to survive. The fundamental tragedy of the situation is that the order itself, although entailing strict measures, was a routine one, directed against the results of the phenomenon rather than considering its causes. Yet Eisenbach's statement, that the Polish Government in Exile in London, as well as the underground press in occupied Poland, passed over the extermination of Polish Jews in silence, cannot be upheld. The list of relevant government documents, as well as of publications, is long enough.[10]

Some footnotes make insinuations, or are simply too vague. For example, the massacre of Praga in 1794 by Suvorov's army, probably affected more than just the Jewish population. It is not clear, why Katyń was 'of interest' to the anti-semitic 'reptile papers' published by the Germans. Eisenbach also fails to explain clearly the connection between the 'incorporation of the Western Ukraine and Byelorussia into the USSR' in 1939 and the growth of anti-semitic feeling among Poles. It is not clear, whether informers, blackmailers and *szmalcownicy* were actually punished, or whether such punishment was just suggested by the *Kierownictwo Walki Zbrojnej* (Command of Military Struggle) and never carried out.

There are several gaps in the footnotes. No views are expressed about the *Jüdische Ordnungsdienst* (Ghetto Police), although the author quite correctly condemns the *Granatowa Policja* (Navy Blue Police). Ringelblum's statement, that the radical nationalists aimed at the physical extermination of Jews even before the war is not commented on, even though Jan Józef Lipski, who investigated this question, found no evidence to support such a view.[11] To interpret the efforts of the Catholic Church to save Jewish children as 'hunting for souls' is, to put it mildly, a great oversimplification. The state of our knowledge today does not allow such a conclusion.[12] Suggestions that Stefan Starzyński's radio speeches had an anti-semitic tone need to be verified by the appropriate documentation.[13]

Eisenbach's notes have a characteristic approach. Ringelblum's critical, often over-severe, views, are backed up, with no attempt being made to verify them. However, his much rarer favourable remarks about Poles have not been developed in a similar way. The language used in the editorial commentary is not all that might be desired. The huge bibliography available for the subject has been used very selectively. The absence of W. Bartoszewski's works, whose conclusions may be debatable but have been thoroughly researched, should not pass unnoticed, nor those of M. Edelman and R. Zimand.

Despite the evident intentions of the editor, his commentary, paradoxically, somewhat diminishes the significance of the essay. What we seem to have been presented with is a version prepared for the first edition of the late 1950s, merely altered in some of its details, but not in its overall tone. It is true, that the forty years since the war have seen a change in judgement on Polish society's attitudes towards the Jews during the war, but it is hard to assume that we have now come full circle. The longstanding debate about Polish behaviour in the face of the Holocaust, has at last entered the stage when facts and real arguments mean more than subjective opinions and emotions. It is too bad that this important publication owes more to the old conventions of the discussion, especially as the English edition of Ringelblum's essay is much less emotional and more balanced in its views.

NOTES

1. E. Ringelblum, *Stosunki polsko-żydowskie w czasie drugiej wojny światowej. Uwagi i spostrzeżenia* (Warsaw, 1988); this text was published earlier in the *BŻIH* no 28-31 (1958-59), and in English by Yad Vashem (Jerusalem, 1974).
2. For interesting remarks on this topic see W. Mędrzecki, *Wojewodztwo wołyńskie 1921-1939. Elementy przemian cywilizacyjnych, społecznych i politycznych* (Ossolineum, 1986), pp.180-3.
3. cf. W.T. Drymmer, 'Zagadnienie żydowskie w Polsce 1935-1939', *Zeszyty Historyczne*, 13 (1968), pp. 55-77.
4. M. Gilbert, *Atlas of the Holocaust* (London, 1982), maintains, that 36 were killed, yet even this number is not properly documented.
5. *Czas*, the organ of the conservative party, in no. 230 (22 August 1934) contained an introductory article entitled 'Parę słów prawdy o polityce żydowskiej' (Some true words about Jewish politics): We have often fought anti-semitism in our paper ... We fight anti-semitism for the sake of domestic peace and to maintain a modern, western state and in the name of Catholic ethics, which certainly cannot be reconciled with racist doctrines or race hatred. Every reader of the Bible is clear and has no doubts over how relations between our religion and the Jews should be conducted.'
6. A. Ciołkosz, 'Dzielnica żydowska obozu w Jabłonnie', *Zeszyty Historyczne*, 20 (1971), pp. 178-199.
7. A. Ciołkosz, 'Broń dla getta Warszawy', *Zeszyty Historyczne*, 15(1969), pp. 15-44; ibid., 'Letter to the editors of *Zeszyty Historyczne* about Ringelblum's essay

published by J. Kermish and S. Krakowski', *Zeszyty Historyczne*, 32 (1975), pp. 226-8.
8 R.C. Lukas tried to evaluate this problem, *The forgotten Holocaust. The Poles and Jews under German Occupation 1939-1944* (The University Press of Kentucky, 1986), pp. 152-181, but he barely touched on it, far less solved it.
9 Cf. I. Caban & Z. Mańkowski, *ZWZ i AK w okręgu lubelskim 1939-1944*, Part II, Documents (Lublin, 1971), p. 517; the original in *Studium Polski Podziemnej* in London, Portfolio 3, no 3, 11.
10 B. Chrzanowski, 'Eksterminacja ludności żydowskiej w świetle polskich wydawnictw konspiracyjnych', *BŻIH*, 1-2 (1985), pp. 85-104;A. Friszke, 'Tuż przed Zagładą', *Więź* no 4 (1986), pp. 98-9; M.M .Drozdowski, 'The Attitude of Sikorski's Government to the Tragedy of the Polish Jews (1939-1944), *Acta Poloniae Historica*, 52 (1985), pp. 147-170.
11 J.J. Lipski, 'Antysemityzm ONR "Falangi"', *Myśl* (Warsaw, 1985), passim.
12 E. Kurek-Lesik, 'Udział żeńskich zgromadzeń zakonnych w akcji ratowania dzieci żydowskich w Polsce w latach 1939-1945', *Dzieje Najnowsze*, 18 (1986), fasc. 3/4, pp. 249-278. See also her article in *Polin*, vol III, 'The Conditions of Admittance and the Social Background of Jewish Children Saved by Women's Religious Orders in Poland from 1939-1945.'
13 This is not confirmed by Starzyński's biographer, M. M. Drozdowski, *Stefan Starzyński, prezydent Warszawy* (Warsaw, 1980); also no information of this type is to be found in L. Landau, *Kronika lat wojny i okupacji*, vol. 1, Warsaw 1939. The recordings of Starzyński's speeches are quoted in extenso by M. J. Kwiatkowski, *Wrzesień 1939 w warszawskiej rozgłośni Polskiego Radia*, Warsaw 1939; and their summaries are to be found in the volume *Cywilna obrona Warszawy we wrześniu 1939*, Warsaw 1964. In none of them have any accents, which could be interpreted as anti-semitic, been found.

RECENT PUBLICATIONS ON THE PLIGHT OF THE JEWS IN OCCUPIED POLAND

Adam A. Hetnal

Although the Nazis were deeply hostile to the Jews from the birth of their movement, only the assumption of power in Germany, Austria, Czechoslovakia, Poland, and other parts of Europe enabled them to put their racial theories into practice. The occupation of Poland was of particular importance in this respect. Pre-war Poland possessed the single largest Jewish community in Europe. The Polish census of 1931, and the estimates for September 1939 enable scholars to see the greatest, though not the only, genocide of our century in proper perspective. According to the Polish census of 1931, 3,130,581 citizens of pre-war Poland declared themselves to be of the Jewish faith. It is assumed that there were 3,474,000 Jews in Poland on September 1, 1939. They represented ten per cent of the country's total population, a percentage much higher than in any other country of Europe.[1]

About 120,000 Polish Jews participated in the September campaign of 1939. 32,216 died in action and 61,000 were taken prisoner. Yet they were not accorded prisoner-of-war status, and most of them perished.[2] Because of the Nazi-Soviet pact of August 23, 1939, which partitioned Poland, some 2,000,000 Jews fell under Nazi rule in September 1939, a number which grew to 2,800,000 after the German invasion of Soviet Russia in June 1941.[3] When Nazi rule over Poland ended in 1945, only perhaps some 100,000 Jews survived. Out of 18 million Nazi victims of all nationalities, 11 million perished on the territory of pre-war Poland, including about 3 million ethnic Poles. Some 89.3 per cent of pre-war Polish citizens perished in executions, reprisals, pacifications, or in the ill-famed concentration camps.[5]

In spite of the time that has elapsed since the agonizing years of Nazi rule, questions relating to the Nazi policy of genocide, the attitude of the Jews themselves and that of the rest of the world continue to be raised in many countries and in numerous languages. The captured Nazi records, the gradual opening of the archives in the West, and the recollections of the survivors or the witnesses of those dreadful events have enabled scholars to provide a better and fuller picture of the Jewish tragedy. At the same time, the topic continues to be highly emotional and controversial, with feelings running high at the expense of an unbiased and professional approach.

Among books on the genocide in occupied Poland, three recent titles deserve special attention. Two are recollections based on reminiscenses of survivors, while the third is based largely on records in the Ringelblum Archive (*Oneg Shabat*).[6] Dr. Emanuel Ringelblum (1900–1944), was a student of the great historian, Professor Marceli Handelsman (1883–1945), himself a victim of the Nazis. Ringelblum and his collaborators decided to collect, examine and preserve oral and written testimonies of witnesses of Nazi brutality. In addition to analyzing the Nazis' anti-Jewish policies, and passing vital information to the West through the intermediary of the Polish Home Army, Ringelblum and his team succeeded in hiding their archive in trunks and milk containers within the Warsaw Ghetto. Luckily, most of these were recovered in the post-1945 period. The records contained in them (or copies) are now housed in the archives of the Jewish Historical Institute in Warsaw and in Israel.

Józef Gitler-Barski, the author of *Przeżycia i wspomnienia z lat okupacji* [Experiences and Recollections of the Nazi Occupation of Poland], was born in 1898 and very early developed leftist leanings. He became actively involved, after 1922, in the Joint Distribution Committee (known as Joint), a philanthropic body organized and sponsored by American Jews. He was also active in the *Centrala Towarzystwa Opieki nad Sierotami i Dziećmi Opuszczonymi* [Relief Centre for Orphans and Abandoned Children] known as *Centos*. Barski continued his political and social activities in the Warsaw ghetto, from which he escaped to the 'Aryan' side in January 1943. After hiding in Warsaw for some time, Barski was sent to a concentration camp at Bergen-Belsen near Hanover, where he remained until the liberation in mid-April 1945. Although conditions at Bergen-Belsen left much to be desired, Jews there received better treatment than elsewhere, because many of them held foreign passports and were to be exchanged for German nationals. On pages 95–96 of his diary, kept at Bergen-Belsen, Barski writes: October 5, 1944, Morning scene [at Bergen-Belsen]:

> In a small corner between our bunks and the lavatory, I have been studying *The Epoch of the Renaissance in Rome* (I have got it from Szenkier) all morning. On the bed in front of me Szajn is playing cards with somebody. Nearby, young Berger is tutoring a boy in arithmetic on a board taken from a bed. A bit further away from us a group in *talitim* are praying loudly. On a neighbouring bed Tomkiewicz is studying English, and near him, Bojman and Lindberg French. In another corner a prisoner-physician is examining a companion in distress. Nearby, Ajerman is bargaining with Prajs, from

whom he wants to buy clothes for bread. On the upper bunk, Dąb is binding up his boils, and close to him, Degenszajn is picking lice out of his shirt ... all this is taking place in an area of about 2.5 square metres. This is more or less a typical morning in our barrack.[8]

Although many Jews at Bergen-Belsen were sent to extermination camps, Barski and his immediate family survived the ordeal of Nazi rule and returned to Poland,[9] where he held responsible positions until the age of seventy. The present volume is composed of articles published between 1948 and 1980, some new ones, and Barski's diary that he kept at Bergen-Belsen, now published without any abbreviations.

The late Professor Henryk Makower (1904–64)[10] made a name for himself in microbiology and in the study of viruses, first at the University of Wrocław and then at the Wrocław Medical Academy, where he worked until his untimely death in 1964. Between October 1940 and January 1943, Makower, his wife and immediate family were in the Warsaw ghetto. Although Makower, who was an excellent physician, enjoyed special treatment within the ghetto, he lost his mother and his immediate family. The same happened to the relatives of his wife, who were also sent to Treblinka. After his successful escape from the Warsaw ghetto in January 1943, Makower and his wife hid with Polish friends until the liberation. It was while in hiding that Makower wrote his memoirs.[11] Forty years later, his wife Dr. Noemi Makower, decided to edit her late husband's recollections, adding her own introduction, conclusion, and two chapters. She is thus more than a simple editor and could be considered co-author.[12]

Both Barski and Makower were in an excellent position to witness the tragedy of Polish Jews in general, and that of the Warsaw ghetto in particular. This became for a while the single largest concentration of Jews in Europe. Within an area of 307 hectares, its population reached some 460,000 people in April 1941. This meant unusual overcrowding, with 150,000 helpless, terrorized, and panic-stricken people per square kilometre.[13] The Warsaw ghetto was surrounded by a wall, and was cut off from the surrounding world. It was strictly forbidden to leave the area, which was heavily guarded. Although well-to-do Jews or speculators were able to draw upon their savings or even make money, the poverty-stricken had almost nowhere to turn for help. The death rate was exceptionally high, and some 100,000 people died in the Warsaw Ghetto prior to the Nazi decision (taken in January 1942) to exterminate all the Jews.[14] The humanitarian doctor and the social and political activist, as well as many others, did their best to alleviate the plight of the old, sick, and of the children. Both record many examples of compassion and humanity among those who were condemned to die. They also cite numerous examples of help coming from the Poles on the 'Aryan' side, many of whom were ready to risk their lives, as well as those of their loved ones, to hide or to assist the inhabitants of the ghetto. Anti-Jewish feelings diminished, and there were even cases of former anti-semites violating the Nazi decree adopted in October 1941 which laid down that any Pole assisting a Jew would be executed.[15] This barbaric law was often enforced.

In spite of the inhuman conditions, starvation, and every kind of hardship imposed upon the Jews within the Warsaw ghetto, many managed to survive. There were impressive examples of self-sacrifices for children, the sick, and the needy, though cases of total indifference to the starving could also be seen. Devoted doctors, nurses, social workers, and humanitarians did their best to care for the ghetto children and others. There existed an enormous will to survive the atrocious conditions that initially many had thought to be temporary. There was no food or medicine, but people learned how to smuggle in what was needed and life began to organize itself. It was at a moment when many hoped that the worst was behind them that the Final Solution began to be applied. When the head of the Jewish Council, Adam Czerniakow, learned about the new 'resettlement policy', which in reality meant the murder of the Jews in Treblinka and other gas chambers, he committed suicide on 23 July, 1942. Realizing that his policy of placating the Nazis had failed, he refused to participate in the physical destruction of his own people.

Both Barski and Makower describe how skilfully the Nazis acted. By terrorizing the Jewish Council, and by making promises to the Jewish Police (*Ordnungsdienst*), they were able to exterminate over 300,000 people between July and October 1942.[16] At first, it was the Jews who selected their own people for the 'resettlement' (read 'the gas chamber'), and then, when the Warsaw Ghetto was largely depleted in numbers, SS-men, Ukrainian auxiliaries, and others entered directly into action. The Nazis acted with regard to the Jews in a deceitful way. No promises were kept, and the number of exempted people was systematically reduced. How could it be otherwise since the Nazis did not consider the Jews as fellow human beings. An SS-man, for example, told a Jew: 'You are neither a man, nor an animal. You are just a Jew'.[17] Consequently, even people who served the Germans, such as members and employees of the Jewish Council and Jewish policemen were all destined for extermination.

Both Barski and Makower express a degree of respect for the Nazis' diabolical skill. They knew how to handle the crowd, how to play upon hopes, and how to encourage others to do the dirty work for them. Both think that the Nazis must have made use of able psychologists, who knew how to handle large crowds.[18] For a long time most Jews in the ghetto resigned themselves and were unprepared to offer any physical resistance. It was largely the younger generation, many of whom were adolescents at the beginning of the occupation, that decided to resist the Germans at any cost. They also punished some of the collaborators. The first show of armed resistance took place in January 1943. Amazed by this, the Nazis withdrew for a while in order to decide their future action. When they came back in April 1943, the Warsaw Ghetto rose in insurrection. Those who took part knew that they had no chance, but they were determined to make a stand. Of course, neither Barski nor Makower witnessed the final tragedy of the Warsaw Ghetto. Both were by then in hiding on the 'Aryan' side.

The third work under review, *Dwa etapy. Hitlerowska polityka eksterminacji Żydów w oczach ofiar* [Two stages. The Hitlerite policy of exterminating the Jews in the eyes of the victims], has been prepared by Dr Ruta Sakowska, a researcher at the Jewish Historical Institute in Warsaw, the author of *Ludzie z dzielnicy zamkniętej. Żydzi w Warszawie w okresie hitlerowskiej okupacji, październik 1939 – marzec 1943* [People from the Closed Quarter: Jews in Warsaw under Nazi Occupation, October 1939 – March 1943] (1975), and editor of *Archiwum Ringelbluma. Getto Warszawskie, lipiec 1942 – styczeń 1943* [Ringelblum's Archive: The Warsaw Ghetto, July 1942 – January 1943] (1980).

In her historical sketch, which occupies almost half of her present book, Sakowska stresses the importance of the Warsaw Ghetto. It represented a kind of model for all the other ghettos in occupied Poland and was the largest Jewish settlement in the occupied territories (in comparison, the Łódź ghetto, which ranked immediately after, contained at its peak some 160,000 inhabitants within an area of 4 square kilometres).[19]

Sakowska and other authors have stressed the problem of starvation and the totally inadequate housing in Jewish ghettos. Even those who were entitled to food rations only received an amount of 184 to 230 calories per day.[20] The 130,000 resettled Jews from the *Reich* and other regions, presented the Warsaw ghetto with its greatest problem. These people suffered most, and death visited them most often.[21]

The author also differs from most authorities on the periodization of the treatment of Jews under Nazi rule. She does not see a great difference between the period of the Final Solution and that which preceded it. She proposes her own periodization – distinguishing between the period of indirect and direct extermination. The first lasted more or less from September 1939 until the invasion of Soviet Russia in June 1941, while the second had already begun in the fall of 1941.[22] Sakowska stresses that in the first stage, Jewish property was plundered, compulsory and exhausting labour was introduced for all Jewish males between 14 and 60,[23] Jews were gradually eliminated from social and economic life, locked up in isolated ghettos, and enjoyed no human rights. They could not even congregate and pray together. Direct extermination meant the total elimination of Jewish settlements in the *Reich*, occupied territories, and satellite countries. Sakowska stresses that the situation changed from one occupied region to another. Often (e.g. in the Warsaw and Łódź ghettos), the two policies were applied simultaneously.[24]

The records selected by Sakowska provide heartbreaking examples of human cruelty and bestiality interwoven with self-denial, readiness to assist others regardless of the risk, and many cases in between. It is impossible to remain indifferent, while examining these three works. The great Russian novelist, Fyodor Dostoyevsky, wrote that man was neither good nor evil but could turn either way. The terrible years of Nazi rule showed the people at their best and also at their worst. When one was ready to conclude that God is dead, and that human feelings no longer exist, one could suddenly see examples which contradicted this pessimistic viewpoint and *vice versa*. Only in times of trial can human nature be seen in its essence.

The three books are also important because of their authenticity. Two of the authors witnessed many events, and Sakowska's own family certainly must have suffered under Nazi rule. The three authors understand the reality of the situation. They do not seek scapegoats for the Jewish tragedy, but describe honestly, though not without passion, the events that they have either witnessed or investigated. They do not excuse those Jews who were indifferent to the plight of others, or who showed an unusual eagerness to obey Nazi orders, regardless of their nature. One can also see cases of Poles who tried to exploit the impossible situation of the hunted Jews, particularly those who desperately tried to survive on the 'Aryan' side. Some such individuals were executed by the Polish Underground.[25] Each society has some percentage of ignoble individuals who not only lack compassion and humanity, but are even ready to exploit someone's misfortune. Many Poles did not remain indifferent to the plight of the Jews and tried to assist them. However, themselves terror-stricken, undernourished, not safe in their own apartments, or homes, there were limits to what the Poles could do. Desperate messages were sent to the West, but several of these were treated with disbelief, even by members of Jewish communities.[26] What the Nazis did was so atrocious, that reasonable and logically thinking people took many true facts for simple exaggerations. In short, only a strong, concerted action could have saved more Jews, but the Nazis were very strong, and the West had other priorities at this stage of the war.[27] Little real help came from Soviet Russia, itself engaged in a mortal struggle with the Nazis. To sum up, the greatest tragedy of our century cannot be undone. But at least one hopes that humanity will derive proper lessons from it. In some respects, people are more compassionate now than then.

To return to the three books under review, one can regret that Barski's and Makower's recollections have not been provided with indexes. Otherwise, all three make a contribution to our knowledge of many aspects of the dehumanizing Nazi rule. It would be good to have them translated into English, so that more people could examine them.

NOTES

1 Władysław Bartoszewski and Zofia Lewinówna, eds. *Righteous Among Nations: How Poles Helped the Jews 1939–1945* (London, 1969), p. XVI; *ibid.*, *Ten jest z ojczyzny mojej. Polacy z pomocą Żydom 1939–1945*. 2nd and revised edition (Kraków, 1969), p. 7.
2 Bartoszewski and Lewinówna, *Ten jest z ojczyzny mojej*, pp. 8–9; *Righteous Among Nations*, p. XVIII.
3 Bartoszewski and Lewinówna, *Ten jest z ojczyzny mojej*, p. 9; *Righteous Among Nations*, pp. XVII-XVIII.
4 Bartoszewski and Lewinówna, *Ten jest z ojczyzny mojej*, p. 9; *Righteous Among Nations*, p. XVII.
5 Norman Davies, *God's Playground. A History of Poland*, 2 vols. (New York, 1982), 2: 463. According to Davies, some 100,000 Polish Jews perished under Soviet occupation between September 1939 and June 1941, see Davies, *God's Playground*, 2: 451.
6 Józef Barski, *Przeżycia i wspomnienia z lat okupacji* (Wrocław, 1986); Henryk Makower, *Pamiętnik z getta warszawskiego październik 1940–styczeń 1943*, Noemi Makower ed. (Wrocław, 1987); Ruta Sakowska, *Dwa etapy. Hitlerowska polityka eksterminacji Żydów w oczach ofiar. Szkic historyczny i dokumenty* (Wrocław, 1986).
7 For some data on Barski, see *Przeżycia*, pp. 5–7; Abraham Shulman, *The Case of Hotel Polski: An Account of One of the Most Enigmatic Episodes of World War II* (New York, 1982).
8 Barski, *Przeżycia*, pp. 95–96.
9 Shulman, *The Case of Hotel Polski*, p. 215, provides a very plausible reason for Barski's survival. Between pages 161 and 167, Shulman provides excerpts from Barski's diary. There are some discrepancies in dates between the Polish original and Shulman's excerpts. Incidentally, Shulman provides one entry which is missing in Barski's original, p. 163 'April 27, 1944. An unusual event – a German guard in one of the watchtowers lowered a loaf of bread on a string together with a slip of paper in which he expressed, in Polish, his wish for peace'.
10 For biographical information relating to Makower, see *Pamiętnik z getta*, pp. 5–7. This is a reprint of a short biographical sketch on him in the *Polski Słownik Biograficzny*, vol. 19.
11 *Ibid.*, p. 211.
12 *Ibid.*, p. 6.
13 Sakowska, *Dwa etapy*, p. 11.
14 *Ibid.*, pp. 13–14.
15 Bartoszewski and Lewinówna, *Righteous Among Nations*, p. 632.
16 Bartoszewski and Lewinówna, *Righteous Among Nations*, p. XXV.
17 Sakowska, *Dwa etapy*, pp. 140–141. 'Du bist kein Mensch, kein Tier, du bist Jude.' SS-man Schultz to a Jew.
18 Makower, *Pamiętnik z getta*, pp. 206–207; Barski, *Przeżycia*, pp. 46–9.
19 Bartoszewski and Lewinówna, *Righteous Among Nations*, p. XIX.
20 *Ibid.*, p. XXII, speaks about 184 calories per day, while Sakowska, *op.cit.*, p. 13, writes about 230 calories. There is, therefore, some discrepancy between the two above studies.
21 Sakowska, *Dwa etapy*, p. 13.
22 *Ibid.*, pp. 8–9.
23 *Ibid.*, pp. 10–14.
24 *Ibid.*, pp. 8–9.

25 Bartoszewski and Lewinówna, *Ten jest z ojczyzny mojej*, pp. 393–99; *Righteous Among Nations*, pp. 670–71.
26 Bartoszewski and Lewinówna, *Righteous Among Nations*, pp. 524–543.
27 For a detailed discussion concerning the situation in the West, see Yehuda Bauer, *American Jewry and the Holocaust: The American Jewish Joint Distribution Committee, 1939–1945* (Detroit, Michigan, 1981).

RESISTANCE TO TYRANNY
M. R. D. Foot

Władysław Bartoszewski, *Herbst der Hoffnungen*. 4th ed., Freiburg im Breisgau: Herder. 1986. Pp. 144.

Id, *Uns eint vergossenes Blut*. Frankfurt am Main: S. Fischer. 1987. Pp. 299.

Id, *Das Warschauer Ghetto – wie es wirklich war*. 2nd ed., Frankfurt am Main: S. Fischer. 1986. Pp. 141. Trans. by Stephen G. Cappelari as *The Warsaw Ghetto*: a Christian's testimony, Boston, Massachusetts: Beacon Press. 1987. Pp. x, 117.

Id, *Wer ein Leben rettet, rettet die ganze Welt*. 2nd ed., Freiburg im Breisgau: Herder. 1987. Pp. 141.

Four books by that prolific historian, the elder Bartoszewski, happen to be available at once, all in German; one accompanied by an English translation; all on a similar theme, resistance to tyranny. This subject was not new 'when Israel was in Egypt's land', or later when Xerxes, King of Persia, tried to subdue Greece early in the fifth century before Christ; it is still a current problem today. Stanisław Lem, in a foreword to the translation, gives Professor Doctor honoris causa Władysław Bartoszewski his full titles, and remarks on his extraordinary luck in coming through the world war alive: for Bartoszewski, Warsaw born and brought up a Polish Roman Catholic, spent most of the years 1939–45 trying to help his Jewish fellow-countrymen – then and there, inside the Gouvernement-General, a capital offence. The Germans arrested him early (in a 1940 round-up of Polish intelligentsia), and put him in Auschwitz, whence by a stroke of blind luck he was released, to resume work for the Red Cross. He fought through, and survived, the Warsaw Uprising of 1944; rearrested at the end of it, he was with a small party who were allowed to slip away into whatever fresh identities they could create for themselves. Released from German domination by the USSR's advance across prostrate Poland, he then tried to follow a career as an independent intellectual: with the consequence to be expected under a regime subservient to Stalin: he was again put inside. Altogether he has seen Christmas nine times from behind bars. In a brash, superficial, pushful age he has a virtue rare among historians who appeal to a wide public – modesty. He even struck his name off a list of those Polish Christians who tried to help the Jews trapped in Warsaw's ghetto; Lem restored it.

The Germans did their best to cut the ghetto off entirely from the rest of the city, as they did in every other city or town in eastern Europe where they set up a ghetto; the inhabitants, who had been taken for granted as part of the urban scheme of things for centuries past, gradually had it borne in on them that there was to be a total block between the Jewish and the non-Jewish sectors. Bartoszewski's testimony about the Warsaw of his childhood in the nineteen-twenties is eloquent on precisely this point, of how normal it seemed to everybody (Jew and Gentile alike) that there were Jews about who dressed differently and worshipped differently, but who were men, women and children exactly on a par with their Christian fellows; even though they tended to keep themselves to themselves. To the Germans life did not seem to be that shape – or at any rate to the convinced Nazis, who continually denounced the Jews as *Untermenschen*, sub-men not worthy of humane treatment. Even to pass a mug of water to a Jew dying of thirst might – sometimes did – bring in the Warsaw of the early nineteen-forties immediate execution.

This is an example, vivid enough, of how much grimmer the war was in eastern than in western Europe. The burning of a single village in France resulted in cries of protest that have resounded for decades; in large tracts of Poland, the Ukraine, parts of western Russia there was hardly a village left unburned. Similarly, awful as some of the privations of prisoners in Vichy's camps were, at least they were not habitually used by the guards for target practice, nor were they marched off by platoons to be gassed. The reviewer spent a hundred days as a prisoner of the German armed forces, during which time he lost about a third of his body weight, but he was so lightly interrogated that he was able to keep his identity as an army intelligence officer to himself; he was never tortured; he was never handed over to the secret police; and he is fully aware that all he went through was as nothing compared to what Bartoszewski had to put up with in a single week in Auschwitz. There, as a treat, the SS paraded the inmates on Christmas eve in front of a Christmas tree, decked out with coloured lights, round which they had piled in lieu of presents the corpses of those prisoners who had been slaughtered during the day: the SS's idea of a joke.

Even there, the extreme strictnesses of the regime did not always apply; in Warsaw, the noose round the ghetto was not drawn as absolutely tight as the SS would have wished. Even so long after the event, the author is able to describe most vividly how it was possible to keep up some degree of communication between the beseiged and their fellows outside who sympathized with them: a task in which he often had a role to play himself. It called for prodigious feats of memory and of patience, both of which he had abundantly. Though cruelty is one of his themes, endurance is another.

Again, as an intellectual, he brings out the part that bright men and women can play in a secret or semi-secret context, working against an oppressor. Those who can read, write and figure easily ought to be well qualified to get jobs as clerks; as clerks, they can watch what passes under their eyes, and make sure that word gets out to interested parties; or they can look for holes in the bureaucratic machinery of their overlords, and help friends to hide in them – or even creep through them to entire safety elsewhere.

He stresses the stupidities of bureaucracy; which paled in turn beside the stupidities inherent in the Nazi system, or lack of system, for putting *Untermenschen* into their necessarily (so Nazi doctrine had it) inferior spots. *The Warsaw Ghetto* is a straightforward history, amply buttressed by contemporary documents, which explains in detail how the ghetto was enclosed, how the restrictions placed on its inhabitants became so unbearable that in 1943 it exploded in a half-armed rising, and how that rising was crushed. Some of the testimony he quotes is his own; and the ghetto's rising seems to him a symbol of the need to stand up against tyranny, even when to do so is quite clearly hopeless: a necessary part of human dignity.

At the time, through the underground press (for which he wrote himself) and through personal contacts, Poles tried to spread word about what was happening to the Jews, who were already disappearing into the fog of *Nacht und Nebel*, the wall of official silence behind which the Third Reich carried out its utmost savageries. The Poles are proud, for their part, of never having had a Pétain or a Quisling: there was no sort of official co-operation with the Nazi occupiers. Yet Bartoszewski is honest enough to admit that there were sub-strata in the population of Poland who did collaborate with them: criminals, both Jew and Gentile, who thought they saw their way to easy money by plying various trades of trickery. This is a side of life in occupied Europe that has not yet been much ventilated in public; not a creditable one for anybody.

Wer ein Leben rettet contains a connected series of essays on the borderland between history and morality. In it the author discusses the age-long familiar problems of guilt and blame, in the light of his own generation's experiences, particularly – without being at all self-centred – of his own. He is sure that historians must speak out about the truth as they see it: indeed his tone sometimes recalls the heroic child in the fable of the Emperor's clothes, as he drags into print some aspects of history quite overlooked at the time. He remarks for example on the extent of Soviet aid to Germany during the currency of the Ribbentrop-Molotov pact (24 August 1939 to 22 June 1941); then kept quiet because the deals were between two secretive regimes, subsequently kept quiet because to reveal them would have been embarrassing to Stalin and all Stalin's admirers.

He opens up also themes covered in the other two books. *Herbst der Hoffnungen* goes through his prison experiences, both under Nazi and under communist governments. Its cover shows, appropriately enough, an apple on a snow-covered tree. It took a Stalinist jailer to hold him for eighteen months completely isolated, with no touch with his family or the outside world, not even a newspaper. Here memories of Auschwitz were of some help to him: at least he could console himself with the thought that he was not bound for the crematorium at Birkenau. He survived seven days' and seven nights' continuous interrogation, by teams of Stalinist officials; having nothing to say, he said it. Released and rearrested, he found himself sharing a cell with a monk and an SS *Hauptstürmführer*: examples of the eccentric company he had to keep.

Eventually they let him out. He happened to get back to Warsaw at a moment when Kafka's *The Trial* was on the stage, saw it, and was struck dumb with how appropriate it was, to what had been happening in Poland's prisons: how had Kafka known, how had he foreseen? No wonder the play is rarely performed in eastern Europe.

Uns eint vergossenes Blut – 'The blood shed unites us' was the title of an English translation of an earlier version – covers Jewish-Polish relations during the Nazis' attempt to wipe out European Jewry altogether. Bartoszewski takes the title from a poem by Władysław Broniewski, put into German by Karl Dedecius, dedicated to the memory of Szmul Zygielbojm who tried in London in 1942 to get the world to listen to the tale of mass murder he had to tell. As is only too well known, the world did not want to know. Bartoszewski goes clearly and carefully through the events that led up to the catastrophe. He starts with the grouping of Jews in Poland before ever the war began, over three million of them in the 1931 census, a tenth of the country's total population, nearly a third of that of Warsaw and of several other cities. He describes the forming of the ghettoes by the Nazis, and annihilation of the Warsaw ghetto in 1942, its refilling from elsewhere in Poland, the secret attempts made to arm it, the fresh battle there in the spring of 1943, and the persecution of those outside it who tried to help. Over two million Gentile Poles were victims of the Gestapo, besides the millions of Jews. From study of their fates, he believes some good can come for the future of mankind.

The book is written in the certainty that those who have experienced such a disaster must bear witness to it, lest future generations forget. Yet, agonizing though the details are of what he describes, he writes without anguish, but with the proper detachment of a scholar. In his own case, he believes he owes his survival to help from Jews – given because he himself had helped Jews; he advocates therefore Jewish-Polish, even German-Polish amity. He has seen enough of hate, and wants no more of it. He describes himself as a patriot, but not a nationalist. And, being human, he cannot abandon hope. These books make inspiring reading: mankind at its best as well as at its worst.

NAZI SOCIAL POLICIES
Michael Burleigh

Beiträge zur nationalsozialistischen Gesundheits- und Sozialpolitik, eds Gotz Aly, Jochen August, Peter Chroust, Klaus Dorner, Matthias Hamann, Hans-Dieter Heilmann, Susanne Heim, Franz Koch, Christian Pross, Ulrich Schultz, Christine Teller: Vol.1. *Aussonderung und Tod. Die klinische Hinrichtung der Unbrauchbaren.* Pp. vi, 189; Vol.2 *Reform und Gewissen 'Euthanasie' im Dienst des Forschritts.* Pp. vi, 196; Vol.3 *Herrenmensch und Arbeitsvölker. Ausländische Arbeiter und Deutsche 1939–1945.* Pp. vi, 189; Vol. 4 *Biedermann und Schreibtischtäter. Materialien zur deutschen Täter-Biographie.* Pp. vi, 207; Vol.5 *Sozialpolitik und Judenvernichtung. Gibt es eine Ökonomie der Endlösung.* Pp. vi, 188; Vol.6 *Feinderklärung und Prävention. Kriminalbiologie, Zigeunerforschung und Asozialenpolitik.* Pp. vi, 214. Rotbuch Verlag. Berlin. 1987–1988.

These studies focus upon the following areas of Nazi health and social policy: the treatment of foreign forced labour during the war; the genesis, extension, and legitimisation of the euthanasia programme; the persecution of Sinti, Rom and others categorised as 'asocial'; and finally, the question of whether the *Endlösung* was simply a 'means' of hastening the modernisation of overpopulated, subsistence economies in eastern Europe, rather than the consequence of ideological race-hatred. They are the work of freelance writers, doctors, social workers and the unemployed, collectively dissatisfied, apparently, with the impersonal and over-conceptualised approach of much academic writing on this period. The emphasis in these overtly empirical, and much-researched volumes is upon the gulf of unknowing which separated the educated professionals who put their intelligence, energies, and careers at the disposal of the Third Reich, and the poor, ill-educated and sick people who were their victims. By focussing upon hitherto obscure agencies and individuals, the authors seek to show how high level decisions were translated into someone else's permanent misfortune. Hence there is much attention to the actual processes of encompassing and categorising the régime's victims, and considerable stress upon how skill and knowledge was instrumentalised in the service of the Nazi's unique racial utopia. In contrast to some recent North American writing, the psychological dilemmas of Hitler's scientific soldiers receive short shrift. The voices one hears in these volumes are arrogant, careerist, brutal, and matter-of-fact: 'I think that one must regard the Polish question without feeling, purely biologically. We must exterminate them, otherwise they will exterminate us. Therefore I am glad about every Pole who is no longer alive', the professor of anatomy at the 'Reichsuniversität Posen', Heinrich Voss, wrote in his diary on 2 June 1941. In fact, taken severally, these studies go some way to recreating Nazi Germany as daily reality, with fifty years of evasive self-exculpation stripped away like so much rotting plaster. Ethnic comrades are served first, the rest queue for what might be left over; swimming baths open to Dutchmen or Danes, but not Poles and Russians; films playing to eighteen million Germans about the state's right to kill the sick; armies of foreign labourers in the factories, on the land, and clearing up the rubble; the Gypsies who decamped in the night, leaving their wagons behind them; and the 'Jewish' business suddenly under new, 'Aryan' management. It is all here in almost indescribably bleak detail.

While the authors' concern with the often obscure lives of the régime's victims is admirable, the studies are not without some major drawbacks. Although their collective desire not to allow the régime to be objectified and 'contextualised' as just another, unfortunate, historical experience is understandable, their concern with its imprint on social policy in the conservative Federal Republic leads them into the dangers which beset all historical parallels. Notwithstanding the insensitivity and ineptitude of many of the Republic's politicians (one forebears to speak of some of West Germany's historians), the Nazi régime had rather more extended objectives than the cost-cutting concerns of fiscal neo-conservatives. No doubt 'rationalising' the allocation of resources was part of the régime's rhetoric, but the fundamental assumptions of Hitler or Himmler were utterly different from those of, say, Heiner Geissler. The men who, in these studies, hanged young Polish workers for racially defiling German women, or who slaughtered the occupants of Soviet lunatic asylums, were not motivated by any desire to equalise the cost:benefit ration, but by an obsession with racial purity. Their victims were seen as a threat to the latter: that is why they were killed. It was a question of *Rassensäuberung*.

It seems invidious to single out particular contributions to a series which is clearly the product of much collective discussion, but some of the work is outstanding. In two related essays (Vol.6), the East German writer Reimar Gilsenbach examines the configuration of individuals and agencies which put Germany's Sinti and Rom on the road to Auschwitz. Pre-existing police harrassment, and the prejudice of ordinary citizens, designed to make the Gypsies someone else's problem, was invested with racial-scientific certitude which justified wiping out the Gypsies entirely. The crucial contribution here came from criminal-biological experts like Professor Robert Ritter, who by classifying 90 per cent of Germany's Gypsies as a racially-impure and criminal Lumpenproletariat, prepared the way for whatever measures the state took against them. This meant *inter alia* isolation, the fragmentation of families, sterilisation, and finally disappearance into the sub-universe of the concentration camps. While it would have been interesting to learn more about the part played by ordinary citizens in the earlier stages of persecution (e.g. in the initial quarantining of the Gypsies prior to the 1936 Olympics), Gilsenbach does not neglect the ultimate role of Hitler in the Gypsies collective tragedy. Himmler's eccentric desire to keep a few 'specimens' around as a living ethnic curiosity was firmly quashed by Bormann as the mouthpiece of his typically laconic leader. After the war, the racial scientists discussed by Gilsenbach experienced few difficulties in finding posts as psychologists dealing with disturbed adolescents. As Ursula Körber shows, the surviving Gypsies quest for compensation was another matter. Until 1965 the federal authorities refused to accept that prior to the execution of the deportation order to Auschwitz on 1 March 1943 the Gypsies had been the victims of racial persecution. This meant implicit acceptance of the Nazi's categorisation of the Gypsies as 'asocial' and hence, retrospective legitimisation of the 'police or security measures' taken against them from 1936 onwards.

Most of the studies of the euthanasia programme focus upon the individuals involved, or the extension of the categories of victim to include those with chronic TB or whose sanity had vanished because of bombing. By contrast, Karl Heinz Roth (Vol.2) gives a fascinating account of films commissioned by Himmler which were designed to overcome widespread popular and clerical disquiet occasioned by the 'T4' programme and hence to legitimise past, and prospective, killings. Extraordinary care was taken by the agencies involved, and their film-making assistants, to develop a story-line which would sow doubt about the moral issues involved, while avoiding the sordid reality. Thus the documentary approach – e.g. contrasting photogenic hopeless cases with a few carefully selected 'luxury' asylums – was shelved in favour of melodrama. The result of months of discussion and extensive re-writing was Wolfgang Liebeneiner's *Ich klage an*, the story of a pioneering scientist who, faced with the limits of his own ingenuity, resolves to overdose his incurably ill wife. Lest the tears shed by the audience occluded the message, this was rehearsed through the device of a courtroom drama at the end. In the best propaganda tradition, the régime's position was not articulated by its token representative on the jury, but by the spokesmen of consensus. A retired Prussian major contrasts the resources expended 'to keep a few pitiful creatures alive' at a time when it was hard to keep the healthy in health and 'to care properly for mothers and their new-born children'. The reality behind the film's ponderous reasonableness is chronicled by, *inter alia*, Matthias Hamann's chapter (Vol.1) on the murder in German asylums of the entirely healthy children of Polish or Soviet female forced labourers.

If there was widespread concern about the euthanasia programme and its possible extension to ever-wider categories of people, the population seems to have adjusted quite smoothly to the presence of seven million foreign workers in their midst. No one seems to have objected to the fact that many of them had been kidnapped from cinemas or churches, or that once in Germany, they were classified along racial lines. 'West workers' did skilled jobs; 'eastern workers' heavy and dirty manual tasks. These distinctions were further cemented by the régime, with draconian penalties for fraternization between Germans and either Russians or Poles. Something of racialism as daily experience, and practice, is conveyed through Jochen August's use of the reminiscences of former Polish forced labourers (Vol.3). In his case, most of the Poles concerned worked on the land. The matter of for whom was resolved at a human cattle market, with German farmers testing their muscles, and slipping bribes to the labour authorities to secure the fittest 'specimens'. Although life on the farms was safer than in camps situated near factories, the Poles were the victims of much peasant mean-mindedness. The issues that rankled included separate tables and less food at mealtimes while the *Herrenmenschen* ate their fill, or the word 'bitte' only attached to orders the day before the American troops marched in. The fate of those *Ostarbeiter* who fell seriously ill, had breakdowns, or simply became pregnant – they were relocated to Hadamar or its equivalents rather than repatriated – is described in Vol.1.

Given the depressing frequency with which racial theories and practice figure in these studies, it is odd to discover Götz Aly's attempt to convert his and Susanne Heim's earlier work on the social planner Helmut Menhold (*Ein Berater der Macht*, Hamburg 1986), into a general explanation of the *Endlösung* as a 'means' of restructuring the class relations and economies of eastern Europe. Since this thesis, in so far as it posits a consensus among the 'planning intelligentsia', has been subjected to a thorough critique by Christopher Browning, only a few points will be made here. While Aly's intellectual dissatisfaction with both the freeflowing 'machinery of destruction' and incomprehensible 'catastrophe' approaches to the *Endlösung* is understandable, to confuse whatever pseudo-rational gloss a few economists put upon it with the complex reality of what took place is plainly unsatisfactory. The Jews were murdered, not because they were an obstacle to the 'modernisation' of Poland or Russia, or because they were a 'health' or 'security' risk, as other sets of 'experts' reported, but because they were Jews. That alone explains the régime's unrelenting efforts to locate and eliminate them *all* throughout the *whole* of occupied Europe, regardless of whatever consequences this had for either the economy of the Reich, or the local economies concerned. That is why, to answer a question Aly formulates but does not answer, the deportation in June 1944 of 2,200 Jews more than two thousand kilometres from Rhodes to Auschwitz took priority over evacuating troops and material from the island. And that is why some of the Jew-hating economists he cites, like Peter Heinz Seraphim, were subsequently appalled when they came face to face with the consequences of ideologically-motivated mass murder which totally ignored their own imperatives. In the end, racial ideology over-ruled any rational calculations; it was this, after all, which distinguished Nazi Germany from any other regime.

Taken severally, these studies represent a major contribution to our knowledge of how Nazi policy, particularly as it affected marginal groups, was given definition, and translated into action, by an army of middling to minor functionaries. Because of the narrow focus of investigations after the war (not to speak of collusion) most of the men and women discussed in these books evaded any form of retribution. The studies also reveal much about the responses of the population at large to government policy, which itself was a sort of dialogue with prejudices latent in ordinary people. Most valuably, these studies recover traces of people whom the régime reduced to digits and racial formulae on index cards and then brutally murdered. This last, modest, achievement certainly makes the whole venture worthwhile.

HISTORY, HOLOCAUST, AND GERMAN NATIONAL IDENTITY
Alexandra Reiche

Ian Kershaw, *The 'Hitler Myth'. Image and Reality in the Third Reich*. Oxford: Clarendon Press. 1987. Pp. ix, 297.

Charles S. Maier. *The Unmasterable Past. History, Holocaust, and German National Identity.*, Cambridge, Mass., and London: Harvard University Press. 1988. Pp. xi, 227.

These books raise questions about German responsibility for the rise of the Third Reich. Kershaw's book is an account of the relationship between German society, Hitler and Nazism, while Maier's book examines the relevance and importance of these questions in contemporary German society. Both discuss the changing significance of the persecution of Jews and the Holocaust; as Kershaw points out this was low on the list of priorities for the average German during the war itself, but has since become the focal point of West German historiography. Maier examines the recent debate in West Germany which has revealed the desire amongst some historians to reverse this by relativizing the Holocaust and by creating a national identity from a selective view of history, of which the Germans 'can once again be proud'. Both Maier and Kershaw discuss the origins of Nazism, of its structural rootedness in German society at large, and of Germans' broad responsibility for the crimes committed by the National Socialists.

Kershaw explores the creation and development of the popular image of Hitler or what he calls the Hitler myth. The image of Hitler was a propaganda masterpiece created largely by Goebbels, who considered it to be his greatest achievement. The myth was based largely on heroic leadership ideals. Hitler was seen by many to be the personification of the nation, whose lack of corruption and unselfish motives were detachable from the scandalous greed and hypocrisy of the Party functionaries. He was seen to be personally sincere and moderate, the representative of popular justice and the upholder of popular morality against the enemies of the people. An example of the early success of this image is seen in the public reaction to the massacre of Rohm and members of the SA by Hitler. As the head of government he openly accepted responsibility for what amounted to the cold-blooded murder of his colleagues, but in the eyes of the majority of the population his stature actually increased. Thereby, the people who had been threatened by the unruliness, arbitrary violence and public outrages of the SA even believed that Hitler had acted quickly to eliminate them in the public interest, making the ludicrous assumption that it was not Hitler himself who had originally sanctioned the SA activities. During his Reichstag speech in which he admitted responsibility for the killings he referred to the 'ulcer of the SA subversion' which had made it 'necessary' for him to 'burn down to the raw flesh'. This was greeted not with scepticism but with admiration and gratitude, as Hitler's intervention was widely regarded as liberation from strongly felt oppression.

Kershaw points to many examples of Hitler's resounding popularity, particularly before the war. The image was so successful that even in July 1944, when it had become clear to most Germans that the country was losing the war and when, according to secret Gestapo reports, Party popularity was decreasing rapidly, the attempt on Hitler's life outraged the majority of Germans. The plotters themselves, hundreds of whom were to be killed by Hitler, were generally regarded as traitors who had acted against the interests of the country. The general public persistently distinguished between Hitler who was seen by most to be beyond reproach, and the Party members, who were frequently criticized. The attitude that 'Hitler would be all right but his underlings are nothing but swindlers' was common. Given this relationship between Hitler and his followers, Kershaw asks what significance this held for the development and outcome of actual policies in the Third Reich. Of particular interest here is the relationship between the Hitler myth and the Holocaust.

It is clear that anti-semitism was central to Hitler's world-view, but was it important in forming the bond between him and the German people? Kershaw shows that the barrage of Nazi propaganda after 1933 extended and deepened already existing anti-semitic attitudes in Germany and that by 1939 most Germans believed that Jews had been a 'harmful influence' in German society. Despite these discriminatory attitudes, however, the vast majority of the population did not remotely match Hitler's anti-Jewish paranoia or the activist Jew-baiting elements in the Nazi Party. For most Germans the 'Jewish question' was, between 1933 and 1945, 'of no more than secondary importance for shaping popular opinion in the Third Reich'. Hitler became increasingly popular in the 1930s despite the fact that he mentioned Jews infrequently. In spring of 1933, summer of 1934 and above all in autumn of 1938 the 'Jewish question' was high on the public agenda but at other times the interest in it was relatively low except amongst Party activists. According to Kershaw the discrimination against the Jews was not the reason why Hitler came to be so popular with the general public.

A speech given by Hitler in January 1939 was the first of a series of speeches in which he made brutal references to the 'destruction of the Jewish race in Europe'. In direct contrast to his pre-war stance, Hitler began to be openly connected with his anti-Jewish policies. Typically, though, his references to the actual fate of the Jews were vague, for although he seemingly had a desire to make his work manifest in the eyes of history, he had agreed with Rosenberg in late 1941 that 'it was inappropriate to speak of extermination in public'. By late 1942, Bormann was anxious to end rumours circulating about the 'Final Solution' in the east. Kershaw points out that the contrast between Hitler deliberately flaunting hints of the mass-murder of the Jews and the suppression of 'hard' information about the actual mechanics of this 'mirrors the manner in which Hitler, as the driving force behind genocide, even privately combined massive threats against the Jews with a taboo on the details of extermination'. Even during this time Hitler's comments on the Jews were received with little interest in comparison for example, to news from the front; and Hitler's Jewish policies remained a marginal interest in Germany until after the war. In retrospect, the general lack of interest in the fate of the Jews is startling, for although Hitler couched the systematic destruction of European Jewry in vague terms, calling it a 'struggle against the immense power of world Jewry', and although he advocated increasing levels of 'legal' discrimination against the Jews rather than 'illegal measures', it is surprising that so few Germans asked themselves what exactly this undefined 'menace of world Jewry' was, or queried why 'legal' discrimination was necessary at all. The German lack of overt resistance to these preliminary measures gave the Nazis an extensive sphere of autonomy free from constraints of popular disapproval which, in the long run, enabled them to adopt ever more radical measures against the Jews, ending in the murder of millions.

While Kershaw points to Germans' lack of interest in the fate of the Jews during the war itself, Maier shows how it has become the central issue in West German historiography. Since the Second World War Germans have been faced with the question of how to perceive their national identity in the aftermath of the Third Reich. After 1945 they had the choice of identifying with the victors or with the vanquished; for obvious reasons both Germanies chose the victors. The East Germans aligned themselves with the international communist movement in which national identity was seen to play no part. Consequently questions of responsibility for crimes committed during the Second World War were simply never voiced. In the West, Germans attempted to cast off the burdern of recent history and to regard themselves not primarily as German, but as members of the Western community of nations, thereby avoiding coming to terms with many aspects of Nazism. The nineteenth-century insistence on a 'separate road' or *Sonderweg* in German history and the rejection of the Western European political and intellectual heritage which had earlier been central to both extreme and anti-nationalistic historians was thus muted in an age in which West Germany saw its fate as inseparably linked with that of its NATO allies. Unlike in East Germany issues of guilt or shared responsibility were not ignored outright; however, Nazism was perceived as an aberration, and Germans were largely able to avoid coming to terms with it, dedicating their energies instead to rebuilding the country.

For almost four decades the Federal Republic lived 'by bread alone', pursuing its economic vocation with success and single-mindedness. West German nationhood has meant production. This is not a new phenomenon for Germans; in the period leading up to unification under Bismarck and through the first decade of nationhood economic union and expansion also served as sinews of German cohesiveness. But periodically the economic vocation has failed to absorb German energies, whether because growth has faltered, or because its successes no longer seemed compelling. This, Maier suggests, is what has happened in the Germany of the 1980s. Faced with changes in the climate of East-West relations, economic security, and generational changes, Germans have once again begun to question what their national existence really means.

For most countries the search for national identity could well involve looking to past heroes of national triumphs for role models; indeed the nineteenth-century German historians saw the creation and maintencance of the proud nation state as their *raison d'être*. In contemporary Germany, however, looking into the past has necessarily meant confronting the crimes committed under Nazism. The latest controversies in West Germany, in particular the *Historikerstreit* and the Museum debate, are representative of attempts to come to terms with this problem.

Maier's book concentrates on these recent debates in West Germany, and he has identified two different approaches to the troublesome past. The first approach involves dealing honestly with the German responsiblity for both the Holocaust and for crimes committed by the Germans against other peoples between 1933 and 1945. The second approach involves the relativization of these crimes, and its authors believe it will allow history to become 'normalized' so that Germans can once again be proud of their national identity. More particularly the debates centre on the perception of the Holocaust. Lines have been drawn between those who see it as a unique event, and those who see it as comparable to other twentieth-century atrocities. If the Final Solution remains non-comparable, the 'relativists' argue, the past may never be 'worked through', the future never normalized, and German nationhood will remain forever tainted.

Maier presents a complex analysis which carefully weighs the merits of each approach. He does not reject the idea of comparing the Final Solution with other atrocities as long as it is not claimed that one has caused the other, or that one somehow excuses the other. In this context he attacks Ernst Nolte's thesis that the Holocaust might be understood as a defensive response which was misconceived but which was provoked by fear of the 'Asiatic deed' (the phrase borrowed from Erwin Scheubner-Richter's description of the massacre of the Armenians by the Turks in 1917), a term used by Nolte to describe the menace of possible Bolshevik massacres which Hitler 'might have felt' could befall the Germans. He also attacks the idea that Chaim Weizmann's 1939 declaration of Jewish support for Britain was seen by the Germans as a declaration of war which could explain the internment of Jews in German held territories. Maier points out that Weizmann's declaration was issued in 1939, when German Jews had already suffered six years of persecution under the Nazis – the original boycotts and violence of 1933, the exclusion from the professions, the Nuremberg laws of 1935, and the destruction, arrests and confiscations which followed *Kristallnacht* in 1938. He correctly asks 'who had declared war on whom?'

There may be a connection between the Final Solution and the Gulag; however, Stalin's killing would have been an indirect precedent and could hardly explain the different forms and targets of Nazi killing. A more likely precedent lay in the euthanasia programme which had already exploited the chilling concept of *lebensunwertes Leben* (life unworthy of life), to terminate 60,000–80,000 German lives.

Maier follows the critique of Nolte with his own comparison of the Soviet and German mass murders. He maintains that it is very important to keep the issue of numbers of deaths in mind, no matter how stupefying, because the death tolls of both the Germans and the Russian regimes were so massive that the issue of uniqueness cannot be decided on this alone. What sets apart the National Socialist crime – not necessarily making it 'worse' but making it different, and appalling and unassimilable – is ultimately the murder of Jews. This was Hitler's deed not Stalin's. Without the Jews, hundreds of thousands would still have died in the concentration camps but the extermination centres in Poland – Auschwitz-Birkenau, Bełżec, Chełmno, Majdanek, Sobibór, and Treblinka – would not have been established. Without the Jews the mass shootings at Babi Yar, Kamieniec Podolski, Riga, Rovno, Odessa-Dalnik, and elsewhere would not have taken place. Stalinist terror had also targeted broad groups of victims who were defined by category, such as 'Kulaks' whose status was passed on to children with no regard for actual socio-economic conditions, but important differences still persist between the persecution of these groups and of the Jews. Annihilation of the Jews was to be total, whereas no Soviet citizen had to expect that deportation or death was inevitable by virtue of his ethnic origin or any other criteria. Nor did the Soviets establish facilities purely for extermination. Soviet labour camps were so lethal that only a quarter of prisoners might survive, but no extermination camps existed which were designed only to kill masses of human beings on arrival. The Soviets did not dedicate such resources to the destruction of their victims, unlike the Germans who continued to destroy the Jews even at the expense of the war effort. For these reasons, Maier maintains, the Holocaust is unique.

There are those who would question this view. For example Richard Lukas has argued that, with the German invasion of 1939 the Poles became the first people in Europe to experience the Holocaust and that historians have so far chosen to interpret the tragedy in exclusivistic terms – namely as the most tragic period in the history of the Jewish Diaspora. (see review in *POLIN* vol. 2, pp. 372–90). Maier agrees that the Poles were treated brutally and that if the Germans had remained in Poland many would have been wantonly starved, shot, and otherwise reduced to a sort of agrarian slavery. He also agrees that Polish Christian attitudes towards the local Jewish populations are not usually treated with the careful differentiation merited. However, despite the fact that millions of Polish citizens suffered under the Germans, only the Jews amongst them were to be pursued at all costs and were to be ruthlessly exterminated. The suffering of other groups under the Nazis may have been great, but in the end only the Jews and the gypsies were singled out for total destruction.

Maier concludes that the Germans cannot create a national identity based upon a version of history which denies the uniqueness of the Holocaust and which somehow excuses Germans for the responsibility for it. Attempts to relativize the Holocaust in order to make German history more palatable to the next generation are misguided at best. Some historians who suggest the comparability of the Final Solution to other genocides may be opening the way to apologetics and may facilitate a literature of evasions. On the other hand not all use of comparison is out of the question; in terms of historical method, some comparisons are possible, as such studies may open the way to important discussions about historical responsibility and national consciousness. Historians should make comparisons when they are justified, and not use them when they are misleading.

Germans must also attempt to come to terms with other crimes committed during the Nazi period. They must recognize that the Holocaust was a unique event, but only one aspect of the regime. Most Germans were not directly involved with the conception and implementation of the extermination of the Jews, and as Kershaw points out in *The 'Hitler Myth'*, the issue of the 'Jewish question' was low on the priority list for an average German during the Third Reich. This does not excuse the Germans from responsibility for the crimes committed under National Socialism, because of their participation in the creation and continuation of conditions which made these crimes possible. After the attempted assassination of Hitler in July 1944 many Germans were outraged at the 'traitors'; this demonstrates the strong identification of the Germans with their leader. Germans must question their involvement in a regime in which Auschwitz and a 'normal life' could coexist. The belief of some Germans that relativizing the Holocaust by claiming for example that its inspiration was derived from Bolshevik terror could lead to a 'problem-free', 'normal' history is not only misguided in itself, but also ignores other aspects of the Nazi killing programme, such as the murder of gypsies, Poles, Soviet POWs, and homosexuals. These issues must all be faced openly, and the silences of Germans in the post-war period must be broken if the Germans continue with the attempt to base their sense of identity in history, honesty in facing the past should be its cornerstone.

But one must ask whether history is enough to create such an identity. Apparently many historians have taken it for granted that national identity is no more nor less than the product of national history. But there are limits to their craft, and the moral implications of crimes such as the Holocaust should not simply be left to the historians but should be discussed by the entire nation. National identity cannot simply be 'taught', but requires an active commitment and the willingness of the nation to accept responsiblity for the past as well as for the present and future.

A LOOK AT THE LAST JEWS OF POLAND
Jack Kugelmass

Yale Strom, *The Last Jews of Eastern Europe*.
Illustrations by Brian Blue and Yale Strom. New York: Philosophical Library. 1986. pp. 51, [150] p. of plates: i 11.

Małgorzata Niezabitowska, *Remnants: The Last Jews of Poland*. Photographs by Tomasz Tomaszewski. New York: Friendly Press.1986. Pp. 272.

Not long ago, two Warsaw Jews arrived in New York and paid a visit to YIVO. They stopped in front of my office door and read the cartoon one of my students had posted there. The drawing depicts a group of 'natives' scrambling to hide their television, stereo and various other modern appliances. Another native peers out of the window and, spotting two white people approach the hut shouts frantically, 'Anthropologists! Anthropologists!' My visitors commented that with the constant flow of Jewish tourists to Poland they have begun to feel just like those natives, frequently being scrutinized by others on their performance of Jewish rituals.

Tourism is a highly ideological phenomenon. It is closely intertwined with political and economic developments that throughout history have made tourism a movement from the powerful toward the weak; the rich toward the poor. Moreover, the movement is ideological in the sense that it contains within it a notion of where the subjects of tourism, the natives, stand in relation to the tourist and his or her home society. The subjects of tourism are expected to function as a living historical museum for the dominant society. Although for some subjects this may be a very heavy load to bear, others may respond much like the natives in the drawing; they may, realizing the economic power of the representatives of the dominant power, do what is necessary to recreate themselves in the image called for by the tourist. This phenomenon has implications for Jewish Studies in general; for the moment it particularly affects the study of Polish Jewry.

Jews, it seems to me, have become one of the great tourist people of the modern world. Whole industries have grown up to serve the Jewish passion for travel, many of which cater to the ceaseless pleasure Jews have in encountering first-hand their more primitive co-religionists as if the tourist were actually encountering an ancestor rather than a contemporary. Since tourism serves an entertainment or leisure function, there are constant changes probably stimulated by marketing strategists in which groups of Jews get 'discovered'. In the 1960s it was Marranos in Spain and Portugal; in the 1970s it was Jews in Morocco; in the 1980s the Jews of Eastern Europe. Invariably the phrase 'the last Jews of . . .' precedes the name of the country, clueing prospective clients in to the theme of the encounter as a chance in a lifetime (somewhat akin, I would think, to a circus barker) to catch a glimpse of an almost extinct species.

The recent re-awakening of interest in Polish Jewry undoubtedly has much to do with trends in tourism, currency fluctuations, and the genealogical craze that has swept America since the screening of the television series *Roots*. Although I do not have any figures on the scale of Jewish tourism to Eastern Europe, the fact is that no visitor to the area, and to Poland in particular, can look through his camera viewfinder and be assured that another American or Israeli will not suddenly appear to mar the 'pristine' view. Indeed, a walk to the market square in Warsaw's Old City already indicates how much Jewish tourism has affected even the local Polish economy: paintings, sometimes caricatures on Jewish themes such as 'ghetto rebbes', a match-seller and even a Shylockian moneylender counting his gold coins are readily available for purchase, made not by Jewish but by non-Jewish artists. In the summer of 1987, a government folk-art store in Kraków had in its window a wooden Jewish figurine holding an actual piece of *Torah*! Although these figurines have their roots in peasant culture, at 5,000 złoty – the equivalent in 1987 of a week's salary for the average Pole – the figurine is clearly intended for the tourist market.

Polish Jews have also been affected by this interest in them. Any number of tour groups now make their way to places such as the Nożyk synagogue in Warsaw and the Remu synagogue in Kraków. On some Saturdays the number of worshippers would turn many an American synagogue administrator green with envy. And community hangers-on now use the advent of the tour buses as an opportunity to do business – to rent an apartment, to change money or to ask for donations. In a country where the average monthly wage is less than $20 US the American dollar is pretty powerful; the proceeds from a single tour bus can provide the recipient with substantial capital. Whether true or not, rumours abound that not all who relate their tales of tribulations at Nożyk are indeed Jews.

A good indication of the extent to which the Jews of Eastern Europe currently occupy the primary place of interest among American, European and Israeli Jewry is the increasing number of articles that appear in Jewish newspapers documenting individual journeys to that part of the world. In addition there are photographic exhibitions on related subjects at both Jewish and non-Jewish institutions and there are films including a recent one on an American *Bar Mitzvah* held in Kraków which was screened at the Margaret Mead Film Festival in New York. The same director is currently working on a film retracing a young *klezmer*'s five-month visit to Eastern Europe.

In 1986, two photo books were published in America about Eastern European Jewry. *The Last Jews of Eastern Europe* by Brian Blue and Yale Strom is a rather ambitious project and includes separate chapters on the USSR, Poland, Czechoslovakia, Hungary, Romania, Yugoslavia and Bulgaria. There are six pages of text devoted to Poland covering Warsaw, Kraków, Wrocław, Dzierżoniów, and Wałbrzych. The text contains a capsule history of Polish Jewry followed by descriptions in each of the localities of individuals and their lives. The photographic section, which forms the bulk of this volume, incorporates black and white images from all the countries visited arranged not by location but by topic, including social institutions, ritual needs, prayer, synagogues, cemeteries, education, children, and so on. The tone of the book is optimistic, and though the photographs are not inspiring as images they do make the point that East European Jewry, though fragile as a community and very small in numbers, continues to exist and will probably go on doing so for a good long time to come. I find the overabundance of photographs unfortunate since editing could have highlighted the stronger images and avoided visual overkill.

The other book, entitled *Remnants: The Last Jews of Poland* by Małgorzata Niezabitowska and Tomasz Tomaszewski is the work of a writer and photographer husband and wife team. In the course of five years the couple interviewed and photographed some of the remaining 5,000 Jews of Poland. Their work has led to a feature magazine article in *National Geographic*, exhibitions in Poland, the United States and Israel, and a book of text and colour photographs which has already sold over 11,000 copies in hardback.

Despite the colour photograph on its cover and the 51 colour images printed inside the book, *Remnants* is primarily a text rather than a photo essay. It is divided into eight chapters, including an Introduction examining the origins and reasons for this project and the connection of the authors to the subject. Since both are non-Jews, the book is somewhat unusual among Jewish books and the self-reflexive tone of the Introduction – a technique that is very much *en vogue* in anthropology and journalism – answers some of the inevitable questions about why non-Jews would undertake such a project. The authors answer the question with a sense of moral mission 'to break the silence' and reveal that 'something is still there ... even if it is only the last chapter in the nearly thousand-year-long history of the Polish Jews.' The mournful tone of the book is also revealed in the Introduction where the author indicates that despite the varied fates of the 5,000 remaining Jews in Poland, 'they all share the consciousness that something is irrevocably coming to an end, which gives their lives a tragic dimension.'

This tragic dimension is apparent throughout the book. The first chapter, entitled 'Lublin: In Search of a Minyan', sketches the current lives and life histories of disparate members of a *minyan* which includes observant Jews, communists, a woman writer, a war hero, and a convert to Catholicism, among others. The second chapter, 'The Long Way Home', looks at two young men, both from solid communist backgrounds, who have become active proponents of Jewish life and values in Poland. The third chapter, 'I Could Have Been a Billionaire', examines the life of an older Jewish butcher from Warsaw who was hidden among peasants during the war and retains intense loyalty and a sense of duty to demonstrate hospitality and reciprocity to the village and its inhabitants. The fourth chapter is a portrait of Szymon Szurmiej, the *Sejm* representative and artistic director of Warsaw's permanent Yiddish theatre. The fifth chapter examines the community of Kraków and features the head of the community, a Yiddish teacher, a well-to-do attorney, an artist, a tinsmith and a man whose life task has become the documenting of the Remu cemetery and the biographies of famous Kraków rabbis. The sixth chapter, 'The Seedling', looks at a mixed-marriage family in which one of the sons has become interested in Judaism and has trained for *Bar Mitzvah* with an Orthodox member of the Warsaw community. The final chapter, 'No Fear in Me', is an interview on Polish-Jewish relations during and after the Holocaust with a leading Jewish scholar, Szymon Datner.

I find this book admirable in many ways, yet deeply troubling in parts. But let me turn first to its strengths. *Remnants* is very broad in its scope and touches upon a number of issues that are central to the Jewish experience in twentieth-century Poland, particularly the problem of pre-war anti-semitism, the behaviour of Poles (both good and bad) during and after the war, including the post-war pogroms. The book mentions the existence of a lingering anti-semitism and the common view in Poland of Jews as manipulators, betrayers of Poland, communist oppressors, and cowardly. All of these issues emerge either through dialogue between the author and her informants or through the characters she has selected, which include a very broad range of people, both communists and non-communists, rich and poor, xenophobes and love-thy-neighbour types, refugees and war heroes. Implicitly, the book makes a clear statement against stereotyping Polish Jewry.

The author evidently makes extensive use of life-history interviews and what I assume are segments of those interviews constitute the basis of the text. The technique, which filters history through the prism of individual experience provides a lively, personal account of the past and current situation of Polish Jewry. But life history has its limits. And it falters badly when it takes the place of more general observations. Although it is true that the author is a journalist and not an anthropologist, while reading this text there were too many times when I felt I would rather be reading something else. These life histories are too short, too scattered. The interviews peter out before they really gather steam, and one gets the impression that they are edited to get maximum emotional mileage. Take, for example, the following exchange between Ms Niezabitowska and a Lublin Jew who bemoans his daughter's having married a *goy* (non-Jew):

'Because all Poles hate Jews.'
'All Poles hate all Jews? Mr Szmulewicz . . .'
The tailor, however, will not be reconciled. As we talk, the door opens every so often. Clients walk in for fittings, and friends to chat. The shop grows crowded, so I edge toward the exit. Right in front of the door I notice a large photograph hanging over the sewing machine: several laughing people sitting around a table on a terrace.
'What's the picture?' I ask.
'That's the forester's house where I hid during the war,' Szmulewicz answers.
'And who are they? Jews?'
'Jews? What Jews? Those are the foresters, the Poles who saved my life.'

Why does Ms Niezabitowska stop here? Is her point that this man is blind to reality, and ungrateful? Is she providing a glimpse of the complexity and profound ambivalence of contemporary Jewish life in Poland? Or does she think that an ambiguous ending has great artistic value? If it is the last, there is a literary pretentiousness here that I find very disconcerting. In truth, I suspect the answer has more to do with the voice of the Polish narrator, a superior, knowing voice still very much bewildered by the Otherness of her subjects. I do not fault Ms Niezabitowska for her bewilderment. I fault her, rather, for not expressing it, for muting her own voice and letting it emerge through the ambiguous sentiments of her subject.

This same muted Polish voice is apparent earlier on in the text when the author writes about herself:

When I began, I never dreamed of how difficult it would turn out to be. Above all because taking up such a painful and complex subject required me to begin with myself: to overcome my own ignorance as well as my own unconscious presuppositions and stereotypes not only about both Jews and Poles but also about their mutual relations.

It was difficult because it also meant — and this is the reverse side of the same problem — overcoming the mistrust of many Jews still living in Poland and gaining acceptance in the closed circles where a *goy* is always an outsider and every Pole is an anti-Semite.

Neither Tomasz nor I are anti-Semites or, for that matter, philo-Semites. We are normal. Or at least we try to be. And we managed to convince many of the people we met of this. Otherwise, this book would have been impossible.

This is much too simple. Ms Niezabitowska makes no attempt to examine the subtleties of culture and the ethno-narcissism that colours one group's reaction to another, particularly when the two groups are co-territorial and even more particularly when there is unequal access to power. It's not only true for Poland, it's true, too, for the United States. Can a white American declare himself to be free of racism? The very arrogance of such a premise also leads to an artistic flaw, namely that this book doesn't move either concretely, that is to greater levels of knowledge, or figuratively, that is emotionally. As the narrator, Ms Niezabitowska places herself on an equal footing with the subject of her research, an approach that distances her from the reader and weakens the emotional appeal of the actual process of reflection and self-reflection. Although she claims to have learned much through her research, the process of discovery is absent in the text. I do not find any genuine dialogue with her subjects here or any real intellectual engagement. The reason for this, I believe, is partly a result of the weakness of the narrator's voice and partly a result of the book's episodic structure. Characters never reappear. How much better this book would be if the central characters were better defined and allowed to reappear now and then to assume a certain authorship of the text and act as genuine guides to Ms Niezabitowska's quest for knowledge. The result would also be a deepening relationship between the author and her subjects. I don't find that here, and because I don't, I have considerable trouble believing that what I am reading is as good as it could be. So I come back to the interview with Mr Szmulewicz. What do we learn from one interview? How do narratives change in the course of repeated performances with fresh questions, greater familiarity and developing trust between the researcher and her subject? Whatever such probing might contribute toward the ultimate truth of the material, it would also permit a relationship to emerge between the subjects and the reader. Instead, I find the narrative cold and distant despite its sensitive patina.

This coldness is considerably amplified through the photographs which, despite the fact that they are in colour and technically good, have surprisingly little emotional depth. Those that do have an emotional appeal tend toward either the sentimental or the bizarre. The image of this community is presented through lenses that either distort the subjects or limit and restrict our vision. I keep turning pages of this book desperately seeking a view of Poland. There are only two. For the most part, these people could be anywhere – in the Bronx, or London's East End. I miss here the beauty of the Polish landscape, its people, its houses and its cities. I also miss family and community portraits. What is lacking here is the outer world, the full life that Polish Jews lead together with the tragic one of their inner reflections. Photographically a balanced picture would give this essay strength, a sense of reality, familiarity and perhaps even beauty, though undoubtedly of a subtler kind than either Mr Tomaszewski chose to depict, or that his editors selected for this volume.

The preoccupation with the inner world underlines the other problems of the text. The most striking deficiency is how little general observation there is here of people interacting with one another. The book is constructed out of people's heads, as if people live entirely as remnants, through the past rather than the present. Indeed, the only description Ms Niezabitowska provides of an event is the following description of a community *seder* in Kraków:

> The tables are arranged in a horseshoe pattern and covered with white tablecloths. They are set with a holiday service; with candle-holders and lighted candles, heaps of matzo sent from Hungary, and bottles of sweet Israeli wine. During the Pesach holiday as well, the Kraków community is noisy and festive. Delicious, fragrant *seder* dishes cooked home-style are served instead of canned food. The man sitting beside me says with gentle melancholy, 'Just a little bit like it used to be . . .'
>
> The banqueters are dressed *en fête*, with Old World elegance. Not a single young face can be seen; except that at the end of the table, under a window, a girl and two boys are sitting. These are American students, Jews in Kraków over the holiday. At first everyone gathered around them. When it turned out, however, that they did not know Yiddish, it ended in smiles and hearty claps on the back. And so once again there is no one from the younger generation to ask, according to tradition and in the words of the *Haggadah*: 'Why is this evening different from all others?'
>
> Somewhat earlier, during the holiday prayers in the Remu synagogue, the men quarrelled. First there were nervous whispers from the direction of the *bimah* and then the voices grew more distinct until the exchanges, all in Yiddish, turned into a loud argument. Five old men in tallises crowded close together. They waved their prayerbooks in violent gestures. The rest of those present looked on in silence.
>
> 'Everybody wants to say a different prayer,' Czesław Jakubowicz, the president of the community, explained to me. After a moment he

added, 'I could feel it coming to this. There's no one left in Kraków who knows how to pray.'

'Couldn't you settle it?' I asked.

Jakubowicz shook his head. 'How, since I don't know either?' (pp. 156–7).

I read this passage and I want what we call in anthropology 'thick description'. I want to know about Jewish rituals and synagogue life in Poland. What is observed and how are rituals invented to meet the needs of these particular people? Who is counted in the *minyan*? Who presides? How long are services? What language is used? Do services vary according to the presence or absence of Jewish tourists? But these are questions only an anthropologist would raise, and in asking them I come to the grey area between journalism and ethnography. And I come, perhaps, to what underlies my problem with this book.

To its credit, *Remnants* was made with good intentions and it is evident that the author has gained considerable knowledge of the area she has chosen to investigate. Moreover, the book stands head and shoulders above what generally passes for reportage on Jewish life. I can commend Ms Niezabitowska and Mr Tomaszewski on having brought the news that there are still Jews in various nooks and crannies in Poland and that their work will encourage others, and I hope scholars in particular, to do the more in-depth observation that will help us create an ethnography of Jews in contemporary Eastern Europe. Although the truth is that by the time such studies are done, Polish Jewry may have long become tired of the constant pointing of cameras and barrage of questions by ever curious Jewish tourists, journalists and academics. But what I am even more afraid of is that the Jews of Poland will learn to become like the natives in the cartoon posted on my door and give the curious observer the pristine native with his curiously anachronistic rituals that he or she has come to see. The best way to prevent that from happening, I believe, is for all of us to accept the fact that the remaining Jews of Poland are not pristine survivors. And if we do study them, with either camera or notebook, that we look at them with the larger view of Poland in mind and their continuing place within it. If we do that, the metaphor for it will not be remnants, for this conveys too much the image of something abandoned and cast off, and this, I believe, is an inaccurate sense of who these people are. Let us remember that they are mostly people with all the foibles and nobility of any other segment of mankind. Indeed they are remnants only in the sense that *we* have assigned them the task of carrying on the tradition of our parents and grandparents who formed the once great Jewish community of Poland.

REPORT

SCHOLARLY CONFERENCE – 500 YEARS OF JEWISH SETTLEMENT IN PODLASIE
Anna Izydorczyk and Ewa Pankiewicz

The conference took place on 14–17 September 1987 in Białystok. Its aim was to present and discuss – according to present research, the fundamental problems of Jewish history in Podlasie, beginning from the 15th century to 1943, and to expand our knowledge of the subject. There were many Jews living in Podlasie and they played an important role in its cultural, economic and political life. The conference also aimed to develop cooperation and to establish links between Polish and Jewish historians.

The conference was organised by the Białystok branch of the Warsaw University Institute of History together with the Institute of Jewish History and the Białystok Academic Society and Tykocin Museum. It was supported by the Białystok municipal authorities and by the president of the town in particular, Mgr Z. Zdrojewski, who entertained the participants at the so-called *Domek koniuszego*.

Four papers were given and 29 reports, 61 people took part in the discussion. Three further papers were given in sessions at Tykocin.

Taking part were academics from Poland, Israel, Australia and France. The conference was also attended by many people interested in the subject. On the whole, 50–80 people attended, depending on the theme of individual papers. Apart from historians, there were also architects, ethnographers and even members of opposition movements.

On Monday, 14.09.87 at 9.00, Professor A. Wyczański opened the conference. The subject that day was the history of Jews in Podlasie during Old Polish times. Dr A. Leszczyński (*ŻIH*, Warsaw) gave a paper entitled 'The history of Jews in Podlasie 1487–1795'. He was followed by Dr A. Cygielman (Ber Sheva), who spoke on the Bocki *kahal pinkas* as a source of the activities of the commune towards the end of the 18th-century. He was followed by Professor J. Goldberg of Jerusalem who spoke on the theme of Jews and taverns in Podlasie in the 18th century. During the afternoon session Dr M. Nadav (Jerusalem) spoke very vividly about the Tykocin *kahal* in pre-partition Poland (on the basis of the 18th century Tykocin *pinkas*). Professor Dr Z. Guldon (*WSP*, Kielce) gave a critical analysis of the figures concerning the Jewish population of the towns in the province of Podlasie at the end of the 18th century. The architects M. and K. Piechotkowie held a slide show at which they showed Podlasie synagogues and commented on the style and building materials employed in specific areas.

During the papers and discussions following them it emerged that there was a great deficiency in historical knowledge concerning various problems under discussion. The historians proposed the publication of sources in the languages of the congress and stressed the necessity for young Polish historians to learn Yiddish and Hebrew in order to develop the research of Jewish history in Poland. The participants were particularly interested in the village Jews in Podlasie who, as tenants, were basically temporary inhabitants of the villages (Prof. Goldberg). According to Doc. S. Alexandrowicz, leasing was also very convenient for the magnates in larger and smaller towns and often practised within the Grand Duchy of Lithuania also. The question of the privilege *de non tolerandis Judaeis* also aroused interest (Prof. Bardach, Mgr Piechotka, Doc. Dr Senkowski, Prof. Goldberg, Dr Leszczyński). It was stated that this privilege meant the town had a right not to accept Jews but was not obliged to realize this right and concerned a ban on residence rather than on conducting a trade. The phenomenon of Jewish oligarchy within the communes was also looked at – to see if it was a typical or occasional phenomenon. Demographic questions received the most attention, concerning the Jewish population of Poland over the centuries. On the one hand, the high figures were questioned, on the other it was unanimously agreed that the growth rate of the Jewish population was greater than that of the Poles. Reasons for this were looked for, among other things, in the postulates of the Jewish religion and habits arising from these, which stressed the importance of the family in society. Dr Nadav noticed, for example, that Tykocin *pinkas* records that the Tykocin *kahal* gave dowries to poor girls. Dr Cygielman added that in the 16th to 18th centuries the rabbinical courts forced youths over 20 who had not yet married to do so and also ordered widowers, even those of 60 or 70, to marry again.

The first part of the second day's session was devoted to visiting Knyszyń and Tykocin. The conference participants visited the Jewish cemetery in Knyszyń. At one time there were dams here dividing lakes – a style of park landscaping dating from the time of Zygmunt August who agreed to allow the establishment of a Jewish cemetery here. This was not accidental – the water was meant to symbolize purification. On one of the old dams there were monuments commemorating the 19th century, and a little further up, later ones which were erected up to, and during, the Second World War. The participants then visited Tykocin which had been inhabited by Jews for centuries, as the presence of the synagogue, built in 1642, testifies. It has now been restored and very carefully refurbished. It is run by the Białystok Regional Museum's branch in Tykocin. The interior is furnished with many objects typical of a building of this kind, together with a gallery of paintings on Jewish themes. Further papers were given in a building housing a museum which was formerly a Talmud House. The conference continued in two separate halls. The Old Polish section took place in one room. Dr J. Maroszek (Białystok) spoke on village Jews in Podlasie in the 16th-18th centuries. Doc. J. Senkowski (Warsaw) spoke on the judiciary of Crown Jews, with particular reference to Podlasie. Dr Daniel Tollet (Paris) spoke on the legend of the one-day king in Poland. The discussion was dominated by the theme of jurisdiction over the Jewish people in the old Republic (Prof. Goldberg and Bardach, Doc. Senkowski, Dr Cygielman, Mgr Piechotka). The participants also discussed the principles under which the *kahal* courts functioned as well as the provincial judiciary. In the other hall were the 19th and 20th-century historians. Doc. A. Dobroński (Białystok) began the proceedings with his paper: 'The history of the Jews in Białystok from 1795–1918'. He was followed by Dr P. Wróbel (Warsaw), whose subject was the Jews in Białystok in the inter-war years. According to Dr Wróbel's statistics, in the Second Republic Jews constituted 42.6 per cent of the population and therefore constituted a large community in the town's 100,000–strong population. It should also be added that this was a smaller percentage than that existing during the partitions, when the Jewish population constituted 70 per cent of the population (1895). The speaker stressed that of 100 pre-war industrial concerns, 95 were owned by Jews, although these were small enterprises in the main. The next speaker, Prof. M. Mishkinsky (Tel Aviv), spoke of the role of Białystok during the formation of the Jewish workers' movement.

Although the papers raised many different issues, it was obvious that the question of Polish-Jewish relations aroused most interest. Mgr J. Adelson spoke on Jewish attitudes to the problem of independence. He stated that one should not measure Jewish patriotism by looking at Jewish participation in uprisings but according to their contribution to the development of the Polish economy. The listeners' opposition was roused by the pessimistic vision of Białystok before the war as a poor and shabby town. The author of the paper in this case had been influenced by the work of Maria Dąbrowska. Mr J. Gorzała (Warsaw) joined the discussion at this point emphasising the incompetent policies of the pre-war government in relation to national minorities, including the Jews, which led to conflict, especially in educational institutions. Dr E. Pankiewicz (Białystok) pointed out that in many states before the war and also in contemporary ones, relations between nationalities present difficulties and that the press often reports conflicts and even acts of terror. If the problem is viewed from this perspective, less emotional evaluations arise. So far as the beauty of Białystok was concerned before the war, the town according to inhabitants of that time had well-cared for and charming districts and artefacts. Alongside these there were also obviously areas in which both the Jewish and Polish poor were concentrated. Dr A. Cygielman confirmed that Polish-Jewish conflicts had taken place in Białystok; nevertheless, an indelible feeling of local patriotism and ties with the local commune had remained.

In the afternoon, back in Białystok, Dr J. Oppenheim (Beer Sheva) gave a paper entitled 'National Democracy and the Jewish question 1895–1905'. He was followed by Dr Z. Abramowicz on the names of Białystok Jews from 1886–1939. Mgr J. Adelson spoke on the socio-professional structure of the Jewish population in Suwałki, based on general records from 1921 and 1939. A paper on the Jewish press from 1918–1939 by Doc. M. Fuks (Warsaw) was read. Dr Z. Sokół (Białystok) discussed the libraries and Jewish reading habits in Białystok and M. Taboryski (Warsaw) took up the theme of the role of Jewish workers in the workers' movement in Białystok from 1918–1931. Finally, Dr Z. Zaporowski from Lublin spoke on the Jewish population in Biała Podlaska from the time of the Second Republic. During the subsequent discussion various opinions were voiced regarding the general number of Jews in inter-war Poland, the numbers participating in the workers' movement and the communist movement in general. According to the calculations of Mr Taboryski this was a group of a few hundred members – including members of the party together with the activists supporting them. Prof. J. Bardach noted that Mr Zaporowski had underemphasised the activities of student corporations, as the *Endecja* strongly influenced the mood among the young. He also maintained that during this time policies were implemented which limited the Jews' economic activity. Dr Z. Abramowicz's paper aroused much interest. During discussion, the author explained that she had drawn names above all from Jewish birth certificates. Dr O. Goldberg (Jerusalem) drew attention to the fact that the most popular names chosen by Dr Abramowicz were taken from the Bible: Abraham, Izrael, Sara, Chaja.

On Wednesday (16.09) the participants laid wreaths at the foot of the monument commemorating the victims of the Tsarist pogrom of 1906 at the cemetery at Wschodnia Street. Dr A. Dobroński outlined the historical background to this event. Next, there was a tour taking in Zabłudów, Narew, Hajnówka, Białowieża, Orla, Bielsk Podlaski. J. Maroszek conducted the tour discussing the historical buildings and Dr W. Szerszunowicz the symbolism of the Jewish cemeteries around Białystok.

The fourth and final day of the conference began with the laying of flowers at the statue of the Heroes of the Ghetto, at the memorial tablets of the Great Synagogue, and the statues of Ludwik Zamenhof and Icchok Malmed. The conference then continued in different sections with the following papers: Sections II and III were presented by Antony Murkies (Brighton – Australia) on Jewish education in pre-war Białystok. Dr O.

Goldberg (Jerusalem) and Dr E. Fryś-Pietraszkowa (Kraków) spoke on Polish-Jewish links in the folk culture of Podlasie; the first speaker's area was customs and traditions, and that of the second speaker was crafts. The Student Educational Circle spoke on the theme 'Jewish society in Christian eyes with reference to Ciechanowiec'.

During the fourth section the fate of the Jews of Białystok during the last war was discussed. Doc. M. Gnatowski (Białystok) described the main problems concerning the fate of the Jews during the German occupation. Sara Bender (Tel Aviv) spoke about the Białystok ghetto. Bronka Klibańska (Jerusalem) described the preparations for armed uprising in the Białystok ghetto (from November 1942 to August 1943). Doc. Sz. Datner's paper was also read on the rebellion of the Jewish police in the Białystok ghetto. Next, Mgr W. Monkiewicz drew the attention of the participants to the extermination of the Jewish population in the Białystok area.

During the discussion conflicting opinions emerged regarding the above questions. First, the question of aid to Jews was discussed. Everyone agreed that it existed, but argued over its extent. The members of the Jewish opposition in Białystok claimed that certain questions have not yet been researched, for example, the organisation of food supplies or arms to the ghetto: in sum, little is known about the uprising.

B. Klibańska added that the organisers of the resistance were not concerned with survival as such as this would have been unethical given the situation in which others were dying. The actual nature of the role of the *Judenrat* was also questioned – and again opinions diverged. An attempt was made to ascertain more precisely the number of Jewish victims of the Hitler terror. B. Klibańska spoke of the great feeling of isolation on the part of those taking part in the uprising. She stated that help organised from the Polish side of the resistance was weak and that help was lacking from Jewish society as a whole. Dr Pankiewicz compared this situation to the Warsaw uprising, which took place in isolation before the eyes of the whole world. The circumstances of Malmed's death were discussed and Róza Michalak (a member of the Białystok opposition movement) stated that he had voluntarily given himself up to the Germans in order not to jeopardise others.

In the afternoon the following participants gave papers: Mgr M. Leszczak ('The Holocaust and the Jewish population of Siemiatycze during the Second World War'); Mgr W. Monkiewicz ('Aid to Jews in the Białystok region during the Second World War' – co-author Dr J. Kowalczyk); Mgr T. Wiśniewski ('The Białystok Ghetto cemetery 1941–1971'). This reconstruction of the history of the Jewish wartime cemetery was much appreciated by the participants. They expressed their disapproval of the destruction of this cemetery in 1971. Questioned on the sources for his paper, W. Monkiewicz presented a series of examples of aid to Jews in the Białystok region based on materials gathered by the Regional Commission for the Study of Nazi Crimes in Białystok. He also described the preparations for pogroms in the area of Grajewo. Their author was a *Volksdeutsch*.

In the concluding section of the conference, Dr D. Tollet spoke, among others. The conference had convinced him of the special character of Podlasie as far as the role and size of the Jewish minority was concerned. In his opinion, during the interwar years Jewish-Polish relations here were rather more peaceful than elsewhere. He proposed that the history of the Jewish minority should be studied against the background of the complete social structure of this area. Prof. M. Mishkinsky thanked the organisers and Israeli participants who had spoken with affection of the Podlasie region. He declared that it was to have been expected that the conference would have an emotional element. But one should not fear emotion here. 'Points of view were not always divided according to nationality, and that is a very good thing', he stated.

Taking leave of the participants of the conference, Prof. A. Wyczański summed up its results and postulates. In his opinion, the conference had initiated research in a number of areas concerning the history of the Jews of Podlasie and had also presented a number of postulates for further research in the area of demography, Jewish laws, the role of Jews in the villages, their participation in the workers movement, Jewish-Christian cultural relations, links between the world and the Jews of Podlasie, society in Podlasie towns, the fate of Jews during the Second World War, and finally the preservation of Jewish historical monuments. The conference undoubtedly extended historical knowledge in the specified area and the same time inspired many new themes for research. It also confirmed the principle that the history of the Jews in Poland is an inseparable part of Polish history as a whole. It is therefore necessary to maintain and deepen the cooperation of Polish and Jewish historians and to preserve the monuments of Jewish culture in our country.

CONTRIBUTORS

Gerson C. Bacon is Senior Lecturer in Jewish History at Bar-Ilan University. Among his publications are *The Jews in Poland and Russia: Bibliographical Essays* (Indiana University Press, 1984) and *Studies in East European Jewry: Bar-Ilan Annual*, Vol. 24–25 (1989), edited with Moshe Rosman. He and Rosman are the co-authors of the forthcoming *Sefer Gezeirot Tah*.

Israel Bartal is Senior Lecturer in modern Jewish history at the Hebrew University of Jerusalem. He is the author of several articles on Eastern European Jewish history and on the history of the pre-Zionist Jewish community in Palestine. His monograph 'Non-Jews and Gentile Society in East European Hebrew and Yiddish Literature 1856–1914' will soon be published by Hebrew Union College. He is currently preparing a revised edition of the minute book of the Council of the Four Lands, as well as a book on the revolt of 1863 in Jewish and Polish literature, together with Magdalena Opalski.

Władysław Bartoszewski is a writer and historian and was a Secretary of the Polish PEN Club (1972–1988). He holds honorary doctorates from the Polish University in exile (London) and Baltimore Hebrew College. From 1973 to 1985, he was Visiting Professor at the Catholic University of Lublin. Since then he has been Visiting Professor of Political Science at Munich, Eichstätt and Augsburg Universities. He has written some 20 books on the Second World War, Nazi crimes and the destruction of the Jews, amongst them *Warsaw Death Ring, 1939–1944* (Warsaw, 1968), *Righteous Among the Nations, How Poles Helped the Jews 1939–1945* (with Z. Lewin, London, 1969), *1859 dni Warszawy* (1859 Days of Warsaw, Kraków, 1974), *Dni walczącej stolicy. Kronika Powstania Warszawskiego* (Days of the Fighting Capital: A Chronicle of the Warsaw Uprising, London, 1984). Four of his other books are reviewed in this volume of *POLIN*. He was co-founder of the Council for the Aid to Jews (*Żegota*) and recipient of the title 'Righteous among Nations' (Yad Vashem 1963). In 1986 he received Peace Prize of the German Publishers' and Booksellers' Association. He is Vice-President of the Institute for Polish-Jewish Studies, Oxford.

Władysław T. Bartoszewski is a Research Fellow at St Antony's College, Oxford, and Associate Editor of *POLIN*. He is editor of Samuel Willenberg, *Surviving Treblinka* (Oxford, 1989).

Stanislaus A. Blejwas is Professor of History at Central Connecticut State University, where he also co-ordinates the University's Polish Studies Program. He works in both Polish and Polish American history. He is the author of *Realism in Polish Politics: Warsaw Positivism and National Survival in Nineteenth Century Poland* (1982), and co-editor of *Pastor of the Poles: Polish American Essays*.

Andrzej Bryk is a lecturer at the Institute for Constitutional History of the Jagiellonian University of Cracow. He has written articles on the history of political ideas and Polish-Jewish relations.

Michael Burleigh is a Lecturer at the Department of International History, London School of Economics and Political Science. He is the author of *Prussian Society and the German Order* (1984) and *Germany Turns Eastwards* (1988).

Andrzej Chojnowski is a Docent at the Historical Institute of Warsaw University specialising in the political history of twentieth-century Poland. He is the author of *Koncepcje polityki narodowościowej rządów polskich w latach 1921-1939* (The Political Conceptions of the Nationality Policies of Polish Governments, 1921-39, 1979) and *Piłsudczycy u władzy. Dzieje Bezpartyjnego Bloku Współpracy z Rządem* (The Pilsudski-ites in Power. A History of the Non-Party Bloc for cooperation with the Government, 1986).

Norman Davies was born in 1939 in Bolton (Lancs.). He is Professor of Polish History at the School of Slavonic and East European Studies, University of London and has been visiting Professor at McGill, Hokkaido and Stanford Universities. He is an M.A. (Oxon), Ph.D. (Kraków) and Fellow of the Royal Historical Society. His books include *White Eagle, Red Star, the Polish-Soviet War 1919-20* (1972); *Poland Past and Present – A Bibliography of Works in English on Polish History* (1976); *God's Playground: A History of Poland*, 2 vols. (1981) and *Heart of Europe: A Short History of Poland* (1984).

David Engel is Senior Lecturer in Jewish History at Tel Aviv University and co-editor of the journal *Gal-Ed: Studies on the History of Polish Jewry*. Among is many publications is *In the Shadow of Auschwitz: the Polish Government-in-Exile and the Jews, 1939–1942* (1987).

M. R. D. Foot, born in 1919, was an officer in the British Army 1939–1945, reaching the rank of major. He was for six years professor of modern history at Manchester, and his dozen books include a study of resistance and a short history of SOE.

Tomasz Gąsowski is a lecturer at the Historical Institute of the Jagiellonian University in Kraków, specialising in the social history of nineteenth-century Poland and especially in Polish-Jewish relations. He is currently preparing for publication a study of the Jewish question in autonomous Galicia and had written many articles on the history of that province and on the Jews there.

Frank Golczewski has since 1983 been Professor of Modern History at the University of the German Federal Armed Forces in Hamburg. He was born in 1948 in Katowice, Poland, and obtained his doctorate (1973) and habilitation (1979) in Cologne. His publications include *Polnisch-jüdische Beziehungen 1881–1922. Eine Studie zur Geschichte des Antisemitismus in Osteuropa* (1981) and *Kölner Universitätslehrer und der Nationalsozialismus* (1988).

Adam A. Hetnal is Assistant Professor of history at the Southern Utah State College. He received his M.A. degree from the Jagiellonian University of Cracow, and his doctorate from the Vanderbilt University. He is the author of *The Polish Question During the Crimean War 1853–6* (forthcoming), and over fifty articles and two hundred book reviews relating to Polish, Jewish, German, Russian and French history.

Julian Ilicki is a researcher in Jewish social studies at the Department of Sociology, University of Uppsala, Sweden. He left Poland in 1969 due to the anti-semitic campaign there. He has published articles on Jewish identity, Middle East conflict and Israel. His Ph.D. thesis deals with the changes in the self-perceived national identification among the younger generation of Polish Jews who immigrated to Sweden in 1968–1972.

Iwona Irwin-Zarecka is Assistant Professor of Sociology and communication studies at Wilfrid Laurier University in Waterloo, Canada. Having grown up in Warsaw, she left for Canada in 1973, later to pursue her graduate studies at the University of California, San Diego. Her current work includes a project dealing with the process of transmitting and transforming Polish-Jewish relations in the context of Canada's multiculturalism. She is the author of *Neutralising Memory: The Jew in Contemporary Poland* (1989).

Krystyna Kersten is a Docent at the Institute of History of the Polish Academy of Sciences, Warsaw. Her main interest lies in contemporary Polish history and her works are devoted to the social and political history of Poland after 1944 and to the movements of the population during and after the war. She is the author of *Repatriacja ludności polskiej po II wojnie światowej* (The Repatriation of the Polish Population after the Second World War, 1974) and *Polska 1943–1948. Narodziny systemu władzy* (Poland 1943–48. Origins of the System of Government, 1986).

Stefan Kieniewicz is Professor Emeritus at the University of Warsaw. He has written extensively on Polish history in the nineteenth century. His books include *Społeczeństwo polskie w powstaniu poznańskim 1848* (Polish Society in the Poznań uprising, 1848), *Historia Polski 1795–1918* (The History of Poland 1795–1918) and *Powstanie styczniowe* (The January Uprising).

Leszek Kołakowski was for many years, until 1968 when he was expelled for political reasons, Professor of the History of Philosophy at the University of Warsaw. He is a Fellow of All Souls College, Oxford and Professor of Philosophy at the University of Chicago. In 1977 he was awarded the Peace Prize of the German Publishers' and Booksellers' Association, and in 1983 the Erasmus Prize. His publications include *Husserl and the Search for Certitude* (1975), *Main Currents of Marxism* (1978) and *Religion* (1982).

Paweł Korzec, former professor of the Łódź University (until 1968), since then researcher in the Centre of National de la Recherche Scientifique in Paris. His most important book is *Juifs en Pologne* (1980).

Shmuel Krakowski is the Director of the Yad Vashem Archives in Jerusalem and was a lecturer on the Holocaust at the Tel-Aviv University. He is the author of *The War of the Doomed* and many other works dealing with the Holocaust, mainly of Polish Jewry.

Jack Kugelmass is Assistant Professor of Anthropology and Folklore at the University of Wisconsin-Madison. He is currently working on a series of essays on the culture of New York City and editing a volume of the *YIVO Annual* devoted to Jewish tourism and the concept of the 'old country'. He is the author of *Between Two Worlds: Ethnographic Essays on American Jewry*, *The Miracle of Intervale Avenue*, *Aging with Dignity in the South Bronx*, and co-editor of *From the Ruined Garden: The Memorial Books of Polish Jewry*.

Anna Landau-Czajka is a researcher at the Historical Institute of the Polish Academy of Sciences in the section of contemporary history. She was educated at Warsaw University where she obtained her doctorate (1988) for a thesis on social and political thought of the radical right-wing nationalists in Poland, 1926–1939.

Sergiusz Michalski is an art historian with an interest in Jewish history. He obtained his doctorate from the University of Warsaw where he was a lecturer (1973–1984). Since 1984 he has been a lecturer at the University of Augsburg. He researches on Mannerism, the Reformation and Art and French painting of the 18th century. He is the author of *The Protestants and Art* (Warsaw, 1989).

Magdalena Opalski teaches at Carleton and York University in Ontario, Canada. She is the author of *The Jewish Tavern-Keeper and his Tavern* (1986), and co-author, with I. Bartal, of a forthcoming comparative study on the legend of 'Polish-Jewish brotherhood' in 1863 in Polish and Jewish literatures. She also edited a special issue of *The Polish Review* devoted to Polish-Jewish cultural relations (1987).

Antony Polonsky is Reader in International History at the London School of Economics and Political Science and editor of *POLIN*. He is the author of *Politics in Independent Poland 1921–1939* (1972), *The Little Dictators* (1975), *The Great Powers and the Polish Question 1941–45* (1976) and co-author of *A History of Modern Poland* (1980).

Eugenia Prokopówna teaches modern Polish literature at the Jagiellonian University of Cracow. Her major essay 'Kafka w Polsce międzywojennej' (Kafka in interwar Poland), originally published in Polish in *Pamiętnik Literacki*, will soon appear as a monograph in the series *Studies on Polish Jewry* in Jerusalem.

Peter Pulzer is Gladstone Professor of Government and Public Administration at the University of Oxford and Fellow of All Souls College. He is the author of *The Rise of Political Antisemitism in Germany and Austria* (revised edition in 1988), and *Jews and State in Germay 1848–1933* (forthcoming).

Anna Radziwiłł has been a teacher since 1959. In 1966 she obtained a doctorate for a thesis on the educational ideology of the *Sanacja*, which was never published due to political censorship. In 1989 she was elected to the Polish Senate on the Solidarity's list. She is the author of *Ideologia wychowawcza w latach 1949–1956* (The ideology of education in the years 1949–1956, 1981).

Alexandra Reiche is a doctoral student at the University of Oxford. She studied at the University of California, Berkeley and at the University of Göttingen. She is presently working on a thesis about German national identity.

Murray J. Rosman teaches Jewish history at Bar-Ilan University. Educated at the Jewish Theological Seminary of America and Columbia University, for the past 10 years he has resided in Israel. His book *The Lord's Jews: Magnates and Jews in the Eighteen Century Polish-Lithuanian Commonwealth* is being published jointly by the Harvard Ukrainian Research Institute and The Harvard Center for Jewish Studies.

Michael C. Steinlauf is Assistant Professor of East European Jewish History at Brandeis University, and a Fellow of the Ukrainian Research Institute of Harvard University. In 1983-84 he spent a year in Poland as a Fulbright Fellow. He devotes himself to Polish Jewish cultural history and Polish-Jewish relations in the nineteenth and twentieth centuries. He is currently studying the development of Yiddish theatre in Poland, and translating works by Y. L. Peretz into English.

Jerzy Szapiro is a Professor of Neurosurgery. Until 1968 he was the Chairman and Director of the Neurosurgery Clinic of the Medical Academy in Łódź. He retired in 1984. He has written over 100 articles on neurosurgery and is the author of many essays – mainly meta-scientific reflections on the human condition. He is a founding member of the Polish Association of Neurosurgeons and a corresponding member of the American Association of Neurological Surgeons and of the Société de Neurochirurgiens de la Langue Française.

Jean-Charles Szurek is a researcher in the Centre National de la Recherche Scientifique in Paris. He has written *Aux origines paysannes de la crise polonaise* (1982) and a number of articles on Jewish-Polish relations.

Janusz Tazbir is a Professor at the Historical Institute of the Polish Academy of Sciences, Warsaw. He is the editor of the annual *Odrodzenie i Reformacja w Polsce* (Renaissance and Reformation in Poland). He works on the history of Polish culture in the sixteenth and seventeenth centuries and of religious movements in this period. Among his publications are: *A State Without Stakes. Polish Religious Tolerance in the Sixteenth and Seventeenth Centuries* (1973), *Geschichte der polnischen Toleranz* (1977), *Le République nobiliare et le monde, Etudes sur l'histoire de la culture polonaise a l'epoque du baroque* (1986). He is a co-author of *History of Poland* (edited by S. Kieniewicz, 1968).

Nechama Tec is Professor of Sociology at the University of Connecticut, Stamford. A Polish Jew who lived through the Nazi occupation, since 1977 she has been conducting research about compassion, altruism and Jewish rescue during the Second World War. She is a member of the Educational Committee of the US Holocaust Memorial Council and recipient of Hadassah's Myrtle Wreath Award (1987). She is the author of five books and over 30 articles.

Chava Turniansky is Professor of Yiddish and Head of the Department of Yiddish at the Hebrew University, Jerusalem. She is the author of several works, including *Sefer Massah U'Merivah by Alexander Den Yitshak Pfaffehofen*.

Roman Zimand, a historian of literature, is Researcher at the Polish Academy of Sciences in Warsaw. Among his publications is *'Dziennik' Adama Czerniakowa – próba lektury* (1979).

OBITUARY

Shmuel Ettinger

Shmuel Ettinger, a distinguished Jewish historian, died suddenly in London, on 22 September, 1988, while on a brief visit to England. He was sixty-nine years old. With his death passed away the most important Jewish historian of Eastern Europe. He was born in Kiev in June 1919, to a distinguished Hasidic family, and at the age of five his parents settled in Leningrad, whence in 1936 they succeeded in migrating to Palestine.

Ettinger as a student was very active in the Students' Federation, and later on, for a few years, was a prominent member of the Palestine Communist Party. After the Second World War, he was the leader of one of the splinter groups of the Palestine Communist Party, and was sent by that group in 1946 to Eastern Europe to enlist the support of the Communist Parties there for the policies advocated by his group, *Emet*. He visited Rumania, Czecho-Slovakia and Poland, where he spent a number of months. What he saw there quickly disillusioned him in communism, and he was deeply shaken by the flourishing anti-semitism in Czecho-Slovakia and Poland, inspired by the Governments and Party leaderships, and which found ready fertile ground among the ordinary people. He returned to Palestine, immediately left the Communist Party, and resumed his studies at the Hebrew University. As a student he already acquired a reputation of being a walking encyclopaedia, and he could talk with great learning on many topics. His mastery of Slavic languages was most impressive.

He did his doctorate under Professors Ben-Zion Dinur and Israel Halpern, on the colonisation of the Ukraine by Poles and Jews in the second half of the 16th century. His research broke new ground by establishing the number of Jews in the Ukraine and their role in the management of the estates of the nobility. Of great significance was his analysis of the number of Jews killed by the Ukrainian Cossacks led by Bogdan

Chmielnicki in 1648-1649, in which he reached the conclusion that the figures given by the Jewish chroniclers of the time, like Nathan Hannover, and others are greatly exaggerated. Ettinger's concluding figure of one hundred and twenty five thousand Jews massacred, and not over a quarter of a million as stated by the chronicles, has been accepted by all Jewish historians. His analysis was based on a very careful checking of the poll tax and other taxes paid by Jews to the government. His enormous knowledge of the sources showed him a master of the subject. The chapters of his doctorate which he published he published in '*Tsion*' – the leading Jewish historical quarterly, have been recognised as classic.

On completion of his doctorate, he was appointed to the teaching staff of the Department of Jewish History at the Hebrew University of Jerusalem, and joined the editorial board of '*Tsion*', at the express invitation of the editors: Yitzhak Baer, Ben-Zion Dinur and Israel Halpern. After the death of the original editors he became the editor-in-chief.

From 1958 on, Ettinger began to publish a series of articles which attracted much attention among many scholars, to mention only a few: 'The Jewish influence on the "Judaisers" in Eastern Europe at the end of the fifteenth century' (1961, in the *Festschrift* for Yitzhak Baer), which provoked a leading Soviet historian, S. Lurye, to polemise with him. Ettinger showed conclusively that Lithuanian Jews had an influence on the Russian 'Judaisers' at the time of their trial in the 1480s. His profound knowledge of old Russian helped him to recognise part of the Eighteen Benedictions in the texts on the basis of which they were accused of heresy.

In the same year, he published in English his study, 'The Beginning of the Change in the Attitude of European Society towards the Jews' (*Scripta Hierosolymitana*, vol. 7). He showed that, after the Reformation, antisemitism began to shift from purely religious motives to social, cultural and political ones; society in Western Europe was divided between a minority of thinkers who saw the Jews in a more positive light and those who subscribed to the popular, stereotypic image of them as the killers of Christ. The first to develop a positive view was the French political philosopher Jean Bodin, for whom the book of Deuteronomy revealed an ideal commonwealth, and this, he argued, required a new understanding of the Jew. This led Ettinger, subsequently, to make a detailed study of the English Deists, who advocated a natural rational religion, and saw Judaism as a religion of egoism, negative to society, a view which was shared by the French Encyclopaedists, and especially Voltaire. Ettinger stressed the more positive view of the Jews by Montesquieu, and those writers in England like Toland, and others who championed the naturalisation of the Jews in 1753 (the so-called 'Jew-Bill') ('*Tsion*', 1964, this article also appeared in English).

An article which created a major new discussion was his study of the early Hasidic leadership (1964, and published in English in 1968 in the

Journal of World History, volume 11). He argued against the other scholars of the Hasidic movement that the early leadership of the Hasidim did not orignate from poor, oppressed protest groups of Jews in the Ukraine, in Podolia and Volhynia, but from groups similar to their opponents, the *Mithnagedim*. He showed that the Hasidic movement created a new sort of leadership, in which power and influence was centred in the spiritual leader – the Tsaddik – rather than in the lay leadership which had been characteristic of the Jewish communities prior to the rise of *Hasidism*.

From 1967 on, Ettinger published a series of seminal papers on anti-semitism in Russia and Germany. Of great importance are his studies on anti-semitism in Russia, particularly on 'The ideological background to the appearance of the new anti-semitic literature in Russia' ('*Tsion*', vol. 35, 1970); 'The roots of anti-semitism in modern times' ('*Tsion*', 1973); 'The permanent and changing aspects of anti-semitism in our time' (1970 as a separate booklet)' 'The discussion of on Jewish exploitation in Russian public opinion in the beginning of the 80's in the 19th century' (1980 in the *Festschrift* for Yakov Katz), in which he examined the writings of the Slavophiles, the radicals and populists, and other publicists on the Jews. He showed the many layers of their hatred towards the Jews: religious, secular, social, in all seeing the Jews as parasite, an exploiter, and especially as an alien in the Russian midst. They are of crucial importance for the understanding of anti-semitic currents in Russia and their persistence to the present day.

Ettinger's study of the phenomenon of anti-semitism covered not only Russia, but the writings of the Left Hegelians in Germany, and the roots of the anti-semitism of Karl Marx's anti-semitism. In his papers, he left a large draft of a history of anti-semitic ideas in modern times.

In 1969, Shmuel Ettinger published his major text book *History of Jews in Modern Times* (which was part three of the *History of The Jewish People*, edited by H. H. Ben Sasson). It became a basic text book for all universities in Israel. It has been reprinted several times and translated into English, German, Russian and Japanese. Written without footnotes, in limpid prose, concise, full of facts and brilliant analysis of movements and ideas.

In all his studies, such as his masterful monograph on Henrich Graetz as a Jewish historian, Ettinger, like his teachers Yitzhak Baer and Ben-Zion Dinur, saw the Jews as one people and not only as a religious community, a nation dispersed but still a nation. A nation that hoped, dreamt all through its history to return one day to its land of origin, and rebuild there a new national centre. He viewed anti-semitism as primarily a major element in European society, whose features varied according to the conditions prevailing in each country in a given time. From this angle, he was not surprised at the revival both of Jewish national sentiments among Jews of the Soviet Union, and at the persistence of anti-semitism in many layers of Soviet society. Hence his very active participation in campaigns on behalf of Soviet Jews. He was the central moving figure in the Jewish Historical Society of Israel, responsible for its many publications in historical studies. To a number of these, he wrote very impressive introductions full of deep insight into Jewish historiography. He encouraged and planned many new enterprises in historical research.

Chimen Abramsky

www.ingramcontent.com/pod-product-compliance
Ingram Content Group UK Ltd.
Pitfield, Milton Keynes, MK11 3LW, UK
UKHW022242230426
12048UKWH00018BA/1407